Learners with Mild Disabilities

A CHARACTERISTICS APPROACH

Fourth Edition

EILEEN B. RAYMOND

The State University of New York at Potsdam

Boston   Columbus   Indianapolis   New York   San Francisco   Upper Saddle River
Amsterdam   Cape Town   Dubai   London   Madrid   Milan   Munich   Paris   Montreal   Toronto
Delhi   Mexico City   São Paulo   Sydney   Hong Kong   Seoul   Singapore   Taipei   Tokyo

KH

Vice President and Editor in Chief: Jeffery W. Johnston
Executive Editor and Publisher: Stephen D. Dragin
Editorial Assistant: Jamie Bushell
Vice President, Director of Marketing: Margaret Waples
Marketing Manager: Weslie Sellinger
Senior Managing Editor: Pamela D. Bennett
Operations Supervisor: Central Publishing
Operations Specialist: Laura Messerly
Senior Art Director: Jayne Conte
Cover Designer: Suzanne Behnke
Cover Art: Fotolia
Photo Researcher: Lori Whitley
Full-Service Project Management: Sumit Makarh/Aptara®, Inc.
Composition: Aptara®, Inc.
Printer/Binder: Edwards Brothers, Inc.
Cover Printer: Lehigh-Phoenix Color
Text Font: Times

Credits and acknowledgments borrowed from other sources and reproduced, with permission, in this textbook appear on appropriate page within text.

Every effort has been made to provide accurate and current Internet information in this book. However, the Internet and information posted on it are constantly changing, so it is inevitable that some of the Internet addresses listed in this textbook will change.

Photo Credits: PhotoAlto/Alamy, pp. 3, 108; Jupiterimages/Creatas Images/Thinkstock, p. 35; Gabe Palmer/ Alamy, p. 55; David Young-Wolff/PhotoEdit Inc., p. 81; Fotolia, LLC - Royalty Free, p. 126; Anthony Magnacca/ Merrill, p. 150; Getty Images - Stockbyte, p. 171; Creatas/Thinkstock, p. 191; Christy Thompson/Shutterstock, p. 224; Big Cheese Photo LLC/Alamy, p. 254; Catherine Ursillo/Photo Researchers, Inc., p. 282.

Library of Congress Cataloging-in-Publication Data
Raymond, Eileen B.
   Learners with mild disabilities : a characteristics approach / Eileen B. Raymond.—4th ed.
     p. cm.
   Includes bibliographical references and index.
   ISBN-13: 978-0-13-706076-4 (alk. paper)
   ISBN-10: 0-13-706076-9 (alk. paper)
   1. Learning disabled children—Education--United States.   2. Children with mental disabilities—Education—
United States.   3. Hyperactive children—Education—United States.   4. Problem children—Education—
United States. I. Title.
   LC4705.R39 2012
   372.92'6—dc22

                                                                                      2010048478

10 9 8 7 6 5 4 3 2 1

www.pearsonhighered.com

ISBN 10:   0-13-706076-9
ISBN 13: 978-0-13-706076-4

10/4/11

ABOUT THE AUTHOR

Eileen Raymond taught for 22 years in college programs preparing special educators, after teaching for 10 years in public schools as a special educator and raising a son with a learning disability. During her term (2005–2009) as Associate Dean in the School of Education and Professional Studies at the State University of New York at Potsdam, Dr. Raymond had primary responsibility for the university's assessment program and served as the NCATE coordinator. She collaborated with colleagues at two colleges to establish new special education preparation programs based on collaborative models of service and focused on learner characteristics rather than categories. She was awarded Professor and Associate Dean Emeritus status upon her retirement from the State University of New York at Potsdam in 2009. From 2009 to 2010, she served as a Fulbright Scholar at Nelson Mandela Metropolitan University in Port Elizabeth, South Africa, where she taught and helped revise the programs related to inclusive education. Her current research interests include issues relating to serving diverse students with disabilities, with special interests in universal design for learning, global inclusive education initiatives, and language diversity. She is an active member of the Council for Exceptional Children, serving on their national Board of Directors from 2009 through 2011. She also serves on the Board of Program Reviewers for the Council for Exceptional Children.

PREFACE

Learners with Mild Disabilities is designed for use at the undergraduate and graduate levels as the main text in courses addressing manifestation of disability in the milder range of impairment, including intellectual disabilities, learning disabilities, attention-deficit/hyperactivity disorders, emotional and behavioral disorders, and autism spectrum disorders. Such courses are typically the first specialized courses taken as part of a special educator preparation program. This text should be especially useful to students preparing for careers in noncategorical generic special education.

NEW TO THIS EDITION

This fourth edition of *Learners with Mild Disabilities* retains many of the distinctive features found in the previous editions, but with significantly updated content throughout:

- Unit I has been reconfigured and condensed from five chapters into three to sharpen the focus on issues related to classification, assessment, instruction, and placement.
- A new chapter has been added to address the increasing numbers of learners with autism spectrum disorders in the mild range of impairment.
- In the 2010 edition of their definitional manual, the American Association of Intellectual and Developmental Disabilities (AAIDD) formally adopted the term *intellectual disabilities* and changed its name from the American Association on Mental Retardation. AAIDD now encourages the preferred use of the term *intellectual disabilities* in place of *mental retardation*. In 2010 the U.S. Congress also adopted the new terminology in federal programs and legislation. In light of this guidance, this text now uses the new terminology and definition throughout.
- Response to intervention (RTI) has become a widespread philosophy and practice since the third edition of this book; consequently, this edition has increased coverage of this concept significantly, especially in Chapters 2, 5, and 6.
- The principles of universal design for learning (UDL; see www.cast.org) have been reformulated since the third edition of this book. This revised framework of multiple and flexible options for presentation, expression, and engagement is more flexible and relevant in classroom settings. In light of this, the Universal Design for Learning in Action boxes in Chapters 2, 9, 10, 11, and 12 have been redone, with new, functional examples of pedagogical practices that are consistent with the new formulation of the UDL principles.
- The case studies at the end of each chapter have been updated to reflect the revisions to formal tests such as the WISC-IV. This provides current material for reader practice.
- All data tables have been updated with the most recent information from the *28th Annual Report to Congress on the IDEA* and other federal databases.
- The On the Web references have been updated and are now integrated within the text to encourage readers to pursue topics as they encounter those concepts within the text.
- References cited throughout the text have been updated, with about 40 percent being new to this edition. These current resources provide readers with options for further study of particular topics.

FEATURES OF THIS EDITION

This edition retains a number of features from previous editions that are designed to facilitate the active learning of readers. The juxtaposition of the traditional categorical approaches to mild disability and cross-categorical and noncategorical approaches helps highlight the complexity of determining student needs. It provides current and potential special educators with the knowledge needed to understand both approaches and then challenges them to synthesize this information into a more functional approach to identification, planning, and programming. It also challenges the simplistic notion that merely determining the correct label or finding the perfect definition is the most important task in designing interventions and supports. Throughout, the text does not avoid conflicting philosophical perspectives but instead uses such apparent discontinuities to stimulate readers' analytical skills.

Learners with Mild Disabilities includes a number of updated case studies drawn from the experiences of real children and teachers, thereby providing practice material that is both realistic and relevant. These cases are longer and more complex than is common in books of this type. Because they are composites based on actual experiences, they are realistically messy and unfinished. They present challenges to readers' analytical skills and provide the basis for interesting class discussions, promoting the disequilibrium necessary for learning, as Piaget theorized. Discussions based on the questions accompanying each case provide opportunities for significant active learning in cooperative learning groups and whole-class instruction.

Learners with Mild Disabilities provides a variety of approaches to thinking about disabilities. In addition to the IDEA disability definitions, Unit II discusses alternative definitions of high-prevalence or mild disabilities, including these:

- The 2010 AAIDD definition of intellectual disabilities
- The NJCLD definition of learning disabilities
- The *DSM-IV-TR* definitions of ADHD and autism spectrum disorders
- The Mental Health and Special Education Coalition definition of emotional or behavioral disorders

Throughout *Learners with Mild Disabilities*, the following structural features are used to highlight the chapter topic and assist student learning:

- *Questions to Guide Your Study* serves as an advance organizer.
- *Opening vignettes,* accompanied by challenging discussion starters, set the stage for the content in the chapter.
- *Spotlight on History* boxes present adapted original texts as contextual elements (Chapters 1, 4, and 6).
- *In the Classroom* boxes help illustrate concepts with realistic short stories of learners with disabilities (Chapters 3, 9, 10, 11, and 12).
- *Universal Design for Learning in Action* boxes provide suggestions for supporting student learning (Chapters 2, 9, 10, 11, and 12).
- *Diversity in Focus* sections within each chapter highlight the issues related to diversity that are presented in the chapter content. Although *Learners with Mild Disabilities* infuses the entire text with discussion of linguistic and cultural diversity—rather than isolating this discussion within a single chapter—these Focus sections highlight the most significant issues of language and culture in relation to chapter content.
- *On the Web* margin notes throughout each chapter provide access to a variety of websites to extend readers' consideration of chapter content.
- *Extended case studies* at the end of each chapter have been updated and revised to challenge readers to apply the concepts presented in the chapter.

ORGANIZATION OF THIS EDITION

Learners with Mild Disabilities departs from the exclusively categorical approaches to disability that are found in other texts. This text is based on an awareness that the notion of discrete disabilities has not been well supported by recent experience and philosophical discussions in special education. Consequently, the text develops an alternative model to prepare special educators for careers in the complex world of mild disabilities, while still equipping them to discuss categorical issues intelligently. *Learners with Mild Disabilities* looks first at the high-prevalence disabilities from the conventional, categorical perspective and then presents readers with a variety of alternative conceptual frameworks for looking at these learners from the perspective of individual strengths and needs. *Learners with Mild Disabilities* also uses person-first language throughout the book when referring to individuals with disabilities, modeling for readers the use of appropriate and accurate language. The principles and rationale for person-first language are presented in Chapter 1.

Unit I has been reconfigured to provide a more concise and focused context for the study of disability and issues of classification, assessment, identification, curriculum, instruction, and placement of students with mild disabilities, providing a summary of key provisions of the 2004 IDEA reauthorization.

Unit II describes learners with high-prevalence learning and behavioral conditions—intellectual disabilities, learning disabilities, emotional or behavioral disorders, and other conditions, including attention-deficit/hyperactivity disorders. Since lower-incidence conditions sometimes manifest in the milder range of impairment and since these learners are frequently placed in general education and resource programs, this edition has added a new chapter on autism spectrum disorders, clarifying the differences among learners with classic autism and increasingly common conditions such as high-functioning autism and Asperger's syndrome. Each chapter explains the development of the definitions for these conditions that are currently found in IDEA, as well as others proposed by organizations such as the American Psychiatric Association. Each chapter identifies a variety of concerns about the adequacy of these definitions, as well as the causes, prevalence, and signature characteristics of each disability. Readers are given the opportunity to apply the current disability definitions through extended case studies designed to help them identify critical issues related to these conditions.

In Unit III, readers consider the characteristics of learners with mild disabilities—their cognitive, linguistic, academic learning, and social–emotional characteristics. *Learners with Mild Disabilities* develops conceptual frameworks related to learner functioning, illustrating the use of these frameworks to analyze a particular child's difficulties and strengths. Moving beyond the categorical perspective, *Learners with Mild Disabilities* focuses on the learner characteristics that may be related to each learner's particular difficulties. Readers are guided in applying conceptual frameworks to analyze any learner's skills and deficit areas, regardless of the labeled condition. Extensive use of short vignettes in Unit III and the extended case studies help readers apply the frameworks to individual learners as an aid to diagnosis and instructional planning.

This edition of *Learners with Mild Disabilities* develops the current knowledge base needed to serve all learners, including those from varying cultural and linguistic backgrounds. Given an increasingly diverse school population, educators are expected to provide instruction that is culturally sensitive. *Learners with Mild Disabilities* highlights the need to focus on the learner, not on a category and not on a particular language or ethnic group. By becoming sensitive to the varying characteristics of individual learners, educators will be better able to identify the needs of students with unique cultural and linguistic backgrounds, as well as those with a variety of disabilities. Readers should be able to use this information to design more effective and relevant instruction for all students.

PHILOSOPHICAL BACKGROUND FOR THE STUDY OF MILD DISABILITIES

Throughout history, disability has been conceptualized primarily as deviance. Individuals with disabilities have been diagnosed, labeled, and treated in accordance with that deviance. Disability services have been justified by determining that an individual met the criteria for one of the established disability categories and was in need of special treatment. For those disabilities with medical etiologies and a profound effect on the functional ability of the individual, this approach may have been appropriate.

However, as society began to demand higher levels of literacy and reasoning, increasing numbers of children began to struggle in school. These learners presented milder and more diverse cognitive and emotional disabilities, compromising their success in school. As local communities began to serve learners with an increasing variety of mild disabilities under the terms of the Individuals with Disabilities Education Act, it became increasingly apparent that it was difficult to identify many youngsters as belonging to one and only one category. The cost of evaluating youngsters for eligibility escalated over the years, while the utility of the diagnoses themselves was called into question.

Increasingly, schools investigated alternatives to categorical service delivery models, particularly for the large group of learners with milder forms of disability. Special education teachers now frequently serve students in a variety of categories, students who share a variety of common needs. In the years to come, special educators will need to be able to accurately and comprehensively describe students' strengths and needs, rather than just applying diagnostic criteria to categorize learners. *Learners with Mild Disabilities* provides the special educator of the future with an understanding of the definitions currently in use and a variety of alternative definitions, as well as the limitations of these categorical processes. This book also develops the conceptual frameworks needed by educators as they identify and interpret a broad range of student behaviors from a noncategorical perspective.

ACKNOWLEDGMENTS

No effort of this kind would be possible without significant support from a variety of individuals. In particular, I want to express my continuing appreciation for the support of my colleague John W. Marson, who provided detailed feedback on preliminary drafts of the text and the field testing of the final drafts in our co-taught classes. Many of the instructional activities in the ancillary materials are derived from our collaborative teaching efforts. I also wish to thank the students in the special education program at the State University of New York at Potsdam for their feedback on drafts of this work.

This book would not have been possible without the stories that students and fellow educators have shared with me over the years. The vignettes and case studies are fictional composites, but they are based on the collective experiences of real learners and real teachers in real school settings. This basis in reality provides readers with many useful application experiences, and I appreciate everyone who has shared a story with me.

As with any writing project, editorial assistance is critical. I thank the following peer reviewers, who read and commented on the manuscript: Morgan Chitiyo, Southern Illinois University–Carbondale; Lydia Conca, St. Joseph College; Diane Miller, Emporia State University; and Christy Roberts, Lewis University. My appreciation also goes to Steve Dragin, Sheryl Langner, and Jamie Bushell for their assistance in producing this edition. Their support, encouragement, and feedback have been critical to completing this project.

Finally, I want to thank my family and friends for their encouragement and forbearance during this long and continuing project. I am especially grateful to Donna for her support and understanding during the completion of this revision.

BRIEF CONTENTS

CONTENTS

BOXES

SPOTLIGHT ON HISTORY

DIVERSITY IN FOCUS

UNIVERSAL DESIGN FOR LEARNING IN ACTION!

IN THE CLASSROOM

Setting the Stage

Educators in contemporary society face many challenges. Schools are expected to provide solutions to myriad social problems by preparing the next generation of citizens to assume their adult roles more competently than previous generations have. We ask that our schools educate all children, and we voice the philosophy that all children can learn. We recognize that our classrooms are filled with learners representing significant diversity, including students who differ from one another with respect to gender, race, ethnic background, language, socioeconomic class, religion, sexual orientation, and ability. It is the specific issue of diversity in learning ability that this book addresses.

To develop an understanding of classification, diagnosis, and interventions for children who differ from others in their age group, we need to gain a perspective on the nature of ability and disability as well as on the historical development of our attention to persons with disabilities. A visit to any classroom will confirm that in any group of children, no two learners are alike. They differ from one another on a wide variety of variables, and this diversity presents challenges to instructional staff seeking to help each learner master critical skills and knowledge.

The concept of disability develops from the determination by various persons within society, and finally by the community itself, that the degree to which a particular individual's behavioral characteristics differ from those of others in the group is unacceptable, that the behavior is deviant to the extent that special attention is warranted (Speece & Harry, 1997). By extension, the individual is then seen as being significantly different so that differential treatment is needed; frequently, this leads to the identification of the individual as having a disability.

Chapter 1 considers the meaning of disability and some of our reasons for focusing on mild disability. The chapter first considers contemporary responses to schoolchildren with disabilities, both by the U.S. Congress and by those advocating in the courts for the rights of children to appropriate educational services. It looks back at the way in which individuals with disabilities have been viewed and treated during certain periods of history, with a specific focus on United States history. The chapter also discusses the process by which some students become classified as learners with disabilities, and it explores the ramifications of such classifications. Finally, it considers the impact on an individual's life of being determined to have a disability.

Chapters 2 and 3 explore some of the implications of the 2004 Individuals with Disabilities Education Act (IDEA) for assessment, identification, curriculum, instruction, and placement of learners with disabilities. Specifically, the following issues are considered, questions that will continue to be discussed and answered by special educators in the future:

- How can we best assess student learning, especially when that learning may be hindered or obscured by a mild disability?
- Is categorical identification the most useful process for understanding a learner and for making programming decisions?
- How do students with disabilities relate most appropriately to the general education curriculum?
- Are there instructional practices that are equally effective for those students with and without disabilities? Are there practices that are effective only with students with disabilities?
- What accommodations are appropriate and useful in providing access to the general education curriculum?
- What do we really mean by *inclusion?* Is it appropriate for all learners?

It is important to note that Unit I identifies a number of issues important to the field of education today. All of them are beyond the scope of this book to address fully. The reader is encouraged to continue to acquire information about such issues, practices, and strategies by reading widely in the current research in the field.

CHAPTER 1

Perspectives on Disability

Questions *to Guide Your Study*

- What is a disability? What is a handicap? Why is the difference important to you as a teacher?
- Why is it important to study *mild* disabilities specifically?
- Why might it be useful to study high-prevalence disabilities together?
- What are the advantages of and problems with using categories to classify students with disabilities?
- What are the major requirements of IDEA?
- In what ways have the attitudes and values of a society or a time in history determined how people with disabilities are viewed and treated?
- What trends do we see in the history of services for students with disabilities?

Meet Clarence

The first day she kept an especially close eye on the boy called Clarence. Clarence was a small, lithe, brown-skinned boy with large eyes and deep dimples. Chris watched his journeys to the pencil sharpener. They were frequent. Clarence took the longest route around the room, walking heel-to-toe and brushing the back of one leg with the shin of the other at every step—a cheerful little dance across the blue carpet, around the perimeter of desks, and along the back wall, passing under the American flag, which didn't quite brush his head. Reaching the pencil sharpener, Clarence would turn his pencil into a stunt plane, which did several loop-the-loops before plunging into the hole. . . . Clarence noticed things. He paid close attention to the intercom. His eyes darted to the door the moment a visitor appeared. But he paid almost no attention to her lessons and his work. It seemed as if every time she glanced up, Clarence wasn't working. . . . The other children were working. . . .

   Chris had received the children's cumulative records, or "cumes." . . . Clarence's cume was about as thick as the Boston phone book. . . . One teacher whom Chris trusted had described him as probably the most difficult child in all of last year's fourth grade classes. Chris wished she hadn't heard that, nor the rumors about Clarence. . . . She'd try to ignore what she had heard, and deal with the problems as they came. Clarence's were surfacing quickly. He came to school the second day without having done his homework. He had not done any work so far, except for one math assignment, and for that he'd just written down some numbers at random. . . .

On the third day of school, a Friday, several children including Clarence came in without homework, and Chris told them they were in for recess. . . . Clarence objected to the news about being in for recess. He threw an eraser at one classmate and punched another. . . . She called him to her desk. He came, but he stood sideways to her, chin lifted, face averted. She told him, in a matter-of-fact voice that wasn't very stern, that he could put someone's eye out by throwing things, and that he could not hit anyone. He didn't say a word. He just stared away, chin raised, as if to say, "I'm not listening to you." . . .

He did a little work after lunch, but he came to a full stop when, late in the day, she asked the class to write a paragraph and draw some pictures to describe their visions of the lives of Native Americans. . . . All the other children got to work, quite happily, it seemed. Clarence said he didn't understand the assignment. She explained it again, twice. . . . The other children bent their heads over their papers, working out their impressions about Indians. Chris saw Clarence take out his ruler, and put it on top of his pencil. Grinning, he tapped the ruler with his finger. It spun like a helicopter blade. . . . Chris watched the ruler spin. She understood this as defiance. The lines were being drawn. . . . Clarence is an angry child, she thought. Angry at the whole world. Worst of all was that stony, averted face he wore when she tried to talk to him. How could she ever get close enough to reason with a child who put up a barrier like that? . . . On his first report card he'd flunk everything, and that would tell him the same old news, that he didn't have to do the work because he couldn't.

THINKING QUESTIONS

What have you learned about Clarence from this story?

If you were his teacher, what else do you think you would need to know to decide what action to take to help Clarence?

Source: Excerpts from *Among Schoolchildren* by Tracy Kidder. Copyright © 1989 by John Tracy Kidder. Reprinted by permission of Houghton Mifflin Harcourt Publishing Company. All rights reserved.

Have you met Clarence or a student like him? Our focus in this book will be on students with milder forms of disability. Schools and teachers are increasingly called upon to serve a variety of children with mild disabilities, students with difficulties in learning, thinking, and behavior . . . students like Clarence.

Historically, special education and services for people with disabilities in general have dealt almost exclusively with more severe levels of disability. As a result, the vocabulary and practices that have emerged over the years have focused on the significant differences that these individuals exhibited when compared to typical individuals (Council for Exceptional Children, 1997b). These children and adults called attention to themselves because of their physical and behavioral differences, and the resulting classification system solidified these differences into categories and labels.

This system, based on difference, failed to consider those students who differed less dramatically from the typical child. Learners with milder physical, learning, or behavioral problems were either overlooked entirely or were counseled into less demanding academic and vocational pursuits. In a society that needed a large supply of unskilled labor to work in fields and factories, unschooled labor had value, and milder levels of disability did not restrict people from performing productive work. For much of history, mild levels of disability were neither identified nor considered to be problematic.

As our schools and larger society began demanding higher levels of academic functioning and skills in the 20th century, the classification system was steadily extended upward to include those youngsters with milder problems. Children who fell outside the "typical" mold found themselves identified with classifications indicating their dysfunction. Words like *defective, retarded, impaired, disadvantaged, disturbed, disabled, handicapped,* and *disordered* were used to describe more and more children who "just didn't fit in."

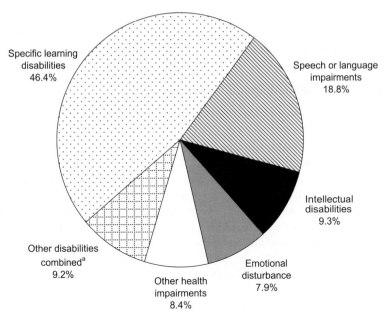

FIGURE 1.1   Distribution of Disabilities

Source: From *28th Annual Report to Congress on the Implementation of the Individuals with Disabilities Education Act, 2006* (Vol. 1, p. 41) by U.S. Department of Education, 2009, Washington, DC: USDOE.

With the advent of universal special education services in the United States in 1975, students with milder levels of disability, as defined by the schools, began to account for a significant majority of students receiving special services (MacMillan, Keogh, & Jones, 1986). These learners were described by MacMillan et al. as "inefficient school learners," students who were characterized by problems in school achievement and social adjustment so different from those of their peers that specialized interventions were deemed necessary. The authors noted that typically these youngsters were unremarkable in appearance and lacked obvious physical manifestations of disability; in short, they looked much like all the other students. Depending on the accounting method used, students identified as having mild disabilities now account for 70 percent to 95 percent of all learners receiving special education services (Gartner & Lipsky, 1987; Reynolds & Heistad, 1997; Salend, 2001; U.S. Department of Education, 2009). (See Figure 1.1.)

Since the mid-1980s, increased awareness of and concern for students who fail to successfully complete the minimum educational program have spawned a new category of learners, the *at-risk students,* those who are perceived to be potential school dropouts. In the tradition of social concern that gave us students with *economic and cultural disadvantage* in the 1960s and 1970s, schools have set up new identification procedures and special programs for these students, many of whom test and perform just above the cutoff line for eligibility for special education services. When the learning and behavioral characteristics and needs of these students are enumerated, it is apparent that they often are very similar to those of students with mild disabilities (Reynolds & Heistad, 1997).

For the following reasons, it seems useful to focus on the needs of all such students, those with mild disabilities as well as those like Clarence who remain unclassified but who nevertheless present significant problems in school:

- The majority of students being served by special education are in the mild range of disability.
- Since the classification system used to categorize learners with mild disabilities evolved upward from the terminology developed to connote more severe disabilities, and since this classification system often does not adequately describe these learners and their capabilities, study of this population by itself may be more useful (MacMillan, Siperstein, & Gresham, 1996).

- Students with mild disabilities are often similar to others who have problems learning, so understanding the life experiences of those with milder levels of disability may help us also serve similar but not-yet-classified learners.

STUDYING HIGH-PREVALENCE DISABILITIES

The primary focus of study in this book will be on the high-prevalence disabilities served by the Individuals with Disabilities Education Act (e.g., learning disabilities, mild intellectual disability, and emotional or behavioral disorders), as well as on other disorders such as attention-deficit/hyperactivity disorder (ADHD) and certain low-incidence disorders that can manifest as milder levels of impairment (e.g., autism spectrum disorder). It is important to note that although ADHD is not specifically identified for services under IDEA, children with ADHD are frequently served in special education programs because they qualify for another disability. (See Chapter 7 for more discussion of this seeming paradox.) Together these conditions account for about 90 percent of all children served under the provisions of IDEA, depending on the degree of overlap among and between these categories and the category of speech and language impairments (see Figure 1.1 and Table 1.1). Students with learning disabilities account for close to 50 percent of all students in special education, whereas intellectual disabilities and emotional disorders account for close to 10 percent each (U.S. Department of Education, 2009).

The definitions for these areas of disability are not now and never have been distinct enough to establish sharp boundaries among and between the categories (Truscott, Catanese, & Abrams, 2005). These learners may all exhibit learning and academic difficulties, problems with cognitive processing of information that includes attention deficits, problems in social–emotional adjustment, and language-related deficits. As was noted by the President's Commission on Excellence in Special Education (2002), these high-incidence disabilities present significant identification

Table 1.1   Students Served in Special Education, by Disability Category (Fall 2004)

Condition	Headcount by Age		Percentage of Population by Age	
	3–5	6–21	Percent of 3–5	Percent of 6–21
Specific learning disabilities	13,736	2,839,694	.11	4.24
Speech/language impairment	333,290	1,151,260	2.77	1.73
Intellectual disability	22,636	567,780	.19	.84
Emotional disturbance	5,853	484,488	.06	.73
Multiple disabilities	8,434	132,033	.07	.20
Hearing impairments	7,824	71,712	.07	.11
Orthopedic impairments	8,599	64,910	.07	.10
Other health impairments	12,838	508,085	.11	.77
Visual impairments	3,322	25,504	.03	.04
Autism	25,929	166,424	.22	.25
Deaf-blindness	259	1,725	.00	.00
Traumatic brain injury	1,054	23,248	.01	.04
Developmental delay	258,175	74,377	2.18	.11
All conditions	701,949	6,118,437	5.87	9.16

Source: Data from *28th Annual Report to Congress on the Implementation of the Individuals with Disabilities Education Act, 2006* (Vol. 2, Tables 1-2, 1-3, 1-11, 1-12) by U.S. Department of Education, 2009, Washington, DC: USDOE.

challenges due to the subjectivity of evaluation along a continuum of human variation. As Hobbs (1975a) predicted, we seem to have learned from our experience in serving youngsters with mild disabilities that knowledge of the classification alone rarely, if ever, provides enough information to plan programs effectively. Given this awareness, it is reasonable to consider the usefulness of looking at the specific characteristics of individual learners as an alternative to categorical services and as a means of achieving more effective program development.

The overlap in characteristics among and between these categories has led many school systems and states to serve these learners with milder levels of disability together in noncategorical or cross-categorical programs, with instructional strategies selected to meet a particular learner's needs. From the 1970s to the present, there has been a steady movement from categorical to noncategorical/multicategorical teacher certification (Cranston-Gingras & Mauser, 1992; Geiger, 2002, 2006; Reynolds & Heistad, 1997). By the 2000s a significant majority of states had some form of noncategorical certification, with remaining categorical certification primarily for teachers of students with hearing and visual impairments (Hardman & McDonnell, 2008).

MILD DOES *NOT* MEAN "NOT SERIOUS"

When the degree of disability is described as mild, moderate, or severe, those levels indicate the extent to which the person differs from others. The more similar the students are to typical students, the fewer the modifications needed to accommodate them in the standard curriculum (Hoover & Patton, 2005). The word *mild* is commonly interpreted as meaning "not a lot." By extension, it is often interpreted as meaning "not serious." A mild cold means you have the sniffles, but basically you are expected to go about your day as usual; it's "not serious." A learner with a mild disability is frequently perceived to require few or minor accommodations to facilitate access to the general education program.

However, before we conclude that a mild disability is less serious than a more severe one, we must consider the effect of being "almost like everyone else." When students look and act similarly to their age peers, parents and teachers tend to have similar academic and behavioral expectations of them. For the most part, milder disabilities tend to be invisible. These students bear none of the physical characteristics that elicit understanding, assistance, or empathy. Physically they appear as if they should be able to learn and behave like typical students. These students can approximate age-appropriate behaviors, but their disabilities may cause them to be enough "off the pace" to compromise their success. When a disability even slightly impairs this ability to function, it can lead to failure in ordinary activities and have disastrous effects on self-esteem and sense of competence (Snell et al., 2009). Let's consider some examples:

Meet John and Jim

John is a student with a severe behavioral disorder. His aggressive behaviors are so severe that he has been placed in a restrictive residential program. There he is served in a structured behavior program and receives counseling and social skills training. No one expects him to function in an ordinary classroom. In fact, no teachers will have him in their classrooms.

Jim, on the other hand, has a mild behavioral disorder. He has problems with impulse control. Most of the time, he functions like the others in his sixth-grade class. When frustrated, however, he is apt to lash out without thinking about the consequences. His teacher tends to respond to him as if his behaviors are volitional and so reacts to these outbursts with punishment. Since Jim looks like the other students, his teacher feels justified in treating him like the others and doesn't believe he needs help with his impulse control disorder. Jim has come to internalize this "bad boy" image.

Meet Jane and Jamie

Jane's birth was a difficult one, resulting in a period of anoxia that left her with cerebral palsy and a severe intellectual disability. As a 16-year-old, she must have all her personal needs met by others. Her special program is designed to increase muscle control and teach her basic daily living skills like self-feeding. Rightly or wrongly, expectations for Jane are low because of her intellectual disability.

Jamie, on the other hand, looks like any other 16-year-old girl. Her mild level of intellectual disability has made learning academic tasks difficult. She can read at about the fourth-grade level and is served in a vocational education program. Because she looks like everyone else and can carry out basic tasks, her parents, teachers, and peers expect her to be able to exercise the social judgment required of a teenager. They were all astonished when she allowed a group of boys to have sex with her, resulting in her becoming pregnant.

When we think of mild disabilities, we must consider the problems of these students as serious and worthy of our understanding and assistance. We must understand that constantly being *almost* able to compete credibly in common activities is very difficult to accept. We must acknowledge the significant effect on a student's self-esteem of not being able to do what everyone else finds easy and of not knowing why. We must seek to understand the effect on a student's ability to function when it is not easily apparent what can be done to change the situation. This awareness should result in an appreciation of the reason so many learners with mild disabilities develop learned helplessness or other inappropriate social behaviors (e.g., noncompliance) when faced day in and day out with expectations that they can't meet and aren't helped to meet. Being "just a little different" can indeed be very serious.

THE POWER OF LANGUAGE

Human beings are distinguished from other animals by our use of a complex symbol system (i.e., language) to communicate with one another. Through language we exchange information, and we communicate our ideas, emotions, feelings, and even our prejudices. As Christensen (2004) observed, "Language reflects our perceptions, beliefs, and understandings of our world. It also helps shape those perceptions. Thus language can exert a powerful influence on social processes which help shape human lives" (p. 17). Language has often been used to categorize and stigmatize groups of people. For example, the use of terms like *retarded* to refer to an entire group of people makes it easier to lose sight of their unique characteristics and to think of them in a devalued way. Because words can mean different things in different contexts, we need to be aware of the effect our words can have.

This book pays special attention to the effect of the words we use to describe these learners, especially the difference between a disability and a handicap. A *disability* is a condition that a person possesses; it is, however, only one characteristic of that individual. A disability is identified when an expected, specific human ability is curtailed or absent. Quite simply, it is the lack of an ability, and it is a describable, measurable condition. By itself, it implies absolutely nothing about the ability of the individual to carry out desired life functions.

A *handicap,* on the other hand, results from the interaction of that condition with the environment. A handicap results when the environment cannot or will not be modified to permit the individual to carry out certain functions. It is this problematic interaction that results in interference with the individual's ability to carry out a desired function (American Psychological Association, 2010; Russell, 2008; Vermont Developmental Disabilities Council, 2007).

For an example of the difference in these two terms, consider Ellen, who has myopia, which results in a measurable lack of distance vision. In fact, her unaided visual acuity is over 20–200 in both eyes. We would be accurate in saying that she has a visual disability since she lacks the visual ability we expect people to have. However, since her vision is amenable to correction and she has been provided with glasses, she is not handicapped in tasks such as acquiring information from text or in mobility (e.g., driving a car). If she broke her glasses or if her vision was uncorrectable with glasses, she would be handicapped in acquiring information from text or in moving around—unless she or her friends or family were able to find another way for her to carry out those functions. Environmental accommodations that would eliminate the handicap might include listening to books on tape or riding to school with a sighted driver. When we think about Ellen, it is quite apparent that the lack of an ability (i.e., having a disability) does not necessarily mean the lack of a function and a resulting handicap.

A related term, *handicapism,* refers to the beliefs and practices that promote differential, unjust, or unequal treatment of a person based solely on an apparent or presumed disability. It involves taking actions on behalf of an individual based on the assumption that the presence of a disability necessarily implies a handicap. Handicapist attitudes or actions include viewing persons with disabilities as victims, as afflicted with their disabilities; pitying persons with disabilities; seeing only the disability and not the person; avoiding people with disabilities; seeing people with disabilities as automatically valiant and brave; and speaking *about* individuals with disabilities in their presence rather than speaking *to* them.

As we work with learners with disabilities of various kinds, we should always use language thoughtfully, communicate accurately, and avoid reinforcing the stereotypes of helplessness and victimization. Some suggestions for more appropriate use of language include these:

- Avoid using shorthand terms like "the handicapped" or "the disabled" to refer to a group of people with disabilities; these terms imply incorrectly that all individuals with that characteristic are alike, that all members of the group are identical in their abilities and needs.
- Avoid using the word *handicapped* as a generic term to refer to people with disabilities; this word implies that a person with a disability is handicapped in functioning, an assumption that is not necessarily warranted.
- Put the person first in sentence construction; this emphasizes the positive individuality of the person. For example, when we say "a student with a learning disability" rather than "a learning disabled student," we imply that the disability is but one attribute of that student.
- Use the active voice rather than the passive voice to diminish the implications of helplessness and victimization. For example, say, "Joan uses a wheelchair for mobility" rather than "Joan is confined to a wheelchair." In addition, avoid using such terms as *victim, suffering,* and *affliction* to refer to the person or to the disability.
- Avoid the use of state-of-being verbs in sentence construction. Say, "John has a learning disability," rather than "John is learning disabled." The first sentence indicates that John possesses a particular characteristic (among many), whereas the second implies a status. If this seems like a minor point, consider whether it would make a difference if you were to say, "John is cancerous," instead of the more usual wording, "John has cancer."

Even the name of the U.S. legislation that governs our work with children and youth reflects the increasing awareness of the potential of language to stereotype. P.L. 94–142, originally titled the Education for All Handicapped Children Act, was renamed the Individuals with Disabilities Education Act (IDEA) in 1990, putting the person first and removing the assumption of handicaps.

LABELING, CLASSIFYING, AND IDENTIFYING

Bogdan and Taylor (1976, 1994) have provided a first-hand view of the life and thoughts of a person with a disability. Ed Murphy is an adult who was classified as a person with an intellectual disability as a child and who subsequently spent a number of years in a state residential school for individuals with intellectual and other severe disabilities. Listen to Ed's own words on labels:

A lot of people are like I was. The problem is getting labeled as something. After that you're not really a person. It's like a sty in your eye—it's noticeable. Like that teacher and the way she looked at me. In the fifth grade—in the fifth grade, my classmates thought I was different and my teacher knew I was different. One day she looked at me and she was on the phone to the office. Her conversation was like this, "When are you going to transfer him?" This was the phone in the room. I was there; she looked at me and knew I was knowledgeable about what she was saying. Her negative picture of me stood out like a sore thumb. That's the problem with people like me—the schools and the teachers find out we have problems, they notice them, and then we are abandoned. That one teacher was very annoyed that I was in her class. She had to put up with me. I was putting her classwork behind. If I were to do it over again, I think I would try harder to make it in school. (pp. 33–34)*

Ed Murphy believed that the classification, or label, he received and the special treatment that followed were caused by the fact that he and his problems in school stood out, that had he tried harder to be like everyone else, he could have avoided being singled out and pushed out of school.

The classification issue is far from simple. Labels affect those who receive the labels, those who give the labels, those who use the labels, and those who live with those who have been labeled. The classification system is designed as a vehicle for communication about a person's disability, although it frequently implies some degree of stigma (Hobbs, 1975a). It affects all future interactions with the individual. Blackman (1989) discussed learners in special education classes as having "been assigned a disability" and referred to them as students with "negative school labels" (p. 459). Norwich (2007) observed that we are faced with a "dilemma of difference." Such classifications have the positive effect of focusing on the individual's needs; however, they also have the negative effect of reflecting lowered status and perpetuating inequality and unfair treatment.

DIVERSITY IN FOCUS 1.1

This chapter highlights a critical issue in the consideration of human diversity and cultural differences—the degree to which we as human beings perceive each other as different, name those differences, and then isolate ourselves from those who are perceived to be different. Our use of language to categorize people—whether by race, ethnicity, language, gender, sexual orientation, socioeconomic class, or ability—carries with it the power to stigmatize and segregate. Our recent history with identifying children as being at risk shows us that when we confront a problem, we tend to attempt to solve it by creating a group to epitomize the problem. We then develop interventions to "fix" that group, that is, to remove or diminish their differences, with limited effectiveness (Brantlinger, 2006).

Our challenge as educators in the 21st century is to assure that programs like IDEA, which were put in place to help solve problems for groups of learners, do not have the unintended outcome of further marginalizing them. We have seen the problems that were created when we provided only segregated services for those with disabilities, and we are moving toward more inclusive practices. However, as long as children are viewed as special education students rather than as students with special learning needs, we have not solved the problem. The history and current practice of special education have tended to see diversity and cultural differences as part of the problem, resulting in actions that further divide human beings. Educators must instead work to be able to answer the only important question: Once placed in special education, do the services students receive enable them to learn more effectively, and is the achievement gap between students reduced or closed (Artiles, Kozleski, Trent, Osher, & Ortiz, 2010)?

The line between typical and exceptional is far from being an absolute. As we will discover when we consider the historical development of the concept of disability, the values and needs of a society or culture determine what constitutes deviance, who is determined to be an outsider, and what response is called for to deal with deviance (Kauffman & Landrum, 2006). The creation of categories of difference serves to define and even reify the boundaries between what is acceptable and typical in that society and what is not (Hobbs, 1975a). Classification can be used to create groups of individuals who are viewed as stigmatized or threatening, and it allows the culture to establish a barrier between those individuals and the "normal" members of society. The barrier between groups can be physical (e.g., an institution wall), or it can be psychological, as when we subtly reduce our expectations of an individual.

To Classify or Not to Classify

A number of justifications have been advanced to support the utility of disability classifications, as have arguments against the use of such categorical labels (Greenspan, 2005). Reasons often given for classifying students with disability labels include these:

- Classification by disability is currently required to qualify a child for services. If we don't place the youngster in a category, the child cannot receive special education services under IDEA.
- Funding schemes generally require reports of children served by category in order to allow for the flow-through of funding; the categories justify the funding. Through classification we are able to control allocation of resources and govern access to them.
- A classification attached to a particular individual may indicate why the individual has been experiencing difficulties in learning and other areas of functioning; it may hold the prospect that specialized help may remediate the problem.
- Some classifications have educational or medical relevance for treatment.
- Categories are useful in conducting educational research, since the classifications are used to define groups for study. Without clearly defined categories for groups of individuals, it is more difficult to combine the research done by different investigators in order to discover useful patterns.
- Classification helps establish justification for specialized professional service providers to interact with that group of individuals; those being served are thought to require special services that can be provided only by professionals with special credentials.
- According to Hobbs (1975a), labeling allows society to maintain stability by identifying and subsequently isolating deviant members—a more subtle explanation.

On the other hand, many problems and unintended outcomes have been attributed to the use of classifications or categories, including the following (Greenspan, 2005; Lipsky & Gartner, 1996):

- Categories tend to rigidify thinking about the prospects for a given individual. They affect teacher and parent expectations of the student, usually in a negative way. Once it is known that a student has a disability, the classification can explain the lack of progress; efforts to help the child learn may be affected in the belief that the child is achieving as well as can be expected and that additional efforts at remediation may not be useful (Lipsky & Gartner, 1996).
- Classifications are often stigmatic. Negative associations with a particular category can be extended to an individual, even when those characteristics are not displayed by that person.
- The individual can "become" the classification, living up or down to the stereotypes carried by that label.
- Classifications related to etiology or medical treatment are frequently of little value for school program planning decisions, as Stevens and Birch argued in their historic 1957 discussion of the terms used to refer to individuals with learning disabilities.
- Psychometric thresholds on tests used to make classification decisions falsely imply sharp demarcations among disabilities and between disability and ability.

- Disability classifications do not convey the specific information needed for designing programmatic interventions, although it is frequently assumed that they do. When a child is identified as a student with a learning disability, parents and teachers may assume that the child displays letter and number reversals and sees words backwards. Such assumptions lead to particular ideas about appropriate interventions, which may have little relevance to a learner's actual problems. When a learner is identified as one who is in need of special education services, we still know very little about the specific manifestations of the given disability until we describe that student's specific characteristics (Greenspan, 2005).
- Funding incentives based on differential funding for certain disabilities or levels of severity may lead to inappropriate or erroneous classifications. If classifying a child gets funding and services, a child whose diagnosis is questionable may be classified simply to justify services. If more funding accrues to particular placement options, children may be placed in settings that are not consistent with their needs. The 1997 IDEA recognized this possibility when it required funding practices to result in neutral effects on placement (Council for Exceptional Children, 1998a; Mahitivanichcha & Parrish, 2005; National Association of State Directors of Special Education, 1997).
- Categories tend to reinforce the notion that the reasons for school failure lie primarily within the student, relieving schools and teachers of responsibility and downplaying the importance of teacher–student interaction in achieving success in school learning.
- Categories tend to serve as explanations for problem behaviors rather than as descriptors of that behavior.

It may be useful here to differentiate between classification and diagnosis. *Classification* is the systematic formation of groups and subgroups based on shared characteristics or traits. The classification does not mean that all members of the group are identical, just that they share some specific characteristics or traits. Classification refers to the formal and systematic conceptual schemes for naming individuals and their problems (Fletcher, Lyon, et al., 2002; Hobbs, 1975a), forming the basis for identification of members of the group.

Diagnosis, on the other hand, refers to the process of determining the nature and impact of a specific individual's disease, condition, or manner of functioning. It is the analytical and descriptive process undertaken to determine etiology, current manifestation of a condition, treatment requirements, and prognosis for the child's condition (Hobbs, 1975a; see Spotlight on History 1.1). Going far beyond the simple act of classification, diagnosis actually determines the factors that are unique to an individual and that are useful or essential in planning an intervention program.

SPOTLIGHT ON HISTORY 1.1

Nicholas Hobbs and the Project on Classification of Exceptional Children

The Project on Classification of Exceptional Children was undertaken in the early 1970s at the direction of Eliot Richardson, U.S. Secretary of Health, Education, and Welfare. He voiced concern about the serious consequences of inappropriate classification of children as *delinquent, retarded, disordered,* or *disturbed.* Noting that there were problems with diagnostic procedures used to classify children, he charged the project team with reviewing the practices and consequences of labeling and with developing recommendations for improving professional assessment practices (Burke & Ruedel, 2008; Kauffman & Landrum, 2006).

The combined efforts of 10 agencies in the Department of Health, Education, and Welfare resulted in the publication of three volumes. *The Futures of Children* (Hobbs, 1975a) summarized the findings of the task force and formulated policy recommendations. The accompanying source books—*Issues in the Classification of Children,* Volumes 1 and 2 (Hobbs, 1975b, 1975c)—contained articles by participants in the study, providing a comprehensive summary of the thinking at the time about problems associated with classification processes.

Hobbs's (1975a) classic discussion of these problems at the beginning of the P.L. 94–142 era made a strong argument for a process based on a description of each individual child's abilities and deficits, revised frequently. He called for a state and federal funding system based on the needs of students rather than on classifications. Concluding his discussion of the categorizing process, Hobbs stated:

> Classification, then, is not a simple, scientific, and value free procedure with predictably benign consequences. Rather, it arises from and tends to perpetuate the value of the cultural majority, often to the detriment of individual children or classes of children. The majority has made the rules, determined what is good, normal, or acceptable, and what is deviant, exceptional, or unacceptable. Classification seeks to identify children who do not fit the norms, who are not progressing normally, and who pose a threat to the equilibrium of the system, so that they may be changed or isolated. Seen in this light, classification becomes a mechanism for social control. It institutionalizes the values of the cultural majority, governs the allocation of resources and access to opportunity, protects the majority from undue anxiety, and maintains the status quo of the community and its institutions. Clearly many of the negative consequences and abuses . . . can be understood and remedied only within this broader cultural context. (pp. 40–41)

> Each child is unique, the center of a unique life space. To design a plan to help him grow and learn requires much specific information about him and his immediate world. The best way we have discovered to get the information needed for good program planning is to construct a profile of assets and liabilities of the child in a particular setting and at a particular time. The profile should describe physical attributes, including salient features of a medical, psychological, and educational evaluation. It should specify what the child can do and what he cannot do, what he can be taught to do, and what is expected of him. It should include the people who are important in his life: parents, brothers and sisters, teachers, a social worker perhaps, or a physician, other children, other significant adults, and also the people who make the profile and plan and carry out a program to help him. Settings are important too: the neighborhood, community center, church, the child's school, sometimes an institution. In effect, a profile of assets and liabilities describes the transactions between the child and people significant in his life, always in particular settings and at particular times. . . . The profile should be the basis for specification of treatment objectives and of time limits for accomplishing goals. (pp. 104–105)

Hobbs criticized simplistic labeling systems for their lack of information capacity and value. For example:

> Jane shows up on summary school records and state reports as "mentally retarded, educable." What is not recorded is that Jane cannot read, that she is attractive and pleasant, that she needs dental care, and that she is very good with children and has held a child care job with a family for five years. There is no record of services needed. (pp. 106–107)

Hobbs asserted that even this simple sketch conveyed far more useful information than the bureaucratic category of "mentally retarded, educable." He held that the current federal and state accounting systems were responsible for "encouraging the neglect of individual differences among children and obscuring their individual service requirements" (p. 108). He concluded:

> When a skilled teacher or therapist or child-care worker undertakes to help an individual child, categories and labels (in their familiar and gross form) recede from the picture. They poorly fit the complex reality of the living child; they provide meager guidance for what to do for him; they are an inherent encumbrance in the educational or treatment process. A stigmatizing label may have to be dealt with as one of the child's problems, but it is essentially useless in the design of a program for him. (p. 113)

To use an example from medicine, the classification process for determining whether a person belongs to the group with diabetes is a blood sugar test. That test, among others, establishes that the person belongs to the general group of people with diabetes. This classification helps the doctor decide about additional diagnostic tests. However, each person with diabetes is unique. Factors such as age, gender, body weight, physical activity level, degree of disability, and emotional adjustment are all investigated and considered as the doctor plans a treatment plan that may include insulin supplementation, diet, physical activities, and other therapies. It is the diagnostic process that guides treatment planning, not the classification of diabetes.

The tendency with disabilities is to stop with classification. Persons working with individuals with an intellectual disability or any other disability often act as if all their clients have identical needs and expectations. Nothing could be further from the truth. The needs of each learner in a special education program are as unique as the needs of individuals with diabetes. We wouldn't dream of giving all persons with diabetes the same dosage of insulin. In a similar way, we must base programming for learners with disabilities on their unique needs, not on their classification.

Another problem with tying programming decisions solely to a classification relates to the observation that learning and behavioral needs lie on a continuum, not in dichotomous or discrete groups. Many schools operate under the assumption that students who do not have a classification are all typical learners and that it is reasonable to expect them all to learn and behave in the same environment. We know that this is not true, but since we do not utilize diagnostic procedures regularly with all children, classified or not, many children struggle in classrooms with instructional programs that do not meet their unique needs. The recent move to classify some students as at risk testifies to this fact. The creation of yet another category is consistent with the assumption that we do not need to provide differentiated programming unless a child is first classified as different. Educators need to examine the logic behind this phenomenon and consider the feasibility of designing diagnosis-based plans rather than using only classification-driven programming. The President's Commission on Excellence in Special Education (2002) suggested reducing the 13 current categories to 3: sensory disabilities, physical and neurological disabilities, and developmental disabilities (Truscott et al., 2005). It is clear that the debate will continue.

Additional Thoughts on Labeling

In response to national concern about educational reform and standards in the 1980s, the Council for Exceptional Children (1997b) developed a policy on labeling and categorizing children that addresses many of these concerns (see Appendix). This policy emphasizes the importance of planning an educational program that is appropriate for a child, based on the learner's individual learning needs and strengths rather than on a label or other external factors. Furthermore, the Council's policy highlights the valuable skills that special educators bring to education reform, namely the knowledge and expertise that enables teachers to provide appropriate, individualized instruction to a variety of learners. This policy underscores the fact that all learners can benefit from an education system that focuses on the educational needs and capabilities of students rather than on a label or category.

Two position papers developed by the National Association of School Psychologists (NASP; 2009a, 2009b) respond to concerns about labels and educational placement. Such policies support alternatives that safeguard the rights of all students while providing for supports based on a student's needs, not on a category of disability (Truscott et al., 2005). In suggesting the possibility of moving toward a unitary system of service delivery, NASP recognizes that although IDEA mandates educational services for students with disabilities, it does not necessarily require a separate special education system (Lipsky & Gartner, 1996). These policies are also in line with IDEA 2004, which supports the use of response to intervention as a planning tool and which requires the use of evidence-based strategies.

THE HISTORICAL CONTEXT OF DISABILITY

The degree to which persons with disabilities are included in social environments is always set in the context of a particular society and time. Economic and social conditions have always defined and driven decisions about the role education plays in a society and about society's response to disabilities and deviance of any kind (Bogdan & Taylor, 1994; Hollenweger, 2008; Kauffman & Landrum, 2006; Safford & Safford, 1996; J. D. Smith, 1998). Changes in social climate have led to changes in the perception of individuals with disabilities. Historical events are a product of the existing social forces, mediated by the personal values and beliefs of the participants. At times it seems that the response of a society to those who differ may serve as an indicator of that society's social progress. Throughout history we see documented trends (although not without some backward steps) toward a greater appreciation of the basic humanity possessed by all members of the society, moving from initially rejecting and neglecting, to tolerating and protecting, and finally to accepting and appreciating those with differences.

The issues surrounding our response to disability and difference have changed over the years. Today we debate issues related to the naming of differences, as we discuss labeling and noncategorical approaches (Kauffman & Landrum, 2006). We consider the degree to which special education may have been used as a tool to keep individuals with disabilities "in their place," as we discuss alternatives in assessment and placement. We make plans and develop programs to address the needs of individuals throughout their life spans and in various contexts, making use of such programs as early intervention, family support mechanisms, transition and vocational services, accessibility programs, and adult services. We now recognize the need to develop the professional skills of teachers and other support personnel, roles not even imagined in previous ages.

To help us understand how we have come to this point, it is useful to review examples of pivotal events in prior eras and ages. Our review will be somewhat cursory as it is impossible to include in a single chapter all of the important events and movements throughout human history. For more detailed treatment of these topics, the reader is referred to the work of Kauffman and Landrum, 2006; Safford and Safford, 1996; and Winzer, 1993, as well as to the special issue of *Remedial and Special Education* (J. D. Smith, 1998). The historical overview here will create a context within which to begin to appreciate our progress as well as to identify continuing challenges as we seek to create a social environment in which all can contribute.

EARLY HISTORY OF DISABILITY

In the classical civilizations of Greece and Rome, noticeable levels of disability were generally viewed as a threat to the economic and cultural vitality of the society. Child abandonment and exposure were widely practiced, usually resulting in the death of the infant. Such practices continued until shortly before the beginning of the Common Era, as a way of ensuring the development of a capable citizenry. When allowed to live, persons with developmental disabilities sometimes served as jesters and clowns.

In the classical period, when treatment was available, it took the form of medical intervention rather than education (Apter & Conoley, 1984). Under Hebraic law, the response to persons with disabilities was more likely to take the form of benign protection. During this early period, those with very severe birth defects would not have survived since the medical knowledge needed to save them did not yet exist. It is also true that only persons with the most severe levels of disability would have been identified as different. In an era when literacy skills were uncommon, persons with milder levels of intellectual disability would simply have merged into the population. By not calling attention to themselves, they would have escaped being singled out for harsh treatment.

THE MIDDLE AGES, THE RENAISSANCE, AND THE ENLIGHTENMENT

During the early years of the Common Era through the Renaissance and the Reformation (100–1700 CE), treatment of persons with disabilities was largely shaped by religious beliefs (Safford & Safford, 1996). The phenomenon of cloistering grew out of the general monastic movements within early Christianity and provided some protection to those with visual or intellectual disabilities. This benign outlook was not shared by Calvin and Luther, who held the belief that society had no responsibility for the welfare of such people. The period of the Reformation was generally characterized by the persecution of persons with disabilities and a return to demonology and superstition. The belief that emotional disorders were the result of demonic possession or other supernatural forces frequently led to severe and abusive treatment of persons with emotional disorders, including torture, exorcism, and witch hunts.

During the Enlightenment (1700s and 1800s), large institutions called madhouses, lunatic hospitals, bedlams, or asylums were established in Europe and America. These facilities were created in response to the higher visibility of persons with significant disabilities (e.g., intellectual disability, mental illness, blindness, deafness, orthopedic disabilities), as well as to house the poor, the widowed, the orphaned, and those with such infectious diseases as tuberculosis. These institutions were created largely to protect society from all those defined as deviant. No therapeutic interventions were available; punishment was the only "treatment" provided.

The French philosophers of this period ushered in a new era (Winzer, 1998). They gave voice to a belief in the natural goodness of human beings, asserting that the ideal society would be one in which everyone's rights were protected. They set about changing the way society viewed itself as well as the individuals who constitute society. In particular, the philosophies of Rousseau and Locke laid the foundation for equal rights for all people, including children and persons with intellectual disabilities (Safford & Safford, 1996).

Philosophers of the Enlightenment focused attention for the first time on the effect the environment can have on an individual's development (Kauffman & Landrum, 2006; Locke, 1690; Safford & Safford, 1996). The experiences that help human beings develop were seen as critical, and it was asserted that society had the power to enhance those experiences through education and training. By the end of the 18th century in Europe, special education was an accepted idea, if not a major force, and psychology and psychiatry had emerged as separate disciplines of medicine. Phillipe Pinel (1745–1826), a French physician and one of the first psychiatrists, literally unchained patients at the Bicetre Hospital in France in 1793 and instituted a regimen of more humane therapeutic treatment. Pinel is credited with introducing the notion of habilitation and rehabilitation (Safford & Safford, 1996; Zigler, Hodapp, & Edison, 1990).

Jean-Marc Gaspard Itard (1774–1838), a student of Pinel, carried out a series of instructional experiments with Victor, a wild boy found wandering in the forest and now assumed to have had an intellectual or an emotional disorder (Lane, 1976; T. E. C. Smith, 1998). Itard published an account of that work, *Wild Boy of Aveyron,* in 1801 (see Spotlight on History 1.2.) His experiments with systematic instruction indicated that persons with conditions such as intellectual disabilities could be taught, although Itard himself was disappointed that he achieved only limited success in teaching Victor to speak (Graham, 1991).

Building on the work of Pinel and Itard and committed to the belief that all children could learn if they were well taught, Edouard Sequin helped to establish schools in France in the 1830s and 1840s for children referred to as "idiots." He brought those principles to the United States in 1848. Throughout this period, the focus remained on individuals with more severe levels of disabilities. With the development of philosophies that supported the educability of human beings and with a growing sense that disabilities might be alterable, the foundation was laid for more supportive services for all persons identified as needing assistance to function more fully in society.

SPOTLIGHT ON HISTORY 1.2

Itard and the Wild Boy of Aveyron

A wild boy—found running in the woods and foraging in the fields in the south of France in 1797, was captured, and then escaped—focused the attention of the professional community and the world on the nature of difference and disability. In many ways, the story of the Wild Boy changed how society then and now thinks about people with disabilities. The boy was finally apprehended and taken to Paris, where he was placed at the Institute for Deaf-Mutes because of his apparent sensory and language deficits. Jean-Marc Gaspard Itard, a French physician, met the Wild Boy of Aveyron there at the end of 1800, and against the advice of colleagues, Itard took on the challenge of educating the "savage." Itard set five goals for his training of the child:

1st aim.   To interest him in social life by rendering it more pleasant for him than the one he was then leading, and above all more like the one he had just left.

2nd aim.   To awaken his nervous sensibility by the most energetic stimulation, and occasionally by intense emotion.

3rd aim.   To extend the range of his ideas by giving him new needs and by increasing his social contacts.

4th aim.   To lead him to the use of speech by inducing the exercise of imitation, through the imperious law of exercise.

5th aim.   To make him exercise the simplest mental operations upon the objects of his physical needs over a period of time, afterwards inducing the application of these mental processes to the objects of instruction. (pp. 10–11)

Sometime later, Itard writes of the naming of the boy:

> One day when he was in the kitchen occupied with cooking potatoes, two people had a sharp dispute behind him, without his appearing to pay the least attention. A third arrived unexpectedly, who, joining in the discussion, commenced all his replies with these words, "Oh, that is different!" I noticed that every time that this person let his favorite "Oh!" escape, the Savage of Aveyron quickly turned his head. That evening when he went to bed, I made some experiments upon this sound and obtained almost the same results. I went over all the other simple sounds known as vowels, but without any success. This preference for "O" obliged me to give him a name which terminated with this vowel. I chose Victor. This name remains his, and when it is called, he rarely fails to turn his head or run up. (p. 29)

Itard's work with Victor is the first detailed account of a therapeutic and instructional program designed to alleviate the effects of a disability. It is the story of a real child with a disability, a real child with a name . . . Victor!

Source: Quotations from Itard (translated by Humphrey/Humphrey), *Wild Boy of Aveyron,* © 1962 by Prentice Hall, Inc. Reproduced by permission of Pearson Education, Inc.

DISABILITY SERVICES IN THE UNITED STATES (1800–1950)

Public special education in America had its roots in the establishment of universal public education in 1837 in Massachusetts. Free public schools were established for the express purpose of socializing all children into the common culture. Even so, it would not be until 1909 that the first compulsory school laws for children with disabilities were enacted in America (Winzer, 1993; Yell, Rogers, & Rogers, 1998).

In the late 1700s in America, Benjamin Rush advocated that corporal punishment and other cruel forms of physical discipline be abandoned in the treatment of children with emotional disorders (Apter & Conoley, 1984; Kauffman & Landrum, 2006; Winzer, 1993). Through these efforts, people of the time began to view mental illness as something to be treated instead of an immutable result of sin (Safford & Safford, 1996; Winzer, 1993). Institutions were slowly established throughout the 1800s to serve youngsters with disabilities too severe for the public schools to serve, including learners with hearing and/or visual impairments as well as those with intellectual disabilities (Apter & Conoley, 1984; Winzer, 1993; Zigler et al., 1990). By 1900 there were 37 residential schools for the blind in the United States, some serving deaf students as well.

In 1848 H. B. Wilbur established a private treatment center in Massachusetts for individuals with intellectual disabilities. At the same time at the Perkins School for the Blind, Samuel Gridley Howe established an experimental program for training individuals with intellectual disabilities (J. D. Smith, 1998; Winzer, 1993). In 1854 the New York legislature asked Wilbur and Sequin to begin a new state school for youngsters with intellectual disabilities. These experimental projects firmly established the residential institution as the treatment of choice for youngsters in America with intellectual or sensory disabilities (Zigler et al., 1990). By 1890 fourteen states had organized institutions designed to serve children with intellectual and developmental disabilities, justifying these institutions on the grounds of expedience, charity, and duty. Concern for the needs of these youngsters with severe disabilities, combined with the inability of the newly forming public schools to handle them and the prevailing emphasis on the medical aspects of disability, led to the establishment of institutions as the predominant provider of special education services beginning in the 19th century.

Isolation from community life in mainstream settings characterized these schools. For the most part, they were set apart from major population areas and were guided by the premise that country living would be the most healthful environment (Winzer, 1993). Promoters of institutionalization during this period said that persons functioning as "mentally subnormal" must be protected and cared for as children, and the "schools" took on the character of asylums.

By 1900 a number of issues were being raised. The cost associated with institutionalization was becoming harder to justify when improved functioning failed to result (Safford & Safford, 1998). The physical and social isolation of the facilities themselves heightened the sense of difference, deviance, and dependency of the persons residing in them. There was discussion about the right to an education for all children and whether or not there were indeed limits to that right. Children and youth like Ed Murphy were institutionalized when their deviance or disability led to problems that could not be accommodated in their schools and communities (Bogdan & Taylor, 1994).

These issues led to the establishment of a two-track system of public educational services—one for typical children, the other for children with disabilities. In particular, children whose disabilities were in the area of behavior usually found themselves outside the schoolyard fence (Apter & Conoley, 1984). Educators frequently found it easier to expel them or to leave their fate to the courts. Learners with deviant behaviors were among the first young people to be provided with education in separate classes (Safford & Safford, 1996). A special education class for "truant, disobedient, and insubordinate" students was opened in 1871 in Connecticut for the purpose of removing difficult or recalcitrant children from regular school programs so that regular classes could proceed without impediment. At the beginning of the 20th century, large institutions served persons with severe disabilities, such as severe intellectual disabilities, emotional disorders, and visual and hearing impairments. Those with less severe disabilities stayed at home. Few attended special education classes.

Eugenics in Europe and the United States

Events in Europe laid the foundation for what was to come in the United States. Charles Darwin's *Origin of the Species* (1859) outlined his theory of natural selection, leading to the articulation of the principles of social Darwinism that heredity alone was responsible for the nature of an individual and that defects could be prevented by eliminating "imperfect people." Francis Galton's *Hereditary Genius* (1869) stated that individual traits, notably intelligence, are inherited and are normally distributed in the general population (Safford & Safford, 1996). In 1883 Galton further refined his theory of *eugenics*, a word he derived from the Greek words for "good stock." In discussing the interaction of nature and nurture, Galton and the eugenicists maintained that society has the power to alter the inborn qualities of future generations by restricting the reproduction of those with defective physical or mental qualities.

Attempting to substantiate these theories, Henry Goddard (1912) traced the genealogy of a girl he called Deborah Kallikak, who resided at the Vineland Training School in the early 1900s (see Spotlight on History 1.3). Goddard was convinced that this work supported the idea that the condition called feeblemindedness was hereditary and that persons with disabilities should not be

SPOTLIGHT ON HISTORY 1.3

H. H. Goddard and the Kallikaks

H. H. Goddard's (1912) historic, though seriously flawed (J. D. Smith, 1985), study of the Kallikak family sought to answer the question of the inheritability of intelligence. As superintendent of the Training School at Vineland in New Jersey, Goddard supervised the Department of Research, established to determine the mental and physical characteristics of children identified as "feeble-minded" (the term for intellectual disability at the time), as well as to determine the cause of such intellectual disability.

Goddard began by relating the story of Deborah Kallikak, who arrived at Vineland from the almshouse at the age of 8. He followed her progress over 14 years, making many behavioral observations, including the following:

> disobedient . . . graceful . . . knows a number of words . . . good in entertainment work . . . plays the cornet . . . played hymns in simple time . . . excellent worker in gardening class . . . helps make beds and waits on table . . . is quick with her work, but very noisy . . . her mind wanders . . . is good in number work . . . her attention is hard to keep . . . knows how to use a sewing machine . . . can write a fairly good story, but spells few words . . . (pp. 2–7)

He concluded with these observations:

> This is the typical illustration of the mentality of a high-grade feeble-minded person, the moron, the delinquent, the kind of girl that fills our reformatories. They are wayward, they get into all sorts of trouble and difficulties, sexually and otherwise, and yet we have been accustomed to account for their defects on the basis of viciousness, environment, or ignorance. It is also the history of the same type of girl in the public school. Rather good looking, bright in appearance, with many attractive ways, the teacher clings to the hope, indeed insists, that such a girl will come out all right. Our work with Deborah convinces us that such hopes are delusions. . . . Today, if this young woman were to leave the Institution, she would at once become a prey to the designs of evil men or evil women and would lead a life that would be vicious, immoral, and criminal, though because of her mentality she herself would not be responsible. The question is, "How do we account for this kind of individual?" The answer is, in a word, "Heredity"—bad stock. We must recognize that the human family shows varying stocks or strains that are as marked and that breed as true as anything in plant or animal life. (pp. 11–12)

Goddard then described the research methods by which his conclusions were reached. Field workers from Vineland collected family tree data on residents over a several-year period.

> Our field worker occasionally found herself in the midst of a good family of the same name, which apparently was in no way related to the girl whose ancestry we were investigating. . . . These cases led to the conviction that ours must be a degenerate shoot from an older family of better stock. (p. 16)

(Continued)

The outcome of the investigation of the Kallikak family led to the compilation of "data" going back seven generations that Goddard believed showed how the defective strain entered this family. He traced the family tree to an illegitimate child born of the "mating" of a Revolutionary soldier named Martin Kallikak with a "nameless feeble-minded girl," a barmaid. Using suspect data (J. D. Smith, 1985), Goddard contended that all the 496 descendants of Martin's marriage to a "respectable girl of good family" were "normal people, including doctors, lawyers, landholders, educators. . . . in short respectable citizens" (pp. 29–30). In contrast, Goddard reported that there were 480 descendants of Martin's liaison with the nameless barmaid, of whom 143 were "conclusively" feeble-minded, 43 were normal, and the rest were doubtful. Goddard also counted 36 illegitimate births, 33 sexually immoral persons, 24 alcoholics, 3 epileptics, 3 criminals, 8 who kept "houses of ill fame," and 82 who died in infancy (pp. 18–19).

This study was used as validation for the eugenics movement, leading for many years to the routine sterilization of persons with intellectual disabilities. According to Goddard's line of reasoning, the only hope for society was to keep such individuals from reproducing and to keep those who *were* born in a protective ghetto so that they could not fall prey to the ills of the environment. He wrote:

> A scion of this [respectable] family, in an unguarded moment, steps aside from the paths of rectitude and with the help of a feeble-minded girl, starts a line of mental defectives that is truly appalling. . . . Fortunately for the cause of science, the Kallikak family in the persons of Martin Kallikak and his descendants are not open to question. They were feeble-minded and no amount of education or good environment can change a feeble-minded individual into a normal one. (pp. 50–53)

Source: Excerpts from *The Kallikak Family: A Study in the Heredity of Feeble-Mindedness* by H. H. Goddard, 1912, New York: Macmillan.

allowed to marry or reproduce. Although Goddard's results have subsequently been discredited on the basis of serious methodological flaws (J. D. Smith, 1985), his efforts and ideas led to the enactment of a number of laws between 1907 and 1958 resulting in the forced sterilization of large numbers of persons with intellectual and other disabilities (Winzer, 1993). The successful enacting of eugenic measures was due less to the power of the argument than to the social and political context of the times: Immigration, two world wars, and the Great Depression raised concern about the future of society. By the 1940s, the popularity of these practices was declining, in part because of the horror generated by the reports coming out of Hitler's Germany (see Figure 1.2), and the use of sterilization as a social tool was largely abandoned.

The Testing Movement in Europe and the United States

The testing movement began in France in 1905 when Alfred Binet and Theophile Simon, at the request of the French Ministry of Public Instruction, developed an instrument to determine mental age (Kauffman & Landrum, 2006; Payne & Patton, 1981). They sought to identify students who were not likely to succeed in the regular school program (Safford & Safford, 1996). Believing that intelligence was a fixed trait, Binet and Simon developed a test to predict a prospective learner's probable success in school and to screen out those who would not benefit from schooling. In 1916 Lewis Terman revised Binet's test for use with Americans. The Army Alpha and Beta Test, the first group intelligence test, was developed in 1917, based on earlier work with individual testing. The results of the widespread use, or misuse, of this test with military recruits suggested that intellectual disability was much more prevalent than once thought, raising alarm about the direction in which society was moving.

Over the next three decades, the Vineland Social Maturity Scale, the Stanford-Binet Intelligence Test, and the Wechsler Intelligence Scale for Children (WISC) were published in the

FIGURE 1.2   A World War II German Propaganda Poster
Source: From *Death and Deliverance: "Euthanasia" in Germany c. 1900–1945* (p. 188) by M. Burleigh, 1994, Cambridge, England: Cambridge University Press.

United States. All of these tests found an enthusiastic audience in the American public because they appeared to provide definitive and simple answers to the difficult questions "Can this person learn? If not, why not?"

One outcome of easily available norm-referenced tests was that there was now a marker for mild disability. Educators could use test results to rank-order children and define a line between "normal" and "disabled." Youngsters did not have to have an obvious disability in the moderate to severe range to be identified by educators as deviant, and students in the milder ranges of disability were identified in ever-increasing numbers. Testing programs and more rigorous school demands made it less possible for students with disabilities to escape notice.

Serving Children Identified as Having Disabilities

By the end of the 19th century, Samuel Gridley Howe and later Alexander Graham Bell had both voiced concern about the effect of serving children in settings that allowed youngsters to associate only with peers with similar disabilities (Winzer, 1993). Howe and Bell believed that this type of residential segregation tended to reinforce and exaggerate disabilities, and both advocated for contact with typical peers to the largest extent possible. They further argued against the removal of children from their family homes unless absolutely necessary. The work of Skeels and Dye (1939) indicated that environmental factors such as attention and interaction significantly affect intellectual outcomes, suggesting the importance of environmental factors in the development of intelligence. This research began to counterbalance the philosophical effect of the eugenicists.

Compulsory school attendance laws were enacted and enforced during the early 20th century in response to increasing numbers of children in the community, notably due to the influx of immigrant children and restrictions on child labor (Safford & Safford, 1996; Yell et al., 1998; Winzer, 2007). The public schools were faced with new challenges from children not previously served in formal educational environments. School districts increasingly addressed these challenges by establishing separate special classes so that students perceived as difficult would not disrupt or interrupt the learning environment in general education classes, nor lower the school's standards for achievement. In many cases, the main purpose of these classes was to manage students who did not conform to the school's behavior standards. Many of these learners probably looked much like learners from diverse cultural backgrounds who still find their way into programs for students with mild disabilities today.

Public school special education classes became more common in the early 20th century as laws mandating education for children with disabilities were passed in a number of states. During the first half of the century, public schools saw school enrollments grow as well as the number of special education classes. Many of the teachers serving these classes had originally been employed in institutional teaching positions. The curricula they implemented in public school special classrooms frequently included heavy emphasis on crafts and manual training activities, similar to the focus in programs they had used in the institutions. In addition, special education curricula often contained a strong component of "social training" designed to teach desired school behaviors.

During this same period, the field of special education was established within the teaching profession. In 1922 Elizabeth Farrell organized a group called the International Council for the Education of Exceptional Children, and the profession of special education came into its own (Kauffman & Landrum, 2006; Safford & Safford, 1998). The Council for Exceptional Children (CEC) has grown from a membership of 50 that first year to over 35,000 today.

DISABILITIES IN THE UNITED STATES FROM 1950 TO THE PRESENT

By midcentury, parents increasingly became active as advocates for their children with disabilities. Disability-specific parent organizations were formed to lobby schools and government for the rights of family members with disabilities. Among these groups were the National Society for Crippled Children (1921), the United Cerebral Palsy Association (1949), the Association for Retarded Citizens (1950), and the Association for Children with Learning Disabilities (1964). These organizations supported families dealing with difficult issues, established local schools and services to meet immediate needs, and fought in the courts and legislatures across the country for governmental support for publicly funded programs. Their tireless efforts and the power of their message were largely responsible for the progress made in the last half of the 20th century (Yell et al., 1998).

Another pivotal influence from Europe was the publication of a monograph by Wolfensberger (1972), describing the concept of normalization (Zigler et al., 1990). Based on concepts developed earlier by Bengt Nirje and other Scandinavian writers, *normalization* refers to the practice of "making available to the mentally retarded and other disabled individuals the patterns and conditions of everyday life which are as close as possible to the norms and patterns of mainstream society" (Nirje, 1969, p. 181). Such practices were believed to reduce the stigmatizing discrepancies between persons with and persons without disabilities. Lloyd Dunn (1968) discussed in similar terms the services being provided to students with mild intellectual disabilities. He questioned the segregation of these students for special treatment, and he called for educators to consider delivering general education services in a more normalized environment (see Spotlight on History 1.4).

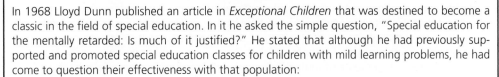

SPOTLIGHT ON HISTORY 1.4

Lloyd Dunn

In 1968 Lloyd Dunn published an article in *Exceptional Children* that was destined to become a classic in the field of special education. In it he asked the simple question, "Special education for the mentally retarded: Is much of it justified?" He stated that although he had previously supported and promoted special education classes for children with mild learning problems, he had come to question their effectiveness with that population:

> A better education than special class placement is needed for the socioculturally deprived children with mild learning problems who have been labeled educable mentally retarded. Over the years, the status of these pupils who come from poverty, broken and inadequate homes and low status ethnic groups has been a checkered one. In the early days, these children were simply excluded from school. Then . . . with the advent of compulsory attendance laws, the schools and these children "were forced into a reluctant mutual recognition of each other." This resulted in the establishment of self-contained special schools and classes as a method of transferring these "misfits" out of the regular grades. This practice continues to this day, and unless counterforces are set in motion now, it will probably become more prevalent in the immediate future. . . . The number of special day classes for the retarded has been increasing by leaps and bounds. . . .
>
> This expensive proliferation of self-contained special schools and classes raises serious educational and civil rights issues which must be squarely faced. It is my thesis that we must stop labeling these deprived children as mentally retarded. Furthermore we must stop segregating them by placing them into our allegedly special programs. . . .
>
> Regular teachers and administrators have sincerely felt they were doing these pupils a favor by removing them from the pressures of an unrealistic and inappropriate program of studies. Special educators have also fully believed that the children involved would make greater progress in special schools and classes. However, the overwhelming evidence is that our present and past practices have their major justification in removing pressures on regular teachers and pupils, at the expense of the socioculturally deprived slow learning pupils themselves. . . . Homogeneous groupings tend to work to the disadvantage of the slow learners and underprivileged. Apparently such pupils learn much from being in the same class with children from white middle class homes. (pp. 5–6)

Dunn also questioned the efficacy of self-contained classes for children with mild disabilities. He cited several studies that indicated that children with mild intellectual disability and emotional disorders did as well or better in regular classes than in special classes. He made the following proposal:

> Existing diagnostic procedures should be replaced by expecting special educators, in large measure, to be responsible for their own diagnostic teaching and their clinical teaching. In this regard, it is suggested that we do away with many existing disability labels and the present practice of grouping children homogeneously by these labels into special classes. Instead, we should try keeping slow learning children more in the mainstream of education, with special educators serving as diagnostic, clinical, remedial, resource room, itinerant and/or team teachers, consultants, and developers of instructional materials and prescriptions for effective teaching. (p. 11)

Dunn called for a moratorium on the expansion of special classes. He envisioned a cadre of specialized educators who would develop curricula and take referrals for diagnostic evaluations, resulting in the development of educational prescriptions. He saw these special educators being available

(Continued)

to help any child who was experiencing difficulty, not only those who had received a disability label. He closed with the following charge:

> The conscience of special educators needs to rub up against morality. In large measure, we have been at the mercy of the general education establishment in that we accept problem pupils who have been transferred out of the regular grades. In this way, we contribute to the delinquency of the general educations since we remove pupils that are problems for them and thus reduce their need to deal with individual differences. The entente of mutual delusion between general and special education that special class placement will be advantageous to slow learning children of poor parents can no longer be tolerated. We must face the reality—we are asked to take children others cannot teach, and a large percentage of these are from ethnically and/or economically disadvantaged backgrounds. Thus much of special education will continue to be a sham of dreams unless we immerse ourselves into the real environments of our children . . . and insist on a comprehensive ecological push—with a quality educational program as part of it. (p. 20)

Even though Dunn's language is somewhat dated by current sensitivities, his message sounds hauntingly familiar. Many of the arguments he raised in 1968 are still being raised today. IDEA sought to respond to these issues, but it remains the task of all educators to find ways to effectively help all children learn.

Source: Quotations from "Special Education for the Mentally Retarded: Is Much of It Justified?" by L. M. Dunn, *Exceptional Children, 35,* 1968, pp. 5–6, 11, & 20. Copyright 1968 by The Council for Exceptional Children. Reprinted with permission.

Another influential movement begun in the latter part of the 20th century has been the general education initiative, or inclusion. Fueled by Madeleine Will's (1986) paper on shared responsibility (see Chapter 3), significant progress has been made toward including learners with disabilities in general education environments for some or all of the school day, and toward delivering their needed accommodations within the general education program (U.S. Department of Education, 2009). The principle of inclusion holds that the general education classroom is an appropriate learning environment for all (or most) children and that special education services can often be delivered more efficiently and effectively in that environment (National Center on Educational Restructuring and Inclusion, 1994). Such a model of service is designed to avoid the fragmentation of services that Will observed in noninclusive special education and compensatory programs. Although the debate about the effectiveness and appropriateness of inclusion for students with disabilities is far from over, it has significantly affected special education in recent years and will likely continue to do so. (See Chapter 3 for more discussion of this topic.)

Legislative and Legal Supports

Changes were also occurring within the political and governmental sphere. By 1952 forty-six of the forty-eight states had passed legislation providing educational services for learners with intellectual disabilities, although these laws did not require educating *all* learners with disabilities. The Elementary and Secondary Education Act (ESEA) of 1965 provided a framework for federal mandates and support of educational programs in local public schools. With the inclusion of support for children in state-supported schools for students with disabilities, the effect of ESEA on special education services went far beyond the funds it provided.

In 1972 the Pennsylvania Association for Retarded Citizens (PARC) successfully sued the state of Pennsylvania on behalf of children with intellectual disabilities for their right to a normalized free and appropriate public education. In the consent decree ending the *Pennsylvania Association for Retarded Citizens (PARC)* v. *Pennsylvania* case, the parties agreed that it was the right of all children in the state, even those with intellectual disabilities, to receive a free and appropriate public education. The provisions of the consent decree formed the basis for the provisions of the federal Education of All Handicapped Children Act in 1975 (Yell et al., 1998).

In 1973 the passage of Section 504 of the Amendments to the Vocational Rehabilitation Act guaranteed equal access for persons with disabilities to all programs and services supported by federal funds, prohibiting discrimination based solely on disability. The act required that reasonable accommodations be made to permit access to programs by people with disabilities. This vital civil rights law remains a basic protection for children and adults with disabilities today (Yell et al., 1998). The Americans with Disabilities Act (ADA) of 1990 later extended these civil rights protections to all persons with disabilities, asserting their right to access to all public services, not merely those receiving federal support.

The 1975 passage of the Education for All Handicapped Children Act (P.L. 94–142) mandated a free and appropriate public education (FAPE) for every school-aged child with a disability in the United States. It established the principle of least restrictive environment (LRE), based on the principle of normalization articulated by Wolfensberger (1972) and requiring that learners be served in those environments in which they can succeed and which are most typical of the environments in which typical peers are educated. Additionally, the law required local districts to assertively attempt to identify all children in their region who might need special education services. "Child Find" efforts in local communities are designed to identify preschool children and others who may not have come to the attention of the schools but who could benefit from special educational services in order to develop maximally.

With the passage and implementation of the Education for All Handicapped Children Act came renewed discussion about classifying and labeling children with disabilities. Because the act tied federal support of special education services to the numbers of children identified with disabilities, there was concern about the effect of labeling on increasing numbers of children. As Hobbs (1975a) stated,

> By *classifying* we mean the act of assigning a child or a condition to a general category or to a particular position in a classification system. . . . By *labeling* we mean to imply more than the assignment of a child to a category. We intend to include the notion of public communication of the way a child is categorized. (p. 43)

Overview of the IDEA Principles

As we begin our study of learners with mild disabilities, it may be useful to outline the major provisions of the Individuals with Disabilities Education Act. The passage of the original legislation in 1975 made identification of and services for students with disabilities the responsibility of schools, districts, and states. In the years since, there have been modifications and additions to the law, including the reauthorization of IDEA in 2004, which continues to provide the foundation for services to children regardless of the severity of their disabilities.

Prior to the passage and implementation of IDEA, fewer than half of the children with disabilities were being served in school programs, and the appropriateness of those programs was debatable (Turnbull, Stowe, & Huerta, 2007). Since the full implementation of P.L. 94–142 (now called the IDEA) in 1978, school districts have been held accountable for assuring that all children are provided with a free and appropriate public education. This provision established the principle of zero reject in public education. No longer could a child be barred from school and educational services because a disability was too severe, because the school didn't have a class or teacher able to handle students with a particular disability, or because the child had not accomplished certain developmental milestones, such as toilet training. All children and youth in the designated age range for school attendance were entitled to a free public education. It became the responsibility of the district and state to determine how to provide that education. In addition to the guarantee of a free and appropriate public education, IDEA established five additional principles to help achieve the aims of the law:

- Nondiscriminatory evaluation
- Individualized education programs (IEPs)

DIVERSITY IN FOCUS 1.2

Throughout history, services for people with disabilities have been determined by the culture and beliefs of the times. In Western cultures, deviance was first feared, then pitied, then avoided (Kauffman & Landrum, 2006). However, as racial groups in the United States began to assert their claim to full civil rights, they laid the foundation for the disability rights movement. Gains made by African Americans in *Brown* v. *Board of Education* provided the basis for legal action to obtain access to quality public schooling for children with disabilities.

Unfortunately, children from racially diverse groups have not always benefited from this increased access. Assessed with discriminatory instruments, African American children and those with limited English proficiency often found themselves classified as students with disabilities when their difficulty in public schools was actually related to cultural and linguistic differences. A series of court cases, including *Diana* v. *State Board of Education* and *Larry P.* v. *Riles,* provided mandates for nondiscriminatory evaluation, including testing in a child's primary language. The courts also required multiple sources of data to support classification decisions. The Education for All Handicapped Children Act codified these rulings into educational law.

However, early in the 21st century, we still see evidence of disproportionality in classification, suggesting that we do not yet have a culturally responsive process for designing appropriate educational programs (National Center on Educational Restructuring and Inclusion, 1994; Skiba et al., 2008). Each year the *Annual Report to Congress on the Implementation of the Individuals with Disabilities Education Act* indicates that there are disproportionate risk indices associated with the race of students (U.S. Department of Education, 2009).

- Least restrictive environment (LRE)
- Parental participation
- Procedural due process

Nondiscriminatory evaluation procedures were mandated for determining eligibility and placement in specialized educational programs. Assessments must include a variety of valid and reliable measures of a child's abilities, the instruments used must be culturally fair and age appropriate, and testing must be in the child's primary language. All evaluations must be performed by appropriately trained personnel, and the child's parents or guardians must give consent for and be informed of the results of the evaluation.

When the evaluation process confirms the presence of a disability requiring special education services, IDEA requires that an individualized education program (IEP) be developed. The purpose of the IEP is to assure that the education provided is appropriate to the learner's needs. Educators and parents collaborate on the IEP team to translate the assessment results into a plan of goals that will guide the student's educational program for the coming year (Turnbull et al., 2007).

Once an IEP has been developed, the team determines the setting most likely to provide the opportunity to achieve those outcomes. IDEA requires that school placements be in the least restrictive environment possible—the setting that most appropriately meets the student's identified educational needs and that maximizes contact with learners without disabilities. A model for thinking about placement decisions is the continuum of services, ranging from the general education classroom to residential placements (Deno, 1970; Reynolds, 1989; Ysseldyke, Algozzine, & Thurlow, 2000). The planning team moves a student in the direction of increasingly restrictive settings only as far as necessary. The team then develops a program of support and instruction that will enable the student to develop the skills and behaviors needed to move as quickly as possible back into settings that are less restrictive and that provide a more normalized school experience.

National data indicate that 52 percent of all students with disabilities are now educated in the general education classroom for 80 percent or more of the school day, another 26 percent are out of the general education class for 21–60 percent of the day, and 17 percent are removed from general education for more than 80 percent of the time. Only 4 percent are served in segregated facilities or

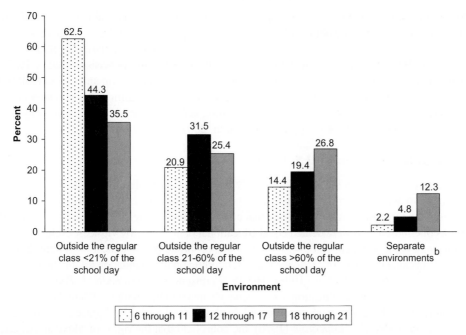

FIGURE 1.3 **Percentage of Use of Placement Options Outside the General Education Classroom, by Age Group (2004)**

Source: From *28th Annual Report to Congress on the Implementation of the Individuals with Disabilities Education Act, 2006* (Vol. 1, p. 53) by U.S. Department of Education, 2009, Washington, DC: USDOE.

residential placements (U.S. Department of Education, 2009). The national trend over the 1984–2006 period has been increasingly to serve students with disabilities in the general education classroom and in regular school buildings (see Figure 1.3 and Table 1.2). However, a troubling trend revealed by the same data indicates that African American students are more likely than their peers in other racial groups to be placed in more restrictive educational environments (Skiba, Poloni-Staudinger, Gallini, Simmons, & Feggins-Azziz, 2006).

Throughout the evaluation, planning, and placement process, IDEA holds that parents are central to all decisions. The procedures reaffirmed in the 2004 IDEA reauthorization assured that parental participation would be an expected event, recognizing the importance of different perspectives in understanding the needs of a particular student. Parents are viewed as an important source of information about the strengths and needs of a learner and as essential partners in the delivery of services.

The Education for All Handicapped Children Amendments of 1986 extended the act's provisions to children from birth to age 5. In addition, the amendments added a requirement for transition planning during the adolescent years to aid in the transition to postschool environments. In

Table 1.2	Percentage of Students with Disabilities (Ages 6–21) Educated in General Education Classrooms and School Buildings (1986–2004)					
	1986	**1990**	**1994**	**1998**	**2002**	**2004**
General education classroom for more than 80% of the day	26.4	32.8	44.5	47.4	48.2	52.1
General education school building	93.9	94.4	95.7	95.9	96.0	96.0

Source: Data from U.S. Department of Education annual reports (2001, p. III-2; 2006b, p. 33; 2009, p. 51), Washington, DC: USDOE.

ON THE WEB

**Building the Legacy:
IDEA 2004**
(http://idea.ed.gov/) is a
U.S. Department of
Education portal to
information about IDEA
2004, including early
intervention, special
education, and related
services for infants and
toddlers with disabilities,
from birth to age 2 (Part C),
and for children and youth
ages 3 to 21 (Part B).

1990 Congress changed the name of the special education law to the Individuals with Disabilities Education Act, reflecting the philosophy of considering a person first before a given disability. In 1997 and again in 2004, Congress amended this landmark legislation, clarifying its provisions and bringing IDEA into alignment with key No Child Left Behind provisions. IDEA 1997 included requirements governing access to the general education curriculum and accountability for learner progress. IDEA 2004 added language concerning teacher qualifications and strengthened the requirement that the response to early intervening services be evaluated before considering special education (Council for Exceptional Children, 2007; Mandlawitz, 2006).

History of Rights Won in U.S. Courts

The modern civil rights era began when the U.S. Supreme Court ruled in 1954 that racially separate education was inherently unequal and, by implication, inferior. In *Brown* v. *Board of Education,* the Supreme Court established that education was the right of every child, stating that the rights of children who were denied equal educational opportunity by virtue of exclusion or segregation were being violated. Access to a free and appropriate public education for children with disabilities became the focus of subsequent cases, building on the foundation established by *Brown* v. *Board of Education* (Yell et al., 1998). The 1972 consent decree in *PARC* v. *Pennsylvania* established the right to public education for all Pennsylvania children with intellectual disability.

Other cases dealt with inappropriate and discriminatory testing and placement procedures. In *Diana* v. *State Board of Education* (1970), the court held that the rights of Mexican American students had been violated when they were placed in classes for students with intellectual disabilities on the basis of intelligence tests that were culturally biased and were not given in the students' primary language. In 1984 the courts ruled in *Larry P.* v. *Riles* that Larry's school district had violated the rights of African American students by using culturally biased intelligence tests as the sole indicator for placement (MacMillan & Forness, 1998). The court substantiated this claim with data showing that disproportionate numbers of minority children were being served in special education classes in San Francisco schools.

In *Mills* v. *District of Columbia Board of Education* (1972), the court heard a case on behalf of seven children with disabilities who had been excluded from attendance because the school district asserted that it could not afford the cost of the services required by these children. The court stated that the burden of funding shortages could not weigh more heavily on students with disabilities than it does on those served in regular education. This case provided the foundation for the due process components of IDEA (Yell et al., 1998). See Table 1.3 for other cases that have upheld the basic rights of children with disabilities to equal educational opportunity (Yell, Ryan, Rozalski, & Katisyannis, 2009).

TRENDS IN HISTORY

The history of special education, according to Reynolds (1989), has been characterized by a degree of progressive inclusion. He noted that even though there are still many children with disabilities in the world who receive no education at all, children with disabilities in the United States have progressively received more education, and they have received it closer to home and more often in the company of their typical peers. He identified four progressive, albeit gradual and as yet incomplete, trends in the history of special education, including the following:

- Moving from distal to proximal arrangements
- Shifting from separation to integration
- Changing the purpose of evaluation from making decisions about selection and rejection, to making placement decisions and designing IEPs
- Shifting from the use of program options that might be characterized as "two-box arrangements" (e.g., special education vs. general education) to service delivery in a single "one-box" system, including an integrated continuum of services for all students

Table 1.3   Additional Court Cases Supporting Equal Access to Educational Services

1972   *Wyatt* v. *Stickney (AL)*

Institutionalized persons have a right to treatment, including education, based on their 14th- and 8th-amendment rights.

1979   *New Mexico Association for Retarded Citizens* v. *New Mexico*

New Mexico violated Section 504 by failing to include all school-age children in an appropriate educational program; this ruling led to New Mexico's agreeing to adhere to P.L. 94–142.

1982   *Board of Education* v. *Rowley*

Districts are responsible for procedural due process under the Education for All Handicapped Children Act, but mandatory services are limited to those required in order to provide educational benefit to a child.

1984   *Irving Independent School District* v. *Tatro*

Medical treatment (e.g., clean intermittent catheterization) needed for a child to attend school is a related service that schools must provide.

1984   *Smith* v. *Robinson*

Parents must exhaust remedies through IDEA before pursuing court action under other statutes; this decision was later overturned by act of Congress clarifying the nonexclusivity of actions taken under special education law on behalf of a child with a disability.

1988   *Honig* v. *Doe*

Suspension or expulsion represents a change of placement for students with disabilities. If the behavior that resulted in the removal from school is deemed to be the result of a disability, the multidisciplinary team must determine a more appropriate service plan.

1989   *Daniel R. R.* v. *State Board of Education*

To ensure placement in the least restrictive environment, schools must determine (a) whether services can be provided in a general education classroom with supplemental aids and (b) whether the child has been mainstreamed to the maximum extent possible.

1989   *Timothy W.* v. *Rochester (NH) School District*

Regardless of the severity of a disability and the amount of expected benefit, every child is entitled to a free and appropriate education.

1993   *Oberti* v. *Board of Education*

Placement in a general education setting must be offered prior to consideration of a segregated setting; a student cannot be excluded just because modifications are required.

1993   *Florence County School District 4* v. *Carter*

Parents are entitled to reimbursement for private tuition if the private school provides an appropriate education and the public school fails to do so.

1999   *Cedar Rapids Community School* v. *Garrett F.*

Students requiring intensive and continuing (nonphysician) health services to enable them to attend school must have those services provided as related services, regardless of their cost.

2005   *Schaffer* v. *Weast*

The party seeking relief under IDEA bears the burden of persuasion.

2006   *Arlington Central School District Board* v. *Murphy*

Plaintiffs may recover fees only for legal representation, not for expert consultants.

2007   *Winkelman* v. *Parma*

Parents and children both have enforceable rights under IDEA; this ruling affirms the importance of the parental role.

The transition from distal to proximal services is exemplified most clearly by the shift from historical placement in large, isolated residential institutions to the more common practice in recent years of placing children in the neighborhood schools they would be attending if they had no disabilities. This move normalizes the life experiences of children with disabilities by keeping them in their neighborhoods and communities so that they can engage in all their expected family and friendship relationships (Winzer, 2007).

In previous centuries and generations, children with disabilities were separated from their typical peers either by death or by placement in institutions. Even when kept at home, children with disabilities were closeted, hidden from view. They had no contact with mainstream society, and they had little or no access to peer role models displaying typical behaviors. Increasingly, such children are now integrated within their neighborhoods and schools (Mitchell, 2004). The principle of least restrictive environment increases the probability that they will spend at least part of their day in integrated mainstream settings and that they may even receive all of their support services in such settings.

Early public special education efforts operated on a selective basis. Children with disabilities were tested and then may have been denied access to education programs based on their level of impairment. Likewise, children were selected into special programs based on a variety of evaluation criteria. Programs with an educational mission selected only those who they thought could benefit from those programs. Adapting programs to meet individual needs was not a common occurrence. Children whose disabilities were too severe could have been denied access even to special education. With the implementation of IDEA, assessment is now used to determine the most appropriate placement and program for children, not to exclude them from participation. Placement teams interpret the available information, determine the likelihood of success in a particular setting, and determine what supports will help students be successful in those settings.

Reynolds's fourth trend is the most incomplete at this time. Traditionally, we have had a two-box system, general education for most learners and special education for those who don't fit into the general education program. Over the years, the special education box has changed its configuration from a large, isolated institution to a special school, to a special class, to a resource room. However, educators still seem to believe that a student with a disability is the responsibility of the special education program and staff. The general education initiative (GEI), or inclusion, encourages special and general educators to look at their roles differently, to see themselves as professionals within a unitary system with a continuum of services available to all children who need them. Educators are also being asked to consider the possibility that the presence of a disability is related more to the context than to some innate characteristic of the individual, and that disability may not be a chronic state.

Summary

A significant majority of students served in special education programs today have intellectual disabilities, learning disabilities, attention-deficit/hyperactivity disorders, or emotional or behavioral disorders. Each of these high-prevalence conditions is characterized by difficulties with cognition, learning, language, and behavior. An integrated perspective on these conditions allows educators to have a more comprehensive understanding of the students they serve.

The majority of learners with disabilities have milder forms of disability. Nevertheless, mild disabilities still cause significant problems for students. Often the disabilities go undetected, leaving the students to struggle on their own. In addition, the students are often blamed for their lack of achievement or their problem behavior. Studying various aspects of mild levels of disability can also be helpful in working with learners whose problems are not severe enough to be classified as a disability.

The language we use to describe students with disabilities conveys much about our view of them. Consistent use of person-first language requires us to consider the individual a person and not a disability. Classifying and labeling raise complex philosophical and political issues with positive and negative implications. Central to this discussion is the fact that IDEA currently requires that students be classified in order to receive services. IDEA, however, contains procedural requirements (nondiscriminatory evaluation, LRE placement, IEP development, due process, and parental participation) that reduce the negative implications of labeling.

In our review of the historical contexts of special education, we have seen societal responses change from rejection to protection, to isolation, to integration. In each case, the response of society to those with disabilities has been determined by the demands and values of their times. During the 20th and 21st centuries in the United States we have moved steadily toward more integration and education in normal environments. We have found ways to provide effective education in normalized environments, and we have committed ourselves through our federal and state governments to doing so. We have seen treatment of those with disabilities make the transition from distal, segregated services for those who qualified, to more proximal, integrated services for all based on their needs. We are moving toward the day when a unitary society will include all its citizens and will meet the needs of each individual as fully as possible.

....

A Case Study • Ed Murphy

For the most part, the historical record of special education has been told through the words of those providing services. Recently, as we have sought to expand beyond our own limited experience of what it is like to be deemed different, we have begun to seek out the perspectives of those judged to be exceptional themselves (Safford & Safford, 1996). Through autobiography and ethnographic interviewing, and following in the tradition established by Edgerton (1967), Bogdan and Taylor (1976, 1994) sought to see the world from the perspective of those thought of as "other," specifically through the eyes of two individuals labeled as having intellectual disabilities. Bogdan and Taylor sought to understand the interactions of these individuals in their cultural milieu, and to reveal the degree to which those interactions defined the individuals, both in the eyes of others and in their own eyes. As the life stories of these two individuals unfolded, it became clear to Bogdan and Taylor (1994) that the participants viewed the programs designed to help them somewhat differently from the way those providing the services saw the programs. The authors also became aware that it was the perceptions of the participants that really determined the outcomes.

When Bogdan and Taylor first met Ed Murphy, he was working at a sheltered workshop. As they got to know Ed better, they sensed the richness of the story he had to share. Over several years, they recorded numerous extended interviews with Ed, which they reproduced in their book *The Social Meaning of Mental Retardation*. It is from this book that the information in this case study is drawn.

Ed was born in 1948 with a variety of developmental disabilities. His mother was told he would probably not live and certainly would never walk. Nevertheless, she refused to give up on him, and in 1954 he began school. At age 11, he was finally removed from regular class and placed in special education. His parents died when he was 15, and after a brief period living with neighbors and in foster care, Ed was placed in a state residential training school for individuals with mental disabilities. He remained at "Empire State School" for almost 5 years. After an additional 4 years of "family care," he moved to a boarding house, and shortly thereafter, at age 25, he began working in a nursing home.

As one reads Ed's story, the power of his story and his perceptiveness shine through. Ed credits his language ability to being a good listener and to hours spent listening to television. The editing of the interviews may be responsible for some of the strength of the narrative, but Bogdan and Taylor assert that they have faithfully represented the man in his own words.

Despite the level of his functioning, the psychologists assigned Ed the label of mental retardation. The diagnosis was justifiable given the standards of the time, since Ed's intelligence test scores ranged from only the high 40s to the low 60s over the years. To put perspective on these scores, here are Ed's own words about what the label *retarded* has meant in his life:

There is discrimination against the retarded. There are people out of ignorance who have hurt retarded children. It really doesn't help a person's character the way the system treats you. One thing that's hard is once you're in it, you can't convince them how smart you are. And you're so weak you can't convince them how smart you are. And you're so weak, you can't really fight back. Some of the help you get isn't help. Like the way they talk to you, "I'll help little Eddie . . . you're so nice." Not that I'm saying that they intentionally treat you that way.

I'm talking like an expert. I had to live it. Shit, I'm not really different. I only had different experiences in my life than you. When you are talking about state schools you need experts. Experts are people who have lived it. I'm not taking anything away from scholars who have sat for years in offices and know the problem. But I know the problem too. (pp. 29–30)

I don't know how old I was when I started talking. It takes time to learn little things when you're handicapped. It's not easy to learn to tie your shoe. Not to know these little things when you're young and everyone else knows them is hell. (p. 31)

My family had problems and it was all over the block that I was this kind or that kind of kid. In school, growing up, it was the same kind of thing. It's very annoying because it follows you around. My mind was slow. I can't deny that. A lot went on when we were kids. My mom and dad weren't really ready for us. They got in over their heads. The family was bogged down. (p. 32)

In elementary school my mind used to drift a lot. Concentrating was almost impossible. I was so much into my own thoughts—my daydreams—I wasn't really in class. I would make up stories in my head. I would think of the cowboy movies. The rest of the kids would be in class and I would be on a battlefield somewhere. The nuns would yell at me to snap out of it, but they were nice. That was my major problem all through school, that I daydreamed. I think a lot of people do that. It wasn't related to retardation. I think a lot of kids do that and are diagnosed as retarded but it's nothing to do with retardation at all. It really has to do with how people deal with people around them and their situation. I don't think I was bored. I think all the kids were competing to be honor students but I wasn't interested in that. I was in my own world—I was happy. I wouldn't recommend it to someone, but daydreaming can be a good thing. I kind of stood in the background—I kind of knew I was different—I knew that I had a problem, but when you're young you don't think of it as a problem. (p. 33)

The way the other kids treated you was a kind of invisible meanness. The meanness you have to look carefully to see. I would get pretty upset when I was teased, but then I learned I had to keep control of myself. It's a lot harder to do that when you're weak. The teasing was one thing, but here was this meanness that you couldn't see that kept after you. (p. 36)

Looking back on it now, when I was in special classes—it really wasn't fair a lot of things that happened. One thing that I remember is that we didn't have a representative on the school senate. We should have been able to vote. We weren't represented. If we had representatives we could have had the advantages the others had. There was a time that everyone voted.

The big thing to get to understand is what the hell is going on around you. They kept us away from the others. The important thing when talking about teaching the retarded child is that we have to teach him to do it for himself. That is real hard. (p. 37)

If you're going to do something with a person's life you don't have to pay all that money to be testing them. I had no place to go. I mean here I am, pretty intelligent, and here are six psychologists testing me and sending me to the state school. How would you feel if you were examined by all those people and then wound up where I did? A psychologist is supposed to help you. The way they talked to me, they must have thought I was pretty intelligent. One of them said, "You look like a smart young man," and then I turned up there. I don't think the tests made any difference—they had their minds made up anyway. . . .

When the psychiatrist interviewed me he had my records in front of him—so he already knew I was mentally retarded. It's the same with everyone. If you are considered mentally retarded there is no way you can win. There is no way they give you a favorable report. They put horses out of misery quicker than they do people. It's a real blow to you being sent to the state school. (p. 40)

Your first day at the institution is an unusual day. It's not like any other day in your whole life. The thing that's so different is, you are different. You're different, the people you are going to be with are different. Going there makes you feel different. I couldn't describe it, but I do think that. I think I almost knew what I was in store for, but on the other hand, I had no idea. I did know about Empire before I went, but I didn't know what it was. When I got to Empire the word "retarded" was something I had to deal with. I had my own way of thinking about myself—I had my own little world. Looking at it from that point of view, I don't know if I looked at myself from the point of view of me being retarded. I knew I had problems when I went to Empire, but I wasn't sure how I thought about it. (p. 42)

I almost didn't make it. . . . I don't like the word "vegetable"—but in my own case I could see that if I had been placed on that low-grade ward I might have slipped to that. I began feeling myself slip—they could have made me a vegetable. If I would have let that place get to me and depress me I would still have been there today. Actually it was one man that saved me. They had me scheduled to go to P-8—a back ward—when just one man looked at me. I was a wreck. I had a beard and baggy state clothes on. I had just arrived at the place. I was trying to understand what was happening. I was confused. What I looked like was P-8 material. There was this supervisor, a woman. She came on the ward and looked right at me and said: "I have him scheduled for P-8." An older attendant was there. He looked over at me and said, "He's too bright for that ward. I think we will keep him." To look at me then I didn't look too good. She made a remark under her breath that I looked pretty retarded to her. She saw me looking at her—I looked her square in the eye. She had on a white dress and a cap with three stripes—I can see them now. She saw me and said, "Just don't stand there, get to work." (pp. 43–44)

It's funny. You hear so many people talking about IQ. The first time I heard the expression was when I was at Empire State School. I didn't know what it was or anything but some people were talking and they brought the subject up. It was on the ward and I went and asked one of the staff what mine was. They told me 49. Forty-nine isn't 50 but I was pretty happy about it. I mean I figured that I wasn't a low grade. I really didn't know what it meant but it sounded pretty high. Hell I was born in 1948 and 49 didn't seem too bad. Forty-nine didn't sound hopeless. I didn't know anything about the highs or lows but I knew I was better than most of them. (p. 55)

The narrative continues with Ed's account of his transition to adulthood, including living arrangements and jobs. In closing the narrative, Bogdan and Taylor (1994) recorded Ed's reflections on the issue of disability and handicap at that point in his adult life:

I never thought of myself as a retarded individual, but who would want to? I never really had that ugly feeling down deep. You're not knowledgeable about what they are saying behind your back. You get a feeling from people around you—they try to hide it, but their intentions don't work. They say they will do this and that—like they will look out for you. They try to protect you, but you feel sort of guilty. You get the feeling that they love you but that they are looking down at you. You always have a sense of a barrier between you and the ones that love you. By their own admission of protecting you, you have an umbrella over you that tells you that you and they have an understanding that there's something wrong—that there is a barrier.

As I got older, I slowly began to find myself becoming mentally awake. I found myself

concentrating—like on television. A lot of people wonder why I have good grammar—it was because of television. I was like a tape recorder—what I heard, I memorized. Even when I was ten or twelve I would listen to Huntley and Brinkley. They were my favorites. As the years went by, I understood what they were talking about.

People were amazed at what I knew. People would begin to ask me what I thought about this and that. Like my aunt would always ask me about the news—what my opinions were. I began to know that I was a little brighter than they thought I was. It became a hobby. I didn't know what it meant, that I had a grasp on a lot of important things—the race riots, Martin Luther King in jail—what was really happening was that I was beginning to find something else instead of just being bored. It was entertaining. I didn't know that meant anything then. I mean I didn't know that I would be sitting here telling you all this.

When you are growing up, you don't think of yourself as a person but as a boy. As you get older it works itself out—who you are deep down, who you ought to be. You have an image of yourself deep down. You try to sort it out. What is happening to it? You know what you are deep inside but those around you give you a negative picture of yourself. It's that umbrella over you.

The fact that you have a handicap follows you around. People don't like the word. We persecute people. The child goes through everything, and all of a sudden—you're marked with a big "R." By the time you reach the situation you're going to grow into, there isn't too much difference with what people are going to say about you.

People tell you you are handicapped in different ways. You're in a restaurant and you may see people watching you eat and people make excuses for you. They go over and talk to them. They say, "The kid is retarded." Make an excuse for him. I've seen that. I've heard them say it, but you love them so you put up with it. For some reason you put up with it.

It makes me sad to see someone who is forty years old taking a child's lunch box to work. It almost makes me want to cry. It's not easy, because parents don't want to let go. Right now schools discriminate against the retarded. You can mix handicapped with regular kids, but they won't do it. Parents of normal kids don't want the retarded kids in their school. I think if they got the kids in there when they were younger, then they would grow up being used to each other. The rest of the world can think of you as retarded, but you don't have to think of yourself as retarded. (pp. 86–87)

Ed Murphy reveals himself to be a knowledgeable informant about the nature of the social context from which the construct of intellectual disability is drawn. His story helps us see the contradictions involved in dividing people into two groups: the "normal" group and those with intellectual disabilities. He helps us see that in many important ways, the notion of disability or handicap is derived from how each of us sees ourselves and others.

Discussion

If the only information available to you was that Ed Murphy had the label of mild-to-moderate intellectual disability based on measured IQ scores in the range of 40 to 60, what would you actually know about Ed Murphy? Make a list.

Next, make a list of what you know about Ed Murphy from these excerpts from his life narrative as recorded by Bogdan and Taylor. Then, compare the two lists, and discuss the implications of this information and analysis with respect to the process of diagnosis and classification.

CHAPTER 2

Issues in Assessment and Identification

Questions *to Guide Your Study*

- What are the IDEA assessment and identification requirements?

- In what three ways can students with disabilities meet the requirements of state and district assessment programs?

- How can accommodations on high-stakes tests be used in a valid manner?

- For what four purposes are assessments generally conducted?

- How do norm-referenced and criterion-referenced assessments differ? What are the advantages of using other assessment techniques such as performance assessment and portfolios?

- What is the purpose of grading? How might that purpose best be achieved?

- What is meant by the phrase *social construction of disability*?

- What does the term *noncategorical alternative* to identification mean? What are the implications of a noncategorical process for identifying and serving youngsters with learning and behavioral differences?

- How does response to intervention (RTI) support

Meet Jeffrey

Jeffrey is an active student in Mrs. Greene's third-grade classroom. He has struggled academically since the beginning of the year, but even more troubling to Mrs. Greene is his behavior. He seems to always be doing something other than what he is assigned to do. She says that if he would mind his own business as much as he minds everyone else's, he'd be fine. She is concerned that he is not learning and that his behavior is beginning to affect the learning of others.

Mrs. Greene finally decides to pick up a special education referral form from the office. Filling it out, she describes the central problem this way:

Jeffrey's academic performance is significantly lower than that of the other students in the class, with specific problems in reading. He is struggling with the second-grade reader. His lack of attention leads to his not doing assignments or to doing them incorrectly. He shouts out in class, disturbs others, and engages in a variety of other off-task behaviors.

Screening by the special education teacher determined that Jeffrey should receive a full evaluation to determine whether a disability existed. After securing his mother's permission, the school psychologist administered a series of tests including assessment of cognitive ability and academic achievement. She also administered the Formal Reading Inventory and had

both identification and instructional planning? How does RTI support prevention efforts?

Mrs. Greene complete the Connors Teacher Rating Scale as well as the Behavior Rating Profile. Finally, the special education teacher conducted a direct observation of Jeffrey in Mrs. Greene's class, coding instances of inappropriate behavior during three 1-hour periods.

The multidisciplinary team determined from the testing that Jeffrey had a delay in acquiring basic academic skills, particularly in reading, but that the problem was not severe enough to classify him as having a learning disability. The behaviors, although certainly bothersome, did not appear to be significantly different from those of other children, and since his academic performance was not significantly affected, he did not meet the criteria for placement as a child with a behavioral disorder.

Mrs. Greene was puzzled. She and Jeffrey needed extra help, but it appeared that they would not be able to get it through the special education process. What was she to do now?

THINKING QUESTIONS

What additional questions might you ask to supplement the data that was gathered during Jeffrey's formal evaluation? What might No Child Left Behind (NCLB) and IDEA suggest as a next step in using assessment to address Jeffrey's difficulties?

ASSESSMENT AND EVALUATION REQUIREMENTS IN IDEA

An appropriate place to begin this consideration of assessment and identification of learners with mild disabilities is with a discussion of the assessment requirements in U.S. special education law. In the IDEA amendments of 1997 and 2004, Congress sought to clarify and modify the basic IDEA requirements established in 1975, with the aim of improving the quality of programming for children and youth with disabilities. Congress focused attention on outcomes for student learning and on increasing the accountability of states and districts for outcomes related to high performance standards for all students, including those with disabilities. Assessment continues to play a major role in serving youngsters with disabilities today (Council for Exceptional Children, 1998a, 1998b, 2010; Fletcher, Coulter, Reschly, & Vaughn, 2004; Hardman & Dawson, 2008; Holdnack & Weiss, 2006; National Association of State Directors of Special Education, 1997, 2004; Yell & Shriner, 1997). Schools must use a variety of procedures to assess students' abilities and disabilities prior to identification and placement and to monitor students' progress toward their IEP goals and objectives after placement (Fletcher & Vaughn, 2009; Fuchs & Fuchs, 1986). Technically sound assessment instruments must be used when evaluating students' abilities in such areas as cognitive functioning, behavior, physical capabilities, and developmental progress. Such tests must be normed on a population appropriate for the purpose and must not discriminate against students on the basis of such variables as race, cultural background, language, or disability. Assessments must be provided in the child's primary language (e.g., Spanish, Russian) or mode of communication (e.g., sign language, motoric responses). Schools are specifically directed to gather and use information about progress in the general education curriculum for all students considered for or served in special education programs.

The effect of a disability on a student's involvement and progress in the general education curriculum must be evaluated and addressed by an IEP team. Multidisciplinary teams must consider all existing data, including data supplied by parents, in making determinations of disability and in designing educational plans. The team is expected to identify and accommodate strengths as well as deficits in designing an individualized education program (van Swet, Wichers-Bots, & Brown, in press).

Reevaluations of student performance must occur at least every 3 years. It is, however, no longer required to repeat all previous testing or to gather additional data unless parents or teachers feel it is necessary. Reevaluation is now a process of reviewing existing information and gathering additional information only if necessary to determine whether a disability still exists.

Teachers must report to parents regularly and in a meaningful manner on student progress. This makes periodic and routine performance assessment even more of a necessity. The parents of each child in special education should be provided with a progress report related to the child's

IEP goals as frequently as parents of students in general education classes are provided with their children's progress reports. In the case of parents from diverse linguistic backgrounds, reports must be in a language they can understand.

The 1997/2004 IDEA amendments posed one new requirement for students with disabilities (Ysseldyke et al., 2004). As of 1997, states had to ensure that all children with disabilities were included in state and district assessment programs, with modifications as appropriate. States are also required to establish performance goals for all learners with disabilities, and annual performance assessments must be reported to the U.S. Secretary of Education and to the public. These reports provide an indicator of the effectiveness of special education programs and the state's progress toward meeting the goals set for youngsters with disabilities, just as annual assessment reports do for students without disabilities. This inclusion in state and district assessments applies to all learners unless it can be shown that no portion of the general education curriculum is applicable to that student. Those few students for whom participation in the general education curriculum is inappropriate because of the severity of their disabilities must be provided with an alternative standardized assessment process.

Accountability for student outcomes is now the goal of the law. According to the U.S. Department of Education (2006b), by 2002–2003 forty-nine states had developed guidelines for participation in assessments, use of accommodations, and use of alternate assessments. It is clear from these initiatives that students with mild disabilities are expected to participate fully both in the general education curriculum and in state and district assessments, and also that schools are responsible for seeing that all learners have the opportunity to learn (Yell & Shriner, 1997).

These new requirements have met with some concern. For many years, it has been conventional wisdom that such tests are inappropriate measures of the achievement of students with disabilities. IEP teams have routinely waived participation of students with disabilities in state and district testing programs, substituting the individual assessments associated with the students' annual reviews (Council for Exceptional Children, 1998b). In IDEA 1997, however, Congress established only three acceptable means to demonstrate progress toward meeting state, district, school, and individual goals for students with disabilities:

- Students can participate in the regular state and district assessments without any modifications or accommodations.
- Students can participate in the regular assessments with accommodations as necessary to ensure that the results are valid indicators of student achievement (Cox, Herner, Demczyk, & Nieberling, 2006; Fletcher et al., 2006; Ketterlin-Geller, Alonza, Braun-Monegan, & Tindal, 2007). Acceptable accommodations relate to the way in which a test is administered, not to the content of the test, and can include some or all of the following (Edgemon, Jablonski, & Lloyd, 2006; Heumann & Warlick, 2000; Salend, 2008):
  - *Flexible settings* (e.g., testing in a separate room, in a small group)
  - *Difference in timing or pacing* (e.g., splitting the test into sections, rearranging the sequence of test sections, allowing extended time to complete sections of the test)
  - *Alternative presentation formats* (e.g., having test questions read aloud, paraphrasing or demonstrating directions, using taped questions or a sign language interpreter)
  - *Alternative response formats* (e.g., oral responses, use of a computer, use of a scribe for written essays)
  - *Linguistically based accommodations* (e.g., translating tests, clarifying vocabulary, using understandable or familiar language)
- Students for whom no part of the general education curriculum and assessments is deemed appropriate because of the severity of their disabilities must be assessed using specially designed alternative state assessments (Elliott & Roach, 2007; Kohl, McLaughlin, & Nagle, 2006; Towles-Reeves, Kleinert, & Muhomba, 2009).

In addition to the mandate that all children participate in state and district assessments, IDEA 2004 stipulates that states and districts "shall, to the extent feasible, use universal design principles in developing and administering assessments" (IDEA 2004, 118 Stat. 2688). The

ON THE WEB

The **National Center on Educational Outcomes** (http://education.umn.edu/nceo) provides resources for assessment of students with disabilities, with a specific focus on state- and district-level assessment programs.

purpose of requiring universal design in preparing assessments is to assure that the test will measure the content and/or skills it purports to measure and not an unrelated ability affected by the student's disability (Acrey, Johnstone, & Milligan, 2005; Meyer & Rose, 2006; National Joint Committee on Learning Disabilities, 2004). This requirement increases the likelihood that the tests will actually measure the target knowledge and skills, rather than having the results obscured by a learner's disability. For example, a science test should assess science content knowledge and not a student's ability to read. By employing universal design principles (see Chapter 3), schools and states increase the number of students who can participate in these assessments without accommodations. (See also Universal Design for Learning in Action 2.)

UNIVERSAL DESIGN FOR LEARNING IN ACTION 2

Supporting Assessment of Student Learning

The purpose of assessment is to determine whether a student has achieved the goals of instruction. If a student's difficulty in reading or writing presents problems in completing an assessment task, then the purpose of assessment has not been achieved. If a student is unable to work quickly enough to complete a task, one cannot be sure whether he/she lacks the skill or just needs more time. Although it is possible to use accommodations to retrofit assessments to match the needs of particular students, it is more efficient and effective to design the assessments so that most students can complete them as presented (National Joint Committee on Learning Disabilities, 2004). The Center for Applied Special Technologies (CAST; 2008) suggests planning assessments to provide multiple and flexible means of expression. Specifically, CAST notes the value of designing assessments that provide options for physical responses, varying levels of expressive skills, fluency of responses, and organizational/executive functioning.

In designing assessment content, consider the following:

- The characteristics of the students who will complete the assessment
- The backgrounds of the students in the class, avoiding terms that are likely to be outside their experience
- The content that was taught and for which students can reasonably be held accountable, avoiding aspects that were not taught or that are irrelevant to the content (National Joint Committee on Learning Disabilities, 2004)
- The level of assessment demands, ensuring that core content is clearly assessed
- The addition of challenge items to assess the learning of more advanced learners (Wiggins & McTighe, 2001)

In designing assessment methods, wherever possible include the following:

- Different types of tasks related to the same instructional goals
- Choices in the manner in which students can demonstrate content or skill competence (e.g., individual or small group; in class or outside of class; flexible time to complete; nature of the task itself)

In designing assessment materials, follow these suggestions:

(Acrey et al., 2005; National Joint Committee on Learning Disabilities, 2004):

- Use simple, clear, direct language, with special emphasis and care in composing directions.
- Design materials to be clearly presented, simple and straightforward.
- Review materials for readability (e.g., font style and size; use of white space; clear directions and sectional breaks).
- Consider the time available for task completion; time constraints increase anxiety, and the resulting performance often poorly reflects students' actual competencies.

IDEA 2004 added response to intervention (RTI) as an additional indicator of the need for special education services, building on the general IDEA requirement that students should not be found to have a disability if they have not had the opportunity to learn (Bradley, Danielson, & Doolittle, 2007; Council for Exceptional Children, 2007; Fletcher & Vaughn, 2009; Zirkel & Krohn, 2008). RTI holds that the first step in meeting learner needs is to provide high-quality general education, followed by progress assessment. The results of that assessment can be used to identify the effectiveness of the instruction as well as to determine which students appear to be candidates for more intensive early intervening services within general education.

RTI also assumes a new role in identifying learning disabilities (see Chapter 5). In response to Jeffrey's story at the beginning of this chapter, IDEA 2004 would now specify that, as part of the referral process, his teacher should describe the effectiveness of the early intervening services that were provided, the extent to which Jeffrey's response differs from that of other students, and the extent to which his underachievement is unexplained.

PURPOSES OF ASSESSMENT OF STUDENTS WITH SPECIAL EDUCATIONAL NEEDS

When assessing students, we are most interested in methods for acquiring information that can be used to describe learners' current functional capabilities in a variety of areas and that can be used over time to monitor their progress. Educators use such information for several purposes:

- Classification: To determine whether a learner has a disability (American Association on Intellectual and Developmental Disabilities, 2010)
- Diagnosis: To provide specific information about the impact of a child's disability in order to design appropriate individualized interventions and supports (American Association on Intellectual and Developmental Disabilities, 2010)
- Formative evaluation of progress: To document student growth or progress as the basis for determining the effectiveness of the learning activities provided and for making changes if improvement is not indicated (Boston, 2002; Dorn, 2010; Espin, Shin, & Busch, 2000; Fuchs & Fuchs, 1986; Mitchell, 2008; Stecker, Lembke, & Foegen, 2008; Volpe, Gadow, Blom-Hoffman, & Feinberg, 2009)
- Summative evaluation of progress: To make decisions about a learner, such as whether a learner has demonstrated sufficient mastery of skills to move to another level or grade (Whitelock, 2010)

TYPES OF ASSESSMENT INSTRUMENTS AND TECHNIQUES

To most effectively achieve the purposes just listed, educators must utilize a variety of instruments and procedures. In fact, IDEA requires that multiple sources of information be used for all special education determinations (Holdnack & Weiss, 2006). Because a full discussion of these practices is beyond the scope of this text, the reader is encouraged to consult current texts and journals on assessment for a more detailed description (e.g., McLoughlin & Lewis, 2008; Overton, 2009; Taylor, 2009; Venn, 2007).

Norm-Referenced Assessment

Some purposes of assessment require that the evaluator compare the performance of a specific learner to typical children of that age or grade. Norm-referenced tests permit such comparisons (Dykeman, 2006). In creating a norm-referenced test, a new or revised test is given to a significant number of comparable individuals (the normative sample), and those scores are then used to derive standard scores that describe typical performance among the sample participants. The test is then given to other students, and the scores of those students are compared to the derived sample scores. From this comparison, a determination is made about the degree to which a specific student performs less well than, the same as, or better than others of the same age or grade. Examples of norm-referenced tests include these:

- Intelligence/aptitude tests (e.g., WISC-IV, Stanford-Binet 5, KABC-II)
- Achievement test batteries (e.g., K-TEA-II; PIAT-R; WIAT-III)
- Diagnostic achievement tests (e.g., Test of Written Language 4; KeyMath 3)
- Adaptive behavior scales (e.g., AAIDD Diagnostic Adaptive Behavior Scale; Vineland-II)
- Behavior rating scales (e.g., Behavior Rating Profile–2; Burks Behavior Rating Scales–2)

Norm-referenced tests are useful for these purposes only if the technical qualities of the instrument are adequate. IDEA and good practice require that tests used to determine the presence of a disability must be normed on populations similar to the individuals being tested if the conclusions drawn from those comparisons are to be valid. This suggests that the normative sample should be inclusive of the racial and language groups in the general population and that individuals with disabilities should be explicitly included in the normative sample if we are to assume that the test is valid for testing such learners. If the test is being given to a learner who uses a language other than English, the test must have been normed in the translated version as well as in the English version. Tests must be *reliable* (i.e., yield similar scores on repeated administrations) as well as *valid* (i.e., measure what they say they measure).

Norm-referenced instruments are useful when comparable measures of performance or aptitude are required, such as for identification and classification or for general placement in graded curricula. Such tests are based on the notion that there is a general body of knowledge and skills that all children, wherever they live and regardless of the schools they attend, should have learned by a certain age. However, these tests are not generally useful in providing the specific information needed for program planning. It cannot be assumed that the test content matches and measures accurately the learning experiences provided in any particular classroom or school curriculum. Additionally, those administering such assessments must be familiar with and observe the standards for fair and responsible testing and interpretation as outlined by the American Educational Research Association (1999), the Joint Committee on Testing Practices (2004), and the National Joint Committee on Learning Disabilities (2004).

ON THE WEB

Fair Test: The National Center for Fair and Open Testing (www.fairtest.org) works to eliminate bias in testing and supports the use of authentic assessment in place of standardized measures.

Criterion-Referenced and Curriculum-Based Assessment

Criterion-referenced or curriculum-based assessment is an alternative to norm-referenced tests that is generally more useful in diagnosis and program planning. Rather than comparing an individual to others as norm-referenced tests do, criterion-referenced tests are designed to determine whether a learner has achieved mastery of specific skills or learning objectives.

Criterion-referenced assessment is particularly useful when combined with task analysis, the process of identifying the subskills required to ultimately achieve a terminal objective (Childre, Sands, & Pope, 2009; Wiggins & McTighe, 2001). After identifying the subskills essential to the desired outcome, the evaluator can devise a series of measures to determine whether a student has achieved the prerequisite and component skills identified in the task analysis (see Table 2.1). Criterion-referenced tests are most often created by teachers or teams of teachers to assess curricular outcomes in a specific district, school, or class, although such tests can also include more formal, published tests. Examples include the state assessment systems required by NCLB/Elementary and Secondary Act (ESEA) to assess learner performance in grades 3–8, the Brigance inventories (Brigance, 2010a, 2010b, 2010c), and the chapter and periodic tests that accompany most reading and mathematics basal series.

Whether criterion-referenced tests are teacher-made or are published in a standardized format, the purposes are the same: to determine whether a student can perform a specific set of skills, to document the amount of learner progress toward a longer-term goal, and to determine whether the student is ready to progress to the next stage of learning. Such instruments can be

Table 2.1 Example of a Task Analysis

Terminal Objective

Given a picture prompt, the student will write a paragraph composed of at least five complete sentences with a clear topic, supporting details, and a concluding sentence.

Task Analysis

Identify parts of a complete sentence (subject and predicate).

Determine whether a sentence is a complete thought.

Write a complete sentence that has a subject and a predicate.

List details relating to a given topic or prompt.

Write a topic sentence.

Write detail sentences.

Write a concluding sentence.

Organize sentences into a coherent paragraph.

used to track progress on social behavior goals as well as academic learning (Volpe et al., 2009). The effectiveness of these instruments in providing useful information depends on how closely they match or are aligned with the instructional activities engaged in by the students in a specific educational program or curriculum (Allsopp et al., 2008; Dykeman, 2006; Roach, Niebling, & Kurz, 2008; Stecker et al., 2008).

Performance Assessment

Concern over the validity of information derived from the traditional processes of norm-referenced and criterion-referenced testing has led teachers, schools, and states to look for other more authentic and valid indicators of student achievement. Increasingly, the new generation of assessments includes items and tasks that require students to demonstrate the ability to apply their knowledge and skills while completing complex and extended tasks, rather than simply choosing answers on multiple-choice examinations. Students are now sometimes asked to develop free-response answers and to work with others.

Performance tasks generally require a learner to use more complex thinking and reasoning and to construct answers. They also often involve direct observation of the student completing relevant, meaningful tasks similar to those found in the real world. These assessments provide evidence of academic learning but also allow assessment of a learner's ability to transfer knowledge and skills to real-world settings. Such assessments emphasize meaning and involve the performance of tasks perceived to have intrinsic value. Through observation and analysis of performance, teachers can better determine the nature and quality of the thinking processes employed by a student (Coutinho & Malouf, 1993; Dykeman, 2006; Schnitzer, 1993). Performance tasks are believed to have stronger validity, especially with learners from diverse cultural and linguistic backgrounds as well as with students whose various disabilities may prevent them from performing accurately on more typical standardized assessments (Darling-Hammond & Friedlaender, 2008; Dean, Salend, & Taylor, 1993; Johnson, Penny, & Gordon, 2008).

Portfolio Assessment

Portfolio assessment combines performance assessment with evaluation of permanent products. A portfolio is a collection of student work gathered over a period of time and intended to show the full range of student endeavor and accomplishment (Gorlewski, 2010). Such collections have been used for many years in performance areas such as art and music, but they are now also finding their place in the battery of general assessment techniques (Salend, 1998). In addition to deciding which work they will include in their portfolios, students are usually asked to select what they believe to be their "best piece" and to explain why.

As Mills (1996) related in his description of the implementation of a statewide system of portfolio assessment in Vermont, assessment guidelines must be established to permit the use of portfolios in place of current standardized tests for accountability purposes. Scoring rubrics can be devised to evaluate portfolio artifacts and to reveal more clearly what students have learned in comparison to what they were expected to learn. Trained evaluators use the rubrics as they review the portfolios to determine whether the evidence supports the claim that students have achieved their learning objectives.

Functional Behavioral Assessment

ON THE WEB

The **Center for Effective Collaboration and Practice** (http://cecp.air. org) focuses on improving assessments of and services for students with problem behaviors. The **Center on Positive Behavioral Interventions and Supports** (http://www.pbis. org) provides technical assistance to identify, adapt, and sustain effective schoolwide positive behavioral supports.

Functional behavioral assessment is the process of gathering information about a learner's behaviors in order to determine the purpose of a problem behavior in addition to its antecedents and consequences. IDEA 1997 instituted this requirement for any student who exhibits problem behaviors, regardless of the defined disability (Barnhill, 2005; McConnell, Hilvitz, & Cox, 1998; Ryan, Halsey, & Matthews, 2003). By identifying the purpose of a behavior and describing its context, teams are able to design more effective behavioral interventions, including positive behavioral supports (Shippen, Simpson, & Crites, 2003; Strout, 2005; Sugai, Horner, & Sprague, 1999). Key to this process is developing a hypothesis about the function of the behavior, determining what need the behavior may be fulfilling for the student. Common purposes include seeking or avoiding attention, escaping difficult or painful situations, or gaining control of some element in one's environment. Plans for effective positive behavioral support use the results from the functional behavioral assessment to identify alternative and acceptable ways for a student to meet personal needs (Simonsen, Sugai, & Negron, 2008). To be effective, these behavioral plans must be based on recent, meaningful assessment data properly collected and interpreted (Etscheidt, 2006).

REPORTING ON STUDENT PROGRESS: GRADING

The report card is a long-standing tradition in U.S. schools. Every 6 to 9 weeks, students take home a card on which a teacher has recorded symbols that are presumed to indicate the level of achievement attained by the students during that marking period. The ritual of showing the card to parents or guardians (or of trying to find a way not to!) is a common experience of childhood.

Common, that is, except for students with disabilities who have not always participated fully in this rite of childhood. Being excluded from general education classroom settings has sometimes meant that a student's work is not assessed/graded as the work of others is and that parents do not receive regular progress reports on their child. Sometimes a brief narrative note or an alternative grading system is used, but often the annual IEP review replaces more frequent periodic reporting. Special educators often view the typical listing of academic subjects along with letters or numbers as irrelevant for their students with disabilities.

Now that IDEA requires that parents of children with disabilities receive information on their children's progress as often as other parents do, schools and teachers are faced with the challenge of constructing a reporting system that communicates useful information to these parents. The purpose of grading—and report card grading in particular—is the central issue. Grades are meant to be communication vehicles (Carpenter, 1985; Guskey, 2002; Munk & Bursuck, 2004; Stanley & Baines, 2004). Thus, any system of grading must be clear and precise if it is to be useful. If the message intended by the recorder of the grade is not interpreted correctly by the receiver of the report, then the purpose has not been met.

Studies of grading practices with students with disabilities (Bursuck et al., 1996; Munk & Bursuck, 1998, 2004) indicate that teachers often believe that adaptations to grading are reasonable, but a majority also believe that adaptations should be available as needed to students with or without disabilities. Responsibility for grading is often shared between general and special education teachers. Such shared responsibility should support the necessary communication between general and special educators and help ensure that teachers are using the symbolic system in a uniform way, enhancing communication with parents.

There are a variety of methods for communicating information regarding learner progress, with many writers suggesting use of multiple-symbol grading systems, which use separate symbols to convey different messages (Glasser, 1990; Jung & Guskey, 2007, 2010; Munk & Bursuck, 2001a, 2001b, 2004; Salend, 2001; Salend & Garrick Duhaney, 2002; Silva, Munk, & Bursuck, 2005; see Table 2.2). Good practice suggests that each symbol should be clearly defined and should convey only one piece of information. If grades are based on modified standards, the report must be clear about the level of the work being assessed if the communication function is to be realized (Jung & Guskey, 2007, 2010).

Table 2.2 Examples of Options for Reporting on Student Progress	
Letter or Numeric Averages	Symbols are used to summarize student performance on tests and other indicators.
Pass/Fail (or No Grade) System	P/F grading denotes mastery of objectives; "no grade" option indicates work still in progress.
Multiple Symbols	Separate symbol systems indicate ability, achievement, and/or effort.
Grade-Level Symbols	Achievement symbol is paired with the symbol indicating the grade level at which the student is working.
Weighted Grading Systems	Learning activities are given varying weights in computing a final grade; this can be varied to meet student learning styles.
Personalized Grading Plans	Student, teacher, and parent design an individual grading system that reflects communication needs and individual differences (Munk & Bursuck, 2001a).
Improvement Grades	Grades are based on changes in performance from period to period.
No Progress Grades	Option for performance not yet indicating mastery (Glasser, 1990).
Competency Checklists	Objectives are rated as "completed," "in progress," or "not attempted."
Narrative Reporting	Teachers provide narrative comments on student learning activities and progress; these comments may supplement letter/numeric grades or serve as the sole reporting system.
Portfolio Grading	Grades are based on evaluation of a portfolio and are guided by a rubric.
Contract Grading	Grading is based on a teacher/student contract identifying standards and requirements for specific grades.
IEP Reporting	Grades are based on accomplishment of IEP objectives; status relative to mastery of objectives is reported.
Combination Systems	This system uses a variety of these practices to better communicate to parents and others.

Sources: Based on Bursuck, Munk, and Olson, 1999; Carpenter, 1985; Cruz and Petersen, 2002; Glasser, 1990; Jung and Guskey, 2007; McMillan, Myran, and Workman, 2002; Munk and Bursuck, 2001a, 2004; Salend, 2001; Salend and Garrick Duhaney, 2002; Silva, Munk, and Bursuck, 2005.

BEST PRACTICES IN ASSESSMENT OF CHILDREN AND YOUTH WITH DISABILITIES

From this discussion and a review of the assessment literature in general, a number of principles emerge that help define best practices in assessment and evaluation of all students, including those with mild disabilities. Frequent and ongoing assessment of student achievement toward established goals is critical to good educational planning and program delivery. The use of formative curriculum-based assessment helps guide educators in determining when learning has occurred and when additional instruction and support are required (Dorn, 2010; Fuchs & Fuchs, 1986; Mitchell, 2008; Stecker et al., 2008).

Use of multiple tools is necessary, since each type of assessment yields only a portion of the information and not all children respond maximally on all kinds of tests (Holdnack & Weiss, 2006). The recent emphasis on the results of norm-referenced tests is likely to be ineffective because such tests relate only in the most general way to any particular curriculum. Teachers, districts, and states must create valid and effective criterion-referenced performance measures, as well as portfolio and performance assessments, to document student achievement, and all such measures must relate directly to the curriculum as taught.

Attention must be paid to the validity of all assessment measures with diverse learners. Students from differing cultural and linguistic backgrounds may not be well served by some standard assessment techniques. Learners with various disabilities may not respond well to certain types of assessment even though they have the skills and knowledge being tested. Some types of tests interact poorly with certain types of learners (e.g., timed tests with students with learning disabilities or ADHD; tests in English for students whose primary language is not English). Increasingly, teachers and administrators are finding that extended performance tasks and portfolio assessment enable many students to more adequately demonstrate what they have really learned. Finally, as IDEA 2004 requires, use of the principles of universal design will help make assessments more accessible, valid, and reliable for all learners (National Joint Committee on Learning Disabilities, 2004).

Now that students with mild disabilities will be taking mandated state and district tests, with or without modifications, attention should be paid to the curriculum provided to these learners as well. Good practice requires that the curriculum, teaching techniques, and assessments be aligned, ensuring that the curriculum established for the children of the state or district is the curriculum that is taught and tested (Hoover & Patton, 2005; Roach et al., 2008). Caution should be used with materials designed for remedial purposes to assure that they support the general curriculum outcomes fully.

When IEP teams design modifications for state and district tests for particular students, the goal is to identify the accommodations that will allow each student to demonstrate what he or she really knows and can do. It is important for special educators to know their students well enough to suggest appropriate accommodations and to be able to explain and sometimes defend the legitimacy of those modifications to others. Tests must measure the learners' skills and content knowledge, not their disabilities (Ketterlin-Geller et al., 2007).

ISSUES IN IDENTIFICATION

The task of identifying students in need of special education services by using an appropriate classification system is far from simple, as we will discover in Chapters 4–8. The definitions used to develop operational criteria for identifying students with specific disabilities have been and still are subject to frequent debate and change, as well as to uneven implementation, particularly for conditions in the mild ranges of impairment (Aebi, Metzke, & Steinhausen, 2010; Dombrowski, Kamphaus, & Barry, 2006; Flanagan, Ortiz, Alfonso, & Dynda, 2006; Fletcher, Lyon, Fuchs, & Barnes, 2007; Kavale, Spaulding, & Beam, 2009; Merrell & Walker, 2004; Nelson & Kauffman, 2009; Polloway, Patton, Smith, Lubin, & Antoine, 2009; Solanto & Alvir, 2009; Wahlstedt, Thorell, & Bohlin, 2009).

The instructional groups resulting from these classification processes are far from being the homogeneous groups that researchers and educators had envisioned, much as Dunn (1968) foresaw so many years ago (see Chapter 1). The needs of students with mild disabilities are extremely variable. Learners vary in their cognition, language, academic performance, and social–emotional adjustment. The attributes of two students within the same classification may differ significantly, whereas two learners in different disability categories may present very similar profiles of strengths and needs. Identifying a specific learner as being within a classification falsely implies a similarity of that learner to others in the classification, resulting in the possibility of inappropriate intervention planning. As an alternative, the use of simple, direct assessment of progress is recommended as a way of determining which students are in need of more intensive assistance to maintain adequate progress (National Association of School Psychologists, 2009a, 2009b).

Susan and William Stainback (1987) asserted that when we actually look at the data about the performance of individual children, we find that the actual information available is much more specific and precise than any categorical label can be and that categories are of limited use in educational planning. These authors maintained that the only purpose of the categorical system was to rule some students eligible for assistance while denying others, a situation that may militate against a coherent plan for meeting the needs of all youngsters.

Studies of instructional practices in self-contained special education classes (Algozzine, Morsink, & Algozzine, 1988; Morsink, Soar, Soar, & Thomas, 1986; Vannest & Hagan-Burke, 2010) reported that special education teachers in general use a variety of pedagogical techniques associated with effective teaching and learning. No significant differences were identified among teachers with respect to the category of students on their caseloads. Instruction in classes for students with learning disabilities was similar to that in classes for students with emotional disorders and in classes for students with mild intellectual disabilities. Although learners in a particular category do share some attributes, they differ on others (Reid, Epstein, Pastor, & Ryser, 2000; Sabornie, Cullinan, Osborne, & Brock, 2005; Sabornie, Evans, & Cullinan, 2006). For this reason, the categories to which learners may be assigned seem to be of limited information value in educational planning, and the overlap of characteristics across categories is often more significant than the average differences among groups. Educators should proceed with caution in assuming that a category designation can be used as a guide to planning.

Since 1975 many writers have questioned the need for and validity of creating two dichotomous groups of students, one special and one regular, or "normal" (Gartner & Lipsky, 1987; Reynolds, 1989; Reynolds & Heistad, 1997; Stainback & Stainback, 1984; Will, 1986). These writers have asserted that all students are individuals with multiple characteristics that vary on one or more continua. Disability definitions create an arbitrary cutoff point on one or two of those characteristics at the most and, in so doing, designate some learners as deviant and in need of special services, whereas others like Jeffrey are found to be ineligible.

This focus on deficits as the defining characteristic of an individual concerned Madeleine Will (1986), former U.S. Assistant Secretary for Special Education and Rehabilitative Services. Will questioned a system that restricted special assistance to only those students who demonstrated serious levels of disability, saying that such a system focused only on failure. She noted that the very language used within special education is a "language of separation, of fragmentation, of removal" (p. 412), and she called for all levels of government and both general and special education to find ways to resolve these problems. Jenkins, Pious, and Peterson (1988) noted that programs based on a categorical identification of students with a variety of difficulties in school are often disjointed and fragmented, with duplication and conflicting methods sometimes employed with the same child. The same concerns persist today (Frattura & Capper, 2006).

Concerns about the validity of defining categories of students are reinforced by questions about the validity and reliability of many of the norm-referenced instruments used in the

Table 2.3   Percentage of the Student Population (Ages 6–21) Served Under IDEA, by Disability and Race/Ethnicity (Fall 2004)

Disability	American Indian/ Alaska Native	Asian/ Pacific Islander	Black (Not Hispanic)	Hispanic	White (Not Hispanic)	Total Population (Ages 6–21)
Learning disability	7.50	1.73	5.65	4.74	3.86	4.2
Speech/language disability	2.29	1.24	1.82	1.58	1.77	1.7
Intellectual disability	1.04	0.41	1.87	0.59	0.69	0.8
Emotional disturbance	1.13	0.21	1.38	0.43	0.69	0.7
All disabilities	13.67	4.57	12.44	8.33	8.65	9.0

Source: Data from *28th Annual Report to Congress on the Implementation of the Individuals with Disabilities Education Act, 2006* (Vol. 1, pp. 42, 47) by U.S. Department of Education, 2009, Washington, DC: USDOE. Retrieved from http://www2.ed.gov/about/reports/annual/osep/2006/index.html.

identification process. The validity of the content of achievement tests is of concern because of the likelihood that either the content itself or the way it is presented and tested does not align with the specific curriculum to which a learner has been exposed (Roach et al., 2008). If the tests are not valid or reliable, it is legitimate to ask how their cutoff scores can be used meaningfully to classify some learners as having disabilities.

The identification of a disproportionate number of students from diverse racial and linguistic backgrounds as needing special education (see Table 2.3) gives further cause for concern (Artiles, 2003; Artiles et al., 2010; Kalyanpur & Harry, 2004). Disproportionate representation is defined as "the extent to which membership in a given group (ethnic, linguistic, or gender) affects the probability of being placed in a specific disability category" (Oswald, Coutinho, Best, & Singh, 1999, p. 198). Disproportionate identification patterns have also been studied with respect to gender and socioeconomic backgrounds (Coutinho & Oswald, 2005; Oswald, Best, & Coutinho, 2006). Identification procedures that purport to be objective and scientific nevertheless result in the identification of students in numbers that are significantly different from the demographics of the general population. This finding suggests that the tests and identification procedures may be responding to gender, socioeconomic, cultural, or linguistic differences rather than identifying legitimate differences in learning abilities and needs. Green, McIntosh, Cook-Morales, and Robinson-Zanartu (2005) suggested that as implementation of response to intervention becomes more widespread, the flexibility of the academic environment to meet students' needs may improve, and the inappropriate disability identification of African American students and others experiencing problems in learning may decrease.

Finally, the effect of differential funding patterns on the rates of identification and decertification in various states suggests that the procedures used for confirming the existence of a disability do not form an objective science. Some state funding schemes reward districts for more restrictive placements or penalize districts for decertifying students who appear to no longer need full services (Council for Exceptional Children, 1997b; Mahitivanichcha & Parrish, 2005). To underscore this concern, IDEA now specifically addresses this issue by requiring states to revise any funding policies that have rewarded districts for placing learners in settings that are more restrictive than the students need. States are required to ensure that funding policies have a neutral effect on identification and placement decisions.

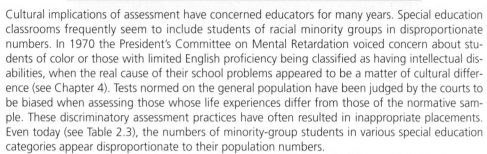

DIVERSITY IN FOCUS 2.1

Cultural implications of assessment have concerned educators for many years. Special education classrooms frequently seem to include students of racial minority groups in disproportionate numbers. In 1970 the President's Committee on Mental Retardation voiced concern about students of color or those with limited English proficiency being classified as having intellectual disabilities, when the real cause of their school problems appeared to be a matter of cultural difference (see Chapter 4). Tests normed on the general population have been judged by the courts to be biased when assessing those whose life experiences differ from those of the normative sample. These discriminatory assessment practices have often resulted in inappropriate placements. Even today (see Table 2.3), the numbers of minority-group students in various special education categories appear disproportionate to their population numbers.

Educators will need to continue to address these issues. For example, consideration must be given to the differences in acceptability of certain behaviors in the general environment as compared with a learner's specific culture. In addition, consideration must be given to the extent to which the behaviors of concern may be related to forms of bias, including sexism, racism, and homophobia (Kauffman & Landrum, 2006).

Use of more authentic assessments may provide more accurate and valid indications of students' strengths and needs. Working with families and members of the community may also provide important insights into the behaviors and learning problems faced at school by children from diverse backgrounds, allowing educators to better determine whether patterns of troubling behavior represent dysfunctionalities or are simply related to cultural differences (Fox, Vaughn, Wyatte, & Dunlap, 2002; Kalyanpur & Harry, 2004). In addition, the interaction of socioeconomics, race/ethnicity, gender, and a host of community variables presents educators with significant challenges in attempting to understand the underlying issues related to apparent disproportionalities (Oswald, Coutinho, Best, & Nguyen, 2001). One may perhaps focus most productively on the question: Will the identification of a learner as having special educational needs lead to effective interventions?

Categories as Social Constructions

A concern raised by some writers about virtually all of the mild disabilities is whether these disabilities are socially constructed, used to exclude some learners and/or dismiss difference. What part does the social context play in identifying and describing a disability? Murphy and Hicks-Stewart (1991) discussed learning disabilities and ADHD, in particular, from an environmental–interactionist point of view. They noted that the social expectations of society define which behaviors are acceptable and which are deviant. When children, for whatever reason, fail to learn in school and violate the rules of the community, they may be determined to be different, deviant, and in need of special accommodations. Thus, one may make a case for the definition of disability with reference to the degree of adaptability in a social context (Reid & Button, 1995; J. D. Smith, 2003).

Skrtic (2005) contrasted this contextual perspective of disability with the more dominant biological or cognitive frameworks. He challenged the definition of disability as intrinsic pathology, suggesting instead a focus on the external processes by which human variability is socially constructed and represented as disability. Social categories (e.g., gender, class, race/ethnicity, sexuality, and disability) have very real social consequences.

This discussion builds on an early description of the "six-hour retarded child" phenomenon (President's Committee on Mental Retardation, 1970; see Spotlight on History 4.1), as well as on Bogdan and Taylor's (1976, 1994) ethnographic work with persons labeled as having intellectual disabilities (see Chapter 1). It continues with similar arguments about learning disabilities (Dudley-Marling, 2004; Murphy & Hicks-Stewart, 1991; Reid & Button, 1995; Sleeter, 1986), attention-deficit/hyperactivity disorder (Armstrong, 1995; Danforth & Navarro, 2001), and emotional or behavioral disorders (McIntyre, 1993; Reid & Button, 1995; Reilly, 1991). Some of the questions include these: Are these real differences? Are they merely a variation in human behavior that we find inconvenient? Are the behaviors of concern a response to the ecology in which the child lives? Do we need to account for diminished performance by using a disability rubric? Such questions come from all parts of the political spectrum, addressing the centrality of "goodness of fit" between an individual and the environment.

At the central core of the discussion is concern about the validity of the concept of classification. To what extent do educators and researchers focus on the individual as the locus of the problem and the solution (Kalyanpur & Harry, 2004)? Are there alternative explanations that situate the discussions about disability within the context of social relations and cultural practices? Given inconsistent prevalence rates across population groups and regions, coupled with the observation that interventions often relate only weakly to specific classifications and are frequently used across disability categories, questions continue to be raised about the validity of discrete disability classifications and categories. Those preparing to enter the field of special education will need to consider these and other questions for which there are no easy answers.

Are Noncategorical Models of Service an Alternative?

One frequently proposed solution suggests that students who are experiencing difficulty in school environments should be identified by their needs, and programming should be designed to build on their strengths and ameliorate their deficiencies. Proponents of these noncategorical approaches argue against expending time and money to define a category of disability when categories alone are insufficient for designing interventions. The CEC policy statement about the labeling and categorizing of children raises clear concerns about the labeling process (Council for Exceptional Children, 1997b; see Appendix). Those who see disability from a social constructivist point of view suggest that focusing on the problem within a social context, rather than looking for a fault in the individual learner, is more likely to result in understanding the problem and coming up with a resolution (Dudley-Marling, 2004; Rose & Meyer, 2002; Skrtic, 2005).

This discussion is not a recent one. MacMillan, Siperstein, and Gresham (1996) suggested that the nature of mild intellectual disabilities, in particular, differs significantly from that of the more severe levels. They observed that mild intellectual disabilities are defined chiefly by the interaction between the individual's cognitive inefficiencies and the demands of the environment and also that there is rarely an identifiable biomedical cause. They further noted that it is often difficult or impossible to make an accurate or definitive discrimination between mild intellectual disabilities and learning disabilities, and that the categories of learning disabilities, mild intellectual disabilities, and ADHD are used interchangeably, depending on the degree of acceptability to the various members of the multidisciplinary team. Their point is that contextually situated forms of mild disability are frequently more similar to each other and more variable than more severe disorders are, and that attempts to discriminate among them seem futile.

Reynolds and Heistad (1997) took this reasoning one step further. They proposed "to drop the partitioning practices that have become so pervasive in schools" (p. 447), which they claimed have immobilized special education in many schools. They claimed that the cost of making determinations about subgroups of students with milder levels of disability is unacceptable, suggesting that the distinctions do not improve instruction and the funds could be more effectively used in direct services. These writers proposed that schools use direct assessment of progress in school learning as an indication of the need for intervention, as a measure of program efficacy, and as an aid in answering two questions: What are the learners' educational needs? and How can schools best meet these needs? With the focus of NCLB/ESEA and IDEA 2004 on responsiveness to intervention as a critical diagnostic variable, we are beginning to seek those answers.

IDEA also addresses this issue by recognizing that it is not always useful to try to definitively determine the specific category of impairment, particularly in young children. Since 1997 IDEA has allowed school districts the option of serving youngsters between the ages of 3 and 9 under the generalized rubric of developmental delay (Yell & Shriner, 1997). This option allows schools to focus on providing early intervention services without first having to satisfy specific disability criteria. In young children, the degree of deficit is often not severe enough to meet the formal criteria used to place children in categorical programs, potentially delaying useful formal interventions. Comments recorded in Senate deliberations on the 1997 IDEA amendments noted:

> The use of a specific disability category to determine a child's eligibility for special education and related services frequently has led to the use of the category to drive the development of the child's IEP and placement to a greater extent than the child's needs. In the early years of a child's development, it is often difficult to determine the precise nature of a child's disability. Use of "developmental delay" as part of a unified approach will allow the special education and related services to be directly related to the child's needs and prevent locking a child into a disability category which may be inappropriate or incorrect. (Council for Exceptional Children, 1998a, p. 13)

Recent meta-analyses have suggested that even though there are some differences among groups of students with disabilities, such as low IQ scores for students with intellectual disabilities, those differences are not strong enough to allow educators to plan instruction for an individual student based on knowledge of the category alone, and focusing on the students' individual characteristics is a better guide to instructional needs (Sabornie et al., 2005; Sabornie et al., 2006). Hallahan and Kauffman's 1977 recommendation for task-centered instruction based on behavioral characteristics continues to be an appropriate approach to educating students (see the introduction to Unit III).

RESPONSE TO INTERVENTION: A NONCATEGORICAL STRATEGY FOR ASSESSMENT AND IDENTIFICATION

The identification of a disability during the last 4 decades has focused primarily on the characteristics of a student without reference in any significant way to the environment in which learning occurs. In actuality, the source of any learning problem may lie (a) within the child, (b) within the instructional environment, or (c) in both (Speece, Case, & Molloy, 2003). The President's Commission on Excellence in Special Education (2002) found that "many children who are placed in special education are essentially instructional casualties and not students with disabilities" (p. 26).

Fuchs, Fuchs, and Speece (2002) proposed an alternative diagnostic model—response to intervention (RTI), a treatment-validity model based on the principles of curriculum-based assessment or measurement. This model looks for a dual discrepancy: (a) the comparatively lower performance of a student when compared to that of peers and (b) a significantly slower learning rate (Kovaleski & Prasse, 2004). The central focus is on the student's lack of responsiveness in the learning environment, defined by Gresham (2002a) as "the change in behavior or performance as a function of an intervention" (p. 480). RTI helps identify the learning needs of a learner, guides the implementation of evidence-based quality interventions, and assesses the learner's responses, providing data for understanding the nature of the learner's continuing challenges.

A related construct is dynamic assessment, focusing on the process of learning (Lidz & Elliott, 2000). Building on Vygotsky's (1978) theory of learning within zones of proximal development (ZPD), dynamic assessment is an interactive assessment model in which a teacher interacts with learners in an attempt to determine their potential for the next learning. The teacher observes the effect of different kinds of scaffolding on each learner's performance. These assessment activities are most useful if they are precise in measuring skill level, can be administered frequently, and are sensitive to change (Ysseldyke, Burns, Scholin, & Parker, 2010).

Response to intervention (RTI) is generally described as a three-tier process of increasingly intensive interventions followed by valid assessment of student response to determine the effectiveness of the interventions. Analysis of these results is used to determine whether there is a learning problem and, if so, whether more targeted intervention or special education may be indicated (Bradley et al., 2007; Brown-Chidsey, 2007; Fletcher et al., 2004; Fletcher & Vaughn, 2009; Fuchs & Deshler, 2007; Gresham, 2005; National Association of School Psychologists, 2009a, 2009b; National Association of State Directors of Special Education, 2006).

TIER I: UNIVERSAL HIGH-QUALITY INSTRUCTIONAL STRATEGIES AND SUPPORTS

This stage provides high-quality, evidence-based instruction and supports for all students in the general education classroom and determines the average rate of growth of learners in the class. Tier I also involves universal screening to identify at-risk students before they have failed and continuous progress monitoring to detect nonresponders. If the learning rate in the class is generally low, then a different classroom intervention should be employed with the whole class to improve the learning environment for all learners.

TIER II: TARGETED SMALL-GROUP INTERVENTIONS AND SUPPORTS

If the overall classroom learning rate is acceptable, Tier II identifies those children not responding to Tier I strategies and those exhibiting a dual discrepancy (lower level achievement and lower rate of learning). The next step is to identify more intensive, targeted interventions that may better address the needs of these learners in the general education environment. These interventions are then implemented along with continued Tier I supports, progress is tracked, and dynamic assessment is used to determine the learners' responsiveness to the alternative teaching strategies (Swanson & Howard, 2005).

TIER III: INTENSIVE, INDIVIDUALIZED INTERVENTIONS AND SUPPORTS

If a dual discrepancy persists, special education services might be more effective for the learner. This possibility can be evaluated through a diagnostic trial with special education services. The learner should be considered for special education only if this evaluation suggests that such placement and/or services are indicated and would be beneficial for the student.

ON THE WEB

For more information on RTI and the IDEA federal regulations, visit the **National Research Center on Learning Disabilities** at http://www.NRCLD.org and the **U.S. Department of Education's IDEA** website at http://idea.ed.gov.

Responsiveness to intervention becomes the context in which a special education diagnosis can be made. Kavale, Holdnack, and Mostert (2006) suggested that RTI is most appropriately viewed as the first step in the identification process. Tier I strategies generally meet the needs of about 80 percent of students. Tier II interventions, following Tier I strategies, are generally effective with another 15 percent of the students. Tier III interventions are needed for only about 5 percent of all students, those who may benefit from the individualized services commonly found in special education (see Figure 2.1). These multiple tiers of increasingly more intensive interventions, combined with continuous monitoring of the progress of all learners, are the foundation for a more data-driven, decision-making system to evaluate learners for possible special education needs (Zirkel & Krohn, 2008). This data gathering supports the IDEA requirement that multidisciplinary teams make use of data related to student response to instruction and gathered over time, providing a measure of a learner's progress and a pattern of strengths and weaknesses.

The RTI model suggests that a learner with a disability is in essence a *nonresponder* to generally available educational methods and curricula (Vaughn & Fuchs, 2003). Benefits of this approach to identification include the following:

• It supports the use of a criterion that has always been part of the federal disability definitions but has rarely been considered, namely, that the student has had an opportunity to learn but has failed to benefit from adequate instruction.

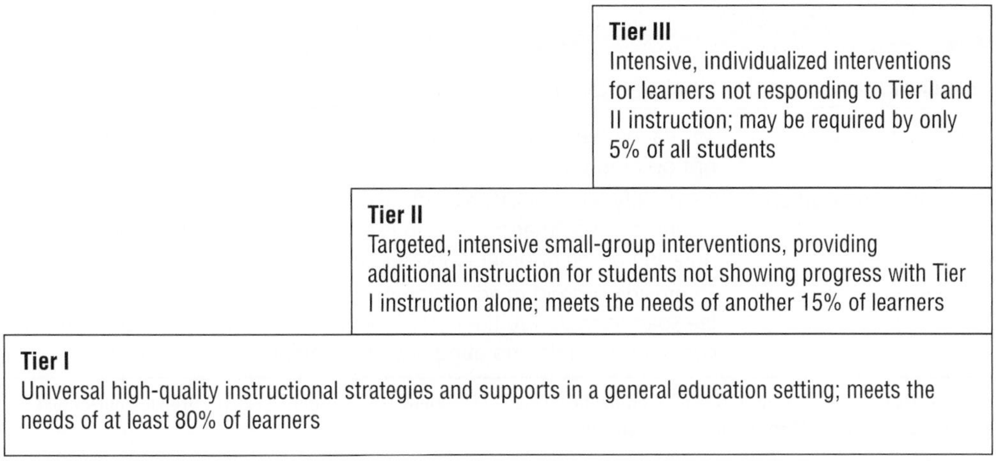

Tier III
Intensive, individualized interventions for learners not responding to Tier I and II instruction; may be required by only 5% of all students

Tier II
Targeted, intensive small-group interventions, providing additional instruction for students not showing progress with Tier I instruction alone; meets the needs of another 15% of learners

Tier I
Universal high-quality instructional strategies and supports in a general education setting; meets the needs of at least 80% of learners

FIGURE 2.1   Framework of Response to Intervention

- With supports for students throughout the learning process, early intervention is built into the model; it avoids the waiting-to-fail syndrome associated with discrepancy identification models (Brown-Chidsey, 2007; Dykeman, 2006; National Joint Committee on Learning Disabilities, 2005; Will, 1986).
- The emphasis on progress monitoring benefits all learners.
- This focus on data may reduce the bias related to teacher referrals.
- The model has the potential to improve the general education learning environment for all learners.

Questions and issues that must be addressed before these benefits can be fully realized include the following:

- The perception that RTI suggests that learning disabilities are merely instructional casualties
- Determination of whether, how, and at what point a disability diagnosis is appropriately made (National Joint Committee on Learning Disabilities, 2005; Reschly, 2005)
- The need for research to assure that assessments and interventions have sufficient validation of effectiveness (Fuchs & Deshler, 2007)
- A definition of *intensive* as applied to interventions
- Personnel preparation to work effectively in an RTI model

Special and general educators must ask whether responsiveness to intervention will be the answer to more effective educational planning for all children, including those who "fail to thrive" in general education classrooms. The jury is out, but the potential is there.

A PREVENTION FRAMEWORK AS SUPPORT

One of the most convincing arguments for classification is that knowledge of a cause may lead to effective prevention in the future and to more effective services for a specific youngster. As we discuss various disabilities and possible causes, it is useful to consider any implications that, once identified, certain conditions may be preventable or that the severity of their effect may be alleviated with interventions specific to the conditions. With increasing knowledge about mild disabilities and their causes, educators have identified some ways to prevent those conditions or to at least reduce their effect on an individual's ability to function. Central to application of this prevention framework is effective performance assessment, indicating clearly when learning and development are not progressing as expected in response to high-quality instructional interventions.

ON THE WEB

The **National Center on Response to Intervention** (www.rti4success.org) provides a variety of resources on the RTI model, including general information, training tools, and intervention and assessment tools.

Table 2.4 Levels of Prevention and Their Goals	
Level of Prevention	**Goal of Prevention Efforts**
Primary prevention	To change the conditions associated with the disability so that it does not occur in the first place
Secondary prevention	To identify the disability as early as possible and change the environment so that the person is affected as little as possible and the duration of the disorder is shortened
Tertiary prevention	To provide support in educational and social environments over the life span to maximize the person's level of functioning and prevent the condition from deteriorating any more rapidly than necessary

Sources: Based on American Association on Intellectual and Developmental Disabilities, 2010; Brown-Chidsey and Steege, 2005; Rowitz, 1986; Scott and Carren, 1987.

A three-tier model of prevention efforts—including primary, secondary, and tertiary levels—may be useful in conceptualizing action plans designed to ameliorate the effects of a variety of conditions and disorders (see Table 2.4). Such a prevention framework also serves as a guide to the design of therapeutic supports (American Association on Intellectual and Developmental Disabilities, 2010; American Association on Mental Retardation, 2002; Rowitz, 1986; Scott & Carren, 1987).

Conditions that are amenable to primary prevention are those that have a known causal agent that can be eliminated so that the condition never occurs. Examples of such conditions are disabilities resulting from maternal rubella infection or maternal alcohol consumption. Effective immunization programs that reach all women before childbearing years can eliminate rubella as a cause of intellectual disability and other defects in infants. In other cases, education campaigns that inform prospective mothers about the dangers of alcohol consumption and abstinence counseling during pregnancy can reduce the use of alcohol in expectant mothers and therefore reduce the incidence of fetal alcohol syndrome and other birth defects in newborns.

Secondary prevention efforts require (a) knowledge of the causal agent, (b) an efficient means of screening for the condition in potentially affected individuals in the early stages, and (c) effective treatment for the condition. Phenylketonuria (PKU) and lead poisoning are examples of such conditions (American Association on Intellectual and Developmental Disabilities, 2010). PKU is a known genetic defect that can be identified in newborns by a simple blood test. Dietary treatment is virtually 100 percent effective in preventing the intellectual disability associated with this condition. In the case of lead poisoning, high levels of lead in the blood may result in intellectual disability, learning disabilities, or ADHD. High-risk populations such as preschool children who live in high-lead environments can be routinely screened for lead. Once lead is detected, medical interventions can lower the level of lead in the blood, and environmental actions can eliminate the source of the lead, preventing recontamination and future intellectual damage.

Tertiary efforts are appropriate when there is no known cause or no procedures to remove the cause or cure the condition. In such cases, we must manage the environment to maximize the development of the child in spite of the condition. Individuals with Down syndrome respond well to tertiary efforts. Although we know the condition is related to chromosomal abnormalities, we do not usually know why it happens, nor can we alter the chromosomal makeup of the affected individual once it occurs. Education efforts across the life span, beginning with infant stimulation and early intervention in preschool, reduce the effect of this condition and allow the child to develop to the maximum extent possible. Another example is the close monitoring of infants who have a sibling with autism; this effort results in identifying early signs of the condition and providing more early intervention services when their effect will be greatest. In both cases, tertiary prevention is clearly a form of support (American Association on Intellectual and Developmental Disabilities, 2010).

This prevention framework can be applied to any disability or condition. In later discussions of intellectual disabilities, learning disabilities, attention-deficit/hyperactivity disorder, emotional or behavioral disorders, and other conditions in the mild range, it will be useful to consider the extent to which primary, secondary, and tertiary prevention actions can be identified to eliminate or lessen the impact of those conditions. To the extent that knowledge of a cause allows effective prevention efforts to be mounted, classification and diagnosis are a useful venture.

Summary

IDEA reinforced requirements for assessment and identification of learners with mild disabilities by stating that evaluations must include multiple measures conducted with technically sound instruments valid for the given purposes. Learners must be evaluated in their primary language and cannot be determined to have a disability if they have not had the opportunity to learn the skills being assessed. Assessments must relate to progress in the general education curriculum, and students with disabilities must participate in all mandated district and state assessments. However, students may have modifications in those assessments as approved by the multidisciplinary team. For the small number of students with very severe disabilities for whom no part of the general education curriculum is appropriate, state-level alternative assessments have been developed that must utilize the principles of universal design. Parents must be provided with progress reports as often as parents of children in general education classes are.

The complexity of determining the presence of a specific disability makes the task far from simple.

Disability definitions are subject to frequent debate and change, as well as to uneven implementation. An additional issue related to the identification of students with disabilities is the extent to which mild disabilities may be socially constructed, or defined by the context in which the identification takes place. Using noncategorical approaches may be an alternative for identifying students who are not making progress in the general education curriculum while still providing assistance to them but without identifying a discrete condition. IDEA 1997 took a step in this direction by allowing states to serve children between the ages of 3 and 9 in a general category called *developmental delay*.

IDEA 2004 endorsed responsiveness to intervention (RTI) as an assessment approach and a general education strategy for intervening early in the course of a learning problem, beginning with high-quality universal instruction and support in the general classroom for all students. Use of RTI also focuses the attention of educators on primary, secondary, and tertiary prevention functions as needed to support the learning and development of all learners.

A Case Study • Sharon

Sharon is a 15-year-old repeating freshman in a large urban high school. She is functioning well below grade level in all academic areas. She failed to move on to the sophomore level this year because of excessive absences and poor academic performance last year. She does not work well independently, hates school, and rebels against all forms of authority. Sharon responds to adults and peers in a very defensive and defiant manner. She frequently uses abusive language in her interactions with peers and adults. If she misplaces her papers, pencils, or books, she attempts to shift the blame to someone else. She seldom accepts personal responsibility for any of her inappropriate behaviors.

According to her parents, Sharon has been in a perpetual state of motion since she was very young. As a young child, she seldom slept long enough at any one time to give them relief from her active, disturbing behaviors. As she grew older, Sharon continued to respond impulsively to situations, regardless of the consequences. Her parents tried all the "parent things"—scolding, spanking, denying privileges, sending her to her room, promising rewards for good behavior—in their attempts to change her behavior. They say that nothing they have tried has had any effect, and they are at their wit's end.

Referral for psychological evaluation had been considered often by school personnel, but it wasn't until Sharon was caught with drugs on the school grounds that her case was finally scheduled for formal consideration by the multidisciplinary team. Sharon's parents had previously talked with a private clinical psychologist who agreed to work with Sharon on a weekly basis, but she refused to see the psychologist—until she was threatened with expulsion from school following the drug incident.

When educational testing was finally completed, it was reported that Sharon had achieved an intelligence score in the superior range on the Stanford-Binet 5 (IQ of 124). Sharon's scores on the Peabody Individual Achievement Test–Revised revealed that her general performance in reading recognition, reading comprehension, spelling, and general information was similar to that of students at the fifth-grade level, significantly below her current ninth-grade school placement. The school psychologist noted in the evaluation that these scores might be lower than her true skill levels because of Sharon's resistance to the testing activities.

Informal observations by regular and special education teachers confirmed that her low level of academic performance on the standardized tests was apparent in actual classroom settings as well. Her teachers reported that Sharon completes work hurriedly, if at all, and that her accuracy in the work she does finish suggests a low level of mastery. In contrast, Sharon is an avid reader at home, withdrawing from those around her by reading novels by writers like Stephen King, Dean Koontz, and Anne Rice.

Sharon has consistently refused to participate in school and classroom activities. She has been cutting classes and skipping school entirely since she entered middle school in sixth grade. Even the promise of a car next summer if she attends school regularly and does well has not altered this behavior pattern. When she is in school, she often refuses to do assignments or participate in class. For example, one day in math class, the teacher passed out a test. Sharon sat there doing nothing. When the teacher asked why she was not working, Sharon said she had no paper. When the teacher gave her a piece of paper, Sharon still refused, saying, "You know I don't do math."

Her classmates also seem to view Sharon in a negative manner. A recent sociogram drawn from the answers to the question "Who would you like to work with on the science project?" showed that no students selected Sharon to be in their group. The two students Sharon chose to work with, Susan and Cathy, are capable students who seem to be well accepted in their class, but Sharon had had little previous contact with them at school or in the neighborhood. Shortly after the sociogram was administered, Sharon did approach Cathy about working with her on a class assignment. Since then, Mrs. Jones, the classroom teacher, has continued to assign them together on projects with some success. Sharon seems to respond positively to the opportunity to work with a student perceived as academically and socially successful.

The multidisciplinary team decided that Sharon met the state criteria for classification as a student with a learning disability and that placement in a self-contained classroom program for students with learning disabilities at the high school would be the most appropriate for her. They cited her low level of academic progress in spite of her above-average intellectual ability as the reason for this decision. They believed that remediation in the self-contained classroom would increase Sharon's academic skills so that ultimately she would experience more success in school, with a resulting improvement in her behavior. Her IEP was developed to address reading, math, and writing skills, coupled with a self-monitoring program for on-task behavior and attention. It was decided to delay her change in placement until the new semester began in January to ease the transition.

One morning just before the semester break, Sharon was gone when her father went to wake her for school. Her duffel bag, suitcase, and clothing were missing. Her parents called the police and the friends with whom she often cuts school. Everyone was mobilized to find her. Fifteen hours later, she was found in a hangout area in the woods, and she reluctantly returned home. She was hungry, cold, and tired. Sharon's parents felt as if they were back to zero.

Discussion

Identify Sharon's strengths and needs. Then sort those characteristics into two groups:

- Academic learning characteristics
- Social–behavioral characteristics

Given your list, what might be the outcome of identifying Sharon as a student with a learning disability and placing her in a self-contained classroom for students with learning disabilities with the goal of remediating her academic weaknesses?

In considering the implications for placement and programming, as presented in the case study, how useful is it for the teacher to know that Sharon meets the criteria for students with learning disabilities? Is there any evidence that knowledge of the classification had any effect on the intervention plan developed by the team?

Issues in Instruction and Placement

■ What does the word *curriculum* mean in the context of IDEA?

■ Give examples of the explicit, hidden, and absent curricula. Why might these differences be important to you as a teacher of students with mild special learning needs?

■ What is the difference between curriculum and instruction? What does this difference imply to you as a teacher?

■ Describe the appropriate use of universal design for learning/instruction. How does UDL/UDI differ from making accommodations for learners with special needs?

■ How does an alternative curriculum differ from the general education curriculum?

■ What are the implications of IDEA's use of the term *individualized instruction*?

■ What two factors does IDEA identify as critical with respect to determining placement options for students with mild disabilities?

■ What is the appropriate sequence of tasks in making programming and

Meet Enrico

Enrico has been identified as a student with a learning disability since third grade. As he prepares to enter ninth grade in the fall, the multidisciplinary team has convened to evaluate his IEP and progress thus far. As with many students with learning disabilities, Enrico's academic performance is most seriously affected by his lack of reading skills. He has been taught with alternative reading curricula and instructional materials since his initial special education placement. Every year he makes modest progress, but when September rolls around, he seems to have lost most of the skill he had gained and must essentially begin anew. Depending on the measure used, his skills in reading are equivalent to those of an average third grader. He reads in a halting, word-by-word manner, and it appears that he is just saying the words with little indication that he expects to derive meaning from them. His special education teacher continues to work with him on basic decoding skills, using an alternative reading curriculum based on instruction in synthetic phonics. In the general education classroom, Enrico is frequently observed to be off-task during reading activities, although he shows adequate attention and participation in class discussions.

    The team is concerned about Enrico's lack of progress and suspects that it indicates that the alternative curricula and instructional approaches used in the past have not served Enrico well. As they look

placement decisions for learners with disabilities? Why is this important?

■ What does least restrictive environment mean to you as a teacher?

■ Describe the continuum of services model. How can it be used to guide the placement process?

■ What is inclusion? How does the philosophy of inclusive education relate to IDEA requirements today?

ahead to his high school years and to the postschool transition, they begin to consider other options. Mr. Thompson, the special education teacher, reminds the team that IDEA 2004 states that they must consider the general education curriculum first in developing the IEP and that Enrico will be required to participate in the statewide assessments. Mr. Thompson notes that alternative curricula are appropriate only when no portion of the general curriculum is applicable to the student. Enrico's class participation in nonreading activities indicates that he is able to derive benefit from the general education curriculum.

The multidisciplinary team reviews the data and makes the following decisions: Enrico should be able to benefit more from the general education curriculum with the support of taped textbooks in the content areas. Participation in Mr. Thompson's Learning to Learn elective class will teach him reading strategies designed to enhance his ability to profit from grade-level materials. The general education teachers should receive support from the consultant teacher in making any necessary modifications to the activities and demands of the classroom. It is decided that these supports will help ameliorate Enrico's needs while recognizing and developing his strengths in learning and that this program of goals and services will better prepare him for the statewide assessments and his future.

THINKING QUESTIONS

What else do you think a teacher might have done when Enrico was failing in elementary school that might have changed the situation we see today? Do you think the new plan will be effective? Why or why not?

CURRICULUM AND LEARNERS WITH MILD DISABILITIES

A central theme in IDEA is the designation of the general education curriculum as the starting point for all instructional planning considerations. In 1997 Congress removed the emphasis on location when considering the meaning of least restrictive environment. Disassociating the concept of curriculum from a discrete physical location has placed the primary focus on the educational program itself, wherever and however it is delivered (Council for Exceptional Children, 1998b; Karger, 2006).

This emphasis on the general education curriculum has presented significant challenges for special and general educators over recent years. In a 1995 study by Sands, Adams, and Stout, over 50 percent of the teachers surveyed believed that each student receiving special education services must have an individual curriculum, believing that the IEP goals served as the basis for each child's curriculum; only 15 percent of the teachers believed that the general education curriculum served as the primary curriculum for their students. Ten years later, in 2006, Idol reported on a study of eight schools following implementation of inclusion of students with disabilities in the general education program. This program evaluation indicated that a significant majority of the teachers then held positive attitudes about including learners with disabilities in general education programs, although they were still working on how best to support learners and teachers.

Whenever educators discuss curriculum, it quickly becomes clear that they assume that everyone means the same thing by the word *curriculum*. It soon becomes equally clear that there are a variety of meanings represented in any such discussion (Richardson & Anders, 1998). To compound the problem in special education, the terms *curriculum* and *individualized education program* are frequently used interchangeably (Abell, Bauder, & Simmons, 2005; Sands, Adams, & Stout, 1995). Since 1975, IDEA has required the development of an individualized education program, or IEP, for each student found to be in need of special education services. Parents and educators alike have generally regarded the IEP as "the curriculum" for each student with a disability (Abell et al., 2005; Bouck, 2004). Prior to 1997, IEPs typically focused only on special education services and goals, with little or no consideration

---

IN THE CLASSROOM 3.1

Curriculum in Special Education Classes

As the Johnson Central School District prepared for the visit of state special education auditors, Ms. Perkins, the Director of Special Education, spoke with the district's special education staff to ensure that everyone was ready for the visit. When Ms. Perkins met with Mr. Clark, a resource teacher at Johnson Elementary, she asked him what curriculum he used with his students. He confidently replied that he used an alternative curriculum, comfortable that this was the desired answer. Ms. Perkins responded quickly, "No, you use the general education curriculum. Your students are learning the same things all other students are; you just give them different ways to learn them." Mr. Clark was puzzled; after all, didn't the law require that "specially designed instruction" be provided to students with disabilities? How could the general education curriculum be appropriate for his students?

---

given to the general education curriculum. Multidisciplinary teams described in the IEP only those services specifically related to special education. Some voiced concerns that this exclusive focus on special education services in curriculum planning frequently resulted in fragmented programs, with little or no consideration of the interactions between special and general education (Will, 1986; Yell & Shriner, 1997).

Instructional materials, including textbooks and basal series, are frequently the most obvious indication of the explicit curriculum in place in classrooms and schools. When general education classroom teachers report that the curriculum used for their students with disabilities is the same or mostly the same as that provided to other students, they often mean that all students use the same textbooks. On the other hand, special education resource teachers (see In the Classroom 3.1) frequently say that their students use a curriculum that is different from the one provided in general education classes, meaning that they use materials that are different from the ones other teachers use (Deno, Maruyama, Espin, & Cohen, 1990; Simmons, Kameenui, & Chard, 1998). Often the process of making modifications for students with special learning needs focuses only on adapting or supplementing the textbooks used by other learners.

In addition to the problem of achieving consensus on a basic definition of *curriculum*, educators must address the multidimensional nature of implemented curricula (Hoover & Patton, 2005; Richardson & Anders, 1998). Curricula can be viewed from at least three perspectives:

- The explicit or public curriculum—the curriculum as written and tested
- The hidden or enacted curriculum—the curriculum as taught
- The absent curriculum—the curricular content that is not taught

The *explicit curriculum* is the formal, written curriculum that teachers and schools are expected to follow. It is the public curriculum that schools say they are providing to students. Increasingly, it refers to the state's learning standards, those learning goals that have been identified as critical for all students to achieve. It also relates to the curriculum as tested in district and state assessment programs. Complications arise when the curriculum as written and the curriculum as tested are not congruent.

The *hidden curriculum* is the actual curriculum implemented in any classroom. It results from the interaction of the explicit curriculum with organizational decisions made by teachers (e.g., grouping practices, time allocation) and with the teachers' selection of pedagogical approaches to teaching content. The hidden curriculum also relates to the implicit values of teachers and students that guide those decisions and the degree to which certain behaviors and values are rewarded and supported (Myles & Simpson, 2001; Richardson & Anders, 1998). The manner in which varying cultures, languages, genders, lifestyles, abilities, and disabilities are handled within any classroom is a significant component of the hidden curriculum. Thus,

ON THE WEB

The **IDEA Partnership** (http://www.ideapartnership.org/) provides comprehensive information on IDEA on such topics as instructional practices, placement, RTI, UDL, and autism, intended for teachers, administrators, policy makers, parents, and advocates.

the hidden curriculum results in a number of important learnings, most of which are not explicitly intentional. The hidden curriculum varies from class to class and school to school despite a seemingly uniform explicit or public curriculum.

The *absent curriculum* includes those topics or learnings that are not included in classroom instruction. Content may be left out of the explicit curriculum by the curriculum developers (e.g., certain topics in sex education). Alternatively, specific content may be left out by individual teachers as the hidden curriculum evolves because of time constraints, personal preferences, or assumptions about what students already know and can do. One issue related to the absent curriculum in most general education programs, and one that is of considerable importance to students learning English as an additional language, is the omission of survival skills in English academic language. This occurs because of the widespread assumption that all students understand English sufficiently to profit from instruction. Comprehension is assumed unless a student's performance indicates that there is a problem. As Cummins (1999) noted, the absent curriculum often includes skills related to cognitive academic language proficiency (CALP), particularly if a student appears to have developed basic interpersonal communication skills (BICS) in the language of instruction (see Chapter 10).

As policy makers, parents, and others seek changes in school practices to allow more successful inclusion of students with disabilities in general education programs, all educators must pay attention to the hidden and absent curricula as well as to the explicit, public curriculum. Such efforts frequently fail if they consider only the explicit curriculum. The classroom procedures and expectations that are central to the hidden curriculum must be made explicit to teachers, students, parents, and support staff so that these important learnings can be made more intentional. In addition, identifying elements of the absent curriculum may be crucial to the success of certain learners in the general education curriculum. The identification and teaching of content and skills that are omitted or assumed can improve the match between individual students and the curriculum. This is particularly true when teachers use this knowledge to supplement the implemented curriculum with crucial cognitive strategies or prerequisite skills that students with special learning needs may lack. Specific awareness of the characteristics of individual learners is critical to this analysis.

ALTERNATIVES TO INSTRUCTIONAL ACCOMMODATIONS

According to NCLB/ESEA, the *general education curriculum* serves as the foundation for the education of all students in a district or state. It consists of the set of skills and knowledge that a graduate of the system is expected to know and demonstrate. In many cases, these expectations are clearly defined and written down; they are specific, measurable, and tested. In other cases, the published curriculum may be a vague sense of what a child should learn, sketched in broad generalities and determined by textbook selection. However it is described, the general education curriculum delineates the competencies expected of adults in that community. For this reason, it is appropriate to view the general education curriculum as the primary guide for the design and delivery of all educational services for all learners (Karger, 2006).

Until recently, it was commonplace to assign a student with a disability to a general education setting and then attempt to design accommodations to respond to the learning difficulties related to the learner's disability. In effect, educators attempted to make the child fit the classroom rather than expanding the classroom options to include the child. This often resulted in awkward and inefficient retrofits of curricular materials and classroom activities. It also often led to isolating the student within the classroom, particularly when a paraprofessional was assigned to assist an individual student while the teacher worked with the rest of the class (Giangreco, Edelman, Luiselli, & MacFarland, 1997; Giangreco, Yuan, McKenzie, Cameron, & Fialka, 2005).

In the 1990s, curriculum researchers and developers began investigating alternatives to making such after-the-fact accommodations. They considered the common architectural philosophy and practice of designing structures to be usable by the widest variety of people without special accommodations being added, an architectural practice called universal design (Meyer & Rose, 2006; Wilkoff & Abed, 1994). Today, no architect would design a new public building without elevators and accessible entrances and bathrooms. Rather, new buildings are routinely constructed on the assumption that some people who use the facility will have special accessibility needs and that planning for them from the beginning is more efficient and economical, as well as being generally helpful to others.

Curriculum developers with interests in the growing field of digital learning materials soon began to consider which learner characteristics might prevent a student from using computers and other digital resources effectively. Rose and Meyer (2006) posed these questions: "What if all learners had genuine opportunities to learn in inclusive environments? What if we recognized that our inflexible curricula and learning environments are 'disabled' rather than pinning that label on learners who face unnecessary barriers?" (p. vii). A variety of changes in hardware and software made digital materials more flexible and accessible to all individuals, with minimal or no retrofitting required. These flexibilities, referred to as assistive technology, included new ways to input data, display information, and interact with technology auditorily, visually, and physically. CAST, the Center for Applied Special Technology, was founded in 1984 to develop technology-based educational resources and strategies. Today, CAST and its National Center on Universal Design for Learning websites are rich resources for technology-based solutions to common curricular challenges.

To increase access to learning materials, IDEA 2004 further mandated that states and schools use the National Instructional Materials Accessibility Standards (NIMAS) to evaluate by 2006 their purchases of accessible, alternate-format instructional materials (Meyer & Rose, 2006; Pisha & Stahl, 2005). IDEA 2004 also established the National Instructional Materials Access Center (NIMAC) as a source for publisher-supplied digital curricular materials.

As buildings and technology responded to a variety of essential accessibility issues, the discussion broadened throughout the 1990s to consider other applications of the principles of universal design in educational settings (McGuire, Scott, & Shaw, 2006). This initiative is now referred to as universal design for learning (UDL) or instruction (UDI). IDEA 2004 required the use of UDL principles in developing and administering assessments of student learning and directed that research be undertaken to determine ways that UDL principles could be applied to the development of standards, assessments, curricula, and instructional strategies as well (Mandlawitz, 2006; Orkwis & McLane, 1998). To support this work, the U.S. Office of Special Education Programs partnered with CAST to develop new curricula, strategies, and educational policies to support educational access for all learners.

Access to learning is enhanced by implementation of three core UDL principles for curriculum development and instructional planning (CAST, 2008; Rose & Meyer, 2002; Rose, Meyer, & Hitchcock, 2006; see Table 3.1):

- *Representation*—multiple and flexible means of presenting/representing information, including ways to reduce perceptual or cognitive barriers
- *Expression*—multiple and flexible means for learners to express or demonstrate competencies, including practices that reduce motoric, linguistic, and cognitive barriers
- *Engagement*—multiple and flexible means for learners to engage effectively in the learning environment, including a variety of resources and activities that provide support and challenge, as well as novelty and familiarity, and are of developmental and cultural interest

Scott, McGuire, and Foley (2001) added two more UDI principles that specifically address the affective and social/emotional support for learning:

- *Community of learners:* Establishing an instructional environment that promotes supportive interaction and communication among students and between students and educators

ON THE WEB

The **Center for Applied Special Technology** (www. cast.org) provides a theoretical and practical introduction, as well as resources, on universal design for learning, with an emphasis on digital solutions; it also provides ideas to make the general education curriculum more accessible to students with a broad range of abilities and needs.

ON THE WEB

NIMAC: National Instructional Materials Access Center (http://www. nimac.us/) is an electronic file repository created under IDEA 2004 to make NIMAS publisher files available for the production of core print instructional materials in specialized formats. Designated users in each state use these source files to produce accessible media products for eligible individuals with disabilities.

ON THE WEB

Universal Design for Learning Guidelines, Version 1.0, can be downloaded from CAST's website, http://www.cast. org/publications/ UDLguidelines/version1. html.

Table 3.1 Principles of Universal Design for Learning/Instruction (UDL/UDI)	
I. Use multiple and flexible means of representation[a]	Learners differ in the ways in which they are able or prefer to comprehend information provided to them; no single means of content representation is optimal for all students and all learning. Variety and options in representation of content support optimal student learning.
II. Allow multiple and flexible means of expression[a]	Learners also differ in the ways that they can best express what they know and can do; no single means of expression allows all students to demonstrate what they know and can do. Providing options for demonstration of learning increases the likelihood that assessment will be a valid measure of that learning.
III. Provide multiple and flexible means of engagement[a]	Learners differ in the ways in which they can or prefer to be engaged in activities needed to practice new knowledge and skills, as well as in their sources of motivation to learn. Providing options in the nature and the intensity of active engagement with learning activities supports effective practice and persistence in learning activities.
IV. Create a community of learners in the classroom[b]	Learners' motivation for learning is enhanced by creating instructional environments that promote interaction and communication among students and between students and teachers. Such communities of learners support effective scaffolding in support of learning.
V. Establish a positive instructional climate[b]	Learning is enhanced by instruction that is designed to be welcoming and inclusive. Learners are more likely to be motivated to persist in learning activities if they perceive the learning goals and expectations as being challenging but reasonable.

Adapted from (a) Center for Applied Special Technology (CAST), 2008, and (b) McGuire, Scott, and Shaw, 2006.

- *Instructional climate:* Designing instruction to be welcoming and inclusive, even as it espouses high and appropriate expectations for all students

So the question remains: How do teachers provide equitable access for all students in their classrooms? UDL/UDI proponents are very clear that the word *universal* does not imply that one optimal solution fits everyone. Rather, it reflects an awareness of the unique nature of each learner and the need to accommodate differences. UDL recommends creating within every learning environment a variety of learning experiences that allow learners to select those that are the best fit and that maximize their progress (Lee, Wehmeyer, Soukup, & Palmer, 2010; McGuire, Scott, & Shaw, 2006; Orkwis & McLane, 1998; Rose & Meyer, 2006; Rose, Meyer, & Hitchcock, 2006; Sourup, Wehmeyer, Bashinski, & Bouvaird, 2007; Wehmeyer, Lance, & Bashinski, 2002).

Each teacher needs to plan instruction with the knowledge of the potential range of abilities and characteristics that may exist among the students in one class (Jackson & Harper, 2006). The UDL/UDI-oriented educator appreciates that

- Students with disabilities, like students with higher abilities, fall along a continuum of learner differences, rather than constituting a separate category.
- Teacher adjustments for learner differences should occur for all students, not just for those with learning problems. These flexibilities should ideally be built in as choices/options throughout a lesson and a school day, and they should be accessible to all students, not only those with disabilities.

DIVERSITY IN FOCUS 3.1

It is not uncommon today for diverse students and their families to report feeling uncomfortable in classrooms because of a lack of fit with the curriculum or the pedagogical approaches in use. This discomfort may be related to a number of factors such as the individual's race, ethnicity, language, religion, socioeconomic class, disability, gender, or sexual orientation. Among the principles of universal design for instruction (McGuire, Scott, & Shaw, 2006) is the assertion that instruction should be designed to be welcoming and inclusive of all students (Sapon-Shevin, 2008). Teachers who strive to create classroom climates that convey their comfort with diversity in the classroom also communicate to their students a deep respect for diverse talents. This principle is critical to assuring that all learners feel safe enough in the classroom to devote their full energies to learning.

Although the principles of universal design for learning/instruction are certainly pertinent to curriculum and instruction for learners who differ with respect to ability, they also mean that the curriculum and instruction should be as inclusive as possible so that all students find relevance in it. UDL/UDI focuses on building a community of learners. It suggests that students of diverse backgrounds and learning preferences should find support for how they learn best, not as an add-on or special event or intervention, but as an everyday occurrence. Even though individual accommodations will still remain necessary from time to time, adherence to universal design principles will sharply reduce that need and include more students as a matter of course (U.S. Office of Special Education Programs, 1999).

The final concern about curricular and instructional flexibility relates to students who are learning English as a second language (Christensen, 2008). Their ability to understand instruction is a critical factor in the amount of time needed to learn. Educators must consider the learner's effectiveness in comprehending and expressing curricular content and then develop curricular supports as needed. Such supports may include intensive English as a second language (ESL) instruction or other means for students to be provided with content instruction (e.g., bilingual education). Teachers cannot assume that students understand what is being said just because they appear to be listening. Frequently, students with difficulty comprehending spoken English will pay very close attention but will still miss significant amounts of content. Students who have acquired basic interpersonal communication skills (BICS) will not necessarily have acquired cognitive academic language proficiency (CALP; Cummins, 1999). Regular assessment of student understanding is critical, especially when competency in the language used for instruction is a noted need for a particular learner.

- Curriculum materials should be varied and diverse, including digital and online resources wherever appropriate, rather than centering on a single textbook.
- Instead of remediating individual students so that they can learn from a set curriculum, the curriculum should be made more flexible to accommodate all learner differences. (Council for Exceptional Children, 2005a)

In making the instructional program more flexible for all learners, Hitchcock, Meyer, Rose, and Jackson (2002) identified four areas where flexibility could be increased:

- Goals can be differentiated to provide appropriate levels of challenge to all students, while assuring that core competencies are developed.
- Materials used to present content should be varied and flexible, providing choices in how students receive content within and across lesson periods.
- Instructional methods should be flexible and diverse, providing challenge, choice, and support to all students as they engage in learning activities.
- Assessments should be flexible enough to provide information that helps teachers and students alike accurately monitor learning and make adjustments where needed.

The central premise of UDL/UDI is that the curriculum and classroom instruction work best when a variety of alternatives are used in widely varied learning contexts to make learning accessible and appropriate for individuals with differing backgrounds, learning paces and styles, and abilities and disabilities. To begin this process, a teacher needs first to understand the range of characteristics that may be present in any classroom (Jackson & Harper, 2001). As we pursue our study of the characteristics of learners with mild disabilities, we must be alert to attributes that may suggest educator actions in line with UDL/UDI theory and principles. For example, if a teacher understands that students in the class read at a variety of levels, then that teacher might plan a whole-group lesson on strategies to determine the main idea of a piece of text and follow the lesson with practice activities at a variety of reading levels. This approach allows all students to work on the same core objective but at levels that challenge rather than frustrate them. See Universal Design for Learning in Action boxes in Chapters 9–12 for additional examples of UDL/UDI practices that are responsive to particular learner characteristics.

As we consider ways to introduce flexibility into curriculum design and resources, the practice of curriculum differentiation, or slicing, may be helpful in understanding how curriculum itself can be made more flexible (Hall, Meyer, & Strangman, 2006; Schumm, Vaughn, & Leavell, 1994; Wiggins & McTighe, 2001). This model focuses on differentiation of content and suggests that teachers ask three questions in considering what should be taught to whom (see Figure 3.1; Deshler, Ellis, & Lenz, 1996):

- What must all students learn?
- What else should most students be able to learn?
- What content might some students benefit from or be interested in learning?

In conducting this type of analysis, educators identify the knowledge and skills that are most critical to successful future learning, as well as those that might be of a more supplemental nature in response to individual student interests and needs. When learning efficiency is impaired by a disability, it is generally more important to focus on helping all students learn those most critical concepts and skills that build a strong foundation for later learning, while also providing additional opportunities for students who are interested in acquiring more advanced learnings. This framework keeps open the possibility that learners may acquire more than minimum skills but also assures that at least foundational learning will be attained by all.

An instructional framework that is closely aligned with UDL is *differentiated instruction*. When teachers seek different ways to vary classroom instruction in response to the range of

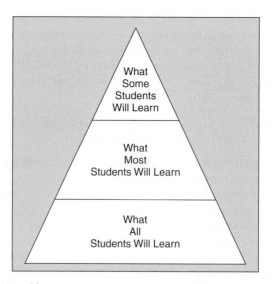

FIGURE 3.1 Planning Pyramid

Source: From *Teaching Adolescents with Learning Disabilities* (2nd ed., p. 429) by D. D. Deshler, E. S. Ellis, and B. K. Lenz, 1996, Denver, CO: Love. Copyright © 1996 by Love Publishing Company. Adapted and reprinted with permission,

strengths and needs among learners, they are using the principles of differentiated instruction. Teachers may differentiate to better meet their students' needs, strengths, and interests in these general areas:

- *Content:* What is most important for all students to learn, and what may be desirable for some to encounter?
- *Process of learning:* Are there varying ways for learners to encounter the content?
- *Products of learning:* In what ways can students practice and demonstrate what they have learned?
- *Learning environment:* How can the classroom environment best be arranged to support varied academic and affective learning needs?

As with UDL, it is not necessary that all students learn the same things in the same ways and demonstrate those learnings in a single, uniform assessment (Hoover & Patton, 2005; King-Sears, 2008; Rock, Gregg, Ellis, & Gable, 2008; Tomlinson, 2000; van Garderen & Whittaker, 2006). Even when learners are functioning significantly below grade expectations, teachers using differentiated instruction can find the right mix of differentiated curricular goals, methods, materials, and assessments to provide meaningful learning experiences (Giangreco, 2007). Focusing on the specific strengths and needs of every student leads to an enriched and positive learning environment for all.

INSTRUCTIONAL STRATEGIES TO ENHANCE CURRICULAR ACCESS

As we consider ways to provide more effective access to the general education curriculum for students with disabilities, it is useful to look at some of the instructional practices that have been shown to be effective with students in both general and special education classrooms. Increasingly researchers are finding that practices that work with one type of student are also effective with others (Bickel & Bickel, 1986; Bost & Riccomini, 2006; Cannon, Idol, & West, 1992; Feldman & Denti, 2004). This finding supports the premise that an integrated delivery of the general education curriculum is feasible and likely to be more effective and efficient than maintaining separate programs.

In an investigation of instructional practices useful with learners who are at risk or who are experiencing failure, Bost and Riccomini (2006) identified effective teaching principles that are related to the academic success of such learners and that are also generally applicable to others:

- Actively engaging students (time on task) and increasing opportunities to learn
- Providing meaningful opportunities for successful learning
- Grouping for instruction (whole class/small group/individual)
- Scaffolding instruction
- Addressing all forms of knowledge—declarative, procedural, conditional (see Chapter 9)
- Organizing and activating knowledge
- Teaching strategically
- Making instruction explicit
- Teaching *sameness* or the connectiveness of knowledge

Although it is beyond the scope and purpose of this text to discuss specific pedagogical techniques in detail, it may be useful to identify a few practices that have been identified as being effective in both general and special education.

Explicit Teaching

Explicit teaching, or direct instruction, is a set of teaching behaviors that have been validated in research over 3 decades (Brophy & Good, 1986; Englert, 1984; Pressley, Mohan, & Raphael, 2007; Rosenshine, 1986; Rupley, Blair, & Nichols, 2009; Tarver, 1999). Referred to variously as *direct instruction, explicit teaching,* or *effective teaching principles,* these behaviors include six instructional functions: (a) reviewing and reteaching as necessary; (b) explicit presentation of new content by the teacher; (c) guided initial practice; (d) feedback and correction; (e) independent practice; and (f) regular reviews to support maintenance. In general, research on explicit/direct instruction indicates that the teacher should play an active and direct role in the instructional process, providing clear content and relevant practice and verifying that learning has occurred before moving on. Although these practices are particularly useful in teaching lower-level skills to all students and in teaching any skill to students who find learning difficult, explicit/direct instruction has been found to be useful in both general education and special education and for a wide variety of levels of learning tasks.

Related to research on explicit/direct instruction is the body of work that looks at how time is used in classrooms (Brophy & Good, 1986; Carroll, 1963; Denham & Lieberman, 1980; Rangel, 2007; Vannest & Hagen-Burke, 2010). Academic learning time is defined as the time a student spends actively involved in a learning task with a high rate of success. Academic responding time is defined as the amount of time learners actually spend in responding to academic tasks and challenges, as opposed to waiting or engaging in task management activities (Lee, 2006). Unfortunately, classroom research and informal classroom observations, in both general and special education settings, indicate that a significant amount of student instructional time does not meet the criteria of either academic learning or academic responding time. Maximizing use of time for learning is critical to the success of learners with mild disabilities.

Peer Tutoring

Reviews of effective practices in inclusive classrooms serving heterogeneous groups of students have indicated that peer tutoring is associated with significant gains in learning by students with disabilities. These gains are seen on learning tasks involving a variety of skills, such as mastering math facts or spelling words (Bownam-Perrott, 2009; Fisher, Schumaker, & Deshler, 1995; Gardner, Nobel, Hessler, Yawn, & Heron, 2007; Harper & Maheady, 2007; Maheady, 2003; Mastropieri, Scruggs, & Berkeley, 2007; Stenhoff & Lignugaris/Kraft, 2007). In peer tutoring arrangements, one student is trained to provide skill practice and feedback to another. Peer tutoring can be an effective way to increase the amount of individualized instructional attention. Improvement in student learning is attributed to the increased opportunity for academic responding time coupled with immediate feedback.

Peer support networks and "peer buddies" have also been associated with more effective social integration of students with disabilities (Copeland et al., 2002). The purpose of these structured peer relationships is primarily nonacademic; they provide an opportunity to support the development of social skills and social relationships among students with and without disabilities.

Cooperative Learning

Cooperative learning refers to a family of instructional practices characterized by the use of groups of learners who stay together for a period of time to support academic learning (Fore, Riser, & Boon, 2006; Johnson, Johnson, Holubec, & Roy, 1984; Johnson & Johnson, 1996; McMaster & Fuchs, 2005; Murphy, Grey, & Honan, 2005). Cooperative learning is structured so that positive interdependence is fostered while individual accountability is retained. Instructional objectives are selected to include both academic content learning and group work skills. Attention is given to actively teaching and coaching these critical work skills so necessary for effective everyday functioning. The efficacy research on cooperative learning among learners in general is substantial and robust (Johnson et al., 1984; McMaster & Fuchs, 2005). Positive changes have been observed in study after study, including increased academic learning for most students regardless of ability, increased skill in higher-order problem solving, and positive social skill development (Johnson et al., 1984). Pomplun (1997) found that, in general, students with disabilities were able to participate and learn effectively in such groups, with the exception of some students with behavioral disorders or intellectual disabilities. Outcomes with these latter students suggest that some students with disabilities may need more specific assistance in developing appropriate and useful group work skills prior to involvement in cooperative learning environments.

Cooperative learning is well suited for supporting learning in inclusive and heterogeneous classrooms (Fisher et al., 1995; Pomplun, 1997; Villa & Thousand, 1988). One of the strongest and most versatile models, developed by David and Roger Johnson (Johnson et al., 1984), makes use of heterogeneous teams that stay together for a period of time. As students interact on the team over time, they support each other as their complementary skills allow; through peer tutoring and mutual support, they work to achieve higher levels of learning for all students in the group. Cooperative learning is frequently cited as a way for classroom teachers to provide more relevant practice and feedback, to accommodate individual differences, and to obtain enhanced learning for all.

Cognitive Strategies

Cognitive strategies can assist students in learning how to learn—for example, self-instruction, self-questioning, self-monitoring, self-evaluation, and self-reinforcement. Such strategies help students become self-regulated learners, allowing them to direct and evaluate their own learning. Cognitive strategy instruction is particularly useful with middle school and secondary students as they attempt to deal with more complex, independent learning tasks. Cognitive strategies are generally developed incidentally by successful learners, but research indicates that they are often missing from the repertoire of students experiencing academic difficulty (Deshler et al., 1996).

One example of a cognitive strategies instruction program, the strategies intervention model (SIM) developed at the University of Kansas, includes a collection of learning strategies that can help students acquire information, store and retrieve facts and skills, and express knowledge in a variety of ways (Deshler et al., 1996; Fisher et al., 1995). Other examples of approaches that address cognitive strategy development include cognitive behavior modification techniques such as self-instruction and self-monitoring (Brigham, Berkley, Simpkins, & Brigham, 2007; Hallahan, Kauffman, & Lloyd, 1999; Meichenbaum, 1977), mnemonic strategies such as keyword techniques (Brigham & Brigham, 2001; Mastropieri & Scruggs, 1991), and content enhancement strategies such as graphic organizers and guided notes (Ellis & Howard, 2007; Lenz, Bulgren, & Hudson, 1990).

ON THE WEB

The **Center for Research on Learning** (www.ku-crl. org) contains information about learning strategies and the strategies intervention model for adolescent learners with learning challenges.

Positive Behavioral Supports

IDEA requires that IEP teams design behavioral intervention plans that include positive behavior supports for any student with a disability who is experiencing problems with behavior (Arter, 2007; McConnell et al., 1998). Positive behavioral supports include changes to antecedents and consequences of the problem behavior so that the triggers are diminished. They also include schoolwide curricular strategies and instructional supports that may increase the ability of all students to resolve problems and interact socially in an acceptable manner, while also limiting the need for and occurrence of the problem behavior. Critical to the success of such a plan is the identification of alternative ways for students to meet the personal needs that seem to be related to the problem behavior (Hendley, 2007; Sugai et al., 1999). The strength of positive behavioral supports as a proactive schoolwide or classwide intervention lies in the potential for primary prevention—preventing problem behaviors from occurring by creating supportive environments that allow all students to meet important needs with socially acceptable and personally satisfying behaviors (Conroy, Sutherland, Snyder, & Marsh, 2008; Fairbanks, Simonsen, & Sugai, 2008; Sugai & Horner, 2002).

INSTRUCTION AND INDIVIDUALIZED EDUCATION PROGRAM PLANNING

IDEA 1997/2004 amendments reemphasized that the IEP is to be developed around both the strengths and the needs of the child, with parents and school personnel actively participating in the planning. IEPs should focus on a student's participation in the general education curriculum, be developed with the assistance of the general educator, and be linked to the state's learning standards. Major provisions of IDEA 1997/2004 include the following (Council for Exceptional Children, 1998a, 1998b, 2004, 2005b, 2010; Gartin & Murdick, 2005; Mandlawitz, 2006; U.S. Department of Education, 2006a, §300–320; Yell & Shriner, 1997):

- The IEP team should include at least the following people who have knowledge of the child and the school:
  - The child's parent
  - A general education teacher
  - A special education teacher
  - A representative of the local educational agency/school (LEA)

One member of the team needs to be able to interpret assessment information, and the student is encouraged to participate as appropriate.

ON THE WEB

The **Alliance for Technology Access** (www. ataccess.org) provides resources related to assistive technology, including a wide range of tools that can increase the independence of people with disabilities.

- Present levels of performance are to include information about the child's academic achievement as well as functional behavior and should focus on the child's strengths as well as areas in need of improvement.
- As required by No Child Left Behind, students with disabilities must be included in state and district assessments; any accommodations needed by the student must be included in the IEP to assure that such assessments produce meaningful results.
- The IEP team must consider the following factors that may impede a child's progress: behavior problems, language needs, communication needs of students with sensory disabilities (e.g., Braille, sign language), and assistive technology needs.

The discussion in this chapter has suggested a potentially contradictory set of requirements, both of which are contained within IDEA. On the one hand, the law requires that each student with a disability be provided with an IEP. On the other hand, Congress has dictated that the curriculum provided to students with disabilities should be the general education curriculum, with accommodations as needed. How can IEP teams and teachers accommodate these seemingly opposing requirements?

The answer lies in differentiating between curriculum, or the content of education, and instruction, the methods used to develop content and skill competence. One legitimate goal of education is to achieve independence in functioning (Dever & Knapczyk, 1997); the role of teachers then becomes assisting learners in the process of growing up to be productive, contributing, and independent members of society. This curricular goal is clearly applicable to all children and youth, whether they have disabilities or not. Even the hierarchical listing of subskills needed to attain independence would be applicable to all. The fact that some learners will not make as much progress toward that goal over a year or a school career is irrelevant; the goal remains the same (Dever, 1990).

If we consider the difference between this curricular goal and the instructional methods and practices used to achieve the goal, the resolution of the apparent contradiction becomes clearer. As teachers and schools work to develop independence in learners, they will employ a variety of activities, and they will pace those challenges in accordance with learner responses. It then becomes obvious that it is the instructional practices that are to be individualized or personalized, not necessarily the curriculum.

In discussing some of the issues involved in individualizing instruction, Lloyd (1984) concluded by observing that there are some methods of instruction that have been empirically demonstrated to be effective with a variety of learners, including those with and without disabilities and those who have cultural and linguistic differences. Lloyd agreed that educators should base their instruction on the specific learning characteristics of their students, rather than on disability categories. "We cannot know that special education is better for students [with disabilities] and regular education is better for [other] learners. . . . It may be that special education would benefit [students without disabilities] just as much as it does special education students" (p. 13). Lloyd suggested that all teachers should individualize instruction on the basis of the skills students have yet to learn and by using a variety of instructional methods that seem to match the individuals' learning patterns and needs. Lloyd and others have implied that this approach would constitute effective instruction for all students: "Whatever is special about special education has relevance for all effective teachers" (Aber, Bachman, Campbell, & O'Malley, 1994, p. 50).

From this reasoning then, the resolution of our apparent contradiction becomes clearer. Learning problems appear to result most directly from the failure of teachers to modify instruction to better match learner characteristics. Instruction in general education (and frequently in special education as well) suffers from too little variation and adaptation for all learners.

Alternative Curricula and Assessments

Our discussion thus far has focused on the general education curriculum and frameworks for increasing access to that curriculum. But what about alternative curricula? Isn't that what special education provides? According to IDEA 2004, alternative curricula and assessments are appropriate only for that small percentage of students with disabilities so severe that no portion of the general education curriculum is applicable. Such students are frequently provided with a curriculum that includes self-care and daily living skills not generally considered part of the K–12 curriculum. Because reading, writing, mathematics, science, and social studies are not generally relevant to these students' needs, an alternative or substitute program of studies is necessary. However, for all other students, including most students with mild/moderate disabilities, some level of competence in the general education curriculum should be a viable goal. The challenge for general and special educators alike is how to provide meaningful access to that general curriculum.

IDEA 2004 AND THE LOCATION OF SERVICES

P.L. 94-142 was passed in 1975 to provide procedures for addressing three main questions:

1. Which students require assistance in order to benefit from their educational programs?
2. What educational objectives or learnings are appropriate for each student at a particular point in time?
3. Where and with whom can those learnings best be achieved?

In practice, the sequence in which these three questions have been answered has not always supported the best practice in serving learners with disabilities. The most commonly observed scenario at IEP planning meetings is shown in the vignette about Stephen (see In the Classroom 3.2).

Stephen's story illustrates several of the major concerns addressed by Congress as they passed the IDEA 2004 amendments. First, the team and the process focused only on identifying Stephen's areas of deficit. Although it is likely that Stephen possessed some areas of strength, the whole process was focused on determining what his problems were, whether their severity was enough to warrant special education, and where his special education needs could best be served. In IDEA 2004 Congress explicitly stated that the whole child must be considered, strengths as well as deficits, academic achievement as well as functional performance.

Second, in the process described in the vignette, the team moved directly from identification to placement, matching Stephen's deficits with the service models available. The team

Placement and Planning Process in Action

Stephen's behavior had become more disruptive as the year progressed. By February Ms. Scott had submitted a referral for special education evaluation. Following the evaluation process, the team met and learned that Stephen exhibited aggressive behaviors toward peers significantly more often than others in his seventh-grade classes did. His educational progress had been virtually nonexistent for about 2 years, as indicated by state and individual assessments.

Regular behavioral interventions within the classroom had not affected the problem behaviors. Consequently, the team found that he met the criteria for identification as a child with an emotional disturbance. Based on that determination, team members reviewed the available placement options and determined that the self-contained classroom was the least restrictive environment that could address his demonstrated problem behaviors. Finally, they addressed what Stephen should be expected to achieve during the next year, and they drafted an IEP with appropriate goals and objectives. These goals and objectives were consistent with the programs already in place in Mr. Reynolds's special education classroom, and Stephen was reassigned to that class beginning the following week.

---

determined that the restrictive environment of the self-contained special class was most compatible with the disability category assigned to Stephen. In fact, if this district is like many, the mere fact that Stephen was identified as having an emotional disturbance probably assured that the only placement given serious consideration was the special classroom. In IDEA 2004 Congress stressed that the focus of discussion must return to the needs of the child, particularly as those needs relate to the general education curriculum. Placements and plans must be based on students' needs, not on their disability categories. As we will discuss in Units II and III, youngsters with the same disability label can vary significantly from one another in their needs. Plans based exclusively on a classification rarely address the individual needs of children adequately.

Third, Stephen's IEP was developed after the placement had been determined. This common sequence of decisions increases the likelihood that the content of the IEP will relate more to the curriculum already in place in that particular special education classroom than to Stephen's needs and strengths. This is also in conflict with the central premise of IDEA. The only valid educational reference points for educational planning, according to IDEA 2004, are the general education curriculum and the child's needs. The fact that here we have discussed educational planning and curricular issues prior to discussing placement options highlights the process intended by Congress to ensure that services are delivered in the least restrictive environment, as is demonstrated in Brandy's story (see In the Classroom 3.3).

Implementation of IDEA 2004 affirms and supports the following sequence for program planning for youngsters with disabilities:

- First, the team makes a careful assessment of the learner's strengths and needs with respect to participation in the general education curriculum, resulting in a full and detailed description of the student.
- Second, the interaction of those strengths and needs is evaluated with respect to the general education curriculum, and then goals and objectives are developed that will enable the student to progress in that curriculum.
- Finally, decisions are made about where the services should be provided and who should provide them, based on the premise that services should be provided in the environment that gives the most access to the general education curriculum and to settings in which other learners are served. Placement in a general education classroom, with UDL principles in place and supports as needed, should always be considered first.

> ### IN THE CLASSROOM 3.3
>
> #### Example of an Appropriate Placement Discussion
>
> Brandy is in fourth grade and has been identified with a specific learning disability for 2 years. She participates in the general education curriculum in all subject areas but until now has been receiving her reading and spelling instruction in the resource room. At the IEP meeting, her fourth-grade teacher and the resource room teacher agreed that she has made some progress in reading, having just completed the 2–2 level of the basal series used in the school, but her difficulties in spelling persist. Brandy's teachers observed that although she listens with good comprehension and has reasonable comprehension in silent reading, her oral reading and spelling have remained problematic. They concurred that Brandy's strengths in conceptual understanding and visual forms of language have enabled her to function fairly well this year in the fourth-grade content. Her needs in the curriculum are related to her need to acquire independent study skills in content-area reading and to be able to write independently with accurate spelling.
>
> The team decided that the rich context of the fourth-grade content was an asset to Brandy and that her IEP objectives should focus on effectively using context clues for silent reading comprehension. In addition, since spelling is a tool skill that she was having trouble developing, it was decided that an objective related to efficient use of word processing would be appropriate at this point. After considering a few more areas of curricular concern, the team turned to the placement issue. Although this instruction could certainly continue to be provided in the resource room, it was determined that the goals could be met equally well within the general education class, and Brandy would not be missing ongoing instruction while traveling to and from the resource room. It was determined that next year Brandy would be best served by receiving indirect and direct services from the consultant teacher in the fifth-grade classroom, with instruction and support in developing study skills and word processing expertise.

LEAST RESTRICTIVE ENVIRONMENT

The concept of placement in the least restrictive environment (LRE) was originally defined in 1975 as part of P.L. 94-142 (now IDEA). This general principle remains in place in federal statute and state regulations today, guiding our special education practice. IDEA mandates that free and appropriate public education be provided for all children and requires that states and localities ensure the following:

> To the maximum extent appropriate, children with disabilities, including those in public/private institutions or other care facilities, are educated with children who are not disabled, and special classes, separate schooling, or other removal of children with disabilities from the regular educational environment occurs only when the nature and severity of the disability of the child is such that education in regular classes with the use of supplementary aids and services cannot be achieved satisfactorily. (P.L. 108-446; 118 Stat. 2677)

Since 1975, IDEA has required that states and districts ensure the availability of "a continuum of alternative placements to meet the needs of children with disabilities for special education and related services" (U.S. Office of Education, 1977b, p. 42497). A full continuum of services should include a variety of supplementary aids to support general education classroom placements, such as the services of consultant teachers, resource rooms, and itinerant instruction, as well as services in special classes and special schools, homebound and hospital instruction, and residential placement. The "overriding rule . . . is that placement decisions must be made on an individual basis" (U.S. Office of Education, 1977b, p. 42497).

One of the first consequences of the implementation of P.L. 94-142 was the review of all placements of learners in residential and day facilities that were distant from their home

ON THE WEB

The **U.S. Office of Special Education and Rehabilitative Services (OSERS;** http://www2.ed.gov/about/offices/list/osers/index.html) is the federal office charged with overseeing special education services; it provides direct access to all governmental resources concerning IDEA and LRE.

communities. New services were established in local districts, and many children were "brought home." One of the most frequently used placements at that time was the self-contained classroom, and many of these students were returned to self-contained classes or special schools nearer their homes. Earlier, Lloyd Dunn (1968) had questioned this reliance on special classes for students with intellectual disabilities (see Chapter 1). He suggested that the needs of students with milder levels of impairment might be served more effectively by keeping them in general education classrooms and using diagnostic, clinical, remedial, resource, itinerant, or consultant teachers to support the instruction they received there. He believed that such support personnel, functioning within the general education environment, would help develop programs of remediation that more closely matched the individual needs of the learner. Seven years later, in 1975, Congress agreed, and local school districts have been working on achieving those ends ever since.

Data submitted by school districts and states indicate that from 1984 through 2004, patterns of services for students with disabilities changed significantly. Over that period, use of general education class placements (defined by the federal government as being served outside the general education classroom for less than 21 percent of the school day) increased from 24.6 percent to 52.1 percent. During the same time, there was a corresponding decrease in the use of more restrictive settings (U.S. Department of Education, 2006b, 2009). Other patterns were also found in the IDEA data: When placement options for 2004–2005 were analyzed by age, 62.5 percent of all elementary children with disabilities were served in general education settings, but only 44.3 percent of students in the adolescent years, with a corresponding increase in more restrictive placements. Placement rates varied by disability as well, as presented in Table 3.2, with students with intellectual disabilities, emotional disturbance, and autism more likely to be served in restrictive settings. Finally, when the placement data were analyzed by race, it became apparent that students from racial groups other than white were more likely to be served in more restrictive settings (see Table 3.3).

In most school districts, a variety of placement options are available for consideration by the IEP team. Once a team has considered how a student's strengths and needs might interact with the general education curriculum, the team determines how to best support the student's learning. "Benefit from their educational program" was the standard established for appropriate services by

Table 3.2   Placement Rates by Disability for Students Ages 6–21 (2004–2005)

Primary Disability	General Education Class	Resource Room	Separate Class	Separate Environment
Learning disabilities	51.6	35.4	12.0	1.0
Speech/language impairments	88.3	6.6	4.7	0.5
Intellectual disabilities	13.8	29.3	50.5	6.4
Emotional disturbance	32.4	22.0	28.4	17.2
Other health impairments	53.9	29.2	13.6	3.3
Autism	29.1	17.7	41.8	11.3
All disabilities	52.1	26.3	17.5	4.0

Notes:
General education: Less than 21% of the day outside the general education classroom
Resource room: 21–60% of the day outside the general education classroom (part-time special class)
Separate class: Services outside the general education classroom more than 60% of the day
Separate environment: Includes public and private special day schools, residential facilities, and home or hospital environments

Source: Data from *28th Annual Report to Congress on the Implementation of the Individuals with Disabilities Education Act, 2006* (Vol. 1, p. 54) by U.S. Department of Education, 2009, Washington, DC: USDOE.

Table 3.3	Placement Rates by Race for Students Ages 6–21 (2004–2005)			
Disability	**General Education Class**	**Resource Room**	**Separate Class**	**Separate Environment**
American Indian	50.9	33.0	13.2	2.8
Asian/Pacific Islander	50.3	22.5	23.3	4.0
Black	41.0	27.2	26.2	5.5
Hispanic	49.7	25.9	21.3	3.1
White	56.8	26.1	13.3	3.7
Total population	52.1	26.3	17.5	4.0

Notes:
General education: Less than 21% of the day outside the general education classroom
Resource room: 21–60% of the day outside the general education classroom (part-time special class)
Separate class: Services outside the general education classroom more than 60% of the day
Separate environment: Includes public and private special day schools, residential facilities, and home or hospital environments

Source: Data from *28th Annual Report to Congress on the Implementation of the Individuals with Disabilities Education Act, 2006* (Vol. 1, p. 55) by U.S. Department of Education, 2009, Washington, DC: USDOE.

the U.S. Supreme Court in *Board of Education of the Hendrick Hudson Central School District* v. *Rowley* (Turnbull, Stowe, & Huerta, 2007; Yell, Katsiyannis, & Hazelkorn, 2007). For many students with disabilities, it will be deemed appropriate to provide supports within the general education classroom to allow them to benefit from their educational programs. For some, it will be necessary to provide additional instruction related to some components of the general education curriculum in a resource room or special class setting. For only a small number of students with the most severe disabilities will it be determined that, even with supports, no part of the general education program is appropriate or possible, and placement in a more restrictive setting (e.g., special class, special school, or residential setting) will be necessary.

DIVERSITY IN FOCUS 3.2

Issues of culture and diversity have historically played a central role in discussions about where children should receive their educational services. Segregated schools were the norm in parts of the United States until the 1954 *Brown* v. *Board of Education* Supreme Court decision declared that separate is inherently unequal. Placements within special education have followed this pattern as well. Early special education services were in segregated and isolated facilities. As sensitivities changed, placements became less restrictive, with more than half of all students with disabilities today being served in general education for more than 80 percent of their day.

However, not all students with disabilities have benefited from this trend. The rates of inclusion in general education are significantly lower for students with disabilities who are identified as African American (U.S. Department of Education, 2009). They also have higher rates of placement in separate classes for more than 80 percent of the school day. These disproportionate placement rates are of concern since it is possible that the system is affected by institutional racism endemic to our evaluation instruments and our referral and decision-making processes (Salend, Garrick Duhaney, & Montgomery, 2002). It has been hypothesized that lack of cultural awareness may lead some educators to see normative cultural behaviors as problematic and in need of special education. Disproportionately low numbers of educators of color compound the problem. Future special education professionals must attend to these concerns to assure that all students receive needed services and that special education is not used to exclude students who are characterized as being culturally diverse.

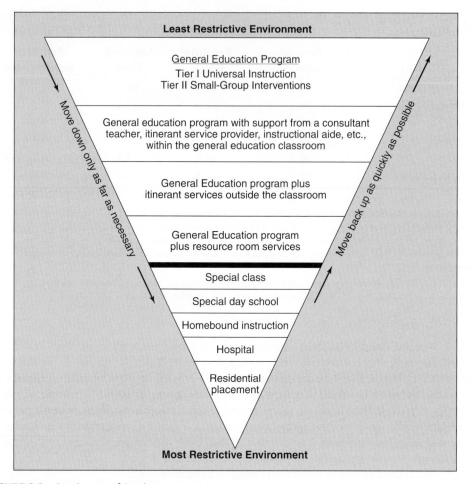

FIGURE 3.2 Continuum of Services
Source: Based on Deno, 1970; Reynolds, 1989; Ysseldyke, Algozzine, and Thurlow, 2000; Fuchs, Fuchs, and Stecker, 2010.

Implementation of a continuum of services is illustrated in Figure 3.2 (Deno, 1970; Fuchs, Fuchs, & Stecker, 2010; Reynolds, 1989; Ysseldyke et al., 2000). The relative size of the elements of the figure is intended to suggest that many more students will be appropriately served at the higher, less restrictive levels than will need to be placed in the lower, more restrictive settings. The IEP team is required to consider the educational needs of a child to identify the learner's instructional goals and objectives and then to move only as far down the continuum as necessary to find an appropriate placement. Once a placement has been identified for a learner, it is the responsibility of each of the student's teachers to provide services and supports that will make movement back to a less restrictive environment possible in the future.

MODELS OF SERVICE COMMONLY USED FOR STUDENTS WITH MILD DISABILITIES

Decades of serving learners in a manner consistent with the guidance of IDEA and the courts suggest that most learners with mild disabilities can be appropriately served at the upper levels of the continuum of services, including the following:

- For some students, the evaluation process identifies accommodations that can be employed within the general education class, allowing the student to progress in that curriculum without direct service by special education personnel. In such cases, the special educators generally provide consultation services (indirect services) to the general education teacher, who in turn delivers the instructional program to the student.

- For other students, it is necessary to provide direct assistance in the classroom through a special educator, related services provider, or instructional aide for parts of the school program (Causton-Theoharis, 2009). Such assistance might involve coteaching and monitoring by the general education–special education team to develop the student's skills needed in that environment (Lee et al., 2010). Sometimes an instructional aide assists a learner in staying on task or with reading support (Appl, 2006; Devlin, 2008; Giangreco et al., 1997)
- Some students with very specific educational needs may require out-of-classroom services several times a week from an itinerant provider (Sunderland, 2004). Examples include speech and language services, vision or hearing supports, physical and occupational therapy, and other related services. Such activities target specific skill deficiencies in areas needed for success in the general education curriculum. Specific training in articulation, for example, can allow a student to participate in the general education language arts program with typical peers.
- Other learners have specific developmental needs (e.g., reading, written language), and although the general education curriculum may be appropriate for them, the pacing and type of instruction may not be. In these cases, the general education curriculum in those specific areas may be delivered in a resource room, although the learner spends the majority of the day in the general education classroom. This type of part-time special class can be disruptive to a student's adjustment and learning and should be used only when appropriate instruction cannot be achieved within the general education class.

For a significant majority of learners with mild disabilities in learning and behavior, one of these options should be appropriate to meet their needs, allowing them to receive educational benefit from the general education curriculum. In all cases, however, the placement decision must be based on the needs of the individual student, not on a diagnostic category and not on the availability of particular services in that school or district. On occasion, the nature and severity of a specific problem might suggest short-term placement in a more restrictive setting, yet still with the goal of providing intensive intervention and returning the learner to a less restrictive environment as soon as possible. (See In the Classroom 3.4.)

Finally, with the IDEA 2004 emphasis on responsiveness to intervention, the lines between special and general education responsibilities have become somewhat blurred, as described by Fuchs and colleagues (2010). Until recently, special education and general education operated under very different authorizing statutes and regulations, with clear delineation between the responsibilities of the two groups of educators. Now, however, where general education stops and special education begins is no longer as clear as Figure 3.2 suggests. This development may lay

---

IN THE CLASSROOM 3.4

Uses of More Restrictive Placements

Jim, a student with an emotional–behavioral disorder, exhibits a period of severe problem behavior, making continued placement in the general education class inappropriate for him or others for the time being. The team is considering a temporary placement in a special class, day school, or even a residential setting where Jim can get intensive short-term counseling and behavioral interventions to prepare him to return to his home school and class.

Jane, a student with a mild intellectual disability, recently fell on the ice, resulting in a severe fracture. She is required to stay in bed for 2 months while it mends. Her physical needs dictate that homebound instruction is appropriate so that her progress in the general education curriculum is not disrupted.

the foundation for finally moving into the integrated single-box system that Reynolds (1989) envisioned (see Chapter 1). Who is responsible for services in Tiers I, II, and III? How can special and general educators work together most effectively and where? What special expertise will each contribute to the collaboration in an RTI environment? Fuchs et al. concluded that it is time for all educators to create a service delivery model that will resolve the current uncertainties, ambiguities, and blurred roles—one that will capitalize on the strengths of all in a unitary system.

INCLUSION: A CONTINUING ISSUE IN SPECIAL EDUCATION

As educators and policy makers consider the implications of providing services in the least restrictive environment, the discussion often turns to inclusion, which has been one of the most hotly debated topics in special education since the early 1980s (Kauffman & Landrum, 2006; National Center on Educational Restructuring and Inclusion, 1994). Articles appear regularly in special education literature, some advocating full inclusion of all students with disabilities, others urging the preservation of separate and specialized educational services. As noted in Fuchs et al. (2010), researchers and advocates are attempting to sort out what blurring the roles and the settings really means. These discussions are also taking place in the context of a growing international commitment to Education for All (UNESCO), to meaningful access to education for children with special educational needs as outlined in the Salamanca Statement (World Conference, 1994). Booth and Ainscow (2002) with the Centre for Studies on Inclusive Education continue to work on supporting inclusive schooling worldwide by developing standards and guidelines for effective practice.

One reason for the continuing debate is the fact that different words and definitions are used interchangeably (see Table 3.4). Some incorrectly view *inclusion* and *mainstreaming* as synonymous terms. *Mainstreaming* generally refers to the philosophy that children with disabilities should be educated with children without disabilities to the maximum extent possible; the term is related to the principle of normalization (see Chapter 1). It generally refers to the placement of

ON THE WEB

UNESCO's Education for All initiative *(http://www.unesco.org/en/efa/)* seeks to build global capacity to provide education to all children and youth around the world by 2015.

Table 3.4   Mainstreaming, Least Restrictive Environment, and Inclusion

Mainstreaming

The temporal, physical, instructional, and/or social integration of children with disabilities with typical peers. In general, children with disabilities are mainstreamed into environments where their disabilities present few impediments and where the need for accommodations is minimal. Special education services are still generally provided outside the mainstream environment.

Least Restrictive Environment

The term used in IDEA to refer to the principle that children with disabilities should be educated with their typical peers as often as possible, and that removal to more specialized (restrictive) settings should occur only when it is not possible, even with the provision of supplementary aids and supports, to serve the students' needs in general education settings. The term refers to the principle that services should be delivered in settings as similar as possible to the general education classroom.

Inclusion

The practice of providing all of the educational services for students with disabilities within the general education program. Support services required by any student are integrated into the general education program.

Partial Inclusion

A variant of the inclusion model in which most of a student's program is delivered in general education settings with supports, but in which students may also be removed from the general classroom for specialized services as dictated by their individual needs.

children in activities unaffected by their disabilities. However, it implies little beyond physical proximity, although the possibility of modifying the classroom program to accommodate mainstreamed children is frequently discussed. Even though the term does not appear in IDEA, many educators and parents continue to believe that the law requires mainstreaming.

Inclusion refers to some degree of actual integration of the two systems, ranging from collaboration and partial integration to a fully unified system. The term initially arose in the 1980s in the debate about the efficacy and morality of a dual system of education (Gartner & Lipsky, 1987; Lipsky & Gartner, 1996; Reynolds, 1989; W. Stainback & S. Stainback, 1984; Wang, Reynolds, & Walberg, 1986; Will, 1986). Drawing from the reasoning of the Supreme Court in *Brown* v. *Board of Education* (1954) that separate is inherently unequal, these writers questioned the morality of a dual system composed of special education and general education (Biklen, 1985; Zigler et al., 1990). Some suggested that special education in segregated settings is indefensible and inherently discriminatory, even if it can be shown to be effective, just as the Supreme Court found "separate but equal" education for black and white students to be inherently unequal. In addition, special education at that time had not yet demonstrated that it was able to achieve the kind of improvements that disability advocates were projecting from an individualized, universally available, separate educational process. Inclusion proponents attributed part of the efficacy problem to the continued separation of special education from real environments and curricula, creating low expectations for students. As Lipsky and Gartner wrote in 1987:

> In education, not only have students with handicapping conditions been ignored in the recent flood of national reports, but the belief persists that they are incapable of learning and behaving appropriately. This leads state education departments, school systems, and the courts to excuse them across the board from the academic, social, and behavioral expectations and standards held for other students. (p. 70)

Lipsky and Gartner went on to call for "changing the mainstream, and making general education flexible, supple, and responsive—educating the full range of students" (p. 72).

Madeleine Will (1986) addressed these issues in *Educating Children with Learning Problems: A Shared Responsibility*. She began with the assertion that the special education system supports the premise that children with disabilities cannot be effectively served in general education settings, even with modifications and supports. She held that reliance on a variety of separate or pull-out programs leads to further separation. Will stated that this system creates the sense that poor school performance is a reliable indicator of disabilities, and she faulted the system for being set up to assist students who have already failed badly, rather than preventing their failure in the first place. Noting that the U.S. educational system was failing more students than ever before, Will urged that attention be directed to developing ways to use our existing resources more efficiently, supporting all children who are having difficulty learning. In closing, she advocated creating a system in which special education and general education worked in partnership—

> to cooperatively assess the educational needs of students with learning problems and to cooperatively develop effective educational strategies for meeting those needs. . . . It does mean the nurturing of a shared commitment to the future of all children with special learning needs. (p. 415)

Such calls for the general education program to stretch and take in students with disabilities have led to two supportive perspectives relative to inclusion. One group sees nothing short of the elimination of the special education system, with all its categories and special settings, as the way to resolve the issue. They envision the return of all children to the general education classroom, regardless of the severity of their disabilities. And they look forward to a day when all education will be "special," when the individual characteristics and needs of all children are addressed as a matter of course, and when all children are included.

The other group of inclusion proponents takes a more considered approach, one that is more closely aligned with IDEA's concept of least restrictive environment and that is consistent with Will's call for shared responsibility. These educators believe that full-time or part-time placement in the general education setting is possible for more children than are now being served there, even though some students still need services that can be provided only in special classrooms and schools. They call for IEP teams to consider more carefully the possibility that the supports currently provided in resource and special classes might be made available in the general education classroom, permitting more students to participate full-time in the general education environment while still receiving special educational benefit. This perspective is best exemplified by the policy statement of the Council for Exceptional Children (1997a) regarding inclusive schools and community settings (see Appendix). The CEC called inclusion a meaningful goal, stating that educators could make the general education classroom a viable alternative for more children if general education settings were strengthened with additional supports and resources. The application of UDL principles holds out the promise that this goal could become a reality (Friesen, 2008; Hall, Strangman, & Meyer, 2009; Hitchcock et al., 2002; Kortering, McClannon, & Braziel, 2008; Meo, 2008; Orkwis & McLane, 1998).

One of the most frequently heard challenges to the efficacy of inclusion and other placement models, such as resource rooms, is that there is no convincing evidence of the effectiveness of the various placement models. Support for or opposition to inclusion tends to be founded more on philosophical rather than empirical grounds (Frattura & Capper, 2006; Kauffman, Landrum, Mock, Sayeski, & Sayeski, 2005). As noted by Vaughn and Schumm (1995), most professional and advocacy organizations have issued position statements on the question, ranging from the unqualified support of the Association for Persons with Severe Handicaps (TASH) to support for inclusion as one element within a full continuum of services (Council for Exceptional Children, 1997a). Some other parent groups fear that inclusive education will deprive their children of needed supports.

Despite these expressions of support for one model or another, the existing research base remains plagued by small samples and experimental designs that lack the power to detect differences, much less establish causal links. Researchers frequently have to work with intact groups, comparing children with disabilities served in general education classrooms with those served in resource rooms—learners who are unlikely to be similar enough for statistical comparisons. Comparing the progress of children in inclusion models with the progress of their counterparts in resource or self-contained classroom settings frequently produces unconvincing results, simply because the groups were not initially comparable. Most of the empirical research related to inclusion and other placement models reports on attitudes and attitude change of teachers or students or on the effectiveness of professional development for implementation (Idol, 2006). Other studies report on the differential effects of techniques like peer tutoring or coteaching (McDuffie, Mastropieri, & Scruggs, 2009), but not on the effect of the placement model on student performance. Only time and experience will sort this out.

Summary

IDEA 2004 provides guidance for instructional planning with the requirement that an IEP be organized around the needs of the learner as they relate to accessing the general education curriculum. The team must consider the strengths a student possesses as well as the deficits. It is important to understand that Congress intends *curriculum* to refer to the general education curriculum. In planning, special educators must be knowledgeable about the explicit or public curriculum. However, it is also important to consider the planning implications associated with the hidden curriculum, or curriculum as taught, as well as with the absent curriculum, which refers to those skills that are not taught but that students with disabilities and others may need in order to benefit from instruction.

Although the curriculum is expected to be the same for all students, that does not mean that all students will benefit from the same instructional activities. Universal design for learning provides a useful framework for making classroom activities flexible enough to provide all students with meaningful access to instruction. Flexibility in presentation, in expression, and in engagement allows all students the opportunity to learn in the way that best matches their strengths and needs. Teachers also need to be knowledgeable about research-based strategies for assisting all of their students to learn, including differentiated instruction, direct instruction, cooperative learning, peer tutoring, cognitive strategies instruction, and positive behavioral supports.

Individualized instructional planning is required for students with disabilities. This does not mean one-to-one tutoring but rather selecting educational services to meet a child's specific needs. By using the principles of universal design for learning, teachers can individualize instruction for all students.

The placement provisions of IDEA 2004 direct educational practice back to the original intent of the law. IDEA states that the only valid considerations in planning are the general education curriculum and the interaction of the learner's characteristics with that environment. Determining where services will be provided is the third step in the process, coming after the student's strengths and needs have been identified and the curriculum objectives have been determined. *Least restrictive environment* (LRE) refers to the provision in IDEA that students shall not be removed any further from the general education classroom than is necessary to meet their needs.

Since the 1980s, discussions have continued on the concept of inclusion. Concern for the lack of efficacy of special education services and the observed fragmentation of services has led some to call for the creation of a unified system, one that meets every child's learning needs without classification and segregation. One thing is clear: Place alone does not ensure a quality program or good outcomes. The setting, or placement, is merely the context in which services are provided. The critical variable is how the settings and services interact to address a student's needs and to increase positive outcomes.

A Case Study • Angie

Angie, a fourth grader in Ms. Allison's class, receives special education services in Ms. Peter's resource room. Angie began kindergarten in a suburban school. She made normal progress in the kindergarten curriculum, which was based on language development, content knowledge enrichment, and academic social skills. Her problems began in first grade with the early reading curriculum. She just didn't seem to be able to associate letters with sounds, and throughout the year she fell further and further behind. Her first-grade teacher told her mother that Angie was careless and unmotivated. Her teacher said that Angie's problems in the reading curriculum were undoubtedly due to these motivational factors, since Angie was obviously capable of learning. Frequently, Angie had to stay in for recess and revise reading worksheets that she had done incorrectly.

Angie was retained in first grade after her teacher suggested that another year might allow Angie to catch up developmentally with the others in her class. But Angie's primary problem areas in reading and spelling continued the following year; it was as if she had decided, "If you think I'm dumb, I'll just show you how dumb I am." She sat back and basically did as little as she could get away with. Yet despite her lack of effort, she made enough progress to move to second grade the next year. As the second-grade curriculum broadened into more complex math skills and the beginning study of science and social studies, Angie began to blossom—as long as she didn't have to read. Her teachers still believed that motivation was her problem; since she did well in the subjects she liked, it must be that she wasn't working hard enough in reading and spelling.

The next summer, the family moved to Littletown, where Angie entered third grade. Her new teachers noted that she had very specific problems in reading, making slow progress in the basal reading curriculum. Her most significant difficulties in reading seemed to be related to difficulty with phonetics. Somewhere along the way, she had become convinced that the goal in reading is to precisely and accurately sound out all the words. Angie tried hard to please her teachers and to prove to them that she wasn't lazy, but her approach to reading and her motivation to achieve resulted in her reading in a very labored way, a behavior that appeared to compromise her comprehension. Phonics deficits also showed up in her difficulty with spelling. She showed little growth in response to the reading and spelling interventions in the resource room.

In fourth grade, her classroom teacher suggested that Angie be referred for possible special education needs. Her full-scale IQ score on the WISC-IV was 119, and she achieved the following standard scores on the Peabody Individual Achievement Test-R:

Total Reading Composite	90
Written Language Composite	93

Subtest Scores	Standard Score
Reading Recognition	85
Reading Comprehension	95
Written Expression	95
Spelling	90
General Information	129
Mathematics	120

Based on the reports from the classroom teacher and this testing, the multidisciplinary team determined that Angie met the district's criteria as a student with a learning disability, and she began to receive special education services in spelling and reading. Angie worked hard in the resource room, but the teacher could tell that she was bored by the repetition and by the low cognitive level of the material she was given to read. Progress was very slow.

In the general education classroom, Angie continued to excel in her math and science work. Her teacher, Ms. Allison, noted that Angie really loved science. She loved doing experiments, she loved to use scientific words (the bigger, the better), and she was excited about learning about computers. Her scores on a math achievement test indicated that she was significantly above her peers in math. On the most recent statewide achievement testing, she scored in the 85th percentile in math and science, receiving an award for her achievement. Her speaking vocabulary and expressive language skills were also both highly developed.

Ms. Allison was glad that Angie was successful in these areas, and now that her reading and spelling were being taken care of by the special educator, those problems were of little concern to Ms. Allison in the general education program. Angie's reading and spelling difficulties faded from concern, and she learned how to effectively compensate for her learning disability. Throughout all this, Angie's mother was a significant support, telling her that she could do anything and that she knew Angie would figure out her own way to get tasks done.

Ms. Peters, the resource room teacher, described Angie as a shy child who tended to become scared at times. Angie was not very secure with herself, and her self-esteem was not as high as it could be. Despite her demonstrated areas of high achievement, the difficulties in reading and spelling led others, and sometimes Angie herself, to believe that she wasn't very smart. Ms. Peters was puzzled by this. She knew that the resource program was not challenging enough for Angie and that because of her problems in reading, she was also not exposed to some of the more challenging opportunities in the general education curriculum. Ms. Peters decided to investigate the possibility of Angie's participating in the district's honors program in fifth grade, while still receiving her learning disability services. The teacher in the honors program said she had heard of students who were bright and also had learning disabilities, but she had never worked with one. She wasn't even sure she believed they existed. In addition, she said that the criteria for the honors program were "very strict," so the idea was never pursued. Ms. Peters now wishes that she had pushed it. Angie shows such good thinking, and her oral skills reflect a much higher level of functioning than is indicated by her spelling and reading scores. Despite all the assistance Angie has received, it seems to Ms. Peters that something is still missing.

Discussion

From the perspective of the general education curriculum, analyze the information provided about Angie. Have her teachers provided her with access to that curriculum? How? To what extent does it appear that the basic skills remediation Angie has received in the resource room has been effective? Can you identify other approaches or instructional strategies that might increase her participation in the general education curriculum? What effect might these strategies have on her overall performance? Consider the implications for instruction and curriculum of a student's having significant intellectual strengths in addition to having a specific learning disability. How might UDL benefit a student like Angie?

Who Are the Learners with Mild Disabilities?

Who are the learners with mild disabilities? How do we identify a child with a disability? How prevalent are learners with mild disabilities? In considering these questions, we undertake one of the most basic of human cognitive activities (Bruner, 1990). Human beings are driven to seek meaning related to people, things, and events by grouping them with like entities. The field of special education has likewise endeavored to create order within the universe of human ability and difference. As individuals were identified who differed from their peers in one or more ways, the central, most prominent characteristics of those individuals were enumerated. Those with sufficient similarities were grouped into categories, giving rise to the disability categories we use today (Sabornie et al., 2005; Sabornie et al., 2006). The challenge then becomes developing definitions or rules to determine whether a particular individual belongs to that group.

> Definitions cannot be right or wrong, or true or false, but only useful or not useful. A useful definition . . . would aid in the classification system that has two major goals: (1) to benefit those classified by being helpful to their clinicians and service providers, and (2) to bring much-needed order to the field, while directing workers to important issues in need of further study. (Zigler & Hodapp, 1986, p. 63)

In this unit, we will consider some of the issues related to conceptualizing a variety of high-incidence conditions at milder levels of impairment, those most likely to be served within the general education program, either in inclusive settings or in part-time special education:

- Mild intellectual disabilities
- Learning disabilities

- Emotional or behavioral disorders
- Attention-deficit/hyperactivity disorders
- Communication disorders

In addition, we will discuss some low-incidence disabilities that can also be manifested in milder ranges of impairment:

- Sensory impairments (e.g., hearing and visual impairments)
- Physical impairments
- Health impairments
- Autism spectrum disorders (e.g., high-functioning autism [HFA] and Asperger's disorder)

In light of the information provided in Chapters 4–8, the reader is encouraged to consider whether our efforts to date have been effective in responding to the goals posed by Zigler and Hodapp in 1986 by answering the following questions:

- What benefits do learners derive from being classified within our current systems?
- Do our current systems bring order to the field and facilitate the delivery of services?
- Are there issues we must continue to address as we seek to support the learning and living of all children and youth?

CHAPTER 4

Learners with Intellectual and Developmental Disabilities

Questions *to Guide Your Study*

- Why has the name for this area of disability changed over time?
- What does the history of intellectual disabilities teach us?
- How do we define *intellectual disabilities*?
- How does the 2010 AAIDD definition differ from previous definitions?
- What are the current issues in defining intellectual disabilities?
- How can we most usefully designate the levels of severity of intellectual disabilities?
- How prevalent is the condition we call intellectual disabilities?
- What conditions place a learner at risk for intellectual disabilities?
- What are students with intellectual disabilities like?

Meet Caroline

Caroline entered a small, rural public school as a kindergartner. She was a pleasant child, anxious to please. Her parents were very supportive of their children and the school, always coming in for conferences and asking how they could help. Caroline's teachers in kindergarten and first grade observed that it seemed to take her longer than the others in the class to learn key concepts, but she worked hard. They appreciated the efforts she made and felt that she would eventually catch on.

In second grade, her teacher noticed that Caroline was continuing to have difficulty learning, particularly when attempting to learn more abstract concepts. Although she got along well in the social environment of the classroom and worked hard to keep up with the lower math and reading groups in the class, her teacher decided to refer her for evaluation of a possible disability in need of special education services.

The psychological evaluation determined that Caroline had an IQ of 64 and that, although her functional and social behaviors and skills were adequate for second grade, she qualified for services as a child with mild intellectual disabilities based on her IQ. Her IEP was developed to provide resource room support as needed, particularly in reading and mathematics.

Initially, Caroline went to the resource room an hour a day for extra help, but the resource room teacher quickly determined that the time she was out of the primary classroom setting seemed to be interfering with her skill development. Because of her strong work habits, Caroline seemed to benefit more from staying in the classroom than from receiving special education services outside the general classroom. The resource room teacher continued to monitor her progress, providing indirect services through Caroline's classroom teachers.

Over the next 3 years, Caroline continued to make adequate progress in basic academic skills, and her good social and work adjustment continued. In fifth grade, however, Caroline began to struggle in reading again. The vocabulary and stories became more abstract and were not related to her daily life experience. Her effort and coping skills were no longer adequate to maintain progress, and she began to fail. Resource room services were reinstituted, with additional instruction in vocabulary development and comprehension skills. This extra support enabled Caroline to hold her own through sixth grade.

As the time neared for her to move to the secondary level, her resource room teacher met with Caroline's parents to plan her IEP for seventh grade. They discussed her progress and then talked about her ultimate goals once her school years were completed—thus beginning the process of IDEA-required transition planning. They discussed her strong social and work skills and her difficulties with abstract levels of learning. Although her grades did not preclude her remaining in the typical academic track in junior high, the team decided that it would be better to develop a program for Caroline that supplemented the academic work with involvement in the school's prevocational program, concentrating her academic program on functional reading, writing, and mathematics skills.

Today, Caroline is an independent young adult. She works as a cashier in the local grocery store, has a social life outside of work, and manages her own financial affairs.

THINKING QUESTIONS

Once Caroline was classified as having intellectual disabilities, how did the classification help her get what she needed? Could these benefits have been provided in another way? What might have been the outcome of this support?

NAMING THIS GROUP OF LEARNERS

ON THE WEB

The **American Association on Intellectual and Developmental Disabilities** (www.aaidd. org) provides resources for professionals serving individuals with intellectual disabilities, including information on definition and identification, a useful publications link, and a section for new professionals.

Various terms have been used over the past 2 centuries for the learners we will be discussing in this chapter—*idiocy, feeblemindedness, mental deficiency, mental handicap, mental subnormality, mental impairment, mental disability, mental retardation.* Throughout the 1st decade of the 21st century, organizations, schools, families, and advocates engaged in active discussions of alternative terminology for the disability that had been generally referred to as mental retardation during the preceding 2 decades (Wehmeyer et al., 2008). A consensus was building that the term *mental retardation* needed to be replaced; it portrayed a deficit orientation and was a stigmatic label. In 2007 the primary organization for professionals serving this group of individuals formally changed its name from the American Association on Mental Retardation (AAMR) to the American Association on Intellectual and Developmental Disabilities (AAIDD), signaling the shift in terminology. AAIDD also used the term *intellectual disability* in the 2010 edition of their definitional manual. Use of the term *intellectual disability* is growing in use outside the United States (World Health Organization, 2001, 2007a), and major U.S. organizations such as The Arc have also adopted it as their term of choice. Nevertheless, IDEA and a majority of states (n = 34) still use the term *mental retardation* in the language of the law, although some states have begun using a variety of new terminologies (Polloway et al., 2009; Schalock et al., 2007; Wehmeyer et al., 2008). With the signing of Rosa's Law in October 2010, the term *intellectual disabilities* should now replace *mental retardation* in most U.S. statutes (Diament, 2010).

One of the primary reasons given for making this change was to respond to the perception of stigma associated with the term *mental retardation* and the preference of affected individuals for the new term. Consequently, we will be using the term *intellectual disability* throughout this book. As was noted in the 11th edition of the AAIDD definition manual (2010), this term refers to the same individuals who were previously referred to as having mental retardation, and an existing diagnosis of mental retardation is equivalent to a classification of intellectual disabilities. For consistency, we will use the term *intellectual disability* even when referring to individuals in earlier time periods when other terminology would have been common.

HISTORICAL FOUNDATIONS OF INTELLECTUAL DISABILITIES

Caroline's story is reflective of the time in which she lives and indicative of the way mild intellectual disability is conceptualized today. Her story would likely have been quite different had she lived in other times—or in the future. The way people with intellectual disabilities have been treated—and whether persons with milder intellectual impairments would have been identified at all—has been determined more by the attitudes and values of the times in which they happened to be born than by any objective criteria (Payne & Patton, 1981).

As was discussed in Chapter 1, the variable treatment of persons with disabilities such as intellectual disabilities prior to 1700 reflected a general lack of understanding, characterized by confusion and lack of knowledge (Stainton, 2008). Such individuals were treated as buffoons, clowns, and jesters or as demons or as beings capable of divine revelations. Only those with the most severe levels of disability were even noticed in those largely preliterate societies.

With the Renaissance and its focus on humanism, society awakened to the idea that all people had rights. This awareness led to the development of a climate of support for those with deficits in intellectual functioning. The 1800s saw the development of optimism about the ability to improve the functioning of those with intellectual disabilities, a result of research conducted almost exclusively by physicians. They focused on individuals with moderate and severe levels of impairment as well as on those with accompanying physical disabilities (Verstraete, 2005). The work of Down and Sequin in the mid-1800s resulted in differentiation of types of intellectual disabilities and an awareness that insanity and retardation were indeed different conditions. Through the work of Itard, Sequin, Dix, Howe, Wilbur, and others, a variety of residential treatment programs were established, all with hope that a cure for intellectual disability would be found in these educational efforts (Graham, 1991).

When these efforts failed to provide the envisioned cures by the late 1800s, states modified more institutions into custodial facilities, and training programs were phased out. Persons with moderate and severe intellectual disabilities were destined to live out their lives in these isolated institutions. The public perception was that the residents of these institutions were dangerous, and calls for segregation of this population from the larger society were heard throughout the country. However, those with milder levels of intellectual disability like Caroline continued to blend into a society that valued manual and unskilled labor more than reading and writing.

With the advent of the testing and eugenics movements, society had new tools to identify, isolate, and eliminate this perceived "social menace." New immigrants were believed to be a source of mental deficiency as well, resulting in discrimination and harassment of new arrivals to the United States. Despite this climate of fear, however, a few public school day classes were established for children with intellectual disabilities.

From 1930 to 1950, research continued. A major breakthrough in investigating causes of intellectual disabilities occurred in 1934 when Folling discovered the cause of the condition called phenylketonuria (PKU). This discovery provided impetus for research designed to identify other genetically determined forms of intellectual disability and held out the possibility of effective early interventions. Skeels and Dye (1939) published a study that indicated that the environment also appeared to affect mental development. The testing movement produced new assessment instruments, laying the groundwork for more specific identification and diagnostic procedures for those with suspected intellectual disabilities (Safford & Safford, 1996). The 1950s saw a renewal of advocacy on behalf of persons with intellectual disabilities. The founding of the National Association for Retarded Children (now The Arc of the United States) helped to create a climate for public advocacy and action.

ON THE WEB

The Arc of the United States (http://www.thearc.org) provides resources for families, as well as for local chapters of The Arc, one of the earliest parent advocacy groups working for community access for individuals with intellectual disabilities.

The nature-versus-nurture debate continued. In response to the eugenicists of the early part of the century, Masland, Sarason, and Gladwin (1958) published *Mental Subnormality*, making the connection between social/cultural variables and intellectual disability and highlighting the nurture component of the debate. Jane Mercer's (1973) work on the sociological definition of intellectual disability further underscored the importance of accurately assessing a person's ability to function in social contexts before making a diagnosis. During the same period, Arthur Jensen (1969) reasserted the nature side of the argument with a controversial article arguing that genetic factors were more important in determining intelligence than environmental factors were.

John Kennedy established the President's Panel on Mental Retardation in 1961 to provide a forum for discussion of issues in this field, sparked by his experiences with his sister who had an intellectual disability. Edgerton's *Cloak of Competence* (1967) helped persons with mild intellectual disability tell their own stories for the first time, just as Bogdan and Taylor (1976, 1994) were to do later with Ed Murphy (see the case study in Chapter 1). The work of Edgerton, Bogdan, and Taylor supported the concept of intellectual disability as a social construction, underscoring the extent to which this disability is defined by the social context of the individual. Edgerton helped expose the extent to which the stigma associated with this condition leads individuals to pull on a "cloak of competence," to deny their disability, and, more importantly, to seek the full benefits of life in society as others do. Lloyd Dunn in his classic article (1968) questioned the efficacy of existing segregated services for students with mild intellectual disability (see Spotlight on History 1.4).

At the end of the 20th century, professionals still debated the construct of intellectual disability, discussing ways to identify those in need of services and focusing attention on functional aspects. The efficacy of many programs was questioned. Lack of appropriate community services threatened the movement toward deinstitutionalization and normalization. Special education professionals and advocates were called on to find ways to ensure that students with intellectual disabilities would continue to advance in the future as they had in the past. Advocates for inclusive education and noncategorical supports took the stage.

DEVELOPMENT OF THE DEFINITION OF INTELLECTUAL DISABILITIES IN THE UNITED STATES

In 1919 the American Association on Mental Deficiency (AAMD/AAMR/AAIDD) established the Committee on Classification and Uniform Statistics and charged it with the responsibility of developing a system of classification to aid in providing differentiated treatment programs for individuals with deficits in intellectual functioning. Diagnostic manuals produced over the next 4 decades provided doctors and other professionals with a common language to discuss the variety of conditions and syndromes presented by their patients and clients.

The 1959 edition of the AAMD/AAIDD manual (Heber, 1959) provided uniformity in terminology for the first time. It also introduced a dual classification system, describing both medical and behavioral aspects of intellectual disability. The behavioral section addressed both intellectual and adaptive behavior levels. This manual changed the IQ criterion for classification from two to one standard deviation below the mean, effectively raising the IQ criterion for diagnosis from 70 to 85. This edition also added an adaptive behavior criterion to the diagnostic process, with the expectation that adding the adaptive behavior deficit criterion would reduce the possibility of overidentification due to the higher IQ criterion. However, there was considerable concern in the field about identifying such a large segment of the population (potentially about 16 percent) as possibly having intellectual disabilities, and in 1973 the IQ level was restored to the pre-1959 level of two standard deviations below the mean (Grossman, 1973). These changes in criteria between 1959 and 1973 illustrate the arbitrariness of such determinations (Hobbs, 1975a; Zigler & Hodapp, 1986). As illustrated in Figure 4.1, with the stroke of a pen in 1959, an additional 14 percent of the population was eligible to be labeled as having intellectual disabilities. However, the 1973 definition effectively removed the threat of that label from the same 14 percent of the population (Bogdan & Taylor, 1994; Kavale et al., 2009).

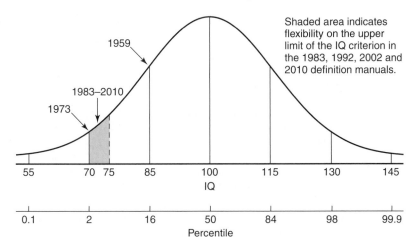

FIGURE 4.1   Effect of Changes in IQ Criterion in the AAMD/AAMR/AAIDD Definition

The 1973 AAMD/AAIDD manual also more explicitly defined deficits in adaptive behavior, providing illustrations of various levels of deficit as guidelines. However, there were problems obtaining standardized measures of adaptive behavior since adaptive behavior scales at the time were normed on institutionalized individuals. The 1983 AAMD/AAIDD manual (Grossman, 1983) clarified the use of IQ testing for classification by emphasizing that the IQ score criterion was a guideline only. Diagnosticians were reminded that they should take into account the standard error of measurement on any test used for classification purposes and should use clinical judgment in interpreting all data. In particular, diagnosticians were reminded to use adaptive behavior assessments in conjunction with IQ in making classification decisions.

IDEA DEFINITION OF INTELLECTUAL DISABILITIES

The definition of *intellectual disabilities/mental retardation* included in IDEA 2004 is the definition published in 1983 by AAMD/AAIDD, which reads as follows:

> Mental retardation [intellectual disabilities] refers to significantly subaverage general intellectual functioning existing concurrently with deficits in adaptive behavior and manifested during the developmental period. (U.S. Office of Education, 1977b, p. 42478; Grossman, 1983, p. 1)

Key terms used in this definition include these four (Grossman, 1983):

• *General intellectual functioning:* Defined operationally as the results obtained from an individually administered intelligence test with appropriate psychometric properties (e.g., Stanford-Binet, the K-ABC, and the Wechsler family of tests: WPPSI, WISC, WAIS).

• *Significantly subaverage:* Defined as an IQ score of about 70 or below (or two standard deviations below the mean for the test used). The manual emphasized that the score of 70 was intended as a *guideline* only, and that it could be extended upward to 75 depending on the reliability of the test used and other relevant data. The IQ guideline of 70 is derived from the normal curve (see Figure 4.2), which implies that individuals with scores of two or more standard deviations from the mean should probably be considered as part of another population, in this case the population of persons with intellectual disabilities. Diagnostic manuals repeatedly caution, however, that clinical judgment and multiple sources of information, including adaptive behavior measures, must always be used in interpreting the meaning and validity of any intelligence measure.

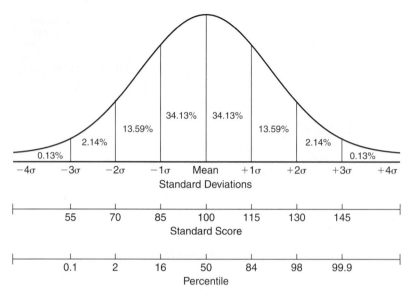

FIGURE 4.2 Normal Distribution of the Population

• *Deficits in adaptive behavior:* Defined as displaying significant limitations in ability to meet age-appropriate cultural standards in conceptual, social, and practical skills—all the things people do to take care of themselves and interact effectively with others in daily life. Although these skills are often evaluated informally by comparing an individual's everyday functioning to that of peers, formal evaluations of intellectual disabilities typically include the use of one or more standardized measures of adaptive behavior. Some of the more commonly used adaptive behavior scales are listed in Table 4.1.

• *Developmental period:* The period of time between conception and age 18. When individuals develop impairments in mental functioning due to trauma or nervous system deterioration after development has been completed, the extent to which previous learning and life experiences affect the nature of rehabilitation services must be considered. It would therefore be inappropriate to classify these individuals with the same diagnostic label used for those whose impairment disrupted typical developmental experiences during childhood and before learning could occur.

To summarize, applying this definition to the classification process with an individual below age 18 requires an IQ score and a standardized evaluation of the individual's adaptive behavior or functioning. These two criteria (see Figure 4.3) are used to determine whether an individual meets both requirements for classification as a child with an intellectual disability.

It is important to note, however, that despite the use of the 1983 AAMD/AAIDD definition in IDEA, a survey of state criteria for classification (Polloway et al., 2009) found that only 34 states used some version of the IDEA definition, whereas 12 others used an adaptation of the later AAIDD definitions, and 4 states used still other definitions. A majority of states did not specify use of all three criteria. Bereron, Floyd, and Shands (2008) reported variation among the states in cutoff scores for intellectual functioning measures, including differential use of the

Table 4.1 Adaptive Behavior Measures in Common Use
AAIDD Diagnostic Adaptive Behavior Scales (DABS; 2010)
Adaptive Behavior Assessment System, Second Edition (ABAS; 2003)
Scales of Independent Behavior—Revised (SIB-R; 1996)
Vineland Adaptive Behavior Scales, Second Edition (2005)

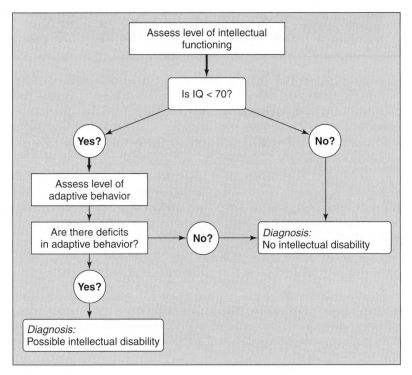

FIGURE 4.3   Classification Protocol for Determining the Existence of Intellectual Disability Using the IDEA Definition

full-scale and part scores derived from assessment of intelligence. Even though all states but one required adaptive behavior assessment, there was significant variation in the application of the adaptive behavior criterion. Some states required only the global assessment scores, whereas others considered the patterns among subdomains. Few states required adaptive behavior to be assessed in multiple settings. In addition, 18 states had specific criteria for the level of severity, with most using mild/moderate/severe/profound. (See Spotlight on History 4.1 for a discussion of other classification issues.)

ADDITIONAL PERSPECTIVES ON DEFINING INTELLECTUAL DISABILITIES

The New Generation of Other AAMR/AAIDD Definitions

In 1992 AAMR/AAIDD's new classification manual shifted the focus from intelligence measures and instead defined intellectual disabilities primarily by the presence of "substantial limitations in present functioning" (1992, p. 1), requiring deficits in at least 2 of 10 adaptive skill areas. Some writers in the field suggested that this definition, by focusing on present functioning, represented a paradigm shift in the conceptualization of intellectual disabilities (J. D. Smith, 1994). By shifting the focus from looking at intellectual disability as a personal trait, AAMR/AAIDD was conceptualizing it as an expression of the interaction of the abilities of an individual and the environment in which that person must function (Wehmeyer et al., 2008).

The implication of the 1992 definition was that the degree of intellectual disability was not a fixed intrinsic trait but in fact might change over time and between environments (Wehmeyer, 2003). Most importantly, it implied that the level of disability might be significantly affected by the level of supports commonly available in the environment. If an individual needed only those supports that were commonly available to all individuals, then no special supports were needed, and the diagnosis of intellectual disability would be deemed inappropriate.

The Six-Hour Retarded Child

To more fully understand the effect and importance of the adaptive behavior criterion as a necessary precondition for classification of intellectual disability, we can look to the report issued by the President's Committee on Mental Retardation (1970), entitled "The Six-Hour Retarded Child." Responding to the concern that children from varying economic and cultural backgrounds were being placed in classes for children with intellectual disabilities in disproportionately large numbers, the conference participants looked closely at the practices that might be related to this phenomenon. One participant said:

> We now have what may be called a 6-hour retarded child—retarded from 9 to 3, five days a week, solely on the basis of an IQ score, without regard to his adaptive behavior, which may be exceptionally adaptive to the situation and community in which he lives. (President's Committee on Mental Retardation, 1970, frontispiece)

The report quoted Wilson Riles, then Associate Superintendent of the California State Department of Education, as asking:

> The rate of placement of Spanish surname children in special education is about three times higher than for Anglo children; the Negro rate is close to four times the Anglo rate. . . . The question must be raised: to what extent are children classified as mentally retarded when the true nature of their learning disabilities stems from environmental factors? (p. 2)

This report underscored the need to include an evaluation of adaptive behavior in a variety of environments in order to better understand the child's strengths as well as weaknesses. The participants called for an assessment of children's behavior in their homes and neighborhoods. The committee members further asserted that when the results of the behavioral assessment were not consistent with the obtained IQ score, the child should not be labeled as having intellectual disabilities but should still receive educational services tailored to the child's strengths and deficits. They believed that this understanding was critical to designing a helpful learning environment for a particular child. In particular, the participants called for a reexamination of the present system of intelligence testing and classification. James Allen, then U.S. Commissioner of Education, asked:

> Is it possible that the term [*intellectual disabilities*] is no longer of any value to an educator? Do we need to find a new concept of education for children with special needs—one that does not carry with it the surplus meaning which is threatening to parents and detrimental to children? (p. 15)

> Leo Cain of the President's Commission observed: "When we attach a number to a child, we conveniently put him in a slot where we say a program has been devised to fit that particular number" (p. 15). Panel members also questioned the basic assumption that programs adequately match labels and test score criteria, and they cast doubts on the utility of the classification process itself.

Source: From *The Six-Hour Retarded Child* by President's Committee on Mental Retardation, 1970, Washington, DC: U.S. Government Printing Office.

This definition was not, however, without its critics. Their concerns as summarized by MacMillan, Gresham, and Siperstein (1993, 1995) included these: (a) that the more flexible IQ guideline (70–75) might lead to increased numbers of inappropriate classifications; (b) that it would be difficult to measure the 10 subdomains of adaptive behavior, given the current lack of validated instruments; and (c) that it would be difficult to reliably determine the intensities of the levels of support needed by an individual. The AAIDD definition and criteria have to date been adopted by 12 states (4 using the 1992 version and another 8 using the 2002 definition) to determine whether a student has intellectual disabilities (Denning, Chamberlain, & Polloway, 2000; Polloway et al., 2009).

In 2002 AAMR/AAIDD revised its manual again in response to the concerns raised with the 1992 version, redefining intellectual disabilities as follows:

> Intellectual disability is characterized by significant limitations both in intellectual functioning and in adaptive behavior as expressed in conceptual, social, and practical adaptive skills. This disability originates before age 18. The following five assumptions are essential to the application of this definition:
>
> 1. Limitations in present functioning must be considered within the context of community environments typical of the individual's age peers and culture.
> 2. Valid assessment considers cultural and linguistic diversity as well as differences in communication, sensory, motor, and behavioral factors.
> 3. Within an individual, limitations often coexist with strengths.
> 4. An important purpose of describing limitations is to develop a profile of needed supports.
> 5. With appropriate personalized supports over a sustained period, the life functioning of the person with intellectual disabilities generally will improve.*

The 1992, 2002, and 2010 AAIDD definitions underscore the importance of considering an individual's current functioning in environments typical for that person before making a determination of limitations in intellectual functioning. AAIDD also emphasizes the importance of sensitivity to the effects of cultural differences when function is assessed. Finally, the AAIDD definition points out the need to consider individual strengths as well as needs in identifying the appropriate supports.

This approach addresses many of the concerns of the President's Committee on Mental Retardation (1970), as described in Spotlight on History 4.1 (Wehmeyer, 2003). It is also responsive to concerns today about the disproportionate identification of students from culturally diverse backgrounds as students with intellectual disabilities (Artiles et al., 2010; Patton, 1998; Salend et al., 2002).

Developmental Disabilities and Delay

Alternative terms are sometimes used to indicate problems during normal development, including *developmental disabilities* or *developmental delay* (J. D. Smith, 2002). Use of these terms has received mixed reception. For some, the terms are preferred because of their lack of potential for stigmatization. *Developmental delay* is often the term of choice for many early intervention programs in which it is not always possible or desirable to apply classification schemes used with school-age children because of the limited language abilities and unstable traits of preschool children. IDEA 2004 allows the use of *developmental delay* as a generic term for children through age 9 whenever children are experiencing delays significant enough to require intervention in one or more of the following areas: physical development, cognitive development, communication development, social or emotional development, or adaptive development.

The term *developmental disability*, on the other hand, has a more specific legal meaning, and those who seek to use it as a more generic-sounding alternative to *intellectual disabilities* need to be aware of this. The Developmental Disabilities Assistance and Bill of Rights Act of 2000 defines a developmental disability as severe, chronic, and generalized impairment in functioning:

> The term "developmental disability" means a severe chronic disability of an individual five years of age or older that (a) is attributable to a mental or physical impairment or

ON THE WEB

The **President's Committee for People with Intellectual Disabilities**, established by President Kennedy in 1961, continues today to advise the President and the Secretary of Health and Human Services on issues that impact people with intellectual disabilities, seeking to improve service delivery and quality of life (http://www.acf.hhs.gov/programs/pcpid/).

---

*Reprinted with permission from *Intellectual Disability: Definition, Classification, and Systems of Supports* (11th ed., p. 1) by American Association on Intellectual and Developmental Disabilities, 2010, Washington, DC: AAIDD.

combination of mental and physical impairments; (b) is manifested before the individual attains age twenty-two; (c) is likely to continue indefinitely; (d) results in substantial functional limitations in three or more of the following areas of major life activity: (i) self-care, (ii) receptive and expressive language, (iii) learning, (iv) mobility, (v) self-direction, (vi) capacity for independent living, and (vii) economic self-sufficiency; and (e) reflects the individual's need for a combination and sequence of special, interdisciplinary, or generic services, individualized supports, or other forms of assistance that are of lifelong or extended duration and are individually planned and coordinated. (Developmental Disabilities Assistance and Bill of Rights Act of 2000, P.L. 106-402, 114 Stat. 1678 § 102[8][A], 2000)

From this definition, it is apparent that the legal definition of this term implies severe and multiple disabilities of a long-term nature. Thus, it applies only when there are very significant deficits in functioning. It is estimated that there are more than 3 million individuals who have developmental disabilities in the United States (U.S. Office of Vocational and Adult Education, 2010). Estimates also indicate that only about half of the individuals currently identified as having intellectual disabilities would meet the more stringent criteria of the Developmental Disabilities Assistance Act (American Association on Mental Retardation, 2002). Although the term would be applicable to some individuals with intellectual disabilities and the term appears to represent a less stigmatizing label, it would be inappropriate to apply it generically to all persons with intellectual disability, and its use would certainly exclude a number of those currently receiving services for mild intellectual disabilities.

An Alternative Definition with an Instructional Perspective

Although the currently used definitions of intellectual disabilities may define for administrative purposes the limitations of persons with intellectual disability, the definitions provide weak guidance to those involved in providing instruction to students with intellectual disability. Dever (1990) developed an instructional paradigm that teachers and caregivers may find more useful. This instructional definition was not intended to replace more formal classification/administrative definitions but rather to complement them. Dever's purpose was to provide a more useful delineation of the degree of deficit in intellectual functioning of individuals who have been identified as having intellectual disabilities. He sought to develop a definition that would be more useful in describing the nature of the disability with respect to instructional goals, proposing the following definition as a supplement to formal classification processes:

> [Intellectual disability] refers to the need for specific training of skills that most people acquire incidentally and that enable individuals to live in the community without supervision. (p. 149)

Dever further clarified the meaning of *independence* as follows:

> Independence is exhibiting behavior patterns appropriate to the behavior settings normally frequented by others of the individual's age and social status in such a manner that the individual is not seen as requiring assistance because of his/her behavior. (p. 151)

In discussing the implications of looking at intellectual disability from an instructional perspective, Dever identified the following assumptions:

- Persons with intellectual disabilities can learn.
- The central issue in identifying intellectual disability is the need for instruction.
- The degree of intellectual disability is related to the amount and intensity of instruction needed to achieve the goal of independent living; the more intense the need for instruction, the more severe the level of disability.

Table 4.2 Levels of Intellectual Disability	
Level of Intellectual Disability	**IQ Ranges**
Mild intellectual disability	50/55 to approximately 70
Moderate intellectual disability	35/40 to 50/55
Severe intellectual disability	20/25 to 35/40
Profound intellectual disability	Below 20/25

Source: Data from American Association on Mental Retardation, 2002; American Psychiatric Association, 2000; Grossman, 1983.

- If an individual achieves the goal of independent living, the designation of intellectual disability is no longer applicable since it is the need for instruction/support that defines the condition.
- The aim of instruction (i.e., independent adult living) is the same for everyone; however, individuals will differ in their ability to attain that goal.
- Some persons with intellectual disability will not attain the goal of independence despite instruction; therefore they will continue to be described as persons with intellectual disability as adults.

LEVELS OF SEVERITY

Once a learner has been classified as having an intellectual disability, using the IDEA criteria of deficits in intellectual functioning and adaptive behavior, educators then generally use the measure of intellectual functioning to determine the level of intellectual disability, taking into account the standard error of measurement of the tests (see Table 4.2). The use of a range of numbers as the upper and lower limits implies that clinical judgment based on an evaluation of the individual's actual ability to function is necessary to establish the level of impairment (Grossman, 1983).

Educational Terminology

Schools began universally serving students with intellectual disability after the passage of the Education for All Handicapped Children Act of 1975 (now IDEA). Prior to that time, many schools routinely excluded those students who were not deemed to be "educable." This differentiation led to the establishment of a level-designation system used to determine placement in school programs. These levels were based on the estimate of ultimate school outcomes and roughly corresponded to the IQ levels established by AAMR/AAIDD (see Table 4.3).

Students placed in "educable" classes were assumed to have the ability to become literate at a basic level and to acquire the basic vocational skills necessary for independent adult living. Students placed in "trainable" classes were expected to develop self-care and daily living skills but not reading and mathematics skills beyond a simple survival level; they were thought to be capable of working only in sheltered environments. Those at the severe/profound level were expected to need custodial care throughout their lives, and their educational program, if any, was

Table 4.3 Terms Used Historically by Schools for Students with Intellectual Disabilities		
Obsolete Educational Terms		**Comparable AAIDD Terms**
EMH/EMR	Educable class	Mild intellectual disability
TMH/TMR	Trainable class	Moderate intellectual disability
PMH/PMR	Severe/profound class	Severe and profound intellectual disability

designed to develop basic communication and mobility skills, as well as simple self-care skills such as eating and using the toilet.

The use of this terminology has largely been phased out, replaced in most schools by the designations of mild, moderate, and severe disability or similar designators indicating the intensity of supports or the type of curriculum needed by the students in the program. Use of the terms *educable* and *trainable* today is generally viewed as offensive and professionally inappropriate.

Supports and Intensity of Support Needs

In 1992 AAIDD replaced the use of such global terms to designate the level of intellectual disability with a supports framework. Acknowledging that each individual possesses strengths and weaknesses among and within the various adaptive skill areas (i.e., conceptual, social, and practical), AAIDD (2010) proposes using these strengths and weaknesses to determine the intensity of supports an individual requires to function optimally. This paradigm provides a guide to planning that is designed to resolve mismatches between an individual's characteristics and environmental demands. The AAIDD framework assumes that if appropriate levels of support, including instruction, are provided, a person will be assisted in carrying out life functions, and over time these supports should enable the person to function with fewer supports (see Figure 4.4). The level of severity, determined primarily by an IQ score, is seen as neither global nor chronic but rather as a guide to providing appropriate supportive services at a given point in development (Brown, Ouellette-Kuntz, Bielsks, & Elliott, 2009; Thompson et al., 2002, 2004, 2009). This perspective is similar to and consistent with the instructional paradigm proposed earlier by Dever and Knapczyk (1997).

It is important to note that, unlike the previous global indicators of severity, this process expects that each adaptive skill area will be evaluated separately and that the supports provided will be tailored to meet those specific needs (J. D. Smith, 1994; Thompson et al., 2002, 2004, 2009). It is very likely that individual students may require differing intensities of support in various skill areas. To provide more or less support than is needed in a particular skill area is potentially to compromise the individual's progress toward more effective functioning over time.

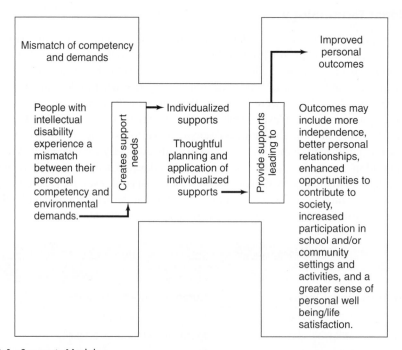

FIGURE 4.4 Supports Model

*Reprinted with permission from Intellectual Disability: Definition, Classification, and Systems of Supports (11th ed., p. 112) by American Association on Intellectual and Developmental Disabilities, 2010, Washington, DC: AAIDD.

Supports may be needed only on an intermittent basis (as needed and short-term), or they may be of a limited, extensive, or pervasive nature, ranging from low to high intensity (AAMR/AAIDD, 2002). Thompson and colleagues (2002, 2004, 2009) noted that by focusing on the functional characteristics of an individual learner, educators can more successfully support the learner in performing the needed tasks, thus increasing levels of independence.

This framework approaches intervention planning more appropriately from a developmental perspective rather than from the older medical "curative" model. It asks the question, What does this learner need in the way of support to function as well as possible and to improve future functioning? The release of the AAIDD Supports Intensity Scale shifted assessment of adaptive functioning from determining what an individual can currently do to assessing the pattern and intensity of supports that will allow him/her to derive satisfaction from and engage more competently in everyday activities in the future (Thompson et al., 2004). The scale assesses potential supports in relation to support needs in seven areas of human functioning: organizational systems (community resources and procedures); incentives; cognitive supports; adaptive/assistive tools; physical environment; knowledge/skills; and development of inherent abilities (Thompson et al., 2009). Such supports may include instruction, socialization/befriending, financial planning, employee assistance, behavioral supports, home living assistance, community use and access, and/or health assistance. To use the supports model, educators and other support personnel should use the following process:

1. Identify desired life experiences and goals.
2. Assess support needs to work toward goals (i.e., type and intensity of supports).
3. Develop and implement an individualized development plan.
4. Monitor progress toward goals.
5. Evaluate outcomes.

Progress for an individual will depend on attention to quality of life indicators within the individual, the immediate family and social group, and the community (Bronfenbrenner, 1979).

PREVALENCE OF INTELLECTUAL DISABILITIES

Determining the prevalence of intellectual disabilities, or the number of cases at a given time, is directly related to the way intellectual disability is defined. Most researchers and epidemiologists estimate the prevalence of intellectual disability as ranging between 1 percent and 3 percent with 2–3 percent being the most frequently cited figure (Polloway, Lubin, Smith, & Patton, 2010; Zigler & Hodapp, 1986). Since the definition of intellectual disability is tied most closely to an IQ score, which itself is based on the normal curve, it would be expected that slightly more than 2 percent of the population would fall below two standard deviations (see Figure 4.2 on page 86). In actuality, the figure is somewhat greater than 2 percent, because some cases of intellectual disability result from organic influences rather than from normally distributed human traits. Causes shown to result in impairment of mental functioning—such as infection, injury, and toxins—affect the individual only in a negative direction, thus increasing the prevalence at the negative end of the normal curve and boosting the overall number of persons functioning in the range associated with intellectual disability (Dingman & Targan, 1960; Zigler & Hodapp, 1986).

Individuals with milder levels of intellectual disability are generally estimated to account for about 80–90 percent of the population of persons with intellectual disabilities (Snell et al., 2009). Moderate levels of impairment affect about 10 percent, whereas those with severe and profound levels account for an additional 5 percent (American Psychiatric Association, 2000). The precise numbers vary because of the effect of adaptive behavior assessments, as well as environmental effects on intellectual functioning. Individuals with less ability may be able to function in environments that place few demands on them but may be noticeably unable to function in more stressful and demanding environments. Since it is the inability to function independently that results in a person's being assessed for possible intellectual disability, prevalence levels would be expected to be somewhat higher in more difficult or demanding environments.

Table 4.4	Change in Numbers and Percentages of Students with Intellectual Disabilities and Learning Disabilities, 1976–2004				
	Intellectual Disabilities		**Learning Disabilities**		**All Disabilities**
School Year	**Number of Students**	**Percent of Students with Disabilities**	**Number of Students**	**Percent of Students with Disabilities**	**Number of Students**
1976–1977	782,713	25.1%	820,290	23.8%	3,288,553
1990–1991	500,877	12.0%	2,117,087	50.5%	4,191,177
1995–1996	585,308	11.5%	2,597,231	51.2%	5,070,658
2000–2001	612,978	10.6%	2,887,217	50.0%	5,775,722
2004–2005	555,524	9.1%	2,789,895	45.6%	6,118,437
Change from 1976 to 2004	**−227,189** **(29% decrease)**		**+1,969,605** **(240% increase)**		**+2,829,884** **(86% increase)**

Source: Data from U.S. Department of Education, 1992, 1997b, 2002b, 2009.

The highest number of new cases of intellectual disability are identified during the school years. The clinical diagnosis of mild intellectual disabilities appears to be particularly age dependent, with most cases being diagnosed once school activities make new demands on children that prove difficult for them to meet. Severe intellectual disability is apparent much earlier because of the more defined gap between an individual's functional level and typical developmental milestones, as well as the frequent presence of additional physical disabilities. For these reasons, identification of new cases of severe/profound intellectual disability is generally higher in the preschool years, whereas milder levels are often not identified until elementary school (Snell et al., 2009).

Since the passage of IDEA in 1975, the prevalence of intellectual disability among U.S. school populations has declined, while the number of students with learning disabilities has increased significantly (MacMillan et al., 1996; Polloway et al., 2010; J. D. Smith, 1997). From 1976 to 2004, the percentage of students with disabilities identified as having intellectual disabilities has dropped 29 percent to about 1 percent of the school population, while the percentage of those with learning disabilities increased 240 percent. It is important to note, however, that most of this change occurred during the first 15 years of the period (1976–1990), likely because of the settling in of IDEA coverage and implementation (see Table 4.4). In addition, the changing numbers are likely affected by increases in numbers of previously unidentified students, as well as by the establishment of learning disabilities as a separate category in 1975 and the addition of autism and traumatic brain injury as separately defined categories in 1990. The identification of some students with ADHD as part of the other-health-impaired category likely also accounts for some of the shifts since 1990. Because one measure of a valid classification process is that it results in stable rates of identification, these patterns do raise concerns about the validity and utility of the identification process itself.

As noted in Chapter 1, concern continues about the patterns of disproportionality with respect to intellectual disability identification. The concerns raised in "The Six-Hour Retarded Child" report (President's Committee on Mental Retardation, 1970) are still raised today. In 2004, child count data (ages 6–21) indicated continued disparate patterns of risk associated with identification as students with intellectual disabilities when analyzed by race (U.S. Department of Education, 2009; see Table 4.5). Data from 2004 indicates that the incidence of intellectual disability is highest among African American students (14.9%) and lowest among Native American students (7.4%).

Table 4.5	Distribution and Risk Factors Associated with Students Identified as Having Intellectual Disability, by Race/Ethnicity (Fall 2004)		
Race/Ethnicity	**Percent of Students with Intellectual Disability**	**Risk Factor for Having Intellectual Disability**	**Risk Factor for Having Intellectual Disability Among All Other Groups Combined**
American Indian/ Alaska Native	8.0	1.04	0.84
Black	14.9	1.87	0.66
White	7.6	0.69	1.09
Hispanic	7.6	0.59	0.90
Asian/Pacific Islander	4.4	0.41	0.86

Source: Data from *28th Annual Report to Congress on the Implementation of the Individuals with Disabilities Education Act, 2006* (Vol. 1, pp. 46–50) by U.S. Department of Education, 2009, Washington, DC: USDOE.

Over the first 4 decades of IDEA services to students with disabilities, the pattern of disproportionate representation of disabilities among racial groups has persisted, puzzling and concerning many (see Diversity in Focus 4.1). Patterns of overrepresentation (U.S. Department of Education, 2009) have continued year after year for some disabilities and some groups while underrepresentation for other disabilities and other groups has also been noted. The theories abound to explain these patterns, but one thing is quite clear: There is no simple answer! Race is but one factor that can impact the contexts leading to a diagnosis of intellectual disability or any other condition. A search for an answer must consider geographical location, language backgrounds, cultural values, school curricula and resources, family structures, and socioeconomic status among many variables; explanations are probably as individual as each learner (Artiles, 2003; Artiles et al., 2010; Skiba, Poloni-Staudinger, Gallini, Simmons, & Feggins-Azziz, 2008). A related and important question concerns the effectiveness of the educational services students receive after identification.

DIVERSITY IN FOCUS 4.1

The issue of disproportionate representation of students from diverse cultural backgrounds in classes for students with intellectual disabilities has been on the table since before 1970. The President's Committee on Mental Retardation (1970) questioned the adequacy of standard assessment practices in determining whether students from diverse cultural or linguistic backgrounds had intellectual disabilities. Two early court decisions, *Larry P.* v. *Riles* (1972, 1979, 1984) and *Diana* v. *State Board of Education* (1970), held that assessment practices using tests that were not culturally fair or that were not presented in the student's primary language could not accurately determine whether the child had an intellectual disability. The central concern related to the validity of instruments commonly used to determine intelligence and the apparent bias of those tests; because their use resulted in a significant overrepresentation of students of color in special education classes, it was suggested that the tests were not adequately assessing the abilities of children from culturally and linguistically diverse backgrounds.

The U.S. Department of Education (2009) confirms that the problem has not lessened in recent years. In 2004–2005, African American students were still much more likely to be identified with intellectual disabilities than would be predicted by their prevalence in the school population, whereas students from Hispanic or Asian/Pacific Islander backgrounds were less likely to be so identified. In addition, African American and Hispanic students were more likely to be placed in more restrictive settings once identified. These data suggest that we do not yet have a culturally sensitive assessment and placement process and that students with intellectual disabilities are continuing to be disproportionately represented by race in special education (Ferri & Connor, 2005; Salend et al., 2002).

CONDITIONS ASSOCIATED WITH RISK OF INTELLECTUAL DISABILITIES

The issue of causation is a difficult one with regard to intellectual disabilities, as it is with many other disabilities. Most writers report that only in about a quarter of cases does the reduced intellectual functioning appear to be related to a specific biomedical condition. In the remainder, a single cause cannot be positively identified, although there are frequently multiple environmental risk factors—including social, behavioral, and educational factors—that appear to be related to the intellectual disability (AAIDD, 1992, 2002, 2010; Hodapp, Burack, & Zigler, 1990).

The fact is, however, that even when a specific biomedical condition is identified as a risk factor (e.g., Down syndrome, fragile X, or prenatal drug exposure), it is also true that there are generally a variety of additional risk factors that interact in complex ways to produce a particular level of functioning (AAIDD, 1992, 2002, 2010). The presence of any particular condition generally associated with intellectual disabilities does not indicate that any particular level of functional impairment is inevitable; instead, function is impacted by the complex interaction of biomedical, social, educational, and behavioral risk factors over time (Chapman, Scott, & Stanton-Chapman, 2008). Any particular condition may result in a wide variety of functioning levels, including having no impairment at all. Simply knowing a cause rarely provides definitive guidance in planning differential treatments.

Nonetheless, it is helpful for special education professionals to be knowledgeable about the terms describing various conditions so that they may be discussed appropriately with parents, other teachers, and medical personnel and so that interactions among risk factors may be considered in the design of primary, secondary, or tertiary prevention and support efforts once the presence of an intellectual disability has been confirmed. In the following discussion of conditions associated with intellectual disabilities, it will be useful to consider the extent to which we can identify prevention efforts that will eliminate or lessen the impact of those conditions. (See Table 2.4 for an outline of the prevention framework.)

Biomedical Risk Factors

Conditions associated with biomedical risk factors are present in only a minority of individuals with intellectual disabilities. In such cases, pathology is present and identifiable, and the intellectual impairment is more likely to be severe, although we are increasingly finding that the level of severity can be reduced by appropriate programming and levels of support, particularly during the early years. For example, recent experience working with individuals with Down syndrome has shown that previous assumptions of severe impairment in these individuals were not justified. With effective early intervention, many individuals with Down syndrome are able to function independently, needing only limited or even intermittent supports in many life skill areas.

GENETIC AND CHROMOSOMAL ABNORMALITIES   Disorders resulting from genetic and chromosomal abnormalities comprise one group of biological risk factors. Phenylketonuria (PKU) is a genetic condition in which a child inherits a defective gene responsible for the production of the enzyme that helps break down phenylalanine in the body. Left untreated, the lack of this enzyme allows phenylalanine to build up in body tissues, causing progressive brain damage. Fortunately, this condition is now easily and routinely tested for at birth, and affected children are placed on a restrictive diet throughout the growing years, virtually eliminating the intellectual disability.

Intellectual disabilities related to chromosomal anomalies occur when there is damage to an entire chromosome and disruption of a number of genes. There may be missing or extra chromosomes, or damaged ones. These anomalies are thought to be caused by genetic mutations, radiation, drugs, toxins, viruses, and other environmental factors. Other genetically determined conditions that include the potential for intellectual disabilities include Down, Williams, fragile X, and Prader-Willi syndromes.

Down syndrome is the most widely known of the chromosomal conditions. Described by Langdon Down in 1854, it was originally associated with moderate to severe intellectual disability as well as a host of physical abnormalities. It is more common in children born to older mothers, but it can occur in any birth. Prominent characteristics of individuals with Down syndrome are upward slanting of the eyes, epicanthic folds, flat broad faces, furrowed protruding tongues, and short broad hands, as well as physical defects in the cervical area, the heart, and the digestive tract. As with all syndromes, few individuals have all of the noted characteristics. Current experiences with children with Down syndrome have drastically altered the expectations for these youngsters. Although the chromosomal abnormality cannot be corrected, with aggressive medical intervention to correct heart and digestive problems, persons with Down syndrome can reasonably expect to live a normal adult life span. The level of intellectual disability has also been lessened for many by effective infant stimulation and early intervention programs. Increasingly, these children are functioning in the milder ranges of intellectual disability or sometimes in the normal range.

Fragile X syndrome (Santos, 1992) is a chromosomal disorder that came to light in the 1980s. It has been described as the most common inherited cause of intellectual disability. Associated with a fragile site on the X chromosome, it is related to intellectual disability as well as other learning and behavioral problems. Physical attributes include an elongated face, large ears, and hyperextensible finger joints. Because of its association with the X chromosome, fragile X syndrome is far more prevalent in boys than in girls, and the effect on girls is less pronounced. As with Down syndrome, the condition cannot be corrected, but with supportive environments, functioning levels can be improved, sometimes dramatically.

ON THE WEB

The **National Down Syndrome Society** (www.ndss.org) provides comprehensive information sources on Down syndrome, with special attention to parent needs.

BIRTH DEFECTS INVOLVING THE NEURAL TUBE   Neural tube defects can affect an infant's mental functioning as well. Anencephaly is a severe defect in the neural tube in which the tube does not close during prenatal development and the brain does not form, leading to death shortly after birth. Spina bifida is another neural tube defect in which a portion of the neural tube in the cervical area or spinal column does not close, generally resulting in paralysis below the lesion. Unless hydrocephalus is also present, children with spina bifida have physical disabilities but generally display normal intelligence. Hydrocephalus occurs when cerebral fluid does not drain normally from the brain, and the resulting buildup of fluid pressure results in brain damage. Surgery to install a shunt can usually relieve this problem before significant levels of brain damage occur. With appropriate medical treatment, children born with neural tube defects today rarely have any intellectual impairment, exemplifying the effectiveness of secondary prevention efforts. Research also indicates that the primary preventive strategy of adding folic acid to the diet of prospective mothers prior to pregnancy appears to be associated with a decreased risk of neural tube disorders.

INFECTIONS   Infectious diseases during both the prenatal and the postnatal periods account for another group of risk factors associated with intellectual disability. Prenatal infection occurs when a mother is infected during pregnancy. Although the placenta protects the fetus from many harmful agents, certain viruses, bacteria, and parasites can pass through the placenta, affecting the fetus. The resulting damage can be very severe, especially if it occurs during the first trimester of pregnancy. Rubella, the best known of these viruses, can lead to intellectual disability, deafness, blindness, cerebral palsy, and heart defects in the fetus. Primary prevention efforts, including routine immunization of children, should render this an obsolete cause of intellectual disability, but the full benefit will not be realized until all women of childbearing age have been immunized before becoming pregnant. Other maternal infections that are implicated in intellectual disability include cytomegalovirus, toxoplasmosis, congenital syphilis, and HIV infection. Postnatal cerebral infections, or encephalitis, related to childhood illnesses such as measles, mumps, rubella, meningitis, and influenza can result in damage to the brain and reduced levels of intellectual functioning. Secondary prevention efforts involving effective and immediate treatment of childhood illnesses can prevent or lessen some of these possible complications.

TOXINS   The ingestion of toxic substances, such as drugs and other chemicals, by a pregnant mother can adversely affect the fetus. Current practice is to carefully monitor all drugs used by pregnant women, prescribing only those that are necessary to preserve the life of the mother. There are also a number of common substances that have been shown to have a toxic effect on a fetus. Alcohol, even in moderation, is implicated in what is now called fetal alcohol syndrome (FAS) or a milder form, fetal alcohol effects (FAE). Children born to mothers who consume alcohol during pregnancy can be born with intellectual disabilities, drooping eyelids, and other facial abnormalities, heart defects, reduced physical size throughout life, and other evidence of central nervous system dysfunction (Duquette, Stodel, Fullarton, & Haggland, 2006; Miller, 2006; Ryan & Ferguson, 2006).

In addition, smoking by expectant mothers can contribute to low-birth-weight babies and the potential for some degree of intellectual disability. Other drugs (e.g., crack, cocaine, and heroin) can also complicate pregnancy and may leave the newborn addicted. Damage during gestation can result from a mother's drug use. In addition, going through the withdrawal process as a newborn can result in brain damage and intellectual disability.

Lead poisoning affects the mental growth of a fetus as well as that of a young child. Common sources of environmental lead are dust from lead-based paint, lead given off by brake linings, and lead in water systems. Young children should be regularly monitored for blood lead levels if there is any reason to suspect that environmental lead is a problem. If caught early, the effects can frequently be reversed; in the more severe stages of toxicity, severe intellectual disability and even death can result.

BRAIN INJURIES   Injury to the brain, either at birth or in childhood, can result in intellectual disabilities. Trauma to a fetus during birth can occur when the baby's position makes normal vaginal delivery difficult or when labor is prolonged or precipitous. Fetal monitoring combined with surgical deliveries are reducing or preventing this type of brain damage. Hypoxia, or lack of oxygen to the brain due to respiration failure, is also implicated in brain injury, with compression of the umbilical cord during delivery a common cause of hypoxia. Anytime that breathing or respiration is stopped, brain injury is a possibility, and impairment in mental functioning can result. Primary prevention involves good prenatal care and fetal monitoring during labor and delivery.

Childhood traumatic brain injury accounts for additional cases of intellectual disability. Injuries to children unrestrained in cars account for a significant portion of these cases. New regulations regarding child safety restraints and the use of seat belts should reduce this cause. Injuries due to child abuse and neglect also represent preventable biomedical cases of intellectual disability.

PREMATURITY   Infants who are born prematurely or who have low birth weights are at risk for various birth defects and intellectual disability. Preterm infants are often born with underdeveloped nervous systems and may not be able to make that development up after birth. Infants who are full term but whose birth weights are low may also show lack of sufficient neurological development. Low birth weight can be attributed to maternal malnutrition, smoking, alcohol or drug use, or other causes. Teenage mothers have a higher rate of premature and low-birth-weight babies who are at higher risk for developmental delays and disabilities (see Jennie's case study at the end of this chapter). In many cases, good prenatal care can avert these causes of intellectual disability (Chapman et al., 2008).

Environmental (Social, Behavioral, Educational) Risk Factors

In the majority of all cases of intellectual disability, including most of those with milder levels of disability, there is no evidence of specific organic disease or pathology. Such cases are presumed to be related to complex interactions among various adverse environmental influences during the prenatal, preschool, and school years (Zigler & Hodapp, 1986). AAIDD (2010) cites a variety of social, behavioral, and educational factors that appear to interact and increase the risk of intellectual disabilities. Social factors include domestic violence, maternal malnutrition, lack of prenatal care, family poverty, and lack of adequate stimulation. Behavioral risk factors include parental smoking, alcohol or drug use, parental abandonment, abuse and neglect, lack of safety measures, and difficult child behaviors. Educational risk factors include parental cognitive functioning deficits, inadequate early intervention/special education, and lack of family supports.

It is generally acknowledged that both innate ability *and* a stimulating environment conducive to learning are necessary prerequisites to intellectual development. Adverse environmental conditions associated with intellectual disability are often related to poverty, including inadequate nutrition during the prenatal period or during the periods of rapid development of early childhood, lack of regular health care and immunizations in infancy and childhood, and infections related to poor sanitation. Children growing up in environments that provide insufficient intellectual and language stimulation in the preschool years often appear to have intellectual disabilities once they begin school. Since delay in acquiring age-appropriate language is often seen as an indication of reduced mental ability, a diagnosis of intellectual disability is frequently the outcome. As James Allen observed:

> Although many children from the slums score low on intelligence tests and their academic achievement is comparably low, we doubt that it is all due to low intellectual ability. Despite the uncertainties of how and why learning does or does not take place, one thing is clear: No child can be expected to learn satisfactorily in a hostile environment. We are gravely concerned with the thought of children growing up in an environment ridden with health hazards, where rodents carry disease from house to house, where infectious diseases are unchecked, where malnutrition is a way of life. We should be equally concerned with impoverished and dangerous educational environments, where discouragement is a way of life and the infectious diseases of apathy and disinterest interfere with normal educational growth and development. (President's Committee on Mental Retardation, 1970, p. 3)

Cultural differences between a family environment and a school environment can compound the problem. If these two cultures differ significantly in their expectations, a child enters school without the adaptive behaviors teachers expect, and the child is at a disadvantage in the school environment (see Spotlight on History Box 4.2). Since deficits in age-appropriate adaptive behaviors are also an indicator of intellectual disability, the child is treated as if he or she has an intellectual disability unless educators are sensitive to the child's skills within the child's own cultural milieu. As Gordon noted, "Educability has been defined less by actual potentials of persons and more by the levels of society's demand for people of certain levels of function" (President's Committee on Mental Retardation, 1970, p. 2).

Nature or Nurture?

This discussion leads naturally to the perennial conundrum: Are mental ability and intellectual functioning determined by and related more to nature or nurture? Is an individual's intellectual ability determined by genetic (and therefore presumably immutable) factors, or is it determined by the environment (and therefore presumably alterable)? The work of eugenicists and Goddard's flawed study of the Kallikaks (Spotlight on History 1.3) asserted that deficiencies in mental functioning were largely inherited and that the answer to intellectual disability was to prevent those judged to have mental deficiencies from reproducing. On the other hand, Blanton's (1975) review of the research on the relative effect of genetics and environment on intellectual functioning indicated that support for the theory of genetic control of traits like intelligence is weak at best.

SPOTLIGHT ON HISTORY 4.2

Rena Gazaway in the Appalachian Mountains

Rena Gazaway spent two years in the 1960s living with the inhabitants of an isolated Appalachian hollow she calls "Duddie's Branch." During her stay, she recorded her observations from the perspective of an anthropologist, and her work reveals the extent to which her stay there challenged her beliefs about intelligence as a fixed trait reflected in adaptive functioning. Her observations, documented in *The Longest Mile,* underscored the importance and validity of multiple perspectives on the functioning of individuals within and outside their cultures in determining intellectual capability:

> Isolation is not selective; it attacks the young as well as the old. For the first six or more years of life the child is utterly dependent on those who care for him. During that time he acquires deeply rooted social habits in terms of communication, self-awareness and other characteristics that are passed on to him through the social order and biological nature of his being. Since each Brancher interacts only with others of the same kind, the child is doomed to become a carbon copy of the products of his community. He is accustomed to the intensely personal interactions of his immediate family and associates and is incapable of analyzing and developing his attributes. He speaks and walks later than other children, has far less curiosity and imagination, and learns more slowly. The only thing he grasps is the routine of crisis. The result of these experiences tends to glue him to his tradition and to his family. He is passive and shy, and regards the outside world and school as sinister places. Estranged from the outer community, he is committed to a lifetime of nothingness in a mile-long hollow of emptiness. (Gazaway, 1969, p. 70)

Gazaway commented on the lack of response to such special events as a circus or opportunities to visit museums or hear a symphony in the city. As she tried to share her experiences in the world outside the hollow with the Brancher children, she observed:

> The willingness to share my knowledge has little meaning, it serves no worthwhile purpose. Sharing sometimes hinders my relationship with those so removed from the world about them. They are unable to understand and I am unable to impart meaning to strange experiences. . . . (p. 71)
>
> Not many of the young people aspire to any kind of achievement that would permit them to become part of the outer society. They cannot read, they cannot write, they cannot draw. In fact they are unfamiliar with most educational materials because they receive little in the way of education. The state law requires school attendance through sixteen years of age, but there is scarcely any enforcement in the rural areas. . . . Parents, too, are responsible for creating an air of indifference among the children. They have not had the advantage of an education and they question its value. The youngsters are not encouraged to make a serious effort because their mothers and fathers cannot appreciate the applicability of what is taught. (p. 72)

Gazaway concluded that the isolation of the Branchers' life assured that few would escape this cycle. She observed that "isolation is to tread backward in time" (p. 73). But as she continued her stay in the hollow, her perceptions changed drastically. She continued with this story:

> Isolation is also selflessness, and ingenuity, and devotion. I was heading out of the hollow at 2:00 a.m. when suddenly I lost control of the jeep station wagon; it somehow turned over in a space scarcely wide enough to admit an automobile. I was stunned. When I regained consciousness I was aware that my hollow friends had come to my assistance. . . . The Branch was so narrow that the jeep doors could not be opened. Sie lost no time in figuring how to get the back door open and came "sneakin'" through to help me. Water was running six inches deep, and I was cold and wet and sore.

"If'n you's not bad hurt, you's bound t' live," he comforted. "Hit's better fur you's if'n you's kin worm out. If'n I's t' pull on you's, I might break off'n somethin' if'n hit 'ud be jist hangin' by skin." I worked my way out, but could not stand. My skinny, undernourished friends were undaunted. "Sittin's hard anywhar in this branch, but we's plannin' sittin' you's outts warter."

With all the skill of a trained first aid crew, they placed me on a board and moved it "jist fur 'nuf so's you's feets hain't warshin' in 'em warters." The women hovered about and covered me with their threadbare coats that provided little warmth. They made me lean against their scrawny, shivering frames. "You's gonna be feelin' bones, but they's not 's hard's rocks a-pushin' through you's meat.". . . .

The next project was to get me dry. "Hit 'udn't be fi ttin' t' take off'n you's wet clothes exposed t' seein' men," Jemima whispered, so the women kept changing the various articles of clothing with which they had covered me. "We's plannin' t' soak you's duds mostly dry by seepin' 'em out int' our'n." It worked. (pp. 73–74)

Gazaway continued her account, describing the ingenuity by which the Branchers extricated her jeep from the Branch and finally got her to the hospital. After evaluation by the doctor, her friends carried her back to Duddie's Branch to recuperate. Solicitous attention continued throughout her convalescence. Healing potions were offered, as well as precious gifts of coal. She concluded her account with this observation and a renewed awareness:

These are the isolated, the "undesirables," the primitives. These are the ones who are destined to live a life of poverty. These are the ones who are excluded from the good things of life, but who do not complain. These are the ones who cannot speak a language that we can understand because it is an idiom that originates from the heart and not the mind. These are my friends. (p. 77)

Source: From *The Longest Mile* by Rena Gazaway. Copyright © 1969 by Rena Gazaway. Used by permission of Doubleday, a division of Random House, Inc.

Angoff (1988) presented a different perspective on this question. He suggested that heritability may not be the most useful issue to address, but rather that the central issue is changeability. When we consider that some of the effects of conditions that are clearly genetically based (e.g., PKU) can be changed dramatically through medical intervention, we must draw the conclusion that *heritable* does not necessarily mean *immutable*. Conversely, when we consider how resistant to change certain environmentally induced conditions or habits can be (e.g., smoking, drug use, or nail biting), it becomes obvious that there is little useful connection between heritability indices and the degree to which a behavior is alterable.

It may be more useful to consider the complex interactive effects of nature and nurture, or heredity and environment. Each person comes into the world with a unique set of genetic instructions. How those instructions will affect development depends in most cases on the extent to which the environment supports the development of those characteristics. Genetically directed traits have a reaction range, a potential range of expression. The manifestation of any hereditary trait depends primarily on the presence or absence of favorable environmental conditions (Zigler & Hodapp, 1986). A favorable environment causes an individual to manifest the trait at the upper limit of the range, whereas a deficient environment results in the trait being restricted to the lower limits of the range (see Figure 4.5).

Since we can never be sure what those limits may be for any individual or trait, the ethical course of action is to maximize the environment for every child. This suggests that as a society, as parents, and as teachers, we should provide good nutrition, health care, and educational opportunities for all children so that they will reach their fullest stature and enjoy vigorous good health. Educators and parents should seek to provide rich and intellectually stimulating environments for all children so that they will be enabled to function at the upper limits of their ranges of mental aptitude, whatever those may be.

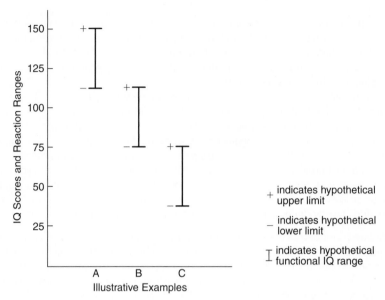

FIGURE 4.5   Reaction Range

TYPICAL CHARACTERISTICS OF PERSONS WITH INTELLECTUAL DISABILITIES

The process of classification (i.e., identifying a person as being part of the population of people with intellectual disabilities) implies little about an individual's specific ability to function or the supports that an individual may need from the environment. Without carefully evaluating individual strengths and weaknesses in each functional domain and then determining the appropriate levels of support, we can assume virtually nothing. There are an infinite number of possibilities in the degree to which an individual exhibits deficits in intellectual functioning and adaptive behavior. Some individuals have additional physical disabilities or disordered psychological states that further restrict their ability to function independently and that affect their need for habilitative and supportive services. Thus, the one sure statement about persons with intellectual disabilities is that they are a very heterogeneous population, especially at the milder end of the range. The nature of an individual's characteristics is determined largely by the interactions among three factors: the general level of intellectual functioning, the age of the person, and the favorableness or adaptive fit of the environment (Wehmeyer, 2003).

Learning characteristics are the most obvious concern for persons with mild intellectual disabilities. In general, they have more in common with their peers who have lower IQs that are nonetheless above the guideline for a diagnosis of intellectual disability (Greenspan, 2006; Shaw, 2008; Snell et al., 2009). A continuing debate addresses the question of whether persons with intellectual disability learn in the same way as others, although more slowly, or whether there is a qualitative difference in their learning patterns that requires unique teaching methods (Hayes & Conway, 2000). As a group, learning is slower and less efficient among these students than it is among a group of learners without intellectual disabilities. The efficiency of learning is affected by the degree to which the individual learns incidentally from environmental input. Students with intellectual disabilities tend to respond better to direct, consistent instruction and to learn poorly or inaccurately from unstructured environmental stimuli and incidental learning experiences (McCormick, Campbell, Pasnak, & Perry, 1990).

As difficult as learning may be, Snell and colleagues (2009) made the case that those with mild intellectual disabilities have even more difficulty with thinking. They may have difficulty flexibly applying what they know in response to environmental demands. Compounding this is that many such students receive their formal education in more restrictive settings and so lack experience in dealing with complex social demands. Such students learn to depend on external control rather than developing a sense of personal responsibility and competence. When not in their restrictive setting, they may attempt to "pass" as not having a disability, much as Edgerton (1967) observed so long ago.

The development of self-determination is an essential step in achieving successful adult status (Wehmeyer, 1992). All adolescents typically question authority, rely on peers, and move toward more independent decision making. Young people with intellectual disabilities have the same needs, but frequently they are not provided with the experiences needed to exercise the decision making necessary for self-determination because caretakers and teachers question the ability of young people with intellectual disability to act effectively and independently (see Chapter 11).

Social and emotional characteristics are also affected by deficits in learning. A number of studies have confirmed that adolescents with intellectual disabilities tend to exhibit social skills deficits, particularly at school, and that they tend to be neglected or rejected in school and to display lower levels of personal efficacy (O'Reilly & Glynn, 1995; Siperstein & Leffert, 1997). These deficits persist into adult life and are believed to be a major factor in problems with postschool adjustment. The outer-directedness of these individuals may leave them vulnerable to peer pressure in certain environments (Greenspan, 2006) as they move into the teen and adult years.

Social judgment is an area of significant concern both for students with mild intellectual disabilities and for those in the borderline range of ability as well. These students are often unmindful of risks and may benefit from careful and consistent instruction in evaluating risks and making decisions. Because these students often appear to others as ordinary teens and young adults but engage in problem behavior due to their naïveté, they may find themselves in legal difficulty (Snell et al., 2009).

Children and youth with intellectual disabilities have social and psychological needs similar to those of other youngsters (Maslow, 1954). Characteristics commonly observed are trying to please others and being overly trusting and even gullible; like others, they desire to be accepted and to be liked (Greenspan, 2006; Snell et al., 2009). They may experience loneliness, depending on the level of their socialization supports. When educators and parents help them meet their needs for physical security, emotional security, and acceptance, these students are more likely to develop a stronger sense of self, which is a necessary prerequisite to an internal locus of control and learned competence. (See Chapter 11 for additional discussion of these characteristics.)

Physically, these students present significant variations in characteristics. At the mild end of the spectrum, there may be few or no observable physical differences. Slight motoric immaturity or slowness to develop may be the only sign of developmental problems. As the level of disability increases, however, especially when there are biological or pathological causal factors present, there may be facial differences (e.g., with Down syndrome), sensory disabilities (hearing or vision deficits), or seizures or cerebral palsy resulting from brain injury. If a lack of adequate nutrition is implicated as a causal factor, physical stature and robust health are likely to be compromised. Throughout life, individuals with intellectual disabilities may have higher instances of injury due to accidents and increased susceptibility to infections. Health and safety education, in addition to appropriate levels of environmental supports, can help ameliorate these problems.

As individuals with intellectual disabilities become adults, the focus of concern shifts from learning and school environments to concerns about employment, independent living, and the use of leisure time. Although children with intellectual disabilities have been routinely provided with educational programs since 1975, unemployment, underemployment, dependence on governmental services, dependent living arrangements, and inadequate social skills still characterize their adult years (T. E. C. Smith & Puccini, 1995; Snell et al., 2009). Individuals with intellectual disabilities have needs and interests in recreational or leisure activities that are similar to those of other adolescents and adults. However, studies indicate that they participate in these activities less frequently than do their peers without disabilities. Hoge and Datillo (1995) suggested that this may be due to a lack of leisure education and to problems in securing access to interesting activities. As these individuals increasingly live typical life spans, communities must provide preparation for adult living during the school years and address the continuing needs for support into the adult years.

Summary

Intellectual disability, particularly at the severe levels, has been a subject for societal study, concern, and action for centuries. More recently, mild intellectual disability has been defined and addressed by services and supports in public schools and communities. In current theory and practice, persons with intellectual disabilities are viewed as individuals with a variety of strengths and needs, and they are served in more normalized and inclusive settings.

Intellectual disability has been conceptualized for more than 50 years as a condition defined by significant limitations in intellectual functioning and in adaptive skills (cognitive, social, and practical) that manifest themselves during childhood and adolescence. The AAIDD (2010) diagnostic processes suggest that our primary concern is most appropriately placed on the current ability of the individual to function in various settings. The diagnostic process assesses adaptive behavior strengths and needs, with an understanding that intellectual disability does not necessarily affect all facets of a person's life equally. It also suggests that the levels of support required to enable a person to function (including instruction, training, and coaching) should be factors in the diagnostic determination. Appropriate levels of support might indeed result in improved functioning over time and in other settings.

The terms used to refer to the severity of intellectual disability include at least three levels of impairment: mild, moderate, and severe/profound. Current conversations concerning the AAIDD definitions suggest that it may be helpful to focus on the relationship between supports and needs as a better description of the impact on the individual.

Intellectual disabilities are believed to affect 2 to 3 percent of the population, with most cases falling in the mild range. Only about 25 percent of the diagnoses relate to known or suspected biomedical causes, whereas the majority of cases are generally attributed to the impact of environmental factors (e.g., social, behavioral, and educational impacts). Debate is ongoing about the relative impact of nature and nurture on the development of human abilities; the reaction range model helps to conceptualize the interaction of genetic and environmental factors.

Individuals with intellectual disability are a heterogeneous group. There are an infinite number of possibilities in the degree to which an individual may manifest deficits in intellectual functioning and in any of the adaptive behavior skill domains (i.e., conceptual, social, and practical). The diagnosis of intellectual disability suggests concerns in learning and cognitive functioning, as well as in social–emotional behaviors and physical ability. Even though generalized reduction in functioning is present, educators must be aware of an individual's profile of abilities and needs to guide program planning.

A Case Study • Jennie

Jennie is 8 years old, the eldest of four children. She lives at home with her mother and siblings in Section 8 housing in a small midwestern city. Her father has been an infrequent part of their lives due to repeated convictions for drug offenses.

Jennie was born prematurely after a difficult pregnancy. Her mother has had the support of a "Mentor Mom" since before Jennie was born. The Mentor Mom program was established in their area to assist young, inexperienced mothers who otherwise would have few supports in caring for their babies. The Mentor Mom's role is similar to that of grandmothers, mothers, and aunts in times when extended families were able to help new parents learn to parent their own children. The Mentor Mom has helped Jennie's mother with child-rearing information and problem-solving support over the years. Jennie frequently spends time with the Mentor Mom at her home in the country. Jennie's mother has been participating in adult basic education programs and counseling for several years, and she wants to make life for her children better than hers has been. Frequently she depends on the Mentor Mom when the demands of living with four young children overwhelm her.

In kindergarten Jennie was tested by her school system for possible identification as a child in need of special education services. This evaluation was prompted by her low skill performance levels and her history of prematurity, neurological problems, and environmental disadvantage. At 8 months of age, she developed a seizure disorder for which she is currently on medication. The following in-

formation from Jennie's school file was compiled almost 3 years ago as part of Jennie's original referral to special education.

Jennie   **Age: 5 years, 11 months**

Referral and Background Information

Jennie was referred for evaluation because of behavioral and academic concerns. From age 3–4, Jennie attended a preschool program for children with developmental delays. Upon her completion of the preschool program, a multi-disciplinary team determined that she was not eligible for special education and should enter the 4–K kindergarten in her home school district. She is presently enrolled in the 5–K kindergarten program.

The referral noted that she engages in frequent self-stimulating behaviors such as rocking and making noises and that she interacts minimally with the other children. Her language skills are significantly delayed in both receptive and expressive areas. She does not speak much in class or attend well to group instruction. She is seated near the teacher in the classroom to reduce distractibility.

Jennie was cooperative and appeared to try to do her best throughout the evaluation. Her speech was difficult to understand at times because of faulty articulation. It was difficult to understand Jennie when she said the proper names of her family members. Jennie could give her name, address, and age but did not know her birthday or telephone number. Some mild tremors were noted in her arm when she was engaged in writing and drawing tasks. She was able to hop on both feet and to hop on her left foot quite well, but not on her right. She could not walk heel-to-toe and had trouble balancing on her left foot with her eyes closed.

Test Results:

Stanford-Binet Intelligence Scale

IQ.   68   M.A.   4–6

Test of Visual-Motor Integration (VMI)

Standard Score   74   Age Equivalent   4–3

Draw-a-Person Test

Estimated Mental Age: 4–5

Vineland Adaptive Behavior Scale (Classroom Edition)

Domain	Standard Score	Adaptive Level
Communication domain	70	Moderately low
Daily living skills domain	80	Moderately low
Socialization domain	67	Low
Motor skills domain	60	Low
Adaptive behavior composite	67	Low

Discussion of Test Results

Jennie was found to be functioning within the significantly-below-average range of intelligence on the Stanford-Binet Test. She was able to match pictures of animals and shapes, to discriminate pictorial likenesses and differences, and to identify pictures in terms of their functions. She could not answer comprehension questions at the 4-year level. She simply repeated the questions rather than responding with an answer. At the 5-year level she was able to identify pictures in terms of similarities and differences and to copy a square. Jennie's drawing of a person, copying of the VMI shapes, and mental age on the Stanford-Binet were all at the level of age 4.0–4.5. This indicates a general 2-year delay in the areas of functioning assessed by these tests.

In terms of skills, Jennie was able to rote count orally to 12 but could not correctly count objects beyond 5. She could recognize only the numerals 1 and 2. She could match the correct quantity of crayons only to the numerals 1 and 2. She could not identify any letters of the alphabet by name, but she was able to sing the alphabet song with only one error. She could not print her name but did print a series of letters that looked like J, N, and E when asked to write her name. Jennie was able to identify 10 basic colors correctly. Behaviorally, Jennie's teacher noted that there are problems with constant fidgeting, humming, making odd noises, being inattentive, being easily distracted, and crying often and easily. To a lesser degree there are problems with being restless, overactive, excitable, impulsive, overly sensitive, disturbing other children, and having quick and drastic mood changes. She further described Jennie as tending to isolate herself from other children, appearing to be easily led, and interfering with other children's activities. Her attitude toward authority was described as submissive and on the shy side. The teacher indicated that Jennie has very poor socialization skills, that she doesn't assert herself, and that when she does try to interact with others, it tends to be inappropriate.

Summary and Recommendations

Jennie has a long history of developmental delays, evidently related to prematurity. She also has a seizure disorder for which she takes medication. Jennie was found to be functioning within the range of intelligence associated with mild intellectual disability, with developmental levels generally around the 4.5-year level in terms of her cognitive ability and physical skill development. She appears to be a child with global delays who very likely does not understand much of what transpires in her kindergarten classroom. Her inattentive and distracting behaviors are possibly a reaction to her inability to compete and perform at a level that is comparable to that of the other children in the class. Her teacher comments that Jennie's socialization skills are similar to those of younger children. It appears that Jennie would benefit from a smaller, structured classroom situation in which she can receive individualized work at her instructional level. She could benefit from a program with a heavy emphasis on the development of socialization and communication skills. She appears to meet the criteria for an individualized education program (IEP) as a child with mild intellectual disability.

Recently Jennie was seen at the neonatal neurological clinic that has been following her since birth because of her history of prematurity and her subsequent seizure disorder. The report noted that Jennie continues to receive speech and language therapy twice weekly at school, once in a group setting, the other individually. Jennie's mother reported that the speech teacher is working on improving Jennie's grammar and articulation. The clinic report noted that she engaged easily in conversation. She was able to follow all simple one- and two-step directions. She exhibited some difficulty with using correct verbs in sentences. Phonological errors were present but were still within expectations for her age. Although grammar errors were evident in her conversational speech, her ability to convey

meaning appears to be appropriate for her overall developmental levels. The clinic recommended that Jennie continue to receive speech and language therapy at school as it appeared to be addressing all appropriate speech/language developmental goals.

When Jennie turned 8, an observational report was prepared by an independent educational evaluator to assist Jennie's mother and the Mentor Mom in preparing for her triennial review. Both Jennie's mom and the Mentor Mom had voiced their concern that Jennie seemed to be making little progress despite all the years she has been in school. They were looking for information to support their request for a full triennial evaluation, including a repeat of the ability and achievement testing done 3 years earlier.

Observational Report   Age: 8 years

At the request of Jennie's mother, an observation was conducted in Jennie's special education classroom to determine whether her current placement in a primary class for youngsters with mild intellectual disability appeared appropriate for her. It was apparent from watching Jennie's performance in her classroom that she had great difficulty with tasks like naming and writing letters and numbers, especially when these tasks were presented without context.

In contrast, in preparation for a parent program the following week, she recited a long poem from memory and without prompts. She appeared to function as well or better than most of her classmates.

Jennie's class behavior was attentive and conforming. It appeared that the majority of class time was spent on counting, reading color words, and naming and writing letters. The teacher mentioned that use of whole language had been suggested but that she didn't think that method was appropriate for students at this functional level. The teacher based her program on acquisition of basic skills such as counting and naming and writing letters. Until the students had mastered those skills, the teacher felt it was inappropriate to move on.

In a subsequent diagnostic teaching session outside of school, Jennie was presented with a whole-word approach to decoding words, using picture cues and repeated self-drill. She quickly learned six words she had selected from a book. She seemed to benefit from the meaningfulness of the words and the picture cues. She was taught to drill herself on these selected words using single-concept picture cards that she and the evaluator had created; she also learned to congratulate (reinforce) herself when she was correct. The process appears to have promise for getting her started on reading.

A second activity was the making of pies for a picnic. As the pie was being made, Jennie and the observer wrote down the steps of the recipe. After each step, the full recipe to that point was read and reread. With the repetition and meaningful activity, Jennie was able to read the entire recipe at the end of the project.

Next, Jennie picked up a book that had been read to her previously. She said she would read it to the observer. She then commenced to "pretend read" the book as many young children do. The difference was that she carefully hid the pages from the observer so that it would not be apparent that she was not actually reading the page. It appeared that Jennie had already decided that she was supposed to be able to read, knew she could not, and was trying to hide that fact. This behavioral pattern was particularly troubling since it suggested that she would be increasingly resistant to real attempts to teach her to read.

Behaviorally, Jennie has developed a talent for getting what she wants and avoiding what she doesn't want to do. She bargains with those around her: "Let me do/have this, then I'll do that." The problem is that she frequently resists the less desired activity after having received her reward, refusing to comply. It is essential that any behavior program established for Jennie place the reward *after* the compliance action has occurred.

From all of these observations, it appears that Jennie is a child with a variety of strengths and weaknesses. She is clearly delayed in developing skills typically expected of an 8-year-old. It appears that she is a child who would benefit from more holistic, experiential forms of teaching. These actions are recommended:

- Her reading instruction should focus on whole words and real language. Appropriate methods might include language experience activities, repeated rereading of trade books with the teacher or parent (perhaps using Reading Recovery or the Fernald multisensory method for learning whole words). For now, focusing on individual letters and sounds should probably be avoided.
- Story reading to and with Jennie may help reduce her anxiety about not reading.
- Consistent use of manipulatives in math instruction, using a curriculum such as *Math Their Way,* is essential if numbers are to begin to have meaning for Jennie.
- Her delays in oral language are obvious. Good models and structured language training should be continued.
- Behavior interventions should pair low-interest activities with high-interest activities (rewards); rewards should be contingent on her completing the required behavior before the reward is received.

Discussion

Using this information on Jennie, collected over a 3-year period, determine whether the classification as a child with intellectual disability appears appropriate. First, analyze the data using the current IDEA criteria (see p. 000), and then reanalyze the case using the AAIDD (2010) framework with its focus on present functioning in conceptual, social, and practical skills. Where you lack information for a full determination, draw tentative conclusions, make a list of the additional information you would need to complete the evaluation, and describe how that information would be of value.

CHAPTER 5

Learners with Learning Disabilities

Questions *to Guide Your Study*

- How did the concept of learning disabilities develop?

- How did we define and identify learning disabilities from 1975 to 2004? What were the issues with that definition?

- Why is the concept of discrepancy problematic?

- How did IDEA 2004 change the way we identify children with learning disabilities? What challenges do these new guidelines present to educators?

- In what ways is the response to intervention process consistent with the conceptual definition of learning disabilities?

- How common are learning disabilities? What explanations can you give for the increases in the numbers of students with learning disabilities since 1975? What are the implications of changes in the prevalence rates since 1990?

- What hypotheses have been formulated about conditions that may be associated with the risk of developing learning disabilities?

Meet Peter

Peter looks like a typical teenager. He has a growing CD collection, he loves his computer video games, and the condition of his room is a source of constant "conversation" with his mother. At age 15, he pores over the driver's license manual, looking forward to the day when that magic card will free him from the constraints of parental transportation and curfews.

But Peter differs from his peers in some significant ways. Although he is alert, appears to be knowledgeable about many things, and is apparently no different from others in his school who are planning on college in a few years, he struggles with basic reading and writing and may not be able to pass the state-mandated competency tests required for high school graduation. What makes this so hard for Peter, his family, and teachers is that Peter "looks smart." In fact, he has a measured IQ of 113, well into the average to above-average range. Yet school has always been hard for him.

What makes Peter different is that he was identified in second grade as a student with a learning disability. Peter failed to learn to read from the basal program used by his school, and his handwriting and spelling were very poor. At first, his teachers and parents felt he just wasn't trying, and he was alternately cajoled and punished in an attempt to get him to exert the effort needed to "live up to his potential." His second-grade teacher, trying to find a way to help Peter become a successful learner, sought the help of the school's resource teacher.

After a period of prereferral intervention, it was determined that more information was needed. The evaluation by the school psychologist provided the answer: Despite normal sensory and intellectual abilities, Peter's achievement lagged significantly behind his potential. Since no other reason could be found for this lag, it was determined that Peter had a learning disability.

Throughout the next few years, a number of interventions were tried. He learned well when information was provided orally in class discussions. He was able to demonstrate his knowledge in oral recitation and various projects that did not require reading and writing. The skills of reading and writing, however, remained problematic. In middle school, compensatory modifications were initiated. He was provided with books on tape, and tests were given in the resource room, with oral responses permitted. These modifications allowed him to keep learning, but they failed to address his reading and writing deficiencies.

Now Peter is in high school. His inability to read at a functional level has impeded his progress. He is unable to demonstrate his knowledge and understanding through written work and tests. He is having more difficulty with the academic-track coursework, and his teachers wonder if he wouldn't be better served by a general vocational program.

His new special education teacher noted that he seemed to lack the cognitive strategies needed for learning, and in an attempt to help him keep his graduation and college options open, his teacher has begun a program of learning strategy instruction. Peter's general intellectual ability suggests that with help and accommodations for his disability, he should be able to complete college. For now, Peter reads his driver's manual and looks forward to driving!

> ■ What characteristics are commonly found among students with learning disabilities? What reasons can you give for this heterogeneity of functional attributes?

THINKING QUESTIONS

How might Peter's teacher determine whether his hypothesis about the nature of Peter's disability is correct? How can he use this teaching trial to provide useful diagnostic information?

NAMING THIS GROUP OF LEARNERS

Students like Peter have puzzled teachers for years. These students seem smart but fail to learn. They are the students identified today as having learning disabilities, but it hasn't always been so. The field of learning disabilities is still relatively young, although it is now apparent that there have always been individuals who would now be identified as having a learning disability. Terms used initially had a distinctly medical/neurological orientation, terms such as *word blindness, brain-injured, perceptually handicapped, minimal brain dysfunction, aphasia,* and *dyslexia.*

The term *learning disabilities* itself has been in use only since 1963, when it was adopted by the parents who formed the Association for Children with Learning Disabilities (ACLD/LDA). At that initial meeting, Sam Kirk noted that the terms *brain-injured* and *neurological impairment* implied that the problem was a medical one. He suggested that a term more related to teaching and learning would be more useful to these parents in acquiring educational services for these children:

> Recently I have used the term "learning disabilities" to describe a group of children who have disorders in the development of language, speech, reading and associated communication skills needed for social interaction. In this group I do not include those who have sensory handicaps such as blindness or deafness because we have

methods of managing and training the deaf and the blind. I also exclude children who have generalized mental retardation. (Kirk, 1963, p. 3; Kirk & McCarthy, 1975, p. 9)

Congress agreed on the use of the term *specific learning disability* in 1969 with passage of the Specific Learning Disabilities Act to support the development of services for this group of learners and to differentiate this disability from other conditions such as intellectual disabilities. Even though the term has now been in use for nearly 50 years, controversy continues as schools and parents seek to understand just what the name means and how these learners differ from others with mild school-related disabilities. This chapter will consider some of these issues.

HISTORICAL DEVELOPMENT OF THE CONCEPT OF LEARNING DISABILITIES

In the 19th century, Gall, Broca, and others investigated the hypothesis that certain human functions were governed by specific parts of the brain and that injuries to specific areas of the brain were related to specific disorders in functioning, with particular emphasis on language usage. Early 20th-century neuropsychologists continued this line of research. Hinshelwood described a condition called "congenital word blindness" in 1917 (Anderson & Meie-Hedde, 2001), and Goldstein studied the characteristics of soldiers with brain injuries in the 1930s. All of these efforts suggested a relationship between brain injuries and specific functional impairments (Hallahan & Mercer, 2002).

The focus on brain differences continued with the work of Orton (1937), who hypothesized that language abilities were controlled by one side of the brain and that children with language disabilities had not achieved hemispheric dominance. Gillingham and Stillman (1940) developed remedial phonetic strategies based on Orton's work, while Fernald (1943) developed a whole-word, multisensory approach (VAKT) for students with problems in reading and writing. Werner and Strauss identified two distinct behavioral clusters among the persons institutionalized with intellectual disability (Werner, Garside, & Murphy, 1940). Those individuals whose intellectual disabilities were associated with apparent birth trauma seemed to exhibit a specific cluster of distractibility, hyperactivity, and perceptual–motor characteristics, including erratic and inappropriate behavior, disproportionate motor activity, poor behavior organization, faulty perceptions, and awkward motor performance (Mercer, 1987; Stevens & Birch, 1957).

Strauss and others developed prescriptive remedial teaching methods to respond to individual differences (Strauss & Kephart, 1955; Strauss & Lehtinen, 1947). During the 1950s, there was considerable interest in matching specific areas of deficit with interventions to remediate those deficits. Lehtinen concentrated on manipulating the environment in which these students learned, whereas Kephart (1960) focused on perceptual–motor development. Cruickshank continued this work with learners with cerebral palsy but normal intelligence, recommending that such children be educated in a highly structured environment to help focus their attention (Cruickshank, Bentzen, Ratzeburgh, & Tannhauser, 1961).

By the early 1960s, the foundation for the concept of learning disabilities had been established. Attention was focused on the unique learning difficulties exhibited by students who had a history of brain injury or by those who displayed similar characteristics but who had no history of brain injury. However, since the term *brain injured* commonly used with all of these students suggested a medical diagnosis and treatment, educators remained largely uninvolved in either the identification or the treatment of learners with these disorders.

During the 1960s, general dissatisfaction grew with the concept of brain injury as an explanation for the problems experienced by children with seemingly normal abilities who were not learning well in school (Fletcher et al., 2007). The term implied severe and permanent disabilities, providing no guidance for educators. Seeking a name for this condition that was increasingly associated with unexplained underachievement, parents, educators, and others began using such terms as educational handicaps, language disorders, perceptual handicaps, clumsy child syndrome, and hyperkinetic syndrome. Without a clear description or understanding of the condition, parents sought help

ON THE WEB

The **Learning Disabilities Association of America** (**LDA;** www.ldanatl.org) is an advocacy group for persons with learning disabilities, founded as the Association for Children with Learning Disabilities in 1963; it provides publications, fact sheets, and position statements on issues.

from other parents in dealing with schools and with their own frustrations, forming a variety of organizations including the Association for Children with Learning Disabilities (ACLD, now LDA).

During the 1960s and 1970s, there was increased governmental activity on behalf of these learners. Task Force I, chaired by S. D. Clements, was established by the U.S. Department of Health, Education, and Welfare to study this condition. Using the term *minimal brain dysfunction* to refer to these children, the task force identified 10 characteristics typically observed in these learners, including hyperactivity, impulsivity, perceptual–motor impairments, attention problems, and difficulties in language and other academic skills (Clements, 1966). Although the term *minimal brain dysfunction* minimized the implication of severe organic damage and mental disability, it still had many of the same limitations of the earlier work in brain injury. Thus, the term *learning disability* gradually became the term of choice for identifying these puzzling students.

Throughout the 1960s, researchers continued to study educational interventions for these students. Kephart (1960) advocated perceptual–motor training as a remedial technique. Kirk and colleagues published the Illinois Test of Psycholinguistic Abilities (ITPA) in 1961, designed to assess the specific components of sensory and psycholinguistic processing (Kirk & Kirk, 1971; Kirk, McCarthy, & Kirk, 1968). In 1964 Frostig developed testing and training materials for remediation of visual perception disabilities. However, none of these approaches demonstrated sustained effectiveness.

In 1968 the National Advisory Committee on Handicapped Children (NACHC; 1968) was formed by the U.S. Office of Education, chaired by Kirk, and charged with developing a definition of *learning disabilities*. The Specific Learning Disabilities Act (1969) included the definition that is still used in federal programs today. With the passage of the Education for All Handicapped Children Act (P.L. 94-142) in 1975, the disorder called specific learning disability was firmly established as a disability. Schools then faced the challenge of identifying and serving these children. Federal regulations in 1977 included the unexpected underachievement criterion, stating that the individual must display significantly lower achievement than would be expected for the learner's age and ability (U.S. Office of Education, 1977a, p. 65083).

From 1975 to the present, as increasing numbers of children have been identified as having learning disabilities, the challenge to schools has been to find effective strategies to educate them (Lloyd & Hallahan, 2005). It was initially reasoned that because learning disabilities were presumed to be related to deficits in psychological processing, remediation of those process deficits should enable these children to eventually profit from regular instruction. However, it soon became apparent that the deficits themselves did not seem to respond to these programs and that academic deficits remained even if the remedial programs seemed to be ameliorating the process deficits (Council for Learning Disabilities, 1987b; Kavale & Mattson, 1983; Lloyd, 1984). By the end of the 1970s, educators had become critical of the efficacy of psycholinguistic and perceptual–motor models of teaching, and attention turned to the use of direct instruction and behavioral reinforcement strategies, working directly on the academic deficits rather than the implied processing problems (Treiber & Lahey, 1983).

During the 1980s and 1990s, research refocused on cognitive approaches to teach these students how to manage their own learning. Researchers investigated the effectiveness of metacognitive strategies such as self-questioning, self-instruction, self-monitoring, self-evaluation, and self-reinforcement. It also appeared that students might benefit from combining cognitive approaches with skill instruction using behavioral approaches. This period saw growing concern regarding adolescents and adults with learning disabilities. Alley and Deshler confirmed a gap between the demands of the secondary school program and the skills students with learning disabilities brought to the learning process. This laid the groundwork for the development of cognitive interventions with adolescent learners and a confirmation that learning disabilities persisted over the life span (Alley & Deshler, 1979; Deshler et al., 1996).

Identification issues continued into the 2000s, with efforts devoted to defining more clearly the differences among such mild disabilities and conditions as ADHD, mild intellectual disability, Asperger's syndrome, and other language-related disorders. In 2004 IDEA was modified once again to support the use of response to intervention as part of the diagnostic process and to remove the requirement that an achievement/ability discrepancy must be identified. The debate continues today, with questions remaining concerning identification, interventions, and service delivery options (Lloyd & Hallahan, 2005).

IDEA DEFINITION OF SPECIFIC LEARNING DISABILITIES

The IDEA definition used to identify this population of learners states:

> The term "specific learning disability" means a disorder in one or more of the basic psychological processes involved in understanding or in using language, spoken or written, which disorder may manifest itself in an imperfect ability to listen, think, speak, read, write, spell, or do mathematical calculations. Such term includes such conditions as perceptual handicaps, brain injury, minimal brain dysfunction, dyslexia, and developmental aphasia. Such term does not include a learning problem that is primarily the result of visual, hearing, or motor disabilities, of mental retardation, of emotional disturbance, or of environmental, cultural, or economic disadvantage. (IDEA Amendments of 2004, §602[30], p. 118)

The IDEA 2004 definition includes the same five components that have been part of the federal definition since 1968:

- *Disorder in basic psychological processes:* The presumed source of the learning difficulty, based on the theory that the individual does not process information as efficiently or effectively as others do. Throughout the history of this field, researchers have taken this to refer to perceptual/perceptual–motor processing, psycholinguistic processing, or cognitive functioning. However, this criterion has yet to be defined in a way that leads to valid, reliable, and practical assessment procedures. The presence of disorders in processing can be inferred only from observation of learning behaviors. Medical diagnostic tools such as magnetic resonance imaging (MRI) have provided some evidence that the brains of individuals with learning disabilities appear to differ from those of typical learners (Joseph, Noble, & Eden, 2001; B. A. Shaywitz et al., 2000). However, this criterion contributes to a conceptual definition of learning disabilities rather than being a diagnostic indicator (Fletcher et al., 2004; Speece, 2008).
- *Language component:* The centrality of disorders in understanding or using language. These disorders are manifested as deficits in the receptive language areas of listening and reading and/or in the expressive language functions of speaking and writing. This component also refers to difficulties in language processing, including cognitive language processing (i.e., "inner language").
- *"The imperfect ability to . . ." clause:* Generally regarded as the primary operational diagnostic indicator. Very simply, a student who has had adequate instruction and shows indications of having the ability to function at an acceptable level but who fails to do so may be viewed as having a learning disability. In other words, the achievement deficits are unexpected, unexplained (Flanagan et al., 2006).
- *The inclusion clause:* Added to bridge the gap between the IDEA definition and the older terms used for these learners. It is not necessary to have one of these diagnoses to be identified as having a learning disability.
- *The exclusion clause:* Derived from the conceptual definition of learning disabilities; the second operational indicator of a learning disability. The condition now called learning disabilities evolved because there were children who could not read although they could see, could not speak well although they could hear language, could not learn but did not have intellectual or emotional disabilities, and did not do well in school although they had access to opportunities to learn in the school, home, and community. If any of these other conditions were present, the reasoning was that there were existing categories by which to identify these children, as well as classes and methods for serving their needs, and they should therefore be excluded from this

category. Learners classified in this category are defined primarily by what they are not (Lavoie, 1989, 2009). IDEA 1997/2004 reinforced this principle when it stated that if a student has not had an opportunity to learn, the learner may not be identified as having a learning disability (Council for Exceptional Children, 1998a).

ASSESSMENT AND IDENTIFICATION ISSUES

IDEA requires that any student suspected of having a disability receive a nondiscriminatory evaluation using multiple sources of reliable and valid information. The following sources have been used most often for the last 4 decades to determine the presence of a learning disability (National Joint Committee on Learning Disabilities, 1998):

- Measures of ability/aptitude (e.g., individually administered intelligence tests)
- Measures of academic achievement (e.g., individual achievement tests)
- Other indicators of academic underachievement (e.g., report cards, group achievement tests, teacher anecdotal records)
- Screening tests for vision and hearing
- Social and school history information (e.g., interviews with parents and teachers)
- A variety of other sources such as classroom observations and results from prereferral interventions

Prior to the reauthorization of IDEA in 2004, the process of classifying a child as having a learning disability typically included the following steps:

1. Document the presence of serious underachievement in a single academic area—such as reading, mathematics, spelling, or written expression—or in several areas.
2. Determine the severity of the underachievement by comparing achievement measures to ability measures to discover whether the underachievement can be explained by the ability measure; underachievement alone was generally not sufficient for classification in most states.
3. Verify that the underachievement is not primarily the result of another condition (e.g., intellectual disability, visual or hearing impairment) or of the lack of opportunity to learn.

Discrepancy Determination Issues

Even though some version of this diagnostic process has been used in most districts and states since 1965, when Barbara Bateman first introduced the discrepancy concept, its use has not been without controversy (Aaron, 1997; Fletcher et al., 2004; Lyon et al., 2001). Three approaches have been utilized in an attempt to operationalize these criteria in order to determine which students exhibit a performance discrepancy severe enough to be classified as a learning disability:

1. Ability–achievement discrepancy
2. Scatter/variation among abilities possessed by a given individual
3. Low achievement for grade placement

Ability–achievement discrepancies and scatter among abilities represent intraindividual discrepancy determinations, whereas low achievement looks at differences in comparison to others in terms of population norms.

A variety of procedures and criteria have been used by school districts and states to determine the presence of a severe discrepancy and to identify students with learning disabilities (see Bobby's case study at the end of this chapter, for example). This variability has been problematic since the implementation of P.L. 94-142, now the IDEA (D. Fuchs, Mock, Morgan, & Young, 2003). Cut scores of any sort always leave an area of uncertainty related to measurement error or test validity (Fletcher et al., 2004). Studies of state criteria have found significant and continuing variability in diagnostic procedures. Reschly and Hosp (2004) found that the 48 states requiring a discrepancy procedure used varying methods and criteria (e.g., standard score point differences, standard deviation differences, regression analysis). This made it likely that a learner who was eligible for services as a student with a learning disability in one district or state might not be eligible in another, depending on the criteria used. The following represent the variety of procedures that have been used to determine whether a significant discrepancy in academic performance exists (Gresham, 2002a; Mercer, King-Sears, & Mercer, 1990; Reschly & Hosp, 2004):

- *Simple difference model (intraindividual determination):* Using a difference of specific magnitude between an IQ score derived from an individual intelligence test and a standardized individual achievement measure
- *Expectancy formulas (intraindividual determination):* Computing a "severe discrepancy level" (SDL) using scores on individual achievement and intelligence measures in a formula, such as the proposed 1976 federal formula: $SDL = CA[(IQ/300) + 0.17] - 2.5$
- *Use of scatter comparisons (intraindividual determination):* A specified "significant" difference between/among subscales on an individual intelligence or achievement test
- *Deviation from grade level (interindividual determination):* Exhibiting a "significant" deviation from grade-level achievement criteria in one or more academic areas, the amount of achievement deficit being generally determined by reference to achievement test scores (in standard score units or percentiles)

Educators and researchers continue to debate the validity and reliability of discrepancy determination methods, as well as the technical adequacy of the tests on which they are based and the cut scores used for decision making (Fletcher et al., 2004; Fletcher et al., 2007; L. Fuchs et al., 2002; D. Fuchs et al., 2003; Lyon et al., 2001; Truscott et al., 2005). Researchers often find that various procedures or formulas overidentify and/or underidentify individuals with learning disabilities, suggesting that the use of these procedures creates a false sense of objectivity (Aaron, 1997; Algozzine & Ysseldyke, 1988; McLeskey, Waldron, & Wornhoff, 1990). The Council for Learning Disabilities (1987a) issued a position paper opposing the use of discrepancy formulas, recommending that educators use them with great caution if they are required by state regulation.

IDEA 2004 and Changes in Identification Procedures

With the enactment of IDEA 2004 came a major change in the operationalizing of the unexpected underachievement criterion. Based in part on the findings of the President's Commission on Excellence in Special Education (2002), IDEA 2004 states:

> When determining whether a child has a specific learning disability, a local educational agency *shall not be required* [italics added] to take into consideration whether a child has a severe discrepancy between achievement and intellectual ability in oral expression, listening comprehension, written expression, basic reading skill, reading comprehension, mathematical calculation or mathematical reasoning. In determining whether a child has a specific learning disability, a local educational agency *may use* [italics added] a process that determines if a child responds to scientific, research-based intervention as a part of the evaluation procedures. (P.L. 108-446, 118 Stat. 2706)

With this language, Congress ended the mandatory use of severe ability–achievement discrepancy as the primary diagnostic indicator of learning disabilities. By stating that states may not *require* the use of discrepancy criteria and by allowing the use of a response to intervention (RTI) process, Congress opened the door for states and districts to develop multifaceted operational criteria for confirming unexpected underachievement as part of the protocol for learning disabilities identification. Flanagan and colleagues (2006) contended that RTI and norm-referenced testing are not mutually exclusive but could be integrated into an operational definition. Time will tell what the effect of these changes will be on identification rates and the heterogeneity of the students with learning disabilities.

Response to Intervention as an Identification Process

Since the 1960s, identification of learning disabilities has focused primarily on the characteristics of the student without reference in any significant way to the environment in which learning occurs. In actuality, of course, the source of the learning problems may lie within the child, within the instructional environment, or within their interaction (Gallego, Duran, & Reyes, 2006; Speece et al., 2003). The President's Commission on Excellence in Special Education (2002) found that "many children who are placed in special education are essentially instructional casualties and not students with disabilities" (p. 26). L. S. Fuchs and colleagues (2002) proposed an alternative diagnostic model in the mid-1990s, a treatment validity model based on the principles of curriculum-based assessment. This model looks for a dual discrepancy in students' responses to instruction: (a) the comparatively lower performance of a target student compared to peers and (b) a significantly slower learning rate (Kovaleski & Prasse, 2004). The central factor is the student's lack of responsiveness in the learning environment, with response defined by Gresham (2002a) as "the change in behavior or performance as a function of an intervention" (p. 480). D. Fuchs and colleagues (2003) proposed a four-phase process to determine whether there is a learning problem and then whether special education may be helpful:

> *Phase I:* Determine average rate of growth in the general education classroom; if the learning rate is generally low, then a whole-classroom intervention should be implemented to improve the learning environment for all learners. The underachievement of the target student is not "unexpected" if everyone is struggling.

> *Phase II:* If the overall classroom learning rate is acceptable, identify those children with a dual discrepancy (i.e., a lower level of achievement *and* a slower rate of learning).

> *Phase III:* Identify more intensive interventions that may better address the needs of these learners in the general education environment; implement these interventions, tracking their progress and using dynamic assessment to determine the learners' responsiveness to the alternative teaching strategies (Swanson & Howard, 2005).

> *Phase IV:* If the dual discrepancy persists in spite of intensive small-group interventions, evaluate the potential that special education services might be more effective for that particular learner; this may be achieved through a diagnostic trial placement in special education and/or through a psychoeducational evaluation. The learner should be considered for special education only if this determination suggests that such placement/services will be beneficial for the student (L. S. Fuchs et al., 2002).

ON THE WEB

The **National Center on Response to Intervention** (**RTI;** http://www. rti4success.org/) provides resources concerning response to intervention, including a library with documents on a variety of topics, such as learning disabilities identification.

RTI, then, becomes the context in which the extent of unexpected underachievement is confirmed and a learning disability diagnosis is made. RTI is another way to operationalize the current IDEA definition and is most appropriately viewed as the first step in the identification process (Kavale et al., 2006; Kavale et al., 2009). This application of RTI suggests that a person with a learning disability is, in essence, a nonresponder to generally used, high-quality educational methods and curricula (Vaughn & Fuchs, 2003). The benefits of this approach to identification include the following:

- It recognizes a criterion that has always been part of the federal definition but has rarely been considered, namely, that the student must have had an opportunity to learn but has failed to benefit from adequate instruction.
- Because this approach supports students throughout the learning process, it avoids the waiting-to-fail syndrome associated with the current discrepancy models; early intervention is built into the model (National Joint Committee on Learning Disabilities, 2005; Will, 1986).
- RTI has a strong focus on learning outcomes and growth, an emphasis on monitoring progress that benefits all learners.
- RTI has the potential to improve the learning environment in general education for all learners.
- It may reduce bias related to teacher referrals.

Potential concerns that must be addressed to fully realize these benefits include the following:

- How can we avoid the RTI implication that learning disabilities are merely instructional casualties and that learning disabilities aren't "real"?
- When and how would a learning disability diagnosis appropriately be made with respect to RTI (National Joint Committee on Learning Disabilities, 2005; Reschly, 2005)?
- How is *intensive* defined as applied to interventions?
- What research is needed to assure that interventions have sufficient validation of their effectiveness?
- What training is required to prepare personnel to work effectively in an RTI model?

Four decades after the criteria for identifying learning disabilities were written into special education law, we are at a crossroads. It is clear that discrepancy determinations can no longer be a sole indication of unexpected underachievement; we face the real possibility that ability–achievement discrepancy determinations will become a part of special education history. Special and general educators must ask whether RTI will be the answer to more effective educational planning for all children, including those who "fail to thrive" in general education classrooms, those with learning disabilities. The jury is out, but the potential is there.

An Alternative Definition of Learning Disabilities

Definitions are created to explain the nature of a thing and to establish the boundaries between that entity and others that differ from the term being defined. There have been numerous attempts over the last 40 years to more clearly and accurately define the condition we now call learning disabilities. However, the construct of learning disabilities has proven elusive to define, and philosophical differences have continued to occupy the efforts of professionals in the field (Hammill, 1990; Kavale & Forness, 1985, 2000).

Hammill (1990) conducted an analysis of the major components of successive definitions, concluding that, despite the apparent controversies, there are common themes throughout most of the definitions:

- Central nervous system dysfunction as the *presumed* cause of the disorder, whether it can be confirmed or not, making the condition intrinsic to the learner
- Unexpected underachievement as a primary diagnostic indicator
- The persistent effects of the learning disability throughout the life span
- The presence and centrality of problems with language, academic learning, thinking, and reasoning
- The possible coexistence of a learning disability with other conditions
- A sense of the heterogeneity of this condition and its many manifestations

The most referenced alternative definition was compiled by the National Joint Committee on Learning Disabilities (NJCLD) in the 1980s. Although the member organizations were in general agreement with the federal definition, they believed it could be made clearer and more specific. In the 1990 version, they addressed learning disabilities as a life span issue; the elimination of psychological processing as a conceptual element; differentiation among learning disabilities, learning problems, and problems in social behavior; and the exclusion clause, acknowledging the possible coexistence of learning disabilities with other disabilities. The NJCLD definition, which follows, was approved by the majority of the member organizations and therefore represents some degree of consensus among professionals in the field, even though it has not been endorsed by the federal government:

> Learning disabilities is a general term that refers to a heterogeneous group of disorders manifested by significant difficulties in the acquisition and use of listening, speaking, reading, writing, reasoning, or mathematical skills.
>
> These disorders are intrinsic to the individual, presumed to be due to central nervous system dysfunction, and may occur across the life span. Problems in

self-regulatory behaviors, social perception, and social interaction may exist with learning disabilities but do not, by themselves, constitute a learning disability.

Although learning disabilities may occur concomitantly with other disabilities (e.g., sensory impairment, mental retardation, serious emotional disturbance), or with extrinsic influences (such as cultural differences, insufficient or inappropriate instruction), they are not the result of those conditions or influences. (NJCLD, 1998, p. 1)

Hammill (1990) concluded that there is a conceptual consensus on what constitutes a learning disability even if practitioners are not always in agreement about how to operationalize it. Kavale and Forness (2000) suggested that both the conceptual and the operational definitions need to be clearer. The implication of this discussion of definitions is that clinical judgment and good diagnostic data are essential to operationalizing the definition and determining the nature and extent of a child's disabilities in learning. Since it is unlikely that any two students with learning disabilities will ever present the same diagnostic profile, what is needed is documentation of the nature and effect of a specific learning disability, followed by the development of an appropriate, adaptive educational plan to facilitate that student's learning (President's Commission on Excellence in Special Education, 2002).

Finally, it is important to note that the IDEA definition of learning disabilities has not changed. What changed with IDEA 2004 is the flexibility states and districts have in operationalizing the definition. IDEA 2004 permits both discrepancy determinations and RTI as options but also requires multiple sources of information to be used in making decisions. Educators in future years will no doubt continue to work to make this process an accurate and valid one.

PREVALENCE OF LEARNING DISABILITIES

The prevalence of learning disabilities as reported by districts, states, and the federal government is related to two factors: (a) the actual number of individuals with learning disabilities and (b) the methods used to operationalize the definition and to classify learners. Although logically it seems that there should be a discrete number that would address the first factor, in actuality the differences among definitions and diagnostic criteria mean that the reported percentages of children identified as having a learning disability vary widely (Reschly & Hosp, 2004), ranging from a low of 1.88 percent in Kentucky to a high of 5.93 percent in Oklahoma in the fall 2004 (U.S. Department of Education, 2009). The manner in which the criteria are used by a state or district affects the rate of identified children (Hallahan et al., 2007). This phenomenon is particularly apparent in the three high-incidence disabilities: learning disabilities, intellectual disabilities, and emotional disorders (Reschly, 2002).

In studies of the implementation of state guidelines for classifying children as having learning disabilities (McLeskey & Waldron, 1991; Reschly & Hosp, 2004; Ross, 1995), it appears that IEP teams tend to rely most heavily on professional and clinical judgment and on the information provided by the referring teacher. It appears difficult for a multidisciplinary team to ignore the conviction of a concerned teacher that a particular child has a learning disability even when the outcome of a particular method of classification fails to support the hypothesis.

The uncertainty about the prevalence of learning disabilities has a historical aspect as well. Prior to the Specific Learning Disabilities Act in 1969 and the passage of the Education for All Handicapped Children Act in 1975, this disability was not officially defined, and students with learning disabilities were uncounted and generally unserved. Most of these children were sitting in regular classes, often failing, and generally regarded as "slow learners" or unmotivated students. Some other students with learning disabilities were receiving special education services, having been inaccurately classified as having an intellectual disability or an emotional or behavioral disorder. In 1975 it was estimated that perhaps 1 percent to 3 percent of children would fall into this new category.

The number of students identified as having learning disabilities steadily increased between 1975 and 1990. During the first 7 years, the increases were dramatic. Since then, the percentage

ON THE WEB

The **National Joint Committee on Learning Disabilities (NJCLD;** http://www.ldonline.org/njcld), founded in 1975, is a national committee of representatives of organizations committed to the education and welfare of individuals with learning disabilities; this website provides access to a variety of NJCLD position papers and other resources.

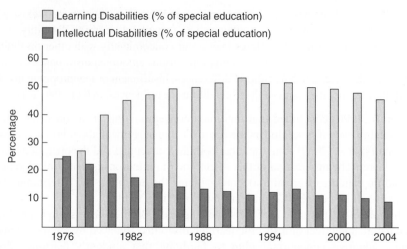

FIGURE 5.1 Percentages of Special Education Students Receiving Services for Learning Disabilities or for Intellectual Disabilities (1976–2004)
Source: Data from U.S. Department of Education, 1992, 1997b, 2002b, 2009.

increases have slowed. Since 1990 each year about 4–5 percent of all students and approximately 50 percent of students in special education have been identified as having a learning disability (see Figure 5.1). There has also been a shift in age distribution, with prevalence among 6- to 11-year-olds declining from 4.6 percent to 3.9 percent, while the percentage of 12- to 17-year-olds increased from 6.1 percent to 6.8 percent.

Several reasons for these trends have been suggested:

- Awareness of the learning disabilities concept beginning in 1975 led teachers and parents to consider it as a possible explanation for a student's failure to learn.
- Improved screening procedures have identified students who would have previously gone undetected as having learning disabilities.
- Learning disabilities as a classification does not seem to have the stigma often associated with intellectual disabilities and emotional or behavioral disorders. Given an ambiguous case, the classification of learning disability might be chosen by a multidisciplinary team rather than a more stigmatic label.
- As cuts have been made in remedial programs for students in general education classes, teachers and parents searching for remedial help for struggling students have sought to utilize the learning disability rubric to get needed help for struggling students.
- Court cases have called into question the use of certain standardized instruments (e.g., intelligence and language tests) in making disability diagnoses for minority students. Coupled with the stigma of intellectual disability, some schools have tended to use that category conservatively and only when the testing is unequivocal. It is likely that a percentage of students with borderline testing results have been labeled as having a learning disability instead of being classified as having mild intellectual disability.
- With the creation of the developmental delay category in IDEA 1997, it is possible that some 6- to 11-year-olds are being identified in that category until age 9.
- With the addition of autism as a category in IDEA 1990, some students at the milder end of the spectrum may now be more appropriately served in that category instead of as students with learning disabilities.

Because learning disabilities primarily affect academic progress, few children are classified as having a learning disability before school age. The numbers rise steadily during elementary school, with the majority of cases identified by the end of elementary school (McLeskey, 1992). By sixth grade, students have been in school long enough to establish the pattern of failure in academic learning required by most placement criteria.

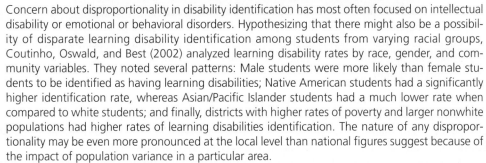

DIVERSITY IN FOCUS 5.1

Concern about disproportionality in disability identification has most often focused on intellectual disability or emotional or behavioral disorders. Hypothesizing that there might also be a possibility of disparate learning disability identification among students from varying racial groups, Coutinho, Oswald, and Best (2002) analyzed learning disability rates by race, gender, and community variables. They noted several patterns: Male students were more likely than female students to be identified as having learning disabilities; Native American students had a significantly higher identification rate, whereas Asian/Pacific Islander students had a much lower rate when compared to white students; and finally, districts with higher rates of poverty and larger nonwhite populations had higher rates of learning disabilities identification. The nature of any disproportionality may be even more pronounced at the local level than national figures suggest because of the impact of population variance in a particular area.

Coutinho, Oswald, and Best (2002) raised several issues to be addressed at the district level: (a) poverty as a risk factor seems to make diverse students differentially susceptible to being identified as having a disability; (b) rates may be affected by bias inherent in teacher evaluation of behavior, with differences in learning and behavior seen as a disability rather than a cultural difference; and (c) districts may not be appropriately utilizing the economic disadvantage exclusion clause, perhaps because teachers see special education as the only available way to get help for a struggling student. In looking at these patterns of disproportionality, Reschly and Hosp (2004) concluded that problems in academic achievement weighed most heavily in the diagnostic process leading to a learning disability decision.

In response to the observed disproportionality, Coutinho, Oswald, and Best (2002) recommended that districts first look at the special education outcome data rather than merely focusing on identification rates, since the most pressing issue may indeed be the quality of services. If students from minority groups do not show a positive response to special education services, then it can be hypothesized that these students are not receiving a free and appropriate education and their placements may not be appropriate. However, if the outcomes are positive, then the placements may also be deemed to be appropriate. Disproportionality may indeed not be the most important issue; the quality of services may be more critical. This complex question will require careful consideration if we are to arrive at the most appropriate solutions (Hallahan & Mercer, 2002).

Often, by the time these students reach adulthood, they fade back into the mainstream population once again, choosing occupations that do not place undue demands on their areas of deficit. Recent studies do confirm, however, that adults with learning disabilities continue to have problems in employment and daily life (Comstock & Kamara, 2003; Morrison & Cosden, 1997; Price & Shaw, 2000). They tend to be underemployed or unemployed more often than their counterparts. They also have more social problems, possibly related to difficulty using language effectively in social situations. The effect of the learning disability may be more subtle, but it remains. Vocational rehabilitation counselors and college academic support offices report increasing numbers of clients who were identified in childhood as having a learning disability and who are now seeking training and accommodation supports in postsecondary education and employment.

ON THE WEB

The **National Association for the Education of African American Children with Learning Disabilities** (www.aacld.org) provides resources for parents and educators for developing quality interventions for African American students with learning disabilities.

CONDITIONS ASSOCIATED WITH LEARNING DISABILITIES

Learning disabilities are generally attributed to presumed causal factors in the environment (extrinsic to the individual) or within the person (intrinsic). As difficult as it has been to agree on what constitutes a learning disability and who has one, it has proven even more difficult to identify causal factors. Studies have used imaging procedures such as MRI studies or PET scans to determine where particular functions are housed in the brain. These and earlier autopsy studies have suggested that human beings differ in brain structure and that those differences appear to correlate with characteristics in mental and motor functioning (Fletcher et al., 2002; Hallahan & Mercer, 2002; B. A. Shaywitz et al., 1997; B. A. Shaywitz et al., 2000). Intrinsic factors that have been implicated in the *Diagnostic and Statistical Manual (DSM)-IV-TR* as causes of learning disabilities include these (American Psychiatric Association, 2000):

- Genetic differences, since there appears to be some tendency for family members to show these problems across generations
- Brain injury (prenatal, perinatal, or postnatal) leading to disruption of a specific brain function
- Biochemical imbalances, hypothesized to affect brain function
- Unspecified brain differences

It is unclear to what extent these intrinsic differences account for unexpected underachievement. Even if they do account for the problems displayed by individual learners, the value of such information for remediation is restricted to diagnosis, since we do not have the capability to make significant repairs or alterations to the brain and nervous system structures.

Extrinsic factors have also been studied. Environmental toxins such as lead have been shown to affect students' ability to learn (American Psychiatric Association, 2000). If caught early enough, the damage may be reversible; if left untreated, it can lead to permanently diminished learning ability or even death. Food and environmental allergens have also come under scrutiny, although research has not supported this line of thought (Kavale & Forness, 1983). Other environmental problems—such as child abuse, neglect, lack of early stimulation, and as discussed earlier, inadequate or inappropriate instruction—have also been targeted as possible extrinsic reasons that some children fail to learn despite apparently normal learning capability.

The fact is that in most cases we cannot infer a specific cause of a learning disability from a child's performance or history. Even in the occasional case when we are able to infer a cause, it rarely dictates specific remedial or preventative actions. The causes of this puzzling disability remain an enigma. The primary difficulty with an inability to reliably pinpoint causal factors is that efforts at primary and secondary prevention are hindered or made impossible. Thus, educators have been left to maximize tertiary prevention efforts in order to improve the functioning of the learner (American Association on Intellectual and Developmental Disabilities, 2010; Rowitz, 1986; see Chapter 2). The focus of IDEA 2004 on RTI may lead to more effective secondary and tertiary treatments with enhanced attention to the context of learning.

CHARACTERISTICS OF STUDENTS WITH LEARNING DISABILITIES

Learning disabilities are characterized by their heterogeneity more than by any other factor. The difficulties these students experience take many forms, and no two students are alike. One way to conceptualize the different types of problems students may exhibit is to use the following framework, dividing the disability into two categories: (a) developmental learning disabilities, or disabilities in functions that are usually considered prerequisites to successful academic learning, and (b) academic learning disabilities, or problems in the more traditional areas of school learning, such as reading, written language, spelling, mathematics (Kirk & Chalfant, 1984; Lerner, 1993). The *DSM-IV-TR* (American Psychiatric Association, 2000) uses a similar framework, identifying disorders in reading, mathematics, and written expression as primary disorders, but noting that there may also be underlying factors related to cognitive processing, such as visual perception, linguistic processing, attention, and memory.

ON THE WEB

The **National Center for Learning Disabilities** (http://www.ncld.org) provides materials on learning disabilities across the life span.

Developmental learning disabilities involve skills related to cognitive processing that develop early in a child's life and are central to later academic success. These include attention, perception, and memory, as well as thinking (or cognitive skills) and oral language (American Psychiatric Association, 2000; Kirk, 1987). One diagnostic indicator of a potential developmental learning disability is a delay in the acquisition of typical language, attention, and/or motor skills when compared to those of other children in the neighborhood or preschool class.

Attention refers to two skills: selective attention, or the ability to select and focus on relevant stimuli, and sustained attention, the ability to maintain that attention over time. A learner who has underdeveloped attention skills will have a difficult time learning effectively and efficiently. (See Chapter 9 for further discussion of attention characteristics.)

Skill in making perceptual judgments is also essential for learning and cognitive processing. Perception involves the interpretation of sensory stimuli and the labeling of those stimuli with meaningful names. Until a stimulus has been named, a student cannot manipulate it cognitively and cannot connect it to other information stored in memory. Visual and auditory perceptual skills, frequent areas of concern for some students with learning disabilities, are essential to later development of reading and written language skills. (See Chapter 9 for more information on perception.)

Thinking, or cognitive, disorders affect a learner's ability to solve problems, to develop conceptual knowledge, and to store and retrieve information in long-term memory. Memory skills include both visual and auditory memory and are likewise central to later reading, language, and mathematics performance. Memory disorders can affect short- and/or long-term memory and may be attributed to problems in storing information and/or retrieving it on demand. (Characteristics related to memory will be discussed in more detail in Chapter 9.)

Oral language skills include young children's abilities to listen effectively and to express themselves orally (American Psychiatric Association, 2000). Difficulties in the use of expressive and/or receptive language skills are often the most obvious indication of a learning disability in a young child. Unlike articulation problems, deficits in oral language affect the ability of a child to learn and interact with others. Oral language problems frequently are followed by later problems in reading and/or writing. (See Chapter 10.)

Academic learning disabilities manifest themselves in school-age learners who have normal learning capacity but who fail to develop age-appropriate skills in reading, written expression, spelling, handwriting, or mathematics (American Psychiatric Association, 2000; Fletcher et al., 2002). Difficulties with language are quite common among these students. Some experience difficulty following what others say to them and comprehending what they hear. Others develop expressive oral language very slowly, with a vocabulary much smaller than that of others their age. Some use very simple or basic syntactic structures and short sentences that are inadequate to express what they need to say. Still others are awkward in their use of social language skills (Owens, 2010).

Some of these students have trouble with the phonological processing needed to make the auditory–visual associations required for success in beginning reading, or they may have difficulty decoding words and blending the sounds. Other students display a serious lack of fluency in reading. Some can read aloud anything put in front of them but may have great difficulty comprehending what they read. Some lack the metacognitive skills needed to monitor their own comprehension, and others find content textbooks incomprehensible both in level of reading and in format (Jenkins & O'Connor, 2002).

Some students with academic learning disabilities find that correct spelling appears to be forever outside their grasp. Others have handwriting even they can't read. Some write in sentences that are shorter and simpler than those of their peers. For others, their writing may be so inaccurate in syntax and spelling that it is incomprehensible. Still other students lack the organizational skills and formatting capabilities to create effective paragraphs and compositions, a condition called *dysgraphia* (Owens, 2010).

It is frequently (and erroneously) believed that mathematics is not a problem for students with learning disabilities; occasionally teachers believe that a student with a learning disability can be identified because of problems in reading as contrasted with good skills in mathematics. The fact is that mathematics does pose problems for a number of these students, leading to a condition called *dyscalculia*. Some struggle unsuccessfully throughout their school years to memorize basic number facts. Others have difficulty organizing the numbers on paper in order to complete the required calculations. Some of these students have difficulty learning and executing the calculation algorithms, particularly when there are many steps, as there are in subtraction with regrouping or in long division. Other students find that their problems in reading interfere with solving story problems, although often the real problem is that they lack the ability to manipulate the numbers in their short-term memory and to see the relationships among them (Miller & Mercer, 1997).

Beyond these academic difficulties, students can have even more basic problems in cognition. They may lack the strategies needed to effectively store information in their long-term memory and then to retrieve it. Or they may lack the cognitive skills of clustering and organizing that make it possible to actively work with a number of concepts at one time. Others lack the self-instructional and self-monitoring skills necessary for effective class participation. Some of these students find taking tests a daunting experience, often because of their anxieties in approaching such tasks and because they do not have strategies for addressing the challenge effectively (Torgeson, 2002).

Finally, many of these students display deficits in social skills. They may have a limited repertoire of social responses, leading them to use the ones they do have frequently and inappropriately and often resulting in other students seeing them as weird. Some students may have learned the necessary social skills but may not be able to use them appropriately. Others may lack the social perception necessary to interpret social cues in the environment and may therefore fail to use an adaptive social response when needed. They may also be physically awkward and may therefore not be desired as playmates.

Assessment of academic disabilities frequently reveals the presence of previously undetected developmental learning disabilities. In effect, the learning disability may always have been there; it may just have been unnoticed because preschool youngsters vary so greatly in their attention, perceptual skills, use of memory, and language abilities. When developmental learning disabilities are found to have evolved into an academic disability, the program of remediation must consider both areas. According to Treiber and Lahey (1983), when developmental learning disabilities are identified in a school-age child, it is more efficient and effective to work on remediating those perceptual, memory, language, or attention disabilities within the context of the academic skill areas.

From this overview of learning disabilities, it should be apparent that this is a very heterogeneous group of disorders with the common theme that the disability affects the student's ability to learn in some way. It has been said that there are so many possible combinations of the many difficulties that may be associated with a learning disability that a teacher is unlikely to ever encounter two students with learning disabilities who have identical needs. This is a critical awareness. Knowledge that a child has been identified as having a learning disability tells us very little about what that child can do and what supports are needed for learning to take place. The teacher's task is to become familiar with the possible problem areas and to work with each student to discover individual needs. Few students with learning disabilities will have all of these problems, and many will have areas of significant strength. They may share the name of the disability, and that may be all that they have in common. We must remember to let each child show us what we need to do; programming must be based on individual student needs, regardless of the disability category.

ON THE WEB

LDONLINE (WETA, Washington, DC; www. ldonline.org) is a comprehensive site with resources related to learning disabilities for teachers, parents, and students with learning disabilities.

Summary

The learning disability construct was initially derived from research from the late 1800s to the 1950s on the relationship between brain injury and impairment of mental functioning. Once the relationship was confirmed, parents and teachers seized on the learning disabilities construct as an explanation for otherwise unexpected underachievement—impaired learning despite apparently normal intellectual abilities. The disability was presumed to be caused by differences or disabilities in cognitive and psychological processing, particularly involving the use of language.

Defining learning disabilities remains a challenge. The key components found in the current federal definition include presumed central nervous system dysfunction and disorders in psychological processing; disorders in the understanding and use of language; unexpected underachievement; and the exclusion of other factors as the primary cause of the learning problem. IDEA 2004 removed ability–achievement discrepancies as a requirement, promoting the use of multiple methods of evaluation including responsiveness to intervention.

Speculation and theories abound about the causes of learning disabilities. Possible intrinsic causes include brain differences of a genetic nature, biochemical imbalances, brain injury, and other unspecified brain differences. Extrinsic causes that have been advanced include environmental toxins such as lead, food allergies, child abuse and neglect, and even inadequate instruction. The fact is that we rarely can know the precise cause, and in any event, knowledge of the cause is unlikely to affect the remediation and support required by the learner.

Learning disabilities are among the most common disabilities, accounting for about 4–5 percent of all school children and almost half of those who receive special education services. Since the passage of IDEA in 1975, the number of students with learning disabilities has more than doubled, although the incidence has leveled off since 1990.

Students with learning disabilities are a very heterogeneous group; any area of functioning may be affected. Problems may be manifested in developmental learning abilities, such as disorders of attention, memory, cognitive processing, language, and/or perceptual–motor skills. Academic learning disabilities account for other manifestations of the disorder—disabilities in reading, mathematics, writing, and/or spelling. The severity varies widely from mild to severe. Because students may possess any combination of these disabilities at any level of severity, no two students with learning disabilities will have the same needs.

A Case Study • Bobby

Bobby is almost 8 years old and lives with his mother, father, and older sister on a small farm outside of town. Bobby's father has a professional career, and his mother works in the home. Bobby has always been an alert and inquisitive child, but his delay in speech development was noticeable by the time he was 3. An evaluation at a local speech clinic revealed that his expressive language lagged considerably behind his receptive abilities. He was placed in an early intervention program for children with speech delays and received intensive speech therapy through kindergarten.

At the end of kindergarten, Bobby's family moved to Moore Central School District. Based on the records Bobby's mother brought with them, the school's multidisciplinary team had determined that Bobby would be best served in a regular first-grade class with one period of resource room services a day and two sessions of speech therapy a week. He made significant progress, although his skills in expressive language and handwriting were still noticeably below those of his classmates. By contrast, his receptive language (i.e., listening) and mathematics skills were very advanced in comparison to those of his peers.

By the middle of second grade, Bobby's classroom teacher felt that he no longer needed special education services because he was making average progress in all areas. She attributed his remaining problems to carelessness; she stated that if he would slow down and work more carefully, he would be successful in school. A reevaluation of his placement was requested, resulting in the following report from the multidisciplinary team, which included the results of evaluation by the school district psychologist.

Multidisciplinary Team (MDT) Evaluation Report

Name: Bobby   Age: 7 years, 5 months (middle of second grade)

Background

Bobby moved to the Moore School District last year, when he began first grade. He has a history of delay in acquiring expressive oral language and received intensive language services throughout his preschool years. Bobby has been receiving assistance in the resource program for children with learning disabilities and assistance from the speech and language therapist for language and articulation since he entered first grade in this district.

Test Results

Throughout the testing session, Bobby paid close attention to the examiner:

WISC-IV			*Wide Range Achievement Test (WRAT-4)*	
Full Scale IQ:	**124**		**Subtest**	**Standard Score**
Verbal Comprehension	120		Reading composite	116
Perceptual Reasoning	125		Word reading	115
Working Memory	112		Sentence comprehension	118
Processing Speed	115		Spelling	113
			Math computation	118
Peabody Individual Achievement Test				
Reading Comprehension	112			

Interpretation of Assessment Results

At this point, Bobby still seems to have articulation difficulties although no other language problems have made themselves known this year to the classroom teacher, special education teacher, or the speech and language therapist. All of Bobby's teachers seem to indicate that his primary problem seems to be related to his being somewhat careless. Bobby tends to complete assignments in as rapid a manner as possible. He fails to check his work and consequently tends to make mistakes.

Current evaluations indicate that Bobby's cognitive ability falls within the high-average range. All of the verbal areas on the ability measure corroborate this. In fact, there was virtually no scatter at all within the areas tested. On the performance subtest, Bobby showed abilities that ranged from average to high average. Bobby's highest ability was in block designs. His lowest measured abilities were in copying symbols for speed and accuracy and in noticing missing details. No measures on the ability tests suggest any sort of difficulty processing information.

All of Bobby's achievement measures suggest that he is able to perform adequately within a regular classroom setting. At this time, he is sometimes able to perform addition and subtraction problems when regrouping is required. Bobby can read one- and two-syllable words. He seems to be able to comprehend at a level commensurate with his ability to decode. In summary, Bobby is functioning at a level that is superior to that of a number of children in the classroom. His primary difficulties appear related to his haphazard work habits and his inconsistency in checking his work.

Recommendations

The Moore Elementary School multidisciplinary team has determined that these scores indicate that Bobby no longer meets the district's criteria for identification as a child with a learning disability. Bobby does not demonstrate a significant enough discrepancy from grade-level achievement to warrant special education services. At this time, his primary disability is related to speech and articulation, and it is recommended that services with the speech/ language therapist continue.

Upon receiving this report, Bobby's parents sought an independent evaluation from a psychologist at the nearby college. They were concerned because his performance, although acceptable, did not appear to be consistent with his ability. They were also concerned that his expressive language deficits would hold him back, particularly as written language demands increased in the upper grades. The independent evaluator produced the following report:

Independent Psychological Assessment

Name: Bobby   Grade: Second (end)   Age: 7 years, 10 months

Bobby was referred for psychological assessment by his parents, who were interested in obtaining an independent assessment of Bobby's cognitive development to assist them in educational planning with his school.

Testing Results

Test of Language Development (TOLD-Primary-4):

Overall language quotient:	105
Picture Vocabulary	13
Relational Vocabulary	13
Oral Vocabulary	14
Syntactic Understanding	10
Sentence Imitation	9
Morphological Completion	9
Word Discrimination	10
Word Analysis	10
Word Articulation	8

WISC-IV

Full Scale IQ:	130
Verbal Comprehension	133
Perceptual Reasoning	121
Working Memory	110
Processing Speed	112

Peabody Picture Vocabulary Test (PPVT-4)

Standard score (receptive language):	104

Wide Range Achievement Test (WRAT-4)

Subtest	Standard Score
Reading composite	107
Spelling	104
Math computation	108

Discussion of Test Results

Intellectual Functioning: Bobby's performance on the WISC-IV suggests that he is functioning within the very superior range of intelligence. His performance scores suggest that his potential ability level may be even higher than presently estimated.

   Achievement: Bobby's present achievement, as measured by the WRAT-4, suggests that he is performing academically at the beginning third-grade level in the three areas measured by the test. Although his performance appears to be in the average range for his age and grade placement, there appears to be a substantial discrepancy between his present intellectual functioning level and these achievement levels. If, as the assessment of his performance on the WISC-IV suggests, his potential intellectual functioning level is somewhat higher than presently obtained, then the discrepancies between achievement and ability would be even greater than estimated here.

   Language: Bobby's performance on the TOLD-P-4 suggests average language development. All subtest scores fall within the average range except oral vocabulary, which fell within the above-average range. He did somewhat better on the subtests involving semantics than on ones involving syntax. The results of the PPVT-4 substantially agree with the results of the TOLD-P-4 and reinforce the finding of average language development.

Discussion

Based on the present assessment of intellectual functioning, Bobby appears to be a child with very superior intelligence who probably should be viewed as potentially intellectually gifted. Bobby appears to be a child who possesses the ability, academic skills, and study habits needed to perform satisfactorily in the general education program. During this testing, Bobby seemed to enjoy the tasks assigned to him. His work habits appeared adequate although he did at times respond too quickly. While it was difficult at times to understand him because of his articulation errors, he appeared to comprehend instructions without any difficulty.

   In summary, Bobby appears to be a child with very superior mental ability although he experiences relative difficulty with tasks involving concentration and manual dexterity. Although he presently functions within expectations for his age and grade placement, a substantial discrepancy exists between his obtained ability and achievement levels. Should his potential ability be somewhat higher than measured, the discrepancy between ability and achievement would be even greater. Consequently, it appears that Bobby is a child who meets the criteria used to identify a child with a mild learning disability.

Recommendations Based on Testing

Bobby will continue to require the services of the speech/language therapist. Bobby's full-time placement in general education should be continued, but he should be carefully monitored to determine whether special education services will again be necessary. In particular, his written language skills should be carefully monitored to ensure that past delays in expressive language do not reoccur. Finally, because Bobby appears to meet the ability criteria for classification as an intellectually gifted child, his progress should be carefully monitored for possible referral to that program.

Discussion

Using the information from these two separate evaluations, determine whether you think the classification of Bobby as a child with a learning disability is justified. Specifically, consider the reasons these two psychologists came to somewhat different conclusions and how those conclusions might be related to the method used to determine the discrepancy. Now that response to intervention has been proposed as a possible diagnostic tool, how might this district use RTI to resolve this conflict instead of relying on discrepancy for identification?

CHAPTER 6

Learners with Emotional or Behavioral Disorders

Meet Nicki

When Nicki entered first grade, her teachers saw a quiet, somewhat re-served child. Her appearance, clothing, and hygiene were typical for this rural community. It wasn't long, however, before her teacher, Mrs. Smith, became concerned. Nicki seemed tense and jumpy, avoiding the physical touches so casually given in a primary classroom. She also was very pos-sessive of school materials and toys, frequently laying claim to as many as possible and refusing to allow others to play with them. She struggled to acquire initial reading and mathematics skills. Mrs. Smith submitted a special education referral in March.

The evaluation for special education eligibility confirmed the fol-lowing: Nicki was exhibiting long-standing and significant problems in building and maintaining satisfactory interpersonal relationships, and she was having difficulty learning despite an IQ in the average range (i.e., 94); the social work evaluation of the home environment revealed an authori-tarian parenting style in the father, with suspected physical and emo-tional abuse. The multidisciplinary team (MDT) agreed that Nicki met the criteria for identification as a child with an emotional disturbance and developed an IEP for services in the resource room.

For the next 3 years, Nicki went to the resource room an hour a day, re-ceiving help with her academic skills. However, her behavior in the general education classroom worsened. She was increasingly aggressive toward other students and had difficulty staying on task and completing independent work. At the end of fourth grade, the MDT determined that services in the self-contained classroom for students with emotional disturbance would be beneficial, including group and individual counseling as well as a consistently administered behavior modification program.

Nicki remained in that class for the next 2 years, and her behaviors appeared to become more controlled. Her teacher felt that Nicki was responding well to the menu of rewards and punishments and that she was learning to avoid unacceptable behaviors to earn her rewards, although she still seemed to struggle to hold back hostile feelings. In seventh grade, Nicki moved to the junior high school's self-contained classroom, where her problems escalated. In February the teacher denied Nicki the right to go to recess after lunch because of rule infractions in the morning. Nicki responded by hitting the teacher, resulting in Nicki's immediate removal from her school program and referral to an Alternative Interim Educational Placement. The MDT immediately reconvened, determined that she was a danger to others, and recommended her transfer to the residential treatment program at the state hospital, where she stayed for the next 9 months. In the safe environment of the hospital, Nicki blossomed, handling seventh-grade mathematics work and making gains in reading as well. The activity program at the hospital provided her with access to social activities, the first time she had participated in such activities outside of school. Her therapist helped her explore issues relating to her family and others. She was making progress in developing her sense of self. She thrived. Unfortunately, work with the family was minimal because the father refused to participate.

In November Nicki returned home to a special education classroom with a new teacher. Unfortunately, nothing had changed at home, and the school program continued to focus on academics and work habits. Work begun at the state hospital on Nicki's emotional issues was abandoned. Two months later, Nicki exploded, hitting the teacher again over a minor disagreement. This time the school authorities pressed criminal charges, and Nicki was assigned to the custody of the juvenile court system as a youth with social maladjustment.

THINKING QUESTIONS

How might Nicki's story have turned out differently if her teachers had considered her responsiveness to interventions as a diagnostic tool?

TERMS TO REFER TO THIS GROUP OF LEARNERS

Unlike intellectual and learning disabilities, emotional and behavioral disorders still have no universally agreed-upon term to refer to learners like Nicki. The federal designation for such a disability is *emotional disturbance,* as defined in IDEA 1997. However, terms used in school programs vary from district to district and state to state.

Writers and professionals in the field over the years have used various combinations of words. Kauffman and Landrum (2009) observed that states, educators, and writers in this field seem to combine one or two terms describing the nature/source of the condition (e.g., behavioral, emotional, social) with a term indicating the condition itself (e.g., disorder, disturbance, handicap, impairment, maladjustment) to create a variety of descriptive names for this disability. The authors demonstrated how this process leads to a large number of possible combinations and terms, each used to define the same group of learners and each with subtly different implications. The professional literature and legislation have included a variety of such terms:

Emotional disturbance	*Emotional and behavioral disorder*
Behavioral disorder	*Social and emotional impairment*
Behavioral disturbance	*Social and emotional disorder*
Emotional disorder	*Social and emotional disturbance*
Emotional handicap	*Social maladjustment*
Behavioral impairment	*Emotional impairment*

Generally, professionals select particular descriptive terms for very specific philosophical reasons; this lack of agreement reflects a significant level of debate on major conceptual issues within this field. How can we begin to address the issue of which learners might need services for this disability when the disability itself is conceptualized and even named differently by various authorities in the field?

This book will use the term *students with emotional or behavioral disorders* because that term focuses primarily on the learner and is most reflective of the dual nature of the disability: the internal/intrapersonal nature (emotions) and the external/interpersonal nature (behavior). Following the lead of IDEA 1997, this book will also not use the word *seriously* to modify this term since our focus is on milder levels of impairment within a continuum of severity. In light of stories like Nicki's, it is important to view the entire continuum of behaviors and emotions so that interventions can be developed and implemented before problems have become unresolvable (Bower, 1960; Koyanagi, 2003; Rutherford & Nelson, 1995).

The designation of a student as having an emotional or behavioral disorder implies a lack of fit between the child, the family, and the larger environment. Our focus in this chapter will be on those students who respond to their environment in ways that are socially unacceptable or personally unsatisfying (Kauffman, 1977). The degree of dysfunction or lack of fit may be interpreted as an indication of the extent to which the learner deals with personal, interpersonal, or larger environmental issues and contexts in a maladaptive manner.

HISTORICAL FOUNDATIONS OF EMOTIONAL AND BEHAVIORAL DISORDERS

The existence of individuals with mental illnesses, those thought to be "mad," has been documented throughout history. However, attention to the phenomenon of emotional and behavioral disorders in children did not occur until the 20th century. (See Safford and Safford, 1996, for a more complete treatment of the history of services to children with emotional or behavioral disorders.) Psychological clinics for children began to appear in the United States about 1900, and the term *emotional disturbance* came into use around 1910. Two theories—organic and functionalist—sought to explain mental illness. The organic approach held that disturbances were due to specific brain disorders and physical disease. The functionalist approach focused on a study of behavior as a key to the cause of the mental illness, fueling the mental hygiene movement and providing the impetus for new services for children with emotional or behavioral disorders.

The first psychiatric hospital for children in the United States was opened in 1931. In 1935 Bender and colleagues established a school at Bellevue Psychiatric Hospital in New York for children with psychoses. In 1946 in Chicago, Redl and Wineman opened Pioneer House, an early group home for youngsters with emotional disorders. It was there that they developed the crisis intervention technique called the *life-space interview* (Wood & Long, 1991).

In 1961 Hobbs and colleagues established Project Re-ED programs, comprehensive ecological interventions for youth with emotional or behavioral disorders, including short-term residential programming for learners within the community and focusing on teaching behavioral skills needed in the present as well as in the future (Fields, Farmer, Apperson, Mustillo, & Simmers, 2006; Long & Morse, 1996). These structured residential programs were combined with and followed up by interventions with the learners' families, schools, and communities.

In 1960 Bower published his classic work on the identification of children with emotional handicaps, a definition that was later to be incorporated into the federal definition of emotional disturbance (see Spotlight on History 6.1). Long, Morse, and Newman published *Conflict in the Classroom* in 1965, resulting in the use of the psychoeducational approach as the major program approach for educating children with emotional or behavioral disorders in schools.

SPOTLIGHT ON HISTORY 6.1

Eli Bower and the Classification of Children with Emotional Disorders

Eli Bower's (1960) classic work on the definition of emotional handicaps was the foundation of the federal IDEA definition. Defining students with emotional disorders as those who exhibit one or more problem behaviors to a marked degree and over a prolonged period of time, Bower listed five problem behavior patterns:

1. An inability to learn which cannot be explained by intellectual, sensory or health factors.
2. An inability to build or maintain satisfactory interpersonal relationships with peers and teachers.
3. Inappropriate types of behavior or feelings under normal circumstances.
4. A general, pervasive mood of unhappiness or depression.
5. A tendency to develop physical symptoms, pains or fears associated with personal or school problems. (Bower, 1960, pp. 8–10)

However, unlike the later federal definition, Bower did not include the requirement that school performance be affected in order for a child to be identified as having an emotional or behavioral disorder.

Although Bower's work formed the foundation for the IDEA definition, he took issue with the definition's focus on only those students with "serious" emotional disturbance (Bower, 1982). He noted that failure to treat problems early, before they had become so severe, would compromise the efficacy of those treatment programs and undoubtedly increase service costs. In his version of the definition, he addressed the varying levels of severity or effect as a guide to the design of services. This acknowledgment by Bower that emotional or behavioral disorders vary along the full continuum of severity further differentiates his work from the later federal definition:

> Emotional handicaps may be displayed in transient, temporary, pervasive or intensive types of behavior. To complete the definition, it would be necessary to establish a continuum in which the handicap can be perceived and perhaps estimated, especially as it relates to possible action by the school. One could begin the continuum with: (1) children who experience and demonstrate the normal problems of everyday living, growing, exploration and reality testing. There are some, however, who can be observed as: (2) children who develop a greater number and degree of symptoms of emotional problems as a result of normal crisis or stressful experiences, such as death of father, birth of sibling, divorce of parents, brain or body injury, school entrance, junior high entrance, puberty, etc. Some children move beyond this level of adjustment and may be described as: (3) children in whom moderate symptoms of emotional maladjustment persist to some extent beyond normal expectations but who are able to manage an adequate school adjustment. The next group would include: (4) children with fixed or recurring symptoms of emotional maladjustment who can, with help, profit from school attendance and maintain some positive relationships in the school setting. Beyond this are: (5) children with fixed and recurring symptoms of emotional difficulties who are best educated in a residential school setting or temporarily in a home setting. (Bower, 1960, pp. 13–14)

Another significant difference between the two definitions, noted by Bower himself in 1982, is the IDEA exclusion of youths who are socially maladjusted. He stated that meeting the criteria of his definition and the definition found in IDEA was tantamount to a definition of social maladjustment:

> To differentiate between behaviors that are antisocial or active and the so-called neurotic or personality disabilities of a more passive kind as if they were indeed separate entities is unfortunate and misleading. Moreover, to use a definition that operationally and conceptually defines emotional disturbance by their social maladjustments, then disqualifies them on the same basis, fits Tweedledee's logic, "If it was so, it might be; and if it were so, it would be; but as it isn't, it ain't." (Bower, 1982, p. 58)

Other programming initiatives in the 1960s included pioneering work by Haring, Hewett, and Wood (Nelson & Kauffman, 2009). Haring proposed interventions based on highly structured environments and operant conditioning and the use of data for making instructional decisions (Haring & Phillips, 1962). Hewett (1968) described a therapeutic approach he called the "engineered classroom," which systematized the data collection process for assessing behavior and established a hierarchical program of activities, using token economies for reinforcement. Later, Wood (1975) developed an intervention program called *developmental therapy*, which provided specific activities designed to remediate delays in the development of age-appropriate social and emotional behaviors.

With the passage of P.L. 94-142 in 1975, children with emotional or behavioral disorders were formally brought into the sphere of public school responsibility under the category of "seriously emotionally disturbed." The presence of these children in schools since then has not been without controversy, and they are more frequently served in self-contained classes, special schools, or residential facilities rather than in general education classrooms. Their troubling behaviors are often described as disruptive to the general classroom environment, and referrals frequently lead to their removal to other settings (see Table 3.2 on p. 70).

An ongoing issue deals with the right of schools to exclude youngsters whose severe problem behaviors disrupt ongoing classroom activities. In *Honig* v. *Doe* (1988), the courts ruled that exclusion from school based on problem behavior judged to be related to the student's disability must be considered as a change of placement, and any such removals must be reviewed by the multidisciplinary planning team within the context of that learner's overall treatment plan. IDEA 2004 further clarified the issues of placement and the right of children and youth with problem behaviors to a free, appropriate public education, as we will discuss further in Chapter 12 (Mandlawitz, 2006; T. E. C. Smith, 2005).

IDEA DEFINITION OF EMOTIONAL DISTURBANCE

IDEA defines emotional disturbance as follows:

(i) The term means a condition exhibiting one or more of the following characteristics over a long period of time and to a marked degree, which adversely affects a child's educational performance:

(A) An inability to learn which cannot be explained by intellectual, sensory, or health factors;

(B) An inability to build or maintain satisfactory interpersonal relationships with peers and teachers;

(C) Inappropriate types of behavior or feelings under normal circumstances;

(D) A general, pervasive mood of unhappiness or depression;

(E) A tendency to develop physical symptoms and fears associated with personal or school problems.

(ii) The term includes schizophrenia. The term does not apply to children who are socially maladjusted, unless it is determined that they have an emotional disturbance. (U.S. Department of Education, 1997a, p. 55069)

Note: This definition has been amended twice over the years. The first change deleted autism as an included condition in 1981. (IDEA subsequently established autism as a discrete category of service in 1990.) In 1997, IDEA removed the modifier "serious" from this definition to avoid the pejorative implications of the classification, although Congress intended no substantive or legal significance in making this change (Yell & Shriner, 1997).

As commonly interpreted, this definition requires evidence of the following:

- One or more of the identified problem behaviors is exhibited.
- The behaviors of concern differ significantly or "to a marked degree" from the behaviors of typical students.

- The problem behaviors have been present "over a long period of time" (typically interpreted as 6 months or more).
- Educational performance has been affected.
- The cause of the behavioral problem is not social maladjustment.

Even though "educational performance" is not defined in the law, many districts and states interpret this requirement to mean that the student must be having academic problems as manifested by underachievement and failing grades. The exclusion of students with social maladjustment has been an issue of constant debate, as will be discussed later in this chapter.

The implementation of this definition has been variable at best over the years. States have provided varying levels of guidance to local school districts through statewide regulations. Implementation at the local level introduces even more variance. Studies over the years have indicated that the implementation of the definition has resulted in varying prevalence rates from state to state and that only a third of that variance can be explained by reference to definitional variables (Cullinan, Epstein, & McLinden, 1986; Epstein, Cullinan, & Sabatino, 1977; Olympia et al., 2004; Tallmadge, Gamel, Munson, & Hanley, 1985; Wright, Pillard, & Cleven, 1990). Disorders of emotions and behavior, interpersonal problems, learning difficulties, and deviation from normative behaviors are the elements included most frequently in state criteria, but the implementation of even these selected criteria varies widely. Surveys of state education departments reveals that over the years, states have used varying combinations of the following 11 criteria to identify students with emotional or behavioral disorders (Cullinan et al., 1986; Epstein et al., 1977; MacMillan, 1998):

- Presence of disorders of emotion or behavior
- Problems maintaining satisfactory social relationships
- Presence of achievement or learning problems
- Deviation from normative emotions or behaviors; failing to perform to age-appropriate expectations
- Problems that are long-standing and chronic
- Symptoms that are extremely serious or intense
- Attribution of the problem to a specific etiology
- Problems that have a favorable prognosis if special services are made available
- Exclusions from classification (e.g., intellectual disability, sensory impairments)
- Need for special education services
- Learners meet the criteria through the certification process used to determine eligibility

Social Maladjustment: Definition and Exclusion

The IDEA definition of emotional disturbance (U.S. Department of Education, 1997a) contains an exclusion clause, stating that socially maladjusted youth do not qualify for services unless they are also determined to have emotional disturbance. There has been much debate on this issue over the years (Council for Children with Behavioral Disorders, 1990; Merrell & Walker, 2004; Theodore, Akin-Little, & Little, 2004). It is frequently noted that this exclusion is contradictory because the IDEA definition of emotional disturbance identifies as eligible those students who exhibit "an inability to build or maintain satisfactory interpersonal relationships with peers and teachers, or inappropriate types of behavior or feelings under normal circumstances," characteristics consistent with most conceptualizations of social maladjustment (Bower, 1982). This exclusion has been viewed as so problematic that 10 states have dropped this criterion from their state regulations (Olympia et al., 2004).

In the 1990s, some school districts and states began using this clause to exclude youth with conduct disorders from receiving special education services, taking the position that social maladjustment is equivalent to having a conduct disorder (Cheney & Sampson, 1990). However, a review of the legislative record indicates that the original intent of Congress was to use this exclusion to relieve school systems from the responsibility of serving adjudicated youth who were provided habilitative and rehabilitative services by other governmental agencies (Cline, 1990; Council for Children with Behavioral Disorders, 1990; Nelson, Leone, & Rutherford, 2004).

Central to this debate is the lack of consensus on a definition of social maladjustment. The presence of significant antisocial behaviors is a key diagnostic indicator of conduct disorders (American Psychiatric Association, 2000). Such antisocial behaviors are frequently considered as equivalent to social maladjustment, resulting in the exclusion of many youngsters with conduct disorder diagnoses from special education services (Kehle, Bray, Theodore, Zhou, & McCoach, 2004; Olympia et al., 2004; Walker, Ramsay, & Gresham, 2004).

An alternate perspective holds that social maladjustment describes those individuals who choose to engage in antisocial behaviors—those who could conform to societal expectations but who will not do so (Apter & Conoley, 1984; Theodore et al., 2004). The central issue in this perspective is the aspect of volition. Students who are socially maladjusted are being viewed as those who choose to engage in antisocial actions; students who have emotional disturbance are believed to have no control or choice in their behaviors. Thus, social maladjustment is defined by some as "a pattern of purposive, antisocial, destructive, and delinquent behavior" (Merrell & Walker, 2004, p. 901).

Still others take the position that students with social maladjustment are those with externalizing behaviors as opposed to the internalizing behaviors evidenced by youngsters with personality and anxiety disorders. Students who have social maladjustment are those with excessive problem behaviors who may be viewed as delinquent or predelinquent. They are frequently characterized as having lower moral reasoning than their peers, resulting in antisocial behavior and differences in the attitudinal responses to their offenses (Clarizio, 1992; Theodore et al., 2004). Those who take this perspective assert that students with conduct disorders or social maladjustment are different from those who have emotional disturbance and, although they may need services, should not be eligible for special education as emotionally disturbed. This leaves unresolved the serious issue of how and where these youngsters should get services.

Center (1989) characterized social maladjustment as an etiologic issue, a problem related to the socialization of the young person. He differentiated among various sources and types of socialization problems. Children who have had deficient or inadequate socialization experiences in their homes and/or communities may in turn exhibit undersocialized, aggressive behaviors. Because of a lack of opportunity to develop appropriate social responses and behaviors, they act in ways that hurt others, causing disruption at home and in school. Other children encounter deviant or inappropriate socialization experiences in their homes or environment, resulting in their learning socialized, aggressive behaviors, antisocial behavior in a peer-oriented context (Merrell & Walker, 2004). The antisocial behaviors exhibited by these youngsters are accepted and even expected by the subcultural groups with which they affiliate. In many ways, these behaviors can be viewed as an adaptation to a problematic environment, necessary for the young person to survive. Center's distinction may be useful in understanding the nature of the problems presented to us by these troubled and troubling students, but it still leaves the eligibility question unanswered. The understanding that particular antisocial behaviors might be attributed to different developmental processes may suggest different programs of prevention or rehabilitation; nevertheless, it seems reasonable to assume that both groups of young people will need assistance in developing other more adaptive behaviors and emotional responses.

Gresham, MacMillan, Bocian, Ward, and Forness (1998) found that students with conduct and attention disorders had fewer reciprocated friendships and were at greater risk of a variety of negative outcomes in academic and social domains during school years and into adulthood. Since these children appear to be at greater risk for developing lifelong patterns of antisocial behavior, Merrell and Walker (2004) suggested that we stop spending time and effort trying to clarify these terms for the purpose of excluding some youngsters from needed services. Instead, they called for making all educational services more effective in meeting their needs. The fact that there is significant overlap between the populations of students with externalizing and internalizing behaviors suggests that attending to the needs of learners is the most critical issue. The RTI approach in IDEA 2004 may be the first step in the right direction. Creating supportive learning communities for all students will assist those with the greatest need for help in developing their social and emotional selves.

AN ALTERNATIVE DEFINITION OF EMOTIONAL OR BEHAVIORAL DISORDERS

The Mental Health and Special Education Coalition, composed of over 30 organizations in the fields of special education, mental health and related services, and parent and advocacy groups, was formed in the 1980s to study the existing federal definition and to consider alternative definitions. The coalition identified the following specific problems with the current IDEA definition (Forness & Kavale, 2000; Kauffman & Landrum, 2009; Mental Health and Special Education Coalition, 1991):

- This was the only disability in IDEA that had the modifier "seriously" attached to the name. In all other cases, we identify and serve learners with disabilities ranging from mild to severe if their conditions restrict their ability to receive an appropriate education. By limiting services to those who are seriously emotionally disturbed, we risk losing the opportunity to provide interventions in the early stages, when efforts can be most effective. Although IDEA 1997 dropped the word *seriously* from the terminology, it has been asserted that this change had no substantive implications (U.S. Department of Education, 1997a; Yell & Shriner, 1997). The fact that the incidence of emotional disturbance has not changed since 1997 supports this assertion.
- The term "adversely affects school performance" has been generally interpreted to imply that a child must be having academic problems as evidenced by underachievement, indicated by poor grades and low test scores (Wodrich, Stobo, & Trca, 1998). This narrow definition restricts services for some students who are having serious social and behavioral adjustment problems, since students who are "getting by" academically may not qualify for services even if they display serious problems in social–emotional areas.
- The five criteria or characteristics do not match terminology used by mental health professionals, making cross-disciplinary conversations more difficult.
- The exclusion of students with social maladjustment is problematic for several reasons:
  - Social maladjustment is not defined.
  - Social maladjustment is commonly equated with conduct disorders, and conduct disorders are described by two of the criteria: (a) inability to build or maintain satisfactory interpersonal relationships and (b) inappropriate types of behavior or feelings under normal circumstances. This definition can lead to a learner being identified in one sentence and disqualified in the next (Bower, 1982).
  - Childhood clinical depression frequently coexists with conduct disorders, thus making a child eligible and ineligible at the same time.
- Throughout the history of this definition, the number of identified students has consistently fallen short of the numbers estimated by researchers in this field. In addition, the numbers served vary widely from state to state (Koyanagi, 2003; Tallmadge et al., 1985; U.S. Department of Education, 2009). The variability in prevalence from state to state suggests that students' right to access to services depends more on where they live than on the nature of their disability.

Members of the Mental Health and Special Education Coalition worked for many years to resolve these issues, resulting in the development and adoption of a substitute for the current definition in IDEA. The U.S. Office of Special Education and Rehabilitative Services (1993) published the proposed definition in the *Federal Register*, inviting comment. To date, the definition has been considered but has not been adopted as part of IDEA.

ON THE WEB

The **Council for Children with Behavioral Disorders (CCBD;** www.ccbd.net), a subdivision of the Council for Exceptional Children, provides this site for educators who work with students with emotional or behavioral disorders. CCBD advocates for educational services for learners with emotional and behavioral disorders.

However, based on the general comments and debate about the current federal definition and in light of concerns cited by the Council for Children with Behavioral Disorders (1990), it may be useful to examine the alternative definition. An examination of the definition and the rationale behind its components can help educators better understand the nature of this disability and perhaps help us develop more effective assessment and identification practices. The text of the proposed definition (as revised during the comment period) reads as follows:

> Emotional disturbance refers to a condition in which behavioral or emotional responses of an individual in school are so different from his/her generally accepted age-appropriate, ethnic or cultural norms that they adversely affect educational performance in such areas as self-care, social relationships, personal adjustment, academic progress, classroom behavior, or work adjustment.
>
> Emotional disturbance is more than a transient, expected response to stresses in the child's or youth's environment, and would persist even with individualized interventions, such as feedback to the individual, consultation with parents and families, and or modifications of the educational environment.
>
> The eligibility decision must be based on multiple sources of data concerning the individual's behavioral or emotional functioning. Emotional disturbance must be exhibited in at least two different settings, at least one of which is school-related.
>
> Emotional disturbance can co-exist with other handicapping conditions as defined elsewhere in this law (i.e., IDEA).
>
> The category may include children or youth with schizophrenia, affective disorders, anxiety disorders, or with other sustained disorders of conduct or adjustment. (Guetzloe, 1998, p. 1)

In this definition, the coalition intended to resolve the most troubling issues found in the current federal IDEA definition. (See Table 6.1 for a list of concurring organizations). Specifically, the group made the following points: Use of the words "so different" implies a contrast to typical behaviors without the negative connotation of the word *deviance*. In referencing this "difference" to "age-appropriate, ethnic, and cultural norms," the coalition hoped to establish local normative behaviors as the standard of comparison to lessen the stigmatizing and pathologizing of a learner who is just responding as others in that environment do.

Table 6.1 Organizations Endorsing the Mental Health and Special Education Coalition Definition of Emotional or Behavioral Disorders

American Association for Counseling and Development
American Orthopsychiatric Association
Council for Children with Behavioral Disorders
Council for Exceptional Children
Federation of Families for Children's Mental Health
Mental Health America (formerly NMHA)
Mental Health Law Project
National Association of Private Schools for Exceptional Children
National Association of Protection and Advocacy Systems
National Association of School Psychologists
National Association of Social Workers

Source : From *Fact Sheets* by Mental Health and Special Education Coalition, 1991, Alexandria, VA: National Mental Health Association.

The definition broadens the interpretation of educational performance to include all areas of functioning in a school context. This helps ensure that services will be available to those who are able to maintain passing grades despite significant emotional and behavioral disorders. It recognizes the holistic nature of the school experience and considers a learner's social, vocational, and personal adjustment as important as academic achievement.

The phrase "more than a transient, expected response to stresses in the learner's environment" indicates that special education services should be reserved for students whose problems are unlikely to be resolved by standard school counseling services and other typically available interventions and who require more intensive services. As described in Bower's description of the levels of severity of emotional disorders, the coalition recognized that special education services were most appropriate for learners identified by Bower (1960) as being in levels 3, 4, or 5 (see again Spotlight on History 6.1).

In requiring that the behaviors be "exhibited in at least two different settings," the coalition sought to prevent the identification of a learner based on the idiosyncratic referral of a single person. If the problem behavior is apparent only in one setting, it is more reasonable to study that setting for the answer rather than to place the child in special education. The requirement that the problem behavior be unresponsive to interventions applied in general education was included to underscore the importance of providing effective instructional environments in general education for all children. When Congress added the concept of response to intervention to IDEA in the 2004 reauthorization, it underscored the belief that only when the best that general education can offer in terms of interventions is insufficient is it appropriate to look to special education.

The statement that emotional or behavioral disorders may exist along with such conditions as learning disabilities, intellectual disabilities, speech impairments, substance abuse, and recognized psychiatric diagnoses was included to ensure that all learners, regardless of their classification, would have access to services designed to help them develop behaviors that are personally satisfying and socially acceptable. IDEA 1997 and 2004 recognized this principle as well in requiring that individualized education programs include individualized behavior intervention plans for all students whose behavior is problematic, regardless of a learner's disability classification.

Although the coalition's definition is not fully in force in IDEA, it is nevertheless useful for teachers and other professionals who work with these students to consider the points made in the proposed definition. Special education services will likely be more effective with such students if we collect the information as specified in the coalition definition. Specifically, the routine practice of evaluating students' behaviors from a contextual basis, from a perspective that recognizes the ecological nature of emotional and behavioral disorders, and of determining cultural and age normative behaviors will provide useful data to guide intervention planning (Elliott, Gresham, Frank, & Beddow, 2008; Forness & Kavale, 2000). Using the results of intervention attempts as diagnostic information is now supported in IDEA. Recognition of the possible coexistence of this disorder with other disabilities will allow schools to serve such youngsters earlier and more fully.

ASSESSMENT AND IDENTIFICATION ISSUES

A major reason for the debate about definition in this field is that emotional or behavioral disorders do not exist outside a social context (Elkind, 1998; McIntyre, 1993, 1996; Murray & Greenberg, 2006). Emotional or behavioral disorders exist only to the extent that behavior or emotions are unacceptable or unsatisfying in a particular contextual environment. Any identification of an emotional or behavioral disorder can be made only by comparing an individual's characteristics with existing cultural rules or norms. What is disturbed behavior at one developmental stage or in one context might be considered quite typical and even expected in another. For example, hitting and knocking peers down is generally considered inappropriate, unless the student is on a football team. Only to the extent that a behavior is seen as significantly different from behaviors expected of typical peers and as a threat to the stability, safety, or values of the individual, society, or community is the behavior (and by extension, the person) appropriately considered to be disordered.

Sensory, physical, or intellectual deficits are viewed for the most part as varying along a single dimension, and there are established instruments to measure the degree of functioning and, by extension, the level of deficit. The presence of an emotional or behavioral disorder, on the other hand, can be inferred only by comparing the behavior of the individual to that of others in the social context. It is also important to distinguish between difference and pathology. Although marked differences in behavior may signal a disorder or pathology, the same behaviors may be present in students who are behaving in a manner consistent with cultural norms. It is critical to ask if there are alternative explanations for the behavior.

By implication, then, any assessment of the nature or degree of disordered behavior will be subjective (MacMillan, 1998; McIntyre, 1996). Educators can improve the objectivity of the process by rigorously defining and describing the applicable cultural norms, rules, and expectations and by developing instruments to describe the person exhibiting the problem behaviors as objectively as possible. By comparing the normative behaviors to the observed behaviors, we determine the extent of the discrepancies and increase the likelihood of developing a helpful intervention program. Because one of the conceptual biases used against these students is that their behavioral excesses are volitional, we must also attempt to determine the degree to which a student is making a choice to engage in those behaviors and the extent to which the student could adopt other behaviors if desired (Merrell & Walker, 2004; Peacock Hill Working Group, 1991; Theodore et al., 2004). If it appears that the learner is choosing the problem behavior, it behooves teachers and parents to ask why. What need does the behavior fill for the child? Functional behavioral assessments also are important in determining the function of a particular behavioral pattern for the individual (Barnhill, 2005; McIntosh, 2008; Ryan et al., 2003).

Such a process might begin by using an adaptation of Wood's (1982) model of behavioral assessment, which suggests that problem behaviors be considered from five perspectives:

- *The disturber element:* Who is the focus of the problem? What do we know about the child? What is the learner's gender, age, race, language(s), economic background, sexual orientation? Are there age, cultural, or ethnic norms that help explain (not excuse) the behavior? Are there other disabilities present? What is the home environment like?
- *The problem behavior element:* How do we describe the behavior? How often does it occur? What are the antecedent and consequent events around the behavior?
- *The setting element:* Where does the behavior occur? What are the characteristics of that setting? What are the characteristics of those settings where the behavior does not occur?
- *The disturbed element:* Who regards this behavior as a problem? Who is bothered by the behavior? What are the characteristics of the person(s) who regard the behavior as a problem, or of those who do not see it as a problem?
- *The functional element:* What goal or need does the behavior appear to help the individual meet; are there alternatives available to allow the child to meet that need?

From this starting point and from the general principles of nondiscriminatory evaluation, it is apparent that the only legitimate process for identifying students with emotional or behavioral disorders is a multiphasic one (Elliott et al., 2008; Marchant et al., 2009). Batteries of psychoeducational instruments alone are rarely of much help in identifying the core issues of a problem behavior or in planning interventions. Appropriate use of such instruments means that the evaluator recognizes that the information value of these instruments becomes apparent only as we collect information from a variety of other sources, including observations.

Behavior rating scales—such as the Behavior Assessment System for Children, Second Edition (BASC-2; C. R. Reynolds & Kamphaus, 2004), Burks Behavior Rating Scales (BBRS-2; Burks, 2006), the Child Behavior Checklist (CBCL; Auchenbach, 2001), the Social Skills Rating System (SSRS; Gresham & Elliott, 1990), the Social Skills Improvement System (SSIS; Gresham & Elliott, 2008), and the Behavioral and Emotional Rating Scale (BERS-2; Epstein,

2004)—provide information about the *informants' perceptions* of the extent of the problem behaviors (Fennerty, Lambert, & Majsterek, 2000). A rating scale completed only by the referring person is likely to reflect only the idiosyncratic views of that individual. When a rating scale is completed independently by several individuals who know the child well, one can begin to have more confidence in the results. Rating scales that also provide support to intervention planning are said to have treatment validity as well (Elliott et al., 2008).

Interviewing can also be a valuable source of information. Information can be gathered from parents, teachers, peers, siblings, and even from the learner. Using open-ended questions and seeking clarification of the information obtained can result in information that is rich in diagnostic value and that can lead to more effective interventions. Each interview provides significant information in itself, but when the information from all of these sources is "triangulated," a more accurate understanding of the problem emerges (Spradley, 1979).

Direct observation in a variety of settings and by multiple observers is essential. The observer needs to collect information on the frequency, duration, intensity, and patterns of the behavior. The observer can compare the nature of the problem behavior with the normative behaviors of peers in the same setting. Identifying antecedents and consequences of the behavior helps add meaning to the description of disturbing behaviors and also guides intervention planning. Observing in more than one setting helps sort out the contextual factors that may be involved (Marchant et al., 2009). Accurate recording of observed behaviors is essential in describing the problem behavior and in evaluating the effect of a particular intervention after implementation.

ON THE WEB

The **National Association of School Psychologists** (www.nasponline.org) provides a variety of resources, including position papers on issues related to identifying and serving children and youth with emotional or behavioral disorders.

Response to Intervention

IDEA 2004 provided an additional perspective for identifying learners with emotional and behavioral disorders. Using the concept of response to intervention (RTI), schools today are encouraged to use a process of successively more intensive, evidence-based interventions in the special education referral and identification process. Gresham (1991, 2005) has long proposed using RTI as a means of determining the presence and severity of an emotional or behavioral disorder. He suggested that students with emotional or behavioral disorders can appropriately be described as those whose problem behaviors are resistant to change even when they are provided with well-designed school-based interventions. Factors that affect resistance to intervention include the severity and chronicity of the behavior, as well as the ease with which behavioral changes generalize outside the treatment setting.

Severity ("to a marked degree") includes such factors as the topology, intensity, and frequency of the behavior. If the strength of initial interventions proves insufficient to significantly alter the behavior, then the individual may appropriately be identified as having an emotional or behavioral disorder (Nevin, 1988). Chronicity ("over a long period of time") is a key criterion in both IDEA and *DSM-IV-TR* criteria. Gresham (2005) concurs with the Mental Health and Special Education Coalition that use of chronicity as a criterion is appropriate only when it is applied to long-standing problem behaviors that persist in the face of validated intervention protocols and procedures designed to change behavior. If no valid attempts have been made to alter the behavior within the general education setting, we need to consider whether the real problem is a lack of effective interventions. Marchant and colleagues (2009) proposed the implementation of strong universal interventions (e.g., schoolwide positive behavioral interventions and supports) as a primary prevention strategy.

Many severe behaviors can also be characterized by a failure to achieve generalization of behavioral change. Some behaviors may respond to intervention in highly structured training settings, only to return to previous levels in nonintervention settings. Such behaviors should be viewed as resistant and will require longer periods of intervention, including careful and explicit generalization training and fading. Students with less severe behavioral problems will more easily maintain and generalize the changes following intervention activities.

ON THE WEB

The **Technical Assistance Center on Positive Behavioral Interventions and Supports** (www.pbis.org), established by the Office of Special Education Programs, U.S. Department of Education, provides information and technical assistance for identifying, adapting, and sustaining effective schoolwide disciplinary practices.

In considering the use of RTI as a diagnostic tool, Gresham (1991, 2005) also reminded educators that the response to any intervention needs to be evaluated with respect to treatment effectiveness, strength, and integrity. Failure to respond to an inadequate intervention tells us nothing about the learner. IDEA 2004 reminds us that treatment plans must have research supporting their effectiveness. Interventions must also be implemented at a level of treatment strength that is appropriate to the individual's needs, the behavior, and the setting or environment. Treatment integrity refers to how well the intervention is implemented. This factor is clearly affected by available resources and staff time, as well as staff training in the strategy. Treatment integrity, another key attribute, must be carefully documented if the results are to be viewed as valid indicators of change or resistance to the intervention. Poorly implemented treatments are unlikely to be effective, tell us nothing about the nature of a child's emotional or behavioral problems, and are of little diagnostic use.

LEVELS OF SEVERITY

As previously discussed, IDEA identifies in this category only those students who have more serious levels of emotional disturbance. However, students logically fall on a continuum of severity with respect to their emotional or behavioral disorders. As Bower (1960) delineated in his classic definitional work, these disorders may manifest themselves as transient or temporary problems with limited impact or as more pervasive problem behaviors requiring more intensive interventions. He further defined the five levels of impact according to the intensity of needed services (see once again Spotlight on History 6.1), beginning with those problems that require only temporary support and structure within general education and the home to resolve them. As the level of severity increases, problem behaviors may require interventions by special education and support personnel for extended periods of time to maintain the student in school programs. Bower's most severe level of disability is characterized by the need for residential or homebound services, when the disorders are so serious that school programs are not appropriate until some progress on the behavior is achieved. As we saw in Nicki's story, the level of disability can change over time, depending on the efficacy of the interventions provided (Gresham, 2005).

Emotional or behavioral disorders vary in severity from mild to severe. *DSM-IV-TR* (American Psychiatric Association, 2000) generally uses a framework of mild disorders displaying the minimal number of criteria to make the diagnosis, whereas severe disorders are characterized by many behaviors in excess of the minimum. Clarizio and Klein (1995) surveyed school psychologists in an attempt to determine which factors held the most weight in determining the severity of a disorder. Four factors strongly affected their determination of severity: impairment of functioning, physical danger, frequency, and chronicity.

Finally, severity levels can be described by a student's responsiveness or resistance to intervention, as described previously. The more resistant the behavioral condition is to intervention, the more serious the disorder (Gresham, 2005). Failing to employ effective, well-implemented interventions when disorders first manifest themselves in the general education environment may impair our ability to halt the progression in severity, as we saw illustrated in Nicki's story at the beginning of this chapter.

PREVALENCE OF EMOTIONAL OR BEHAVIORAL DISORDERS

Estimates of the number of youngsters affected by emotional and behavioral disorders range widely. Figures ranging from less than 0.5 percent to 30 percent have appeared throughout the literature and in various government reports, with most estimates ranging from 3 percent to 6 percent (Forness & Knitzer, 1992; Gerber, 2005; Gresham, 2005; Kauffman & Landrum, 2009; U.S. Department of Education, 1997b). One federal estimate held that 7–8 percent of all school-age children may have emotional or behavioral disorders severe enough to require treatment and that one-third to one-half of those would be expected to also display academic difficulties (Forness & Knitzer, 1992; Gerber, 2005; U.S. Department of Education, 1994). These are the students who are believed to be in need of assistance in developing more personally satisfying and socially acceptable behaviors and who may benefit from special education intervention.

According to annual reports to Congress on the implementation of IDEA, however, less than 1 percent of all children are currently served in programs for students with emotional or behavioral disorders (U.S. Department of Education, 2009). Given that the most conservative professional and governmental estimates cite a prevalence rate of 2 percent (Kauffman & Landrum, 2009; U.S. Department of Education, 2001), the fact that special education programs are currently serving significantly less than 1 percent of all children raises serious questions.

IDEA child count data for 2004–2005 also indicate that the percentage of school-age children (ages 6–21) classified as students with emotional or behavioral disorders ranged from a low of 0.12 percent in Arkansas to a high of 1.58 percent in Vermont (U.S. Department of Education, 2009). Within states, districts have historically shown the same variability (U.S. Department of Education, 1994), and a review of state implementation of identification criteria found that about two-thirds of the variance remained unaccounted for (Wright et al., 1990). These observations suggest that there are long-standing problems with the definition itself because an effective definition should generate comparable prevalence rates across comparable settings and time periods.

Another concern with identification rates was identified by the U.S. Department of Education (1994, 2001, 2006b, 2009). The annual reports have repeatedly noted that rates of identification vary significantly across racial, cultural, gender, and socioeconomic groups. Disproportionately high numbers of students from low socioeconomic backgrounds have been identified, and disproportionately low numbers of female students have become classified as having primary emotional disturbances. Rates have varied across racial categories as well (see Table 6.2 and Diversity in Focus 6.1). A task force of the Council for Children with Behavioral Disorders discussed these trends in its position paper on disproportionate representation and culturally sensitive treatment of learners from diverse cultural and linguistic backgrounds (Anderson et al., 2003).

Prevalence by age groups also suggests some interesting comparisons (see Table 6.3). Adolescents account for almost 65 percent of all students with emotional or behavioral disorders, although they account for less than half of all students with disabilities (U.S. Department of Education, 2009). One hypothesis that might explain this finding is that students with milder forms of emotional or behavioral disorders are tolerated within general education when they are younger, but by the time they reach the more turbulent adolescent years, the problems have become serious enough to demand attention and services.

Table 6.2	Percentage of Students with Emotional Disturbance, by Race, Compared to Total Populations (2004–2005)		
Racial Group	**Percentage of Students in Special Education for Emotional Disturbance (Ages 6–21)**	**Percentage of Total Special Education Population (All Disabilities, Ages 6–21)**	**Percentage of Total School Population (Ages 6–21)**
Black	28.42	20.75	15.08
Hispanic	10.46	16.15	17.65
Asian/Pacific Islander	1.17	2.08	4.10
American Indian/ Alaskan Native	1.52	1.51	.98
White	58.44	59.50	62.19

Source: Data from *28th Annual Report to Congress on the Implementation of the Individuals with Disabilities Education Act, 2006* (Vols. 1 and 2, pp. 75, 83, C-10) by U.S. Department of Education, 2009, Washington, DC: USDOE.

With all this said, just what is a reasonable estimate of the numbers of children and youth who may need various levels of support for emotional or behavioral disorders? The most generally accepted estimates suggest that 3–6 percent of the school population may require Tier 2 or 3 interventions in any given year, whereas the federal estimates are widely regarded as entirely too conservative (Forness & Knitzer, 1992; Kauffman, Mock, & Simpson, 2007). Using the IDEA projections as the expectation, schools appear to be identifying only those with the most severe disorders, students who are clearly a danger to themselves and others. This leaves unserved and unnoticed many other students who are not *yet* that severe and who might actually be more amenable to interventions. We may be failing to identify those very students who might be more

Table 6.3 Distribution of Students with Emotional Disturbance, by Age Group, Compared to Total Populations (2004–2005)

Age Group	Percentage of Students in Special Education for Emotional Disturbance	Percentage of Total Special Education Population (All Disabilities)	Percentage of Total School Population
3–5	1.19	10.30	15.20
6–11	28.12	40.76	}63.34
12–17	64.63	44.33	
18–21	6.05	4.61	21.26

Source: Data from *28th Annual Report to Congress on the Implementation of the Individuals with Disabilities Education Act, 2006* (Vol. 2, pp. 7, 8, 14, 17, 20, C-1, C-3, C-4, C-5) by U.S. Department of Education, 2009, Washington, DC: USDOE.

likely to benefit from interventions and improve their ability to function in personally satisfying and socially acceptable ways, enough so that they might no longer require services.

Special educators need to consider why we are so significantly underserving the estimated number of children in need of assistance. Some reasons advanced for this phenomenon include these:

- As one listens to teachers and administrators discuss these students, particularly those with conduct disorders, it quickly becomes apparent that this group elicits few sympathetic responses. The learner is often described as willfully disobedient or aggressive, as an undisciplined child. It is implied or sometimes stated that the children could behave if they wanted to, that they choose not to behave or have never been taught to behave in accordance with school standards. Frequently, the response is that schools and parents could solve this problem by simply disciplining these youngsters more firmly.

- The diagnosis of emotional or behavioral disorders is not one that parents are particularly relieved to hear. Because the stigma associated with the condition is applied not only to the student but also to the parents, the parents are not as likely to accept this as the problem. Society tends to assume that if a child has an emotional or behavioral disorder, it is either because the parents failed to provide appropriate discipline and socialization or because they abused or neglected the child. Parents will frequently argue for any other possible category in order to avoid this implied stigma and blame.

- Students who experience withdrawal or depression symptoms may simply be overlooked, particularly if they manage to achieve passing grades. Teachers may see these students as a little different, but since they cause no disruptions to ongoing classroom programming, they are often allowed to just sit.

- Following the *Honig* v. *Doe* ruling in 1988, some school officials have become reluctant to have a student with acting-out problem behaviors identified as having an emotional or behavioral disorder. They believe incorrectly that the special education label will prevent school staff from using standard discipline practices (including suspension and expulsion) to respond to problem behaviors. The conventional, although erroneous, wisdom is that school personnel can't discipline a special education student for behavior that disrupts school activity and safety, that these students can do anything they want, and that no one can do anything to stop them. The fact is, of course, that these children can be and are subject to various consequences for their actions. The requirement of *Honig* v. *Doe* and IDEA 2004 is that those consequences and changes in placement must be guided by the multidisciplinary team, which must consider what part the child's disability plays in the problem and what actions are most likely to be therapeutic as well as corrective. In any event, students who threaten the health and safety of themselves or others can always be removed, at least temporarily, to an alternative interim educational setting. (See Chapter 12 for a more detailed description of the IDEA provisions regarding discipline issues.)

- Teaching students with emotional or behavioral disorders requires a significant level of skill and training. In addition, the stress associated with serving these children leads to a significant incidence of burnout among professionals working with them. The shortage of specialized personnel can effectively become a cap on identification because once a student is identified, services must be provided.

Because the identification of an emotional or behavioral disorder is so context-driven and because the determination of who does or does not belong in this group is relatively subjective, almost any estimate of prevalence could be justified. It has been observed that the classification of behavioral disorders is a social or ecological construct, based mainly on what we as members of the community view as tolerable or desirable (Kauffman & Landrum, 2009; Knoblock, 1983). The potential for stigma suggests that we need to be sure that the benefit to the learner from being classified as having an emotional or behavioral disorder outweighs the societal burden imposed by use of this category.

CONDITIONS ASSOCIATED WITH EMOTIONAL OR BEHAVIORAL DISORDERS

As with all of the conditions we have discussed to this point, the question that is often asked and that is very hard to answer is "What caused this problem?" With emotional or behavioral disorders, this question implies the additional questions "Who is to blame? Whose fault is it?" As discussed previously, unlike other disabilities, an emotional or behavioral disorder elicits little sympathy or empathy. Indeed, the person with this disability is frequently seen to be at fault; the tendency is to blame the victim. The reasoning employed is that such children choose to act inappropriately and *could* behave appropriately if they wanted to. Alternatively, they are seen as weak and unwilling to help themselves; they could "cheer up" or get better if they just tried. If we don't blame the child, we blame the parents. Suspected inadequate or abusive home environments and perceived deficiencies in parental discipline are easy targets.

Additionally, in discussing causes of emotional or behavioral disorders, as with other disabilities, the implication is that knowing the cause will lead to a cure and that it is not possible to identify an appropriate treatment in the absence of knowledge of the cause. As discussed in the chapters on intellectual and learning disabilities, knowledge of the cause of the disorder rarely points to a unique remedial action. The most effective interventions are based on the observed characteristics regardless of a known or presumed cause.

What must also be understood is that even when home or personal factors may have contributed to the problem, the individual or the parents are often doing the best they can in the context. As we look for factors associated with an emotional or behavioral disorder, our goal should be to use that information to plan interventions, not to excuse school personnel from acting to assist the student. In addition to providing interventions for the learner, it is generally advisable to use this information to support interventions within the family context as well in order to help achieve longer-lasting improvement for the child. Educators can also use such information to develop primary and secondary prevention programs (see Chapter 2) in schools so that fewer learners in the future develop these problems in the first place.

Biological Factors

Biological factors are rarely the sole cause of an emotional or behavioral disorder. It is generally only in the interaction with the environment that biological causes result in specific disorders of emotions or behavior. When such causes can be identified, they tend to be related to more severe disorders, some of which can now be partially treated by use of psychoactive drugs (Forness, Walker & Kavale, 2003). Research on biological causes has been far from conclusive. Brain damage is often believed to be related to subsequent emotional or behavioral disorders, but it is rarely possible to validate this belief. Only the most serious of brain injuries can be definitively shown to affect emotional development, as is found in youngsters who have experienced certain traumatic brain injuries (Mira & Tyler, 1991), conditions now generally responded to within the traumatic brain injury category.

Some serious disorders, such as schizophrenia and clinical depression, appear to have a genetic explanation. Genetic connections are generally viewed as a *predisposition,* which may develop into the disorder in a complex interaction with a particular social environment rather than as a simple Mendelian trait (Plomin, 1995). Fragile X syndrome has been linked with behavioral disorders as well as with intellectual disabilities (Santos, 1992). Still other conditions, such as clinical depression and attention-deficit/hyperactivity disorder, now appear to be related to biochemical abnormalities in the brain (Barkley, 2006). In some cases, using psychoactive drugs can help restore near-normal brain functioning. When medication is used along with psychotherapy, an individual can learn to cope with the disorder and achieve a level of functioning that is more normalized (Forness, Freeman, & Paparella, 2006; Forness & Kavale, 2001; Forness et al., 2003).

Another more indirect biological factor is derived from the research of Thomas and Chess (1977, 1984), who found that children appear to be born with a predisposition toward a particular temperament or behavioral style. Temperament or behavioral style is described as the "how" of behavior rather than the "what" or "why." How an individual responds to environmental stimuli will have a significant effect on that person's life experience. Thomas and Chess identified several primary reaction patterns. This inborn temperament of a child interacts with the characteristics of adult caregivers, affecting these crucial early relationships. The temperament that a child is born with may affect the quality of nurturing interactions the child receives from parents and teachers, which in turn affects the child's behavioral responses, sometimes in problematic ways (Martin, 1992). (See Chapter 12 for a more detailed discussion of the role of temperament in social adjustment.)

Children's physical illnesses and disabilities also place stress on caregivers and affect both the quality of caregiving and the children's perceptions of themselves as competent people (Baker-Ericzen, Brookman-Frazee, & Stahmer, 2005; Gallagher, Beckman, & Cross, 1983; Neely-Barnes & Dia, 2008). Children can exhibit emotional responses (e.g., depression, anxiety) related to necessary medical treatments. These factors, apparently related to biological conditions, can affect the way a child experiences the environment, leading to differential effects on the emotional or behavioral status of the child.

Family Factors

A number of family factors may also affect a child's emotional or behavioral development. Among these are family stress, parenting styles, parental psychopathology, and addiction in a family member. Families today experience significant stresses related to maintaining the family unit (Gallagher et al., 1983; Neely-Barnes & Dia, 2008). Factors often implicated in family and parental dysfunction include poverty, unemployment, marital problems (including separation and divorce), domestic violence, and illness or disability of a family member. As our society has become more complex, the isolation of families has also increased, compounding the potential effects of family dysfunction when dealing with stressful situations.

Although these factors do not in themselves cause children to develop emotional or behavioral disorders, the presence of multiple risk factors and the absence of supportive networks for parents and children significantly increase the risk that a child may develop emotional or behavioral disorders (W. Copeland, Shanahan, Costello, & Angold, 2009; Keogh & Weisner, 1993; Morrison & Cosden, 1997). The issue of risk is complex. Children within a single family may react quite differently to the same environment and stresses; one may develop a behavioral disorder, while another appears resistant or resilient and makes a good adjustment to life. (See Chapter 12 for further discussion of risk and resilience.)

The style of parenting may affect the school and community adjustment of a child (Rodriguez & Eden, 2008). Overprotective parenting may be related to anxiety in a child, causing withdrawal from normal situations that the child perceives as dangerous. Parents who place undue emphasis on the importance of achieving high standards may increase the potential for depression. Abusive discipline has obvious implications for a child's emotional health, although the result is not always predictable. Some children become very conforming, others become overly attached and cling to the abusive parent, whereas still others act out with abusive behavior toward other people or animals. Another potential problem occurs when the parenting style—be it authoritarian, permissive, or democratic—conflicts with the discipline style in the school. This may result in confusion for the learner and in behavioral adjustment problems at home, in school, or both.

Parental mental health and adjustment problems have the potential to disrupt the parent–child relationship (W. Copeland et al., 2009). Parents who have emotional disorders themselves—including such conditions as schizophrenia, depression, or addiction—have fewer resources to allocate to and use in the parenting role. If other healthy caregivers are available to the child, the effect of pathology in one family member may be reduced.

The presence of alcoholism or other drug dependency problems in the family setting also affects many children and families today (Eiden, Edwards, & Leonard, 2007; Jordan & Chassin,

ON THE WEB

The **National Institute of Mental Health** (www.nimh.nih.gov) is dedicated to the understanding and treatment of mental illnesses through research for prevention, recovery, and cure. This website provides resources for understanding the brain and human behavior.

ON THE WEB

The **National Association for Children of Alcoholics** (www.nacoa.org/) provides a variety of print and Web resources for teachers, clergy, parents, and other helping individuals seeking to eliminate the adverse effects of alcohol and drug addiction on families and children.

1998). Every classroom contains some learners whose family nurturing is being distorted by the substance abuse of a family member. Children growing up with an alcohol- or drug-dependent person grow up in a home with different rules (Black, 1981). These children learn three basic family rules:

- Don't talk about what goes on at home, and don't talk about what you're feeling.
- Don't trust others to meet your needs. Adults are unpredictable and unreliable; if you don't trust or hope, you can't be hurt.
- Don't feel, particularly your pain and hurt. Convince yourself that it isn't so bad, that it doesn't matter that significant adults are not reliably available for you.

Children growing up in such homes may develop coping behaviors and assume specific family roles in order to deal with an unpredictable home environment that revolves around the needs of the alcoholic or drug-dependent family member (Wegsheider, 1981). Obviously, some of these roles cause more problems in school situations than others, but all can be destructive to children's ability to fulfill their own unique potential and may result in a variety of emotional or behavioral problems that may become severe enough to require intervention.

Environmental, Social, and School Factors

Although there are many environmental factors that can affect a child's ability to develop personally satisfying and socially acceptable responses to life events, school factors are those that teachers and administrators have the most control over (Wehby, Lane, & Falk, 2003). Next to the family, the school is the most important socializing force in a young person's life. Causal factors directly related to schools include school failure, developmentally inappropriate expectations and discipline, and incongruity between school and home cultures.

School failure is highly correlated with school adjustment difficulties later. It is not always clear whether academic problems lead to behavioral problems or vice versa (Payne, Marks, & Bogan, 2007). What does appear to be clear is that once the cycle is established, it will continue unless effective academic and behavioral interventions are implemented. Failure in school can lead a child to develop a diminished sense of self-esteem. Peer rejection of students who do not meet social and behavioral norms in the community or school accentuates the problem.

Students who experience frequent failure tend to adopt a self-defeating cycle of responses, including setting lower goals and putting forth less effort, which leads to more failure (see Chapter 11). Such youngsters see their efforts as less and less efficacious and come to see their lives as controlled by external forces rather than by their own efforts. When their self-esteem as a learner is under attack, they may respond by giving up, saying, "I don't care; it's not important." Alternatively, a student may fight back, saying in effect, "I won't, and you can't make me." When students see themselves as incapable of succeeding in the tasks valued by teachers, they may attempt to find other activities in which they can be competent or "the best." This may include being the class bully or clown. A student may become noncompliant or disinterested in school tasks that present difficulties. Any of these behaviors, extended over time, may result in a referral for special education evaluation.

Schools and teachers increase the likelihood of problems when they hold inappropriate expectations for a student's age, ability, and culture. The likelihood of school failure, with its associated problems, is increased in an environment characterized by the quest for uniformity at the expense of individuality. Learners need the opportunity to learn and explore in ways that fit their abilities, temperaments, and interests. They also need to learn in environments that validate their particular cultural realities (including differences of race, religion, language, gender, sexual orientation, economic background, and physical and mental abilities). When the options for learning are narrowly restricted, many students will find no place they fit in that environment, and they may then respond in problematic ways to become self-determined individuals. (See Chapter 11 for further discussion of self-determination.)

Classroom management and school behavior codes can be another source of confusing information for students. When management of behavior and classroom life is inconsistent, students are likely to discount rules of community life in general. They come to see all rules as arbitrary or capricious. Use of destructive reinforcement contingencies to achieve behavioral control—such as the use of candy rewards, exemption from homework for good behavior, or corporal punishment for bad behavior—provides little support for the intrinsic motivation that most youngsters have when they begin school. When adults in the school environment provide inadequate or undesirable models of school conduct, it is not difficult to see why the actions and attitudes of learners may fall short of desired behaviors.

One of the most common factors affecting the emotional health and behavior of a child is the conflict between and among the norms of the family, the school, and the culture (McIntyre, 1993). Cultural biases may affect evaluation for behavior disorders when a teacher's norms are at variance with the community and family culture. Children who find that their own culture is devalued in the school environment—and who are not helped to navigate the differences in cultures between home and school—frequently fail to develop the ability to adapt in different settings, and the cycle of disorder begins.

A final environmental factor that must be addressed by our society as a whole relates to the effect of mass media on children today. Frequent episodes of violence and inappropriate expressions of sexuality provide destructive models of behavior for young people. These models establish new norms of behavior and tend to cheapen regard for the feelings of others and even for human life. Families, schools, and communities must address this issue in a concerted way, expanding the dialogue on what it means to be human.

TYPES OF EMOTIONAL OR BEHAVIORAL DISORDERS

There are many behaviors and attitudes that young people can exhibit that might cause their teachers and parents to become concerned. Psychiatrists use the *DSM-IV-TR* criteria (American Psychiatric Association, 2000) to arrive at a diagnosis related to the presenting symptoms. Among the more common (but still rare) psychiatric disorders in children and adolescents are oppositional defiant disorder, conduct disorders, depression, bipolar disorder, anxiety disorders, and schizophrenia and other psychotic disorders (Forness et al., 2003). Even though it may be useful for teachers to recognize these psychiatric diagnostic terms, educators do not have the authority to determine that such conditions exist, nor do these categories generally have significant relevance for educational placement and planning. The usefulness of the *DSM-IV-TR* descriptions for educational personnel is further limited because the manifestations of a number of disorders (e.g., depression) may be different in young people than they are in adults. (See Chapter 12 and references such as Kauffman and Landrum [2009] for more detailed discussions of these maladaptive behavior disorders.)

One of the simplest, most commonly used, and most educationally relevant classification schemes organizes these behaviors and the conditions themselves into *externalizing* and *internalizing* behaviors (Lane, Kalberg, Lambert, Crnobori, & Bruhn, 2010; Walker et al., 2004; see Table 6.4). Conduct disorders are comprised of externalizing aggressive behaviors of both overt and covert varieties. Anxiety-withdrawal-dysphoria disorders include primarily internalizing behaviors. Behaviors categorized as ADHD or immaturity disorders include both externalizing and internalizing behaviors.

There are two benefits of grouping problem behaviors into externalizing and internalizing behaviors. Such categorization helps us focus on the dual nature of behaviors and may help ensure that children with internalizing disorders do not get overlooked in the screening and referral process. In addition, useful interventions and placement options tend to be different for externalizing and internalizing behaviors.

Problem behaviors frequently emerge as stable patterns as early as the preschool and primary levels. Early screening to detect problem behaviors results in an opportunity for intervention in the earliest stages of the disorder, when treatment is likely to be most successful (Rutherford &

ON THE WEB

Parent Advocacy Coalition for Educational Rights (www.pacer.org/ebd) is a Minnesota-based organization that provides information for parents on a variety of disability issues, including dealing with challenging behaviors, functional behavioral assessment, and mental health resources.

ON THE WEB

The **Mental Health America (MHA)** website (www.nmha.org) provides information and fact sheets on topics related to mental health issues, including depression and suicide, as well as information on local chapters.

ON THE WEB

The **National Alliance on Mental Illness (NAMI)** website (www.nami.org) includes research and other resources, a helpline, books, and topical information on issues related to mental illness.

Table 6.4 Examples of Externalizing and Internalizing Behaviors	
Overt, Undersocialized	**Covert, Socialized**
Examples of Externalizing Behaviors	
Fighting	Lying
Being disobedient	Stealing
Being destructive	Being uncooperative
Dominating others	Staying out late
Being disruptive	Being truant
"Blowing up" easily	Setting fires
Hitting	Associating with "bad" companions
Having temper tantrums	Using alcohol or drugs
Refusing to follow directions	Engaging in gang activity
Being boisterous, noisy	Being passively noncompliant
Bullying	Cheating
Swearing	
Examples of Internalizing Behaviors	
Anxious	Fearful
Shy	Timid
Tense	Bashful
Depressed or sad	Hypersensitive, easily hurt
Feeling inferior	Self-conscious
Lacking self-confidence	Easily confused
Crying easily	Aloof
Worrying excessively	Preferring to be alone

Source: Based on *Systematic Screening for Behavior Disorders (SSBD): User's guide and Administration Manual* (2nd ed.) by H. M. Walker and H. H. Severson, 1992, Longmont, CO: Sopris West.

Nelson, 1995). The Systematic Screening for Behavior Disorders (SSBD) process assists teachers in screening all children for early indications of potentially disabling behavior patterns (Walker et al., 1988; Walker & Severson, 1992). The SSBD specifically asks teachers to focus on each student in their classes and to determine which students are the most externalizing in their behaviors, as well as which ones exhibit the highest degree of internalizing behaviors. Using this information, detailed follow-up evaluations can be performed to determine the nature and severity of identified behavioral responses and the need for intervention in either general or special education.

Students who are primarily internalizing in their behaviors generally require different interventions than those who present more externalizing behaviors. Children who are grouped within a single self-contained classroom simply because they are all determined to be eligible for services as students with emotional or behavioral disorders are unlikely to have their needs met very well. Students with anxiety-withdrawal-dysphoria disorders often retreat further into their shells and become unhappier when grouped with students who are acting out and who exhibit externalizing behaviors. The behavioral approaches commonly used with students with conduct disorders are repressive to a child with anxiety symptoms. For these and other reasons, it is more useful to think of students who have emotional or behavioral disorders not as a single group but rather as individual students with very specific personal characteristics.

Since problem behaviors and delays in developing appropriate behavior are not the exclusive property of students with emotional or behavioral disorders, Chapter 12 will discuss in more detail the developmental emotional/behavioral delays and maladaptive behaviors found among all learners with mild disabilities.

Summary

Many different terms have been used over the years to describe learners who have problems with their behaviors and emotions. The term *emotional or behavioral disorders* reflects the dual nature of this condition and also the concern for students across a continuum of severity. This chapter focuses on all students who exhibit behaviors that are personally unsatisfying and/or socially unacceptable to the extent that their emotional and social development is affected.

Historically, little attention has been given to these children. The advent of the mental hygiene movement early in the 20th century signaled the awareness that children develop in their emotions and behaviors and that adults can assist in that development. Public school special education classes and programs have evolved slowly and have generally been spurred on by concerns about the effect that out-of-control children might have on general education classroom activities.

IDEA states that students are eligible for services for emotional or behavioral disorders when they exhibit relatively severe problem behaviors for a significant period of time and when those behaviors affect school performance. Students who are determined to have only social maladjustment are excluded from services. Many components of the IDEA definition have raised concern, including the issues related to underidentification, the definition of educational performance, the exclusion of social maladjustment, and the overrepresentation of students from certain ethnic and cultural minority backgrounds.

Assessment and identification of students must include multiple sources of data. A reliable and valid assessment process includes direct observation in multiple settings and information from a variety of informants (parents, teachers, and the child). Response to intervention is also a valid diagnostic and intervention planning tool.

It has been estimated that as many as 7–8 percent of all schoolchildren may have emotional or behavioral disorders significant enough to require some kind of intervention. Currently, fewer than 1 percent are served in programs for students with emotional or behavioral disorders. The reasons for this discrepancy have been discussed widely and include the inadequacy of the current definition. The Mental Health and Special Education Coalition definition was developed in response to these concerns.

Factors associated with emotional or behavioral disorders are not easy or even always possible to identify. When evident, the cause is rarely helpful in designing the intervention. Three groups of factors may be involved: (a) biological, including brain injury and genetic predisposition; (b) family factors, recognizing the family's role as the first socialization agent in a child's life; and (c) school and other environmental factors.

Emotional or behavioral disorders can be separated into two groups: those represented by externalizing behaviors and those characterized as internalizing. Conduct disorders and anxiety-withdrawal-dysphoria are conditions most typically included in school programs for learners with emotional or behavioral disorders. Specific interventions should be developed in response to the nature of an individual child's behavioral challenges.

A Case Study • Carter

Carter was initially referred for possible special education services in a first-grade compensatory classroom at Browning Elementary School. The compensatory class, a district Tier II intervention, served students who had not reached the criterion score for first-grade placement on the district readiness test. This classroom had only 15 students and was served by a teacher and a full-time aide.

Carter was referred by his mother, who had many concerns about her son. She noted that his progress seemed slow, that he not only had problems with academics but had a lot of trouble paying attention, was impulsive, and had poor motor control. Carter's teacher concurred with the mother's concerns. Carter was having very little success in the classroom and was constantly in motion. This had become a problem even in this developmentally appropriate, alternative first-grade program. He was easily distracted and had trouble delaying gratification. He was impatient and gave up easily. He was easily discouraged, and he complained that he did not have any friends. His teacher reported that Carter voiced fears that were "unusual" for this age group.

Carter was the younger of two children. He had been a large baby (10 pounds at birth), and the pregnancy had been complicated by high blood pressure and toxemia. However, no adverse effects were noted after the birth. His mother described Carter as a clumsy child, with repeated falls and bumps. Normal developmental milestones were somewhat delayed. He did not crawl until he was 8 months old or walk until he was 2. Speech development was interrupted by a loss of hearing at 18 months due to ear infections.

The speech and language evaluation, done at the time of referral, confirmed difficulty with some sound frequencies, and it confirmed deficits in speech and communication skills. Carter was taking Ritalin twice a day, prescribed by his pediatrician for attention and hyperactivity problems (ADHD). Even so, Carter's mother described him as a creative, sensitive, and generally happy child.

At age 6½, Carter was evaluated by the school psychologist, who noted that Carter was able to concentrate more easily on tasks that involved manipulation of objects but was very distracted in auditory tasks. He needed encouragement and reinforcement to sustain effort during the testing. The results indicated the following:

WISC-IV (measure of intellectual functioning):

Full Scale IQ:	105

Composite scores:

Verbal Comprehension	102
Perceptual Reasoning	109
Working Memory	95
Processing Speed	110

Carter also achieved a standard score of 105 (63rd percentile) on the Peabody Picture Vocabulary Test, a measure of receptive language ability, which indicated age-appropriate receptive language skills consistent with the WISC-IV results.

Carter was given two measures of academic achievement:

Diagnostic Achievement Battery-3

Reading	109
Math	94

Wide Range Achievement Test (WRAT-4)

Subtest	Standard Score
Reading composite	112
Word reading	113
Sentence comprehension	110
Spelling	108
Math computation	103

From the evaluation, the multidisciplinary team concluded that Carter was a student of average intelligence who showed no significant strengths and weaknesses. Based on state guidelines, he did not qualify for special education at that time.

Carter went on to second grade, continuing on the Ritalin for his medically diagnosed ADHD. His classroom teacher was very sensitive to Carter's needs and monitored the effects of his medication carefully. Carter continued to show signs of problematic socialization behaviors. He had significant trouble getting along with others, often picking on other children.

In third grade, he moved to another school, where he still received all of his education in the regular classroom program. He returned to Browning Elementary School in fourth grade, where he seemed to be in constant trouble. He was still on Ritalin, receiving the highest dose possible. His mother had sought help and advice from other doctors and agencies, and she was in the process of getting him evaluated by a major regional child evaluation clinic. Carter's behavior at home continued to cause serious problems. He exhibited a lot of unwarranted fears and was obsessed by violence. He could not seem to complete any tasks given to him. For the first time, his math skills fell below grade level. In January of that year, the school support team placed him in the resource room under the new eligibility of "other health impaired" because of his ADHD. He was also receiving counseling at the community mental health clinic.

Carter's problems with attention were causing him difficulties, specifically during transitions, such as from lunch to recess and from recess back to class. Right before lunch, when his morning medication would wear off and before the noon dose would take effect, he was unable to concentrate and do work and was consistently disruptive in the regular classroom. It was suggested that his resource room services could include having lunch with the resource teacher and spending recess in the resource room. This was done for about 4 months, during which careful anecdotal records were kept on his behavior to determine what would be the best placement for Carter. His mother requested that he be reevaluated. He was also scheduled for a brain scan and other diagnostic testing outside of school.

During this period, Carter was being weaned off the Ritalin because he had to be completely off it for the planned brain scan to be accurate. As he came off the Ritalin, his attention quickly diminished. By the time he was completely off the drug, he could not sustain attention for more than 1 or 2 minutes at a time, even on things that he enjoyed, such as computer games. He was unable to do any academic work at that time.

Problem behaviors toward his classmates, teachers, and other people were still very evident. Those behaviors didn't change whether he was on the Ritalin or not. His reevaluation by the school psychologist included additional tests to try to uncover the real source of Carter's problems. The reevaluation and the behavioral records helped clarify the nature and extent of his problems. His new fear of crowds caused him to resist going to the lunchroom and to prefer solitude. He made up stories and talked extensively about violence. He would jump from one thing to another in conversation, not seeming to know whether he was telling true or made-up stories. He seemed not to be able to tell what was real from what was not real. By April of that year, the full team met with his mother to determine how to best meet Carter's needs. He had not made any progress during this school year, and the entire experience had been very frustrating for him, his mother, and his teachers.

Everyone at the meeting was aware that Carter had attention-deficit/hyperactivity disorder. When the team met, the school psychologist reported that the results of the evaluation indicated that Carter's school problems stemmed primarily from his emotional problems, not from the ADHD. The ADHD was a contributing factor, but the primary disability appeared to be the emotional or behavioral disorder. Even when he was on Ritalin, the abnormal behavior continued. The mother and the classroom teacher concurred in this. They saw a special class placement as being the least restrictive environment for Carter at that time, a placement that it was hoped would allow him to resume academic learning and to work on his emotional issues and problem behaviors. However, the teacher of the class for students with emotional or behavioral disorders disagreed, saying that the ADHD was the root problem.

The committee took all the evidence and decided that the emotional problems were the central issue. Those concerns were always there, on or off the Ritalin; therefore, they felt that his emotional problems were the primary cause of his lack of academic success. Carter had never had a successful year since he started school, and because of his past history, it was the committee's sincere hope that intensive work in the self-contained classroom environment would help him finally begin to make progress.

Discussion

Using the given information and the federal definition of emotional disturbance, determine whether the classification of Carter as a child with an emotional or behavioral disorder is appropriate.

How might the diagnosis of ADHD complement or contradict Carter's classification as a child with an emotional or behavioral disorder? (Review your answer to this question after completing your study of ADHD in Chapter 7.)

Specifically, consider possible reasons the team and the teacher of the self-contained class might have come to somewhat different conclusions. How might this school have more effectively used RTI as a diagnostic tool?

Learners with Attention Disorders and Other Conditions

Questions *to Guide Your Study*

- What is attention-deficit/hyperactivity disorder (ADHD)?

- What are the defining characteristics of students with ADHD? How do we identify students with ADHD?

- How are learning disabilities, emotional–behavioral disorders, and ADHD related?

- How are students with ADHD served in the public schools if ADHD isn't listed as a disability in IDEA?

- Why might learners with intellectual disabilities, learning disabilities, and emotional or behavioral disorders also be identified as having communication disorders?

- Low-incidence disabilities tend to be more severe in their impact on the learner. Why is it appropriate to include a discussion of low-incidence disabilities such as traumatic brain injury, physical disabilities, and sensory impairments in our discussion of mild disabilities?

Meet Nancy

Nancy makes an impression, and she always has. As an infant, she was fussy and cried a lot. Despite all attempts to soothe her, it appeared impossible to make her comfortable or happy. Her mother wondered if she would ever sleep through the night. As Nancy grew and as her physical abilities increased, life in the house was devoted to keeping her safe, 24 hours a day. She learned how to climb the bars and get out of her crib by her first birthday. Child safety latches and gates proved inadequate to the task of keeping Nancy and harm apart. When she was 3, her parents were awakened one morning at 4:30 AM to the screams of the family cat. They followed the sound, arriving in the bathroom just in time to prevent Nancy from flushing the cat down the toilet. Her pediatrician felt that Nancy was just an active, inquisitive preschooler and that judgment would come with maturity. Time was the only remedy.

When Nancy was enrolled in kindergarten at age 5, her teacher quickly realized that Nancy was different. Her level of attention was much shorter than that of the other children, and her levels of impulsivity and activity were much higher. She was not benefiting from the kindergarten program, and the decision was made to move her to the prekindergarten class, assuming that with time, she would develop the attention abilities required to be successful in school—she was just developmentally immature. Life was no better in the prekindergarten class. She talked incessantly, grabbed what she wanted, and was in constant motion. Nancy wasn't learning, and neither was anyone else.

Finally, when Nancy was in second grade, the school and her parents concluded that a psychological evaluation was in order to determine an explanation for Nancy's problems. The results indicated normal ability and, surprisingly, normal development of cognitive concepts and language. What stood out was her constant movement and her dangerous and disruptive impulsivity, as well as her academic problems in the classroom. Her performance levels in reading, writing, and math lagged well behind those of her peers. A medical examination was suggested, and the diagnosis was made: attention-deficit/hyperactivity disorder, combined type. Based on the given information and the discrepancy between her achievement and ability, as well as the absence of other disabling conditions, the school's multidisciplinary team determined that she qualified for services as a student with a learning disability.

Today, Nancy is a reasonably successful fourth grader. She still stands out, and she probably always will. A combination of behavioral interventions and psychostimulant medication has brought her behavior under control, although she still has a shorter attention span, is somewhat fidgety, and displays more impulsivity and activity than other fourth graders do. She has learned to self-monitor her attention as a result of cognitive behavior modification interventions implemented by the consultant teacher. Counseling sessions with the guidance counselor have helped her accept responsibility for her actions and not blame her actions on the ADHD or the medication schedule. Nevertheless, her homeroom teacher has a hard time accepting that her behaviors are the result of a disability. Mr. Smith finds it hard to accept that a student who is as capable as Nancy and who *sometimes* pays attention and *sometimes* controls her behavior reasonably well has a "real" learning disability. He suspects that the attention disorder is an excuse for letting Nancy do what she pleases.

THINKING QUESTIONS

How might Nancy's teachers have applied the RTI approach to help them understand and respond to her learning problems earlier? What difference might that have made?

- How do mild physical and sensory disabilities affect student learning?
- What are the effects of traumatic brain injury on a learner's performance and behavior?
- What should educators know about the use of medication in the management of disabilities in the school context?

LEARNERS WITH ATTENTION PROBLEMS

Naming This Group of Learners

Like learning disabilities, attention-deficit/hyperactivity disorders are a fairly recent phenomenon, and, like that of learning disabilities, the history of ADHD is one that tells of struggles to describe and even name the condition (Barkley, 2006; Epstein, Shaywitz, Shaywitz, & Woolston, 1991; S.E. Shaywitz & Shaywitz, 1988). Over the years, the focus of those struggles has shifted from hyperactivity and restlessness characteristics, at times attributed to brain injury or minimal brain dysfunction, to a firmer focus on attention, with or without the overactivity characteristics:

- "Morbid defects in moral control" (Still, 1902)
- Attention problems associated with "brain injury" (Strauss & Lehtinen, 1947)
- "Minimal brain dysfunction" (Clements, 1966)
- "Hyperkinetic disorder of childhood" (*DSM-II*; APA, 1968)
- "Attention deficit disorder" (*DSM-III*; APA, 1980)
- "Attention-deficit/hyperactivity disorder" (*DSM-III-R*; APA, 1987)
- "Hyperkinetic disorders" (HKD) (*ICD-10*; World Health Organization, 2007b)
- "Attention-deficit/hyperactivity disorder" with subtypes (*DSM-IV*; APA, 1994, 2000)

Since the 1980s, physicians, psychiatrists, psychologists, and sometimes teachers and schools have identified increasing numbers of children like Nancy as having attention-deficit/hyperactivity disorder. Schools are increasingly challenged by parents to provide modified programming and accommodations for these students. School administrators and teachers like Mr. Smith frequently question these diagnoses, voicing concern that the disability rubric is being abused. A suspicion exists that the label is being used to relieve children of responsibility for their own behavior (Sciutto & Eisenberg, 2007). The one thing that seems certain about attention-deficit/hyperactivity disorders is that nothing is certain. (Note: Because *attention-deficit/hyperactivity disorder* is the current medical term used for the condition affecting this group of learners (*DSM-IV-TR*; APA, 2000), in the interest of brevity we will use the abbreviation ADHD to refer to the condition.)

Historical Development of the Concept of ADHD

In 1902 Still reported his observations as a physician of children with "morbid defects in moral control," using terms that parallel current descriptions of children with ADHD. Following the 1918 influenza epidemic, children with inattention and overactivity were diagnosed with postencephalitic behavior disorders. Goldstein, Bender, and other researchers and physicians of that period related these problem behaviors to brain injuries or infections of the central nervous system. Werner, Strauss, and Lehtinen described clients with apparent disorders of attention and hyperactivity that they associated with a history of brain injury (Stevens & Birch, 1957; Strauss & Lehtinen, 1947). Clements and the members of Task Force I (see Chapter 5) described a condition called "minimal brain dysfunction," which included children with "various combinations of impairment in . . . control of attention, impulse, and motor control" (Clements, 1966, p. 9).

Beginning in 1968, the American Psychiatric Association (APA) established a new diagnostic category entitled "hyperkinetic disorder of childhood" in the *Diagnostic and Statistical Manual II* (*DSM-II*). The criteria for this disorder included overactivity, distractibility, short attention span, and restlessness (APA, 1968). In 1980 the focus changed to include issues of attention rather than just overactivity (APA, 1980); the *DSM-III* diagnostic criteria for attention deficit disorder highlighted the importance of attention in the learning process and daily functioning, with or without hyperactivity. In 1987 the *DSM-III-R* characterized this disorder as one with developmentally inappropriate and marked inattention (APA, 1987). In the *DSM-IV* (APA, 1994, 2000), the criteria for attention-deficit/hyperactivity disorder focused on the dual nature of the condition, inattention and hyperactivity, and then identified three subtypes: hyperactive-impulsive type, inattentive type, and combined type.

From this brief history, it becomes apparent that the conditions of learning disabilities and ADHD have been integrally intertwined throughout the last century. Their histories were identical in the earliest years and then continued to proceed on parallel tracks after 1980. Through all the changes in names and revised criteria, the fact remains that learners with ADHD have a medically defined condition related to attention and/or activity levels that impairs their ability to function optimally in school. Currently, medication and behavioral approaches are the most common interventions used with these students (Schnoes, Reid, Wagner, & Marder, 2006). Increasingly, however, schools are using cognitive behavior modification, self-instructional strategies, and counseling as well.

ADHD and the IDEA

When the IDEA was reauthorized in 1990, Congress decided not to add ADHD to the list of specific diagnostic special education categories, despite the urging of ADHD advocates to do so. Instead, Congress directed the U.S. Department of Education to conduct a study of the condition and the extent to which these students were being denied needed services and access to a free, appropriate, public education. Subsequently, in 1991 the U.S. Department of Education issued a clarification memorandum, confirming that most children with ADHD were already eligible for services under IDEA if their ADHD impaired their educational performance and prevented them from learning (Davila, Williams, & MacDonald, 1991). The memorandum also asserted that it was not necessary to list ADHD as a separate diagnostic category because these students generally present learning and behavioral problems to an extent that makes them eligible for services under one of the existing categories, most often within the categories of learning disabilities or emotional disturbance.

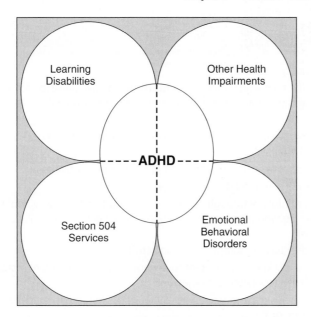

FIGURE 7.1 Ways in Which Learners with ADHD May Be Served

The clarification memorandum continued, stating that since ADHD is a medical diagnosis, youngsters with ADHD may also be qualified for services under IDEA as "other health impaired" if it can be shown that their disorder constitutes a "chronic or acute health problem that results in limited alertness, which adversely affects educational performance" (Davila et al., 1991). The memorandum further noted that children with attention-deficit/hyperactivity disorders may also be determined to be "qualified handicapped persons" under the provisions of Section 504 of the Rehabilitation Act of 1973 if their condition limits their ability to learn or benefit from their educational program. The memorandum concluded that students with ADHD were already being served within the IDEA and Section 504 guidelines if their learning was significantly impaired and to the extent that their characteristics matched the criteria for learning disabilities, emotional disturbance, or other health impairment, and this remains so today (see Figure 7.1).

Current ADHD Definition in the DSM-IV-TR

The American Psychiatric Association's *Diagnostic and Statistical Manual of Mental Disorders, Fourth Edition—Text Revision* (2000) outlines the diagnostic criteria for ADHD (see Table 7.1). The *DSM-IV-TR* notes that a criterion is met only if a behavior is observed to occur considerably more frequently and severely than the behavior occurs in peers of the same developmental level. It is also required that some of the symptoms have been evident before the age of 7 although the diagnosis can occur later. Impaired function should be in evidence in at least two settings—such as home, school, work, and/or social situations—and the problem behaviors must be judged to be interfering with expected functioning. Symptoms must also have persisted for at least 6 months.

Although this definition represents an improvement over prior conceptual definitions, which consisted of a vague sense of overactivity, the *DSM-IV-TR* criteria still lack clear operational procedures for determining that a criterion is met. The evaluation and diagnosis of ADHD requires considerable levels of subjectivity, making this a judgmental category similar to mild intellectual disabilities, learning disabilities, and emotional or behavioral disorders (MacMillan, 1998). Although acknowledging that there are currently no standardized tests that can be used to establish a definitive diagnosis of this condition, the *DSM-IV-TR* does provide some descriptive language for evaluating common behavioral phenotypes. Behaviors may worsen in situations that require sustained attention and mental effort or that are not intrinsically interesting.

Table 7.1 *DSM-IV-TR* Diagnostic Criteria for Attention-Deficit/Hyperactivity Disorder (2000)

A: Either (1) and/or (2):

(1) Six or more of the following symptoms of **inattention** have persisted for at least 6 months to a degree that is maladaptive and inconsistent with developmental level:

Inattention

(a) often fails to give close attention to details or makes careless mistakes in schoolwork, work, or other activities

(b) often has difficulty sustaining attention in tasks or play activities

(c) often does not seem to listen when spoken to directly

(d) often does not follow through on instructions and fails to finish schoolwork, chores, or duties in the workplace (not due to oppositional behavior or failure to understand instructions)

(e) often has difficulty organizing tasks and activities

(f) often avoids, dislikes or is reluctant to engage in tasks that require sustained mental effort (such as schoolwork or homework)

(g) often loses things necessary for tasks and activities (e.g., toys, school assignments, pencils, books, or tools)

(h) is often easily distracted by extraneous stimuli

(i) is often forgetful in daily activities

(2) Six or more of the following symptoms of **hyperactivity-impulsivity** have persisted for at least six months to a degree that is maladaptive and inconsistent with developmental level:

Hyperactivity

(a) often fidgets with hands or feet or squirms in seat

(b) often leaves seat in classroom or in other situations in which remaining seated is expected

(c) often runs about or climbs excessively in situations in which it is inappropriate (in adolescents or adults, may be limited to subjective feelings of restlessness)

(d) often has difficulty playing or engaging in leisure activities quietly

(e) is often "on the go" or often acts as if "driven by a motor"

(f) often talks excessively

Impulsivity

(g) often blurts out answers before questions have been completed

(h) often has difficulty waiting turn

(i) often interrupts or intrudes on other; e.g., butts into conversations or games

B. Some hyperactive-impulsive or inattentive symptoms that caused impairment were present before age 7

C. Some impairment from the symptoms is present in two or more settings (e.g., at school or work and at home)

D. There must be clear evidence of clinically significant impairment in social, academic, or occupational functioning

E. The symptoms do not occur exclusively during the course of a pervasive developmental disorder, schizophrenia, or other psychotic disorder and are not accounted for by another mental disorder (e.g., mood disorder, anxiety disorder, dissociative disorder, or a personality disorder)

Source: Reprinted with permission from the *Diagnostic and Statistical Manual of Mental Disorders,* Fourth Edition, Text Revision (pp. 92–93). Copyright © 2000 American Psychiatric Association.

Symptoms generally decrease or disappear entirely in very controlled situations, such as working one-on-one, or when an activity is particularly interesting, such as video games. The *DSM-IV-TR* further cautions that it may be difficult to distinguish between the behaviors of a child with ADHD and the age-appropriate behaviors of normally active children. (Note: The APA is currently in the process of compiling the *DSM-5,* due out in 2013. There are expected to be some changes to the ADHD criteria at that point.)

Identification of Learners with ADHD

The diagnostic process used to confirm the presence of ADHD is a complex one with the procedures chosen to match the specific situation. The *DSM-IV-TR* provides descriptions of typical manifestations of the diagnostic criteria. Generally the following procedures are used to gather needed information to make the diagnosis (Barkley & Murphy, 2006; National Association of School Psychologists, 2003):

- *Structured clinical interviews with parents, teachers, and the student:* The parental interview gathers information about their major concerns; the learner's development; school, family, and treatment history; peer relationships; and any evidence of other childhood psychiatric disorders. The learner interview covers school functioning, peer relationships, family relations, and general mood. Teacher interviews should address academic performance, classroom behavior, and specific concerns the teacher has about the child's behavior and adjustment in the school setting.
- *Direct observation of behaviors* in a variety of naturalistic settings, followed by comparison of these observed behaviors with those of typical peers: One of the central components of the ADHD construct is that the condition is relatively pervasive. The individual's ability to attend is seen to be impaired at home as well as at school, and at play as well as at work, although the extent of the impairment may vary between settings. This means that even though the symptoms may increase or decrease in particular environments, they never completely vanish. If the symptoms were found to be present only in one setting (e.g., in the classroom with a particular teacher), one would not identify the child as having ADHD but would instead look for environmental conditions in that setting that could be altered to improve the child's ability to function.
- *Psychoeducational examination, including measures of intellectual functioning and achievement:* This evaluation helps identify any negative impact the condition may be having on school performance; it may also identify the existence of another disability, such as a learning disability, emotional or behavioral disorder, or intellectual disability.
- *Rating scales:* Behavior rating scales are one of the principal instruments used to identify children and youth who have problems related to inattention, impulsivity, and hyperactivity that are significantly different from those of their peers. Generally related to the *DSM-IV* criteria, these scales break down the criteria into more specific indicators. By their nature, rating scales are inferential and subjective, with the results influenced as much by the characteristics of the person completing them as they are by the characteristics of the learner being evaluated. Good practice requires that rating scales be completed by as many people as possible who know the child. Although rating scales describe the child's behaviors in comparison to those of a normative sample, more importantly they also give some sense of the variability of the behaviors across settings. Some of the more commonly used scales include the Behavioral Assessment System for Children (BASC-II; Reynolds & Kamphaus, 2004), Child Behavior Checklist (Auchenbach, 2001), Connors Rating Scales–Revised (Connors, 2001), CSI-4: Child Symptom Inventory-4 (Gadow & Sprafkin, 1994), and the ADHD Symptom Checklist–4 (Gadow & Sprafkin, 1997; Sprafkin, Gadow, & Nolan, 2001).
- *Pediatric medical examination, including direct measures of activity level and attending behaviors:* A general physical examination is recommended to determine any medical basis for the condition and to rule out treatable causes. Although ADHD is a condition

ON THE WEB

The *DSM-5* website (www. dsm5.org) provides updates on the process being used by the **American Psychiatric Association** in revising the *Diagnostic and Statistical Manual,* including possible changes to the section on ADHD.

based on a medical diagnosis and is presumed to have a neurobiological basis, it is not generally useful to include a complete neurological examination in the assessment process. Routine neurological examinations usually indicate normal functioning; since the source of the disorder is rather subtle in its manifestation, the absence or presence of neurological findings does not constitute a diagnosis in itself (APA, 2000). It should also be noted that, although a medical evaluation is recommended for diagnosis, schools frequently base their determination of a need for services on other assessment information derived from reports of the educational psychologist and teachers.

Finally, an RTI assessment should be considered, especially if the condition manifests itself primarily in the school environment. Evidence-based intervention strategies should be implemented in the general education classroom, with careful records kept of the effect on the behaviors of concern. The information from such diagnostic trials is useful information even if the problems remain.

Types of ADHD

The *DSM-IV-TR* (APA, 2000) identifies three primary subtypes of ADHD: (a) predominantly inattentive (Zentall, 2005), (b) predominantly hyperactive/impulsive, and (c) combined type. A majority of individuals are found to have the combined type of ADHD. Those who have one of the other types may develop the combined type later and vice versa. In the field test of the *DSM-IV* criteria conducted by Lahey and colleagues (1994), incidence data by subtype, as presented in Table 7.2, indicated that more than half of the field test learners who met the criteria for an ADHD diagnosis were judged to have the combined subtype, while 27 percent of those referred were found not to have ADHD at all.

Levels of Severity

As with other disorders, ADHD may be mild, moderate, or severe in its impact on the ability of an individual to function appropriately. *DSM-IV-TR* (APA, 2000) provides the following guidelines for differentiating among the levels of severity:

- *Mild:* Few if any symptoms in excess of the six indicators required to make the diagnosis; minimal or no impairment in school or social functioning
- *Moderate:* Symptoms or functional impairment intermediate between mild and severe
- *Severe:* Many symptoms in excess of those required to make the diagnosis; significant and pervasive impairment in functioning at home and in school with age peers

Prevalence of ADHD

ADHD has been referred to as a low-visibility, high-prevalence disorder. It is a low-visibility condition because in many cases the youngsters look like and act similarly to their typical peers unless their hyperactivity is at the severe end of the continuum. It is a high-prevalence disorder,

Table 7.2   Percentage of Students with ADHD Subtypes in Field Test Sample

	ADHD Subtypes			
	Inattentive (N = 74)	Hyperactive/ Impulsive (N = 50)	Combined (N = 152)	No ADHD (N = 104)
Percent of students in sample (N = 380)	20%	13%	40%	27%
Percent of students with ADHD in sample (N = 276)	27%	18%	55%	—

Source: Data from "*DSM-IV* Field Trials for Attention Deficit Hyperactivity Disorder in Children and Adolescents" by B. B. Lahey et al., 1994, *American Journal of Psychiatry, 151*(11), pp. 1673–1685.

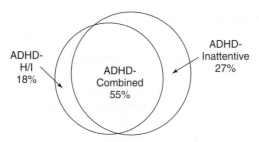

FIGURE 7.2   Illustration of the Relationship Among ADHD Subtypes

however, with the incidence of ADHD in children estimated to be between 3 percent and 10 percent, with 4–7 percent most often cited (APA, 2000; Barkley, 2006; Davila et al., 1991; Pastor & Reuben, 2008; Salend & Rohena, 2003). Varying prevalence rates are obtained in different geographic areas, with the variations more likely due to different ways of conceptualizing and diagnosing the condition rather than to a true variability (Lee et al., 2008; Sciutto & Eisenberg, 2007; S.E. Shaywitz & Shaywitz, 1988). Although students with only the inattentive type of ADHD are at significant risk for school failure without intervention, they are less likely to be referred for services than their peers with the other types of ADHD since their inattention is not combined with the more obvious symptoms of hyperactivity/impulsivity (Epstein et al., 1991; Lee et al., 2008; Zentall, 2005). (See Figure 7.2 for an illustration of the relationship between the subtypes.)

ADHD is more prevalent among males than females, with ratios in the general population found to range from 2:1 to 8:1 in various studies (Barkley, 2006; Pastor & Reuben, 2008; Sciutto & Eisenberg, 2007; S.E. Shaywitz & Shaywitz, 1988). The range of symptoms displayed by boys and girls is similar, but girls have a tendency to display more cognitive, language, and social deficits, whereas the boys exhibit more problems with aggression and impulse control (Lerner & Lerner, 1991; Pastor & Reuben, 2008; Sciutto & Eisenberg, 2007). The lower numbers of girls identified may be attributed to the observation that boys tend to display more characteristics associated with hyperactivity whereas girls appear to manifest symptoms of inattention more frequently; this difference can lead to boys being identified more often because their behaviors are more obvious and troubling. Age is also a factor in prevalence with incidence increasing among older students (Pastor & Reuben, 2008), a factor that may be attributed to older students having been eligible for classification longer. Behaviors that seem within the normal range of activity for young children become less expected among middle and high school students.

DIVERSITY IN FOCUS 7.1

The conditions discussed in this chapter present a number of issues related to culture and diversity, specifically issues of gender, race/ethnicity, and socioeconomic status. Issues of gender seem, appropriately or not, to reflect the effect of societal expectations (based on the dominant culture) of normative behavior for boys and girls. Patterns of disproportionality related to race are also well documented over a period of years (U.S. Department of Education, 2001, 2006b), and poverty has been repeatedly shown to be related as a risk factor for a variety of disabilities.

Males are significantly overrepresented among students with ADHD, particularly among those with the hyperactive or combined types (S.E. Shaywitz & Shaywitz, 1988). It has been hypothesized that females may be underidentified because they seem to be more likely to exhibit the ADHD-inattentive type, leading them to be overlooked for services. This disproportionality by gender suggests that ADHD classifications may be affected to some extent by a disparity between the normative behavior expected by female, middle-class teachers and the activity levels exhibited by boys. Similar concerns have been raised with respect to ADHD identification among culturally different groups. Multidisciplinary teams should consider the possibility that the activity levels observed in students from diverse cultural groups may in fact be normative for that cultural group or the community.

Conditions Associated with ADHD

ADHD is generally regarded to be a chronic neurobiological condition that can interfere with many life functions, disrupting an individual's life at home, school, work, and play. Current thinking holds that both biological and psychosocial factors play a role in the genesis of ADHD (Cooper, 2001, 2005; Graham, 2008; National Institute of Mental Health, 2008). One theory holds that a child's genetic and biological makeup forms the physical basis for the condition but that the specific manifestation and expression of the disorder is related to the environmental context (Coghill, Nigg, Rothenberger, Sonuga-Barke, & Tannock, 2005; Graham, 2008; S.E. Shaywitz & Shaywitz, 1988). In an early review of the literature that included 25 studies of ADHD, Goodman and Poillion (1992) identified 38 separate causal factors in five broad categories: organic causes (including genetic conditions), birth complications, intellectual/developmental causes, psychological issues, and environmental factors.

ON THE WEB

The **National Institute of Mental Health** website provides current, general information on ADHD (http://www.nimh.nih.gov/health/topics/attention-deficit-hyperactivity-disorder-adhd).

The search for a single cause within an individual has not been fruitful. Instead, it appears that the biological causes and behavioral outcomes are mediated by experiential and environmental factors. Seeking to develop a heterogeneous causal model, researchers, educators, parents, and students are moving beyond a purely biomedical model, in which the cause is presumed to be solely within the child and beyond his or her control. With a more psychosocial orientation, the possibility of the learner's developing and exerting some measure of self-control becomes clearer (Cooper, 2001, 2005; Graham, 2008; Tannock, 1998).

BIOLOGICAL FACTORS   There is considerable scientific evidence (Barkley, 2006; Lerner, Lowenthal, & Lerner, 1995; NIMH, 2008; Roccio, Hynd, Cohen, & Gonzalez, 1993; Tannock, 1998) that organic causes (e.g., brain structure differences, chemical imbalances or deficiencies, genetic factors) are correlated with ADHD. Some researchers hypothesize that neuroanatomical or neurophysiological differences resulting from differences in brain structure may play a role in attention and hyperactivity. Others hypothesize that the attention problems may be due to a reduced ability of the brain to produce the required neurotransmitters. The deficits in functioning of neurotransmitters may result in a reduction in stimulation from the brain to the central nervous system, thus disrupting the normal process of activity and inhibition. Still other research studies have implicated thyroid abnormalities or problems with glucose metabolism as causal factors (Barkley, 2006; Coghill et al., 2005; Lerner et al., 1995; B.A. Shaywitz et al., 1997; Tannock, 1998).

There is also evidence that genetic factors may be involved in some cases, with several members of the same family (e.g., grandparent, parent, child, siblings) exhibiting symptoms of ADHD. Learners with conditions such as fragile X and neurofibromatosis often display an increased level of attention and hyperactivity problems. Inheritance patterns of ADHD and Tourette's syndrome suggest interrelated patterns of heritability for these two conditions. Children with phenylketonuria (PKU) seem to have a higher-than-expected incidence of ADHD, indicating a potential relationship with that genetic condition (Barkley, 2006; Coghill et al., 2005; Farone & Biederman, 1998; NIMH, 2008).

Brain injury was implicated early in the history of the syndrome. According to the *DSM-IV-TR*, ADHD is sometimes associated with a history of child abuse, lead poisoning, encephalitis and other infections, prenatal drug and alcohol exposure, and low birth weight, frequently associated with birth complications (APA, 1994, 2000; Pastor & Reuben, 2008). Children with seizure disorders are more likely to also display ADHD, although it is not clear whether the cause is the seizure disorder itself or the antiseizure medications. All of these factors constitute insults to the brain and central nervous system and thus may be implicated as biological causes of inattention, impulsivity, and hyperactivity.

PSYCHOSOCIAL FACTORS   Coghill and others (2005) held that biomedical factors are just the beginning of understanding this complex condition. Psychological causes (Goodman & Poillion,

1992) are increasingly implicated as key parts of the model. Such causes include problematic psychosocial relationships, anxiety, conduct disorders, frustration, and personal space needs. In such cases, it is possible that these conditions are characterized by behaviors similar to those of ADHD, although causal connections have not been established.

The environment has also recently been considered as a contributing factor to ADHD. Coghill and colleagues (2005) and Cooper (2005) called for integrating the environmental and social factors and processes into the genetic and neurobiological frameworks to more fully explain the syndrome. The "goodness of fit" between children and the settings in which they learn, live, and play may be critical in whether a given child is judged to be inattentive or hyperactive. The ability of the cultural contexts to tolerate the levels of inattention and hyperactivity of normally active children is often critical to determining whether a child is viewed as deviant. Additionally, the degree to which the environment provides the opportunity and the need to focus attention and control activity may be a factor (Graham, 2008). One hypothesis suggests that hyperactivity may be a child's response to an environment that lacks sufficient stimulation.

Characteristics of Individuals with ADHD

In addition to the *DSM-IV-TR* diagnostic criteria listed previously, the following characteristics are frequently observed in individuals with this disorder (Goodman & Poillion, 1992; Cooper, 2001, 2005):

- Low frustration tolerance
- Temper outbursts
- Resentment toward family members
- Stubbornness
- Mood lability (i.e., instability)
- Rejection by peers
- Poor self-esteem
- Oppositional behavior
- Lack of effort, "laziness"
- Antagonism and aggression
- Perceived lack of self-responsibility
- Bossiness
- Social isolation
- Psychological dysfunction
- Excessive, insistent demands that requests be met

In 25 percent to 60 percent of cases, the ADHD is an additional disability alongside learning disabilities, conduct disorders, oppositional defiant disorder, depression, and anxiety (Cooper, 2005). The specific manifestations, of course, will depend on the type of ADHD the learner has. Zentall (2005) described learners with the inattentive or combined type as having more pronounced academic disabilities and social unpopularity.

Individuals with ADHD frequently perform more poorly in school, drop out of school more often, and have less vocational success as adults than their typical peers do. Intellectual functioning and development may be affected adversely. Inattention, of course, is a hallmark of this condition (Kofler, Rapport, & Alderson, 2008; Zentall, 2005). The disorder may coexist with a number of other conditions such as mood disorders, learning disabilities, anxiety disorders, communication disorders, behavioral disorders, and Tourette syndrome (APA, 2000; Cooper, 2001; Graham, 2008; NIMH, 2008).

DEFICITS IN BEHAVIORAL INHIBITION One theory about the source of the symptoms of ADHD suggests that the condition may actually arise from deficits in the ability to cognitively process information before acting. Behavioral inhibition allows an individual to make informed choices about proceeding with a course of action and to refrain from carrying out those impulsive actions that, on reflection, would not lead to desirable outcomes.

Barkley (2006) hypothesized that ADHD is better characterized as disinhibition (i.e., a deficit in delay of response) rather than a primary deficit in attention. Barkley related this inability to delay responses to a disruption of basic thought processes, including (a) separating a message into several components (e.g., affect and content), (b) holding a stimulus long enough to perform complex mental operations with it, (c) reflecting on the meaning of a stimulus with the mediation of inner language, and (d) reconstituting the message into a new thought or concept. Barkley suggested that basic thinking processes may in fact be intact in students with ADHD but that behavioral disinhibition does not allow time for appropriate cognitive processing to occur before acting.

Barkley (2006) further suggested that these students have problems with the cognitive processes involved with nonverbal and verbal working memory, emotional regulation, and planning. They do not process information efficiently and therefore have problems inhibiting inappropriate responses, interrupting an ongoing response when the responses of others suggest that would be helpful, or holding thoughts when interrupted. Based on this theory, simply telling such a student to stop and think or to slow down is not apt to be helpful. Such students need help to develop these cognitive skills. (We will return to these issues in more detail in Chapter 9.)

CHARACTERISTICS AT DIFFERENT AGES   ADHD affects individuals differentially at various age levels, with the symptoms undergoing transmogrification, or changes, as an individual moves through the periods of preschool, elementary school, adolescence, and adulthood (APA, 2000; Barkley, 2006; Lerner et al., 1995; NASP, 2003; Teeter, 1991). Research has confirmed that the symptoms vary according to developmental age and that the effects of these symptoms on behavior vary as well. Even though the age at onset and diagnosis may be as early as 3 years of age, the child who is later identified with ADHD is often retrospectively reported to have cried excessively and to have been difficult to soothe in infancy. Excessive sensitivity to stimuli is noted. Temperamental differences may adversely affect the mother–child bonding process.

Preschool children diagnosed with ADHD are frequently described as "always on the go," with excessive motor activity a primary characteristic. Aggressive acts are also frequent, perhaps explained by the behavioral disinhibition that characterizes these children. Their natural childlike inquisitiveness can take destructive turns because they act without thinking about the possibility of damaging property or harming other people or themselves. They also test their parents regularly by exhibiting more noncompliance than do their typical peers.

By elementary school, the motor activity moderates in some children, manifesting itself as fidgeting and restlessness. Problems with organization and task completion are frequently mentioned in referrals. The inability to sustain attention will eventually affect school performance negatively. These children display a low tolerance for frustration. They respond impulsively, often failing to follow directions because they get started on a task before all the directions have been given. They may take undue risks and engage in dangerous acts, either because of impulsivity or as a means to gain the attention of their peer group. They may be reported to be disruptive in class and to display oppositional and noncompliant behaviors. They frequently exhibit social difficulties in maintaining friendships because of their troubling behaviors.

In adolescence, the motoric excesses all but disappear in most individuals, although the young person may talk about being "jumpy" inside. As the years of inattention take their toll, the teenager frequently has growing academic skill deficits. Problems with following rules and achieving self-control are frequently noted by teachers and parents. In fact, at this age, the secondary symptoms of aggression, problems with peer relationships, and problems in school learning become the predominant concerns. Concurrent diagnoses with behavioral disorders such as oppositional defiant disorder or other conduct disorders become more common. There is an increased risk of developing problems with substance abuse and antisocial behaviors, as well as with depression.

ON THE WEB

The **Attention Deficit Disorder Association** (**ADDA;** www.add.org) provides information on adults and young adults with ADHD, including information for parents.

In adults, ADHD is usually a hidden disorder, and the manifestation of the disorder is a result of the cumulative effects over the years. The adult may exhibit problems maintaining relationships, staying organized, or keeping a job. Substance abuse and problems with impulse control can result in abuse of spouses or children, similar to the temper tantrums these individuals may have engaged in as young children. Depression is frequently observed in adults with ADHD who have experienced significant failure in their developmental years. In some cases, the ability to function in the workplace may improve over previous school performance, partly because of the reduction in motoric activity, but also because of the ability of adults to choose a work environment that accommodates their particular ability to function.

A review of the research on the developmental manifestations of ADHD illustrates the continuing effects of ADHD on affected individuals throughout the life span; the effect of ADHD over time leads to increasing problems with learning, conduct, emotional development, and health. Lack of success in school learning and impaired social relationships impact overall development and the ability to function. Treatment plans need to focus on the concerns that are central to the developmental level of the individual. Although the manifestation of ADHD may change over time, the effect on related functioning may well persist throughout the life span. Educators and parents should address these related concerns as consistently as they do deficiencies in attention, time on task, and hyperactivity.

Issue: Should ADHD Be a Separate Category in IDEA?

As indicated previously, ADHD is not currently specified as a separate eligibility category in the federal special education statute. Although Congress failed to add it to IDEA in 1990 and the U.S. Department of Education has determined that children with ADHD can receive services under existing categories, the debate continues. In a study of identification and service delivery, Schnoes and colleagues (2006) verified that significant numbers of students with emotional disturbance and other health impairment have concurrent ADHD diagnoses, with additional cases of ADHD among students with intellectual disabilities, learning disabilities, and speech/language impairment (see Table 7.3). Clearly, special educators need to be knowledgeable participants in these ongoing discussions.

To set the context for this debate, it may be useful to summarize the arguments advanced on both sides of the issue. Children and Adults with Attention Deficit/Hyperactivity Disorder

Table 7.3 Prevalence of Dual Diagnoses Among ADHD Students

Disability Category	A Percentage of Students in Each Disability Category Who Have an Additional ADHD Diagnosis[a]	B Percentage of Students with ADHD Who Have This Additional Disability[a]	C Percentage of Special Education Students in Each Disability Category[b]
Other health impairments	65.8	17.7	8.77
Emotional disturbance	57.9	13.8	5.65
Intellectual disabilities	20.6	12.4	7.34
Learning disabilities	20.2	49.7	38.08
Speech/language impairment	4.5	6.5	40.16

[a]The data in Columns A and B are drawn from a sample of 1419 students (ages 6–12) in the Special Education Elementary Longitudinal Study (2000–2006); 467 of those students were identified by their parents and schools as presenting ADHD characteristics.

[b]The data in Column C are drawn from U.S. child count data for all students (ages 6–11) and all disabilities served in special education in 2004–2005.

Source: Data from (a) "ADHD Among Students Receiving Special Education: A National Survey" by C. Schnoes, R. Reid, M. Wagner, and C. Marder, 2006, *Exceptional Children, 72*(4), pp. 483–496 and (b) *28th Annual Report to Congress on the Implementation of the Individuals with Disabilities Education Act, 2006* by U.S. Department of Education, 2009, Washington, DC: USDOE.

ON THE WEB

Children and Adults with Attention Deficit/ Hyperactivity Disorder (CHADD; www.chadd.org) was founded in 1987 as an advocacy group for children and adults with ADHD and provides information and resources for parents, professionals, and persons with ADHD.

(CHADD), with the support of some professionals in the field, has been among the most vocal proponents of establishing a separate category. Composed primarily of parents and serving as a support and advocacy group for individuals with ADHD, CHADD holds the position that students with ADHD are being denied appropriate services because of the lack of a diagnostic category. CHADD uses the history of disability advocacy (e.g., ARC, ACLD/LDA) as a precedent to underscore the direct connection between formal designation as a separate condition and the provision of services and accommodations in public schools. CHADD contends that individuals with ADHD require specialized and distinctive treatment plans and services. This organization contends that grouping these children with students with other conditions results in their receiving inappropriate services.

On the other side of the debate, the position against establishing a separate category in IDEA was articulated by the U.S. Department of Education in its 1991 clarification memorandum (Davila et al., 1991), as well as by other disability and professional groups. The Division for Learning Disabilities (1991) of the Council for Exceptional Children held that although ADHD is a valid medical diagnosis, appropriate services are already available under current programming options. This position focuses on the premise that special education services should always be designed to meet the individual needs of the child in question and that the label is merely a vehicle for determining that a child is eligible for such an individualized education program, not a design of what that program should include. Others who oppose CHADD's position argue that the services already exist in the schools to assist children in learning and in managing their behavior. Many special education professionals agree that there are no specialized methods that apply only to students with ADHD and that separate programs for learners with ADHD would be redundant.

ADHD AND OTHER HEALTH IMPAIRMENTS   One increasingly popular course of action identified by the U.S. Department of Education is to designate a student with ADHD as a student with "other health impairment." The significant increase in numbers of learners classified with other health impairments since the mid-1990s is largely attributed to inclusion of learners with ADHD (U.S. Department of Education, 2009). Currently, the vehicle for identifying a learner as having ADHD is a medical diagnosis as established by the American Psychiatric Association (2000), making the condition legitimately a medical condition. According to the provisions of IDEA, a health condition constitutes a disability under this law when it results in limited alertness, adversely affecting educational performance. Because deficits in attention affect the alertness needed for learning, the U.S. Department of Education (Davila et al., 1991) determined that students with ADHD may be judged eligible under this IDEA category if their educational performance is affected. IDEA data from 1992 to 2004 show that the percentage of individuals receiving special education services for other health impairments increased from 0.1 percent to 0.8 percent, with districts saying that ADHD diagnoses accounted for most of that increase (U.S. Department of Education, 2006b).

ADHD AND LEARNING DISABILITIES   When "unexpected underachievement" is the primary presenting symptom, use of the learning disability category may be appropriate. Since attention is considered to be a psychological or cognitive process and learning disabilities are conceptualized as disorders in basic psychological processes, a disorder in attention that leads to learning problems would appear to be justification for determining that a student has a learning disability (see Chapter 5). Silver (1990), however, said that although ADHD is not and should not be considered a learning disability, it frequently coexists with a learning disability and that children with ADHD who also have a learning disability could appropriately receive services for both conditions in programs designed for students with learning disabilities.

ADHD AND EMOTIONAL OR BEHAVIORAL DISORDERS   If the primary presenting symptoms relate to aggression, noncompliance, oppositional disorders, depression, and other problem behaviors affecting educational performance, a multidisciplinary team may determine that the instructional needs of the student justify identification as a student with an emotional or behavioral disorder. The most frequent problem behaviors associated with ADHD are antisocial and aggressive behaviors or oppositional/conduct disorders (Graham, 2008). However, multidisciplinary placement teams find that even though identification of a learner as having an emotional disturbance qualifies the student for needed behavioral services, parents often resist this category and refuse services because of the significant stigma the label represents. They hold that the behavioral problems are secondary to the primary condition of ADHD and that if their child is treated for the ADHD, the behavioral problems will be resolved.

ADHD AS A SOCIAL CONSTRUCTION   The positions just described have in common the fact that they accept ADHD as a disabling condition, even though they differ on where and under what rubric services should be provided. The concept of attention-deficit/hyperactivity disorder as a condition, however, is not without its critics. Another position on services for learners with ADHD holds that neither the classification nor the services are needed or justified. The rapid increases in numbers of children identified as having ADHD has raised suspicions that this diagnosis is socially constructed to account for the mismatch between the current behavioral contexts in which children live and learn and the characteristics of normally active children. Others, including some teachers and parents, believe that the diagnosis is being used to explain an undisciplined child (Armstrong, 1995). Those who hold these views make the following points:

- Children learn to control both their attention and their behavior when they are expected to do so. Delays in developing these skills may be attributed to a lack of that expectation of appropriate behavior by parents and teachers.
- Over the last 3 decades, schools have consistently expected children to handle more advanced material and to develop academic skills at ever-earlier years. It is not uncommon now for 3- and 4-year-old children to be expected to sit still and complete reading and writing worksheets and for children to be expected to enter first grade knowing how to read. This raises questions about the developmental match between school expectations and these young students. When children are viewed as hyperactive and inattentive in developmentally inappropriate environments (Elkind, 1981), is the problem with the child or with the setting?
- Children growing up today are presented with a barrage of stimuli from their earliest years. Television programs like *Sesame Street* teach them letters and numbers at a frenetic pace. Some make the argument that young children have come to expect the world to provide the same fast-paced environment for learning and leisure. When schools don't provide that level of stimulation, children lose interest and attention. If attention and reflection are not nurtured in children's everyday environment, where are they to learn it?

These questions and arguments address the issue of the social construction of ADHD. As with all issues of disability, professional educators must always evaluate the rationale used to identify students as deviant and in need of special education services. IDEA 2004 suggests that the label of ADHD should be reserved for only those learners who are most severely affected and that children with fewer symptoms should be supported within the general education program. If a child is identified as having severe ADHD, the child's IEP should be developed to meet his or her specific behavioral and learning needs. The cross- or noncategorical framework proposed by the National Association of School Psychologists (2009a, 2009b; see Chapter 1) provides an alternative rubric for service. IDEA 2004 holds that quality interventions should be available to support all students with mild learning problems, including those whose difficulties are related to inattention, impulsivity, and hyperactivity. As the general education classroom becomes more responsive to the needs of diverse learners, those classrooms will become more effective for all students. Specifically, the focus on building general education programs that create successful learners should help avert the secondary problems of low self-esteem, aggression, and depression.

PHYSICAL AND SENSORY DISABILITIES

Generally, low-incidence conditions identified by IDEA as categories of disability represent significant levels of impairment and therefore are outside the scope of this text. However, some physical and sensory disabilities include students whose level of impairment is in the milder range. These students are usually served in general education classrooms, with the support of itinerant or resource special educators or nurses. Such students may have physical disabilities, health impairments, traumatic brain injury, or visual or hearing impairments, affecting to some extent their ability to access the general education program.

Students with chronic medical conditions or physical or sensory disabilities often have needs beyond their physical and sensory impairments, particularly in social–behavioral learning. Medical conditions often present barriers for children in engaging in typical social interactions, resulting in slower development of these skills. Even when these students have the social skills, they tend to use them inefficiently or inconsistently, limiting their effectiveness (Coster & Haltiwanger, 2004.) If they require a personal assistant, an additional barrier to interaction is erected (Giangreco et al., 1997). Opportunities to develop and exercise self-determination are also critical (Angell, Stoner, & Fulk, 2010; see Chapter 11).

Physical and Health Disabilities

Students with physical or health impairments are a small and very diverse group of students with disabilities. This group consists of students with orthopedic conditions, including impairments in movement due to injury or disease of the bones, muscles, or neurological system. The group also includes students with a variety of health conditions (e.g., asthma, diabetes, cancer, heart conditions, HIV/AIDS, epilepsy) that reduce their alertness for learning, often preventing regular school attendance and therefore affecting their educational performance.

One large group of students with physical disabilities consists of those with cerebral palsy. Most of these learners have cerebral palsy related to an injury during the birth process, typically involving a lack of oxygen to the brain. Others were affected by injury or infection in the early developmental period. The effect of this condition on a child's functioning can range from mild to severe, with most students able to participate in general education with physical accommodations if there is no additional disability (e.g., intellectual disability or sensory impairment).

Other conditions affecting a student's physical abilities include spina bifida, muscular dystrophy, arthritis, paralysis, and amputations (congenital as well as traumatic). In most cases, related service providers—including physical and occupational therapists, adaptive physical educators, and school nurses—provide the support needed for these students to be served in the general education program. The most important understanding for teachers is that this group of students is very heterogeneous and their ability to learn is often largely unaffected by their conditions.

When a student with a physical or health disability is placed in a general education classroom, it is essential that the teacher consult with the parents and the related service providers to learn about that student's specific areas of impairment and the actions required to make the general education program accessible to the maximum extent possible (Heller, Fredrick, Best, & Cohen, 2000; Nabors, Little, Akin-Little, & Jobst, 2008). It is also critical that the classroom environment itself be evaluated with respect to the learner's physical needs, including assistive technology and adaptive equipment so that those needs can be met efficiently, promoting inclusion of the learner in the learning environment (Heller, Forney, Alberto, Schwartzman, & Goekel, 2000; Pivik, McComas, & LaFlamme, 2002; Wadsworth & Knight, 1999).

Sensory Disabilities

Sensory disabilities involve impairment in one or both of the primary sensory systems used for learning. In 2004 students with visual impairments accounted for 0.4 percent of all students in special education, and those with hearing impairments accounted for 1.2 percent (U.S.

ON THE WEB

Division for Physical, Health and Multiple Disabilities (DPHMD; http://web.utk.edu/~dphmd/) is the division of the Council for Exceptional Children (CEC) that advocates for quality education for all individuals with physical disabilities, multiple disabilities, and special health care needs who are served in schools, hospitals, or home settings.

ON THE WEB

The **Epilepsy Foundation** (www.epilepsyfoundation. org) provides educational resources about epilepsy, including first aid, causes, and treatments.

ON THE WEB

The **United Cerebral Palsy Association** (www. ucp.org) provides a variety of links to national resources about cerebral palsy and other disabilities; the organization promotes full inclusion of individuals with disabilities.

ON THE WEB

The **National Association of School Nurses** (www. nasn.org) provides information on the roles and responsibilities of school nurses as well as information on a variety of health issues such as diabetes, asthma, influenza, obesity, nutrition, and emergency preparedness.

Department of Education, 2009; see Figure 1.1 in Chapter 1). In each case, the hearing or visual impairment is significant enough that, even with correction, the student's educational performance is affected unless accommodations and special education are provided. Students with correctible sensory deficits (glasses or hearing aids) are not identified for special education services.

HEARING IMPAIRMENT It is important to differentiate between the criteria used to make a medical diagnosis of a hearing impairment and the functional needs of a learner in a school environment. For school purposes, students with hearing impairments are classified as hard of hearing, or as having a mild to moderate hearing loss, if they have enough residual hearing so that processing linguistic information is possible with amplification and other accommodations. However, this degree of loss reduces the effectiveness of educational programs because of the learners' inaccuracy and inefficiency in processing auditory information, coupled with the extra energy required to do so (Fiedler, 2001). These students can be classified as deaf if the hearing loss is so severe that even with amplification, the individual cannot process linguistic information through the ears alone. Most students with hearing impairments have impairment in the mild-to-moderate range; only a small number have severe and profound hearing losses requiring more extensive accommodations. Language learning is especially important for these students as the typical mode of language modeling is restricted by their conditions (Easterbrooks & Baker, 2001; Friedman-Narr, 2006; Wurst, Jones, & Luckner, 2005). Teachers also need to work closely with related services providers to assist these children in the maintenance and use of their hearing aids. An FM transmitter may be used to help a student receive verbal instruction more effectively from the classroom teacher.

VISUAL IMPAIRMENT As noted for hearing impairments, it is important to differentiate between a medical diagnosis and the functional impact of a visual impairment in a school setting. Students with visual impairments are classified as having a mild-to-moderate visual impairment if they can process print information with the help of visual devices, such as magnifiers. Students with a severe visual impairment are able to use their vision only with difficulty, and a student with a profound visual impairment cannot use vision for educational purposes and must rely on adaptive devices such as auditory media and Braille. Most students with visual impairments fall in the mild-to-moderate range, with only a very small percentage having severe and profound levels of visual loss that require more extensive accommodations for learning. Students with visual impairments may also have mobility needs. Teachers working with students with visual impairments need to work closely with itinerant special educators and mobility specialists as needed in order to assure that such learners have the material and training supports needed for effective learning and mobility (Cox & Dykes, 2001; Griffin, Williams, Davis, & Engleman, 2002).

According to U.S. Department of Education (2009) data, about 56 percent of all students with visual impairments are served in general education for more than 80 percent of the day. About 47 percent of students with hearing disorders are served in general education for more than 80 percent of the day. One aspect of universal design for learning involves the easy access to materials in a variety of formats. Schools are now required by IDEA to adhere to the National Instructional Materials Accessibility Standards (NIMAS) for textbooks and other materials. Having the option of listening to text can be helpful in combating the fatigue experienced by students with visual impairments when required to complete significant amounts of print reading.

Traumatic Brain Injury

In 1990 Congress added the category of traumatic brain injury to the disabilities covered by IDEA. These students have an acquired brain injury due to external force or accident (e.g., a car accident, fall, gunshot wound, child abuse). The results of such injuries are many and variable, including physical impairment, sensory impairment, emotional disturbance, disruption of cognition, and language problems. This small and varied group of students includes about 0.4 percent

ON THE WEB

Alexander Graham Bell Association for the Deaf and Hard of Hearing (http://nc.agbell.org) provides resources and publications related to hearing impairments across the life span for families and professionals; it also provides contact information for support groups and advocacy.

ON THE WEB

Division on Visual Impairments (http://www.cecdvi.org/), a division of the Council for Exceptional Children (CEC) dedicated to the educational needs of learners with visual impairments and those with additional exceptionalities, offers a variety of resources to assist professionals in implementing adaptations for these students.

ON THE WEB

The **National Federation of the Blind** (www.nfb.org) provides links to research and resources about visual impairments across the life span for individuals, parents, and professionals; it also provides links to sources of nonprint media.

ON THE WEB

The **National Center on Accessible Instructional Materials** (www.aim.cast.org), operated by CAST, works with states, districts, and an OSEP-supported network of technical assistance and dissemination projects to support the implementation of NIMAS and effective uses of accessible instructional materials (AIM).

of all students in special education today (U.S. Department of Education, 2009). Their injuries may be temporary or relatively permanent, mild or severe, and no two will be the same.

Unlike students with developmental disabilities such as intellectual disabilities, students with traumatic brain injury typically retain some of the skills they had learned previously. They may return to school after varying lengths of hospitalization and home care, but it is likely that the recovery process will continue for a significant period of time. Successful reentry into the school environment may require adjustments to the environment, the learning/relearning of skills, and the use of various compensatory aides. Socialization will likely have been disrupted by the injury as well.

ON THE WEB

The **Brain Injury Association of America** (www.biausa.org) provides resources and support networks for individuals dealing with traumatic brain injury.

Interventions provided for these students involve rehabilitative services. Special and general educators need to work closely with parents, related services providers, and medical personnel to design the most appropriate program of rehabilitation, maximizing the remaining abilities and working to regain those that were damaged. School professionals must also be prepared for the manifestations of the injury to vary from day to day and for progress to be intermittent and variable (Bowen, 2005; Keyser-Marcus et al., 2002; Witte, 1998).

COMMUNICATION DISORDERS

Communication disorders include disorders in speech as well as language and are high-incidence disorders, generally in the mild range. Communication disorders can coexist with other disabilities, including intellectual disabilities, learning disabilities, cerebral palsy, and hearing impairments (Sunderland, 2004). Speech disorders include those affecting articulation, fluency, and voice quality; they affect the mechanical production of oral language. Language disorders, on the other hand, involve impairment in the understanding or use of the language system, including the spoken or written code, vocabulary, and syntax. Speech, language, and communication needs can also impact learners' cognitive processing involving storage and retrieval of linguistic concepts (Martin, 2005).

Children with speech and language impairments account for 18.8 percent of all students receiving special education services (U.S. Department of Education, 2009; see Figure 1.1). Martin (2005) reports a higher incidence of communication disorders and delays among children from lower socioeconomic backgrounds. Also, some population groups may not use language as a tool in the same way that the school does, creating a communication mismatch when the child enters school. The highest prevalence of speech/language impairment is in early intervention and the primary grades, with most students responding to itinerant speech therapy and no longer needing services by the middle of elementary school. Speech/language therapists today often coteach with K–3 teachers in the general education classroom. We will return to a more extended discussion of language characteristics and disabilities in Chapter 10.

MEDICATION: A PERSISTENT ISSUE

When dealing with conditions like ADHD and behavioral disorders, among others, the issue of medication as part of the treatment plan frequently arises. There is a perception that medication is widely overprescribed for a variety of behavioral symptoms. However, Forness and Kavale (2001) reported on a large-scale study that indicated that medication alone was more effective in changing behavior than behavioral treatment alone, but that using both together produced even greater effectiveness. They observed that, contrary to public perceptions, medication is prescribed less often than would be useful and that based on the neurobiological basis of such conditions, medication may be a valuable part of a scientifically based intervention plan.

In a review of recent studies on the efficacy of pharmacologic treatment versus behavioral interventions with students with ADHD or emotional or behavioral disorders, Forness, Freeman, and Paparella (2006) reconfirmed the finding that both interventions are effective with significant numbers of children. Medication alone helped normalize the behavior of 52 percent of students, whereas behavioral interventions alone helped 32 percent. This means that 48 percent did not respond to medication. Clearly, neither approach is right for all children, and a combination approach helps many but not all. The conclusion is that medication must be considered in intervention planning and that families, teachers, and medical personnel must work collaboratively to find the right intervention plan for a particular student.

Barkley (2006) advocated for continued research into effective nonpharmacological interventions. He noted that not all children benefit from medication and others have unacceptable levels of side effects. He also noted that although medications may help moderate behavior, they are less effective at resolving academic and social deficits. Zentall (2005) claimed that medication is primarily helpful in improving sustained attention but that it does little to address problems of focus, or selective attention.

In considering these arguments, teachers must remember that IDEA prohibits schools from requiring that a child be put on medication as a condition for attending school, being evaluated for possible disabilities, or receiving services (Council for Exceptional Children, 2005b; U.S. Department of Education, 2006a). It is also critical that teachers understand that if a child is put on a medication regimen by a physician, teachers also have responsibilities to the child and parents. These include the following (American Academy of Pediatrics, 2009; Austin, 2003; National Association of School Nurses, 2003):

- Being knowledgeable about any medications students are taking
- Sharing classroom observations with parents so that the effect of medication can be monitored
- Alerting the school nurse and/or parent if there are changes that may be related to the medication
- Responding to parents' queries about their child's progress while on medication

Finally, one should not assume that medication alone will resolve a student's difficulties (Whalen & Henker, 1991). Well-implemented behavioral interventions are important as well. Holding children accountable for their own behavior lessens the likelihood of learned helplessness developing because of dependence on medication.

ON THE WEB

The **American Speech-Language-Hearing Association** (www.asha.org) is the major professional association for speech, language, and audiology; this website provides resources related to disabilities in communication and hearing, as well as referral information.

ON THE WEB

The **American Academy of Pediatrics** website (http://aappolicy.aappublications.org/index.dtl) provides access to a variety of policy documents related to student health issues. The organization's policy on medication in schools can be accessed at http://aappolicy.aappublications.org/cgi/reprint/pediatrics;124/4/1244.

Summary

Teachers today encounter a variety of other disorders in programs for students with mild disabilities. Attention-deficit/hyperactivity disorder (ADHD) is the most prevalent of these disorders affecting school performance. ADHD is currently defined in the *DSM-IV-TR* as a condition in which individuals exhibit significant differences with regard to attention and/or hyperactivity/impulsivity when compared to typical students. It is estimated that approximately 3–7 percent of school-age children may be affected by disorders in the ADHD group.

ADHD is most appropriately diagnosed through a multiphasic assessment process that includes a medical examination, a psychoeducational assessment, and an ecological assessment including direct observations, family history, and teacher rating scales. Multiple sources of data are required to confirm the presence and severity of the disorder and to differentiate it from other conditions.

Students with ADHD display a wide variety of characteristics. Some are predominantly inattentive, whereas others are mainly characterized by their hyperactivity and impulsivity. The symptoms also vary by age and cause a variety of secondary problems in school achievement and social relationships.

ADHD is not identified separately within IDEA. A 1991 U.S. Department of Education study indicated that children with ADHD could be and were being served appropriately in programs for students with other health impairments, learning disabilities, or emotional disturbance, as well as under Section 504. Specific placements and services are dependent on an individual's primary presenting symptoms.

Students with a variety of other conditions in the mild-to-moderate range are also frequently well served in a general education environment with supports. These conditions include physical and health disabilities, visual and hearing impairments, speech and language disorders, and traumatic brain injury. With appropriate accommodations based on their strengths and needs, these students can generally make adequate progress in a general education curriculum.

A Case Study   • Frank

Frank is a relatively new student at Rayberg Elementary School. He lives with both parents and a younger sister. His father is an engineer whose job takes him away from home frequently. His first-grade teacher referred him for evaluation because of concerns that his high levels of distractibility and activity, as well as his short attention span, were significantly affecting his daily classroom performance. Frank seems to be happy, intellectually curious, and very verbal. However, his short attention span affects both his comprehension of directions and his reading skills. He has frequent reversals of letters and numerals when writing and is disorganized in his work habits. He appears easily distracted by his own thoughts. When frustrated and tired, Frank reverts to immature behaviors and baby talk, and he continues to have occasional temper tantrums when he cannot complete a task. His mother has indicated that he sometimes hits himself on the front of his head with his fist when he is frustrated, exclaiming in frustration, "It won't work." His mother has also indicated that Frank has always had difficulty paying attention in school. She said that teachers have expressed concerns about Frank's behaviors since his entrance into kindergarten.

Frank's mother acknowledges that she was under significant stress during her pregnancy because her husband was on military duty at the time. Frank was born following a prolonged period of labor; his mother was on oxygen for the last 8 hours of labor because of a decrease in Frank's heartbeat with each contraction. The first APGAR score taken at birth was abnormally low, but the second at 5 minutes indicated normal neonatal health. Frank reached most developmental milestones within expected time ranges, although he began walking early at 9 months of age.

Frank began kindergarten in Alabama. The family then moved to Kansas last summer where Frank began first grade. In October of that year, the family moved to Indiana for 3 months, before moving in February to their present home in a southern state, where Frank is enrolled in first grade. Each of his teachers has indicated concern about his attention and learning behaviors. Although he has attended four different schools, there have been no excessive absences. Frank's previous teachers thought his difficulties might be due to a hearing problem. Although Frank has had extensive ear infections that required tubes in his ears at age 3, his hearing has recently been checked and found to be normal. Frank also has passed both near- and far-vision screenings. He began receiving speech therapy in first grade in Indiana, and he continues with speech services at Rayberg Elementary School for articulation problems.

Strategies used at his current school to strengthen his school performance have included modified instruction and use of a multisensory literature-based reading program. He also receives math instruction through an activity-based manipulative program. Supplementary texts and materials such as tapes, word cards, and dictated stories have been used to strengthen his reading skills. Frank has also been consistently praised for appropriate responses, and his parents and teacher are in regular communication. These efforts have resulted in sporadic improvements in Frank's academic skills and behavioral responses.

Results of the School-Based Testing

Peabody Picture Vocabulary Test 4

Standard score: 115   Percentile: 84

WIAT-II (Wechsler Individual Achievement Test)

Cluster Scores	Standard Score
Oral language	105
Reading	97
Mathematics	114
Written language	97

Subtest Scores	Standard Score
Listening comprehension	115
Oral expression	95
Word reading	99
Pseudoword decoding	95
Comprehension	98
Written expression	98
Spelling	95
Math reasoning	113
Numerical operations	116

Psychoeducational Evaluation Results

The school psychologist performed a complete psychological evaluation. Frank was attentive to individual activities and seemed to be putting forth good effort. However, he was very bouncy and physically restless, even in the one-to-one setting. Although Frank was fidgety during the assessment, he seemed to be a very pleasant student who wanted to perform well. His speech articulation difficulties were noted throughout the assessment.

The Wechsler Intelligence Scale for Children-IV (WISC-IV) yielded the following results:

Full Scale IQ (FSIQ)	118
Verbal Comprehension (VCI)	119
Perceptual Reasoning (PRI)	112
Working Memory (WMI)	98
Processing Speed (PSI):	100

These results suggest that Frank's overall abilities fall generally within the average to high-average range for his age, with minor weakness in areas affected by attention and processing speed. It is possible that these results may underestimate his true potential to some degree because of his physical restlessness and his distractibility throughout the assessment. Individual subtest scores on the WISC-IV verbal comprehension scale reflected strength in Frank's vocabulary skills as well as auditory processing. The WISC-IV perceptual reasoning scale reflected strength in Frank's visual analysis and perceptual–motor skills. His visual attention to detail within the environment, visual organizational skills, and concentration on a short, structured, pencil-and-paper activity fell within the average range.

An additional assessment of short-term visual and auditory memory (VADS) was given to assess Frank's concentration and immediate recall of auditory and visual cues when he is asked to respond orally and in writing. Frank's responses suggested strengths in immediate memory skills for both auditory and visual cues. When working on the written items of the test, he reversed several numerals. However, he recognized his reversals and asked whether it was all right for the numbers to be backwards. The fact that he recognized his reversals is a positive sign. However, the formation and spacing of his numerals as well as his placement of the forms on the page suggested some impulsivity in his responses.

The Bender Gestalt Test of Visual Perception II (BGTVP-II) revealed five errors involving shape distortion, integration of designs, and figure rotation, yielding an age range equivalent of 7–6 to 7–11 and a standard score of 109, reflecting adequate perceptual motor skills when working with pencil-and-paper activities. However, his use of space and placement of the forms on the page suggested some difficulty in organizing visually unstructured activities. His actual responses also reflected some difficulty in fine-motor control when working with pencil-and-paper activities, although his perceptual skills seemed to be adequate.

The WIAT-II results given here revealed deficits in Frank's academic skills, which are reflected in his classroom performance. His difficulty with basic phonetic skills affects his identification of less familiar words as well as his understanding of content. It appeared that some of his correct answers on the passage comprehension test were achieved by guessing rather than by application of decoding skills. He could not recognize many of the words, and he used pictures as clues to content. He would often shake his head and stand up when working. He constantly looked around the room and reached for materials. His responses on the written expression and spelling subtests reveal both his weak phonetic skills as well as his weak fine-motor coordination skills, affecting his formation of letters. Frank seemed to have difficulty reproducing sounds he heard, and letter reversals were also noted.

Frank seemed to be learning basic math skills more easily than reading skills. In fact, his understanding of math concepts when writing is not involved has developed to a point generally found at the beginning of the second-grade level. He was easily able to add and subtract one-digit numbers without regrouping.

The Attention Deficit Disorder Behavior Rating Scale was completed with information supplied by Frank's mother, revealing significant concerns about Frank's short attention span and impulsivity, as seen by his difficulty completing assigned activities, weak listening skills, poor concentration on difficult activities, high level of distractibility, a tendency to act before thinking, weak organizational skills, a need for consistent supervision, and a tendency to interrupt or speak out of turn. Concerns were also expressed about his academic skills and low self-confidence. Concerns about his activity level were validated through observation of his difficulty sitting still and his fidgeting during the evaluation period. His high activity level was more evident through his restlessness in his seat than by a need for large motor movement. The results of this administration of the ADD Behavior Scale suggested that Frank may be experiencing physiologically based issues that are affecting his attention and control of impulses. He expresses anger when he is frustrated, although he is not a student who gets mad easily or who expresses anger when asked to do something. He does not lose his temper easily. Frank seems to be developing adequate social responsibility and is not generally seen as aggressive with others.

Assessment Summary and Placement Recommendations

The results of this assessment suggest that Frank's overall abilities fall within the above-average range for his age, although the results may underestimate his potential to some degree. By having a greater than 15-point discrepancy between his abilities and achievement, Frank meets one of the eligibility criteria established by the school district for specialized instructional services for students with learning disabilities in the areas of reading and written language.

It appears that his academic delays are primarily due to physiological factors involving attention deficit disorder. Each of his teachers in the three schools he has attended this year has expressed concern about his activity level, listening skills, and weak reading and written language skills. His behavioral responses during the assessment, his classroom performance, and the Attention Deficit Disorder Behavior Rating Scale suggest that Frank's school-related behaviors may be related to attention-deficit/ hyperactivity disorder.

Frank appears to be a student who will benefit from a more detailed medical evaluation to further evaluate his activity and attention. A trial of stimulant medication may be suggested to determine whether this might help control his impulsivity and distractibility. In a recent parent conference, his mother expressed her interest in pursuing this option because of the continuing difficulty Frank is experiencing in school. His teachers will be able to monitor his performance on a daily basis and offer feedback concerning the effectiveness of the medication. His mother has been offered information concerning ADHD and support resources within the community.

Retention in the first grade is being considered because of Frank's academic skills and immaturity. His mother has expressed concern that he may not be successful at the second-grade level, particularly if he continues to have the significant difficulties with distractibility and impulsivity that he is now experiencing. However, a decision on retention will be delayed until closer to the end of this school year, when information has been gathered concerning Frank's responses to instruction in reading and math skills as well as the results of any medication trial. His progress should be followed carefully as he progresses through school to ensure that the programs and services provided for him are meeting his needs appropriately.

Discussion

Using the above information from Frank's evaluation for special education, determine whether it is most appropriate to classify Frank as a child with attention-deficit/hyperactivity disorder or with a learning disability. Specifically, consider the reasons for choosing one category over the other.

How might use of RTI have helped resolve these issues sooner?

CHAPTER 8

Learners with Autism Spectrum Disorders

Questions *to Guide Your Study*

■ Low-incidence disabilities tend to be more severe in their impact on the learner. Why is it appropriate to include a discussion of a low-incidence condition such as autism spectrum disorders in our discussion of learners with mild disabilities?

■ What conditions does the group of autism spectrum disorders (ASD) encompass?

■ How are emotional– behavioral disorders, intellectual disabilities, and ASD related historically?

■ What are the defining characteristics of students with ASD?

■ How do Asperger's syndrome and autistic disorder differ?

■ Which of the autism spectrum disorders might be most likely to be considered among the mild disabilities?

■ What explanations are given for the increasing numbers of learners with ASD?

■ What conditions are related to the risk of developing autism spectrum disorders?

Meet Jacob

When Jacob was an infant, his parents spoke to their pediatrician about their concerns that he showed atypical social behaviors and language use. The doctor dismissed their concerns with "He'll grow out of it." By the age of 3, Jacob was enrolled in an early intervention class with a diagnosis of developmental delay with a focus on language development. In the class, he displayed echolalia, frequently repeating prompts and questions. When the teacher asked, "Jacob, what are you doing?" Jacob repeated, "Jacob, what are you doing?" with the exact same pacing, tone, and inflection. However, when given explicit choices such as "Do you want blocks or computer?" he might respond, "I want computer."

Jacob's social behaviors in the early intervention class were problematic. Transitions and changes to routines elicited echolalic speech, hand flapping, and sometimes aggressive behavior. When directed to clean up after playtime, he was likely to erupt into a tantrum—screaming, crying, kicking, and biting. When he began attending the class, Jacob tolerated no physical contact, but as the year progressed, he sought out hugs from select adults. Based upon these behaviors, the team requested additional assessments to determine whether Jacob fell within the autism spectrum.

Now 8 years old, Jacob grips his pencil tightly, seemingly oblivious to the group of typically developing third graders working around him.

- How do communication and socialization disabilities associated with ASD affect student learning?

- What issues are raised by the growing number of individuals with ASD?

According to his IEP, Jacob receives no resource services because his academic work is above grade level, although his teacher consults regularly with the special educator. His IEP specifies weekly speech/language services, although he seldom receives them. His preemptive observation to the speech therapist, "I don't like you, leave me alone," effectively pushes her away.

Still, Jacob is succeeding academically in this general education setting. His teacher, Ms. George, instills a sense of community and respect in her class. She expects all children to learn successfully and provides high-quality instruction to assure on-task, engaged behavior. Ms. George optimizes every instructional opportunity. She "gets" Jacob; she understands that he can experience as assaults what others might perceive as everyday actions and words. In consultation with the special educator, she has taught him scripts to deal with things he finds problematic. Jacob has a small chart of icons to cue appropriate behavior choices. Ms. George will stroll past his desk, tapping quietly on the relevant icon (e.g., focus, transition soon).

Socially, Jacob remains isolated from most of his peers. Ineffective social filters mar his attempts to interact with other children. However, Jacob enjoys music and especially enjoys TV shows like *American Idol*. He recounts each contestant's history; a few phrases or names can trigger a lengthy monologue. Unable to participate in the conversation, his peers quickly lose interest in the topic. In spite of these challenges, Jacob's peer relationships have improved from his early days in school. Two students expressed an interest in helping him and have received coaching to interact with him effectively. Efforts to include him in their social activities appear to be working; last week, for the first time, another peer invited Jacob to play at his house!

THINKING QUESTIONS

Why do you think the pediatrician might have dismissed Jacob's parents' concerns?

What factors might have suggested to the early intervention team that Jacob should be referred for a special education evaluation?

What else might be done to promote Jacob's success next year in fourth grade?

NAMING THIS GROUP OF LEARNERS

Autism spectrum disorders are a collection of disorders included within the pervasive developmental disorders category in the *DSM-IV-TR* (APA, 2000). Centuries ago, only those with the most severe manifestations of these disorders would have been identified, nearly always judged to have intellectual disabilities or to be insane because of their bizarre behaviors (Koegel, 2008). Over the years, specific conditions within the spectrum have gradually been given their own names.

Autism came into its own in the 1940s in America when Kanner (1943) referred to these individuals as having "autistic disturbances of affective contact," which was also the title of his landmark article. He coined the term *early infantile autism*, describing these children as being unable to relate in ordinary ways to other people and in social situations. Unfortunately, during this period the word *autistic* was also applied to schizophrenia, resulting in confusion about the relationship between these two conditions. "Kanner's autism" continued to be the term used for decades to refer to those children who displayed the patterns of aloofness and avoidance of social interaction that Kanner had described (Benaron, 2008; Frith, 2004).

At the same time in Germany, Asperger (1944) independently described the condition that would come to bear his name. Because of world events of the time, Kanner and Asperger were unaware of each other's work, and Asperger's work remained unknown in the United States until Wing published a paper in 1981 in England based on Asperger's translated work. Although the children in both studies shared common traits, Wing differentiated what she called Asperger syndrome (AS) from Kanner's autism, observing that children with Asperger's syndrome had intact speech along with odd, unilateral social approaches and a strong focus on topics of special interest (Benaron, 2008).

Debate continues about the extent of differentiation between autistic disorder, Asperger's disorder, and atypical autism as currently defined in the *DSM-IV-TR* among the pervasive developmental disorders (PDD) category. Other debates have ensued over the use of the term *high-functioning autism (HFA)* to denote individuals who meet the autistic disorder criteria but who have borderline or average intellectual ability. In recent years, the terms Asperger's syndrome (AS) and high-functioning autism have become familiar to many educators as more learners with milder levels of impairment have been diagnosed on the spectrum and enrolled in general education classrooms.

Since 1994 the American Psychiatric Association (1994, 2000) has included the following conditions within the category of pervasive developmental disorders: autistic disorder, Rett's disorder, childhood disintegrative disorder, and Asperger's disorder. It is expected that changes in the next revision of the *Diagnostic and Statistical Manual* will affect the conditions generally grouped as autism spectrum disorders. Included in these discussions are issues related to the naming of the category and subtypes as well as to refinement of the criteria.

Throughout the relatively short history of autism spectrum disorders, many names have been used for the varied disabilities in this category: autism, Asperger's syndrome (AS), pervasive developmental disorder (PDD), high-functioning autism (HFA), low-functioning autism, atypical autism, and so on. Most commonly today, professionals and parents alike use the term *autism spectrum disorders,* recognizing the core characteristics of deficits in socialization and communication while acknowledging the heterogeneity of the individuals within the classification and across the spectrum.

Consistent with the purposes of this text, our discussion of autism spectrum disorders will focus primarily on those students who manifest mild to moderate impairments in communication and social interaction. (Note: Because *autism spectrum disorder* is the term currently in general use to refer to this group of learners, in the interest of brevity we will often use the abbreviation ASD to refer collectively to the conditions affecting these students.)

ON THE WEB

The **DSM-5** website (www.dsm5.org) provides updates on the revision of the *Diagnostic and Statistical Manual,* with possible changes to the diagnosis of autism spectrum disorders to appear in the *DSM-5,* due to be published about May 2013.

HISTORICAL DEVELOPMENT OF THE CONCEPT OF AUTISM SPECTRUM DISORDERS

For decades, educators and parents reported stories of children who demonstrated behaviors we would now consider part of the autism spectrum. Following his 1943 description of a group of children who displayed communication impairments, social interaction deficits, and repetitive behaviors, Leo Kanner developed specific diagnostic criteria that would aid psychiatrists in diagnosing the condition. Kanner's criteria served as a guide to the field from the mid-1950s until 1968, when the American Psychiatric Association added childhood schizophrenia as a diagnostic category to the *DSM-II*, with infantile autism as a subcategory. However, Kanner continued to advocate for autism to be a separate diagnostic category, noting that unlike children identified as having childhood schizophrenia, the children he identified as autistic appeared uninterested in other people, even from birth (Wolff, 2004). In 1980 the *DSM-III* finally introduced the pervasive developmental disorders category and included within it the autistic disorder subcategory.

Meanwhile in 1944 in Germany, working independently of Kanner, Hans Asperger published his postgraduate thesis, *Autistic Psychopathy in Childhood,* in which he described children with similar characteristics—notably in social interaction and repetitive behaviors—children with autistic personality disorder. Unlike Kanner's subjects, however, Asperger's sample included individuals with a range of intellectual abilities and language use. This range of strengths and needs foreshadowed the concept of the autism spectrum (Frith, 2004; Wolff, 2004).

Nearly 4 decades after Kanner and Asperger shared their work individually with the professional community in their respective countries, Wing (1981) introduced Asperger syndrome to the English-speaking world, identifying similarities and differences in the findings of Kanner and Asperger. Her purpose in distinguishing the characteristics within the autism spectrum and selecting the title *Asperger syndrome* for this higher-achieving group was to facilitate a clearer understanding of each group's distinct needs (Frith, 2004). It was evident that individuals who possessed average or high intelligence and verbal abilities would require different services from those of their less able peers. Noting common core behaviors and variations, Wing also proposed the concept of a spectrum of autistic disorders with varying degrees of severity along each of the defining dimensions of social impairment, communication impairment, and restricted, repetitive behaviors.

International professional recognition of the autism diagnostic category occurred in 1993 when the World Health Organization (2007b) included childhood autism and Asperger's disorder in the *International Classification of Diseases (ICD-10)*. The American Psychiatric Association's *DSM-IV* joined in establishing the diagnosis within the American psychiatric community in 1994 with the inclusion of both autistic disorder and Asperger's disorder under the category of pervasive developmental disorders. Both manuals acknowledged the heterogeneity of these disorders and the fact that autism is manifested in different subtypes (Attwood, 2007). In particular, there was an increasing understanding that the level of functioning could vary considerably, based on additional factors such as intelligence and environment.

For the next 2 decades, theories abounded about the causes of autism, with a commonly held theory that the pattern of social withdrawal that characterized these children was related to unresponsive parenting, termed the "refrigerator mother" syndrome. Bruno Bettelheim was a chief proponent of this now-discredited theory. These children were treated as having a mental illness, families were subjected to psychotherapy, and parents were blamed for their children's conditions (Benaron, 2008; Sicile-Kira, 2004; Wolff, 2004).

Bernard Rimland, a psychologist who was himself the parent of a son with autism, published *Infantile Autism: The Syndrome and Its Implication for a Neural Theory of Behavior* in 1964, asserting a neurobiological cause for the disorder. In the tradition of parent advocacy established by The Arc, United Cerebral Palsy, and the Learning Disabilities Association, Rimland and others founded the Autism Society in 1965, a parent organization established to actively advocate for support for their children (Sicile-Kira, 2004). He also founded the Autism Research Institute in 1967 to bring together individuals from around the world to study issues related to autism and to provide a clearinghouse for information on diagnosis and treatment of individuals with autism spectrum disorders.

When Public Law 94-142 (Education for All Handicapped Children Act, now IDEA) was passed in 1975, it did not include autism as a separate category. The 1975 definition of serious emotional disturbance identified both schizophrenia and autism as included diagnoses (U.S. Office of Education, 1977b). In 1981 autism was removed from that category and formally added to the category of other health impairments, as it was determined that individuals with autism disorders would be more appropriately served in that category (Bower, 1982; U.S. Department of Education, 1981). In addition, depending on the diversity of manifestations of the condition and comorbidity with other IDEA conditions, the learner might also meet the criteria for intellectual disabilities or emotional disturbance. Limited programming and school-based interventions were available initially, primarily because of unfamiliarity with the conditions. Meanwhile, students who struggled socially despite average or above-average academic performance were seen simply as shy, awkward, or strange. Their special needs were generally unseen or disregarded so long as they made acceptable academic progress.

As more students with ASDs began to attend schools, the general public's exposure to these students increased. Their unique characteristics, strengths, and needs became more evident as teachers conferred with other professionals to identify effective interventions for this group of learners. In 1990 the U.S. Congress finally added autism as a separate category of service under IDEA.

As professionals refined their understanding of autism, popular culture was also developing an increased awareness of and interest in the disorder. Popular media such as the hit movie *Rain Man* in 1988 provided opportunities for the general public to get a glimpse into the lives of people with autism. Print media also portrayed more images of individuals with ASD. Dr. Temple Grandin, an expert in animal science who is also a person with autism, has published several

ON THE WEB

Since 1965 the **Autism Society** (www.autism-society.org) has been the leading grassroots autism organization, working to increase public awareness about the issues faced by people with ASDs, advocating for services across the life span, and providing information on autism for professionals and families.

ON THE WEB

Autism Research Institute (ARI; http://www.autism.com/index.asp) disseminates research findings to parents and others, maintains a data bank of detailed case histories of autistic children from over 60 countries, and publishes the *Autism Research Review International*.

best-selling books about her own experiences as a person with autism (Grandin, 2006; Grandin & Johnson, 2005). In addition, she has been featured on National Public Radio, and her life has been portrayed in an HBO film. The award-winning fictional work *The Curious Incident of the Dog in the Night-Time* helped many understand more personally the experience of an adolescent with ASD (Haddon, 2003).

Advocates now regularly use print and electronic media to connect with others to support education, research, and services for those with ASD. Some individuals with ASD, their families, and support groups assert that autism merely represents yet another facet of humanity, advocating respect for "neurological diversity" (e.g., Autistic Self-Advocacy Network). Others call for increased research to prevent, treat, and cure autism (e.g., Autism Speaks).

IDEA DEFINITION OF AUTISM SPECTRUM DISORDERS

Autism was originally included in the Education of All Handicapped Children Act (P.L. 94-142) as part of the category of serious emotional disturbance; in 1981 its status was changed to inclusion as an other health impairment but was not an individually defined disability. Advocates finally secured explicit inclusion of autism as a specific category during the 1990 reauthorization and renaming of the Individuals with Disabilities Education Act (IDEA, P.L. 101-476). IDEA now offers this definition of *autism*:

> A developmental disability significantly affecting verbal and non-verbal communication and social interaction, usually evident before age 3, that adversely affects a child's educational performance. Other characteristics often associated with autism are engagement in repetitive activities, resistance to environmental change or change in daily routines, and unusual sensory experiences. The term does not apply if a child's educational performance is adversely affected because the child has a serious emotional disturbance. (U.S. Department of Education, 1999, p. 12421)

An analysis of this IDEA definition reveals four primary characteristics and one exclusion:

- Autism is a developmental disability usually evident before age 3.
- It includes significant deficits in three areas of functioning:
  - Verbal and nonverbal communication
  - Social interaction
  - Educational performance
- Exclusion: Educational problems are not primarily due to emotional disturbance.

The definition also notes some additional characteristics that may but do not need to be present; interestingly, these optional characteristics are among those most stereotypically associated with individuals with ASD:

- Engagement in repetitive activities
- Resistance to environmental change or change in daily routines
- Unusual sensory experiences and reactions

As is true of the core principle of IDEA and other IDEA definitions as well, this definition specifically requires that the condition interfere with educational performance, in addition to the requirement that the learner exhibit the core behavioral characteristics relating to communication and socialization that are associated with autism. There is no school-based assessment instrument that confirms the presence of an ASD in a learner; as with ADHD and other health impairments, an ASD diagnosis results primarily from a medical process. The school's role in the process is to determine whether there is a negative effect on the learner's educational performance once the learner has been diagnosed medically. For this reason, the release of a revised autism category in the *DSM-5* in 2013 will be of considerable interest and importance to educators, psychiatrists, and parents.

ON THE WEB

ASAN, the **Autistic Self-Advocacy Network** (http://www.autisticadvocacy.org/), is run by and for people with ASDs. Their motto is "Nothing about us, without us!" ASAN provides support to individuals on the autism spectrum while working to change public perceptions and combat misinformation. Their activities encourage inclusion and respect for neurodiversity.

ON THE WEB

Autism Speaks (http://www.autismspeaks.org/) is dedicated to funding global biomedical research into the causes, prevention, treatments, and a cure for autism and is committed to raising the funds necessary to support these goals.

The Psychiatric/Medical Definition of Autism Spectrum Disorders in the *DSM-IV-TR*

The *DSM-IV-TR* uses the umbrella term of pervasive developmental disorders for this group, which includes autistic disorder, Rett's disorder, childhood disintegrative disorder, Asperger's disorder, and pervasive developmental disorder–not otherwise specified (PDD-NOS; APA, 2000). These conditions are generally referred to in professional literature and popular press as autism spectrum disorders (e.g., Wing, 1981; Frith, 2004; Sanders, 2009). Usually becoming evident in a child's early years, the pervasive social, linguistic, and behavioral impairments that are hallmarks of ASD occur across multiple areas of development. Differentiating these disorders requires analyzing the pattern of development and/or regression in language, cognition, social, and motor skills. The *DSM-IV-TR* (APA, 2000) outlines the general diagnostic criteria for pervasive developmental disorders as pervasive impairments or problems in the following areas of development: reciprocal social interaction skills; communication skills; and stereotypic behavior, interests, and activities.

The specific *DSM-IV-TR* criteria for autistic disorders and Asperger's disorder are of primary concern in our study of learners with mild/moderate disabilities. As Table 8.1 indicates, these two conditions share problems with social interactions and with restricted and repetitive patterns of behavior and interests. Both also display functional impairment in a variety of life skill areas. Individuals in each of the conditions present a variety of degrees and combinations of the other listed problem behaviors, but these three criteria—problems with social interactions, restricted patterns of behavior, and functional impairments—comprise the central features of all of the autism spectrum disorders. Communication and cognitive/intellectual functioning pose significant problems for students with autistic disorders, whereas those with Asperger's disorder generally have adequate development of language skills and average to above-average intelligence.

ASSESSMENT AND IDENTIFICATION ISSUES

According to the *DSM-IV-TR* definitions, assessment and identification generally take place from ages 3 to 5, with most cases identified by the age of 8 (Centers for Disease Control and Prevention, 2009; Shattuck et al., 2009). Those children with more severe involvement will be noticed earlier because of their nonresponsive socialization behaviors and deficits in language use. Those who will eventually be identified with high-functioning autism or Asperger's syndrome may at first seem to be developing normally or in some cases, because of their good verbal skills, may be seen as very bright. However, their odd patterns of socialization and rigid preoccupations with special interests eventually create concerns.

Assessment procedures are most effective and reliable when closely tied to a clear definition and criteria. Kanner's criteria, used until the 1980s, provided very strict guidelines for the type of autism he identified. After that point, as understanding of the scope of the spectrum began to develop and widen, the criteria became more complicated. From the 1980s, the challenge has not only been diagnosing a single specific condition, but it has also become increasingly important to make differential diagnoses from among a number of possible conditions with overlapping boundaries (Wing & Potter, 2002), as well as between autism spectrum disorders and the "borderlines of normality" (Wing, 2005, p. 591).

Assessment for individuals with possible ASD presents other challenges as well (Lord & Corsello, 2005). Some children are very young when assessed, making assessment more difficult. Information is needed from many sources. Some behavioral factors may be absent, whereas others are described as odd. Once autism has been eliminated, more assessments are required to confirm Asperger's. There are no clear biological markers to help make the case; the boundaries between levels of behavioral indicators are not clear-cut, and one cannot assume that unobserved behaviors are actually absent.

To effectively evaluate children and youth for potential identification as a learner with autism or Asperger's syndrome, a very detailed and comprehensive evaluation process is

Table 8.1	Diagnostic Criteria: Autistic Disorder and Asperger's Disorder

	Autistic Disorder	**Asperger's Disorder**
	A total of six or more of the following characteristics	A total of three or more of the following characteristics
Social Interaction	Qualitative impairment in social interaction as manifested by two of the following: (a) Marked impairment in the use of multiple non-verbal behaviors such as eye-to-eye contact, facial expression, body postures and gestures to regulate social interactions. (b) Failure to develop peer relationships appropriate to the developmental level. (c) A lack of spontaneous seeking to share enjoyment, interest, or achievements with other people (e.g., by a lack of showing, bringing, or pointing out objects of interest to other people). (d) Lack of social or emotional reciprocity	
Communication	Qualitative impairments in communication, manifested by at least one of the following: (a) Delay in or total lack of the development of spoken language (not accompanied by the attempt to compensate through alternative modes of communication such as gestures and mime). (b) In individuals with adequate speech, marked impairment in the ability to initiate or sustain a conversation with others. (c) Stereotyped and repetitive use of language or idiosyncratic language. (d) Lack of varied, spontaneous make-believe play or social imitative play appropriate to the developmental level.	There is no clinically significant delay in language (e.g., single words used by 2 years, communicative phrases by age 3 years)
Activities and Interests	Restricted and repetitive and stereotyped patterns of behavior, interests and activities, as manifested by at least one of the following: (a) Encompassing preoccupation with one or more stereotyped and restricted patterns of interest that is abnormal in intensity or focus (b) Apparently inflexible adherence to specific non-functional routines or rituals (c) Stereotyped and repetitive motor mannerisms (e.g., hand or finger flapping or twisting, or complex whole body movements) (d) Persistent preoccupation with parts of objects	
Impact on Functioning	Delays or abnormal functioning in at least one of the following areas with onset prior to age 3 years: (a) social interaction, (b) language as used in social communication, or (c) symbolic or imaginative play.	The disturbance causes clinically significant impairment in social, occupational, or other important areas of functioning.
Cognition	May display mild to profound cognitive impairment	There is no clinically significant delay in cognitive development or in the development of age-appropriate self-help skills, adaptive behavior (other than social interaction) and curiosity about the environment in childhood.

Source: Reprinted as adapted with permission from the *Diagnostic and Statistical Manual of Mental Disorders: Fourth Edition, Text Revision.* Copyright 2000 American Psychiatric Association.

required (Klin, Salnier, Tsatanis, & Volkmar, 2005). The process must ascertain the extent of the core markers of social and communication deficits and behavioral rigidities. Since a percentage of suspected cases are also learners with intellectual deficits, it is important that the process also have a developmental perspective and an intellectual functioning frame.

To accomplish this, it is critical to have an interdisciplinary team that is able to function in a transdisciplinary manner. The team should include qualified evaluators in a variety of disciplines. This team must triangulate information from many perspectives to confirm the absence of normative behaviors as well as the presence of aberrant ones; separate assessment reports on discrete functional areas are not helpful in connecting the factors of this complex process. Parents and classroom teachers must also be considered as valuable sources of information on the team.

Assessments in multiple settings facilitate the creation of an accurate picture of functioning. Naturalized settings are critical to assessing social relationships, whereas highly structured environments are needed to assess intellectual functioning. Observations and interviews are necessary to assess the interrelationships of social, communication, and emotional factors. Functional behaviors must be evaluated using culturally valid adaptive behavior assessments. All of these measures must be designed to provide information relative to the diagnostic criteria being used.

In addition to individual intelligence testing (e.g., WISC-IV, WPPSI) and adaptive behavior scales (e.g., Vineland Adaptive Behavior Scales, Diagnostic Adaptive Behavior Scale), a variety of other rating scales and diagnostic instruments are used to gather the required information from multiple perspectives (Lord & Corsello, 2005; Mayes et al., 2009), including autism rating scales (e.g., Gilliam Autism Rating Scale [GARS]); diagnostic interviews (e.g., Diagnostic Interview for Social and Communication Disorders [DISCO]); direct observations using relevant observation guides (e.g., Autism Diagnostic Observation Schedule [ADOS]); diagnostic and behavioral assessments to confirm Asperger's syndrome or high-functioning autism (e.g., AS and HFA Diagnostic Interview); and assessments of pragmatic language, focusing on communication acts in natural and seminatural environments (Paul, 2005).

ON THE WEB

First Signs (http://www.firstsigns.org/) provides information on early detection and early intervention with children with ASD.

IDENTIFICATION ISSUES   Once all the information is gathered, the answers are often still not clear. One challenge is to differentiate among ASDs and other conditions. Among possible comorbid or alternative diagnoses are intellectual disability, developmental language disorders, hearing or visual deficits, obsessive-compulsive disorder, ADHD, Tourette's syndrome, depression, anxiety, and other psychiatric diagnoses. The team must determine whether the individual should be diagnosed with ASD, another condition, or both (Volkmar & Klin, 2005; Wing, 2005)

The second decision relates to the question of subtypes within pervasive developmental disorders/autism spectrum disorders. It has been generally held that there are at least three subtypes: (a) typical autism, with social, communication, and behavioral deficits, along with intellectual functioning deficits in the moderate to severe range; (b) Asperger's syndrome, with social and behavioral characteristics but with adequate language skills and average or high intellectual functioning; and (c) atypical autism included in the PDD-NOS category. Questions remain about the legitimacy of an identification status of high-functioning autism as a separate identified subtype, composed of learners with autistic behavioral characteristics but who also display intellectual functioning in the mild or borderline range (Volkmar, State, & Klin, 2008), questions that will likely be addressed in the upcoming *DSM* revision.

PREVALENCE OF AUTISM SPECTRUM DISORDERS

Autism spectrum disorders are considered low-incidence conditions, with only about .39 percent of the school-age population and 2.8 percent of students receiving special education services classified in this category (see Figure 1.1). The Centers for Disease Control and Prevention (2009) report the current average rate of ASD prevalence among American 8-year-olds as 1 in 110 students. Of particular concern is the fact that the number of students classified in this category increased eightfold from 1996 to 2008, increasing from 34,254 to 292,818 nationwide (U.S. Department of Education, 2009) and prompting many questions as to the cause.

Table 8.2 Educational Placements of Students with Autism as a Percentage of All Students with Autism (1996–2008, ages 6–21)

Year	Percent in General Education (>80% of day)	Percent in Resource Room/ Part-Time Special Classroom (21–60% of day)	Percent in Separate Classroom (>60% of day)	Percent in Separate Environments*	Total Enrollment of Students with Autism
1996	14.28	11.71	53.17	20.83	34,254
1998	20.27	13.19	51.13	15.40	53,675
2000	24.31	15.33	46.38	13.98	80,324
2002	24.65	17.84	45.52	11.99	118,502
2004	29.20	17.74	41.84	11.28	166,645
2006	32.30	18.40	38.70	10.50	224,594
2008	36.25	18.24	35.73	9.78	292,818

Separate Environments: Includes full-time placements in public and private special day schools, residential facilities, and home or hospital environments.

Sources: Data from U.S. Department of Education, 2009: Office of Special Education Programs, Data Analysis System (DANS) 2004, Table 2–5; National Center for Education Statistics, U.S. Department of Education (http://nces.ed.gov); and Data Accountability Center: Individuals with Disabilities Education Act (IDEA) Data (http://www.ideadata.org).

Although autism is generally considered a disorder with more severe effects, an increasing number of these students appear to be those functioning in the milder range of impairment, with diagnoses of high-functioning autism (HFA) or Asperger's syndrome becoming more common (Safran, 2001; Shore, 2001). U.S. Department of Education data indicate that 36 percent of students with autism in 2008 received a significant portion (>80 percent) of their educational services within general education, with 54 percent in general education for 20–100 percent of their day (see Table 8.2). A reasonable assumption is that these placements are due to the students' relatively high levels of academic functioning, allowing them to benefit from activities in the general education classroom with supports.

The placement data in Table 8.2 are of interest for several reasons. Even though the overall increase in students with autism is extraordinary, the changes in placement data are skewed toward more inclusive placements. The percentage of students served in special classes and separate environments—that is, those with no or limited interaction with general education students—declined over the decade 1996–2008. At the same time, percentages in general education and part-time special classes more than doubled. Although we cannot be sure of the reasons for the shifts in service placement decisions, a number of interesting possibilities come to mind (Wing & Potter, 2002):

- Could the overall increases in the autism category be due to the widening of the defined spectrum and identification of more students at the milder end of the spectrum, those who could be most appropriately served in inclusive environments but were previously unidentified?
- What is the effect of Asperger's disorder having been added to the *ICD* in 1993 and the *DSM-IV* in 1994? Given the addition of this diagnostic possibility, should we have expected to see new and/or possibly more accurate identifications?
- Could these numbers be reflective of the same identification pressures experienced within the learning disabilities category during the first 2 decades of IDEA? Could the new IDEA autism category be identifying students who would previously not have been identified or would have been identified less appropriately, and are these students more likely to be at the mild end of the spectrum?
- Could some subtle shifts be occurring among the judgmental categories (i.e., intellectual and learning disabilities, emotional–behavioral disorders, speech impairments, ADHD) at the milder end of the spectrum in favor of identification as a student with ASD? Could these shifts help explain a parallel decrease in intellectual disability over the same time period?

- Could educators be becoming more comfortable and capable of serving these students in general education environments, furthering inclusion and reducing segregation (Loiacono & Allen, 2008)?
- Does this trend indicate a true increase in numbers or cases? If so, why might this be happening?

Some or all of these possibilities could yield explanations for changes in the prevalence of autism generally, as well as for the larger increases at the milder end of the spectrum. Additional population studies and analyses are needed to answer the many questions about the prevalence patterns among students with ASD and in the general population (Safran, 2008).

ON THE WEB

Three sources of autism and special education data include the Centers for Disease Control and Prevention (http://www.cdc.gov/ncbddd/autism/index.html), the National Center for Education Statistics, U.S. Department of Education (http://nces.ed.gov), and the Data Accountability Center: Individuals with Disabilities Education Act (IDEA) Data (http://www.ideadata.org).

Researchers have also investigated a variety of causes for these increases in diagnoses over the past decade, including environmental impacts such as pollutants, diet, allergies, mercury, and the MMR vaccine (*Autism: Why the Increased Rates*, 2001). However, none of these research agendas have confirmed causal explanations for the changes in prevalence (Immunization Safety Review Committee, 2004). Research does suggest that changes in the definition and identification criteria have likely had the most significant impact on identification rates (Wing & Potter, 2002). Another promising research agenda is focused on uncovering suspected genetic links and neurobiological causes.

LEVELS OF SEVERITY

Neurobiological in origin, autism spectrum disorders result in an impaired ability to communicate, understand language, play, develop social skills, and relate to others. However, there is significant variation within the spectrum. Individuals with ASD include those who might not appear to have a disability at first glance as well as individuals whose disabilities are much more apparent. Some individuals possess above-average intelligence yet manifest great difficulty in social interactions; others experience significant cognitive impairments and are nonverbal. Some children with ASDs are characterized as having mild to moderate disabilities, while others are considered to have severe disabilities. In other words, this condition is characterized most accurately by its heterogeneity.

One way to conceptualize the severity of impact of an ASD is to look at the level of intellectual functioning. Intellectual deficits are infrequent in learners with Asperger's syndrome and, if present, are generally mild. Autistic disorders include a range of intellectual impairments, from mild to severe. Those classified as autistic with mild or borderline intellectual impairments are frequently referred to as having high-functioning autism. Severe/profound intellectual and functional impairments characterize the rarer, progressively degenerative conditions of Rett's disorder and childhood disintegrative disorder and therefore are outside the scope of this text. Pervasive developmental disorder not otherwise specified (PDD-NOS) includes atypical autism, which includes learners who meet some but not all of the criteria for the other conditions.

When considering the specific impact of the heterogeneous conditions of Asperger's syndrome and autistic disorder, one must also consider the effect on the learner's communication and socialization skills, which can also range from mild to severe and will impact decisions about educational placement. One way of estimating the relative numbers of students with ASD at the various severity levels is to review the placement data across the 1996–2008 period (see Table 8.2), which show increasing numbers of students served in inclusive environments for at least half of the school day, implying growth in the numbers of students with less severe levels of ASD.

Another indication of the severity of the condition is the percentage of individuals who also have intellectual functioning measures with IQs below 70. Up to the end of the 1990s, it was believed that 70–80 percent of learners with autism also had intellectual disabilities with IQs <70 (Shea & Mesibov, 2005). However, a more recent 2009 study by the Centers for Disease Control and Prevention indicates that the percentages of learners with intellectual disabilities (i.e., IQ <70) in addition to autism have decreased to 30–50 percent, likely reflecting the addition of a significant number of learners at the mild end of the spectrum over the decade. This suggests that at least half of the students with autism now exhibit cognitive functioning in the borderline to average range, also suggesting less severity in the level of impact on intellectual functioning (Hill & Frith, 2003).

That said, however, autism spectrum disorders are so complex and heterogeneous in their impact that no single variable can capture the extent of the impairment or can be used to reliably place learners with ASD into categories of impact. Based on the *DSM-IV-TR* definitions, it may generally be appropriate to consider most learners with Asperger's syndrome at the milder end of the spectrum because of their average to above-average cognitive functioning and language skills, followed by those with high-functioning autism with its intellectual functioning deficits in the mild or borderline range, followed by those with autistic disorder at the moderate to severe end of the spectrum.

CONDITIONS ASSOCIATED WITH AUTISM SPECTRUM DISORDERS

In confronting the effects of a condition like autism, it is natural to ask, "Why?" (Robinson-Neal, 2009). Unfortunately at this point, we do not yet have definitive, useful answers to give to parents and educators. While the search goes on for the reasons that some children develop ASD, it is important to note that at least one theory has been refuted over the years, namely, the hypothesis that autism is the result of distant, unresponsive parenting (Sicile-Kira, 2004). We now know that parents of children with autism have the same range of parenting skills as other parents (National Institute of Neurological Disorders and Stroke, 2010).

Another theory that was pursued vigorously over the past decade related to a specific environmental cause, namely that the children were having an adverse reaction to the MMR vaccine they were given as infants or to the preservative found in other vaccines. As a result, many parents resisted having their children receive those important shots, leaving these children at risk for the devastating effects of the diseases vaccines were created to prevent (Wolff, 2004). Extensive research has now demonstrated that there is no correlation between vaccine use and the development of autism and that parents should feel comfortable giving their children vaccines that will protect them, not harm them (Immunization Safety Review Committee, 2004).

All scientific evidence now supports biological causes for ASDs. The most frequently mentioned potential causes point strongly to genetic factors resulting in brain differences. Research using twin and family studies strongly suggests that some involvement of genetic transmission is probable, with a .90 heritability index associated with ASD in twin studies (Rutter, 2005). The research also suggests that a single gene is unlikely to be the culprit; more likely, it is a polygenic pattern with as many as 10–20 genes acting together to make an individual more susceptible to developing autism or autistic tendencies. The National Institute of Neurological Disorder and Stroke (NINDS, 2010) is supporting the work of the international Autism Genome Project to collect DNA samples from children with ASD and their families around the world. Scientists will use this genetic database to continue the search for genetic explanations of ASD.

Another possible cause is brain differences in general. The symptoms of ASD suggest altered central nervous system functioning. Neurotransmitters are the chemicals that transmit impulses throughout the nervous system, and it is these chemicals that are being investigated to identify differences that may be the source of the symptoms of ASD. A number of neurotransmitters and neuroendocrine systems have been studied, including serotonin, Blood 5-HT, dopamine, norepinephrine, a variety of hormones, and amino acid metabolism. Even though research to date has ended with more negative than positive results, those results still help narrow the field of study to others showing more promise (Anderson & Hoshino, 2005).

Other researchers are studying the impact on brain structure and functioning directly (Schultz & Robins, 2005). There are indications that the hypothesized genetic effect may act on

ON THE WEB

The **National Institute of Neurological Disorders and Stroke (NINDS;** http://www.ninds.nih.gov/) is funded to study a variety of neurological disorders and to provide information and resources on those topics.

the fetus as early as the second prenatal trimester. In particular, there is evidence of reduced functional connectivity during the developmental period, constraining the integrative processing functions needed for complex learning such as language development, problem solving, and socialization. Researchers have also noted evidence of changes in the structure of both white and gray matter in the brains of individuals with ASD. Brain imaging and functional neuroimaging studies hold promise for helping to explain the processes and associated deficits involved in social cognition and perception, which are so central to the functional deficits of individuals with ASD. It is likely that over the next decade, genetic, neurochemical, neurological, and functional neuroimaging research will converge on more definitive answers to these puzzling conditions (Minshew, Sweeney, Bauman, & Webb, 2005).

CHARACTERISTICS OF STUDENTS WITH AUTISM SPECTRUM DISORDERS

It is important to keep in mind the heterogeneity of this group of learners when we discuss their characteristics. At the most impaired end of the spectrum, the learner becomes indistinguishable from those with profound intellectual disabilities, while at the higher end of functioning, it is difficult to distinguish the person from individuals who are merely eccentric. In discussing these complex classification issues, Wing observed that "nature never draws a line without smudging it" (2005, p. 202). The lines between and among the autism spectrum disorders and normality are indeed fuzzy at best. As we discuss the core defining characteristics of ASDs, it is important to keep in mind that each learner will manifest these characteristics in unique ways and that even students without a diagnosis of ASD may display some of these from time to time as well.

Reciprocal Social Interactions and Relationships

All learners with ASDs, by definition, have some level of difficulty in social relationships and interactions. At the milder end of impairment, they may have difficulty reading the social cues of adults or other children in their environment. Pragmatic language skills for initiating, maintaining, and terminating a social conversation are generally undeveloped or awkward (Boutot, 2007). At the moderate to severe level of impairment, a learner may make little or no effort to interact with others.

An early classification of interactional types divided these learners into three groups: aloof, passive, and active-but-odd (Wing, 2005; Wing & Gould, 1979). The aloof group includes those who are most isolated from other human beings. They are most apt to respond negatively to attempts to engage them, and their behaviors represent those most stereotypically associated with classic autism. Speech may be absent or very difficult to interpret. Those in the passive group do not initiate social interaction, but they respond to some degree when others approach them. Speech may be more developed in these children. They are likely to be diagnosed with autistic disorder, but at the moderate level of impairment. The final group is the active-but-odd group, characterized by active initiation of social contact, but in a decidedly odd manner. With behaviors most characteristic of those with Asperger's syndrome, these learners will talk at length about their particular interests, whether anyone is interested or not.

Another commonly observed characteristic of learners with high-functioning autism (HFA) and Asperger's syndrome, like Sara (see p. 186), is general ineptness in social skills (Linn & Myles, 2004; Williams, 2001). The odd behaviors of these students often cause them to be singled out and teased by peers in general education classes. They are naive about social conventions and are relatively unable to cope with changes common in daily social interactions, particularly in the adolescent years. These students also frequently have difficulty conceptualizing and appreciating the thoughts and feelings of others (Barnhill, 2001; Safran, 2001).

Generally displaying clear social skills deficits (see Chapter 12), learners with ASD specifically seem to lack the ability to take the perspective of another person and to modify their behavioral responses to match the situation. The concept *theory of mind* refers to this ability to attribute mental states to others and ourselves; it is the ability that allows learners to be reflective of their own cognition (Hill & Frith, 2003; Perner, 2000). In the context of social relationships, it is the ability to understand the desires and intentions of others in order to predict responses and plan future actions. Deficits in theory of mind characterize many with ASD and result in difficulty reading the emotional messages that others display, particularly with their eyes. With this limited ability to make inferences about verbal and nonverbal messages, persons with ASD tend to interpret messages very literally. Additionally, since they are often without the skill or ablity to put themselves in another's shoes, their responses are often seen as rude or disrespectful (Attwood, 2007). Such deficits are related to social-perspective-taking and social competence (see Chapter 12).

DIVERSITY IN FOCUS 8.1

In considering issues of diversity within populations of learners with special educational needs, the discussion often proceeds primarily from the perspective of overrepresentation within racial minority populations. This is particularly true of the judgmental categories discussed previously in this book. However, as we turn to questions of diversity within the population of learners with autism spectrum disorders, the focus of concern shifts somewhat.

Reviews of population data and studies of learners affected by ASDs indicate that the incidence of ASDs seems to be relatively evenly distributed across all racial, ethnic, and income groups. The variations that do occur across studies appear to be related more to differences in definitions and procedures for identification than to actual disproportionalities (Fombonne, 2005; Morrier, Hess, & Heflin, 2008). Dyches, Wilder, Sudweeks, Obiakor, & Algozzine (2004) discussed at length the complex issues related to defining population groups for analysis, issues that confound meaningful interpretation of autism identification data. On the other hand, for reasons that appear to be related to hypotheses about genetic transmission of autistic susceptibility, there is a consistently higher prevalence among boys, with 4–5 boys for every girl identified with an ASD (Fombonne, 2005; Morrier et al., 2008).

We find another important diversity issue related to the ways families adapt to having a child identified with an ASD. Much of the earliest research into the nature of autism occurred in Westernized, primarily Euro-American environments. The question that educators must answer today is the extent to which we can extend what we have learned from these studies to other population groups within the United States and around the world. To what extent are the generally used treatment plans and interactions with families appropriate and helpful for families who may have differing home values, traditions, and cultural experiences? To what extent is the concept of a disability relevant to a particular family's acceptance of the behavioral characteristics of their child?

Family acceptance of an ASD diagnosis can be a positive or negative stressor, depending on their cultural traditions and values and the severity of the condition (Dyches et al., 2004). Family and community supports and the family's receptivity to and dependence on both or either are other aspects that are affected by each family's sociocultural experiences. For example, one study looked at the experience of three families with children with ASD and found that the response of the school to the children's autism seemed to be in conflict with the parents' Muslim values and Asian cultural traditions, increasing their level of stress (Jegatheesan, Miller, & Fowler, 2010).

Support planning is definitely not a one-size-fits-all issue. In light of the very limited autism research on issues related to identification patterns among culturally diverse groups and the determination of culturally relevant family acceptance and support needs, educators need to be particularly aware that each family and each child may have different needs but also different resources to contribute—that is, each family has its own cultural base. The lack of a cultural frame of reference must be resolved if we are to provide appropriate supports to each family.

Communication

The *DSM-IV-TR* emphasizes the difficulty children with autistic spectrum disorders experience with communication skills. All social language skills can be affected, including use of clear and functional speech. A study by Lewis, Murdoch, and Woodyatt (2007) confirmed that communication performance clearly differentiates typically developing children from those with an ASD diagnosis. However, these authors did not find that there was a significant difference between those with HFA and Asperger's syndrome.

The *DSM-IV-TR* definition puts specific emphasis on language pragmatics (see Chapter 10), especially when assessing those with HFA and Asperger's syndrome. For example, a child with ASD may not access meaning from nonlinguistic or paralinguistic cues; gestures, facial expressions, rate, and tone may appear to convey little or no meaning. These children generally lack skill or interest in initiating or maintaining a social conversation. Unlike those with more severe autistic disorders, who may appear indifferent to social and emotional events, individuals with Asperger's manifest deficits in social reciprocity through an "eccentric and one-sided social approach" (APA, 2000, p. 80). Younger children with ASD may lack the language common to and necessary for imaginative play.

Restricted Interests

Finally, all conditions on the autism spectrum are characterized by restricted and stereotypic interests that often make peer interactions difficult because of a lack of shared interests. However, behaviors related to this characteristic vary considerably over the spectrum. Students with Asperger's syndrome frequently develop an all-consuming interest in a particular topic, about which they acquire as much information as possible and which they often pursue with great intensity. These students frequently become impatient with others who do not share their preoccupation. Those learners at the more severe end of the spectrum become involved with their own sensory experience and repetitive behaviors to the exclusion of all social interaction.

Other Related Characteristics and Behaviors

ACADEMIC PERFORMANCE   Individuals with ASD frequently perform more poorly in school and have less vocational success as adults. The disorder may coexist with a number of other conditions that impact school learning, such as ADHD, specific learning disabilities, sensory impairments, obsessive-compulsive disorder, and intellectual impairments (Wing, 2005).

Students with ASDs generally appear to have deficits in executive functioning (see Chapter 9). Executive functions are those mental actions that orchestrate completion of cognitive tasks, including planning, directing, and monitoring of thought processes. These deficits in executive functions are likely responsible for many of the academic learning problems of these students (Hill & Frith, 2003; Ozonoff & Griffith, 2000).

ADAPTIVE BEHAVIOR   Although neither the *DSM-IV-TR* or the *ICD-10* addresses issues of adaptive behavior among individuals with ASD, many writers have raised concerns in this area of functioning, and adaptive behavior deficits do present major obstacles to adjustment. The abilities related to social competence, described in Chapter 12, are generally all impacted by these conditions. An adaptive behavior evaluation should be part of an assessment process, and the results should be used to design an appropriate social skill development plan.

Characteristics Descriptive of Specific Conditions on the Spectrum

ASPERGER'S SYNDROME   Students with Asperger's syndrome differ from students with other ASDs in that their impairment is primarily within the social interaction and pragmatic language area. They do not display the cognitive and language deficits more common to students with more severe autistic disorders. Instead, they are identified according to the *DSM-IV-TR* criteria by a severe and sustained qualitative impairment related to social interactions, accompanied by evidence of restricted and repetitive patterns of behavior, activities, and interests (APA, 2000).

Although students with Asperger's syndrome generally have average to above-average intellectual ability, they can experience difficulties in academic learning due to their tendency to be literal thinkers. This causes problems when school demands include higher-level thinking skills and comprehension of complex materials (Linn & Myles, 2004; Williams, 2001).

Students with Asperger's syndrome are also frequently characterized by poor attention skills. In particular, they have difficulty focusing on the most relevant stimuli. These characteristics, combined with their obsessive interests in particular topics and their well-developed language skills, often lead teachers to assume that these students could be more successful in school if they just applied themselves. To successfully assist students with Asperger's syndrome in a general education classroom, teachers must understand how these annoying behaviors relate to their condition and then work with the students, their parents, and special educators to design supportive interventions (Barnhill, 2001). Social skills interventions are valuable, particularly when combined with structured teaching strategies (Safran, 2001).

AUTISTIC DISORDER AND HIGH-FUNCTIONING AUTISM High-functioning autism (HFA) presents considerable diagnostic challenge to schools and medical personnel. HFA is often initially confused with ADHD or an anxiety disorder, and controversy continues about whether Asperger's syndrome and HFA are the same or different conditions (Hartley & Sikora, 2009; Mayes & Calhoun 2003). It is generally true that as IQ increases, the severity of autistic tendencies decreases, which often results in a delay of diagnosis until late elementary grades.

One constant issue involves determining whether there is a line between Asperger's syndrome and HFA. Some make the case that there is only the autism spectrum, with a continuum for functional characteristics from low to high functioning. However, others hold that HFA differs from Asperger's syndrome because language development delays are not present in learners with Asperger's. This is one of the debates underway as the *DSM-5* revision proceeds.

ON THE WEB

The **Asperger Syndrome Coalition of the U.S.** (http://aspergersyndrome. org) provides resources for professionals and families about Asperger syndrome (AS).

Summary

Autism spectrum disorders (ASDs) are a collection of disorders identified since the 1940s and now included within the pervasive developmental disorders category in the *DSM-IV-TR*. They include autistic disorder (including high-functioning autism), Asperger's disorder, and several other disorders in the severe range of impact. Autism was added as a separate IDEA category in 1990.

ASDs are developmental disorders affecting social relationships and communication and involving repetitive, restrictive behaviors. For school purposes, they must also have a negative impact on educational performance. ASDs are a medically diagnosed group of disorders, generally based on criteria in the *DSM-IV-TR*. The assessment process is complex and detailed, involving developmental testing, observations, interviews, and rating scales.

Autism is a low-incidence disability, although there has been a significant increase since the mid-1990s. About .39 percent of the population and 2.8 percent of the special education population were served under the category of autism in 2004–2005. An increasing number of these students function in the milder range of the spectrum, and more than half spend a significant amount of their time in general education environments. Less than half of those identified with ASD have IQs <70. The prevalence data continue to raise many questions and concerns.

Based on significant research over the past 10–20 years, autism is now believed to have a biological and genetic basis. Theories concerning unresponsive parenting ("refrigerator mothers") and reactions to vaccines have been refuted as causes.

Primary characteristics of individuals with autism include problems in social interactions, with a specific concern over their inability to empathize with others. Communications disorders are many and varied, but all include deficits in functional or pragmatic use of language. Repetitive and restrictive behaviors are also present but varied. At the milder end of the spectrum, learners may show intense interest in specific topics to the exclusion of all others, and they may talk about those interests incessantly. Academic performance is compromised to a greater or lesser extent, and deficits in adaptive behavior are generally in evidence.

A Case Study • Sara

Sara has just turned 15 and is graduating from Gordon Junior High this year. Because of a history of early neglect and abuse in her biological family, she was placed in a foster home and subsequently in a residential program for 2 years because of her unmanageable behaviors. Sara was finally diagnosed with Asperger's syndrome, and she has lived with her current foster mother for the past 2 years. Her placement in this therapeutic foster home provides the support services she needs to make the transition back to a normalized community setting. Sara loves to swing, spending long periods of time in the family's backyard. She was very disappointed when she found out that her junior high school did not have swings.

Sara's foster mother has noticed some unusual behavioral characteristics. Sara becomes almost hypnotic when she eats; she will continue to eat as long as there is any food available. Her foster mother wonders if this is due to the early physical neglect. When she is asked to slow down, Sara will blurt out, "Well, I'm hungry!" It is becoming problematic as Sara is beginning to gain weight as a result of the nonstop eating.

Sara also seems to have a very high tolerance for pain. One day she was riding down the driveway in the back of a truck and fell off. She was on the ground, her tooth chipped and her face bruised. Her foster mother said that she had a "bizarre look in her eyes," but she didn't shed a tear. Sara seems unresponsive to most physical stimuli. Her foster mother thinks she doesn't express the pain she feels. Once again, her foster mother wonders if this is part of her condition or if it is the result of her early abuse.

Sara is very intelligent, and she can't understand why the other students aren't getting what the teacher is teaching. She doesn't understand that what is obvious to her might not be obvious to someone else. She sees the world only from her own perspective, assuming that everyone sees things the way she does. Sara's foster mother is particularly concerned about her egocentrism and sees it getting in the way of her making friends at school.

Sara participates fully in her general education classes, and with the help of Carol, her one-on-one aide, she makes good grades. Her measured intelligence is in the average range, and she demonstrates grade-level achievement on tests and her report cards. Carol has noticed, however, that Sara needs explicit directions for each task. For example, when the teacher says, "Take out your notebooks," the other children take them out and open them, whereas Sara just takes hers out.

Sara also has a Big Sister named Nancy, a professor at a nearby community college. Sara and her Big Sister share a love of libraries and books. It often seems that Sara would prefer to be alone and to read and write her books. To her credit, she has actually written three stories which she calls her "books."

Sara seems to be a very concrete thinker. One day Sara and her Big Sister were talking about sex. Sara told Nancy that she's never getting pregnant and that "I'm going to wait until I'm 21, and then I'll get married to someone I'm really in love with, and then maybe I'll have sex." But then she added that she guessed she *would* get pregnant. When asked why she thought that, Sara said, "Well, I saw this sign at school that said that girls who play sports don't get pregnant . . . and I don't play sports." Sara also doesn't understand figurative phrases like "You're on thin ice!"

Sara doesn't seem to realize that sometimes people need to do things they'd rather not but that doing them is part of the social contract. One day, her aide asked her if she would throw something in the trash can, and Sara said, "No!" Another day, Sara hurt her foster sister's feelings by criticizing her singing. Sara was puzzled because she thought she was "helping" her sister. Carol takes note of these situations and reports them to Sara's speech therapist. The speech therapist works on social conversational skills like these that most young people pick up by observing others. Then Carol follows up by spending 10 hours a week working with Sara in a community setting, reinforcing the social interaction skills that her speech therapist has been working on. Her foster mother tries to reinforce them, too, but she sometimes tires of being a "24-7" teacher when she would rather just be Sara's mother.

Her foster mother is concerned that at the age of 15, Sara doesn't seem to have a sense of personal boundaries. One day they had a visitor with a beard, something new for Sara. She reached up and pulled his beard and started laughing, even when he reacted with pain. At camp last summer, she met a boy. She was "all over him, hugging and kissing, like a much younger child." She was happy to have a friend, but she doesn't realize which behaviors would be considered appropriate or inappropriate in such social situations.

Recently, her foster mother has seen her become very "boy crazy." Sara is very interested in a boy at school named Bob, but he hardly seems to notice that Sara is there. Sara hates to be ignored, and she can't understand why Bob ignores her. She responds by inappropriately putting her hands on him, often with an altercation ensuing. She doesn't appreciate the subtleties of adolescent interactions, responding much like a third grader who chases another child around the playground to make him be her friend. The problem is that as a young adolescent such behaviors are apt to be seen as sexually inappropriate and definitely odd.

Sara has some long-standing problems with appropriate personal hygiene. She doesn't seem to notice the need to change her clothes or take a shower, even when her clothes are dirty and her body odor has become offensive. She does not appreciate that the changes in her adolescent body require more attention to hygiene if she is to be welcome in social environments. This really bothers her foster mother, who can't understand why Sara would be so oblivious to the appearance she presents. She has noted, however, that recently Sara seems to be developing an interest in her grooming.

Another issue that has surfaced is the constant presence of Carol, Sara's aide, in school and in the community. Recently, Carol has been consciously attempting to step back a bit and let Sara try to handle her own social interactions. However, Carol remains vigilant and intervenes as needed. For example, at graduation practice, Sara was sitting with some other girls, trying to interact with them. Carol became aware that the girls were trying to embarrass Sara by calling Bob over, although Sara was oblivious to their motives. Carol stepped in to stop the teasing. She continues to be concerned that Sara doesn't seem to recognize when others are laughing at her rather than with her. Sara's foster mother knows that Sara will continue to need her aide's help when she moves to the high school next year, but she hopes that the social coaching Sara receives from Carol and the speech therapist will begin to make her

capable of handling the social side of adolescence with fewer interventions from Carol. There seems to be a real deficit in her level of socializing, a deficit that her foster mother fears will continue to cause Sara problems.

Sara's lack of social awareness and skill continues to concern everyone. At the graduation ceremony this week, it was painfully obvious that Sara was not at the social level of the other girls. She wants people to like her, but she stands out in her immaturity. When someone does something she doesn't like, she is apt to respond by pushing or biting, because the other person "wouldn't leave me alone." These behaviors cause others to avoid her. Recently she was at a parade downtown and tried to greet some girls from school. The girls whispered to each other and walked away. Her foster mother wonders how to explain what happened to Sara. She realizes that these might be girls Sara had yelled at inappropriately just the day before.

The questions remain: How might her foster mother and teachers help Sara develop the social competence to match her academic abilities?

Discussion

- From the information provided in this text, identify descriptive elements that suggest that Sara's diagnosis of Asperger's disorder is appropriate and in line with the *DSM-IV-TR* and IDEA definitions.
- From the case study information, make a list of Sara's strengths and needs. Relate these to your knowledge of typical developmental patterns.

What Are Learners with Mild Disabilities Like?

What does it really mean when we say that Jennie has a mild intellectual disability, Bobby has a learning disability, Frank has ADHD, Carter has an emotional or behavioral disorder, or Sara has Asperger's syndrome? Are there other more relevant perspectives from which to view mild disabilities? P.L. 94-142, the Education for All Handicapped Children Act of 1975, had not even been fully implemented when Hallahan and Kauffman (1977) gave voice to growing concerns about the relevance of categorical approaches to instructional planning. They contended that the traditional definitions of conditions such as learning disabilities, intellectual disabilities, and emotional disorders were vague, were subject to a variety of interpretations, and provided little useful information for instructional programming. They noted research evidence of overlapping characteristics among the disability groupings (see Figure III.1). Although social adjustment, intelligence, and underachievement are each primarily associated with specific disabilities, research has failed to support their exclusive use as a defining trait for any one category.

In light of these concerns, Hallahan and Kauffman (1977) and others over the years have recommended that special education services might be more effectively delivered if intervention planning was based on each learner's specific behavioral and academic characteristics and needs rather than on his or her category. Epstein and Cullinan (1983) voiced the opinion that even though categories provided some relevant information, it was nevertheless important to determine the differences and similarities among learners and to base programming decisions on those relevant differences. This perspective implies that educators should work on identifying specific functional deficits and strengths, regardless of the categories used for administrative purposes. Indeed, IDEA 2004 requires this.

MacMillan (1998) made a similar point in his discussion of the variability of categorical determinations by multidisciplinary teams. He

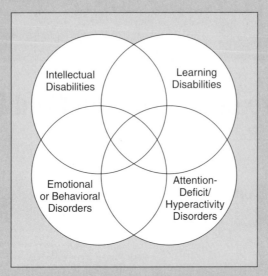

FIGURE III.1 Representation of the Manifestations of Characteristics of Various Mild Disabilities

observed that since the passage of P.L. 94-142 in 1975, eligibility determinations have increasingly had less and less to do with where a child is placed and what services he or she receives. MacMillan found this to be particularly true of the high-incidence disorders, which he referred to as "judgmental categories" because the criteria are subject to professional judgment for interpretation. In addition, his research indicated that school teams were more likely to identify students as having a learning disability, and less likely to use intellectual disability or emotional disturbance, when they knew that it would not affect placement or planning.

Others more recently voiced similar sentiments (Sabornie et al., 2005; Sabornie et al., 2006). Although indicators of differences among the categories are present, there is still enough variation within a category to warrant individualized program planning regardless of the classification decided upon. These writers further observed that we do not yet have clear indications that particular methods work well with one group and not with another. Effective teaching is effective teaching. "Individualized, appropriate assessment and effective instruction regardless of the disability category are still the best practice for students with high-incidence disabilities in special and general education" (Sabornie et al., 2006, p. 104).

In Unit III we will consider the characteristics of all of these learners from the perspectives of their cognitive processing, perceptual abilities, use of language, needs and functioning in academic settings, and social–emotional development rather than their diagnostic category. We will investigate a variety of alternative frameworks for looking at learners' instructional and social needs. These frameworks serve as a useful supplement to the traditional categorical systems for describing children. It is, after all, the specific characteristics of students like Jennie, Bobby, Frank, Carter, and Sara that matter most as teachers and parents work with learners who are experiencing difficulty developing the skills needed for successful living.

CHAPTER 9

Cognitive and Perceptual Characteristics

Questions *to Guide Your Study*

- What are the underlying assumptions of current cognitive learning theories, and how do they apply to our study of the learning of students with mild disabilities?

- What can we learn from the work of constructivists like Piaget and Vygotsky to help us understand the cognitive functioning of learners with mild disabilities?

- How do field-dependent and field-independent learners differ from each other?

- What is the difference between impulsive and reflective learners?

- What are the functions of the three structural components of the cognitive/information-processing model?

- What functions do strategic control components perform in carrying out cognitive activities?

- How do selective and sustained attention differ from one another? How do they relate to cognitive functioning in general?

- What is perception? How does perception relate to overall cognitive functioning?

Meet Robert

Robert is a student in the fourth grade at Smith Elementary School. He is served in his school's resource program for students with learning disabilities. Robert's history is unremarkable. He was adopted shortly after birth and lives with his adoptive family, including his four sisters. His mother does not work outside the home and has tried to help Robert with his academic work all through elementary school. Robert is described as a sweet and quiet child. He enjoys sports and is physically active.

According to Mrs. Peters, his resource teacher, Robert has the most difficulty with the cognitive processing required for reading, writing, and math activities. He does not shift easily from one function to another. For example, he has a problem with listening and then speaking. If Mrs. Peters asks him a question, he needs extended time to process the answer. Sometimes he is not sure enough of himself to even chance an answer. For example, one day Mrs. Peters had worked a math problem with regrouping on the board, and she asked Robert why she put a number in a particular place. It took Robert an extended period of time to process the answer. Mrs. Peters understood Robert's difficulty in processing, so she gave him the time he needed. The length of time it takes Robert to accomplish academic tasks has caused him to fall behind in reading, spelling, and math. He is working with reading and spelling materials at the mid-first-grade level. His math tends to be a little higher; he can add

- Describe visual, auditory, and haptic perception. What are the subskills associated with each type of perception?
- Should a teacher or psychologist attempt to assess a student's perceptual and perceptual–motor functioning? Why? Why not? How?
- What role does executive functioning play in cognitive processes?

and subtract with basic regrouping. He can do basic multiplication tables up to the 7s and 8s, but he has trouble with the processing required to use those facts in problem solving or computation. Robert knows that he has a problem. He recently told Mrs. Peters and his fourth-grade classroom teacher that he wants to know why he can't read like the other kids.

THINKING QUESTIONS

Response to intervention holds that if one strategy is unsuccessful with a child, the teacher should try a more intensive, research-validated intervention. If you had been Robert's first- or second-grade teacher, what might you have tried? Why?

COGNITIVE THEORY AND APPROACHES TO MILD DISABILITIES

To understand the difficulties students with mild disabilities have in school learning environments, it is helpful to consider the complex cognitive processes that must occur in the minds of students like Robert before, during, and after a specific learning event. In this chapter, we will first look at the processes most individuals use to incorporate new information into their knowledge bases. Then we will consider how learners with mild disabilities might differ from more typical learners with respect to their cognitive functioning.

Learning theory holds that learning is an active process that results in lasting changes within a learner's knowledge base and leads to stable changes in behavior. Learning may be conceptualized as the process of "coming to understand" (Benevento, 2004; Paris & Winograd, 1990; Stone & Reid, 1994). Children in classrooms may be most appropriately viewed as apprentice learners who are engaged in a variety of interactive and collaborative activities in meaningful social contexts with both teachers and peers (Reid & Stone, 1991). The expert thinker (i.e., teacher or mentor) provides the support that allows novices to develop their own understandings and cognitive structures.

The following assumptions form the basis for this discussion of the cognitive characteristics of children and youth (Gaskins & Pressley, 2007):

- Learners must be active participants in and responsible for their own learning.
- Learning results when a student effectively relates a new learning to previous learning.
- The way individuals organize and integrate information is critical to their success in learning.
- Although it is possible and useful to study the individual components of successful learning, effective interventions must consider and address the whole learning act.

These basic assumptions apply to all learners, with or without disabilities. However, because research into cognitive approaches to instruction has tended to focus specifically on those children who are experiencing difficulty in the learning process, such research findings have direct application to the learners we are studying. This research indicates that learners with mild disabilities tend to have more difficulty than typical individuals do in cognitively generalizing content and strategies to new situations. They appear to be less able to appreciate the applications of what they have learned, making their learning appear less effective and useful (Gaskins & Pressley, 2007; McFarland & Weibe, 1987; Reid, Hresko, & Swanson, 1996).

Behavioral theories and frameworks have had a significant impact on educational practice for many years. Behaviorists such as Skinner (1953, 1974) view learning as occurring when the individual forms an association between a particular environmental stimulus and a pleasant or punishing event. Stimuli associated with pleasant outcomes result in new learned behaviors; those associated with unpleasant events or with no reinforcement are ignored or rejected by a learner. Teachers are seen as those who provide the stimuli to be learned along with the appropriate reinforcers to ensure the learning of those behaviors or concepts.

Although behavioral approaches are very common in special education, they have generally failed to develop students' abilities to learn independently of the teacher; these approaches do not focus on the holistic act of learning, do not involve the learner actively in that learning, and do not develop the learner's ability to cognitively process information independently and to create his or her own learning (Alley & Deshler, 1979; Benevento, 2004; Deshler et al., 1996). For this reason, we will focus primarily on constructivist and information-processing frameworks, perspectives that may be more helpful in clarifying the cognitive difficulties of students with mild disabilities.

CONSTRUCTIVIST PERSPECTIVES

The constructivists, most notably Piaget and Vygotsky, focused their attention on how children develop, or "construct," knowledge from experiences provided by the environment. With the belief that learning is more complicated than a series of simple stimulus–response sequences, Piaget and Vygotsky developed explanations for the complex learning they saw demonstrated every day by active children, children who were apparently busily constructing new knowledge.

Piaget and Biological Constructivism

Based on his 50 years of observational research on the development of cognitive skills in children, Piaget developed the theory that learning occurs in a sequence of stages related to the maturation of the learner and that learning is self-regulated by learners themselves (Benevento, 2004; Piaget, 1960). Through a combination of maturation and experience, these self-regulated learners construct their understandings of the world, a theory he called *biological constructivism.*

Piaget theorized that learning begins when individuals differentiate among various environmental stimuli, allowing the learners to recognize specific stimuli as new information. Learning occurs as individuals develop schema, or organizational concepts reflecting their perceptions of the world. Learners develop schema by using the cognitive functions of organization and adaptation. As new information is received by learners, they are prompted by their own internal self-regulatory processes to fit the information into their existing organizational structures, to relate it to previous learning (Stone & Reid, 1994). Learners modify their existing schema by adapting their cognitive structures, using assimilation (i.e., adding new and complementary information into an existing schema) or accommodation (i.e., changing existing schema to accommodate the new and contradictory information).

Piaget believed that each new experience tends to create an unsteady cognitive state, or disequilibrium, which the learner seeks to resolve, using the cognitive functions of organization and adaptation to arrive at a new level of equilibrium (see Figure 9.1). With each new attainment of equilibrium, the learner spirals upward to a new level of cognitive understanding. Piaget noted that the quality of cognitive processing appeared to change significantly at certain points in development, leading him to divide cognitive development into cognitive stages (see Table 9.1 and In the Classroom 9.1). He observed that once children had achieved specific critical understandings, they were then able to engage in significantly more complex levels of cognitive processing. Piaget attributed learning problems or deficits to a lag in cognitive maturation. Although learning experiences could be made available to children, Piaget did not believe that learning could be accelerated beyond the limits of maturation.

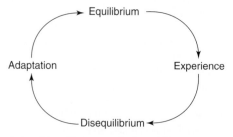

FIGURE 9.1   The Learning Cycle of Equilibrium and Disequilibrium

Table 9.1	Piaget's Cognitive Stages	
Stage	**Age Range (Approximate)**	**Characteristics**
Sensorimotor	Birth to 2	Builds knowledge/concepts through sensory experience and motor activity
Preoperational	Ages 2–7	Begins to think in symbols but is still dependent on direct experience for learning
Concrete operations	Ages 7–14	Begins to use logic to create new concepts, but only those related to the here and now
Formal operations	Ages 14 to adult	Develops ability to think abstractly and logically

The processes described by Piaget take on increasing importance in considering the cognitive characteristics of learners with mild disabilities. First, the process of cognitive development is generally slower for learners with mild disabilities, and these learners may reach a plateau before progressing through all the stages. For example, although learners with intellectual disabilities move through the same Piagetian stages as other children do, they make slower progress and tend to stall at lower stages. Progress through the developmental stages may be disrupted or less efficient in learners with ADHD, learning disabilities, or emotional or behavioral disorders as well. In general, all will need more experiences and careful coaching to arrive at the required insights with respect to fundamental concepts and processes.

The impetus for learning presented by cognitive disequilibrium may have less significance for a child with a mild disability. This learner may not recognize the disequilibrium created by a particular event and therefore may not process it or learn from it. In some learners, the state of disequilibrium may become so constant that they see it as the normal state of affairs, failing to

IN THE CLASSROOM 9.1

Piaget's Stages of Cognitive Development

Sandy is a student in an early-intervention program for children with developmental delays. At age 4, Sandy would be expected to be in the preoperational Piagetian stage. Instead she appears to still be in the sensorimotor stage. She is responsive to sensory experiences of all kinds. She bangs objects on the floor and on each other. She likes to be touched and tickled, and she enjoys touching and tickling others. She will place her hand on another person's hand to "ask for help" and then move that person's hand to what she wants done. It is not clear to her teacher whether she is actually building conceptual knowledge through her tactile and kinesthetic senses, but it is evident that touch and motor activity are involved in nearly all her daily activities and they appear to be the primary means by which she incorporates new information into her knowledge base.

Ricky, a first grader with learning disabilities, appears to still be in the preoperational stage. He uses letters, numbers, and some sign language for communication, but he needs direct experience to understand basic concepts. For example, when he was asked, "If we cut the apple in half, how many pieces will there be?" he was unable to answer. He just shrugged his shoulders and said, "I don't know." The look on his face suggested that he didn't even understand the question. Even when the concept was demonstrated for him, he could not answer the question later without seeing the visual model.

Ben, a middle school student with a mild intellectual disability, seems to be functioning within Piaget's concrete operations stage. He appears to need to connect new information to real-life experiences to give it meaning. During a recent math lesson, he struggled to understand the concept of area until his teacher explained that he might think of area as a floor that needed to be carpeted. With that analogy, Ben was finally able to understand the concept.

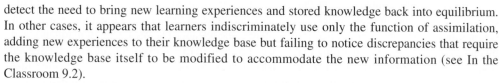

IN THE CLASSROOM 9.2

Accommodation and Assimilation

Danielle is a middle school student with learning disabilities and secondary emotional problems. Her teacher observed that she is unable to relate one idea to another unless it is essentially a duplication or extension of prior patterns of learning. For instance, she has mastered the process of computation with two addends (4 + 9 or 22 + 36) but sees computation with three or more addends as an unrelated process (4 + 9 + 7). She is unable to modify her schema readily to incorporate new or discrepant information. Danielle is able to learn or process information if it is given in small enough chunks and if teacher assistance is provided to perform the accommodation function.

Eugene, a 17-year-old with an intellectual disability, is still at the concrete operations level of cognitive development. Even more importantly, he experiences difficulty with the cognitive function of accommodation. For example, he can play Rummy with his friends and can remember the rules as he learned them from his brother. He understands that a player needs three of a kind to lay the cards down and that if you have the fourth card, you can say, "Rummy." However, for Eugene, the idea of laying down three cards in a sequence is "cheating." He was taught to play the game in a certain way, and that has been reinforced over time. He is not able to accommodate the new information in his schema or add it to and adjust what he already knows.

detect the need to bring new learning experiences and stored knowledge back into equilibrium. In other cases, it appears that learners indiscriminately use only the function of assimilation, adding new experiences to their knowledge base but failing to notice discrepancies that require the knowledge base itself to be modified to accommodate the new information (see In the Classroom 9.2).

Although Piaget did not think that cognitive development could be speeded up significantly, research suggests otherwise (Bruce & Muhammad, 2009; McCormick et al., 1990; Pasnak et al., 1995; Perry, Pasnak, & Holt, 1992; Reid & Stone, 1991). Studies indicate that well-designed, developmentally appropriate teaching activities, using significant exposure to manipulatives and hands-on activities and focusing on developing key cognitive concepts, can increase the rate of cognitive development beyond that achieved solely with good academic skill instruction or incidental learning activities. Researchers have found that concepts such as object permanence, seriation, and classification can be taught, allowing a learner to move more quickly to the next stage of cognitive functioning (Bruce & Muhammad, 2009; Pasnak et al., 1995). Furthermore, Reid and Stone noted that the common practice of structuring remedial instruction in very small increments tends to deprive these learners of the opportunity to note and address discrepancies. Breaking down learning into very tiny steps can result in these learners being unaware of the subtle changes from one concept or skill to the next. This deprives them of the experience of resolving the disequilibrium needed to develop their cognitive functions of accommodation and assimilation.

ON THE WEB

The **Jean Piaget Society: Society for the Study of Knowledge and Development** (http://www.piaget.org) provides an open forum—through symposia, books, and other publications—for the discussion of scholarly work on issues related to the development of human knowledge; a comprehensive list of web links is also included.

Vygotsky and Social Constructivism

Another constructivist approach to learning was developed by Vygotsky (1978, 1987), who theorized that learning occurs through participation in social or culturally embedded experiences. In contrast to Piaget, Vygotsky did not see the learner as a solitary explorer of the world but rather as one who learns through social interactions in meaningful contexts. His theory of social constructivism holds that learning occurs when teachers and others guide learners in developing new understandings. Vygotsky extended the concept of a social context for learning to include the symbolic social context of shared language systems (Trent, Artiles, & Englert, 1998). A model for literacy development with learners with communication impairments (Kaderavek & Rabidoux, 2004) builds on Vygotsky's theory by providing learners with emergent literacy supports within socially guided instruction to achieve gains toward independent literacy.

Vygotsky formulated the concept of a *zone of proximal development* to indicate that range of learning that students can achieve when they are engaged in meaningful activities with competent others. The zone of proximal development is the distance between what individuals can do by themselves and the next learning that they can be helped to achieve with competent assistance (Larkin, 2001; Stone & Reid, 1994; Vygotsky, 1987). According to Vygotsky, learning takes place only in the zone of proximal development. In working with students with disorders in learning and behavior, it is essential to understand that successful learning will be determined first by what the learners already know and then by the nature and quality of the support needed for them to learn the "next thing." Vygotsky believed that the zone of proximal development is a better indication of what a student can learn than tests of acquired knowledge.

Vygotsky also used the term *scaffolding instruction* to refer to the actions of teachers and others in supporting the learner's development and providing support structures to get to that next stage or level. The "teacher" helps students connect the known with the new. As these interactions proceed, the learners increasingly assume responsibility for the task and for problem solving, "appropriating" the goal and the plan for achieving the goal from the teacher or guide (Larkin, 2001; Stone & Reid, 1994). Vygotsky explained that as a learner develops more sophisticated cognitive systems related to fields of learning such as mathematics or language, the system of knowledge itself becomes part of the scaffold, or social support, for the new learning (McFarland & Weibe, 1987; Reid & Stone, 1991).

Youngsters with mild disabilities such as Mary and Kathy (see In the Classroom 9.3) appear to have smaller zones of proximal development in many areas of academic and social learning. They require more scaffolding by their parents and teachers to achieve firm learning. Teachers help by orchestrating learning situations in which there is a gap between where the child is and where the child can be reasonably expected to go with assistance from the teacher (Trent et al., 1998). This framework is particularly critical in working with learners who have difficulty with social interactions. Expectations of appropriate behavior are reasonable only when the skill is determined to be in the child's repertoire or when it is within the child's zone of proximal development and the environment provides the support or scaffolding needed to learn and use that skill.

An awareness of the current levels of functioning of learners in a class, as well as the types of scaffolding or support those learners typically find useful, will be critical to a teacher's success in meeting the needs of all students. Universal design for learning provides an excellent framework for designing effective, accessible scaffolds (Rose & Rose, 2007). In best practice,

IN THE CLASSROOM 9.3

Scaffolding Within the Zone of Proximal Development

Mary is a middle school student with a learning disability. Her zone of proximal development is smaller than that of her peers in English class. The class moves fairly quickly from chapter to chapter in the novel they are reading. Often Mary has not fully comprehended one chapter when the class moves on to the next. She experiences similar frustrations with the English vocabulary lists. More scaffolding would help Mary achieve firmer learning. She needs more time and instruction, as well as more support, than her peers need in order to master this English content before moving on.

Kathy was diagnosed with mild intellectual disability in second grade. She has just begun classes at the high school. Her current math teacher has said that her zone of proximal development is very narrow. Significant scaffolding is required for Kathy to relate new information to previously learned material. She does not assimilate or accommodate new ideas or concepts easily. In math, for example, she does not see the relationship between addition and subtraction, subtraction and division, or division and fractions. She still depends on the scaffolding provided by her teacher's use of manipulatives for basic mathematical operations. She seems to be constantly in a state of disequilibrium, always trying to catch up.

---

materials and support are available as needed and are not designed as an afterthought. It is most effective to have a variety of scaffolds available to deploy as the needs arise and to allow children to learn to make choices and access them independently (Larkin, 2001).

COGNITIVE STYLES RESEARCH

About the time that the term *learning disabilities* came into use to refer to learners with unexpected underachievement, researchers began to look more closely at the way in which these learners approached learning tasks. It was reasoned that there might be differences between typical students and those with mild disabilities and that these differences might be useful in designing remedial activities. This research, focusing on the cognitive styles of these learners, revealed some patterns related to the structure and process of thinking rather than to the content of thought processes (Blackman & Goldstein, 1982; Chinn et al., 2001; Claxton & Murrell, 1987; Sternberg & Grigorenko, 1997). Research indicates that learners with disabilities exhibit less flexibility in completing learning tasks, but their flexibility can be developed through intervention efforts (Chinn et al., 2001). Two cognitive styles shown to have relevance to our work with learners with mild disabilities include (a) field dependence/independence and (b) reflectivity and impulsivity.

Field Dependence/Independence

The degree to which an individual's perceptual and cognitive judgments are influenced by the surrounding environment has been referred to as field dependence/independence. This construct takes note of the extent to which a person interprets perceptual information by independently attending to relevant cues in the environment while discarding irrelevant ones. The degree of field independence is related to the individual's ability to perceive an object or situation without being unduly influenced by or dependent on other information in the surrounding field, that is, the ability to lift the critical information out of the field (Alamolhodaei, 2009; Rittschof, 2010; Witkin, Moore, Goodenough, & Cox, 1977).

The degree of field independence, then, is determined by the extent to which individuals are able to identify critical information independently and to resolve conflicting sources of information by reference to a standard derived from within themselves. That standard of comparison is typically thought to be an individual's stored knowledge. Students who function in a field-independent manner are more likely to use such inner resources as a mediator for information processing in their working memory (Reid et al., 1996; Rittschof, 2010). Field-independent children are more capable of using inner language to mediate their processing of environmental stimuli (Rittschof, 2010; Swanson, 1991). Such learners perform more consistently on school tasks and in other learning environments. It has also been determined that the tendency toward field independence tends to grow stronger with age and that learners with learning disabilities and other mild disabilities tend to remain more field dependent for longer periods of time.

Field dependence, on the other hand, is evidenced when learners' perceptions are largely determined by the prevailing external stimuli and information. Such students experience difficulty structuring the stimuli that they take in, and they rely on teacher-generated cues and hints to identify critical information and to give meaning to what they see or hear (Alamolhodaei, 2009; Reid et al., 1996; Rittschof, 2010). The tendency for field-dependent learners to scan larger portions of the environment for clues may lead to confusion and ambiguity in some learning situations, thereby reducing learning efficiency (Keogh & Donlon, 1972). Many of the studies on field dependence have found a link between field dependence and academic underachievement (Alamolhodaei, 2009; Blackman & Goldstein, 1982). Forns-Santacana, Amador-Campos, and Roig-Lopez (1993) concluded that field independence tends to be less well developed in children from lower-socioeconomic backgrounds, possibly because of the effect of limited learning experiences on cognitive development. These writers also reported that girls in their study tended to function in a more field-dependent manner than the boys did.

The concept of field dependence/independence can be applied in social situations as well as cognitive ones (see Chapter 12). Individuals with a field-dependent social orientation make extensive use of social referents in guiding their feelings, attitudes, and actions. The tendency to view field dependence as undesirable or less adaptive has been questioned by some researchers (Claxton & Murrell, 1987). They noted that some cultures (e.g., Mexican American) appear to place a value on a field-dependent cognitive style, suggesting that the term *field sensitive* may be a more appropriate alternative. They recommended that teachers strive to develop a balance of both cognitive styles in their students, asserting that contemporary life requires individuals who can be field independent and field sensitive as the occasion demands. (See In the Classroom 9.4.)

IN THE CLASSROOM 9.4

Field Dependence/Independence

Mike, a fifth grader with ADHD, has become more field independent since he began taking medication for his ADHD. Sometimes being field independent works to his disadvantage, however. He now tends to do things entirely on his own. If he does not remember the directions, he makes up his own. If he doesn't know an answer, he skips the question. He does not seek the assistance of the teacher when it would be useful to do so. He is proud of being able to control himself now and likes not having to rely on others for support and confirmation. He is happy he can complete his work on his own, whether it is correct or not.

Dennis, a fifth grader with a learning disability, shows signs of both field dependence and independence, depending on the subject or task he is working on. He still exhibits considerable field dependence in writing and spelling. He continually stops to look up the spelling of words when writing a story. When he is told to just write and not worry about the spelling for now, he cannot proceed. He just focuses on the spelling. His teachers have begun having him use a word processor with a spelling checker. When the word processor beeps at an error, he may still ask how to spell it, but he is beginning to try it on his own several times before asking for help. On the other hand, Dennis appears very field independent in math. He considers himself to be a very good math student, and he prides himself on figuring out the answers rather than checking the answers on the cue cards available in his classroom.

	Faster Response Time	**Slower Response Time**
Higher Error Rate	**Impulsive Style** **Faster response time** **Higher rate of error**	*Slower/Inaccurate** *Slower responses* *Higher rate of error*
Lower Error Rate	*Fast/Accurate** *Faster responses* *Lower error rate*	**Reflective Style** **Slower response time** **Lower error rate**

*These cells represent significantly fewer individuals

FIGURE 9.2   Patterns of Reflection and Impulsivity (Response Rate Versus Errors)

Impulsivity and Reflectivity

Impulsivity/reflectivity, or cognitive tempo, is the aspect of cognitive style that refers to the speed with which an individual responds to task demands and the tendency of the individual to consider an action before acting. The critical issue is not the actual speed of taking action but rather the presence or absence of an effective and deliberate decision-making process prior to acting.

Reflective learners evaluate their responses, based on the demands of the task, before answering, whereas impulsive children check their standard of comparison less often and use fewer analytical strategies to evaluate their responses (Keller & Ripoll, 2004; Rozencwajg & Corroyer, 2005; Swanson, 1991). Impulsivity is characterized by quick decisions and a higher error rate, whereas reflectivity is described as a more deliberate decision-making process, usually with higher accuracy (see Figure 9.2). A smaller number of individuals appear consistently in the fast/accurate or the slow/inaccurate groups. Reflective children also seem more capable of adjusting their rate of response with respect to the demands of the task (Kagan, 1965, 1966). This cognitive style dimension is related to our discussion in Chapter 7 of behavioral inhibition among individuals with ADHD (Barkley, 2006; see In the Classroom 9.5).

IN THE CLASSROOM 9.5

Impulsivity and Reflectivity

Elaine is 10 years old and has Asperger's syndrome. She appears somewhat impulsive. She will write down or blurt out the first thing she thinks of, whether it has anything to do with the subject or not. When asked for an explanation of her response, she usually gets defensive and says something like, "It's the best I can do." At times she fails to read the questions or directions before beginning tasks or tests. She does not check over her work unless instructed to do so. She usually finishes an assignment quickly and then immediately wants to hand it in. She states that she doesn't go back to look over her work because "I don't have time." When instructed to do so, she appears frustrated as she notes her errors and must try again.

John's teacher describes him as surprisingly reflective. He is usually the last student to complete an assignment in his high school class for students with intellectual disabilities. In approaching a cognitive task, he consciously and systematically attacks the problem. If he feels rushed for time, he asks the teacher for an extension. Unfortunately for John, his deficits in long-term memory mean that thinking about the task before acting doesn't always result in fewer mistakes.

There is some evidence that impulsivity may be associated with underachievement, but the pattern is not consistent (Blackman & Goldstein, 1982). In their summary of research on cognitive styles, Hallahan, Kauffman, and Lloyd (1999) reported that even though children with mild disabilities can be trained to respond in a more reflective manner using self-instruction techniques, simply getting impulsive learners to slow down does not automatically lead to fewer errors. Also, increased reflectivity in clinical settings does not automatically generalize to classroom-based tasks. Use of language-mediated cognitive behavior modification techniques has had the most success in developing more adaptive and reflective cognitive styles. Such techniques teach a student to engage in self-instruction while carrying out standard cognitive tasks, thereby promoting reflectivity.

INFORMATION-PROCESSING APPROACHES

Information-processing theory provides still another perspective for understanding a learner's specific patterns of learning and thinking. This framework is based on the premise that cognition is a highly interactive, internalized process. It assumes that individuals interpret all newly received sensory input in terms of what they already know, based on the hypothesis that individuals then construct meaning or modify their knowledge bases. The critical factors influencing the success of the learning include a person's selection of stimuli from all the available environmental stimuli and the processes used to give meaning to those environmental stimuli.

Information-processing researchers have studied how human beings collect, interpret, store, and modify information received from the environment and retrieved from their own stored information. A variety of functional models and hypotheses have resulted from this study of these complex cognitive processes. Within this framework, the process of learning is not viewed as qualitatively different from stage to stage or from age to age. Instead, it is related to each learner's ability to process new information efficiently and effectively. Each cognitive action adds new concepts, skills, and insights to an individual's existing knowledge base, resulting in the learner's being able to use that new knowledge in subsequent learning. The learner associates this new input with previous learning and stores it for use in the future, much as computers do.

Models of cognitive functioning generally are composed of three primary components or functions (Reid et al., 1996; Swanson, 1987; Swanson & Cooney, 1991; Sweller, 2004):

- Structural components
- Strategic control components
- Executive functions

The structural components of the cognitive model include the sensory register, the immediate memory (composed of short-term and working memories), and the long-term storage or memory. The strategic control components include strategies for completing specific tasks, such as attention, perception, and the storage and retrieval strategies used to transform information so that it is useful in the next stage of the processing. The executive functions perform a variety of monitoring activities, evaluating the effectiveness of cognitive processing, directing the flow of information, and allocating resources. Executive functions are "self-directed actions by the individual that are being used for self-regulation toward the future" (Barkley, 2006, p. 304; Benevento, 2004; Meltzer, 2007). The relationship of the structural components, strategic processes, and executive functions to the processing of environmental stimuli or information is illustrated in Figure 9.3.

Structural Storage Components

Most models of the cognitive processing of information include a multilevel structural storage component, composed of three types of memory (Anderson, 1983; Stone & Reid, 1994; Sweller, 2004):

- Sensory register or store that receives and stores sensory stimuli very briefly
- Immediate memory, composed of working and short-term memories, which processes information prior to storage or use (output)
- Long-term memory for indefinite storage

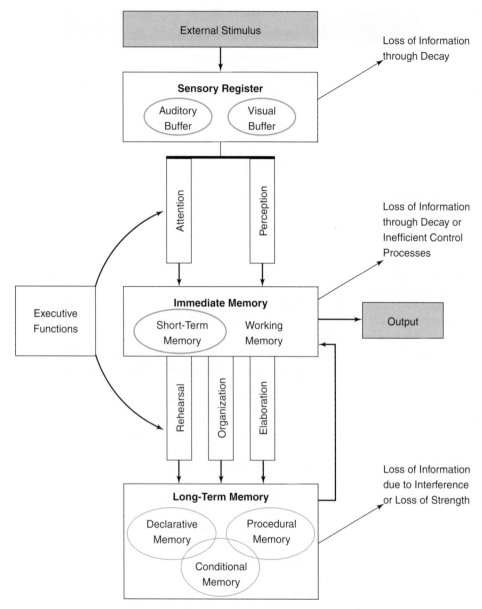

FIGURE 9.3   Model of Cognitive Processing

SENSORY REGISTER   The sensory register is the cognitive storage device for all sensory input (J. R. Hayes, 1989; Wyer & Srull, 1989) and is capable of receiving significant amounts of sensory information. It stores a relatively complete copy of the physical stimulus—much like photographic film—that is available for further processing (Swanson & Cooney, 1991). However, unless captured by the attention control process, this information decays within 3 to 5 seconds. Upon capture, sensory information is scanned and compared against information in long-term memory; if no match is found, the stimulus is deemed not meaningful, and the memory of the stimulus is lost through decay.

The sensory register (see Figure 9.3) is composed of separate stores, or buffers, for the different sensory modalities, including buffers for visual, auditory, tactile, olfactory, and gustatory stimuli. The visual and auditory buffers are most often used in the process of school learning, and they are the only ones that have been studied extensively. These buffers store pure sensory information without complex meaning. Such information is considered

---

IN THE CLASSROOM 9.6

Sensory Register

Billy, a middle school student with a learning and behavioral disability, exhibits both strengths and deficits in his sensory register. It appears that it is easier for him to pick up and process auditory stimuli rather than visual stimuli. He is much more comfortable and efficient in listening and talking than he is in reading and writing. When he is trying to read, he has so much difficulty processing the visual symbols that the stimulus is frequently lost before meaning can be attached. Trying to make sense of a group of visual symbols as a complete thought appears impossible. If he is given the same information verbally, he has little difficulty understanding the concepts. Attaching meaning to auditory stimuli is much more automatic, and his efficiency in processing the auditory stimuli allows him to be more successful in attributing meaning to it as a complete thought.

---

precategorical or unprocessed, without meaning until acted on by the attention and perception functions (Hayes, 1989).

Images stored in the sensory register are operated on by the strategic control process of selective attention, which makes determinations about which stimuli should be captured and used and which should be ignored and allowed to decay. The attention function scans the images, identifying relevant/irrelevant environmental stimuli and filtering out those considered to be irrelevant. Problems for some learners may arise at this stage if relevant images are allowed to decay because of inefficient attention processes or if the filtering system allows irrelevant images to remain active, competing with more useful stimuli for processing space (Stone & Reid, 1994). The attention problems of many learners with mild disabilities (see In the Classroom 9.6) mean that information is often lost because it never makes it past the sensory register.

IMMEDIATE MEMORY   The structural component devoted to active processing of information is called the *immediate memory* and is composed of two complementary functions: working memory and short-term memory (Alamolhodaei, 2009; Gathercole, Alloway, Willis, & Adams, 2006; see Figure 9.3). *Working memory* has been described as a work table for the temporary storage and manipulation of information derived from incoming stimuli and information retrieved from long-term memory. It is a dynamic and active system in which a limited number of pieces of information can be processed rapidly prior to storing or use (Alamolhodaei, 2009; Ashbaker & Swanson, 1996; Baddeley, 2000; Swanson, 1994; Swanson & Saez, 2003; Sweller, 2004). Working memory requires holding on to pieces of information while cognitive operations are carried out (Siegel, 2003).

Immediate memory has another subsection referred to as *short-term memory,* a temporary, passive storage location for information being operated on in the pursuit of a specific cognitive objective (Baddeley, 2000). Short-term memory provides a storage buffer for auditory, visual, or other sensory stimuli, holding information for short periods of time. It also provides a rehearsal stage, serving as a mediator between input, processing, and output (Ashbaker & Swanson, 1996; Reid et al., 1996; Swanson, 1994; Swanson, Cochran, & Ewers, 1990; Swanson & O'Connor, 2009).

The allocation of space in immediate memory to either working or short-term memory is flexible. Some cognitive tasks require more storage, whereas others demand more active workspace to manipulate data. Learners, using their executive functions, determine the optimal allocation of these limited resources for the immediate task. The limitations of both working and short-term memories are their storage and processing capacities. Studies indicate that normally about seven independent pieces, or chunks, of information can be held in working memory at one time without the need to transfer some information into long-term memory or run the risk of losing it

(Baddeley, 2000; Hayes, 1989; Miller, 1956). A chunk is an aggregate of stimuli or symbols that is treated as a unit. For example, words are combinations of letters, treated as a single chunk; sentences are combinations of words and may sometimes be viewed as a chunk. Once the storage limit of the working memory has been exceeded, information becomes lost.

Immediate memory is limited in its storage capacity. Information stored in the short-term memory buffer decays on average within 20 to 30 seconds unless it is retained and renewed by strategies such as rehearsal. The time that a specific chunk remains active and available within the short-term memory buffer is variable and is significantly influenced by the actions and strategies of the individual. Repeating the information over and over or actively working with the information can sustain it for longer than this brief time. An alternative is to transfer the information into long-term memory for subsequent use, retaining clues for retrieving it as needed.

The ability of learners to create and use chunks to increase the limited processing capacity of their immediate memory is dependent on the extent of the prior knowledge they can apply to the situation (Baddeley, 2000; Miller, 1956). Sometimes, rearranging the units can create even larger chunks (e.g., grouping sets of items into categories to aid in recall.) A chunk must be a familiar unit of meaning if an individual is to be able to recognize and handle it as a chunk. When learners are able, based on their prior knowledge, to recognize a pattern in the information being processed, they can treat that information as a single chunk and can therefore increase the capacity of their immediate memory. Effective use of such "chunking" strategies increases the effectiveness of immediate memory, both in the storage (short-term memory) and the processing (working memory) subcomponents.

Learners with mild disabilities frequently exhibit a variety of difficulties in using their working and short-term memories (see In the Classroom 9.7). Problems include difficulty in strategically processing information as well as less frequent or less skillful use of organizational strategies to chunk information. In general, these learners exhibit less mature memory functioning, more comparable to that of younger children (Swanson & Cooney, 1991). The memory strategies and skills of students with learning disabilities often do not match estimates of their general intellectual ability. Such students may present a variety of problems in the use of their working and short-term memories, with some learners seeming to have more problems with the storage facilities whereas others encounter more difficulty in using their executive functions to organize their working memories for efficient processing (Swanson et al., 1990; Swanson, 2002).

Verbal interference appears to seriously compromise immediate memory efficiency in some learners (Webster, Hall, Brown, & Bolen, 1996). Students with mild disabilities frequently encounter specific problems in reading comprehension because of the inefficient operation of their working memory to handle decoding and perceptual tasks simultaneously (Ashbaker & Swanson, 1996; Barkley, 2006; Swanson, 2002). Students with intellectual disabilities are reported to take

---

IN THE CLASSROOM 9.7

Immediate Memory (Working and Short-Term Memory)

Deficits in his immediate memory have had a critical effect on Chris's academic achievement and functioning in his self-contained classroom for elementary students with emotional disorders. Directions for assignments are a particular problem. His teacher gives him specific directions and routinely asks him to repeat them, checking for understanding. Although he looks at the teacher while she is speaking and gives the appearance of listening, he frequently is unable to repeat what she has told him. On other occasions, the teacher gives Chris a specific fact, such as the year he was born, to use on a form he is filling out; when she immediately asks him to repeat what she has said, he is unable to do so. Without the ability to hold information briefly in his immediate memory for use or processing, Chris is unable to perform immediate tasks adequately. He is also unable to add the information effectively to his knowledge base in long-term memory.

longer to achieve automatic and fluent levels of information processing, a factor that compromises the amount of cognitive information they can handle at one time (Merrill, 1990). For many learners with mild disabilities, it is the extent, strength, and accessibility of their knowledge base that are frequently inadequate, compromising their overall cognitive effectiveness.

LONG-TERM MEMORY   Long-term memory, the main storage facility, appears to have virtually unlimited storage capacity. Once information is stored in long-term memory, it is generally considered to be permanent and accessible for a lifetime. Information may be of a declarative, procedural, or conditional nature and is transferred into long-term memory by the use of strategic control processes (Billingsley & Wildman, 1990; Deshler et al., 1996; Sweller, 2004; see Figure 9.3).

Declarative knowledge deals with factual information and the acquisition of related concepts. Factual data are encoded for future use and stored in the declarative memory store, also called the semantic memory. Prior to storage, information is compared with previously stored information and is either assimilated or accommodated based on that comparison and evaluation. If there is interference, or a discrepancy between the new information and the previously stored material, cognitive decisions must be made by the learner about which information to keep or how to modify the knowledge base to accommodate the new data (Benevento, 2004).

The structure of information stored in declarative memory is best described as a hierarchical classification system, with information of a more specific nature stored in relationship to more general or global categories (McFarland & Weibe, 1987; Reid et al., 1996). The learner makes use of various associations or links to store the data, as well as utilizing more general organizational structures or frameworks to organize the memory store as a whole. The stronger the relationship between two facts or stimuli, the more easily the learner will be able to retrieve those facts on demand (Hasselbring, Goin, & Bansford, 1988).

Research suggests that the structure of declarative memory in individuals with mild disabilities is similar to that in other persons, but there is some evidence that the extent and accessibility of that information may differ somewhat (see In the Classroom 9.8). Hayes and Taplin (1993) reported that although the structure of declarative memory in individuals with intellectual disabilities resembles that of those without such disabilities, such learners seem most often to develop new concepts based on references to prototypes (that is, by linking the new concept to a generalized and similar concept already stored). More adaptive learners tend to develop concepts from generic characteristics extracted from experience with a series of exemplars of such concepts. Hasselbring and colleagues (1988) observed that when learners with mild disabilities are unsuccessful in retrieving needed information from their declarative memories, they often rely on strategies in their procedural memory to determine the needed facts (see In the Classroom 9.9). Although this is sometimes effective in recovering the needed information, this process slows down the cognitive processing and can obstruct higher-order thinking.

IN THE CLASSROOM 9.8

Declarative Knowledge

Melissa, a fifth grader with a learning disability, has a difficult time storing and retrieving declarative information in her long-term memory. She is working on learning her multiplication facts by using flashcards with her teacher. She frequently gets "that look" on her face when she appears to know the answer but doesn't answer right away. Her teacher thinks this may be because she has difficulty transferring the information quickly from long-term memory into her working memory and then forming an adequate response. Melissa's teacher wonders if it is because of inefficient organization of concepts within her declarative memory or if ineffective memory strategies used in the storage process are to blame. Melissa appears primarily to use verbal rehearsal strategies, which may not be the best choice for her since she appears to respond more readily to visual and tactile stimuli.

IN THE CLASSROOM 9.9

Procedural Knowledge

Donnie, a sixth grader with learning disabilities, continues to experience difficulties in his math class. He started having trouble in math in second grade when the class began to memorize the multiplication tables. He had always been able to complete addition and subtraction computation and problem solving well. Even though he did not have the facts in memory, he could rapidly count them, and he had a firm grasp of the procedures for doing the calculation. Ever since then, his teachers have been working unsuccessfully on his memory of the multiplication facts. At first he was allowed to use a chart, and he became quite competent in the processes of multiplying and then dividing. Trouble began when his teachers said, "No more chart." Procedural knowledge alone was simply not enough. Donnie's consultant teacher, recognizing his strength in procedural knowledge, has been working with him on the declarative knowledge deficit while seeking to put accommodations in place that will allow him to continue to function in math class with his multiplication chart.

Procedural knowledge includes information about how to perform specific tasks. This knowledge includes basic action sequences, such as how to tie a shoe or how to subtract three-digit numbers with regrouping, as well as the more complex knowledge needed to carry out complex cognitive processing of information (Derry, 1990). Procedural knowledge is generally composed of a system of condition–action rules called productions, similar to a basic stimulus–response framework. These rules permit more automatic performance of complex tasks because each step leads automatically to the next, once the string has been activated (Derry, 1990; Reid et al., 1996). Such procedural memories make use of data stored in the declarative memory but allow more efficient processing of information within working memory and in cognitive information processing as a whole, resulting in a capable individual's being able to carry out a variety of such action sequences simultaneously. Youngsters such as Donnie (see In the Classroom 9.9) sometimes find these action sequences easier to learn, perhaps because of the multisensory aspect of most procedural learning. Once learned, procedural sequences are at times used by the learner to compensate for deficits in declarative memory.

The third component of long-term memory is conditional knowledge, consisting of the knowledge base that is used to determine when or whether to initiate a particular cognitive process. Conditional knowledge provides the strategy knowledge needed to integrate declarative and procedural knowledge. Conditional knowledge also involves the knowledge of appropriate techniques for monitoring and evaluating cognitive events and thus includes the knowledge of how one's memory and overall cognitive processing operate and have operated in the past. These standards, developed from past experiences, enable an individual to make use of prior experiences to support cognitive processing in the present. This is the memory store that is likely to be least well developed in learners with mild disabilities.

PROCESSING WITHIN LONG-TERM MEMORY Long-term memory processing involves the use of three activities (Hayes, 1989; Sweller, 2004):

- Encoding, or putting the information into memory
- Organizing that stored information in an accessible manner
- Retrieving or recovering stored information

Encoding, or preparing the material for transfer into long-term memory, can be accomplished by simple rehearsal. However, in order to effectively fix the information in a form that is strong enough to be easily and reliably accessed later, more complex and elaborative rehearsal techniques are generally more useful. Such strategies involve making a variety of connections with the new information. The more connections that are made, the more likely it is that the material will be successfully and effectively encoded for storage and retrieval. Access to stored material and the effectiveness of both storage and retrieval are largely mediated by mnemonic strategic control functions, such as rehearsal strategies (oral, written, or motoric), organization strategies (e.g., chunking, clustering, using mnemonics, and coding), and use of strategies to elaborate on the meaning of the stimuli being processed (e.g., use of semantic elaboration or imagery strategies).

Access to stored information can be disrupted by either interference or decay. Interference is usually attributed to conflicts with other learning. When the interference is with a prior experience, it is called *proactive interference.* When the interference is from a later learning, it is called *retroactive interference.* Decay often appears to be related to the insufficient strength of the original learning, resulting in a memory trace that is too weak to facilitate recall (Hayes, 1989). The decay effect can be reduced by practicing overlearning strategies or by reviewing stored information periodically. Learners with mild disabilities experience frequent problems in retrieving stored data primarily because of weak original learning. (See Chapter 11 for a more complete discussion of the stages of learning required for robust learning to occur.) These learners also may not monitor their memory stores for possible interference with previously stored information, as was discussed in relation to Piaget and the process of accommodation.

Strategic Control Components

The processing and transfer of information between cognitive structural components is accomplished by the use of strategic control processes, including attention, perception, and mnemonic strategies (see again Figure 9.3 on page 201). The application of these strategic control processes is first evidenced when stimuli are being evaluated in the sensory register. At this stage, the information is scanned quickly, attention is focused on distinctive features, and names are generated for specific bits of information. Almost instantaneously, a decision is made about the usefulness of these stimuli. Unless tagged for further attention, they quickly decay and are lost. Much of what occurs around us fails to pass this initial screening and disappears without notice.

Once information has been given meaning and has passed into working memory, the executive function evaluates it again and calls up an appropriate mnemonic strategy to transfer it to an appropriate location in long-term memory. Finally, strategic control processes may combine incoming stimuli with stored information, resulting in a response to the environment. Such responses may be verbal (oral or written) or kinesthetic (including gestural language as well as physical actions).

ATTENTION   No learning can occur unless the learner is first able to focus on the relevant aspects of a task or concept and focus on them long enough to process the information, giving it meaning and making it usable. *Attention,* the term typically used to refer to this focusing function, has been conceptualized in a variety of ways over the years. Students with intellectual disabilities, learning disabilities, ADHD, ASD, or emotional or behavioral disorders, as well as other low-achieving learners, frequently exhibit problems with attention, or with one or more of its components, as a defining characteristic of their disability (Krupski, 1980, 1986; Richards, Samuels, Turnure, & Ysseldyke, 1990).

Attention is much more than a simple system for taking in information. It is an integral part of the cognitive process. Information previously stored in an individual's long-term memory is utilized by the attention function to determine what is novel or relevant. Difficulties in learning are more likely caused by a fundamental limitation in cognitive functioning as a system rather than by a deficit in any single function such as attention (Krupski, 1986). For example, the adequacy and availability of prior knowledge are significant determiners of what a learner can and will attend to. Information taken in from the environment through the sensory register is joined with information retrieved from long-term memory; if a match is found, a learner is able to give meaning to the stimulus within working memory (Stolzenberg & Cherkes- Julkowski, 1991; see

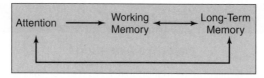

FIGURE 9.4   Interaction of Attention and Memory

Figure 9.4). In this way, the attention function interacts with all aspects of the learning and thinking process as one of the strategic control functions.

Attention has been described as a multifaceted construct composed of several subfunctions. Most frameworks focus on three: (a) coming to attention, (b) selective attention, and (c) sustained attention (Conte, 1991; Keogh & Margolis, 1976; Krupski, 1986; Posner & Boies, 1971; C. R. Smith, 1991). All of these components are involved in identifying relevant information and inhibiting the processing of irrelevant information (Klorman, 1991; Krupski, 1986).

Coming to Attention.   The initial factor in our ability to attend to relevant stimuli is our alertness, or our receptivity to signals from the environment. Our alertness, or capability of being aroused by external stimuli to "come to attention," varies considerably throughout the day, and alertness varies across individuals. Various factors affect alertness or receptivity to stimuli:

- Our physical state (e.g., tiredness, excitement, physical health, hunger)
- External circumstances (e.g., the weather, the type of activity)
- The presence of advance organizers (e.g., information that prompts us to attend)
- The need to allocate attention resources in a setting of conflicting attentional demands (e.g., a crowded room, a busy shopping mall)

All of us exhibit varying levels of alertness over time and situations. Our effectiveness in functioning requires that we moderate our alertness to meet environmental demands (Zentall, 2005). In considering learners with mild disabilities, there is some evidence that their ability to come to attention may be compromised by their conditions. Some children may appear to be underaroused and so engage in "stimulus seeking" behaviors (Conte, 1991; Zentall, 2005); they appear to be very distractible and to have problems attending to a specific stimulus. Other learners seem to be overaroused, resulting in high levels of anxiety and disorganization. The level of alertness becomes problematic when a student exhibits a uniform level of arousal across setting demands (i.e., when the student is uniformly underaroused or overaroused), without the ability to adjust attention responses to meet specific daily living demands. Without this ability to come to attention as needed, functioning is certainly impaired (see In the Classroom 9.10).

Selective Attention.   Once an individual has become alert to the need to attend to incoming stimuli, the next step in the process is "catching and focusing" the attention (C. R. Smith, 1991).

IN THE CLASSROOM 9.10

Alertness or Coming to Attention

Dianne is 9 years old and has a learning disability. Attention appears to be difficult for her. Her deficits appear to lie primarily in alertness, or coming to attention. Her teacher finds it helpful to give her a little extra time (about 30 seconds) when transitioning from one subject or activity to another. Dianne is then able to effectively come to attention. The teacher finds that if she asks her to switch her attention focus too quickly, Dianne "gets lost." She is usually focused on the task she has just completed and needs to have some advance warning of what's happening next. When ample time is given to the transition stage, Dianne comes to attention and maintains attention more effectively for longer periods.

IN THE CLASSROOM 9.11

Selective Attention

Jerry is a third grader with a mild intellectual disability. His teacher has ruled out coming to attention as an area of deficit because Jerry initially appears excited to begin work and seems fully focused. He will immediately make comments about the subject being presented. Difficulties begin with his selective attention. He often seems unaware of the main idea and cannot pick out relevant details. His difficulty in selecting the most relevant stimuli is evidenced during classroom discussion. He frequently provides answers that are off the topic, or he displays little if any recollection of material discussed. In a recent discussion of the four food groups, for example, he responded, "I don't remember hearing about all of them."

Tina is a third grader with a learning disability and ADHD. One day, her teacher was reading aloud as the students followed along. Tina appeared to be paying attention for the first few minutes. However, she had a pencil in her hand that appeared to draw her attention away from the book. When Tina saw or heard the others turn the page, she did so as well. The teacher directed Tina to put the pencil away, and for the remainder of the reading, she appeared to follow along. Her teacher later said that she is unsure whether Tina was unable to sustain her attention on the reading and so turned to focus on the pencil or whether her selective attention left the book and focused on the pencil, shifting her attention away from the more relevant stimulus.

Human beings are bombarded by enormous quantities of stimuli during every conscious moment. It is impossible to attend to and process everything, and many of the environmental stimuli are not relevant and should not be processed. *Selective attention* refers to the ability to focus on the most relevant stimuli without being distracted by irrelevant environmental factors (Hallahan & Reeve, 1980; Zentall, 2005). It requires that an individual identify and maintain attention on the target stimulus for several seconds even when distracters are present. It then requires that the individual engage in decision making about which stimuli are relevant and should be focused on to the exclusion of other stimuli. The first four *DSM-IV-TR* characteristics of inattention relate to selective attention.

Learners with problems with selective attention often appear to attend to central stimuli and incidental stimuli indiscriminately (see In the Classroom 9.11). Several research reviews have indicated that students with mild disabilities frequently have more difficulty with selective attention than other learners do or they may achieve their focus on the central signal more slowly (Conte, 1991; Krupski, 1986; Merrill, 1990). They may also exhibit problems identifying the central stimulus because of problems connecting the stimulus in their sensory register or immediate memory with a concept in their knowledge base or long-term memory. Hallahan and Reeve (1980) concluded that problems in selective attention could be attributed to immature or deficient task-appropriate attending strategies. They noted that repeated studies have failed to demonstrate an increase in attending behaviors when these learners are shielded from distractions. The authors concluded from this finding that such learners may lack the cognitive skills needed to connect sensory images with concepts and images stored in their long-term memory. Nonrelevant factors associated with a learning task (i.e., selective attention to novelty) can create problems in the use of selective attention to complete that task (Zentall, 2005).

Selective attention does not refer to occurrences when learners appear to choose not to attend to something being presented to them. It also does not refer to a situation when a child attends to some stimuli and not to others. It refers to that adaptive attention function of being able to focus on relevant target stimuli and to ignore other distracting or irrelevant stimuli. It represents a decision-making function, but not in the sense of willfulness or disobedience. It involves catching hold of a stimulus briefly and focusing attention on the stimulus for a few seconds, long enough to utilize other cognitive processes of perception and memory to give it meaning. At that point, the ability to sustain or maintain attention takes over.

IN THE CLASSROOM 9.12

Sustained Attention

Martha is in middle school and has been diagnosed as having a mild behavioral disorder. Her main problem is attending to the stimuli presented by her teachers or parents. She cannot always decide what is relevant for her to focus on. Her selective attention has shown signs of improvement since she has learned to check herself on what she should be learning. If she does focus on a relevant stimulus initially, her sustained attention still tends to be a problem; she cannot usually maintain her attention long enough for learning to occur. For example, in English class she verified the story she was to read and began the reading with the others. The teacher checked to see that Martha had begun the task and then went on to another student. Unfortunately, after the first two pages, Martha's sustained attention waned, and when the others had completed the story and were ready to discuss it, she was still on the second page.

Sustained Attention.   If continuous attention to the stimulus or task is required once a stimulus has been caught, sustained attention takes over. To be effective as learners, students must develop the ability to maintain focus on incoming information over a sufficient period of time for effective cognitive processing to occur. During this time, learners must also withhold responses to incidental or nonrelevant stimuli. *Sustained attention* is conceptualized as the ability to exercise vigilance, or the continuous monitoring of stimuli, combined with the evaluative capacity to reject those stimuli that are not relevant to the task at hand. The last five inattention criteria in *DSM-IV-TR* relate to sustaining attention (Zentall, 2005).

Learners should have developed the ability to maintain attention on a task for at least 10 minutes in order to be effective at most school and work activities. Most students with learning disabilities, ADHD, or other mild disabilities seem to be particularly affected by problems with sustained attention and will often be observed making more responses to nontarget stimuli over time (Krupski, 1980,1986; Zentall, 2005; see In the Classroom 9.12). Obviously, the ability to attend for significant periods is typically less developed in very young children. Preschool and kindergarten programs are specifically designed to develop this ability by the early primary grades, because it is so essential to effective learning.

The Nature of Attention Demands.   The ability to sustain attention over time is affected by the voluntary attributes of an attention task. Involuntary attention, the most basic and automatic form of attention, is elicited directly by the particular qualities of the stimulus. Such tasks require only passive attending; they are tasks that an individual cannot avoid attending to. The attention of infants and young children is largely determined by the characteristics of the stimulus, and they primarily exhibit involuntary attention. Involuntary attention demands are more predictably responded to by older individuals as well. One can hardly ignore or fail to attend to a fire licking at one's heels!

Voluntary attention, on the other hand, requires some degree of personal effort on the part of the attender. The individual must act consciously and actively to focus on and control the processing of stimuli. With maturity, individuals generally develop an increasing ability to employ voluntary attention and to exert more personal and cognitive control over stimuli. With experience and training, children usually learn to use personal effort to command their own attention, making voluntary attention more possible and dependable.

The performance of students with deficits in attention will be compromised most on those tasks that present the greatest cognitive difficulty, those that present voluntary attention demands (Krupski, 1986; Zentall, 2005). In addition, because of the increasing demands attention makes on other cognitive functions, such as storage and retrieval from memory, deficits in voluntary attention are frequently found to be linked to problems in other areas of cognitive functioning. For this reason, teachers attempting to evaluate the effectiveness of attention in schoolchildren may discover that attention functioning is confounded by problems in memory storage and retrieval and in other strategic and executive functions (see In the Classroom 9.13).

IN THE CLASSROOM 9.13

Voluntary and Involuntary Attention Demands

John is an 8-year-old with mild intellectual disability and has just completed first grade. He has demonstrated difficulty maintaining attention in areas that he does not find appealing. On most days, he is fidgety and roams around the classroom. In contrast, John was recently able to listen attentively for over 30 minutes to a presentation on rainforests, and later he could recall much of the information that had been presented. Relevance in his instruction helps him maintain attention. This example illustrates the differential performance often seen in youngsters when faced with tasks that present involuntary attention demands as compared to those that make voluntary attention demands. Rainforests for John clearly present involuntary attention demands.

Problems in Attention.   Some writers describe attention as a process by which an individual applies concentration and mental powers to an object or task, a process that mediates virtually all other cognitive activities. Others describe it as the capacity for processing (Merrill, 1990). In this framework, effective allocation of attentional resources is required for success in various cognitive tasks. Problems occur when a learner has difficulty making the associations needed to focus on relevant stimuli and then connecting them to prior learning (Krupski, 1986, 1987).

The lack of sustained attention or vigilance of effort is a central attribute of students with ADHD (Barkley, 2006). In an investigation of the attention capabilities of students with learning disabilities and ADHD, Richards and colleagues (1990) observed that students with ADHD seemed to have more difficulty with sustained attention, whereas those with learning disabilities were more likely to exhibit problems in selective attention. Like Robert at the beginning of this chapter, they seem to need longer response times, indicating a slower speed of cognitive processing in general. These researchers concluded that teachers need to carefully investigate the specific nature of an apparent deficit in attention in order to plan appropriate interventions. Although the source and defining characteristics of an attention problem may differ, the fact remains that deficiencies and inefficiencies in attention create problems in learning and everyday functioning for many learners with mild disabilities. A full diagnostic description of their attention attributes is essential to the development of effective educational plans for these students.

Factors That Affect Attention Availability.   In evaluating the nature of a learner's attention capabilities, it is useful to consider the individual within the ecological context, determining how the attention may be affected by environmental factors. The ability to attend or the quality of that attention is affected by the interaction of three variables: the child, the setting, and the task (Krupski, 1981).

In considering the characteristics of a child that may be influencing attention capabilities, it is important to consider the nature of any disabilities because these conditions frequently reduce the effectiveness of attending behaviors. A history of failure may also affect attention. In addition, regardless of the presence or absence of a disability, physiological factors such as hunger, fatigue, and pain will adversely affect attention, whereas good physical health, nutrition, and rest will tend to enhance the ability to attend.

The more structured the demands and the setting, the more difficult it is for any child to respond with appropriate levels of attention. In a highly structured setting such as a classroom, a child's deficits in attention skills are increasingly noticeable and problematic. Such settings permit little leeway in attention responses and penalize the student who is less consistently attentive.

In evaluating task demands, it is important to determine the extent to which a task requires voluntary attention. The more voluntary the attention demands, the more effort the learner must exert to focus attention. Conversely, the more strongly the task draws the attention of the learner, the less the individual has to consciously pay attention and the easier it is to sustain attention.

Sources of Deficits in Attention.   Some problems in selective or sustained attention may be traced to physiological causes, as was discussed in Chapter 7. In such cases, medication may be prescribed as one component of a total treatment plan. It is important to note, however, that

ON THE WEB

The **National Attention Deficit Disorder Association (ADDA;** www.add.org) provides information on the nature of attention problems and information for parents and for adults with attention deficits.

medication alone is unlikely to solve the problem, because attention interacts with all of the components of the cognitive system. Without development of effective strategic processing, performance is unlikely to significantly improve by the use of medication alone (Stolzenberg & Cherkes-Julkowski, 1991).

There is also evidence that some attention problems may be due to a history of failure, which affects the motivation of a learner. Failure frequently reduces motivation and alertness as well as compromising the knowledge base that is integral to completing the attention process. It is also possible that a learner has never learned the subskills necessary to selectively attend and to maintain attention over time. (See Chapter 11 for more discussion of the effect of failure on learning.)

PERCEPTION   Once stimuli are attended to, they must be given meaning. Perception performs this important bridging function in cognitive processing (Faust & Faust, 1980). Perception is the strategic control process by which stimuli are named and given meaning, allowing the learner to then work with these mental representations. Once the perception function has effectively assigned a descriptive name to a stimulus, the learner can use that named stimulus to create new cognitive concepts and to relate those concepts to others within the individual's memory structures (see Figure 9.5).

Perceptual skills are often discussed in the research literature in relationship to learning disabilities. However, it is important to keep in mind that perceptual functioning is central to all cognitive activity and that deficiencies in perception can be identified in any learner, regardless of diagnostic category. For example, we focus on perception when we consider the social perceptions of youngsters with emotional or behavioral disorders or when we investigate the visual and auditory perceptual functions of students with deficits in reading, regardless of the disability category (Torgeson, Kistner, & Morgan, 1987; Willows, 1991).

THEORETICAL FRAMEWORKS OF PERCEPTION   Using the processes of scanning, selecting, attending to, and categorizing sensory stimuli, perception transforms raw stimuli into meaningful

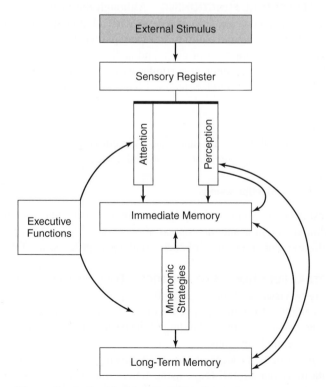

FIGURE 9.5   Role of Perception in the Model of Cognitive Processing

representations. *Perception* is the capturing of stimuli and the matching of those stimuli with relevant representations in long-term memory, thereby giving the stimuli meaning.

Infants are initially unable to perceive their world as a meaningful place because they have no stored representations to match with new stimuli. Gradually, a young child encounters experiences that resemble a previous group of experiences and derives names for those categories of experience. With each concept stored in memory, the process of perception is enhanced. For this reason, perception is most appropriately viewed as an active and constructive process that differs significantly from simple vision or hearing (Dellarosa, 1988).

Torgeson and others (1987) described perception as coding, the process of translating sensory input into a representational form that can be manipulated in a person's working memory and stored in long-term memory. Children with a variety of learning problems seem to be deficient in the speed and effectiveness of this coding process (Torgeson et al., 1987; Torgeson & Kail, 1980).

The following components are related to the process of perception (Carroll, 1976, 1981; Sternberg, 1988):

- Apprehension: Registering the stimulus in the sensory buffers
- Encoding: Forming a mental representation of the stimulus, including its interpretation in terms of attributes, associations, or meanings
- Perceptual integration: Matching the encoded stimulus with a previously stored mental representation

It is important to appreciate the complexity of this interactive role of sensory encoding, storage and retrieval from memory, and cognitive abstraction in performing various perceptual tasks, as indicated in Figure 9.5. Learning problems attributed to perception may actually be related to or exacerbated by difficulties in other areas of cognitive functioning, such as selective attention (sensory encoding), strategic memory processes, or the inadequacy of the working-memory storage area for manipulating information and allowing accurate perceptual matching to occur.

ASSESSMENT OF PERCEPTUAL FUNCTIONING   Although the visual and auditory channels are often discussed and treated as separate entities, the development of perceptual skills is enhanced by the interactions among the abilities. For example, visual and motor development frequently interact to aid the development of each, and auditory perception and visual perception often work together to support learning. In a similar way, a learner's functioning in the area of perception can be best assessed through behavioral observations of everyday activities, such as these (Ariel, 1992):

- Following directions
- Copying letters, including both far- and near-point copying
- Writing, drawing, manipulating various tools and devices
- Listening tasks
- Identifying letters and letter sounds

Careful investigation of all possible hypotheses for a learner's apparent difficulty with perceptual tasks within an actual academic context allows a teacher to plan appropriate assistive supports (i.e., scaffolds). For an example of such a diagnostic process, see Table 9.2.

SPECIFIC PERCEPTUAL FUNCTIONS AND ABILITIES   The general term *perception* refers to the complex processing of visual, auditory, and haptic stimuli. Even though it is important to consider the topic of perception from the perspective of the general cognitive-processing model, it is also useful for teachers to have an understanding of the basic terms used throughout the literature to refer to specific perceptual functions.

Visual perception is the process of ascribing meaning to visual stimuli. Because many school tasks relate to visual stimuli (e.g., using letters, numbers, and words), the ability to

| **Table 9.2** | Example of Appropriate Assessment of Perceptual Functioning |

When asked by her teacher to write her name, Susie falters on the *S,* resulting in distortions of the desired letter shapes, which are frequently reversed. Her teacher wonders why this happens and whether Susie may have a "perceptual disability." Having just learned about the cognitive model and the specific function of perception, her teacher considers a number of possibilities, or hypotheses:

Sensory encoding: *Susie does not recognize that letter shapes differ from each other.*

When given a set of letters, can Susie sort the letters into groups?

When given a set of letters and a card with the letter *S* on it, can Susie pick out the *S*'s from the pile?

Perceptual integration: *Susie cannot determine the essential features that comprise the letter* S.

Can she describe the shape of the letter *S* (e.g., round, two parts of circles)?

Can she pick out the letter *S* from similar letters or numbers (e.g., O, G, C, R, Z, or the number 2)?

Can she identify the reversed letter forms, given a stack of letters?

Memorial storage and retrieval: *Susie cannot retrieve the name and shape of the letter* S *from memory.*

Is the letter *S* stored in her long-term memory?

Has she been taught the letter *S* as a concept or shape?

Does she have a problem retrieving the *S* concept from her long-term memory?

When shown a set of five letters, can she pick out the letter *S*?

Cognitive abstraction: *Susie can identify as* S *only the stimulus letter with which she was taught the letter* S.

Can she identify (name) the letter *S* when it is presented in a variety of forms and sizes?

Motoric output/response: *Susie has a deficit in the motor control needed to produce the letter.*

Can she copy the letter from a model?

Does she have similar copying problems (e.g., shapes, other letters, numbers)?

process visual stimuli is critical to school success. Visual perception can be broken down into subcompetencies:

- *Visual discrimination* is the ability to identify dominant features in different objects and to use that ability to differentiate among a variety of objects. Objects may differ by shape, color, size, pattern, position, and brightness. The ability to discriminate among stimuli based on their distinctive features is an essential first step in visual perception, and visual discrimination of letters and words is crucial to success in learning to read.
- *Visual figure–ground discrimination* is the ability to distinguish an object from its background. Students who have not developed this ability appear easily distracted by irrelevant stimuli.
- *Object recognition* is the ability to recognize the essential nature of an object. Form constancy refers to the awareness that an object generally retains its identity despite its position. Young children learn early in life to use the word *cup* for a round shape with a loop on the side, whether it is right-side up or upside down. This ability is critical to flexible processing of visual stimuli. If a learner is able to identify enough congruency between the stimuli and a stored generalized concept, the image can be named for further processing.
- *Spatial relations* refers to the ability to give meaning to the position of physical objects in space in relation to oneself and other objects. In certain reading and mathematics tasks, form alone is not enough without taking into account relative positions in space. In reading, it is important for a student to develop an awareness that spatial position is related to the identity of some stimuli (e.g., letters like *b, d, p,* and *q*). This understanding is often not

IN THE CLASSROOM 9.14

Visual Perceptual Skills

Nan is a fourth grader diagnosed with ADHD. She appears to be somewhat delayed in the development of visual perceptual skills. Her spelling and reading are affected by problems with visual memory. She has problems revisualizing common words such as *said, went,* and *was,* words she should have mastered by now. She demonstrates adequate visual discrimination and figure–ground discrimination because she can distinguish the dominant features of different stimuli and distinguish them from the background. Nan appears to have a problem with spatial relations, however, which presents itself in her writing, where she frequently reverses the letters *b, p, d,* and *q.*

Joey is a 9-year-old with a learning disability. Recently, when he played Concentration with his tutor, he displayed strong visual memory for pictures. He can also distinguish among items by shape and color, and he can recall the sequence of three objects or pictures. His primary visual perceptual deficit is in the area of spatial relations. In writing he has difficulty determining where to position his letters. They are frequently above and below the line, and spacing between letters and words is erratic. These problems persist even when his tutor provides a model to copy.

Cassie is a 12-year-old girl with mild intellectual disability related to Down syndrome. Her teacher has noted that Cassie experiences recurring problems differentiating between letters that present finer discrimination challenges (e.g., *K* and *R*). Mrs. Green attributes this to problems with visual discrimination. To help Cassie, Mrs. Green taught her some verbalizations to highlight the differences between the visual letter forms, building on her stronger auditory association skills, with positive results.

well established in primary-age youngsters who have previously learned that object identity is a constant, regardless of spatial orientation (Lavoie, 1989, 2009).

- *Visual memory* refers to the ability to recall the dominant features of a stimulus no longer present or to recall the sequence of items presented visually. In school this skill is especially useful in spelling. However, the concept of visual memory has a more generalized function. In order to ascribe meaning to a specific visual stimulus, a learner needs to call up a visual memory with a tag or label. The ability to name a visual stimulus and complete the perceptual process depends on that ability.

- *Visual closure* is the ability to identify figures that are presented in incomplete form or that have unclear elements. Visual closure is related to visual memory because the remainder of a word or sentence is filled in by the mind's reconstruction of a likely match. Visual closure allows capable readers to read a word or sentence without actually processing all of the elements. Without the skill of visual closure, the speed of perceptual processing of written material is slowed because each element must be individually processed (see In the Classroom 9.14).

Auditory perception refers to the ability to interpret auditory stimuli and to attach meaning to what is heard. Because most auditory perceptual skills develop early in childhood, less attention is given to the development of these skills in the elementary classroom. However, early reading depends on a student's ability to make very fine auditory judgments, and difficulties in this area must be identified and remediated. Some of the auditory perception subskills include the following:

- *Auditory discrimination* is the ability to recognize differences between sounds. Initially, a child must make discriminations between distinctly different sounds, but reading and spelling instruction soon requires them to be able to make perceptual judgments between very similar sounds. Phonological and phonemic awareness is an important aspect of auditory discrimination. As children develop the ability to discriminate between the sounds they hear, they also begin to understand the basic structure of language and develop an awareness that language can be divided into words, syllables, and sounds.

- ***Auditory blending*** is the ability to make a complete word by blending the individual phonological elements. Students without the ability to perceive the whole as a combination of parts experience difficulty in reading programs based on synthetic phonetic approaches or in blending letter sounds into words.
- ***Auditory figure–ground discrimination*** is the ability to distinguish a sound from its background. An individual must have the ability to lift the relevant auditory stimulus from its sound background in order to be successful in school.
- ***Auditory memory*** refers to the ability to recognize and recall previously presented auditory stimuli or a sequence of items presented orally. Rote memory of spelling words and other facts (e.g., multiplication tables) makes use of this skill. Even more importantly, auditory memory provides a matching template against which new stimuli can be evaluated.
- ***Auditory closure*** is the ability to identify words and other auditory elements that have been presented in incomplete form or that have unclear elements. Effective auditory closure skills permit perceptual information to be processed more efficiently, especially in lectures and discussion, because a listener does not need to process every phonological element for meaning to be derived.
- ***Auditory association*** is the ability to relate ideas, find relationships, make associations, and categorize information obtained by listening. It is the final stage in auditory perceptual processing and completes the determination of the meaning of a particular stimulus (see In the Classroom 9.15).

Haptic perception refers to the ability to ascribe meaning to tactile and kinesthetic stimuli. The term *tactile* refers to the sense of touch, and the term *kinesthetic* relates to the sensations received through body movement. Information received through the fingers and skin as well as from the movement of parts of the body must be interpreted and given meaning, just as visual and auditory stimuli are handled.

IN THE CLASSROOM 9.15

Auditory Perceptual Abilities

Jeremy is a 10-year-old with an emotional disorder accompanied by ADHD. He seems to have a problem making auditory associations. This causes him significant problems in his regular education class when the teacher is presenting information orally. Jeremy recently experienced problems in a lesson on outlining. He was unable to use the given information to find the relationships in the information he had already assembled and to use that information to compose his outline. Although he understood the words the teacher was saying, he was unable to associate those words with his previous learning in order to perform the task.

Christy is a fifth grader with a mild intellectual disability and continuing speech impairments. Although she has great difficulty pronouncing words that are similar (e.g., *etch* and *edge*), she has no difficulty hearing the difference between these similar words. This strength in auditory discrimination leads her speech therapist to believe that she will eventually be able to articulate the words correctly.

Jonathan is a 14-year-old student in a resource program for students with learning disabilities. His teacher has noted that auditory processing appears to be a strength for him. He can recall information that has been presented to him orally, using his auditory perceptual abilities. In particular, his auditory memory appears to be particularly strong, because he has little trouble retrieving material that was presented days before. His teacher has hypothesized that because Jonathan doesn't have to spend time deciphering each word, as he does in reading, he is able to listen, attach meaning to the words, and then store the information in his long-term memory. For this reason, Jonathan's IEP provides access to books on tape.

IN THE CLASSROOM 9.16

Perceptual Overload

Maggie is a second grader with a learning disability. Her classroom teacher complains that she is always daydreaming and looking out the window. Surprisingly, though, she often seems to know the answer when she is called on. Her resource teacher noticed one day that when Maggie maintained eye contact with her teacher during oral spelling practice, she often made mistakes, but when she was looking sideways at the wall, she was 100 percent accurate. Puzzled, the resource teacher talked to her about it. Maggie's answer was "When I look at the teacher, her face gets in the way of the words."

Perceptual motor integration involves the interaction of perceptual functioning (using any sense) with a specific motor activity. In school we are most concerned with the abilities to integrate perceived visual stimuli with the movement of body parts. The abilities to copy, draw, and write each involve significant visual motor integration.

Two areas in which the processing of sensory stimuli can become problematic include tactile defensiveness and perceptual overload (Lerner, 1993). Tactile defensiveness is characterized by extreme sensitivity and discomfort in response to the slightest tactile stimulation, impeding a student's processing of haptic stimuli. Perceptual overload refers to the tendency in some individuals for information from one sensory input system to interfere with information coming in from another. For example, children like Maggie (see In the Classroom 9.16) can listen or watch but have difficulty doing both simultaneously.

ISSUES CONCERNING PERCEPTUAL ASSESSMENT AND TRAINING   Early in the current special education era, especially in the field of learning disabilities, it was believed that assessment and training of basic cognitive functions such as perception would allow students with disabilities to eventually function similarly to their typical age peers. Consider this seemingly analogous situation: Physical therapy is prescribed for a person who has experienced a physical injury, based on the assumption that if range of motion and strength are regained, the person will once again be able to perform the full range of physical activities impaired by the injury, as well learn new physical skills.

In much the same way, it was reasoned that if perception is impaired, providing therapy should improve those fundamental abilities, allowing the learner to then use these improved perceptual skills to master other skills involving perception, such as reading and writing, without the need for continued therapeutic interventions. During the 1970s and 1980s, special educators, particularly for children with learning disabilities, operated on this deficit-remediation assumption. It was reasoned that identifying and removing the deficit would permit typical levels of functioning to be attained in the future (Wodrich & Joy, 1986).

Experience soon cast doubt on this assumption (Gresham, 2002a; Hessler & Sosnowsky, 1979; Truscott et al., 2005). Meta-analyses of the research on perceptual motor training programs indicated a lack of research support for the "aptitude/treatment interaction" or "processing deficit and remediation" hypotheses (Hessler & Sosnowsky, 1979; Kavale & Mattson, 1983). Despite extensive testing of process skills and intensive remedial programs, there was little or no improvement in overall achievement; and the effort spent on ineffective programs wasted valuable time and resources, leaving these learners even further behind. In 1987 the Council for Learning Disabilities issued a policy statement opposing the continuation of measurement and training of perceptual and perceptual–motor functions (Council for Learning Disabilities, 1987b).

During the 1980s, researchers and practitioners began to experiment with other answers (Torgeson, 1991). A focus on direct instruction techniques and cognitive strategies replaced the earlier process training approaches as treatments of choice. Researchers and teachers looked for alternatives that were consistent with the growing understanding of learning and cognition. Behavioral models of academic remediation (e.g., direct instruction) focused on the academic tasks themselves. It was suggested that direct instruction be used to remediate identified academic deficits while also addressing prerequisite skills for learning (Rosenshine, 1986; Rosenshine & Stevens, 1986; Treiber & Lahey, 1983).

By the 1990s, the focus was returning to the cognitive functioning of students with mild disabilities. Researchers and educators began to use instructional strategies that responded to deficits in cognitive processing, including perception, and to do so in a context that enhanced academic achievement (Torgeson, 1991). Such techniques include instruction in metacomprehension strategies, phonological awareness, and other learning strategies (Benevento, 2004; Deshler et al., 1996). Educators now recognize and understand the complexity of perceptual and cognitive functioning, the context in which cognitive processing occurs, and the interaction of cognitive skills with academic demands, and they use that knowledge to plan effective instruction.

MNEMONIC, OR MEMORY, STRATEGIES   The skills used to encode, process, store, and retrieve information are what most people associate with the word *memory*. These skills and processes involve the efficient and effective application of mnemonic strategic control processes. It is the ability to use these mnemonic—that is, memory—strategies that is implied when we say that a learner has a "good memory" or that a student has "memory deficits." Deficiencies in the use of mnemonic strategies usually lead to academic and other cognitive difficulties. Learners with mild disabilities frequently rely on a small repertoire of strategies or on less flexible ones, such as rehearsal. These deficits in mnemonic strategies compromise learning and functioning.

As mentioned earlier, the mnemonic strategies most often applied include rehearsal (verbal, written, or motoric), organization (including chunking, clustering, categorization, mnemonics, and coding or paired associates), and elaboration (including imagery and semantic elaboration). Rehearsal is the most primitive of the mnemonic strategies and is heavily used in both immediate memory and long-term memory, particularly by less sophisticated learners. It is hypothesized that the short-term memory portion of immediate memory is reserved for use as a rehearsal buffer (Merrill, 1990; Swanson & Cooney, 1991; Torgeson et al., 1987; Wyer & Srull, 1989). The common experience of repeating a telephone number over and over until reaching the phone and dialing it illustrates the application of rehearsal in immediate memory. It seems as if the repetition makes a deeper, more durable memory trace of the concept or stimulus, keeping it accessible for a longer period. Rehearsal can be oral, written, or kinesthetic. In each case, the purpose is to retain an exact copy of the idea or action, much like a photocopying machine.

Rehearsal strategies are useful in preserving a copy of a stimulus, but they are limited in their usefulness in developing more complex cognitive structures or concepts within long-term memory. Used primarily for rote memory of specific facts or automatic performance of specific functions, rehearsal is most applicable to lower-level or convergent thinking, facts, concepts, and actions. Use of rehearsal as a memory strategy does not promote the development of the connections between concepts—connections required for efficient and complex thinking. One might imagine it as a cognitive equivalent of the kitchen junk drawer. Everything is stored in that drawer, but there is no rhyme or reason to the storage, and finding a specific item is often difficult and time-consuming. Learners with mild disabilities tend to rely on simple forms of rehearsal to the exclusion of other strategies, and their learning is consequently less efficient and effective.

Strategies that utilize organization, on the other hand, make use of purposeful connections between items to facilitate their storage and ultimate retrieval. Specific strategies include these:

- Chunking—grouping items that relate to one another in a meaningful way
- Clustering—arranging items in categories or in relationship to a superordinate category or concept

- Ordering—arranging items in some logical sequence
- Paired associates—the connection of a new term with a term already in the learner's repertoire
- Mnemonics—the use of an idiosyncratic or artificially meaningful method of organizing items to be remembered (e.g., "Every good boy does fine" to remember the letters of the treble staff in music)

Organizational strategies are similar to the addition of trays to the kitchen junk drawer to hold specific categories of items (e.g., a tray for screws, a tray for small tools, a tray for glue and tape). Grouping these kitchen items makes finding them again much easier and more likely. It also makes storage of new items faster and more effective. Strategies such as chunking, clustering, and paired associates not only serve the basic memory storage function but also increase the likelihood that the learner will relate the material being learned to other previously acquired material in a meaningful way, fostering the development of more complex concepts within the long-term memory knowledge base. Retrieval is enhanced as well, because the retrieval of one concept or fact tends to open up access to related and connected information. Learners with mild disabilities tend not to utilize this strategy unless provided with explicit instruction in the connection of one concept to another. Their weaker original learning tends to reduce the likelihood that they will build strong categories of knowledge or that they will see the connection of new learning to prior learning.

Elaboration represents the third grouping of memory strategies, creating enhanced images to aid storage and retrieval. Semantic elaboration involves verbal enhancement of the concept(s) to be stored and may include establishing a richer context for the item (e.g., relating the concept to a story, metaphor, or analogy). Imagery involves pairing the concept with a visual image to enhance the strength of the memory trace. In both cases, use of verbal or visual images creates a stronger mental image or representation of the concept. Students with mild disabilities are aided in learning when their teachers help them create rich pictures of the material to be learned or when techniques such as semantic webs are used to connect the material visually in meaningful ways.

When the need for retrieval of stored data arises, these strategies aid the retrieval process in reverse. Using cues (fragments of information), we reconstruct the information after a search of long-term memory. When the fragment or cue connects with a likely item, the individual reconstructs the image and transfers it back to working memory for use. Information cannot be manipulated until it has been retrieved and returned to the working memory area, much as information on a computer's hard drive cannot be used until it has been brought back to the desktop (see In the Classroom 9.17).

Executive Functions

Throughout the entire cognitive process, the use of executive functions, or metacognitive regulation, is the hallmark of an effective learner. Using these executive functions, learners determine the possibility and need to use one or more strategic control components and then monitor and evaluate the effectiveness of the processing. Drawing on their conditional knowledge and the ability to plan, organize, monitor, and evaluate, efficient learners engage in making a series of decisions, including deciding on the best mnemonic strategy for a given task, checking on the implementation of the strategy, and determining the effectiveness of the strategy was. If the strategy is not proving adequate to the task, further decisions are made about alternative strategies (Benevento, 2004; Meltzer, 2007; Reynolds & Horton, 2008; Swanson & Saez, 2003; Sweller, 2004).

Following the development of a few specific cognitive strategies, typical learners usually develop a degree of general strategy knowledge, including the understanding that the use of strategies increases cognitive effectiveness and that effort is required to achieve the full benefit of strategy use. This general strategy knowledge does not develop until some elements of the specific strategy knowledge base are in place (Borkowski & Kurtz, 1987). For this reason, learners such as those with mild disabilities who do not develop and use specific cognitive strategies are also hampered in developing a comprehensive strategic approach to cognitive functioning. As

IN THE CLASSROOM 9.17

Mnemonic Strategies

Barry appears to have average memory skills in spite of his diagnosis of mild intellectual disability. He seems particularly successful with the use of rehearsal strategies in learning math facts and spelling. When he writes his spelling words a number of times each day, he does well on the weekly tests. Other practice activities, such as looking up the words in the dictionary and filling in the words in sentences, seem much less effective. His teacher is concerned that his exclusive reliance on rehearsal strategies limits his overall cognitive development in areas of learning where rehearsal is not an effective strategy. When rehearsal fails to help him store information in memory, he tends to become more field dependent and increasingly depends on his teacher or others to structure his learning.

Organization seems to be Ben's preferred memory strategy. If he can relate something to what he already knows, he tends to remember it well. Rehearsal and elaboration are strategies he still rarely uses effectively. His dependence on only one method of storage and retrieval hinders his cognitive processing.

Amanda experiences difficulties in her work in sixth grade due to problems in the use of mnemonic strategies. Although she makes some use of rehearsal, her use of other strategies, such as elaboration, is largely nonexistent. She does not have the capability to create or enhance the meaning attributable to particular stimuli. In language arts class, when she was recently asked to memorize a short poem, Amanda became upset and said she couldn't do it. The problem was that the task was too much for rehearsal alone, and she lacked other strategies to enable her to do it. Her teacher stepped in and, by using drawings and gestures to accompany the words, provided the meaningful elaboration for her. With these cues, Amanda quickly caught on and was able to successfully complete the memorization assignment. Based on this success, her resource teacher plans to work with her on developing strategic use of elaboration in the future.

learners begin to develop beliefs about their own self-efficacy and the effect of effort, these motivational understandings also become a part of the general strategy knowledge base and increase the likelihood that the individuals will deploy strategies when needed in the future. Such attributional and self-efficacy beliefs are essential for the operation of the system and will be discussed further in Chapter 11.

Tying all of these elements together and providing the oversight required for their use is the job of the executive functions. They develop only when sufficient specific and general strategy frameworks have been established. When faced with an unstructured or ambiguous learning task, a learner must independently evaluate the situation and determine a strategy to be deployed. Executive functions are used to monitor the effectiveness of that strategy use and to refine specific strategy knowledge based on experience; they also aid in the development of self-regulated cognitive behavior in general. Use of such executive functions as checking, monitoring, and revising strategies enhances the strategic knowledge base. The executive functions may be thought of as traffic officers, orchestrating the flow of information and redirecting traffic patterns as needed. They also function as the highway department, which accumulates information on traffic flow and accidents and then uses that information to modify traffic patterns and maintain the highway system.

The metacognitive skills used by learners to determine the effectiveness of their comprehension during cognitive activities are central to efficient cognitive processing. Such skills include self-instruction, self-questioning, self-monitoring, and self-evaluation. Students with intellectual disabilities, learning disabilities, ADHD, ASD, or emotional or behavioral disorders frequently fail to develop these specific strategies and executive functions, or they fail to use them effectively, displaying deficits in control of attention by their executive functions, (Swanson & Saez, 2003). These students also present difficulties in coordination of memory systems, encoding and retrieval strategies, and manipulation of material in the immediate memory

ON THE WEB

The **Center for Research on Learning** (www.ku-crl. org) provides information about learning strategies and the strategies intervention model, which can be used to develop cognitive strategies in students with disabilities.

UNIVERSAL DESIGN FOR LEARNING *IN ACTION* 9

Supporting Cognitive Learning

Principle I:
Use multiple and flexible means of representation[a]

Because learning begins with a student taking in sensory stimuli through the sensory register, ensure that all students can see and hear instructional presentations.

Provide instruction in a variety of modalities, allowing students to depend on their stronger sensory register channel while supplementing it with the weaker channel.

Use clear, multiple examples and nonexamples to help all students build strong cognitive structures in long-term memory.

Teach the use of graphic organizers to provide scaffolds for learning content.

Teach strategies for performing common cognitive tasks.

Model the full process for the completion of cognitive tasks to correct misconceptions students have.

Use note sheets to go along with PowerPoints or lectures to reduce the tendency for students to write less relevant sentences and words, allowing them to follow along with the lesson without losing their focus on the key points.

Principle II:
Allow multiple and flexible means of expression[a]

Provide a list of tasks to be completed by the students, and then allow them to choose the order of completion. This permits students to plan their work in the way that best suits their interests and skills, maximizing attention.

When appropriate, allow learners to choose to complete projects individually or in small groups.

Encourage finding multiple ways to complete tasks such as mathematics problems; reinforce that there are multiple ways to reach a goal.

Principle III:
Provide multiple and flexible means of engagement[a]

Teach the use of a variety of cognitive scaffolds for students to use in learning how to perform cognitive tasks (e.g., paired associate learning, mnemonics); students can then use them as needed.

Post cue cards/posters for common strategies to assist field-dependent students in completing learning tasks more confidently.

Allow students to choose to use computers or calculators to reduce the cognitive load of certain learning tasks.

Monitor students engaged in learning tasks, and provide additional coaching/ scaffolding for those who do not develop learning strategies on their own.

Make computers available for drill and practice, reducing the effort needed to learn basic skills information and providing more immediate feedback.

Principle IV:
Create a community of learners in the classroom[b]

Group students heterogeneously in cooperative learning groups to accomplish cognitive tasks, allowing students with ineffective learning strategies to benefit from the models of effective strategies used by more successful learners.

Design cooperative learning activities with clear group interdependence as well as individual accountability for learning.

Promote use of peer-mediated activities such as paired reading.

Actively encourage students to explain alternative ways to learn content or solve problems; modeling acceptance of such alternative strategies supports respect among learners for each other's attempts.

Provide time to conference with students individually to monitor and assess their use of critical cognitive learning strategies.

UNIVERSAL DESIGN FOR LEARNING *IN ACTION* 9

Supporting Cognitive Learning (*continued*)

Principle V: ***Establish a positive instructional climate***[b]	Clearly identify learning objectives to assist all students in focusing on and sustaining attention to the core content. Differentiate learning objectives to respond to learner capability and needs. Ensure that learning goals provide challenges appropriate to each learner. Recognize learners' creative ways to solve learning problems. Acknowledge learners in attempting difficult tasks.

Principles adapted from (a) Center for Applied Special Technology (CAST), 2008 and (b) McGuire, Scott, and Shaw, 2006.

(see In the Classroom 9.18). As a result, such students are frequently less successful in learning tasks and environments as well as in problem solving (Merrill, 1990; Ryan, Short, & Weed, 1986; Swanson & Cooney, 1991; Torgeson et al., 1987). Instructional assistance in developing such strategies has been shown to be useful in helping learners develop more efficient and effective cognitive functions (Benevento, 2004; Deshler et al., 1996; Meltzer, 2007).

This body of research suggests that what is needed is a focus on the opportunity to learn. As IDEA states, students cannot be identified as having a disability without having had the opportunity to learn, to develop their knowledge base, and to develop the strategic control processes and executive functions necessary for learning. Educators and families must find ways to work together to provide the rich language and learning experiences required for cognitive development and to bridge the worlds of the family, community, and school.

IN THE CLASSROOM 9.18

Executive Functions

Amy's problems in cognitive processing seem to be related to a breakdown in her executive functions. She appears attentive, but her processing is slow, and she tries to pay attention to everything. She has difficulty sorting out which information is relevant. Although she is able to focus on a specific source—for example, the teacher—she cannot easily identify which information from the teacher is most useful or relevant. She tries to process everything the teacher says. Without a useful repertoire of organizational skills to sort the information in her short-term memory, she gets confused. It is not apparent to the speaker that Amy is not following the conversation until she is asked to respond. She can typically answer questions about the first things the speaker said but not the later. As long as information is presented slowly and in small chunks, she seems to be able to work with it rather well.

Ellie seems to have a number of gaps in her executive functioning. Even though she seems to be paying attention and appears to recognize which information is relevant to the task, she seems to lack the ability to determine which strategies to use to relate this new information to what she already knows. She does not have effective executive functioning that will allow her to access her declarative memory efficiently and effectively. When asked what year she was born, she could not answer and was unable to apply any retrieval strategies that might help her find the answer. This suggests a deficit in her executive functioning decision processes, accompanied by difficulties transferring information from both her procedural and her declarative memories to her working memory. Her teachers have been working on short-term memory functions and will begin working on improving organizational and rehearsal strategies to aid storage in and retrieval from her long-term memory. Without further training in general strategy selection and metamemory skills, the specific strategy training is unlikely to be very effective or to generalize to other tasks.

Summary

This chapter has considered the concept of cognitive functioning from a variety of perspectives. The constructivists view learning and cognitive functioning from a developmental point of view. According to Piaget, learning results as children encounter discrepant information and use the processes of assimilation and accommodation to incorporate the information into their cognitive schema. Vygotsky viewed cognitive development from a social constructivist framework, recognizing the importance of a skilled mentor in learning. Cognitive style research looks at the way a learner approaches various tasks. Field dependence/independence refers to the need to depend on cues from the environment in making perceptual decisions. Impulsivity/reflectivity refers to the use of reflection before taking action.

Information-processing frameworks provide another useful theory of cognitive functioning. The cognitive model consists of structural components and strategic control components, coordinated by executive functions. The structural components include (a) the sensory register, which receives all sensory stimuli; (b) the immediate memory, which stores information briefly (short-term memory) for processing (working memory); and (c) the long-term memory, where information can be stored for use at any time in the future.

The structural components are connected by the strategic control components. Attention includes three subfunctions: (a) coming to attention, (b) selective attention, and (c) sustained attention. Perception attaches a name and meaning to stimuli before transferring them to working memory. Memory strategies round out the strategic control components. Coordinating all of these processes and events is the job of the executive functions, which direct the selection of appropriate strategies, monitor ongoing cognitive activity, modify processes to meet cognitive needs, and evaluate the effectiveness of the outcomes.

Individual students with mild disabilities may exhibit a variety of problems in cognitive functioning, all of which can lead to problems in school achievement. Regardless of their diagnostic categories, these students may develop cognitively more slowly than those without disabilities. Educators working with such students will find it useful to fully identify the learners' cognitive strengths and needs so that the most effective remediation and support can be provided.

A Case Study • Charlene

Charlene is a junior at the local high school in the small town where she lives. She has developed considerable artistic talent and hopes one day to be a graphic designer. She appears to be a happy, emotionally stable teenager despite her longstanding learning disability, which is accompanied by her inattentive type of ADHD. Charlene's primary areas of difficulty have involved the use of memory, particularly for auditory stimuli. She also experiences problems in use of expressive language, particularly in the areas of grammar and semantics. It is these areas of concern that initially brought her into contact with special education as a young child.

Charlene was served by special education personnel throughout elementary school and had the services of a one-to-one aide for part of that time. Now she is served by the high school's resource program, receiving supplemental assistance only during study halls. Although this assistance is available on her request, she rarely asks for it. At age 17, she places a premium on independent functioning.

As her resource teacher, Mr. Stewart, reflected on Charlene's current levels of functioning in preparation for her annual review meeting, he made a number of observations. Although Charlene seems to want to act in an independent manner, she actually appears to depend heavily on her surrounding environment for cues to guide perceptual decision making. She needs the reinforcement of having assignments, directions, and procedures written on the board. Often she will check and recheck the directions with a peer before proceeding. Without these guides, she loses confidence and spends extra time going back and checking and rechecking.

Charlene appears to think logically when presented with problem-solving situations, but she often requires the use of manipulatives and other concrete representations of the problem as an aid. With the use of manipulatives, she proceeds to draw her own conclusions. Recently, her American history class was discussing everyday life in the 18th century. It was not until her teacher brought in some actual examples of the tools and clothing used during that time that she was able to understand the difficulty of life in that period.

Mr. Stewart believes that Charlene's problems in memory are related to her disability in attention. She appears to have difficulty focusing on relevant stimuli. She is easily distracted by irrelevant stimuli, such as people in the hall or candy on another student's desk. She seems unable to make the decisions needed to focus on the relevant features of a task or on the teacher's instructions. If, after a number of attempts and cues, she does focus her attention appropriately, she has trouble maintaining her attention for a sufficient period, despite having been on medication for a number of years.

Mr. Stewart has noted some factors that might be affecting Charlene's attention. First, the ADHD diagnosis suggests that problems with various attention tasks are to be expected. Next, it seems that the form of instruction and the tasks assigned by Charlene's teachers do not present strong attention signals. Charlene says that school is boring and that it is too hard to pay attention, an observation that appears related to the repetitious nature of the tasks and Charlene's perception of their lack of explicit value for her everyday life. This lack of attention is particularly evident in her academic classes, in which instruction is primarily in the form of lectures that do not require much active student participation. Activities in the class continue, with or without Charlene focusing on what the teacher is saying. Finally, throughout much of the day, Charlene is in a setting that is fairly unstructured in its demands on her, and Mr. Stewart notices that Charlene's attention lapses often go unnoticed and are not viewed as a problem.

If Charlene is able to focus her attention and remain focused, she appears to be able to transfer information effectively into her memory structure. In art and technical drawing classes, Charlene sees the information as interesting and valuable, and she uses appropriate means to store it in her long-term memory. Interestingly, however, her past annual reviews have noted problems in memory retrieval. In English and social studies, she appears to have difficulty dealing with the large amount of information she is asked to process at one time. She is unable to quickly make the connections needed to save the information, and it rapidly passes from her mind. She most often resorts to rote rehearsal as a memory strategy, a practice that seems to be inadequate in dealing with the large amounts of complex material in the 11th-grade curriculum. Lack of access to information in memory results in poor test scores and inadequate performance on other assignments.

Noting Charlene's dependence on rehearsal, Mr. Stewart suspects that this restricted repertoire of memory strategies is impeding learning. When Charlene uses rehearsal instead of other more appropriate memory strategies, her concept development is hindered and retrieval is compromised. Although Charlene is aware of other ways of dealing with memory tasks, she either fails to use them or uses them so inefficiently that she does not benefit from them.

Mr. Stewart has tried to help Charlene by prescribing particular study strategies as well as by monitoring her completion of tasks. At times, Mr. Stewart even completes portions of the assignment for Charlene, modeling the processes. He believes that this coaching will eventually help Charlene learn to apply these organizational and elaborative memory strategies herself. Mr. Stewart is surprised that Charlene still seems to distrust her own abilities and that she continues to look to her teachers for cues and information rather than beginning to depend on her own cognitive and organizational resources.

Discussion

Review the information about Charlene in the context of cognitive functioning. Specifically, what indications do you see in Charlene's functioning with regard to the following, and what are the instructional implications of these factors?

- Level and process of cognitive development described by Piaget
- The process of cognitive development described by Vygotsky
- Field dependence and independence
- Impulsivity and reflectivity
- Structural cognitive components: sensory register, immediate memory (including working and short-term memories), and long-term memory
- Attention: alertness, selective attention, and sustained attention
- Perceptual abilities
- Memory strategies
- Executive functions

CHAPTER 10

Language Characteristics

Questions *to Guide Your Study*

- What is language? Why is language so important to everyday functioning?

- Describe the three components and the five skills of language.

- Why is it important to assess and develop pragmatics skills in students with disabilities?

- How do the auditory and visual channels of language differ? Why is awareness of this difference important in understanding language difficulties?

- Describe the relationship among the two receptive and two expressive language functions.

- How do the three types of listening differ from one another?

- Why is it important to determine whether reading problems are related to decoding or to comprehension or to both areas?

- Why is it important to determine whether problems in written expression are related to comprehensibility or to mechanics (grammar) or to both areas?

Meet Tom

Tom was initially placed in special education because of his difficulties in first grade. Throughout his years in school, Tom has had difficulties in cognitive processing and the use of language. This fall, he began eighth grade in a class for students with learning disabilities.

Tom tries very hard to listen when spoken to, and Ms. Allen, his teacher, usually describes him as being attentive. He participates well in class discussions and often volunteers to answer questions. When he knows an answer, he responds confidently. When he is unsure of the answer, his response is generally a simple shrug. He seems to have a hard time expressing his uncertainty and has difficulty saying, "I don't know." At times it seems to Ms. Allen that Tom's lack of response may be related to problems with retrieving the words stored in his long-term memory.

Most of Tom's written work is understandable. Although grammatical errors are common in his writing, the meaning of the written message is apparent most of the time. His spelling is generally phonetically correct, although vowel digraphs and other nonphonetic spelling patterns cause him difficulty. Tom takes pride in his very neat cursive penmanship, voluntarily copying over work that he considers messy.

Although he is able in many cases to comprehend what he hears, his expressive and receptive skills in social environments often prove to be unreliable. As a young adolescent, these deficits in social communication are beginning to set him apart from his peers. Ms. Allen frequently notes his misreading of social cues and occurrences of inappropriate social behaviors in Tom's classroom and social activities. Messages conveyed by his nonverbal communication behaviors (e.g., facial expressions, body language) frequently do not match his verbalizations. He frequently moves in too close to the person with whom he is conversing, making casual conversation uncomfortable.

Tom tends to misinterpret what peers intend to communicate to him and others. Last week, he was observing two other students playing around in the classroom before school, calling each other names in jest. Tom joined in but was very puzzled when the other students reacted negatively. He couldn't understand why they were blaming him for what appeared to him to be the same behavior in which they were engaging. He failed to take into account the effect of the existing relationship between the other two students, which formed an acceptable context for their teasing. Such occurrences are increasingly frequent as Tom's lack of social language skills interferes with his ability to develop normal adolescent relationships. He is mystified by his lack of success in this area. Ms. Allen is concerned that if this problem is not addressed, Tom's language difficulties will be compounded by isolation and rejection.

THINKING QUESTIONS

How might Tom's language learning disability be related to the social problems he is experiencing as a young adolescent? What might the outcome be if this is not addressed in his educational plan?

- What special issues are involved in serving learners of English as an additional language?

- What is the distinction between language differences and language disabilities? Of what importance is this distinction to educators, parents, and students?

DEFINITION OF LANGUAGE

Language is that uniquely human behavior that involves the use of vocal sounds and, in many cultures, the corresponding written symbols to comprehend, form, and express thoughts and feelings. The term *language* generally refers to any code employing signs, symbols, or gestures to communicate ideas meaningfully between human beings (Bloom, 1988; Owens, 2010; Pinker & Jackendoff, 2005). As Tom's story indicates, it is also a social tool that is used to communicate meanings, feelings, and intentions by means of a symbol system specifically designed to transmit and receive social messages. Language is an integral part of learning and thinking; it is not merely synonymous with or limited to oral expression.

Language competencies are critical to success as a learner (Bashir & Scavuzzo, 1992; O'Neal & Ringler, 2010; Thatcher, Fletcher, & Decker, 2008). Language is the vehicle by which content knowledge is presented and elaborated on. Success in learning depends in large part on a student's ability to effectively and efficiently process information in spoken and text formats. Language is also the means by which an individual becomes part of a social group. Educators and curriculum designers assume, sometimes incorrectly, that learners bring to learning events basic competencies in the understanding and use of language. Students' ability to share a common language with teachers and other learners is critical to their success in the learning environment. Finally, language is a tool for self-expression, a means by which a young person develops a sense of personal identity as an individual in society.

The word *language* is used throughout this book as a collective noun, referring to all of the varied languages human beings use to communicate with one another. The word *language* does not necessarily refer to English. The concepts developed throughout this chapter can generally be applied to the functional capabilities of most languages and language users, including those who communicate in English, in another language, in sign language, or in a dialect or cultural variant of English (O'Neal & Ringler, 2010). As noted in the section on language differences later in this chapter, learners of English as an additional language do present special concerns in the classroom, and it is necessary to carefully evaluate the language use of such learners to determine whether their language competencies are being affected primarily by a language disability, a difference, or both (Garcia & Tyler, 2010; Gersten, Brengelman, & Jimenez, 1994).

ON THE WEB

The **American Speech-Language-Hearing Association** (www.asha.org) provides resources related to disorders in communication and hearing, as well as referral information.

IMPAIRMENTS IN SPEECH AND LANGUAGE

The American Speech-Language-Hearing Association (ASHA) defines disorders in speech and language as follows:

> When a person is unable to produce speech sounds correctly or fluently, or has problems with his or her voice, then he or she has a **speech disorder**. Difficulties pronouncing sounds, or articulation disorders, and stuttering are examples of speech disorders. When a person has trouble understanding others (receptive language), or sharing thoughts, ideas, and feelings completely (expressive language), then he or she has a **language disorder**. (American Speech-Language-Hearing Association, 2010)

Students with speech and language impairments comprise close to 20 percent of all students served under IDEA (ages 6–21) and almost half of all preschool children (ages 3–5) with disabilities (U.S. Department of Education, 2009). A significant number of students with other conditions (e.g., intellectual disabilities, learning disabilities, emotional disturbance, ASDs, or cerebral palsy) also receive speech/language support as a related service. This makes speech/language disorders among the most prevalent IDEA conditions. In addition, in 2008 English was an additional language (EAL) for 10.9 million public school students (21 percent), with 2.7 million of those speaking English with difficulty (5 percent of all students; National Center for Education Statistics, 2010).

When one considers all of the needs of (a) students with disabilities, (b) learners of English as an additional language, and (c) learners without disabilities who nevertheless need assistance in developing effective communication and literacy skills, it appears likely that language challenges will affect a majority of students at some point during their time in school. The need for all teachers to be language teachers is apparent.

Prevalence data underscore the importance of early intervening language services. Since half of all preschool children with disabilities have speech/language impairments and the number of children with speech/language impairments increases steadily from ages 3 to 8, before dropping off substantially after age 9, it appears that this is a condition that affects young children most dramatically (U.S. Department of Education, 2009). Quality early language interventions have the greatest potential to resolve these difficulties before they lead to other problems. General and special educators who are able to analyze the nature and extent of language barriers during the early childhood years (birth to grade 3) will be in the best position to collaborate on the design of helpful interventions. The remainder of this chapter will focus on diagnostic frameworks to assist in the analysis of learners' language strengths and needs across the grade levels.

LANGUAGE COMPONENTS AND SKILLS

Language is generally regarded as having three components: form, content, and use (Brice, 2004; Johnson & Croasmun, 1991; J. E. Roberts, Price, & Malkin, 2007). Form is related to the rules by which a given communication system, or language, is governed; form is the "how" of language. Content refers to the "meaning" component; it is the "what" that we listen to and read, talk, and write about. Use is the third component and is the reason, purpose, or "why" of language. Language competence depends on the integration of these three components. Bloom (1988) suggests that problems in language may be the result of

- Simple delay in development of language competence
- Disruption in one or more of the three components of language
- Failure to integrate the three components functionally

Language is also composed of five groups of skills that are associated with the components of form, content, and use (Brice, 2004). Form includes phonology, morphology, and syntax; content generally relates to semantics; and use refers to pragmatics (Owens, 2010). Although

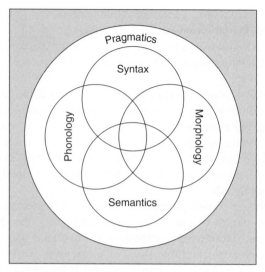

FIGURE 10.1 Functionalist Theory of Language Skills
Source: From Owens, *Language Disorders: A Functional Approach to Assessment and Intervention* (5th ed.), Figure 1.1, p. 9. ©2010 by Pearson Education, Inc. Reproduced by permission of Pearson Education, Inc.

there is obviously a relationship and interaction between and among these skill groups, there is no implied hierarchical nature to this structure. A skillful communicator generally has facility in all five skill groups, although it is possible for a speaker, writer, listener, or reader to have skill deficits within one group while still being able to function to some degree in the others, as we will see in Clark's story at the end of this chapter. It is not expected that these skills will be developed sequentially, but rather that growth in all of the skill groups will generally occur simultaneously and that all five will be integrated to produce functional language. One might also make the case that phonology, morphology, syntax, and semantics must all work together to support pragmatics, or functional language use (see Figure 10.1).

As we consider the language abilities of students with mild disabilities, one of the first areas that should be evaluated is their facility within the various language skill groups and components. Teachers and others should consider how strengths or deficits in any of these language skills may be affecting the overall functional use of language and, by extension, cognitive processing. The centrality of language to all human functioning implies that skill or lack of skill in any of the language components will have a significant impact on a learner's ability to function socially and cognitively. Language is frequently the most observable indicator of the more covert cognitive and perceptual skills discussed in Chapter 9. Deficits in any area of language will likely make the assessment and use of cognitive, perceptual, and social skills more difficult.

Phonology

Phonology is the study and use of the individual sound units in a language and the rules by which these units are combined and recombined to create larger language units. Phonology is of particular importance because it is involved with two of the five major reading skills: phonemic awareness and phonics (Brice, 2004; Ming & Dukes, 2010; National Reading Panel, 2000; U.S. Department of Education, 2002a).

Languages such as English that are based primarily on an alphabetic principle are composed of unique phonological characteristics, rules, and principles that a novice communicator must learn (National Reading Panel, 2000; C. A. Smith, 1991). The smallest unit of sound is called a *phoneme.* There are about 40 phonemes in English, each representing a separate and unique sound used in English speech. The written symbols used to represent these sounds are called *phonograms* or *graphemes*. There are 26 phonograms or graphemes (letters) in the English language, letters that are combined and recombined to stand for the various phonemes and are then combined in various ways to create English words. For learners of English as an additional language (EAL), the phonemic differences between languages can present significant challenges.

By itself a phoneme or phonogram has no meaning, but by using a variety of rules particular to a given language, an individual can combine those sounds and letters to create the words that do convey meaning. For example, in English the letters *p, h, o, n,* and *e* have no meaning in themselves, but we can use the rules governing English words to combine the *p* with the *h* to represent the *f* sound, and we can attach the *e* to the end of a word with an *o* in it to represent the *long o* sound; we can then combine all of these letter/sound units to spell *phone* to refer to a device for talking to distant friends.

Typically, problems in phonology are evidenced first by articulation problems in spoken language, as well as differences in voice, intonation, and fluency; then by decoding deficits in reading; and/or by deficits in handwriting or spelling. The existence and extent of such deficits is most often investigated through careful analysis of spontaneous or prompted samples of language use, spoken or written. Analysis of such samples helps determine the degree to which speech or writing differs significantly from that of age peers and the degree to which the communication calls attention to itself instead of to the message.

Phonological awareness is the awareness of the internal structure of words and involves sensitivity to the segmental aspect of the sound structure of the language. It is the capability of analyzing and manipulating the sound/symbol components of a language without respect to meaning (Jerger, 1996; Owens, 2010; Torgeson, Morgan, & Rashotte, 1994; Troia, 2004). *Phonemic awareness* refers to the ability to analyze the smallest units (phonemes) in a word. Students whose disabilities result in reading delays may experience difficulty segmenting and differentiating speech sounds, blending sounds into words, and accessing phonological information (Lovett, Barron, & Benson, 2003; Ming & Dukes, 2010). There are indications that difficulty in using phonological awareness as an aid to decoding unfamiliar words may be related to inefficient use of the working memory discussed in Chapter 9. In order to complete such tasks, a reader must hold a visual symbol in working memory and match it with the stored phonic information. This may prove difficult for youngsters with underlying information-processing deficits (Baddeley, 2000; Swanson & Saez, 2003).

In addition to concern for the impact of phonological deficits on oral language, researchers are increasingly aware of the relationship between difficulty with phonological processing and success in early reading (see In the Classroom 10.1). A number of studies support the hypothesis that it is necessary to pay attention to development of a child's phonological awareness, letter

IN THE CLASSROOM 10.1

Phonological Skills

Kathy seems to have problems with the phonological processing needed for reading and spelling. She frequently cannot decode words she does not recognize by sight in her reading book; this hinders her ability to attach meaning to the words or the sentence. When she comes to an unknown word, she appears to examine the letters and to begin to "sound it out," but then she abandons the attempt and guesses.

Jonathan began receiving speech/language services in kindergarten. Today at age 13, his speech is still marked by misarticulations. He has particular difficulty with the letters *r* and *l,* so a phrase such as "Let me run" comes out like "Wet me wun." This makes him an easy target for classroom teasing, and he is often picked on by other students since his speech sounds rather babyish. This juvenile speech is particularly incongruent coming from a boy of his physical size.

knowledge, and decoding skills (e.g., speech-to-print matching, spelling, and word decoding) within reading-based activities to effectively support the development of reading skills. Children who are successful with sound awareness tasks as preschool youngsters will find learning to read easier (C. R. Smith, 1998; Troia, 2004; Vandervelden & Siegel, 1997). Troia cautions teachers of EAL students, however, that phonemic and phonological awareness does not necessarily transfer between languages. EAL learners may find some similar factors in English and their primary language, but other relationships will be unfamiliar or even conflicting.

Morphology

Morphology is the study and use of *morphemes,* the smallest units of a language that have meaning, making up a learner's vocabulary (Brice, 2004; C. A. Smith, 1991; Ming & Dukes, 2010; National Reading Panel, 2000). Morphemes are those language units that cannot be further subdivided while still retaining meaning. The morpheme must have a referent for which it clearly stands. In other words, the group of sounds must be recognized as referring to a particular object, action, or idea. For example, *cat* is widely understood to refer to a furry domestic pet that meows, and the pronoun *he* refers to a previously named male person or animal.

Morphemes consist of two types of letter combinations: free morphemes and bound morphemes. Free morphemes are groups of letters (i.e., words) that can exist by themselves and still convey meaning; the collection of free morphemes constitutes the vocabulary used by a learner. Bound morphemes are units that have meaning but that cannot stand by themselves (e.g., prefixes and suffixes); bound morphemes must be attached to a free morpheme to function fully. A word may consist of a free morpheme (e.g., *turn*) or a combination of free and bound morphemes (e.g., *return* or *returning*). Students whose vocabulary is limited or inappropriate for the settings in which they must function can be viewed as having language problems in morphology. Research also indicates that students with problems with morphology in speech will likely have similar problems in reading (Mann, 2003; Ming & Dukes, 2010).

The development of children's vocabulary generally occurs in a reliable sequence (American Speech-Language-Hearing Association, 2010). Initially, a young child acquires single nouns and then verbs that have concrete objects or actions as referents. Throughout childhood, a learner's vocabulary gradually expands to include words referring to more complex and abstract objects and actions. In addition, the limited meanings initially attributed to words within a child's vocabulary develop into richer and more inclusive understandings, including the multiple uses of many common words such as *mother* and *father*. Finally, in later childhood and adolescence, most learners begin to appreciate the symbolic nature of words, moving more easily past literal interpretations of spoken and written discourse as needed.

Vocabulary (i.e., morphology) is another major group of language/reading skills (Ming & Dukes, 2010; National Reading Panel, 2000; U.S. Department of Education, 2002a). For children experiencing difficulty in developing morphological competence, the most common problem is delayed or arrested development of their vocabulary and metalinguistic awareness. Learners with language impairments are more likely to have trouble acquiring new words and maintaining them in their lexicon. Those whose vocabulary is restricted to very concrete words—who are unable to effectively comprehend language unless the explanations are made very concrete—are likely to encounter difficulty in academic classwork (e.g., reading) as well as in social interactions.

Development of facility with use of inflected endings (i.e., bound morphemes) appears to proceed in the same sequence for most children, but those with language impairments tend to develop these skills later and with more difficulty (C. A. Smith, 1991). Such problems also generally affect a student's syntactic competence as well (see In the Classroom 10.2).

Syntax

Syntax is the study of the rules by which a particular language organizes morphemes into phrases or sentences (Brice, 2004; Chomsky, 1965). The relationships among morphemes are governed

IN THE CLASSROOM 10.2

Morphological Skills

Susan is a fourth grader with mild intellectual disability. Her teacher has observed that Susan uses a very limited vocabulary. She is not exposed to a great deal of language at home, and this lack of vocabulary role models has apparently compounded her problems in school. Susan's vocabulary is functional enough to allow her to express her basic needs, but she seems to have too few words to allow her to explain fully and accurately how she is feeling or what problems she is facing. Most of the time she handles this deficit by keeping quiet.

Ivan's teacher has noted his limited vocabulary. He frequently describes objects in terms of their function when he is unable to retrieve the word itself. Yesterday, in a lesson about household objects, Ivan was asked to identify a picture of a light switch. He replied, "The thing that turns the light off." His limited vocabulary is hindering his performance in the general education classroom. Attempts at providing additional supports for learning (i.e., scaffolding) as he deals with the general education curriculum have not been very successful in the past because his vocabulary delay is too large. He attends the classroom reading group for exposure to concepts and ideas and for the group participation and discussion. His resource teacher has started preteaching vocabulary in the resource room, a practice that has begun to show some positive effect on his performance in the third-grade reading group.

by a variety of syntactic rules (i.e., the grammar of the language) that are specific to that particular language. Syntax allows fuller expression of thoughts and ideas by making references to past and future events possible, as well as elaboration on complex relationships. When students use faulty syntax in their expressive functions of speaking or writing, meaning may quickly become obscured. Inability to use syntax as a contextual clue to meaning can impede progress in learning to read. Inefficient working memory capabilities hinder comprehension because a reader may be unable to hold the words long enough to interpret the syntactic relationship between those words and others (Siegel, 2003). Those who attempt to apply the rules of syntax related to other cultural language systems to their study of a new language may also encounter difficulty communicating and comprehending written text (see In the Classroom 10.3).

IN THE CLASSROOM 10.3

Syntactic Skills

Allen is 10 years old and is being served in a resource program for students with learning disabilities. His oral language is often characterized by problems with standard English grammar. His oral syntactical errors are indicative of the immature grammar of younger children (e.g., "He don't have brown hair" or "He runned down the street"). He also frequently makes errors with pronoun usage (e.g., "Me and Willie want to play football"). After talking with Allen's father, his teacher reports that she believes Allen's spoken grammar is a reflection of the language used in his home.

Tara is 13 years old and has been placed in a resource program for students with mild disabilities. She exhibits a variety of problems with her written language. Frequently, her attempts at written sentences include fragments or run-on sentences. She can identify nouns and verbs in grammar exercises, but she doesn't self-evaluate her written sentences to assure that each is a complete and independent thought with a subject and a verb. Although she understands basic grammatical rules, she does not apply them independently. Capitalization and punctuation are erratic, although she can correctly recite the rules for their use. Her teacher sees Tara as having deficits in language performance at the syntactic level but not necessarily in overall competence in language.

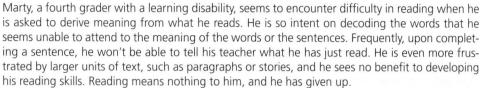

IN THE CLASSROOM 10.4

Semantic Skills

Marty, a fourth grader with a learning disability, seems to encounter difficulty in reading when he is asked to derive meaning from what he reads. He is so intent on decoding the words that he seems unable to attend to the meaning of the words or the sentences. Frequently, upon completing a sentence, he won't be able to tell his teacher what he has just read. He is even more frustrated by larger units of text, such as paragraphs or stories, and he sees no benefit to developing his reading skills. Reading means nothing to him, and he has given up.

Kelly is 10 years old and has an intellectual disability associated with Down syndrome. She has significant problems putting her thoughts and ideas into meaningful sentences, indicating problems with the semantic level of language. Her sentences are quite short, and she rarely develops a thought or a story beyond a single sentence; subsequent sentences rarely relate in any way to the ones before. She does not understand the jokes told by her general education classmates since the play on words that is central to many jokes is lost on her.

Semantics

Semantics is the larger meaning component of language and forms the basis for reading comprehension, another critical reading skill (Brice, 2004; Ming & Dukes, 2010; National Reading Panel, 2000; U.S. Department of Education, 2002a). Language is more than a compilation of single words with direct referents. It consists of complex language patterns such as phrases, sentences, and paragraphs, involving the interactions among a number of words in a given context. Semantics refers to the meaning of the entire communication act. It involves the complex use and decoding of vocabulary in a syntactic context. It includes processing complex semantic structures with understanding—for example, word categories, word relationships, synonyms, antonyms, figurative language, ambiguities, and absurdities. Often students appear to possess skills in the areas of phonology, morphology, and syntax and yet seem to still have problems in the general comprehension of language, in listening or reading. For some it may be an issue of cognitive skills for processing language in their working memory (Federenko, Gibson, & Rohde, 2006), whereas for others it may be related to a lack of experiential knowledge to apply to the communication act (see In the Classroom 10.4).

Pragmatics

Pragmatics is the knowledge and ability to use other language skills functionally in social or interactive situations. Pragmatics combines competence (or knowledge) with performance (or use). Many complex concepts, skills, and abilities are required to become an effective user of language. Pragmatics integrates all of the other levels of language but also involves knowledge and use of the rules governing the use of language in context (Brice, 2004; Owens, 2010; Prutting, 1982; Prutting & Kirchner, 1987).

Language can be correct in form and content but still not be adaptive for the individual. The appropriateness of a communicative act depends on the context in which those linguistic structures and behaviors are applied, contexts that are complex, multidimensional, and ever-changing. Learners must consider the contexts of linguistic interactions if they are to engage effectively in the functional use of language. They must consider the relevant conceptual, social, and cultural knowledge; the previous and concurrent linguistic events; and any nonverbal behaviors involved in the interaction (Bardovi-Harlig & Mahan-Taylor, 2003). Pragmatics builds on the content of the communication, but it goes beyond the simple meaning of the words. Pragmatics considers the manner of communication and the ability of the individual to use social communication rules effectively and appropriately (Brice, 2004; McCabe & Meller, 2004; Owens, 2010; Prutting, 1982).

Whereas the linguist sees language as a collection of sentences following particular rules, the functionalist sees language as a vehicle of social competence. It is our knowledge of pragmatics that causes us to vary our speech and writing to fit particular situations. For this reason, the use of appropriate communication is often identified as the most significant indicator of social competence. Not surprisingly then, social identity is often adversely affected by a pragmatic language disorder. Students like Tom in the chapter opening vignette, who fail to pick up these social language skills and who are not taught them by teachers or parents, are frequently excluded from the very social interactions that would help them become more skillful communicators and social beings. Students with disabilities who are placed in more restrictive school environments may lack exposure to and experience with classmates who use language more skillfully, thus hindering their development of pragmatic language and depriving them of the opportunities to practice pragmatic language skills in natural contexts.

Pragmatics is also the level of language that is least likely to be identified as an area of instruction or to be included as a part of a formal school curriculum or a student's IEP. It is, however, the area most likely to cause continuing problems for learners with mild disabilities like Tom's (Rinaldi, 2003). Language assessments of students with mild disabilities should include evaluations of their pragmatic skills (Hyter, 2007; Paul, 2005). If a learner is found to have deficits in this area, instructional interventions can be designed to develop these skills that are so essential to functioning in a classroom and in the larger society (see In the Classroom 10.5).

PRAGMATIC SKILLS   In order to communicate effectively, students must be able to apply their understandings of the context of language, along with their knowledge of a variety of linguistic and pragmatic skills. Linguistic skills include knowledge of the phonologic, morphologic, syntactic, and semantic relationships that govern the language in use. Pragmatic skills apply to a variety of other aspects of communication, including nonverbal as well as verbal behaviors (see Table 10.1).

Communication participants must be aware of the type of interaction(s) being engaged in and then must be able to tailor their responses to those circumstances. Some of the basic conversation patterns that a communicator may encounter include these:

- *Directive/compliance:* The communication of a personal need or imperative, responded to by an indication of compliance or noncompliance
- *Query/response:* Questioning followed by a response or indication of uncertainty
- *Request/response:* Direct or implied requests followed by appropriate, respectful response
- *Comment/acknowledgment:* A statement or description followed by a statement indicating that the information has been received and is being considered (Prutting & Kirchner, 1987, pp. 118–119)

Table 10.1 Pragmatic Skills for Communication	
Verbal Skills	**Definition, Example**
Topic selection, introduction, maintenance, and change	Skills used to select topics relevant to the context, make relevant contributions to the topic, make smooth and respectful changes in topic, and end the discussion at an appropriate place
Initiation and response	Initiating and responding appropriately
Repair/revision	The ability to repair a conversation that has broken down and to ask for repair when ambiguity and misunderstandings occur
Pause time	Use of pauses that support the purpose of the conversation and are neither too short nor too long
Interruptions/overlap	Avoiding interruptions or talking at the same time as the communication partner unless necessary; using appropriate interruption behaviors if needed
Feedback to speaker	Listener use of verbal and nonverbal means to provide feedback to the speaker
Contingency	Use of responses that relate to partner's previous utterance
Quantity/conciseness	Speaking enough to address topic, but not too much
Nonverbal Skills	**Definition, Example**
Physical proximity and contact	Distance between speakers and amount of physical contact appropriate to relationship and to the purpose of the communication; may be culturally determined
Body posture	Use of body posture that accomplishes purpose of communication (forward lean, etc.)
Foot/leg and hand/arm movements; gestures	Use of movements/gestures to complement verbal communication
Facial expression	Use of facial expressions to complement and encourage verbal communication
Gaze	Maintaining eye contact
Paralinguistic Skills	**Definition, Example**
Intelligibility	Extent to which the utterance can be understood
Vocal intensity	Appropriate selection of vocal volume for the intended purpose
Fluency	Rhythm and flow of the speech
Prosody	Use of varying intonation and emphasis to match message

Source: Adapted from "A Clinical Appraisal of the Pragmatic Aspects of Language" by C. A. Prutting and D. M. Kirchner, 1987, *Journal of Speech and Hearing Disorders, 52*(2), pp. 118–119. Reprinted by permission of the American Speech-Language-Hearing Association.

In each of these communication patterns, it is critical that the speaker's initiating act (i.e., directive, query, request, or comment) be clearly stated and appropriate for the context. It is also incumbent upon the listener to respond in an appropriate manner (e.g., to indicate whether or not a directive or request will be complied with and why). Frequently students with mild disabilities will

- Initiate a conversation interchange in an inappropriate context or manner
- Fail to modify their conversation to fit the relationship with the other person
- Fail to verbally respond to a directive or request in a socially acceptable manner

Learners with mild disabilities also frequently display response deficits, such as not responding at all, being compliant when that is not a useful response, or refusing to comply in a manner that is interpreted by others as being unreasonable or argumentative. Finally, problems can occur when an individual's response repertoire is so limited that there are few adaptive response options available (e.g., the toddler whose only response is a firm no).

THE COOPERATIVE PRINCIPLE   A communicative act is composed of the actions of at least two people reciprocally interacting as both receiver (listener or reader) and sender (speaker or writer). Communication proceeds most effectively on the assumption that when two people are engaging in a communicative interaction, there is a cooperative principle at work (Grice, 1989; Stone & Reid, 1994). This principle holds that the receiver expects that the sender is engaged in conveying a message that is appropriate to the context. Grice observed that conversation is appropriate when it is relevant, true, clear, and only as informative as is required in the situation. The receiver's knowledge of these characteristics and the expectation that they are indeed present provide the motivation to actually attempt to extract meaning from the message. Individuals whose communications do not follow these rules or who do not expect that the messages others send will be meaningful frequently miss the point of the interaction, making their functional use of language unreliable.

SOCIETAL MEMBERSHIP   Another concern related to the development of skill in pragmatic language relates to the role language plays in determining the extent to which an individual is accepted as a functioning member of a society. Ferguson (1994) asserted,

> The purpose of all of our [language] interventions . . . is *to enable all students to actively participate in their communities so that others care enough about what happens to them to look for ways to include them as part of that community* [emphasis in the original]. . . . Satisfying, active contributory membership depends upon fostering the kinds of interest, shared meaning, and relationships upon which socially meaningful communication must be based. (p. 10)

The question that must be addressed by those who live and work with individuals with mild disabilities is the relationship and interaction between communicative skills and societal membership. As in the proverbial chicken-and-egg debate, we must consider the extent to which skill in social communication enhances a person's membership in a social group and the degree to which being considered a member of the group furthers communicative development. As Bruner (1990) wrote:

> When we enter human life, it is as if we walk on a stage into a play whose enactment is already in progress—a play whose somewhat open plot determines what parts we may play and toward what denouements we may be heading. Others on the stage already have a sense of what the play is about, enough to make negotiation with a newcomer possible. (p. 34)

Teachers, parents, and friends all play a role in conferring societal membership on individuals, in initiating new arrivals into the community, and also in helping them develop the social language necessary to participate in that community as a full member. An understanding of an individual's pragmatic language strengths and deficits can help parents, teachers, and friends find effective ways to help the learner develop the pragmatic competence so necessary for full societal participation.

RECEPTIVE AND EXPRESSIVE LANGUAGE CHANNELS

Language use is related to two separate and complementary language channels. Receptive language (i.e., comprehension) is used to receive language communications from the environment.

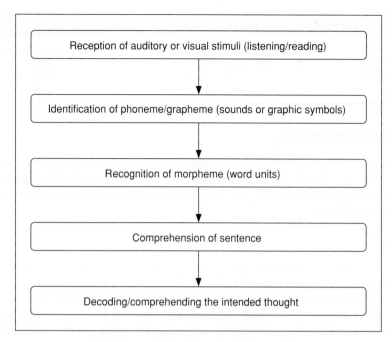

FIGURE 10.2 Process of Comprehension/Reception

This channel functions as a decoder of symbolic information and makes use of the functions of listening and reading. The comprehension channel works as illustrated in Figure 10.2.

Expressive language (i.e., production) is used to relay information about an individual's thoughts and feelings to others. This channel serves an encoding function, making accessible to others the content of a person's covert thinking processes. The production channel makes use of the functions of speaking and writing and is illustrated in Figure 10.3.

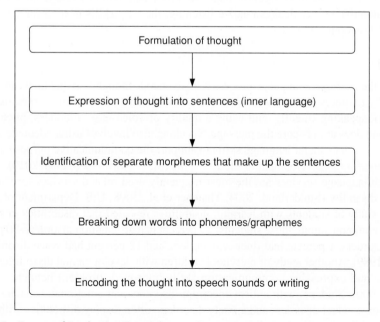

FIGURE 10.3 Process of Production/Expression

Table 10.2 Language Functions and Processing Channels		
	Comprehension/Reception	**Production/Expression**
Auditory/verbal	Listening	Speaking
Visual/written	Reading	Writing

LANGUAGE FUNCTIONS

Each of these communication channels is composed of two functions, one related to auditory/verbal processing, the other to visual/written functioning (see Table 10.2). Comprehension, or receptive functioning, involves listening and reading; production, or expressive functioning, involves speaking and writing.

Listening

Listening is the receptive language process used to derive meaning from language received auditorily. Listening requires that an individual be able to attend to a message, select the main idea, and then, using working memory, recall and relate the ideas to one another and to concepts stored in long-term memory in order to extract meaning. Three types of listening are relevant to activities in schools, each of which makes varying demands on the cognitive functioning of a listener (C. D. Mercer, 1987):

- Appreciative listening for entertainment and enjoyment (e.g., listening to music or a story)
- Attentive listening for the acquisition of information (e.g., listening to a lecture or directions)
- Critical or evaluative listening (e.g., listening to a debate or campaign speech and judging whether the arguments are persuasive)

Problems commonly found among learners with mild disabilities in the areas of attention and cognitive processing (see Chapter 9) frequently also interfere with their ability to perform many listening tasks effectively (McGuinnes, Humphries, Hogg-Johnson, & Tannock, 2003; Swain, Friehe, & Harrington, 2004). Learners may be able to listen appreciatively and still experience difficulty with the more rigorous cognitive processing within working memory that is required for attentive and critical/evaluative listening, the very skills needed for school success (see In the Classroom 10.6).

Speaking

Speaking is the expressive language process used to encode thoughts so that they can be communicated orally to others. Speaking involves accurately making speech sounds (i.e., using correct articulation), speaking fluently, and using a quality of voice (e.g., loudness, pitch) that contributes to and does not obscure the message. Speaking also involves using adequate vocabulary, syntax, meaning, and social language skills to support the communicative purpose and provide the foundation for the development of literacy skills (M. E. Reynolds & Fish, 2010).

Speech/language services are the most frequently used related services for students with all types of disability (Sunderland, 2004; Thatcher et al., 2008; U.S. Department of Education, 2005). One study of students with learning disabilities revealed that disabilities in spoken language were common among those students: 23 percent had articulation disorders, 90 percent had language disorders, 1 percent had fluency disorders, and 12 percent had voice disorders (Gibbs & Cooper, 1989). Another study of preschool children with developmental disabilities noted that as receptive and expressive communication skills improved, problem behaviors decreased (Sigafoos, 2000). Students with autism spectrum disorders and emotional–behavioral disabilities, including conduct disorders and anxiety disorders, often display difficulties with pragmatic or social speech, using inappropriate or ineffective means to convey their wants and needs,

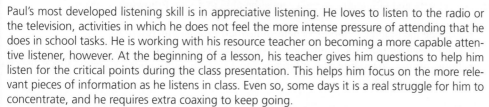

IN THE CLASSROOM 10.6

Listening

Paul's most developed listening skill is in appreciative listening. He loves to listen to the radio or the television, activities in which he does not feel the more intense pressure of attending that he does in school tasks. He is working with his resource teacher on becoming a more capable attentive listener, however. At the beginning of a lesson, his teacher gives him questions to help him listen for the critical points during the class presentation. This helps him focus on the more relevant pieces of information as he listens in class. Even so, some days it is a real struggle for him to concentrate, and he requires extra coaxing to keep going.

Laurie is a kindergartner in a special class for children with language impairments. Listening, particularly attentive listening, is very difficult for her. She does not process verbal directions well and has to be reminded of when and where she should be somewhere. Each day, Laurie gets off the bus, enters school, and needs to be directed step by step through the process of hanging up her coat, storing her lunch, and entering the classroom. At this time, she seems incapable of processing more than single-step listening tasks. Ironically, she seems to be able to listen effectively to more heavily content-laden messages, such as a story or concept presentation. Her teacher is amazed that despite wiggling and failure to make eye contact, she can still answer questions about what was just presented.

whereas children with intellectual disabilities may exhibit speech patterns more common in younger children (Pinborough-Zimmerman et al., 2007; see In the Classroom 10.7).

Speaking competence is important beyond the functionality associated with skillful speech. A study of English- and Spanish-speaking youngsters indicated that oral language proficiency was directly related to reading skill levels (J. F. Miller et al., 2006). Oral and written language skills are also related in students with language learning disabilities; instruction in one function can lead to improvement in the other (Brice, 2004).

IN THE CLASSROOM 10.7

Speaking

Jane is in an early intervention program and is classified as a preschool child with a disability. Her speech is generally unintelligible. The staff members are able to decipher more of her communication when it deals with events in a strong context or with routine matters. When she arrives at school bursting with a new piece of information, the teachers frequently put their heads together to figure out what she might be saying. Her mother and aunt frequently translate; they often know what she wants and needs when her teachers are baffled. Early in the year, the staff members were astonished to hear her mother report on the tales Jane told at home about her day at school, since her speech in class sounds only like sing-song humming. With the help of her speech teacher, she has progressed some during the year. She understands the syntactic meaning of verb tenses and plurals, but she rarely uses these devices in her own speech. Her teacher is working on sentence repetition to give her practice in speaking in syntactically correct sentences.

Jeremy is 11 years old and is in a program for students with emotional disorders. His teacher reports that Jeremy's speech is rapid and soft. He rarely talks in complete sentences, and when he does, he tends to speak in three-word units, despite the phrasing needs of the sentence (e.g., "I dressed for—Halloween as a—Terminator"). At times she says that it seems as if he is saying other things to himself while he is speaking. She says that he frequently adds words or phrases to his story that have nothing to do with what he is trying to tell her. She believes that Jeremy has a lot going on internally. He told her last week that aliens were calling him inside his head. She wonders how he manages to speak at all with such distractions.

Reading

Reading is a receptive language process involving interaction between a reader and the text for the purpose of deriving meaning from the language symbols found in the written text. In order to read effectively and efficiently, a reader must be able to do the following (Cowen, 2003):

- Decode the graphic symbols to determine their morphemic referents
- Infer meaning from the combinations of words, using syntactic and semantic clues
- Perform these decoding and inference functions fluently enough to make this a feasible way to get information

For instructional purposes, these skills are often broken down into two skill components: word recognition and comprehension. However, it is important that the whole reading act be considered when evaluating a student's reading skills and problems. Focusing exclusively on remedial techniques to teach phonetic decoding or sight-word recognition might result in students being able to decode the words accurately while still not being able to achieve the primary purpose of reading, deriving meaning from text (Cowen, 2003).

Problems in fluency are also common among many students with disabilities. Fluency is the bridge between decoding and comprehension. A major component of reading, fluency is present when a reader can decode accurately, efficiently, and automatically enough to focus cognitive energies on comprehension (Dudley, 2005; Hudson, Pullen, Lane, & Torgeson, 2009; Kubina & Hughes, 2007; Ming & Dukes, 2010; U.S. Department of Education, 2002a). Lack of fluency often results in a student's losing the sense of the passage by the end of the sentence or paragraph (McCollin & O'Shea, 2005). Assessing students' reading fluency provides information critical to intervention planning.

The final major reading skill is reading comprehension, an area that is frequently problematic for students with mild disabilities (Diehl, Bennetto, & Young, 2006; Ming & Dukes, 2010; U.S. Department of Education, 2002a). Assessment of reading skills should include several comprehension measures: silent reading as well as oral reading and listening comprehension as well as reading comprehension. Students are frequently capable of complex comprehension skills beyond simple sound–symbol associations (see In the Classroom 10.8). Judging comprehension solely by oral reading checks alone may be misleading since the decoding load may impact comprehension of text. An evaluation of the variety of ways by which students process literary materials may reveal some strengths that can be used to accommodate deficits in word recognition. The key is to determine how students might be helped to see reading as a meaning-based interaction with text. Such a diagnostic profile can then be used to make more appropriate matches between a specific learner and instructional approaches for fostering literacy (Macrine & Sabbatino, 2008).

Students with learning disabilities frequently display specific disabilities in discrete reading skills, whereas learners with intellectual disabilities or autistic disorder may exhibit more generalized lags in developing reading skills commensurate with their chronological ages. In either case, a common remedial approach is to focus on assessing and then developing beginning reading skills related to decoding and oral reading. The assumption has been that these building blocks must be attained before higher-level reading skills can be developed (see Jennie's case study in Chapter 4). However, this process frequently results in youngsters with mild disabilities approaching middle school age still using first-grade materials.

Students with emotional or behavioral disorders frequently experience failure in reading in the early grades, only later being identified with behavior problems. It is unclear in many cases whether the behavioral disorder resulted from the reading failure or whether the behavioral problems contributed to the reading failures (Rivera, Al-Otaiba, & Koorland, 2006). In any case, assessment of the academic and linguistic needs of all students with mild disabilities should give attention to the development of all five critical reading skills: phonological awareness, phonics, vocabulary, fluency, and comprehension (Katims, 2000).

> ### IN THE CLASSROOM 10.8
>
> ### Reading
>
> Randy is a third grader with a learning disability; his reading ability is limited to simple words. He is able to read short stories in the preprimers in his classroom, but he often does not seem to understand what he reads. He basically reads the words, one after the other, in isolation. He is unable to conceive of the meaning conveyed by words as a group. He does have some basic reading vocabulary, and given a strong enough context, he can sometimes figure out an unknown word. He understands initial phonemes and depends exclusively on this skill to help him decode the words.
>
> Tilly is a ninth grader classified as having a language learning disability. Reading is very difficult for her. She has the ability to decode words, but she appears to derive little meaning from them. She even reads aloud with considerable fluency, but when asked fairly straightforward literal comprehension questions after reading aloud, she is unable to provide answers. In particular, she is unable to identify the main idea of a passage with any accuracy.
>
> George, although designated as a fifth grader, continued to experience significant difficulty with simple text reading. His LD resource teacher, Mr. Cohen, had been working with him for several months on the preprimer level of an alternative reading series in an attempt to master the phonologic code but with no significant progress. As the year progressed, George became more frustrated; his efforts were never sufficient. The preprimer material was uninteresting and presented no cognitive challenge to George, who demonstrated that he possessed the ability to process information as well as his fifth-grade peers. Finally, Mr. Cohen decided to make use of this disparity and develop some different approaches. He made books on tape in the content areas of science and social studies available to George, as well as some age-appropriate fiction for more recreational reading. The content of these materials engaged George's mind; he was, for the first time, able to experience the cognitive outcomes of literacy activities. With this stronger meaning base, George began to read along with the tapes, which gradually improved his ability to deal with textual materials. Even more importantly, for the first time he viewed reading as a rewarding, engaging activity.

Writing

Writing is the process of encoding thought into graphemic symbols or phonograms so that communication can occur across time and space. To be effective, a writer must be able to convey meaningful content in an accurate mechanical form that does not detract from the communication. Written expression is composed of the subskills of handwriting, spelling, and composition.

Handwriting problems are common among students with mild disabilities; their writing may either be too slow to be usable or may be illegible because of difficulty coordinating motoric production with the visual–perceptual skills needed for handwriting (Cahill, 2009). Spelling requires the ability to turn phonemes into graphemes, using visual memory and/or auditory discrimination and association skills, which many children with learning disabilities and other mild disabilities find difficult, if not impossible. Written expression involves the use of both of those skills, as well as the ability to organize thoughts and to use vocabulary, syntax, and semantics to communicate, and doing so in a form that follows the mechanical conventions of the language.

Many students with mild disabilities seem to view writing activities as particularly threatening, possibly because writing results in a permanent record of their competence in language and content. This fear frequently results in attempts to avoid any participation in writing activities. When they do write, their work often displays problems in the following areas:

- Lack of fluency; using too few words per sentence or too few sentences
- Limited vocabulary and lack of diversity in their choice and use of words; using only "safe" words
- Problems with syntactic accuracy, including less complexity in sentence structures

- Problems with the mechanical conventions of English (e.g., spelling, capitalization, punctuation, handwriting, and appearance)
- Less originality in content and organization of the written product than is exhibited by their typical peers

Older students frequently lack the organizational strategies required for the more extensive written assignments given by secondary school teachers (Hallenbeck, 1996; Milford & Harrison, 2010). All of these problems interfere with a writer's effectiveness in conveying the intended message to the reader. Problems in written expression can also lead a teacher or parent to significantly underestimate the degree to which a learner has successfully mastered academic content and skills.

As with all language functions, written language involves the components related to form, content, and use (function). When we evaluate a learner's ability to communicate effectively in written form, it is helpful to be clear about the strengths and deficits of each component. Issues of form involve the ability to use legible penmanship, spell with reasonable accuracy, select a range of vocabulary for the task, and use appropriate syntax. Content is concerned with semantics, which is also affected by task-specific organizational strategies. With respect to function, the question is whether a student can use written language to achieve specific purposes, particularly in functional/social written language such as applications and letters.

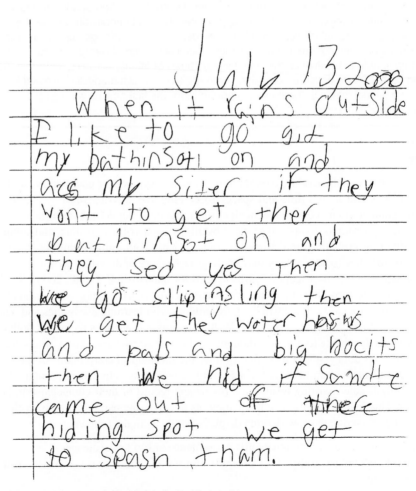

FIGURE 10.4   Writing Sample for Analysis: Todd, Age 11

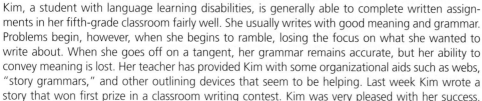

IN THE CLASSROOM 10.9

Written Expression

Kim, a student with language learning disabilities, is generally able to complete written assignments in her fifth-grade classroom fairly well. She usually writes with good meaning and grammar. Problems begin, however, when she begins to ramble, losing the focus on what she wanted to write about. When she goes off on a tangent, her grammar remains accurate, but her ability to convey meaning is lost. Her teacher has provided Kim with some organizational aids such as webs, "story grammars," and other outlining devices that seem to be helping. Last week Kim wrote a story that won first prize in a classroom writing contest. Kim was very pleased with her success.

Jim is a middle school student with a mild intellectual disability. His teachers are very concerned about his writing ability. In preparation for the state test in writing required of all eighth graders, his resource teacher analyzed a sample of his work to determine ways to help him. She noted that all of his errors were in syntax or spelling. She was able to understand his meaning, but she noted that he writes as little as possible to get by and that his main ideas lack development. She finds that if she asks him questions about his writing to get more detail, she can sometimes get him to expand on his first effort. His problems in grammar and punctuation continue to cause serious problems. His teacher plans to introduce him to basic word processing as the next step.

Giordano (1984) proposed a process for analyzing student writing that may be useful in evaluating a student's needs more accurately so that an appropriate developmental or remedial program can be designed. He suggested that teachers perform an error analysis, evaluating the nature of each of the errors a child makes in a piece of writing with respect to the dimensions of grammar and comprehensibility:

- Is the error grammatically correct/incorrect?
- Is the meaning comprehensible despite any mechanical errors?

Tallying the types of errors makes it possible to determine the predominant pattern of errors and strengths and then to use that information to plan interventions. (See Figure 10.4 for a sample of student writing for analysis.)

Some of these written expression deficiencies can be remediated or compensated for by the introduction of basic word processing tools (MacArthur, 2009). Word processing programs support a writer's proofreading skills by assisting in the checking of spelling and grammar. The burden of making editing changes is reduced, encouraging writers with disabilities to modify and improve the accuracy of their work. The final typed copy circumvents the problems associated with illegible handwriting and produces a paper with a more polished appearance. In evaluating a student's written expression abilities, a diagnostic trial with word processing may provide useful information for planning interventions (see In the Classroom 10.9).

COMMON LANGUAGE CHARACTERISTICS OF LEARNERS WITH MILD DISABILITIES

The language capabilities of learners with mild disabilities are frequently affected in a variety of ways by their particular disabilities. These individual linguistic characteristics indicate that the development of language has been impaired in some way and must be considered in the design of effective language learning programs. As a group, learners with mild disabilities frequently experience some degree of difficulty in social communication, regardless of their diagnostic category (Owens, 2010; Rinaldi, 2003). These language difficulties further impair their ability to learn and to perform age-appropriate tasks. As with Tom in the vignette at the beginning of this chapter, there are potentially an infinite number of combinations of strengths and problems that contribute to the language skill or lack of skill for a specific learner, who may exhibit any of the following problems:

- Difficulty in auditory reception and perception, affecting listening comprehension
- Limited facility in use of working memory to handle receptive language tasks
- Difficulty with verbal expression
- Difficulty with word retrieval in spoken language
- Incomplete sentences or thoughts in speaking and writing
- Difficulty comprehending what has been read
- Difficulty in written expression
- Problems in social language interactions and conversation

As a group, children with intellectual disabilities tend to develop language more slowly than their typical peers do (Pruess, Vadasy, & Fewell, 1987; see Chapter 4). They exhibit delays in understanding as well as in using language, with more delay as the level of intellectual impairment increases (J. E. Roberts et al., 2007). Some have specific problems in language production and syntax. Problems with speech intelligibility are also common and can have a serious impact on social language. One hypothesis suggested to explain these delays relates to the inefficiency with which these children make use of incidental learning opportunities critical to early language development. Another explanation relates to insufficient interaction with other children who are more skilled in language use. This problem may be exacerbated by the use of more segregated educational services and the lack of friends without language disabilities. As a child with an intellectual disability grows older, a qualitative difference in speech patterns is frequently evidenced in addition to the rate difference. These youngsters are frequently less effective in social communication, a fact that may be attributable to a lack of social language experiences or skill.

Learners with emotional or behavioral disorders frequently have difficulty using socially skilled language to meet their wants and needs (Rogers-Atkinson, 2003; see Chapter 6). The oral language of students with conduct disorders may be laced with profanity and with argumentative and hostile expressions. Their problems frequently include difficulties with inappropriate content and use rather than with the form of language. Students with anxiety, withdrawal, or immaturity disorders may exhibit difficulty with expression of feelings and needs.

Students with language/communication disorders may display problems in emotional or behavioral development (Ruhl, Hughes, & Camarata, 1992; Sunderland, 2004; see Chapter 7). Students exhibiting problems with expressive language encounter more difficulty expressing ideas, feelings, concerns, and needs and may develop frustration in response. Although they may possess age-appropriate language skills at the phonemic and morphemic levels, they may still display difficulties with syntax, semantics, and/or pragmatics. They appear to be at greater risk of developing emotional or behavioral disorders than those with speech disorders involving articulation.

By definition, students with learning disabilities exhibit problems in the understanding or use of language, spoken or written (see Chapter 5). They frequently display a wide variety of problems with receptive and/or expressive language, as well as with the integrative thought functions of inner language. Deficiencies in cognitive processing can result in difficulties with word retrieval when speaking, as well as inefficiency in decoding the messages presented by the speech of others. These students often present uneven language abilities in both school and social settings; the exact nature of their difficulties depends on the nature and severity of their learning disabilities (Candler & Hildreth, 1990; Dockrell, Lindsay, Connelly, & Mackie, 2007; Schoenbrodt, Kumin, & Sloan, 1997).

Frequently, those with learning disabilities and language disorders are also seen as less effective in social communication. Because of their deficits in processing syntactic and semantic cues, these students may miss the subtle meaning of communication acts employing such devices as jokes, idioms, and sarcasm. They may also lack the ability to understand and use effectively the rules of social language, such as turn taking and topic maintenance. A meta-analysis of studies of the pragmatic abilities of students with learning disabilities indicated that students with learning disabilities displayed more consistent and pervasive difficulty in this area than did their peers without disabilities (Lapadat, 1991). In particular, young people with learning disabilities exhibit more problems in the following:

- Overuse of nonspecific referents in conversation, leading to ambiguity
- Word choices that do not enhance understanding
- Frequent instances of unrelatedness and lack of cohesion in social discourse
- Lack of skill and restricted use of a variety of speech acts
- Inability to consider verbal interactions from a partner's perspective

Furthermore, because of repeated difficulties in social language situations, these learners may gradually develop a communicative role that is predominantly passive and underresponsive.

Although there are few studies of communication skills in youngsters with ADHD, the specific deficits in attention displayed by these learners may inhibit their ability to concentrate on the relevant features of a conversation and may result in their making off-topic contributions that are interpreted by peers as "weird." The language learning of children with ADHD may be delayed because of their problems in attending to environmental stimuli consistently enough to learn the language rules of their culture. In cases in which a learning disability is also determined to be present, language difficulties are likely to be similar to those of children with learning disabilities alone (Javorsky, 1996; McGuinnes, Humphries, Hogg-Johnson, & Tannock, 2003).

Students with autism spectrum disorders are defined by their language differences (APA, 2000) and, compared to typical peers, demonstrate varied linguistic difficulties, requiring a range of language supports in the school setting. Those with Asperger's syndrome display serious problems with use of language for social interaction, lacking an understanding of the skills of pragmatic language. Those classified as having a mild/moderate autistic disorder also exhibit less skilled expressive verbal behavior, including deficits in core language, expressive language, language content, and language memory. However, they may show more competence in receptive language (Lewis et al., 2007).

In looking at the effect of an individual learner's disability on his or her use of language, a variety of functional characteristics may be found to be contributing factors, regardless of the specific disability category. It must be noted, however, that it is unlikely that any two students will have the same problems; even those who have similar deficits in a given area will be found to vary in the severity of those difficulties.

Unfortunately, the instructional practices used by teachers in scaffolding and designing remedial activities may pose significant linguistic demands, causing even more difficulties for learners. Tutors often use multiple and varied words, sentence patterns, and rephrasings to help students develop a skill or concept. Reexplaining a concept multiple times, using different words each time, increases the processing load students must handle (Lavoie, 1989, 2009). If these multiple verbal explanations and interactions are to be successful, students must be able to identify the referents of the words used and interpret the syntactic and semantic structures. These are the very tasks that may prove daunting to learners with language deficits.

LANGUAGE DIFFERENCE OR DISABILITY?

A final concern in the area of language development and linguistic characteristics is raised when this question is asked: Is Juan's difficulty in using and understanding language due to a deficit in his ability to process linguistic information, or is his effective use of English affected by his background of using a different home language? Increasingly, schools in many parts of the country are finding that newly admitted students use languages other than English as their primary means of communication and that their skill in using English for learning is minimal (National Center for Education Statistics, 2004; O'Neal & Ringler, 2010).

According to U.S. government data, the number of U.S. students who speak a language other than English at home—that is, English language learners (ELLs)—increased almost threefold

ON THE WEB

The **National Association for Bilingual Education** (**NABE;** www.nabe.org) supports advocacy initiatives related to bilingual education for learners with limited English proficiency. The **Center for Applied Linguistics** (www.cal.org) provides resources concerning English language learners, including information about ESL and bilingual education. The website of **Teachers of English to Speakers of Other Languages (TESOL),** www.tesol.org, provides resources for professional TESOL educators.

UNIVERSAL DESIGN FOR LEARNING IN ACTION 10

Supporting Language Learning

Principle I: *Use multiple and flexible means of representation*[a]	Use direct instruction to teach common sentence and essay structures. Teach vocabulary clearly and meaningfully. Be sure that environmental print (e.g., classroom posters) is clearly printed in a large, clear font. Use white space effectively to enhance legibility of overheads and handouts. Routinely provide access to reading materials in a wide variety of formats (print, digitized electronic media, audiotape, large print). Access learning materials in a digitized format from the National Instructional Materials Access Center (www.cast.org).
Principle II: *Allow multiple and flexible means of expression*[a]	Provide opportunities for students to demonstrate orally, in addition to writing, what they have learned. If a student's handwriting is difficult to interpret, allow the student to read it to you. Provide the option of using PowerPoint presentation software to present information from individual research projects.
Principle III: *Provide multiple and flexible means of engagement*[a]	Allow students to practice reading-comprehension skills in books they have chosen. Allow use of word processors to reduce the physical effort involved in drafting written work, thereby allowing the writer to concentrate on the content. Create listening-conducive spaces to reduce effort associated with listening. Have quiet work stations available as an option to facilitate work completion of learners who need help focusing on reading or writing activities. Create an accessible writing center with a variety of interesting papers and writing implements for students to access independently. Establish peer buddy reading times.
Principle IV: *Create a community of learners in the classroom*[b]	Use collaborative language projects such as literature circles and group writing projects to assist and engage learners of varying abilities in supported language learning. Use Author's Chair, a community strategy that allows the class to celebrate the accomplishment of a writer.
Principle V: *Support the establishment of a positive instructional climate*[b]	Provide wait time during questioning and discussion activities to assist all students in participating in oral language and listening activities on an equal basis; this tells students that what they want to say is important and models respectful listening for everyone. Work with students to establish meaningful individual literacy goals in reading and writing; track progress on those goals. Create a display area for students to share work they are proud of.

Principles adapted from (a) Center for Applied Special Technology (CAST), 2008 and (b) McGuire, Scott, and Shaw, 2006.

Table 10.3	Students Served Under IDEA, Part B, in the United States and Outlying Areas, by LEP Status and Age Group, Fall 2006			
	Number of Students with Disabilities		Percentage of Students with Disabilities	
Age Group	Limited English Proficient	English Proficient	Limited English Proficient	English Proficient
3–5	41,159	649,726	5.96	94.04
6–21	424,963	5,463,264	7.22	92.78
3–21	466,122	6,112,990	7.08	92.92

Data from http://www.ideadata.org/tables30th%5Car_1-13.htm.

to over 10.9 million from 1979 to 2008, making such students the fastest-growing minority group in the country. By 2008 the percentage of students whose home language was not English had reached 21 percent of the U.S. school population, with about 5 percent of all U.S. students (2.7 million) having difficulty speaking English. About 25 percent spoke Spanish, another 25 percent spoke an Asian/Pacific Islander language, and the remainder spoke other languages (National Center for Education Statistics, 2004, 2010). The prevalence of students with limited English proficiency is higher among special education students, with 7.08 percent of students with disabilities experiencing difficulty learning in English (see Table 10.3).

Teachers are also increasingly recognizing that students with difficulty in speaking, reading, listening, and writing may be students whose primary language is actually a dialect or cultural variant of standard English (i.e., the version of English that is used most widely in public oral and written discourse; Garcia, 1994; O'Neal & Ringler, 2010; M. E. Reynolds & Fish, 2010). Because standard English is the language system used in most U.S. schools as the medium of instruction, those challenged by limited English skills are likely to encounter additional difficulties dealing with the school curriculum and interacting effectively with other students and staff.

Teachers find themselves asking whether the learning problem they are concerned about is a language difference or a disability (Case & Taylor, 2005) since common characteristics of students with language differences often overlap with those of learners with a mild disability. Pronunciation errors could be speech/articulation problems. Confusion between the syntax of the home language and that of English often results in errors in both, affecting both expressive and receptive language. Semantic development in English is the last skill to develop in a student whose home language is not English but is also a characteristic of learners like Tom, native English speakers with learning disabilities.

Cummins (1999) raised another issue that complicates our understanding of student learning needs. His language development model is composed of two stages: basic interpersonal communication skills (BICS), which are used for everyday social discourse, and cognitive academic language proficiency (CALP) skills, which are used for content learning. His research indicates that BICS can be developed in 1–2 years, but CALP can take 5–7 years to develop to functional learning levels. This delay in developing academic language skills can be interpreted as a disability, even when it is actually a language learning difference (Sánchez, Parker, Akbayin, & McTigue, 2010).

A review of the literature by Klingner, Artiles, and Barletta (2006) indicates that more research is needed if we are to fully understand the interactions among learner characteristics, language development, and the learning processes of students who struggle in school because of language differences and who may or may not have a disability. Only when we understand these factors can we begin to make valid determinations about difference vs. disability and to design and provide appropriate programs for those learners who struggle to read and use language effectively. Until then, teachers must continue to use techniques like response to intervention to identify strategies that are more effective with learners like these.

In the past, students learning English as an additional language were automatically placed in general education classrooms until their failures became severe enough for them to be referred for possible special education classification. Once referred, they would likely have been assessed using standard English-based instruments, even though IDEA and various court decisions have held that students with limited English proficiency must be assessed in their primary language (e.g., *Diana* v. *State Board of Education*, 1970; *Jose P.* v. *Ambach*, 1979). The courts have also ruled that evaluations must use instruments that are culturally appropriate and are designed to avoid disproportionate placements of children from minority cultural groups in special education (e.g., *Larry P.* v. *Riles*, 1979, 1984).

Once placed in special education, such children would rarely have been provided with a program that was appropriate to their needs. English-based special education programs frequently did not accommodate the special needs of students who were learning English as an additional language and who may also have had differing cultural and linguistic backgrounds.

Today the scenario might be somewhat different, particularly in larger cities with significant numbers of learners with language differences. In addition to special education services for those children found to also have disabilities, some schools and districts have established alternative programs to help students with different language backgrounds learn to function within an English learning environment as well. Two approaches are (a) bilingual education programs, which provide content instruction in English and in the target language (e.g., Spanish and English instruction for Spanish-speaking students), and (b) English as a second language (ESL) programs designed to teach standard English as quickly and effectively as possible so that these students can begin participating fully in content classes in English (Cummins, 2009). Students who are learning English as an additional language today may be automatically assigned to such programs, based on the assumption that children with different language backgrounds need only to be taught English and that they are by definition not in need of special education services.

The irony, of course, is that the automatic use of either of these placement procedures (special education or bilingual education/ESL) is likely to result in programming errors if applied across the board without regard to the educational and developmental needs of each individual learner. In some cases, children are hindered in learning and using standard English only because they learned their first language in a non-English environment or within a different cultural environment. Their skill in understanding and using their primary language or a cultural variant of English indicates that they have an intact ability to learn language. Their needs are predominantly related to learning the new language code referred to as standard English while maintaining proficiency in their home language and developing literacy skills in both. These children have a language difference, and IDEA 2004 states that a student may not be placed in special education if the learning problem is determined to be due to the student's limited English proficiency (Turnbull et al., 2007).

Other learners of English as an additional language may have language disabilities that are related to a primary disability, such as an intellectual disability, a learning disability, ADHD, autism, or an emotional or behavioral disorder. Their difficulties in developing, understanding, and using language and literacy skills exist in their primary language system as well as in English. The challenges of functioning in an English-speaking environment may result in a lower level of competence in English than they currently display in their primary language system, but there is evidence of impaired language learning in both communication systems. These students have language disabilities in addition to language differences. Disabilities can coexist with a language difference, and the IEP team must consider related language needs in their planning if the learner is found to be a child with a disability (Klingner et al., 2006; Salend & Salinas, 2003; Sánchez et al., 2010; Turnbull et al., 2007).

To illustrate the implications of the interaction of a disability with language learning, consider the following example: Many students with learning disabilities whose primary language is standard English find that, with support, they are able to cope with many of the demands of a high school and postsecondary curriculum, with the exception of foreign language requirements. One of the most frequently sought curricular waivers is exemption from second language study. Even though students with learning disabilities might well be able to function in the United States without mastering Spanish or French, the situation would be quite different if they suddenly found

IN THE CLASSROOM 10.10

Tony: Language Difference, Language Disability, or Both?

Tony was born in the Caribbean and moved to New York City as a toddler. His parents speak only Spanish, and Tony had no English skills when he entered first grade. Throughout elementary school he learned a little English, and although his oral Spanish is fluent, he has not learned to read in either language above a very basic level. Exposure to dangerous levels of lead and life with his abusive father led to his deriving little benefit from his elementary schooling. Pushed from grade to grade, he was finally classified as having a learning disability at age 13. His adolescence was marked by time spent in a juvenile facility, traumatic times at home when he and his father became violent with one another, and eventual placement in a state correctional facility for armed robbery at age 18. While in prison, Tony has been enrolled in adult basic education classes because of his low level of English literacy.

Tony told Mr. Samuels, his new teacher, that the little English he knows he has learned since coming there. His spoken Spanish is much more fluent, and he uses it whenever he can. However, he was never given the opportunity to learn to read and write in his home language, so he has to get the help of a friend to write letters home to his mother and girlfriend. He uses the teaching assistant as a translator when he wants to share something with his teacher. When Tony tries to communicate in English, his syntax is often more similar to that of Spanish. His listening skills are also better in Spanish than in English. He has difficulty processing his teacher's English directions, and again the teaching assistant is pressed into service to translate. Tony's oral and written English competencies are poor, as are his reading and writing skills in both English and Spanish. He explains that he hears the English, tries to translate it into Spanish, and then responds in whichever language seems most accessible at the time.

Mr. Samuels, Tony's teacher, reports that in the classroom, Tony's behavior is very cooperative, and his pragmatic skills seem functional. However, when he is with Spanish-speaking peers during meals and breaks, he often becomes loud and hostile, speaking only in Spanish. He seems to lose the social behaviors he uses in the controlled classroom setting, reverting to the street culture of his youth.

When Mr. Samuels asks Tony what he wants out of life, he says that he wants to learn to speak, read, and write both English and Spanish and to get his GED. He wants a better life, and he wants to be happy. Mr. Samuels wonders what the likelihood of this is when Tony's problems with language seem to have been overlooked for so long. He is uncertain whether Tony's problems are due to language disabilities attributable to his history of lead poisoning and domestic abuse, or whether they are due primarily to language differences—or both. Mr. Samuels realizes that Tony has not learned either Spanish or English well enough to use them in the world of adult work and wonders whether it is too late for Tony to develop these skills.

themselves living in an area or country in which Spanish or French was the main vehicle for communication. Learning the second language would then not be optional; it would be a necessity, and it would be very difficult. Their language disability would impair their learning of the second language, and they would require specialized teaching methods in order to be successful.

This is the situation faced today by those students in bilingual or ESL programs who also have disabilities affecting their language learning. Those disabilities compound the task of learning the new language. These students (like Tony in In the Classroom 10.10) frequently have not learned their primary language well enough or have not reached the stage of being able to read and write in that language, and these gaps make new language learning more difficult. These students are best viewed as having a language disability, not simply because they lack skill in using English but because they have some level of difficulty in the development and use of language in general.

Distinguishing between students who have language disabilities and language differences, or who have a combination of both, is not always an easy task (see In the Classroom 10.11). But in order to match each student with the most appropriate developmental and support program, it is essential that we make the attempt (Salend & Salinas, 2003). Evaluation of language learning

IN THE CLASSROOM 10.11

David: Language Difference, Language Disability, or Both?

David is a third grader in a school serving students from his Native American reservation. His family uses both English and their native language in the home. When he began school in prekindergarten, he was referred for evaluation because of his language difficulties, particularly in pronouncing English sounds, and he began receiving daily speech services.

By second grade, his teacher voiced additional concerns. David was having trouble with memory tasks in mathematics, as well as difficulty with word recognition and sight word vocabulary. She found that unless concepts were retaught numerous times, he did not retain them. She also stated that David rarely volunteered information; unless she prompted more complete expressions, he communicated mainly in single words or phrases. His speech teacher noted some speech improvement but also observed that he continued to lag behind in vocabulary development as well as with attentive listening. At the end of the year, the multidisciplinary team determined that David met the criteria for learning disability services.

Mr. Johnson, his new teacher in third grade, has voiced the opinion that the phonetic approach to reading does not seem to be effective with David, and he has proposed a Tier II intervention with a meaning-based, whole-language approach. Mr. Johnson notes that David loves to draw and wonders if combining his drawings with stories may help him develop a sense of what reading is all about. Ironically, no one seems to have considered the possibility that some of these problems might be due to the interaction of his native culture and language with the school's mainstream English culture. No one has addressed the differences in these two languages and cultures or discussed the possibility that David might be struggling to reconcile these two linguistic and cultural paradigms.

in children whose primary language is other than English or who use a variant form of English—such as the dialects found in Hawaii, African American communities, or the rural southern United States—should include identification of the primary language, the nature of language dominance, and the level of proficiency in both languages.

Such assessment requires attention to the phonologic, morphologic, syntactic, semantic, and pragmatic aspects of the first language. The level of skill in the first language is a strong predictor of success in English learning (Artiles, Rueda, Salazar, & Higareda, 2005). Critical information about skill in the primary language that is needed for program planning includes answers to the following questions:

- Is the student's vocabulary age appropriate in size and in complexity?
- Does the child use the syntactical rules appropriate to that primary language?
- Does the child use language functionally, following the culture-specific rules for pragmatic discourse, such as eye contact, turn taking, and so on?

Dynamic assessment tasks are more useful than norm-referenced instruments for this purpose—for example, using a test-teach-test format to evaluate a child's response to language learning activities. The teacher focuses on how the child learns, not only on what he or she knows. Through this process, the teacher learns how much the child can learn when given adequate supports. Lack of responsiveness and apparent difficulty with the learning may indicate underlying disabilities in addition to the language differences (Moore-Brown, Huerta, Uranga-Hernandez, & Pena, 2006; Owens, 2010).

It is important to realize, however, that school personnel cannot generally make accurate assessments of a student's level of skill in language learning without seeking the assistance of persons who are familiar with the cultural language used by the child. Gazaway's work (1969) with the adults and children living in Duddie's Branch (see Chapter 4) illustrates this well. By outsider standards, the language used by the residents of that isolated community appeared deficient. As Gazaway spent more time in that community, she became an insider able to appreciate the functionality of their language usage. She became able to evaluate their level of competence more validly, not in comparison to the outside world but by the standards of that community. The children from this community would indeed have been at a disadvantage outside their hollow; they would have required assistance in learning the vocabulary and syntax of standard English. Some of them would have been able to learn that new language system and thus would have been viewed as being affected by language differences. Others undoubtedly would have found the task daunting, possibly because they were also eligible for classification as children with intellectual or learning disabilities. They would have been more correctly viewed as having a language disability in addition to their use of a language other than standard English.

Complex issues are involved in assessing and serving the needs of students whose primary language is not English, students who use a dialectical variant of English, students who have developed oral competencies in their primary language but have not progressed to the written form before beginning the study of a second language, or students who have one of these characteristics in addition to a language learning disability. (See again In the Classroom 10.10 and 10.11). Finding answers for individual learners based on their needs, stages of development, and the nature of their primary language or dialect is critical for their success. In part, those answers depend on our ability to separate disability from difference, to treat each appropriately, and to recognize when both conditions coexist within a single learner. Educators interested in continuing their study in this area could begin with four recent special journal issues on this topic: Gerber and Durgunoglu, 2004; Graves and Alvarado, 2005; McCardle, Mele-McCarthy, Cutting, and Leos, 2005; Silliman and Scott, 2006.

DIVERSITY IN FOCUS 10.1

Title VII of the Improving America's Schools Act of 1994 defined a student with limited English proficiency (LEP) as one who has "sufficient difficulty speaking, reading, writing, or understanding the English language and whose difficulties may deny such individual the opportunity to learn successfully in classrooms where the language of instruction is English" (U.S. Department of Education, 2001, p. II-31). IDEA 2004 directly addressed this issue with the requirements that assessments be conducted in a child's primary language and that students should not be identified as having a disability if their difficulties are primarily related to their limited proficiency in English. Although the goal of these requirements is to halt inappropriate placements in special education, they do not address the academic and language learning difficulties faced by students whose home language differs from the language of instruction. Questions continue to be raised about the disproportionality of students from ethnic and racial minority groups in special education (Artiles et al., 2005).

According to 2006 data cited by the U.S. Department of Education (www.ideadata.org), 7.08 percent of all students with disabilities are also in need of services for limited English proficiency (see again Table 10.3). Many of these students come from families with economic challenges, and their achievement is, on average, lower than that of their English-speaking peers. The dropout rate among students with LEP, like Tony in In the Classroom 10.10, has historically been higher than for speakers of English, and those who complete their education are more likely to leave school with a certificate rather than a diploma, indicating that these students have not received educational services appropriate to their needs (see Table 10.4).

Complicating this issue is the fact that students with LEP may also differ culturally, socially, and linguistically from native English speakers and all three factors can impact the disability assessment process (U.S. Department of Education, 2001). Students with LEP may be referred by teachers who are poorly prepared to provide the needed language instruction and who believe that special educators are more able to provide the support services these learners require to become successful in school. The use of evaluations that were normed on Euro-American, middle class, native English speakers compounds the problem still further, even when they are translated into a child's primary language. Such tests are not able to accurately identify the nature of the problems faced by a student with LEP (Klingner et al., 2006). Appropriate evaluation of and program planning for students with LEP require educators who possess cultural and linguistic sensitivity in distinguishing between language disabilities and language differences and who also have the ability to design appropriate interventions that accommodate all of a learner's needs (Garcia & Tyler, 2010; Sánchez et al., 2010).

Table 10.4	Comparison of School-Leaving Percentages for English Proficient and LEP Students, Ages 14–21, Served Under IDEA Part B, 2006–2007						
	Graduated with Diploma	Received Certificate	Reached Maximum Age	Transferred to Regular Education	Moved, Continuing	Died	Dropped out
English Proficient	33.21	9.35	0.88	9.93	31.55	0.26	14.82
Limited English Proficient	21.99	16.15	0.66	9.18	33.79	0.29	17.03

Data from http://www.ideadata.org/TABLES31ST/AR_4-6.htm (Tables 4.6a and 4.6b).

IMPLICATIONS OF LANGUAGE CHARACTERISTICS FOR THINKING AND LEARNING

As we conclude this discussion of language, it may be useful to return briefly to our discussion of cognition from Chapter 9. In using language symbols, human beings have a powerful tool for communicating to others the results of their cognitive processing of information. We can receive interpretable information from our environment, and we have tools for responding to that information. Clearly, any condition that disrupts the cognitive processing of information or the use of that information through communication will impede the process of development and learning (McGuinnes et al., 2003). By using the frameworks developed in this chapter, along with the cognitive frameworks in Chapter 9, educators can analyze the language capabilities and disabilities of their students to gain clues to the more fundamental aspects of cognitive functioning and then to use that information to develop effective language and cognitive interventions.

Summary

Language is that uniquely human behavior involving the use of a symbol system for the communication of ideas and feelings between human beings. The study of language can be subdivided into three components: form (phonology, morphology, and syntax), meaning (semantics), and use (pragmatics). Development proceeds simultaneously on each of these components, and deficits in any one of them will generally impact overall functioning.

Pragmatics is the area of language that is most likely to be overlooked in assessing language skills and least likely to be included as a part of formal school curricula. Communication achieves its purpose when a message is effectively sent and interpreted. The communicator's ability to use a number of pragmatic skills determines that effectiveness. The degree to which individuals can use appropriate pragmatic skills often determines the extent to which they will be included as members of a group or society.

Language utilizes two separate but complementary channels: comprehension (listening and reading) and production (speaking and writing). Listening involves a hierarchy of behaviors. Depending on the purpose for the listening, individuals utilize appreciative listening, attentive listening, and/or critical listening. Reading is the receptive language function that is used to derive meaning from text materials. Readers must be able to decode word units, infer meaning from the sentences, and do so fluently.

Speaking is the process used to encode our thoughts in sound units and to communicate orally with others. Writing is the vehicle for communicating in a permanent form using written symbols and syntax. Handwriting and spelling are tool skills used to reliably transmit the intended message. Composition deals with the meaning component of written expression.

Learners with mild disabilities frequently exhibit difficulties with language, which impact their ability to learn. No two students present the same profile of abilities and deficits, but it is likely that language difficulties play a role in a youngster's ability to learn effectively. An area of growing concern is the extent to which a learner's problems are due to language differences or language disabilities or some combination of both. Learners affected by language differences are those whose primary language is a language or dialect other than the language of instruction and whose academic progress is affected by that fact. Learners with language disabilities are those whose condition affects their ability to process linguistic information in any language.

A Case Study • Clark

Clark is 16 years old and has just completed the tenth grade. His oral language is somewhat awkward, and he lacks the skills for natural adolescent banter. He has had some difficulty relating to peers over the years and often tends to be isolated. At times, he is teased and picked on, but he tends to accept this treatment with resignation. Clark enjoys spending his time reading, working on his computer, and watching TV—all solitary pursuits. He also enjoys basketball but does not get to play much because of a lack of friends.

Clark was slow to develop language skills and received speech therapy until age 12. His spoken language remains somewhat deliberate and labored. His handwriting is still poor, often quite illegible. His written compositions are not well structured or organized. Although Clark has a history of expressive language difficulties, he is currently being served in honors classes at his school because of his strengths in math and science. He maintains consistent honor roll grades even though he struggles in his English classes.

Clark's spelling, vocabulary, and intellectual functioning are appropriate for his grade, although his handwriting often makes it seem as if he has deficits in these areas. He knows how to use a word processor, but his English teacher is reluctant to let him use it for routine assignments, asserting that he needs to develop his handwriting skills. Written syntax is very problematic. His sentences frequently include problems with verb tenses and subject–verb agreement, as well as pronoun referent mismatches and an inaccurate use of homophones. His written sentences also tend to be short and choppy, although his oral speech reflects use of more complex language. He is able to process very sophisticated language structures in listening and reading.

Clark has problems with the organization of most written assignments, from paragraphs needed for short essay responses on tests to longer compositions and papers. His written work rambles, failing to reflect the complex thinking and reasoning he is clearly capable of. After several attempts with private tutoring failed to improve Clark's writing ability, his parents sought an independent evaluation of his abilities as part of the process of exploring alternative schools to help him function closer to his potential. The following testing was conducted to assist them in determining Clark's current personal and academic capabilities and needs.

Assessment Results

Intellectual Functioning

Wechsler Adult Intelligence Scale (WAIS-IV):

Full Scale IQ 117 (high-average)

Verbal Comprehension (VCI): 108		Perceptual Reasoning (PRI): 111	
Similarities	10	Block Design	12
Vocabulary	12	Visual Puzzles	12
Information	13	Matrix Reasoning	12
(Comprehension)	15	(Picture Completion)	12
Working Memory (WMI): 100		**Processing Speed (PSI): 137**	
Digit Span	9	Coding	18
Arithmetic	11	Symbol Search	16

Clark is functioning in the high-average range of intelligence but with considerable variability among his scores. He is extremely adept at performing rapid hand–eye coordination movements; he displays an excellent capacity for exercising clear and logical judgments; and he has a well-developed fund of general information. His poorest score occurred on a task dependent on auditory learning and spoken response (digit span).

Academic Achievement

Clark is functioning at or above the level of his peers in reading comprehension, spelling, and mathematics. On the Woodcock Reading Mastery Tests–Revised (Passage Comprehension subtest), Clark displayed accelerated abilities, comprehending written material well beyond the capability of his peers (92nd percentile). Consistent with Clark's longstanding difficulties in expressive language, his reading decoding score lags mildly behind his actual grade placement.

On the Test of Adolescent and Adult Language (TOAL-4), Clark attained a general language quotient of 108, in the high-average range. However, his scores on the various subtests varied considerably (10 is the mean score):

Spoken Language	98
Word Opposites	10
Word Derivations	9
Spoken Analogies	10
Written Language	117
Word Similarities	12
Sentence Combining	11
Orthographic Usage	11
General Language	108

Clark's language-related strengths are apparent when his writing is evaluated for ideas as opposed to mechanical competence. His strengths are also apparent when he is asked to define vocabulary words. Relative weaknesses become evident when spoken language and grammar tasks are presented to him.

On the Test of Written Language (TOWL-4), Clark attained a written language quotient of 101, significantly lower than the estimates of his overall intelligence but still in the average range. On this task, Clark created an original and creative story. However, his good descriptive abilities are compromised by his frequent grammatical errors, which detract from his idea development and for which he is penalized in school when written language assignments are assessed. His handwriting is cramped and at times illegible (average subtest score is 10):

Language Quotient (Overall Writing): 101

Contrived Writing	10
Vocabulary	12
Spelling	11
Punctuation	9
Logical Sentences	12
Sentence Combining	10
Spontaneous Writing	11
Contextual Conventions	10
Story Composition	12

Personality Functioning

Clark seems to have a quiet, reserved interpersonal relationship style. He appears to particularly enjoy topics that are more theoretical and scientific rather than those having social components. His declaration that "I am best when a new idea interests me" reflects his efforts to invest himself in safer, theoretical, abstract interests, rather than in those of a more interpersonal nature. Some of his responses suggest that he has not yet developed appropriate ways of releasing his bad feelings but just internalizes them. He admitted to sometimes feeling sad, acknowledging that he often "did not know what to do next" and "felt a little too different." He indicated that he frequently feels helpless and overwhelmed.

Clark has a strong need for acceptance and support. However, he has learned to expect criticism and rejection and attempts to steel himself against the hurt and frustration associated with others' rejection. He has developed a wall of indifference to insulate himself from social hurts, but this tactic reinforces his sense of loneliness and isolation. His social avoidance and withdrawal actually limit opportunities for gaining the degree of social attention and fulfillment he craves. His emotional distress may soon deplete his energy and optimism and may interfere with his ability to carry out the tasks and responsibilities expected of an adolescent.

Summary

Clark demonstrates above-average intellectual abilities. He is particularly adept in his mathematical skills and has well-developed conceptual and abstraction capabilities. He scores beyond his actual grade placement on most academic tasks but has encountered long-standing difficulties in language-related skills, particularly in spoken and written expression. On personality testing, he displays significant feelings of inadequacy and insecurity, relying on avoidance, withdrawal, and fantasy activities in an attempt to maintain an indifference to the slights and rejections of others.

Discussion

- What have you learned regarding Clark's abilities in the following language skills:
  - Phonology
  - Morphology
  - Syntax
  - Semantics
  - Pragmatics
- What information do you have about his relative abilities in the four language functions of listening, speaking, reading, and writing? What are the implications of those differences? How does Clark's language functioning affect other areas of his life?
- How might the classroom application of the principles of universal design for learning help alleviate his difficulties while supporting his strengths?
- What concerns and implications for intervention might you derive from this analysis?

CHAPTER 11

Academic Learning Characteristics

Questions *to Guide Your Study*

- What is learning? Identify the goal of each of the five stages of learning.
- How might a student's deficits in cognitive functioning interact with classroom and academic expectations in problematic ways?
- What is the difference between extrinsic and intrinsic motivation? Give examples of the three sources of intrinsic motivation.
- What is the difference between an internal and an external locus of control?
- How might students' attributions of success or failure affect their performance in the classroom?
- What special concerns are associated with adolescents with mild learning and behavioral disorders in the school environment?
- How does the need to achieve self-determination interact with the way schools provide services to students with disabilities?

Meet Barbara

Barbara is an 8-year-old student in Mr. Taylor's special education classroom. She was classified as a student with a mild intellectual disability about 4 years ago when her prekindergarten teacher noted the language delays that continue to present serious problems for her today. Barbara has recently begun to experience some success in school. When she accomplishes a desired task, she seems very pleased with herself, and she is likely to continue working hard to refine her skills. Her achievements appear to be motivation enough to keep her trying. She tries very hard to please Mr. Taylor. Unfortunately, he notes that when she fails after attempting a difficult task, she generally pulls back and will not try again. The amount of new information Barbara is able to handle at one time is limited, and her zone of proximal development is narrow. Mr. Taylor finds it sometimes difficult to judge how much of a challenge Barbara is ready to attempt.

Barbara learns most effectively when Mr. Taylor makes the learning objective, as well as the activities themselves, very concrete. She requires many attempts and careful monitoring over a period of days and even weeks to reach mastery on basic reading and math tasks. Once she seems to "have it," she still needs much more practice to make the skill automatic. She also needs to be prompted to use her new academic and daily living skills in settings other than the classroom where they were taught. It is as if she doesn't recognize that she can apply her new reading skills to books and reading tasks other than the basal reader.

Barbara has recently developed a behavioral pattern that concerns Mr. Taylor. Increasingly, she is unwilling to complete an activity unless Mr. Taylor tells her that the part she has already completed is correct. Yesterday, Mr. Taylor assigned a reading activity that involved reading several short stories and writing a good title for each. After each story, Barbara raised her hand and would not continue until Mr. Taylor had confirmed that her answer was correct. Mr. Taylor has also noticed that Barbara is becoming very dependent on the teaching assistant as well. He is concerned that this dependent behavior will keep Barbara from being successful outside the classroom.

THINKING QUESTIONS

How might Mr. Taylor respond to Barbara's new pattern of dependency? How might the strategies Mr. Taylor has found useful for Barbara benefit others as well? How might UDL principles be applicable here?

- How can the theories of learning styles and multiple intelligences most appropriately be used in planning programs for students with mild disabilities?
- What does Carroll's model of school learning suggest to you as a teacher?

WHAT IS LEARNING?

Learning is defined as the process by which experience and practice result in a stable change in the learner's behavior that is not explained simply by maturation, growth, or aging (Akiba & Alkins, 2010). It is the process of going from "not knowing" to "knowing" or "coming to understand" (Stone & Reid, 1994, p. 73). We can only infer that learning has occurred by observing the performance and behavior of the learner. Because this is only an inference, teachers must use caution when making assumptions about the level of learning from any given observation of learner practice.

As educators discuss more inclusive models of service for learners with mild disabilities, a special consideration is the applicability of social learning theory to academic performance. Social learning theory holds that behaviors are learned by observing the behavior of others and by observing the direct consequences of those behaviors (Bandura, 1977, 1986; Grusec, 1992). When making decisions about placements, we must evaluate not only the characteristics of individual student behavior but also the extent to which an environment provides useful supports and models of skillful behavior and the extent to which a student can make use of those models.

Whenever we discuss learning as a topic, we generally think of school learning. For students with mild disabilities, schools certainly present particular problems. However, it is important to remember that much of what we will discuss in this chapter is also applicable to learning in any setting and context, at home and in the community as well as in school. Teachers can use these frameworks to help parents and others work more effectively with these learners.

STAGES OF LEARNING

As just noted, learning is generally viewed as the process of moving from a state of not knowing to a state of knowing and then to a state of using. Teachers frequently assume that once a student demonstrates the ability to perform a skill or demonstrates an understanding, that learning is complete, and teacher and student can move on to the next concept to be mastered. With learners with mild disabilities, this assumption frequently leads to poorly learned content and skills that provide a weak foundation for new learning. It doesn't take many layers of weak learning before the structure collapses and the student is left without the capacity to perform at all.

Weak learning results from the failure to recognize that the learning process must continue past simple acquisition or mastery to proficiency, maintenance, and generalization in order to become firm. With most students, the process of reinforcing prior learning continues rather easily and incidentally as new skills are presented. With students with mild disabilities, however, attention and conscious effort must be applied to ensure that they move satisfactorily

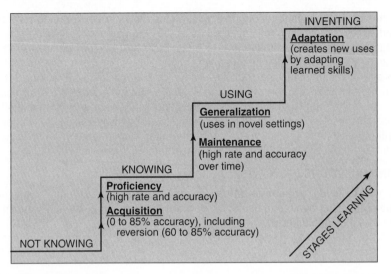

FIGURE 11.1   Stages of Learning

through each of the following stages of learning: (a) acquisition, including reversion, (b) proficiency, (c) maintenance, (d) generalization, and (e) adaptation (Mercer, 1987; see Figure 11.1 and *In the Classroom* 11.1).

Acquisition and Reversion

Acquisition is the stage of learning in which a learner moves from no knowledge to basic mastery, or from no skill to about 85 percent accuracy. Explicit instruction is often a useful teaching strategy at this stage, because it ensures that students are presented with the most accurate information. During acquisition, learners also benefit from actual experience and active involvement with the content or skill, which help to make the knowledge or skill more relevant. At this stage, making learning meaningful seems to be more helpful than making the task simple (Akiba & Alkins, 2010; Gaskins & Pressley, 2007).

Incidental learning, although useful to some learners, can result in inaccurate learning for many students with mild disabilities. Such students are as likely to learn undesirable, unproductive, or unrelated skills or facts as they are to master the object of instruction. Students with attention deficits frequently attend to too many stimuli or pick the least helpful one, both of which approaches impede learning at the acquisition stage. At this stage, frequent and specific feedback, including both positive and corrective feedback, is essential so that students are assured that the learning in progress is accurate.

Throughout the acquisition stage, the goal is accuracy in learning. The performance of students in acquisition is frequently awkward and variable (S. Graham, 1985). In a critical substage of acquisition known as reversion, learners respond correctly enough of the time (more than 50 percent) to indicate some level of mastery but are nevertheless erratic in their accuracy of response. In reversion the goal is to capitalize on beginning skills and to acquire sufficient practice with clear and immediate feedback to finally achieve the desired accuracy in the learning. Through continued instruction, practice, coaching, and feedback, students are gradually helped to define the characteristics of accurate learning and to finally be able to perform the skill accurately at least 85 percent of the time. The biggest danger during the reversion period lies in allowing students to continue extended practice unmonitored without the frequent and specific feedback needed to refine the skill. If this occurs, errors and misunderstandings are likely to be practiced and learned, with inaccurate learning result.

IN THE CLASSROOM 11.1

Stages of Learning

John is a third grader with a language learning disability who spends the majority of his day in the general education classroom. He is an enthusiastic learner, willing to try almost anything. He is one of those students who seem to either get it quickly or not understand at all. He is frequently the first one to respond to questions and to note similarities in content discussions, but he is also the first one to jump to erroneous conclusions. As soon as a skill is introduced, he is most eager, almost impatient, to use it. Because his tendency is to attempt to quickly apply his knowledge, he often appears to think that he has achieved mastery of a new skill after only one or two examples. It soon becomes obvious that his accuracy and understandings are not as strong as his enthusiasm, indicating that the learning is still at the reversion substage. Without careful monitoring, he is apt to end up practicing skills incorrectly. He responds well to corrective feedback, but he seems to be amazed when it is pointed out to him that he doesn't have it right. His teacher's challenge is to keep John at the acquisition stage of learning longer so that learning is accurate, and then to carefully monitor his practice during proficiency to ensure accurate learning.

Heather is a fourth grader with a mild intellectual disability. Her teachers have noted that she seems to move through the stages of learning fairly slowly when compared to typical fourth graders. She frequently needs to have material taught in a variety of ways and to have concepts retaught in the resource room. She benefits from extensive feedback during the acquisition process. Achieving proficiency is also difficult, as Heather needs many more opportunities for practice than other students do. Her exclusive reliance on rehearsal as a memory strategy also impedes her learning. Conscious attention to maintenance activities is necessary. Although Heather had achieved fluency with her multiplication facts, after a period without specific practice with the facts, she has begun to need the multiplication table again to do calculations.

Frank is in 10th grade, although his mild intellectual disability has limited his ability to progress academically. Frank receives significant learning assistance from his teachers, progressing slowly through the acquisition, proficiency, and maintenance stages with each new skill. He has had some success in developing functional reading and math skills to the fifth- and sixth-grade levels. However, he encounters significant difficulty in generalizing learned skills. Last week, the social studies teacher asked the class to find out how many years ago the Civil War ended. Although Frank can subtract multidigit numbers easily, he was unable to see the applicability of that skill to social studies until his teacher showed him how to figure it out. It is difficult for him to transfer skills across situations, settings, and time. Frank's best friend, Tom, a student with no cognitive disabilities, regularly uses basic math skills independently in a variety of settings (i.e., generalization). He enjoys mental math activities in which he manipulates numbers in creative ways to solve computation problems more efficiently than by using pencil and paper. This creative problem solving illustrates that Tom's learning of subtraction is clearly at the adaptation stage, a level his friend Frank is unlikely to achieve.

Proficiency and Automaticity

Once a firm understanding or mastery of the skill or concept has been demonstrated, the learner enters the proficiency stage. The goal of this stage is to develop automaticity or fluency. The advantage of developing proficiency in skills and content is that as performance becomes more automatic, less cognitive capacity is required for execution. As less of a learner's finite cognitive processing capacity in working memory is used for retrieval of facts and execution of basic skills, this capacity can be freed up for higher-level processing (Gray, 2004; Hasselbring et al., 1988).

To be successful and to move past conscious performance of a skill, the learner requires significant amounts of practice so that the skill becomes automatic. The number of trials needed to achieve fluency varies greatly, depending on the general and specific abilities of the student and the strength of prior learning. Students with intellectual disabilities and other cognitive or learning limitations generally require many more encounters with a skill or content to make it their own, and they are vulnerable to failure without concentrated practice (Gray, 2004; Podell, Tournaki-Rein, & Lin, 1992). For example, Hasselbring and colleagues (1988) reported that students with mild disabilities acquire automaticity in recall of math facts significantly more slowly than their typical peers do and are more likely to continue to depend on alternative strategies (e.g., counting on fingers) rather than retrieval from memory to achieve correct answers. This lack of proficiency restricts students from applying basic skills to more complex learning. Samuels (1987) proposed a similar explanation for the reading problems observed in students with mild disabilities. Fluency in reading is an essential goal if learners are to be able to use reading for learning.

Maintenance

During the maintenance stage, the goal is to maintain a high level of performance over time, after the reinforcement associated with instruction ends. Maintenance of skills is necessary if future learning is to build on those skills. This goal requires that students continue meaningful use and practice in functional contexts with appropriate feedback on their performance. Students with mild disabilities generally require extended practice and review to maintain their skill level, particularly in natural contexts. Teachers and parents must keep in mind the fact that if skills are not used and if maintenance opportunities are not provided, the skills will atrophy no matter how firmly they appear to have been learned.

Generalization

The goal of the generalization stage is to extend the use of acquired skills across situations, behaviors, settings, and time. Once learned, a skill should be available to be used in any appropriate setting. It has been stated that generalization is of such importance that if it does not occur, the learning process has not been successful (Ellis, Lenz, & Sabornie, 1987). When a learner recognizes a different stimulus as a prompt to apply a learned skill, generalization has occurred. For example, if Mary learns to add in math class, she should be able to use those addition skills in home economics, shop, and science without prompting. However, learners with mild disabilities often fail to see how a skill learned in one setting might be applied in another. Skills learned in a resource room frequently do not transfer automatically to the general education class unless the teachers work together to prompt the use of the skills in the new setting. Without prompts to use a newly acquired skill, students with learning challenges frequently fail to make the connection or perceive the applicability of the skill to a new situation.

Generalization rarely happens automatically. Initially in this stage, a teacher or parent helps the student see how a skill might apply in a new setting. Preparation for generalization can occur during initial instruction, as the teacher describes the variety of ways and places a new skill might be used (Deshler et al., 1996; Ellis et al., 1987). By using a continuum of generalization techniques, ranging from teacher-mediated to student-mediated, the teacher also increases the likelihood that students will see their own efforts as responsible for their successes and they will develop internal attributions for those outcomes. (The critical role of attributions for success/failure will be discussed later in this chapter.)

Adaptation

The final stage of learning occurs when a student is able to apply a learned skill in a modified way to a new task without help or prompts. When the stimulus to apply a skill is radically different from the training setting, the learner must modify the manner of performance to meet the new demands (Ellis et al., 1987). The basic skill is the same, but the execution varies. In this stage, a student is firm enough in the learning to see how it can be modified to match the demands of the novel situation. In adaptation the learner is also able to discern the larger implications of a skill and assumes personal responsibility for carrying the learning further. As with the generalization stage, coaching and prompting may be needed initially to help students identify the applicability of modifying skills for use in novel situations. Although adaptation is the final stage in learning, not all skills will be learned to the adaptation stage, particularly by students with mild disabilities. Achieving generalization of a skill may be an appropriate end goal for some learnings and some students.

CRITICAL LEARNING NEEDS OF STUDENTS WITH DISABILITIES

Students with mild disabilities exhibit two behavioral patterns that impede their learning efficiency. First, they progress through the stages of learning more slowly than more skillful learners do; they need more time, experiences, and materials to allow for accurate learning. Second, they generally require more explicit teaching and supportive practice. The principles of UDL related to providing multiple and flexible means of representation and engagement are good guides in this respect. The clearer and more direct the teaching, the easier the learning is for all students (Landrum, Tankersley, & Kauffman, 2003). Supportive practice calls for numerous and varied opportunities to apply the target skill, with prompting as needed to use the skill. Corrective feedback is also essential so that learning is practiced accurately.

Analyzing the characteristics of learners with mild disabilities in academic learning environments quickly leads back to the model of cognitive functioning. Within the cognitive model (see Chapter 9), the three areas that most affect students' success in learning are attention, memory, and executive functioning. Learning cannot occur until a student is able to focus on the relevant details in the environment. Students who encounter difficulty in selective attention will almost certainly be viewed as inefficient learners; their attentional problems will interfere with their success in the classroom. Students with learning disabilities along with hyperactivity exhibit significant problems focusing their attention appropriately and effectively (Cotugno, 1987). Such students are more narrowly restricted in their scanning of incoming sensory stimuli and are more likely to be distracted by extraneous input. They appear to lack the cognitive capacity to sort information for relevancy in an efficient manner. Learners with the most difficulty focusing on relevant stimuli need more teacher coaching to develop efficient selective attention strategies.

Students' efficiency in learning is frequently evaluated by the extent to which they are able to store information and retrieve facts on demand. Learners with school learning problems frequently display difficulty memorizing math facts, vocabulary definitions, spelling words, and other content area information (e.g., lists and dates). They also have difficulty demonstrating the basic skills involved in reading and mathematics. With investigation of the strategies these students use to accomplish memorization tasks, teachers frequently discover that such learners differ in their ability to organize information for recall. Strategies such as verbal or written rehearsal, coding (i.e., associating a new item with a concept already in memory), imagery, and mnemonics are absent, immature, or inefficiently used by younger students and by those with mild disabilities (Leal & Raforth, 1991).

Two helpful strategies that are rarely spontaneously utilized by individuals with intellectual and learning disabilities to deal with declarative knowledge learning tasks are paired associates and grouping/clustering. Both organizational strategies depend on establishing relationships between new stimuli and prior learning and are dependent on the strength of that prior learning. For these reasons, students who do not achieve mastery at the maintenance stage or better in prior learning are less able to use these strategies. Without knowledge of a variety of memory strategies, students are inefficient or unsuccessful in accomplishing memory tasks. Since so much emphasis is placed on quick recall in school environments, these students are seen as failures or lazy. Teachers can assist students in developing such strategies by clearly explaining how new learnings relate to old learnings and by modeling ways to store such information in long-term memory.

As was discussed in Chapter 9, declarative memory deals with factual knowledge, whereas procedural memory stores action sequences and procedures. Teachers may find it useful to treat declarative memory tasks differently than procedural memory tasks and to teach learners to deal with them differently, too (Derry, 1990). Declarative memory depends on establishing strong networks among related bits of content information. This is most effectively done in the early stages of learning, during acquisition. As teachers and students discuss new information, they can develop elaborations on the concepts and the connections between the new data and previously stored information (i.e., organization). Students with mild disabilities often fail to see relevant connections to prior learning without assistance. Taking the time during the earliest learning stages to ensure firm learning increases students' effectiveness in the later stages of learning.

Procedural memory differs from declarative in that skills (e.g., calculation skills in mathematics) are stored as action sequences that are best learned by repetition (Derry, 1990). Students with mild disabilities tend to respond quickly during initial skill instruction but then are unable to retrieve the action sequence accurately the next day. Repeated initial demonstration of a skill, particularly with the support of concrete representations, and extended practice with corrective feedback are needed by these students to develop the necessary level of automaticity in procedural knowledge.

Central to efficient cognitive processing and academic learning is the ability to make cognitive decisions about the applicability of particular strategies and the effectiveness of learning (Meltzer, Pollica, & Barzillai, 2007). These executive functions (metacognition) include control of attention, metacognitive regulation (self-instruction and self-direction), metacomprehension (self-questioning and monitoring), and reflection (self-evaluation). When a student exhibits deficiencies in executive functioning or strategic control functions (see In the Classroom 11.2), adults often assume the control and direction of strategy selection, monitoring, and even task completion, resulting in learner passivity, outer-directedness, and learned helplessness (Borkowski & Kurtz, 1987). The lack of specific and general strategy knowledge, as well as deficits in employing executive control functions or metacognitive regulation, can lead to an increasingly negative attitude and avoidance of cognitive tasks. Learners look to others for cues, are less reliant on their own resources for developing solutions, and may distrust their own abilities. The literature about the utility of metacognitive coaching suggests that active interference in this negative spiral by teachers and others is both possible and necessary (Meltzer et al., 2007; Paris & Winograd, 1990). By actively working to help students develop metacognitive awareness of their own thinking, teachers can help develop attributions of effort in their students and can enhance their intrinsic motivation for self-determination, both of which can lead to increased persistence in the pursuit of learning. Later in this chapter, the implications of these issues for the academic success of learners with mild disabilities will be discussed.

IN THE CLASSROOM 11.2

Cognitive Functioning and Academic Performance

Kelly is a sixth grader with learning disabilities and attention deficits. Now that she is changing classes in middle school, she is expected to organize her time, learning, and herself. Her reduced ability to process information affects her academic performance in several ways. Because of her deficits in selective and sustained attention, her teachers must frequently call her back to attention, with resulting gaps in learning. Rehearsal is the only memory strategy Kelly uses independently, and the demands of the middle school curriculum make this an inefficient mode of learning. Kelly's teachers have begun to assist her in developing other memory strategies. They also provide her with study guides and summaries of readings. Unfortunately, she is not yet developing and using the self-monitoring strategies needed to evaluate her own learning, and she is becoming dependent on the aids her teachers provide.

THE ROLE OF MOTIVATION

New teachers are frequently told that they are responsible not only for teaching their students but also for motivating them to learn. Teachers in turn frequently attribute a lack of learning to students being unmotivated or to parents failing to motivate their children. Although it is certainly true that motivation affects the learning process and that, without motivation, learning is unlikely to occur, the converse is not necessarily true. For example, one cannot reason that if learners are motivated, they will be able to learn anything they are asked to or want to learn. Motivation only encourages students to persist in doing something they are already capable of doing. If a learner does not have the aptitude or prerequisite skills to learn or perform a particular skill (e.g., fly out the window or read a story from the basal reader), a teacher could promise that student a million dollars (strong motivation indeed!), and a positive learning outcome would still be unlikely (Lavoie, 1989, 2009).

Nonetheless, learners with a variety of mild disabilities do present significant motivation concerns in classrooms (Mehring & Colson, 1990; Meltzer & Krishnan, 2007; Nichols, McKenzie, & Shufro, 1994; Nunez et al., 2005; Ozonoff & Schetter, 2007; Switzky & Schultz, 1988). These learners tend to develop an expectation of failure and do not believe that they can control their own destiny. They also tend to attribute success or failure to forces outside their control or to see no relationship between task outcomes and their own efforts.

Extrinsic Motivation

Motivation comes from many sources. Extrinsic motivation is provided by sources outside the individual. Examples include rewards that a student earns on execution of a desired behavior or the punishments the student seeks to avoid by performing as asked. Extrinsic motivation rarely leads to robust learning. The tendency for the learning to be tied directly to the reward frequently leads an individual to do the minimum to achieve the reward or to avoid the punishment (Stipek, 1993). Changes in behavior are likely to disappear once the extrinsic reinforcement is withdrawn unless the change of behavior has created its own intrinsic rewards for the student. In addition, learners may come to equate an extrinsic reward with an external control of their destiny, reducing their own sense of self-determination (Grolnick & Ryan, 1990). This can lead to a cycle in which teachers see students as being unmotivated and students become more dependent on external control of their learning and behavior.

The possibility of earning extrinsic rewards may actually result in decreased natural intrinsic motivation and in students' reduced interest in a task. When an extrinsic reinforcer is removed, students may find no reason to continue to perform the task that was previously reinforced with extrinsic rewards (Schultz & Switzky, 1994). Furthermore, it is unlikely that learning based only on extrinsic motivation has the strength to generalize into other settings. This represents the classic "learn it for the test, then forget it" situation (see In the Classroom 11.3). That said, however, a teacher or parent may sometimes find that it is advantageous to temporarily enhance or support a learner's weaker intrinsic motivation with an extrinsic reinforcer. In such cases, parents and teachers must be aware of the dangers of overuse of rewards and punishments; seeking ways to identify and reinforce the learner's intrinsic motivation is preferable whenever possible (Kohn, 1993).

Intrinsic Motivation

Motivation derived from sources within an individual student, referred to as *intrinsic motivation*, appears to have the strongest effect on learning. The amount of intrinsic motivation available to achieve a particular level of learning is affected foremost by an individual's sense of competence. Learners are more motivated to learn something that appears to be possible for them to achieve and that engages them in meaningful activities with others who already possess the skill or knowledge—that is, learning that appears to be within their zone of proximal development (Akiba & Alkins, 2010; Lavoie, 1989, 2009).

Extrinsic Motivation

Darlene is 14 years old and is classified as a student with learning disabilities, although her IQ of 75 indicates that she might also be viewed as having a borderline intellectual disability. Her motivation for learning is affected strongly by her history of failure. When completing class work, she works hard enough to pass, but not to do well. It appears that she exerts enough effort to avoid the punishment of failing grades, but she shows no evidence of working to achieve the competence represented by good grades. Her history of failure seems to have affected her to the extent that she believes that she cannot obtain a good grade, and she sees no point in exerting the effort to try.

At 10 years old, Harry is served in a self-contained classroom for students with emotional disorders. His teachers are concerned with his noncompliance, temper outbursts, and general oppositional behavior. His classroom management system utilizes a point system for earning food rewards, buying items at the school store, and earning privileges. His teachers also utilize response-cost procedures and time-out for problem behavior. These extrinsic motivators are only marginally effective with Harry. He wants to receive the rewards and avoid the punishments and so will try to adjust his behavior only as much as necessary to achieve those ends. However, it is becoming apparent to the staff that these are not strong enough motivators. Harry continues to exhibit his problematic behaviors in spite of the rewards and punishments, and the problem behaviors are persisting outside the school environment.

On the other hand, the uncertainty of prior learning or an experience of failure in that learning frequently leads to reduced motivation for new learning attempts (Nunez et al., 2005). Teaching students how to perform a particular learning task (e.g., comprehension strategy, writing strategy) increases their feeling of competence in performing that task, enhancing their intrinsic motivation as well (Harper & Maheady, 2007; Santangelo, Harris, & Graham, 2007). Students who experience less success in meeting school learning demands can be taught the cognitive learning strategies needed for successful learning, thereby resulting in increased intrinsic motivation for learning simply because they see it as possible (Haywood, 2004).

Additionally, a student's perception that a particular learning activity has meaning or meets an identified personal need or goal affects the level of motivation to participate in the learning activity (Roberts, Torgeson, Boardman, & Scammacca, 2008). Human behavior is an attempt to satisfy basic human needs, including the needs to survive, to belong, to love, to have fun, to gain power, and to be free (Frey & Wilhite, 2005; Glasser, 1990, 1998). What we choose to do is what we think is the most need-satisfying thing to do at the time. Glasser advocated that teachers ensure that there is potential for students to actually meet their basic needs in school settings. This would lead to their being more motivated to adapt their behavioral responses in ways that would make the whole social structure more productive for everyone.

Intrinsic motivation to persist in a variety of human efforts, learning or otherwise, follows from at least three basic needs or goals, including a drive for competence, self-determination, and/or relatedness or affiliation (Adelman & Taylor, 1990; Deci & Chandler, 1986; Stipek, 1993). A student may exhibit one or more of these needs from time to time, but for any given learning or activity, one of the needs is likely to be the primary motivation (see In the Classroom 11.4). Some students are motivated to participate in school activities because learning results in an enhanced sense of competence (Deci & Ryan, 1985; Stipek, 1993). Competence motivation is derived from exposure to activities that extend and enhance the ability to interact effectively with the environment and to master challenges. The competence motivation leads an individual to perform difficult but interesting tasks as well as possible in order to achieve a goal (Banda, Matuszny, & Therrien, 2009). An artist works on a painting, motivated by the drive to achieve a masterpiece that will be recognized as significant by peers and the public. A mathematics student works to

IN THE CLASSROOM 11.4

Intrinsic Motivation

Peter is 12 years old and is served in a program for students with intellectual disabilities. Everyone who meets him is impressed by his eagerness and positive attitude. They wonder what keeps him resilient in the face of his significant learning challenges. In observing him at work in the classroom, they note that he seems very focused and determined to meet his goals. It appears that he gains a sense of accomplishment and recognition from his achievements. His pride is evident when he completes a project or when he sees his work posted in the hallway. It is apparent that he possesses a strong competence motivation and that he gives his all to classroom activities to meet that competence need.

Joanne is 15 and has ADHD and a behavioral disorder. Her need for relatedness, or affiliation, appears to be the strongest motivation for her actions. Unfortunately, this manifests itself in negative ways. She tends to rush through assignments in Mr. Tallon's resource room, with little effort or concern for quality, so that she can interact with her peers. Yesterday she rushed through a math worksheet, completing only as much as she needed to do to receive a passing grade. Mr. Tallon convinced her to finish the worksheet, whereupon she rushed off to interact with one of her friends. Since this relatedness motivation is so strong for her, Mr. Tallon has decided to see if he can structure Joanne's learning activities to take advantage of it.

Seth is 13 years old in a self-contained class for students (mostly boys) with learning disabilities. In this classroom, power struggles are common; and posturing, threatening, and fighting are means of survival. Academic success is not perceived by the students as a way to gain power or control; ironically, it is sometimes even viewed as weakness, indicating that the student has succumbed to the domination of teachers. Arguments among class members involve knowledge of nonacademic subjects such as wrestling, other sports, and snowmobiles. Seth's knowledge in these areas accords him a place of importance in the group and possible power and control. His need for self-determination fuels his desire to learn all he can about sports, allowing him to determine the course of events in these classroom discussions.

prove a difficult theorem, motivated by the challenge of the puzzle to be solved. A high school student works to demonstrate competence in chemistry because achieving the grade of A indicates mastery of the subject—to the student and to others as well. All of these individuals are motivated by the need to achieve, to demonstrate their competence, to climb the mountain because it is there. Competence motivation is often enhanced by the recognition and appreciation from significant others that follows the demonstration of competence, thereby blending intrinsic and extrinsic motivations.

Individuals are also motivated by a need for self-determination; in order to feel self-determined, they must have a sense of perceived control, choice, and autonomy (Deci & Ryan, 1985; Frey & Wilhite, 2005; Stipek, 1993). Learners may be motivated by their perception of the control or choice involved in an activity that appears to give them power or that demonstrates their power over others or over their circumstances (Morgan, 2006). This desire to be in control of their fate often leads individuals to work to achieve new competencies because such skills are essential to managing their environment and being in control of their destiny. Learning how to do things for yourself means that you don't have to ask others for help; you develop increased personal control of your life and become more self-determining. Because you know how to do something better than someone else, you may be hired for a job you're seeking. Having the ability and authority to act competently results in the capability to affect outcomes, to wield power, to determine personal outcomes. We often think of control as a negative, but it is important to remember that depression and helplessness are outcomes of a sense of lack of control or power. Some students are motivated to learn by the need to be self-determining, to have control, so that they don't have to be dependent anymore.

Finally, some students are motivated by the need for relatedness, as evidenced by attempts to develop affiliations or friendships and to achieve a sense of belonging (Frey & Wilhite, 2005; Harper & Maheady, 2007). This human need for belonging and nurturing is well documented in the early work of Maslow (1954) and Skeels and Dye (1939). Frequently, students are motivated to stay with the learning process simply because it enables them to interact with others in interesting ways. Learning new skills may create more opportunities for relating to others. This source of motivation is perhaps the most frequently overlooked of all the possible intrinsic motivations for learning. In fact, it is often seen as a detriment to learning. Teachers chastise students who seem more interested in talking about their learning than in completing the work. The research in cooperative learning (Johnson et al., 1984) and on other peer-mediated strategies (Harper & Maheady, 2007) gives strong evidence of the power of the relatedness motive for learning. When students work cooperatively, they often learn more and better than when they work in individualistic or competitive structures.

As with any human being, any of these sources of intrinsic motivation may exist in learners with mild disabilities. An individual may even exhibit a combination of motivations, depending on environmental and personal factors. In learners with disabilities, the competence motivation is likely to be weaker because of their history of failure. Since the effectiveness of competence in motivating individual actions depends on the individual's belief that success is possible, this belief and therefore motivation are frequently weaker in learners with mild disabilities. Lack of cognitive learning strategies can undermine learning confidence even more, making cognitive mentoring an essential part of the academic program for learners with mild disabilities (Santangelo et al., 2007). Teachers and parents must recognize that the lure of achievement or competence as represented by a good report card may be a weak motivator for these students, as one is motivated to attempt only those tasks that seem possible.

Generally, the motivation stemming from learning as a means of interacting with others or of achieving control or personal power and becoming more self-determining is more influential with learners with mild disabilities (Wehmeyer, 1994; Wehmeyer, Agran, & Hughes, 1998). As we seek to help these students become more successful in academic settings that have not previously met their needs, we need to help them identify how school tasks can help them meet their personal needs of becoming more competent, self-determining, or connected to others. Then we have to address the additional issue of possibility by ensuring that an assigned task is within their zone of proximal development and that an appropriate level of support/scaffolding is available to help them move to the next level of learning. Providing choice in selection of learning materials (e.g., a variety of books for reading lessons) can support motivation and enhance the development of self-determination, which is particularly critical in the adolescent years (Roberts et al., 2008).

Before leaving our discussion of motivation, it is important to consider some reasons that motivations focused on meeting these basic needs might lead learners to engage in destructive behaviors. When considering problem behaviors, we must understand that many instances of misbehavior are related to learners' mistaken, and mostly unconscious, belief that engaging in the problem behavior will achieve for them a measure of control, competence, or connectedness. Central to the studies of problem behavior and aggression is the concept of perceived control of one's life (Adelman & Taylor, 1990; Allen & Greenberger, 1980; Grolnick & Ryan, 1990; Morgan, 2006; Schrunk, 1992). Failure experiences can lead to a low sense of perceived control, which can constitute a threat to self-determination needs and prompt these learners to turn to other, often destructive, means of reestablishing a sense of personal control and self-determination—for example, displaying oppositional and aggressive behavior (Morgan, 2006). In such situations, teachers and parents frequently revert to extrinsic rewards to achieve desired behavior. Ironically, such rewards may be perceived as external control and thus as an additional threat to self-determination, causing students to react against the reward with even less effort or with increased acting out behaviors (Carey & Bourbon, 2004, 2006). This suggests a strong connection between developing competence in students and reducing their need to control their environment through aggressive behaviors. Learning and behavior are clearly related in students with mild disabilities.

LOCUS OF CONTROL AND ATTRIBUTIONS OF SUCCESS OR FAILURE

Two theories found in the literature regarding personal motivation concern locus of control and attribution theory. *Locus of control* refers to the degree to which individuals perceive that there is a connection between their actions and the outcomes achieved. An individual's locus of control is reflected in the explanations that person gives to account for personal successes or failures. Rotter (1966) considered locus of control a relatively stable trait of an individual, characterized by causal explanations defined by the locus of responsibility, internal or external to the individual (Mamlin, Harris, & Case, 2001).

Attribution theory focuses on the variables affecting the expectancy of success or failure, including perceptions of responsibility for the outcome, the cause of the outcome, and the possibility of change to the task or situation (Weiner, 1985, 1986, 2010). Causal attributions depend on how an individual describes the cause of the situation and whether the cause is viewed as stable or unstable. A third element of this theory relates to controllability: Is the focus susceptible to the individual's control or not? Weiner identified four aspects upon which achievement attributions depend: ability, task difficulty, effort, and luck (see Table 11.1). He viewed attributions as pertaining to a particular event and context, making this potentially a more context-specific descriptor than locus of control and not an individual trait.

External Causal Attributions and Locus of Control

When learners indicate that their success or failure is due to factors outside their control or to the actions of others, we say they are exhibiting an external locus of control or that they hold external causal attributions for their success or failure. External locus of control can be generalized or related specifically to academic performance. When students with mild disabilities say that the outcome of a challenge is due to their low level of ability, to luck, to a task that is too hard (or too easy), or to other factors such as the teacher's liking or disliking them (Borkowski, Weyhing, & Turner, 1986), we say they are exhibiting external locus of control. Their motivation is affected by the hopelessness they project about affecting the outcome. Deming and Lochman (2008) reported a correlation of external locus of control with anger, impulsivity, and aggression, as well as depression and anxiety. Students with an external locus of control also tend to adopt failure-avoiding strategies, in which they avoid tasks they view as beyond their ability or environments they see as nonproductive (Stipek, 1993). Young children or those who have developmental delays generally display more dependence on an external locus of control. This may be related to the tendency of these same children to display a more field-dependent cognitive style. (See In the Classroom 11.5.) Although existing research generally indicates that students with mild learning and behavioral disabilities exhibit characteristics associated with an external locus of control, one review of the research indicated that more study is needed since this characteristic may be more variable than has been thought and students with disabilities may be more heterogeneous in their attributions of success and failure than was previously believed (Mamlin et al., 2001).

Table 11.1 Variables in the Attribution Theory Framework

Causal Factors	Locus: Internal/External	Stability: Fixed/Modifiable	Controllability
Ability	Internal	Generally stable	Generally uncontrollable
Effort	Internal	Unstable/modifiable	Controllable
Task difficulty	External	Stable	Controllable/ uncontrollable
Luck	External	Unstable	Uncontrollable

External Attributions of Success and Failure

Diana, a third grader with ADHD, appears to expect failure and has a tendency to attribute her successes to external factors. When her mother asked her how she did on a recent test on time and money, Diana answered that she had failed. Later, her mother found the test in her backpack and said, "You didn't fail; you got a 94!" Diana's response was that she did well only because the teacher had them "do time and money so much at school." She did not appear to believe that her efforts played a part in the success. Diana expects failure, and even when she experiences success in her school program, she attributes it to the actions of others.

Mike is 18 years old and has been served in programs for students with mild intellectual disabilities since first grade. As do many adolescents, he seeks to be in control of his life. Because of his disability, he needs to spend more time on his class work than the typical student does to be successful. Frequently, however, he spends a minimal amount of time studying. When he experiences failure, he generally blames the instructor for making the test too hard or for not telling him what to study. His tendency to blame everything and everyone else for his situation is evidence of his external locus of control, a fact that undermines the development of self-determination for this young man.

Attribution theory and its explanations of success or failure are a bit more complicated. Employing Weiner's three variables of locus, stability, and controllability, the following patterns are associated with less personal responsibility and lower motivation:

- *Ability:* Seen as a stable trait but judged by the individual to be inadequate
- *Task difficulty:* Fixed, set and controlled by someone else
- *Luck:* External, unpredictable, and uncontrollable
- *Efforts:* Reduced because of the other factors, resulting in low performance motivation

Attributions are also related to emotions, with external attributions (including those implying lack of personal control, effort, or skill) related most often to negative emotions such as regret, shame, and hopelessness. Clearly, learners who regularly attribute outcomes to factors outside their personal control have little motivation to exert the effort needed to change the outcomes. External attributions underscore the lack of efficacy these learners frequently experience.

Internal Causal Attributions and Locus of Control

On the other hand, successful learners are more likely to attribute outcomes to their own efforts (e.g., trying hard or not trying hard enough), a characteristic referred to as internal causal attribution or locus of control. Recognition that effort matters is often linked to persistence in the face of difficulty, a factor that is also associated with greater success in learning tasks (Licht & Kistner, 1986). Students who come to believe that effort makes a difference will exert more effort, leading them to persist with difficult tasks and subsequently to learn more (Stipek, 1993). Attributions related to effort are also related to the sense that factors within an individual's control (e.g., personal efforts) are primarily responsible for outcomes. Such learners experience more intrinsic reinforcement from the learning outcomes that they attribute to their own actions. They experience pride in their successes, thereby providing motivation for future efforts (see In the Classroom 11.6).

Effective learning requires internalizing the locus of control and causal attributions if a learner is to move beyond teachers, parents, school, and home to become an independent learner and problem solver. Typically, individuals develop a more internal locus of control and causal attributions as they move into adolescence and adulthood, although this is not as generally true of

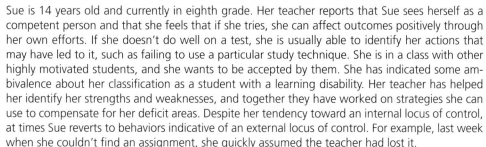

IN THE CLASSROOM 11.6

Internal Attributions or Locus of Control

Sue is 14 years old and currently in eighth grade. Her teacher reports that Sue sees herself as a competent person and that she feels that if she tries, she can affect outcomes positively through her own efforts. If she doesn't do well on a test, she is usually able to identify her actions that may have led to it, such as failing to use a particular study technique. She is in a class with other highly motivated students, and she wants to be accepted by them. She has indicated some ambivalence about her classification as a student with a learning disability. Her teacher has helped her identify her strengths and weaknesses, and together they have worked on strategies she can use to compensate for her deficit areas. Despite her tendency toward an internal locus of control, at times Sue reverts to behaviors indicative of an external locus of control. For example, last week when she couldn't find an assignment, she quickly assumed the teacher had lost it.

Bill, an eighth grader with a mild behavioral disorder, has just been placed in a full-inclusion program. Academically, he is challenged by this new environment. When he is successful on a project, he takes pride in his effort and accomplishment. When he encounters failure, such as doing an assignment incorrectly or losing his temper, his first impulse is to blame others. Last week, he tore up his science worksheet when the teacher asked him to redo a section. At first he blamed the teacher, saying, "He made me do it." After a short period in the time-out area and a discussion with the crisis counselor, he admitted that he had lost control and that he was responsible for the problem and for getting a new worksheet. This development of more internal attributions for events in his life is evidence of the progress Bill is making with the help of his teachers and counselor.

those with disabilities. Students with mild disabilities tend to remain more externally oriented than their typical peers are, leading to less adaptive adult outcomes (Wehmeyer, 1994). It is important to note that merely providing instruction in content and cognitive strategies for learning is unlikely to have much effect. Cognitive mentoring and coaching are required as well to help youngsters with disabilities see that the effort they put forth in applying such strategies can pay off in improved outcomes, that their efforts result in more success. Attribution theory leads to the realization that success is related to the degree to which individuals are able to affect their environments and tasks by exerting more effort, by developing new abilities, and by adapting tasks to reduce difficulty.

Spirals of Failure or Success

From the preceding discussions, it is clear that the manner in which a learner approaches a task affects the outcome. The expectation of success or failure creates a climate that increases the likelihood of the expected outcome (Miller, Heafner, & Massey, 2009). Experiences with failure often result in a learner (and others) setting lower goals and exerting less effort, which in turn may bring about subsequent failures, leading to a downward spiral of ever-lower goals and efforts (Licht & Kistner, 1986; Meltzer, Katzir, Miller, Reddy, & Roditi, 2004; Sutherland & Singh, 2004). Repeated failure erodes a student's motivation to learn, resulting in a lowered sense of personal efficacy, diminished academic self-concept, and more external attributions for all outcomes (see Figure 11.2; In the Classroom 11.7). The student then tends to avoid challenges, giving up at the first sign of difficulty and becoming a passive learner in the classroom (Wong, 1991).

A similar but opposite effect tends to follow successful learning experiences. A sense of competence results when a student exerts effort, takes a voluntary action, and is successful. In such cases, students perceive their efforts as efficacious and have a tendency to exert similar efforts on future tasks, increasing the likelihood of further successes (Meltzer et al., 2004). It is important, however, for students to believe that these successes have been achieved as a result of

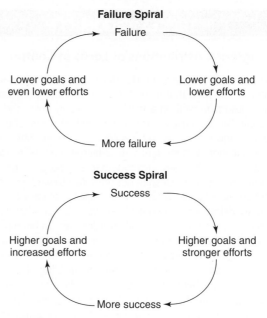

FIGURE 11.2   Failure and Success Spirals

their own efforts. Often, special educators manipulate the learning environment in such a way as to make success inevitable and effortless. In such cases, students are less likely to recognize the effort used or to attribute the successful outcome to their personal effort, but more likely to attribute the success to the teacher's making the task easy. When learners don't confront the possibility of failure and then see personal effort pay off, they are often left helpless in the face of real challenges in the future (Balk, 1983; Seligman, 1975).

IN THE CLASSROOM 11.7

Failure and Success Spirals

Megan is 15 years old and has received special education services, under the classification of learning disability, in three states since second grade. After almost 10 years of significant failure in school, Megan appears to be firmly planted in a failure spiral. She does not invest full effort in academic tasks, responding, "I'm just a 'retard.' I can't do this." When asked a question, she often responds at random with the first word that pops into her head. Her lack of progress appears to have defeated her. Megan recently told her teacher, "There's not enough time left for me to learn. I'll never do it."

Mary, on the other hand, has really benefited from the assistance she has received this fall. Last year was a frustrating one for her, with failing grades in math primarily related to incomplete homework. Her special education teacher this year decided to teach her some organizational and study strategies to help with her content area classes, including math. Mary found that by using the assignment completion strategy for her math assignments, she was able to keep track of her materials better, which encouraged her to actually complete the work. Her teacher reinforced her for handing in her homework, which led Mary to try even harder to be more accurate in the work she handed in and to ask for help when she needed it. This week she received an 87 on her math test, and she attributes the grade to her having done her homework every night for the last 2 weeks. Mary finally appears to be firmly in a success spiral for math.

IN THE CLASSROOM 11.8

Learned Helplessness

Ray, a sixth grader with learning disabilities and ADHD, is placed in an inclusion classroom. He tends to rely on external supports such as teacher prompts and assistance even when he is capable of completing a task independently. He quickly gives up on assignments that are only slightly challenging, saying, "I don't know how to do this." His intrinsic motivation for self- determination and control is in conflict with this learned helplessness. Although he is quick to say he can't do something, he is also quick to dismiss assistance offered by his teachers. They recognize these signs of learned helplessness and are developing an intervention program to help Ray develop more independence.

Learned Helplessness

Learned helplessness, or the generalized belief that one's own efforts will not be sufficient to positively affect outcomes, is a related characteristic affecting motivation that is frequently observed among learners with mild disabilities (Nunez et al., 2005; Stipek, 1993; Sutherland & Singh, 2004; Yates, 2009). Defined originally by Seligman (1975), learned helplessness results when individuals repeatedly experience events that they can't control by their own actions. In other words, no matter what response the learners make in the school environment, they have no expectation that any response will lead to a positive outcome or to more control and self-determination. The experience of repeated failure leads students to believe that effort is ineffective in achieving desired results, undermining their own motivation. Efforts and persistence in learning are reduced; they accept failure as inevitable, adopt a passive approach to their learning, and develop learned helplessness. Their attributions indicate their belief that the situation is unchanging, that they are incapable of changing or controlling the outcomes (see In the Classroom 11.8).

Learners whose mild disabilities affect their learning and adjustment in school settings often receive intensive academic help and guidance, including teachers who monitor and intervene in everything these students do and parents who do their children's homework or make excuses for their achievement problems. This experience of control by others and the students' own lack of personal control and responsibility often convinces them that they are unable to act (or learn) on their own and that everything that happens is related to uncontrollable, external forces, resulting in learned helpless behavior (Seifert, 2004).

Sutherland and Singh (2004) conjectured that the learned helplessness shown by students with emotional–behavioral disorders may be attributed to their response to classroom programs that they perceive as aversive, leading to avoidance/escape behaviors. The degree to which a learner feels that a task or situation presents impossible demands determines how much motivation will be demonstrated; the degree to which a student views a task as possible indicates how much motivation to learn can be mobilized. On the other hand, the loss of freedom and control of one's destiny, particularly when accompanied by the imposition of external controls, often leads to increased motivation to restore the lost freedom. Brehm and Brehm (1981) called this response "psychological reactance." The more important the freedom, the stronger the motivation to regain it. However, they also noted that when individuals become convinced that freedom is irretrievably lost, they generally abandon the quest, leading once again to a condition similar to learned helplessness and depression.

A study of adolescents with mild intellectual disabilities indicated that these students experienced more learned helplessness than their typical peers did (W. M. Reynolds & Miller, 1985). The learned helplessness was attributed to the significant levels of school failure experienced by these students, failure that they could not avoid by their own efforts. Learned helplessness appeared to interfere with their learning progress and was also found to be related to later instances of depression.

Students with ADHD and others who take medication for hyperactivity and inattention frequently come to believe they cannot control themselves without it (Whalen & Henker, 1991). The next step for these learners is to refuse to accept responsibility for their learning or for their behavioral control. It appears that children with disabilities can learn helplessness as surely as they learn competence (Balk, 1983).

ADOLESCENTS WITH DISABILITIES IN BEHAVIOR AND LEARNING

All adolescent students present special challenges to their parents and educators, and those with mild disabilities are no exception. The problems and issues encountered by typical adolescents are compounded for students with disabilities that affect learning and behavior. Challenges associated with identity exploration, self-determination, and biological changes, as well as with the development of social interaction and career skills needed for adult life, are faced by all teenagers. These challenges are often exacerbated by specific issues related to an adolescent's disability, such as

- Poor academic achievement or reaching an academic learning plateau
- Deficits in cognitive processing
- Ineffective study skills and cognitive strategies needed for problem solving and self-regulated learning
- Social skill deficits and other problem behaviors
- Motivational deficits induced by failure, passive learning styles, and learned helplessness

In the 1970s, the Institute for Research on Learning Disabilities at the University of Kansas began investigating the characteristics of adolescents with learning disabilities. As they looked at the experiences of these young people, they discovered some common patterns of behavior among them (Alley & Deshler, 1979; Johnston, 1984):

- Growing discrepancy between ability and achievement, including difficulty in reading, spelling, and/or mathematics
- Reduced ability to retain information; disorganized thinking patterns
- Inability to stay on task, although attention appears to improve
- Poor study habits and inconsistent organization of school tasks
- Continued difficulties with fine motor skills (e.g., poor handwriting), although gross motor skills are improved
- More frequent manifestation of emotional symptoms, including a tendency to overrespond to social stresses
- Tendency to be unaware of their effect on others in social situations
- Tendency for learning and behavioral problems to become more covert as increased maturity masks characteristics more common at younger ages

In addition, researchers confirmed that the demands of a high school environment are significantly different from the demands encountered in elementary school (Alley & Deshler, 1979; Deshler et al., 1996). Secondary teachers routinely expect that students will be relatively independent in their learning skills. High school teachers tend to concentrate instruction on course content, providing less of the cognitive coaching and fewer skill development activities commonly part of the elementary school program. Secondary teachers expect students to be proficient in independently carrying out the following tasks:

- Acquiring information by studying and note taking
- Devising ways to remember information
- Demonstrating competence through complex written formats on assignments and tests

Significant mismatches can occur between the learning profile of a specific student with a disability and the demands of a high school environment, resulting in impaired performance and school failure. One indication of this mismatch is the amount of stress exhibited by these youth and the coping strategies they use to deal with it. In a study of the stresses encountered by young adolescents with learning disabilities, Geisthardt and Munsch (1996) found that these students experienced stressors in similar proportions to those of other students, although they were much more likely to fail a class and less likely to be chosen for a special school activity. Both of these factors have implications for an adolescent's sense of competence and self-worth. These students were also found to respond more often to academic stresses with cognitive avoidance and denial and were less apt to seek help from a friend when faced with a problem. These responses are problematic in the long run, as they increase the likelihood that these adolescents will move into adulthood without the skills to actively deal with problems and without a support network of friends (Wenz-Gross & Siperstein, 1997).

Although these research efforts focused specifically on adolescents with learning disabilities, the patterns and issues have been found to apply generally to students with other mild disabilities as well. Research on students with behavioral disorders indicates that they, too, face significant academic problems in high school. Their academic difficulty also increases as they move from the elementary to the secondary level; academic underachievement is a common characteristic of this group, which places them at risk from the beginning. Students with organizational deficits in

---

DIVERSITY IN FOCUS 11.1

When we consider the academic learning characteristics of students with disabilities, we must eventually consider factors that contribute to making an educational environment feel supportive or hostile to a learner. Unfortunately, today the outcome of hostile school environments is all too evident: Bullies and harassment, school violence, and high dropout rates remind us that a number of students do not find school a place that meets their needs. When students feel excluded, marginalized, or unsafe because of who they are—by virtue of their abilities, race, ethnicity, language, religion, gender, physical attributes, sexual orientation, family structure, or economic status—learning is certain to be compromised and may become impossible. Educators must work to see that every child finds school to be a comfortable place to learn.

High school graduation rates are one indicator of the success of an academic program. U.S. Department of Education (2009) data indicate that 55 percent of students with disabilities graduated with a standard diploma in 2003–2004, but rates were much lower for students with intellectual disabilities (39 percent) and emotional disturbance (38 percent). A significant number of additional students with intellectual disabilities left school with a certificate rather than a diploma.

This report also indicated that Euro-American students with disabilities had a 61 percent graduation rate, whereas only 39 percent of African American students with disabilities graduated with a diploma. Among students with disabilities, dropout rates were highest among Native American students (45 percent), African American students (38 percent), and Hispanic students (35 percent). It is clear that students with disabilities who identify as Native American, African American, or Hispanic are being left behind, although the numbers do not point to a cause. Data are not kept on how many gay or lesbian students fail to complete high school although results of the 2009 National School Climate Survey (Gay, Lesbian and Straight Education Network, 2010) indicate that over 60 percent of gay and lesbian youth felt unsafe at school and 90 percent experienced harassment, with school and class attendance and academic performance thereby affected.

Issues related to family poverty must also be considered in any discussion of academic performance. Poverty has repeatedly been shown to be correlated with academic failure (Coutinho, Oswald, & Best, 2002; Coutinho, Oswald, & Forness, 2002). Unfortunately, students with disabilities whose lives are also affected by poverty and racial or linguistic differences are at significantly more risk of school failure (U.S. Department of Education, 2001). Educators must find out why this is so.

It has been suggested that increasing the number of diverse educators would help address these problems (Salend et al., 2002). One positive response to these findings would be for districts to increase their efforts to diversify their staffs by recruiting educators who represent diverse backgrounds and/or who have had successful experiences working with diverse learners.

ON THE WEB

Teaching Tolerance (www. tolerance.org) provides a number of teaching resources for educators to use in making the elementary and secondary curriculum and schools more supportive of the needs of diverse students. The **Gay, Lesbian, and Straight Education Network,** or **GLSEN** (www.glsen.org), provides access to information, including the biennial National School Climate Survey and other resources for creating safer school environments for all, with particular emphasis on gay, lesbian, bisexual, and transgender youth.

ON THE WEB

The **2009 National School Climate Survey** (www. glsen.org) describes continuing patterns of harassment in schools that is based on sexual orientation, gender identity, race, disabilities, and gender.

	Total Number Exiting	Percent Receiving Diploma	Percent Dropping Out	Other Exit Status*
Learning Disabilities	236,921	59%	29%	12%
Emotional–Behavioral Disorders	49,217	38%	52%	10%
Intellectual Disabilities	47,832	39%	26%	35%
Other Health Impaired	25,438	60%	28%	12%
All Disabilities	392,753	55%	31%	14%
All Students	—	—	10.3%**	—

Table 11.2   Percentage of School Leavers with Disabilities Receiving Diplomas or Dropping Out (2003–2004)

*Includes receiving a certificate, leaving the district (not known to be continuing), reaching maximum age, transferring to general education, and dying.

** Includes all those not receiving a high school diploma or GED.

Sources: Data from U.S. Department of Education, National Center for Education Statistics, 2009, available at http://nces.ed.gov.

managing time, poor test-taking skills, content reading problems, and an external locus of control—traits commonly observed in all students with mild disabilities—also tend to fare more poorly academically (Foley & Epstein, 1992). Kortering and Blackorby (1992) reported that students with emotional–behavioral disorders fail to graduate from high school at a rate that is significantly higher than that of their typical peers or even of students with other disabilities (see Table 11.2). The students who dropped out were characterized as having had frequent school and program placement changes, indicating that their school programs may not have been as appropriate or continuous as one might hope. The picture that emerges of students with behavioral disorders is consistent with the earlier description of those with learning disabilities, and it is reasonable to expect that the same patterns apply in varying degrees to all learners with mild disabilities.

Self-Determination

One of the central developmental tasks facing every young person is self-determination, the condition of "acting as the primary causal agent in one's life and making choices and decisions regarding one's quality of life free from external influence or interference" (Wehmeyer, Kelchner, & Richards, 1996, p. 632). Self-determination develops over the life span, with critical developmental periods in childhood and adolescence. It involves the experience of acting out of choice rather than responding to coercion or obligation (Deci & Ryan, 1985; Wehmeyer, 1992, 1994; Wehmeyer et al., 1998; Wehmeyer et al., 1996; Wehmeyer & Schwartz, 1997; Whitney-Thomas & Moloney, 2001). The opportunity to make choices, express preferences, experience personal control over outcomes, take risks, and assume responsibility for personal actions is a highly valued indicator of becoming an adult. The importance of self-determination is reflected in the amendments to IDEA that require the involvement of adolescents with disabilities in transition planning (Carter, Trainor, Owens, Sweden, & Sun, 2010; Field, Hoffman, & Posch, 1997; Sands & Doll, 1996).

Self-determination is affected by four attributes: autonomy, self-regulation, psychological empowerment, and self-realization (Wehmeyer et al., 1996), all of which present particular challenges to adolescents with disabilities. Students with disabilities frequently have little opportunity to practice autonomous decision-making skills, particularly as the severity of their disabilities increases. This lack of opportunity to develop the skills required by autonomy promotes passive responses, learned helplessness, and dependency, leading these adolescents and others to believe that they are incapable of making their own decisions. Deficits in metacognition result in less skill in the self-examination and strategic knowledge necessary to solve problems, as well as a random or haphazard approach to self-regulation activities. The tendency of youngsters with

---

IN THE CLASSROOM 11.9

Adolescents and Self-Determination

Karen is a 10th grader receiving services for learning disabilities and ADHD. She has developed into a young woman with a strong set of values about what is right and wrong, and she is not easily swayed by others. She says she gets into a lot of fights standing up for her friends or for what she believes. She thinks about possible choices when a problem arises, then goes "with what's right." However, she is influenced by peer pressure in the classroom and frequently will not ask questions for fear of sounding "stupid." Karen says she works hard in school when she has "good days" (meaning Fridays, gym days, soccer days, cheerleading days, and days she isn't fighting with anyone). Her learning results in an increased sense of competence; when she passes tests, she feels good about herself, and she attributes her success to studying and working hard. Failures are often attributed to external forces, such as "The work was too hard," "The teacher didn't read the whole test to me," or "I am stupid." Karen is clearly working on determining her identity; when she is with her friends, she acts in a confident manner, sure of herself; when she encounters difficulty in class, she feels like she is "different."

---

disabilities to be delayed in self-regulation causes them to interact with significant others in ways that lead the others to conclude that these young people are incapable of making choices and must be protected. Psychological empowerment is derived primarily from a perceived sense of control of one's life. However, as noted previously, young people with disabilities tend to develop an external locus of control and to attribute their successes and failures to factors beyond their control. Their experience with failure and negative feedback, as well as with events that appear unpredictable or uncontrollable, affects their persistence and motivation, resulting in a diminished sense of perceived control. The life experience of adolescents with mild disabilities leads them to focus on what they cannot do, building on their experience of failure (Carter et al., 2010; Deci & Chandler, 1986; Wehmeyer et al., 1996; see In the Classroom 11.9).

ON THE WEB

See **The Arc** (http://www.thearc.org) for the organization's position statement on self-determination.

Evaluation of an adolescent's progress in becoming a self-determined adult is a critical factor in creating an appropriate educational program and in planning for transition. Those students who leave their adolescent years without a strong sense of self-determination are more likely to experience problems in employment and self-sufficiency during their adult years (Wehmeyer & Schwartz, 1997). Teenagers with disabilities must be viewed as active participants in planning their educational programs with an eye to transition (AAIDD, 2008). As they play active roles in determining what they need to learn, why they want to learn it, and how they are going to learn it, the likelihood increases that positive outcomes will be achieved and they will grow in their sense of self-determination (Field et al., 1997). Students who participate in their own transition planning become more confident in their self-determined behaviors and skills.

Research indicates that students with disabilities tend to rate their own self-determination skills more highly than either teachers or parents rate them, but they were ranked lower than their general education peers on self-determined behaviors. Students with learning disabilities were ranked more highly on self-determination than those with emotional–behavioral disorders, and both were ranked more highly than those with mild intellectual disabilities (Carter et al., 2010). More research is needed to address these needs, to develop effective strategies for resolving these deficits, and to better prepare secondary students with disabilities for the decisions they will make in the future.

LEARNING STYLES AND MULTIPLE INTELLIGENCES

Early in the history of learning disabilities, it was hypothesized that these disabilities were related to deficits in specific processing modalities or channels. It was believed that a prescription of specific procedures to remediate these deficits would allow these children to function normally in a school environment. This hypothesis, called the aptitude–treatment interaction, or ATI, is predicated on the premise that a specific treatment matched to a specific ability or deficit will result in skill improvement. Subsequent research has failed to support this hypothesis for a variety of reasons: (a) It is not possible to accurately assess many of these aptitudes; (b) it has not been possible to consistently design valid treatments to match specific deficits and abilities; and (c) it has not been possible to measure the interaction, or outcome of intervention, with any degree of confidence (L. S. Fuchs & Fuchs, 1986; Kavale, Hirshoren, & Forness, 1998; Snider, 1992). As noted by Treiber and Lahey (1983; see Chapter 9), even when children developed their skills in the prescribed remedial activities, they were often not able to transfer those skills to related academic tasks.

It is important, however, to discuss two additional theoretical perspectives that are related to diversity among students with respect to learning and that bear some similarities to these earlier processing-deficit theories. The first, learning styles, focuses on the context and nature of instruction, suggesting that the instructional environment and teaching methods should be selected to support the learning style of each student. The second perspective, multiple intelligences, focuses on individual students and their innate and varying abilities to solve problems and to create products that are of value in societal interactions.

Learning Styles

Even though decades of special education research has failed to support processing-deficit approaches to remediation, a similar discussion continues today in general education and special education programs concerning instructional accommodation of different learning styles within instructional settings. Proponents recommend this approach to instructional programming as an answer to underachievement among students in general, and particularly for those students with mild disabilities, despite inconsistent research findings on its general applicability and efficacy (Kavale et al., 1998).

The basic tenet of learning style theory is that individuals possess certain characteristics that interact with specific learning experiences and environments, resulting in enhancing learning or in making it more difficult. Learning style theory is concerned with how students learn, with the personal characteristics they bring to learning tasks, and with the means by which they accommodate and assimilate new information. Specifically, learning style proponents believe that teachers should select methods of instruction that match their students' learning style strengths, increasing the likelihood that instruction will be successful (Carbo, 2009; Dunn & Dunn, 2005). Proponents assert that in making instructional plans, teachers need to consider the characteristics and preferences of learners relative to the physical environment, method of instruction, modality preferences, motivation and feedback, and types of working groups. One common framework suggests that there are three learning styles reflected in the ways individuals prefer to acquire new information: (a) Visual learners are most effective using reading, watching demonstrations, and drawing pictures; (b) auditory learners learn best through listening and participating in discussions; and (c) kinesthetic learners learn most effectively through hands-on experiences with manipulatives and other media (Melton & Pickett, 1997; Slack & Norwich, 2007).

Nevertheless, even though it is generally recognized that all human beings relate somewhat differently to instruction and that the act of learning is affected by individual and environmental variables, the proposal that learning environments must be tailored to those characteristics appears to encounter the same problems that characterized earlier process-deficit and training theories (e.g., perceptual–motor training and psycholinguistic theories) and aptitude–treatment interaction approaches in general (Hessler & Sosnowsky, 1979; Kavale et al., 1998; Snider, 1992). Specifically, the instruments used to assess learning style preferences have been found to have questionable validity and reliability; the teaching methods are only superficially related to any particular style; and the effect of such a match is difficult to measure (Cassidy, 2004; Desmedt & Valcke, 2004). Although there may be some value in the notion that learners approach learning uniquely, it is not necessarily possible or desirable to tailor an individual child's instructional environment to any specific style. Teachers may find it more useful to provide multiple and flexible approaches that all of their learners can use as they encounter and practice the

IN THE CLASSROOM 11.10

Learning Styles

Aaron and Carolyn are eighth graders with mild disabilities. Aaron's resource teacher has noted that he does much better in his mainstream classes when the teacher uses visual media and demonstrations to explain the content. He has more difficulty in history class, in which the teacher uses lecture and discussion methods exclusively. This leads his resource teacher to conclude that Aaron benefits from the use of visual presentation methods and that exclusive use of auditory presentations puts Aaron at a disadvantage for learning. Carolyn, on the other hand, has great difficulty learning from reading but does much better when she can also hear the material. Their teacher concludes that both students would benefit from instruction that included both visual and auditory input and an opportunity for active involvement in learning.

skills and content of the curriculum, and then to guide students in identifying for themselves the ones that are most useful for them (see In the Classroom 11.10). Teachers who plan instruction in accordance with the principles of UDL will make classroom activities flexibly accessible to most learners, despite disabilities or differences in preferred learning styles.

Multiple Intelligences

Related to this discussion of learning profiles is Gardner's theory of multiple intelligences (Gardner, 2006; Moran, Kornhaber, & Gardner, 2006). In the tradition of cognitive styles research, Gardner advanced the theory that each individual possesses at least nine distinct ways of thinking and learning, solving problems, and creating valued products: (a) linguistic, (b) logical–mathematical, (c) musical, (d) spatial, (e) bodily–kinesthetic, (f) intrapersonal, (g) interpersonal, (h) naturalist, and (i) existentialist intelligences (see Table 11.3). Gardner viewed all of these intelligences as having equal standing and hypothesized that each person exhibits a profile of these intelligences that reflects specific intraindividual strengths. He asserted that the intelligences are not discrete entities but rather function in a variety of overlapping and complementary ways in

Table 11.3 Gardner's Multiple Intelligences	
Type of Intelligence	**Description of Specific Skill or Ability**
Linguistic intelligence	Verbal facility; skill in the use of words
Logical–mathematical intelligence	Symbolic reasoning and skill in dealing with abstract reasoning and problem solving, as well as recognizing patterns and order
Musical intelligence	Skill in performance and appreciation of musical forms of expression; sensitivity to pitch, rhythm, and tone
Spatial intelligence	Awareness of the structural components of ideas and objects, and the ability to transform structures mentally; ability to work effectively in a three-dimensional world
Bodily–kinesthetic intelligence	Ability to use movement for learning and expression; skillful use of the body and manipulation of objects to produce a desired outcome
Intrapersonal intelligence	Ability to understand one's own feelings and emotions as a means of self-development and growth
Interpersonal intelligence	Awareness of others and social interactions; ability to apply social understandings to interactions with others
Naturalist intelligence	Sensitivity to and ability to differentiate among living things, as well as sensitivity to other features of the natural world
Existentialist intelligence	Ability to consider phenomena or questions philosophically and beyond sensory input

Source: Based on Gardner, 2006; and Moran, Kornhaber, and Gardner, 2006.

real-life situations. Finally, he proposed that everyone has the potential to develop skills in all nine intelligences (Armstrong, 1994; Moran & Gardner, 2007; Moran et al., 2006).

Gardner (2006) proposed that the difficulties some individuals experience in our current schooling process may actually be due to the fact that their stronger skills and intelligences lie in areas not generally tapped by common school curricula and practices. It has been asserted by some (e.g., Hearne & Stone, 1995) that the preoccupation of schools with linguistic and logical–mathematical abilities may cause other intelligences to be devalued and underdeveloped. Programming decisions for learners that are based almost entirely on their deficits in linguistic and logical–mathematical areas may restrict their development in other areas of strength, and the learners may be disadvantaged in the teaching–learning environment because of a lack of fit. (For an example, see the case study of Sammy at the end of Chapter 12.) Ironically, the development of intelligences other than linguistic and logical–mathematical is seen as necessary for success in many postschool environments. Interpersonal and intrapersonal intelligences are particularly valued in the adult world of work and should be clearly addressed in school programs. Nurturing of students' intrapersonal intelligence is also relevant to the development of executive functioning so necessary for effective cognitive performance (Moran & Gardner, 2007).

Gardner voiced caution, however, in applying the theory of multiple intelligences in a restrictive and prescriptive manner. The multiple intelligences framework suggests that each person varies in the means by which learning happens most effectively and by which achievement is demonstrated most clearly. When considering the theory of multiple intelligences, teachers may want to explore ways of creating learning environments that recognize and value all the intelligences, rather than focusing exclusively on the linguistic and logical–mathematical forms (Akiba & Alkins, 2010; Hoerr, 1996).

Universal Design for Learning

ON THE WEB

The **National Center on Universal Design for Learning** (http://www. udlcenter.org) explains the principles of universal design for learning, including ways to make the general education curriculum accessible to a broad variety of student abilities.

Discussion of these theories and perspectives continues. Even though it is not entirely clear how the frameworks of learning styles and multiple intelligences might affect schooling in general and special education in particular, it is important that educators remember that all students have strengths that must be considered in good educational planning. In fact, IDEA requires that educational plans consider a student's strengths, not merely the deficits. It may well be that developing a student's abilities in a variety of intelligences will also assist in the development of the currently valued linguistic and logical–mathematical intelligences. Helping students identify and use their own strengths in working and learning may suggest ways for educators to design instructional interventions that make use of untapped strengths to support learning. Using more diverse teaching methods and activities will result in more effective learning. As educators develop instructional activities that are consistent with the principles of UDL, the likelihood increases that all students will be able to successfully access their learning environment (see Chapter 3).

INSTRUCTIONAL NEEDS OF LEARNERS WITH DISABILITIES

As we consider the instructional needs of learners with mild disabilities, we need to consider variables that affect how well students learn in school and explore how these variables interact with student characteristics. Carroll (1963, 1989) suggested that students will be successful in learning only to the extent that they actually spend the amount of time they need in order to master a task or concept. In his model of school learning, Carroll defined the time spent by a learner as a function of the actual clock time allowed for learning and the persistence or motivation of the learner to stick with the learning tasks. He further defined the time needed by the student as determined by the quality of instruction, the student's aptitude for instruction, and the student's ability to understand instruction.

The rate and efficiency of learning depend on how effectively the time allocated for learning is used (S. Graham, 1985). If no time is allocated for a learning task, no learning will result. If too little time is spent, the resultant learning will be incomplete. If the time available is devoted to tasks

UNIVERSAL DESIGN FOR LEARNING IN ACTION 11

Supporting Academic Learning

Principle I: *Use multiple and flexible means of representation*[a]	Provide multiple options for students to get information on a unit topic (books, magazines, interviews, Internet, etc.), and help them learn to evaluate and triangulate the information they acquire.
	Use the principles of effective instruction (e.g., direct instruction) to teach most basic skills to those who need a structured approach to learning.
	Use clear examples and nonexamples when teaching new concepts in order to support accurate acquisition of new learning.
	For those students with deficits in learning strategies, teach relevant strategies and coach their use.
	Explore Internet resources for content in the primary language of English language learners; students can then use the first language information alongside the English version.
Principle II: *Allow multiple and flexible means of expression*[a]	Engage students in a discussion about how they can best demonstrate what they have learned in a specific learning activity; pose these questions: How will I know that I have learned ___? How will others know?
	Use continuous assessment to help students monitor their own progress.
	Offer options for assessment, including contracts for performance.
Principle III: *Provide multiple and flexible means of engagement*[a]	Provide multiple ways for students to practice what they need to learn; students need differing amounts and types of practice to achieve proficiency, maintenance, and generalization.
	Challenge students to develop and share their own practice activities.
	Monitor student learning carefully during acquisition to prevent incorrect learning during the reversion substage.
	Use error analysis and share results with individual students to help each see how to improve.
	Offer computerized drill/practice programs to provide flexible opportunities for the practice needed to achieve proficiency in basic skills.
	Have practice materials easily available for those odd bits of unstructured time.
	Plan practice activities with options to respond to differing multiple intelligences.
Principle IV: *Create a community of learners in the classroom*[b]	Remember that practice can be most meaningfully performed in collaboration with others.
	Use strategies such as peer tutoring, partner reading, and cooperative learning to provide an environment for learners to persist in needed practice until proficiency and generalization is achieved.
	Create a supportive environment in which students feel they belong, to enhance student achievement of learning goals.
Principle V: *Establish a positive instructional climate*[b]	Use instructional time efficiently by reducing nonessential effort.
	Understand that all learners have some source(s) of intrinsic motivation that can be applied to learning; find out what matters to particular learners.
	When dealing with students who exhibit learned helplessness, communicate your confidence in them, and require that they make an attempt before asking for help.
	Teach learning strategies to help develop internal attributions for learning and to help students see that effort matters.
	To enhance self-determination, provide opportunities for students to set priorities for learning, engaging them in setting their own instructional goals.

Principles adapted from (a) Center for Applied Special Technology (CAST), 2008 and (b) McGuire, Scott, and Shaw, 2006.

Model of School Learning

$$\text{Degree of learning} = \frac{\text{Time actually spent}}{\text{Time needed}}$$

FIGURE 11.3 Carroll's Model of School Learning

that are incomprehensible to the learner, or if time is spent repeating errors, learning will not proceed with maximum efficiency. Furthermore, if the learner is required to continue a learning activity past the point of mastery and proficiency, no additional learning will occur (see Figure 11.3).

As we consider instructional variables that affect the success and efficiency of learning, it might be useful to discuss each of these elements individually, with particular attention to their relationship to the characteristics of learners with mild disabilities and to the stages of learning discussed earlier.

Time Allowed for Instruction

Learners with mild disabilities generally need more actual time to learn. Given real-world time constraints, it is important to make careful decisions about the allocation of time in order to ensure that the most critical learning has sufficient time allocated to it. Studies of time use in schools indicate that a significant amount of time is used on nonacademic pursuits or in off-task, nonengaged behavior (Vannest & Parker, 2010; Wallace, Anderson, Bartholomay, & Hupp, 2002). Time in school is further eroded when students are pulled from their primary classrooms for remedial assistance, spending significant amounts of time traveling the halls (see In the Classroom 11.11). When one measures the actual academic learning time, or the time spent engaged in learning with a high rate of success, it is frequently meager indeed (Denham & Lieberman, 1980; Johns, Crowley, & Guetzloe, 2008; Vannest & Parker, 2010).

Persistence or Motivation

As noted earlier in this chapter, students are motivated by different goals and needs. Even more importantly, motivation is affected by the quality of prior learning. Motivation alone cannot cause students to do what they lack the preparation to do. Difficulty in maintaining attention on academic tasks also affects a student's ability to stay with a task long enough to complete the learning. Teachers must assess prior relevant learnings for robustness as they evaluate a specific student's zone of proximal development (see Chapter 9). Evaluation of teaching and learning activities with respect to the likelihood that participation will help students meet their goals and needs is also important. Finally, the quality of the attention paid by learners must be assessed, and learning time demands modified to accommodate and develop their attention spans.

IN THE CLASSROOM 11.11

Time to Learn

Gail is in ninth grade and receives resource room services for her learning disability in reading and written expression. Now that she attends the high school, her time in regular classes is not disrupted by these services. In elementary and middle school, she lost instructional time traveling to the resource room and getting back on task when she returned to class. Now, she spends her study hall period in the resource room, where she receives instruction in learning strategies that help her meet the reading and writing demands of her content classes. Her motivation to use this assistance to do well allows her allocated time in the resource room to be fully used in the pursuit of learning.

Pupils' Aptitude for Instruction

This variable requires an accurate assessment of the aptitudes and prior learning that students bring to classrooms, and that teachers can then use to design classroom activities. Obviously, general intellectual functioning is a variable, but teachers also need to understand the ways their students process cognitive information, the nature of their attention capabilities, their motivations for learning, their specific abilities in using and understanding language, and the quality of their prior learning. It is important to also understand that the ability of some students to profit from instruction may be reduced by a variety of social or emotional factors outside the classroom.

Ability to Understand Instruction

The factors that most affect this variable include competence in the use and comprehension of spoken and written language. Students learning English as an additional language will have more difficulty understanding instruction provided in standard English and will need to be provided with supports and additional language instruction to become most effective in learning (see Chapter 10). The ability to understand instruction may also be affected by social or emotional demands that command the energies a student needs for learning (see Chapter 12).

Quality of Instruction

Of all the factors in Carroll's model, this is the one most clearly within a teacher's ability to control. Research (e.g., Christenson, Ysseldyke, & Thurlow, 1989) indicates that a number of critical instructional factors are essential to the learning success of students with mild disabilities. One pedagogical concern relates to the nature of the interaction between a student's individual characteristics (such as cognitive reasoning abilities, language competencies, motivation, and emotional and behavioral characteristics) and the method of instruction used by the teacher. In general, research on effective teaching of students with mild disabilities has suggested that direct instruction is preferable to other methods such as inquiry learning (Ellis, 1993). Mastropieri, Scruggs, and Butcher (1997) confirmed this in their study of student performance on an inductive inquiry task in science. In this study, students with learning and intellectual disabilities were significantly less successful on their own in discovering the principle being demonstrated, and they required much more directive coaching to be successful. This suggests that teachers should use caution in assuming that learning has occurred through nondirective classroom activity; inquiry learning experiences may need to be followed up with additional direct instruction and practice in order for these students to fully learn concepts and skills.

Summary

Learning is the process of moving from not knowing to knowing and using. Five stages mark the progress of a learner: acquisition, proficiency, maintenance, generalization, and adaptation. Learners with mild disabilities tend to move through the stages more slowly and to need more support or scaffolding to achieve each of the goals of the stages. The ability of learners to process information cognitively is critical to their academic success. Deficits in attention, short- or long-term memory, and executive functions present special problems, as teachers tend to assume the control, direction, and monitoring of learning for these students, often resulting in passive learning styles.

Motivation is critical to all human endeavors, including learning. Extrinsic motivation is supplied by rewards or punishments that reinforce learned behaviors. Intrinsic motivation comes from the individual learner's personal needs and drives, such as the need for competence, self-determination/control, or relatedness. Learners also vary in their perceptions of their ability to control learning outcomes. Those who view events as determined by luck or the actions of other people outside their control are said to have an external locus of control. Those who see outcomes as determined by their own efforts are said to have an internal locus of control, which has been shown to be associated with greater learning effectiveness. Significant experiences of failure frequently lead to a failure spiral, whereas successes can result in a success spiral. Students with disabilities who encounter failure in learning tasks frequently develop learned help-lessness, the belief that nothing they do will affect a negative outcome.

Adolescents with disabilities face unique challenges in school learning. Their areas of deficit frequently prevent them from meeting the expectations of secondary teachers. Self-determination, a crucial learning for all adolescents, is the ability to act as the primary causal agent in one's life, to make choices and decisions independently. The effect of a disability may impede the development of the self-determination so necessary for adult independence.

Theories of learning styles and multiple intelligences suggest that students approach the task of learning in potentially unique ways, which seems to suggest the need for tailoring instruction to individual prefer-ences. An alternative approach to meeting individual needs is to plan instruction in accordance with the principles of universal design for learning, providing multiple and flexible ways for all learners to access the educational environment.

In concluding our discussion of academic learning characteristics, it is important to note that knowledge of student characteristics can lead us to make more effective decisions about instructional techniques and the types of environment necessary to be most supportive of student achievement. In addition, each student's opportunity to learn will be enhanced by having the time needed to learn effectively and assuring that instructional decisions are made with the primary goal of increasing learning efficiency.

A Case Study   • Allison

Allison is an 8-year-old girl classified as having a mild intellectual disability. She is presently enrolled in Mrs. Riley's self-contained special education classroom. Allison has been progressing nicely in Mrs. Riley's class for the past 2 months. She has demonstrated particular growth in mathematics. However, Allison is a timid child who has difficulty functioning in large groups. She becomes easily distracted and anxious when surrounded by more than a few other children. She needs extra support and encouragement to interact with her peers.

Allison's mother, Jane Miller, has been very impressed with her daughter's recent achievement in mathematics and suggested to Mrs. Riley that Allison be mainstreamed into a general education classroom for math. In response to her suggestion, Mrs. Riley said that although Allison has demonstrated significant improvements in mathematics, she has difficulty functioning in large groups and may need more time to strengthen her self-confidence and social skills. Mrs. Riley thought that Allison would eventually be ready for mainstreaming, but that it was premature to consider it at this stage.

Disappointed by Mrs. Riley's response, Mrs. Miller met with the Director of Special Education and expressed her strong belief that Allison should be mainstreamed for mathematics. She then asked the director to schedule a meeting of the multidisciplinary team to discuss the situation.

The meeting was scheduled within the week, and Mrs. Miller presented her suggestion to the committee. "I am very pleased with Allison's progress in mathematics," she said. "I am also aware that Allison has difficulty socializing; however, I believe that Allison would benefit, both socially and academically, from being mainstreamed in math. She would have the perfect opportunity to strengthen her social skills with a greater number of students, while getting the more sophisticated math instruction she needs."

Mrs. Riley responded, "Mrs. Miller, I am as pleased as you are with Allison's progress in math. I am not concerned with Allison's ability to succeed academically; in fact, Mrs. Armstrong's first-grade class is covering the same math concepts that Allison is working on. I have considered Mrs. Armstrong's class as a possibility for Allison to eventually be mainstreamed into. At this point, though, I strongly recommend that Allison remain in my class where we can work on her self-esteem and improve her social skills. I am afraid that mainstreaming Allison at this point would be too overwhelming. Allison has a tendency to cry when she is surrounded by a group of children, and it is very difficult for her to function appropriately, let alone do her best, in such an environment. Let's wait before we subject Allison to an environment for which she may not be ready."

Mrs. Miller forcefully explained, "If Allison were mainstreamed, it would be a parent's dream come true. It would go a long way to reducing the stigma of Allison's having an intellectual disability. IDEA requires that a child be educated in the least restrictive environment. Let us at least do Allison justice and give her the opportunity to work in a regular classroom with regular kids! We cannot possibly know that Allison would not be able to function in a regular classroom until we give her a chance."

The decision was finalized at the meeting. Allison would be mainstreamed into Mrs. Armstrong's classroom for mathematics beginning the following Monday. It was agreed at the meeting that a student from Mrs. Riley's class would walk Allison to and from Mrs. Armstrong's class until Allison felt comfortable walking by herself.

On Monday, Allison arrived at Mrs. Armstrong's class with her classmate Jenny. Mrs. Armstrong welcomed Allison warmly and introduced her to the class. One of the students in the class said, "Hi! You can sit next to me. My name is Tracey." Allison held tight to Jenny's hand and didn't take another step. Jenny said, "Come on, Allison. You're going to sit here," and began walking Allison to the empty seat next to Tracey. Allison sat down apprehensively, and Jenny returned to Mrs. Riley's class.

Five days had passed when the following scene took place. It was a scenario that had become common in Mrs. Armstrong's classroom:

Mrs. Armstrong asked, "Tracey, could you please share your crayons with Allison?" Tracey replied, "I'm not sharing my crayons with her—she never gives them back and she puts them in her mouth!"

Peter added, "Yeah, and she always cries like a big baby when you want your stuff back!"

Allison, with tears in her eyes, pleaded, "Let me go back to Mrs. Riley's class—please, let me go!"

Discussion

Discuss Allison's experience with respect to the major topics in this chapter:

- Social learning theory
- Stages of learning
- Cognitive processing and academic performance
- Attributions of success and failure
- Learned helplessness

Based on this analysis, how might this scenario have had a different outcome? What actions might both teachers have taken to make this a more successful experience?

How might planning in accordance with UDL change this picture?

Source: Adapted with permission from "When Mainstreaming Fails" by Karin Otto-Flynn.

CHAPTER 12

Social–Emotional Characteristics

Meet Eddie

Eddie is 7 years old and a first grader in Mrs. Williams's class. He is one of three children, with a younger sister and an older brother. Mrs. Williams has become increasingly concerned about Eddie's tendency to fly into a rage when he encounters frustration. He responds to frustration with behavior more typical of a much younger child by hitting, kicking, biting, and spitting at other children in the classroom and at home. His mother reports that he is particularly violent with his sister.

Eddie's mother has told the social worker that she is unable to control Eddie at home. She seems to be overwhelmed by the care of three young children. When Eddie loses his temper, her only recourse is to remove the other children from the apartment. She reports that Eddie has been abused by two adults in his life—physically by his father, who is no longer in the home, and sexually by an uncle who has been committed to the state hospital.

Eddie was referred to the local mental health agency for an evaluation. The evaluator found that Eddie's intellectual functioning fell within the borderline range of mild intellectual disability, with academic measures below grade level but consistent with his IQ of 72. He found evidence of oppositional and controlling tendencies, which supported a diagnosis of oppositional defiant disorder. The school multidisciplinary team recommended placement in a day treatment program for children with emotional disorders. They felt that Eddie should be able to experience success both at home and in his school environment with appropriate therapeutic interventions to address his emotional and behavioral needs, along with small-group academic instruction.

Meanwhile, Eddie's teacher, his mother, and the social worker have put in place a behavior modification program involving earning privileges and the use of time-outs. They are finding it difficult to carry out the program consistently, however, because of the nature of Eddie's violent outbursts, and the social worker is investigating placement in a therapeutic foster home.

THINKING QUESTIONS

In the case of dangerous behavior like this, what options do teachers and schools have? How might response to intervention have been useful?

■ What are the implications of IDEA 2004 for responding to maladaptive behaviors in schools? How might response to intervention be useful as a critical preventive strategy?

PERSPECTIVES ON SOCIAL–EMOTIONAL CHARACTERISTICS

Behavioral responses are adaptive when they result in socially acceptable and personally satisfying outcomes. On the other hand, social–emotional behaviors are deemed to be problematic when they become socially unacceptable or personally unsatisfying (Kauffman, 1977). Behaviors become problematic in two ways:

- Learners may fail to develop age-appropriate social behaviors or may develop appropriate behaviors more slowly than typical children do, thereby restricting their ability to participate productively in ways that are appropriate for their ages or culture. Learners may also be blocked in the normal developmental progression, diminishing their ability to accomplish later social learnings and leading to accumulating deficits in social behavior.
- Maladaptive behaviors may be present. A learner may exhibit substitute behaviors that are maladaptive responses to environmental events and personal issues and that take the place of more useful behaviors, thus compromising the learner's functioning in critical ways.

The difficulties presented by learners who have problems in identifying, choosing, and using appropriate and adaptive social responses can be considered from two theoretical perspectives that help explain the meaning of the behaviors exhibited by these learners:

- Developmental perspectives, which consider typical social skill progressions observed in learners as they develop age-appropriate levels of social awareness and behavioral responses
- Ecological perspectives, which describe behavior as a result of the interactions among the characteristics of individual learners, the nature of the environment, and the behavioral context in which the behavior occurs.

IDEA 2004 requires that multidisciplinary teams always consider the behavior problems of the learner when developing an IEP, regardless of the individual's specific disabilities (Yell & Dragsow, 2000). The concepts developed in this chapter will be useful in considering the nature and impact of any behavior problem, including those exhibited by learners with intellectual disabilities, learning disabilities, autism, and ADHD, as well as emotional or behavioral disorders. At the end of the chapter, we will discuss some of the most frequent types of maladaptive behaviors presented by learners with mild disabilities.

DEVELOPMENTAL PERSPECTIVES

Developmentalists such as Piaget and Erikson have generally held that behaviors and emotions develop in a predictable manner throughout the life span. Over the years, individuals incorporate learnings from typical life events into their own unique personalities. These theorists have suggested that knowledge about normal development in children, adolescents, and adults is useful as

Table 12.1 Stages of Psychosocial Development		
Stage or Crisis	**Virtue/Goal**	**Time Period**
Basic trust vs. mistrust	Hope	Birth to 12–18 months
Autonomy vs. shame	Willpower	12–18 months to 3 years
Initiative vs. guilt	Purpose	3 to 6 years
Industry vs. inferiority	Competence	6 years to puberty
Identity vs. role confusion	Fidelity	Puberty to young adult
Intimacy vs. isolation	Love	Early adult years
Generativity vs. stagnation	Care	Middle adult years
Ego integrity vs. despair	Wisdom	Late adult years

Source: Based on *Childhood and Society* (2nd ed.) by E. Erikson, 1963, New York: Norton.

a guide when designing instructional interventions for students whose development appears to be following a different path or pace. For this reason, we will begin by reviewing common developmental frameworks and will then discuss how a learner's disability might interact with that developmental process.

Erikson's Theory of Psychosocial Development

Erik Erikson (1963) formulated his theory of psychosocial development based on his concern about the effect of societal and cultural factors on the development of the ego, or self. He identified eight predictable stages of life, each of which is characterized by a particular life challenge or crisis. As individuals work to resolve each of these crises, they develop socially and emotionally. Erikson asserted that the development of a healthy sense of self was dependent on coming to a successful resolution of each of these eight successive crises (see Table 12.1).

Each stage is characterized by two opposite outcomes. Satisfactory resolution of each stage results in a strong sense of the positive quality, appropriately balanced by the negative quality. For example, infants who develop a healthy balance in the trust-versus-mistrust stage come to view the world and other people as generally trustworthy, while maintaining enough mistrust to protect themselves from potential dangers. Children who fail to resolve this crisis in a positive direction in infancy continue to view the world as a scary place and are likely to have trouble forming satisfactory interpersonal relationships until they can be helped to develop trusting relationships with significant others.

In the autonomy-versus-shame stage, a toddler learns to strike an appropriate balance between self-determination and control. The initiative-versus-guilt stage challenges a child to balance the pursuit of goals with appropriate reservations or caution about carrying them out. In the industry-versus-inferiority stage, children develop a sense of competence and value for productive work, as well as a positive but realistic self-concept. Adolescents struggle with the identity-versus-role-confusion stage as they determine who they are and to what they will commit their lives (e.g., careers, values, loved ones). Through this process, teenagers develop a strong sense of self while keeping themselves open to later growth. The final three stages relate to the challenges faced by adults in developing intimacy, productivity, and wholeness. In each stage, Erikson believed that an individual's experience with significant others is critical in determining whether a healthy sense of self will be the outcome.

As we look at learners with disabilities, we can identify several ways in which normal development patterns may be hindered, affecting the ability of these individuals to interact productively with others. Obviously a child whose needs have not been met reliably in infancy is more likely to have problems with trust throughout life, and caregivers will find it difficult to form relationships with such youngsters. Children like Eddie in the chapter opening vignette may exhibit emotional problems in their interactions with others, and it is important to document and address these trust needs (Arent, 1992).

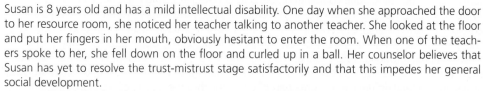

IN THE CLASSROOM 12.1

Stages of Psychosocial Development

Susan is 8 years old and has a mild intellectual disability. One day when she approached the door to her resource room, she noticed her teacher talking to another teacher. She looked at the floor and put her fingers in her mouth, obviously hesitant to enter the room. When one of the teachers spoke to her, she fell down on the floor and curled up in a ball. Her counselor believes that Susan has yet to resolve the trust-mistrust stage satisfactorily and that this impedes her general social development.

Larry, who is 11, has struggled with his reading disability ever since he entered school. The failure he has experienced has undermined his sense of value as a learner and has compromised his resolution of the industry-versus-inferiority stage. He responds to teacher-assigned tasks with the simple response, "I can't." He has developed a strong distrust of his own capability as a learner, and this restricts his ability to recognize the skills he does have. Although he shows signs of beginning to deal with the identity stage (e.g., involvement with his peer group and disassociation from authority), his problems with the industry stage will likely compromise further development.

Erica is 15 and receiving special education services for her learning disability. It appears that she is currently working on resolving the identity stage, as is appropriate for her age. Her teacher observes that Erica is trying to establish herself as an autonomous person with a name. She wants to be recognized by others and works very hard toward that end. Recently, she has become very concerned with her appearance. She wants to look her best. She wants her clothes to match, and she fusses with her appearance before school and after gym. She doesn't like wearing her glasses because she doesn't think they are as stylish as those worn by others. She is very conscious of her peer group and is struggling to balance fitting in with the group while still being herself.

Toddlers whose world is circumscribed by overprotectiveness or restriction may fail to develop the healthy sense of self-determined behavior necessary for later academic and social learning. Children who are reticent and reserved in attempting new tasks or interacting with new people may have been restricted in setting and achieving goals in their early play experiences.

Elementary-age youngsters who find school-valued academic tasks difficult because of intellectual disabilities, learning disabilities, Asperger's syndrome, or ADHD, or whose special education classification is used by others to excuse their failures, may end up struggling with a sense of inferiority rather than developing a positive sense of self-worth as a learner and worker.

Considering current behaviors of children and youth in light of Erikson's theory may provide some clues to the source of problems and may assist in the development of effective interventions, much as Schlesinger (2000/1972) described in her classic article on deaf children. It is also worth considering that the way we serve children in schools may enhance or detract from their psychosocial development (see In the Classroom 12.1). The most obvious implication is that when we classify children, we are confirming their status as problem learners; by pulling them out of the mainstream and placing them in special classes, we may inadvertently communicate to them that they are not capable of the work others can do and that they are therefore inferior—thus compromising their successful resolution of the childhood crisis of industry versus inferiority. Separate placements may also restrict their interaction with typical peers, resulting in delayed interpersonal development (Bradley & Meredith, 1991).

Emotional Development

Because emotions underlie behaviors, it is important to consider the role emotions play in an individual's life. In a review of emotional development as it affects students with learning and behavioral disabilities, Dupont (1989) suggested that emotions develop over time from the interaction of maturation with physical and social experience, proceeding only in interaction with other human beings. He noted that emotions are based on (a) a cognitive analysis of a situation, leading to (b) an alteration of affect (mood, feeling), which is followed by (c) an action or behavior.

The core emotions of joy, anger, guilt, sadness, pride, and fear also serve as important indicators of who we are. Each human being is unique in terms of what he or she has strong feelings about and what is done with those feelings. These feelings and responses change over time, as do the explanations we give for our feelings. From 2 decades of observational research, Dupont (1989) identified a predictable sequence of stages of emotional development based on the explanations we give for our feelings (see Table 12.2).

It should be noted that as emotional development proceeds, the lower stages do not disappear but coexist with and are integrated into the higher stages. For example, individuals who have come to value being self-defined will nevertheless be happy at times simply because of pleasurable experiences. When individuals encounter conflicts between the values of various

Table 12.2 Stages of Emotional Development

Explanations Given by Individuals for Their Feelings

1. Reasons given for emotions appear bizarre and irrational
2. Reasons for feelings relate to simple pleasure or displeasure, comfort or pain
3. Reasons for emotions relate to actions of authority figures and being allowed to get or have things that are desired
4. Reasons for feelings relate to being allowed to "go and do" or to being restricted from doing so by authority figures
5. Reasons for emotions relate to having friends and belonging; conformity is valued
6. Explanations for emotions relate to reciprocal relationships, and involve sensitivity to feelings of others; mutuality is valued
7. Reasons for emotions involve being self-defining and directed; autonomy is valued
8. Reasons for feelings reflect the need to be consistent with values and principles; integrity is valued

Source: From "The Emotional Development of Exceptional Students," by H. Dupont, 1989, *Focus on Exceptional Children, 21*(1), p. 4. Copyright © 1989 by Love Publishing Company. Adapted and reprinted with permission.

stages that have become integrated into their emotional selves, the higher stage takes precedence (e.g., functioning at the more advanced stage of valuing autonomy will lead an individual to resist problematic responses related to blind conformity in instances of peer pressure).

As we consider the social and emotional characteristics of learners with mild disabilities, an awareness of any delays in developing age-appropriate emotional cognitions may help us design more useful cognitive and behavioral interventions. Adolescent youngsters whose emotions still derive primarily from pleasure seeking, freedom from pain, or the responses of authority figures (i.e., explanations typical of younger children) will likely be impaired in the development of age-appropriate emotions and social behaviors. The emotional cognitions that underlie their behavior are similar to those of much younger children, and their behaviors are likely to be less age appropriate as well. Interventions must respect this level of development.

The nature of a disability may also impact the development and manifestation of emotional responses. Learners with autism spectrum disorders are defined by their lack of typical emotional responses and empathy in interaction with others, making it likely that they will be often found to be at the earliest stages of emotional development. Additionally, cognitive delays associated with intellectual disabilities are likely to impact students' abilities to complete the cognitive appraisal process in an age-appropriate manner, impacting their emotional responses as well.

Consideration of the range of emotions expressed by a child or adolescent may also provide important diagnostic information. Children need to develop the ability to feel and express all of the core emotions in appropriate ways. As noted in Chapter 6, children who grow up in homes affected by alcohol or drug dependency or by child or spousal abuse frequently display a very restricted ability to feel anything, often opting for feeling nothing (Black, 1981; Long & Morse, 1996). Attending to the range of expressed emotions and learners' explanations for them can be useful to therapists and others in responding to and assisting the emotional development of such youngsters (see In the Classroom 12.2).

IN THE CLASSROOM 12.2

Emotional Development

Susan is 7 years old and is in a class for children with emotional disorders. She seems to be delayed in emotional development; all of her emotions are apparently related to her own pleasure or freedom from pain (a characteristic of younger children). She goes after the toys she wants, regardless of whose they are; she attends only those mainstream classes that she wants to attend. If she is sent to time-out for problems behaving during group time, she will sit there and cry, saying over and over, "I want to come back." She simply wants what she wants! The feelings or reactions of others have no bearing on the things she desires or seeks to avoid.

Mark is a sixth grader with an intellectual disability and a history of acting-out behaviors. His behavior and emotions depend to a large extent on the guidelines and restrictions placed on him by Mr. Chapman, his teacher. Mark exhibits a lot of resistance when his teacher does not grant a request or demand, but he will usually end up complying. Occasionally he reacts violently and "trashes" the room, blaming Mr. Chapman for these occurrences. He clearly explains his feelings and emotions by what his teacher allows him to do or by reference to other authority figures in his life.

Jill, a seventh-grade student with a learning disability, is served entirely in general education classes with consultant support. She interacts easily with others, and her teacher feels that she has advanced to the stage of emotional development that values interactions with others. Her attitudes on any given day are dictated by how she is feeling about her relationship to her peer group. She seems to be very happy and gets right to work when things are going well between her and her friends. When she has had a disagreement with one of her friends, she becomes uncooperative and unwilling to carry out requests.

Development of Social Perspective Taking

Social perspective taking is a social cognitive skill defined as the ability to relate to the viewpoints of others and to display empathy for the other. It involves the coordination of multiple perspectives both within the self and socially between the self and others (Bradley & Meredith, 1991; Gelbach, 2004; Selman, 1980). For example, in intervening with a child who has just hurt another student, it is useful to consider whether the child has the ability to see the situation from the injured student's perspective, to have empathy. Selman and others have hypothesized that social perspective taking is a developmental process similar to other social cognitions. Human beings make decisions based on their changing perceptions of others, and they act, in a series of qualitatively different stages, on the basis of their ideas about the inherent social nature of behavior (see Table 12.3). In addition to the ability to stand in the other's shoes, the level of social perspective taking impacts the learner's motivation to act to correct a situation or give comfort and is impacted by the environmental context of the event (Gelbach, 2004).

Selman's theory of social perspective taking has several implications for work with youngsters with various mild disabilities. A study of social perspective taking among learners with mild intellectual disabilities found that such youngsters exhibit developmental growth in perspective taking but the rate of growth is slower than that of typical peers, supporting the premise that their development is delayed, not defective (Bradley & Meredith, 1991). As these youngsters grow older, the increasing gap may become problematic in social interactions and in the developmental tasks of adolescence.

Table 12.3   Stages of Social Perspective Taking

Egocentric Perspective Taking (Ages 3–6)
The child relates to others as physical entities; recognizes that feelings and thoughts exist, but does not understand that others may not interpret a particular situation as they do; friends are simply those who are available to play at the time.

Subjective Perspective Taking (Ages 5–9)
The child understands that others have their own feelings and thoughts, although the interpretation of the feelings of others is based on the observer's experience; differentiates between intentional and unintentional acts; assumes that other's feelings and thoughts may be discerned from the physical indicators such as facial expressions; friends are those who do as one wishes.

Reciprocal Perspective Taking (Ages 7–12)
The young person becomes able to put himself or herself in the other's shoes; reflects on one's own actions from the perspective of the other; develops sense of reciprocity of thoughts and feelings, not merely actions; friends are those who like the same things, but friendships dissolve when that is no longer true.

Mutual Perspective Taking (Ages 10–15)
The young person is capable of stepping entirely outside the self and the situation; from this third-party perspective, the individual can simultaneously coordinate the perspectives of self and other; relationships are seen as ongoing systems whereby feelings and experiences are mutually shared.

Societal Perspective Taking (Ages 12–Adult)
Individual understands that all perspectives include multidimensional levels that may affect outcomes; capable of abstracting multiple and mutual perspectives to a societal or moral level shared by others; relationships are viewed as supportive but autonomous.

Source: From "Interpersonal Development: A Study with Children Classified as Educable Mentally Retarded" by L. J. Bradley and R. C. Meredith, 1991, *Education and Training in Mental Retardation, 26*(2), pp. 134–135. Copyright © 1991 by Division on Mental Retardation and Developmental Disabilities of The Council for Exceptional Children. Adapted and reprinted with permission.

Development of social perspective taking may be affected or delayed by other disabilities as well. A study of social perspective taking among children and adolescents with behavioral problems associated with child abuse indicated a significant developmental delay, with the learners tending to remain at the egocentric level longer (Burack et al., 2006). Those with less serious conduct problems seem to be more able to understand that others have their own perspectives. A third study, focused on learners with ADHD, found that this group also exhibits less empathy and more limited social perspective-taking skills, which may be related to comorbid conduct and language problems (Marton, Wiener, Rogers, Moore, & Tannock, 2009). It is possible that learners with attention deficits may not be able to attend to environmental information efficiently enough to incorporate that information into their social schema.

A review of studies of the social perspective-taking ability of children with learning disabilities found evidence that these students also exhibit deficits in perspective taking when compared to typical peers (Bryan, 1991). One hypothesis for this finding is that the difficulty experienced by these students in understanding and using the communication tools needed to develop social cognitive skills may also impede their development of social perspective taking.

Learners with emotional or behavioral disorders frequently display the negative effects of failing to develop age-appropriate levels of perspective taking. They frequently seem not to know, or even care, what others think or feel, and thus their ability or motivation to modify their behaviors and emotions based on this information is impeded. Learners with ASD are defined by their inability to assess and act on the perspectives of others with whom they need to interact (S. F. Diehl, 2003). The degree to which learners are successful in understanding the perspectives of others is crucial to the development of their concept of what it means to be a person, a "self," and to the development of satisfying relationships with others (see examples in *In the Classroom* 12.3). Behavioral and social skill interventions with these students must definitely take into account their level of social perspective taking and any comorbid disabilities that may have compromised their development of this skill.

IN THE CLASSROOM 12.3

Social Perspective Taking

David is a second grader with a learning disability. He seems to see the world solely from his own perspective and consequently has difficulty taking turns. Yesterday he took a ball out for recess and was throwing it up and down. His teacher asked if he wouldn't rather play with Philip, to which he answered, "Yes." However, when he threw the ball, he threw it so that Philip could not possibly catch it and then ran after it and threw it to himself again. He did not appear to be able to envision the game of catch from Philip's perspective. David's teacher believes that he is still in the egocentric stage of perspective taking and that this is hindering his social development.

Vinnie is an eighth grader in a program for students with emotional disabilities. In discussing a watch-stealing incident with Vinnie, Ms. Taylor realized that even though Vinnie appeared to understand that others looked at the theft as a bad thing, he seemed to excuse it because he "needed" the watch. Ms. Taylor also reflected on another incident: Vinnie had struck up a "friendship" with a new student for the mutual purpose of humiliating a third student. As long as they were in accord on this goal, the friendship remained intact; when that common goal ended, so did the friendship. From these incidents, Ms. Taylor believes that Vinnie displays a delay in development of social perspective taking, functioning primarily at the subjective stage, a stage more typical of elementary children.

Marie is an 11th grader who has a language impairment. Most of the time, her teacher notes, she seems to understand that everyone has a perspective and that it might be different from hers. Last week, her class was discussing a piece of poetry. Marie listened intently and took into account each classmate's point of view. She was able to coordinate the different views expressed and to reference those ideas as she explained what she thought, indicating to her teacher that she is functioning within either the reciprocal or mutual perspective stage of social perspective taking.

SOCIAL COMPETENCE AND COGNITIVE DEVELOPMENT

Social behaviors depend on the development of essential social cognitive skills (Bryan, 1991; Kauffman & Landrum, 2009). Social cognition involves the use of thinking skills (e.g., social perspective taking, social problem solving) to coordinate environmental events and social behaviors (Bryan, 1991). It appears that social cognition develops just as other cognitive skills do; thus, a developmental perspective may help explain the social functioning of learners with mild disabilities (Siperstein, 1992). By helping young people develop their ability to cognitively process and act on social information, we give them the tools to manage their own responses to the environment and thereby make it more reasonable to expect them to display increasing levels of self-responsibility.

Students with mild disabilities, as a group, tend to display deficits and delays in developing age-appropriate social cognitive skills and the behavioral repertoire needed to operate in a socially competent manner (Gumpel, 1994; Kavale & Forness, 1996; Vaughn, Zaragoza, Hogan, & Walker, 1993). For example, the concept of the six-hour retarded child (President's Committee on Mental Retardation, 1970; discussed in Chapter 4) identified this inability to function competently in particular social environments as one of the primary indicators of a disability. AAMR/AAIDD (1992) proposed using an evaluation of an individual's social competence as a means of assessing adaptive behavior and confirming the diagnosis of intellectual disability. Although some have questioned that position (McGrew, Bruininks, & Johnson, 1996), it remains true that a variety of competencies are required for effective social functioning and that students with disabilities are judged by the appropriateness of their social behaviors (Warnes, Sheridan, Geske, & Warnes, 2005).

Central to the social cognitive approach is the concept of personal competence, a multidimensional construct relating to an individual's ability to coordinate and effectively use a variety of skills to function in social contexts. A model of personal competence based on a variety of sources is presented in Figure 12.1 to illustrate the complex interactions among the multiple

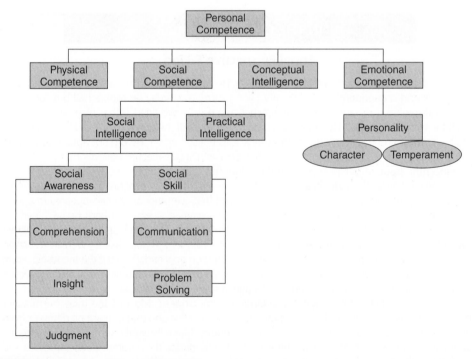

FIGURE 12.1   Model of Personal Competence
Source: Based on AAIDD, 2010; AAMR/AAIDD,1992, 2002; Greenspan and Granfield, 1992; Gumpel, 1994; Mathais, 1990; McGrew and Bruininks, 1990; McGrew, Bruininks, and Johnson, 1996; Thompson, McGrew, and Bruininks, 2002.

abilities involved in personal competence, with each factor contributing uniquely to the ability to function in a socially and personally competent manner.

As Figure 12.1 indicates, a number of specific abilities contribute to an individual's personal competence:

- *Conceptual intelligence:* The intrinsic intellectual ability of an individual; the ability to process information, to solve abstract problems, and to understand and use symbolic processes such as language
- *Physical competence:* Fine and gross motor skills; physical growth and development; general health status; capacity for hearing, vision, or mobility, as well as other physical conditions that can affect a learner's physical competence
- *Emotional competence:* The degree to which an individual is able to maintain an emotional "steady-state"; affected by an individual's personality, including character and temperament; the dimension most often compromised when maladaptive behaviors are present
- *Social competence:* The ability to respond appropriately in social situations and to carry out the functions associated with independent living; composed of two subcomponents
    - *Social intelligence:* The ability to understand social expectations and to interpret the behavior of others, to judge appropriately how to conduct oneself in social situations, and to select and use appropriate social strategies
    - *Practical intelligence:* The ability to deal with the physical and mechanical aspects of life, including daily living and vocational skills, and to solve problems of everyday life

Social Intelligence

Social intelligence is a critical component of social competence. It is the perception that an individual has deficits in social intelligence that most often leads to identification of a disability (Gresham & Elliott, 1987). Low levels of social intelligence are frequently found to be related to functional failures in social settings such as school and work (Greenspan & Granfield, 1992). Teachers and others must not only consider the appropriateness of overt behaviors, but must also explore underlying social cognitive abilities or social intelligence (Bryan, 1997; Gumpel, 1994, 2007; Leffert & Siperstein, 1996; Meadan & Monda-Amaya, 2008, Siperstein, 1992; Thompson, McGrew, & Bruininks, 2002; Warnes, et al., 2005). It is the effectiveness of cognitive processing of social information that provides evidence of an individual's social intelligence.

Social intelligence is composed of two subcompetencies: social awareness and social skill (Gumpel, 2007). Social awareness refers to those cognitive abilities that allow an individual to receive and process relevant social information from the environment. It refers specifically to the comprehension of behavioral cues and to the accompanying insight about the meaning of such information, followed by the exercise of judgment in determining the relevance and value of that information. Adequate social awareness requires that students attend to actions and words around them, view that information from various perspectives, and interpret the cues using the mediator of language. Any one of these steps may prove difficult for students with cognitive disabilities (see In the Classroom 12.4).

Chapter 9 noted that the concept of field dependence applies to social judgment as well. Field-dependent individuals are more likely to attend closely to and make use of social models and frames of reference in their immediate environment, or to be socially field dependent, a concept related to social awareness (Witkin, Moore, Goodenough, & Cox, 1977). There is some evidence that such individuals may make more effective use of eye contact, facial cues, verbal messages, and other social components as a guide to social function. In unfamiliar environments, such behaviors are quite adaptive if they are accompanied by the social cognitive skills necessary to process and give meaning to the information. A field-dependent social orientation can result in individuals' being more attuned to those with whom they interact and therefore more valued as friends. The negative aspect is the susceptibility of such individuals to follow the crowd indiscriminately, sometimes participating in behaviors that are not healthy, safe, or legal.

IN THE CLASSROOM 12.4

Social Intelligence

Linda is a sixth grader with a mild intellectual disability who is served in a general education class for most of the day. Her deficits in social awareness, particularly in comprehension and judgment, affect her adjustment in that environment. One day another girl told her, in a very sarcastic tone and with facial expression to underscore the sarcasm, that her dress looked "real nice." The look on Linda's face made it clear that she wasn't sure what the other girl meant. She noted the discrepancy between voice, words, and actions, but she seemed at a loss as to the meaning of the communication, and she was therefore unable to respond effectively. Incidents such as this have caused her teacher to be very concerned about the effect of social awareness deficits on Linda's overall social adjustment.

Gary is 12 years old and has been placed in a self-contained classroom as a result of his conduct disorder and associated ADHD. Because of his attentional deficits, his overall cognitive functioning has been slowed, including his ability to appraise his emotions and to take the perspectives of others in social situations. He is quick to become frustrated, and his reactions to people and events are impulsive. His repertoire of responses is not well developed, resulting in frequent exaggerated outbursts that are inappropriate to the stimuli. After an outburst, he experiences remorse. His teacher is heartened by his self-awareness in cases in which he has overreacted, believing that it indicates that he is beginning to develop some initial competence in social awareness. His teacher hopes that this cognitive awareness will open up the opportunity for instruction in reading social cues more effectively before he reaches the frustration point, and will ultimately result in the use of more adaptive social skills.

The second component of social intelligence is social skill, or the ability to select and use behaviors that lead to socially acceptable and personally satisfying outcomes (Goldstein & McGinnis, 1997; Gresham & Elliott, 1987; Gumpel, 2007; McGinnis & Goldstein, 1990, 1997). Social skills include learned behaviors (overt and covert) used in interpersonal interactions to achieve an environmental effect and response. Communication skills and problem solving are central to social skill (see again In the Classroom 12.4). Students with mild disabilities often have deficits in social skill, and therefore their responses to events are likely to be unsatisfactory, ineffective, or unacceptable (Kavale & Forness, 1996; Short & Evans, 1990).

Emotional Competence

Emotional competence is related to a number of personality variables, including temperament and character (AAMR/AAIDD, 1992; McGrew et al., 1996). Together, character and temperament constitute personality, or behavioral individuality (DePauw & Mervielde, 2010). Severe deficits in dimensions of personality, as well as in emotional competence in general, are often held to be suggestive of a psychiatric condition or of emotional or behavioral disorders (Greenspan & Granfield, 1992). In fact, emotional competence is frequently defined by the absence of any maladaptive indicators, such as externalizing, internalizing, or other asocial behaviors.

Character is defined as the collection of features and traits that form the individual nature of a person, including moral qualities, ethical standards, and guiding principles. This aspect of personality is viewed as being susceptible to change in response to significant environmental pressures. Character deficits are also frequently viewed as psychiatric conditions, including character disorders and other acting-out forms of psychopathology (Greenspan & Granfield, 1992).

Temperament is an individual's behavioral style in interpersonal interactions. The term relates to the "how" of behavior, focusing on the manner of the behavior and not the actions themselves. Temperament has been characterized as having a variety of aspects or components, most of which refer to the nature of an individual's responsiveness, or reactivity, as well as other self-regulatory tendencies (Thomas & Chess, 1977; see Table 12.4).

Table 12.4   Dimensions of Behavioral Style or Temperament

- Activity level
- Rhythmicity (regularity, predictability)
- Approach/withdrawal tendencies (response to new stimuli)
- Adaptability
- Threshold of responsiveness (or reactiveness to stimuli)
- Intensity of reaction
- Quality of mood
- Distractibility
- Attention span or task persistence

Source: Based on *Temperament and Development* (pp. 21–22) by A. Thomas and S. Chess, 1977, New York: Brunner/Mazel.

Temperament is generally presumed to be an inborn predisposition that is largely neurobiological or genetic in origin and is more stable than other personality factors (DePauw & Mervielde, 2010; Keogh & Bess, 1991). Thomas and Chess (1977) studied the responses of infants and young children extensively, describing reaction patterns of behavior that appeared to be primary and innate. They clustered the core attributes listed in Table 12.4 into four styles: the easy child (40 percent), the difficult child (10 percent), the slow-to-warm-up child (15 percent), and uncertain (33 percent). Children exhibiting the difficult-child pattern may present more acting-out behaviors at home and school. Those who are slow to warm up may present more passive or internalized clinical symptoms.

An individual's temperament, or behavioral style, interacts with the environment, affecting the responses from significant others (Thomas & Chess, 1977). The effect of the interaction of teacher–child or parent–child temperaments depends on the temperamental characteristics of both individuals, or the goodness of fit. There is some evidence that learners' temperaments, as well as their cognitive abilities and motivation, can influence a teacher's opinion about their teachability (Cardell & Parmar, 1988; Keogh & Bess, 1991). When a learner's temperament matches the teacher's expectation of teachability, the match and the interactions are likely to be positive and conducive to learning; when the style is inconsistent with the teacher's expectations, the teacher's evaluation of the learner is more likely to be negative and the interactions less supportive.

Social Cognitive Delay

Social cognition follows a developmental pattern that is similar to that observed among other cognitive abilities. The term *social cognitive delay* refers to a delay in developing age-appropriate, functional social cognitive skills and in applying those skills in social contexts (see In the Classroom 12.5). For a variety of reasons, there are individuals who are delayed in every developmental process, such as learners with mild intellectual disabilities who commonly display social perspective-taking skills that are characteristic of younger children (Bradley & Meredith, 1991).

One possible explanation for the inappropriate or immature behaviors exhibited by children and youth with a variety of disabilities is that they have one or more deficits or delays in general cognitive functioning. When these generalized delays affect social development, a student may simply not have developed the necessary cognitive skills to cope effectively in the social arena. Difficulties in social problem solving may be related to deficits in general cognitive functioning:

- *Attention*—lack of attention to social cues
- *Perception*—misinterpretation of social cues, or attaching incorrect meaning to social cues
- *Memory*—poor memory of social cues as a situation unfolds
- *Strategic control functions*—lack or poor selection of social skill strategies
- *Executive functions*—inefficient management of behaviors in response to input

IN THE CLASSROOM 12.5

Social Cognitive Delay

Carlos is 14 years old and is currently placed in a self-contained class for students with learning disabilities. He is the type of student who wants to be involved in everything that is going on in the room. His teacher describes him as a "neat kid" with a good sense of humor and a caring attitude toward others, who is a good conversationalist with adults. Unfortunately, Carlos does not see these positive qualities in himself, nor do his peers. He has a tendency to turn off his peers, and therefore they do not include him in social conversations and activities unless he initiates them. When he does interact with peers, he tends to engage in impulsive and inappropriate behaviors, similar to those of a younger child. It is common for Carlos to trip or poke other students or to say inappropriate things to them regarding their personality, looks, family, or gender. He will barge into conversations uninvited and then talk above the others to be included. Because this has been going on for so long, most of his peers won't have anything to do with him. Recently his tendency to act inappropriately in order to get attention has increased. When his teacher discussed a recent incident with him, he was unable to see why it was inappropriate. He is unable to differentiate between his actions and those of others. His teacher and counselor are beginning to work with him on social skills, including self-evaluation and self-regulation of his behavior.

Failure to operate effectively in social contexts may be attributed to (a) an insufficient repertoire of skills or (b) deficits in skill selection and performance, including fluency of execution (Gresham, 2002b; Gresham & Elliott, 1987; Gumpel, 2007; Kavale & Forness, 1996). In the first case, a learner may never have developed the required social cognitive strategies, so that the skills are simply not in the learner's social skill repertoire. Such students are appropriately said to have social skill deficits that can be addressed through careful, age-appropriate teaching of prosocial skills.

Alternatively, some students appear to possess the skills and can demonstrate them on cue in role-playing situations or sporadically in natural settings. However, they may not be interpreting and using environmental cues reliably enough to determine when to appropriately use a skill, or they may be awkward or lack fluency when they do use a skill (Gresham, 2002b; Gumpel, 2007). Such students are said to have performance deficits, which can result when skills are taught in isolation in the classroom, making it more difficult for the students to generalize those skills to other appropriate settings (Gumpel, 2007). Learners with performance deficits are frequently punished for their inabilities because it is assumed that they could use the appropriate skills if they wanted to and their failure to do so is a matter of carelessness, choice, or simply a lack of motivation.

Another performance-deficit-related problem concerns the degree to which learners are able to demonstrate the self-regulatory behavior needed for behavioral flexibility, or the ability to adjust behavior to respond to different situations, people, or settings (Gumpel, 2007; McGinnis & Goldstein, 1997). When students with mild disabilities lack the behavioral flexibility to respond to changing situations, their responses may be seen as inappropriate or noncompliant (see In the Classroom 12.6). These students may use fixed or stereotypic responses to situations rather than employing a full repertoire of adaptive social skills. Some learners with deficits in social cognition may exhibit newness panic in change situations, responding to new social demands with resistance or withdrawal or acting out (Redl & Wineman, 1951).

When we note behaviors in a child that are suggestive of a less mature social cognitive stage or of inconsistent behavioral flexibility, we must also address the following questions:

- Does a pattern of delay exist, or is this an isolated instance?
- Are the desired skills present in the training or classroom setting? Is the learner failing to generalize them to other environments?
- Is the learner aware of the inadequacy or inappropriateness of his or her behavioral responses?

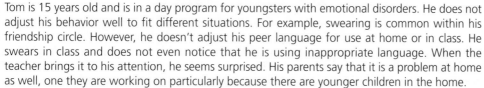

IN THE CLASSROOM 12.6

Lack of Behavioral Flexibility

Tom is 15 years old and is in a day program for youngsters with emotional disorders. He does not adjust his behavior well to fit different situations. For example, swearing is common within his friendship circle. However, he doesn't adjust his peer language for use at home or in class. He swears in class and does not even notice that he is using inappropriate language. When the teacher brings it to his attention, he seems surprised. His parents say that it is a problem at home as well, one they are working on particularly because there are younger children in the home.

Lee is 10 years old and is in a resource program for students with learning disabilities. Her teacher has noted that she uses a very limited number of social skills to deal with social situations; saying "I'm sorry" and hitting comprise her repertoire. Saying "I'm sorry" has seemed to work well for Lee in school, although hitting has not. She has been suspended several times for hitting other students. Nevertheless, she continues to respond to all situations with only those behaviors.

With answers to these questions, we can then hypothesize about how a student's social cognitive development may have been affected. If we use the information we have gathered to design interventions to develop missing or faulty social cognitive skills, we can enable the learner to address future social situations more adaptively. In dealing with social cognitive delay, teachers and parents need to evaluate the development of age-appropriate language and cognitive skills related to the growth of social competence. When deficits are identified, coaching and feedback are required to increase the student's ability to analyze social situations and to choose and implement more effective responses (Cummings, 2010; S. F. Diehl, 2003; Dotson, Leaf, Sheldon, & Sherman, 2010; Meadan & Monda-Amaya, 2008). Training in self-regulation of behavior may be effective in remediating deficits in performance and fluency (Gumpel, 2007). It is important to be aware, however, that punishment is rarely effective when self-regulatory mechanisms are not in the youngster's repertoire.

THE RELATIONSHIP BETWEEN PROBLEMS IN BEHAVIOR AND PROBLEMS IN LEARNING

For students who are served in special education for learning problems, it is assumed that their disabilities are related solely to academic learning areas. However, studies have repeatedly shown that when rated by teachers, students with disabilities of all kinds exhibit higher levels of problem behavior and have more social deficits than do typical youngsters, and they frequently exhibit social deficits along with their academic learning deficiencies (Forness & Kavale, 1991; Pearl, Donahue, & Bryan, 1986). It is estimated that 12 percent of all students in U.S. schools have emotional and behavioral problems that require intervention (J. R. Nelson et al., 2009). To illustrate this fact, consider that three of the most recent alternative definitions of learning disabilities (NJCLD, 1998; ACLD/LDA, 1986; Interagency Committee on Learning Disabilities [ICLD], 1987) refer explicitly to socialization problems (Forness & Kavale, 1991; Hammill, 1990). Problems in social skills have also been central to the definition of intellectual disability since Edgar Doll first defined it as social incompetence due to mental subnormality (Doll, 1941; J. D. Smith, 1997). The *DSM-IV-TR* definitions of ADHD, Asperger's syndrome, and autistic disorder all include social behaviors that are problematic in classroom and social interactions.

In order to understand why learners with mild disabilities often display inappropriate or ineffective social behavior, it is helpful to reconsider the critical features of their disabilities. Central to the functioning of most learners with mild disabilities are their difficulties in understanding, processing, and using language, problems that are related to their cognitive processing of language (as discussed in Chapters 9 and 10). Because language facility appears to be essential to social learning

UNIVERSAL DESIGN FOR LEARNING IN ACTION 12

Supporting Social–Emotional Learning and Functioning

Principle I: *Use multiple and flexible means of representation*[a]	Implement effective social skills training programs to help all students develop their social intelligence, with special assistance as needed. Deliver behavioral directives clearly, directly, and consistently to help students develop social awareness (e.g., insight, comprehension, judgment). When using cooperative learning groups, be sure to preteach social skills that are essential to successful group work. Welcome family and community partners into the classroom to share their interests and time.
Principle II: *Allow multiple and flexible means of expression*[a]	Ensure that all students are attending to important behavioral directives. Use sharing-circle activities to help students develop their social perspective taking.
Principle III: *Provide multiple and flexible means of engagement*[a]	Recognize that students have different levels of comfort in social situations; look for opportunities to prompt social relationship building. Provide opportunities for students to engage in socialization with others in order to build their social competence.
Principle IV: *Create a community of learners in the classroom*[b]	Utilize restitution approaches with problem behavior to help children learn how to make a problem "right" and to increase the likelihood that they won't violate that standard again. Consider how the physical environment may be helping or hindering appropriate behavior; using an ecological perspective, consider whether another room arrangement might enhance the social aspect of the working environment and reduce conflicts. Establish a respectful classroom to help students who are dealing with trust issues. Establish a "no harassment" rule; accept no behavior that fails to respect another.
Principle V: *Establish a positive instructional climate*[b]	Ensure space/voice for each learner. Using principles of functional behavioral assessment, work to ensure that all students have the opportunity in your classroom to have their important needs met. Help students to understand that not everybody has to enjoy the same things or feel the same way when something happens; encourage students to grow in social perspective taking.

Source: Principles adapted from (a) Center for Applied Special Technology (CAST), 2008 and (b) McGuire, Scott, and Shaw, 2006.

and functioning, it is reasonable that disabilities in cognitive processing and language could hinder a child's development of socially skilled behavior. These deficits impair the learning of social rules and strategies generally acquired through observation of appropriate behavioral models.

To compound these problems, language mediates social learning, and social interaction is essential for language learning. This reciprocal process is disrupted by the inability of learners with mild disabilities to process and use language effectively and to demonstrate social competence through the use of pragmatic language skills. Despite this, teachers of students with mild disabilities (like Nicki in Chapter 6) consider academic remediation their primary responsibility.

Teaching skills related to social competence is rarely included as part of a child's IEP. If behavior is addressed at all, it is from the perspective of behavior management and control rather than remediation (Gresham, MacMillan, & Bocian, 1996; Nichols, 1992). The connection between these learners' troubling behavioral problems and their disability-related difficulties in processing language is often overlooked.

Such problems are sometimes exacerbated by the newcomer phenomenon. Students miss bits and pieces of classroom life while receiving services outside the general education classroom. They may also miss important input while in the classroom because of difficulties in attention or in processing oral language. This means that classroom conversations may not make much sense because they are missing specific pieces of background. Too often this leads to avoidance strategies that result in these students staying out of communicative interactions, appearing to be disinterested onlookers. Other students may avoid interacting with such students because their conversation often seems "weird." Since language learning requires interaction, the communicative differences grow. These problems are compounded for students who are learning English as an additional language. Students with disabilities need social skill instruction along with an opportunity to practice skills in real contexts, with feedback to help them develop their pragmatic language skills and to increase their levels of social competence.

BEHAVIOR FROM AN ECOLOGICAL PERSPECTIVE

Social–emotional characteristics and functioning can alternatively be viewed from an ecological perspective. Ecological frameworks hold that the explanations of behavioral or emotional functioning often lie in the interaction between a child and the environment (Bronfenbrenner, 1979; Grusec, 1992; J. R. Nelson, Stage, Duppong-Hurley, Synhorst, & Epstein, 2007; Swick & Williams, 2006). Behavioral ecologists assert that problem behavior is not simply or invariably the result of conflict within an individual, as psychodynamic theorists like Freud believed, nor is it the outcome of inappropriate reinforcement, as behaviorists such as Skinner asserted. Rather, social ecologists believe that behavior results from the reciprocal interactions among and between personal variables, environmental factors, and the quality/nature of antecedent behaviors.

Bronfenbrenner (1979) offered this definition of the ecology of human development:

> [The] study of the progressive, mutual accommodation between an active, growing human being and the changing properties of the immediate settings in which the developing person lives, as this process is affected by relations between these settings and by the larger context in which the settings are embedded. (p. 21)

To illustrate this theory, he outlined a model of nested systems with an individual positioned at the center (see Figure 12.2). Beyond the individual with all of his or her characteristics and

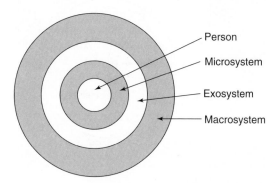

FIGURE 12.2 Bronfenbrenner's Ecological Model
Source: Based on *The Ecology of Human Development: Experiments by Nature and Design* by U. Bronfenbrenner, 1979, Cambridge, MA: Harvard University Press.

experiences lies the microsystem (i.e., immediate influences, such as family and school); the exosystem (i.e., the indirect influences of the larger community); and the macrosystem (i.e., the principles and ideologies that integrate the societal structure). As we consider the social–emotional characteristics of learners today, it is important to also consider how these learners are impacted by and impact this larger ecological context of family, school, community, and society.

Kauffman and Landrum (2009) illustrated these reciprocal interactions in their discussion of Bandura's triadic reciprocality model (1977, 1986), which holds that a given behavior (B′) is the result of the reciprocal interactions among and between an individual's personal traits (P), the environment (E), and prior or antecedent behaviors or events (B):

$$B' = f(P, E, B)$$

Social ecologists believe that observed behaviors (B′) are interpretable only within the context of the mutual and reciprocal effects of relevant personal, environmental, and behavioral variables:

- Personal variables include an individual's thoughts, feelings, and perceptions, as well as other personal traits such as age, disability, ethnicity, language, religion, gender, sexual orientation, appearance, stature, and socioeconomic class.
- Environmental variables include both social and physical factors related to the setting in which the behavior occurs.
- Behavioral variables include the qualities of behaviors or events that are antecedent to the target behavior.

When considering behaviors from an ecological perspective, it is important to understand that most of the time, all three influences are at work to some degree, although in some cases only one or two may be of significance, as indicated by the overlapping circles of the model in Figure 12.3. As we evaluate learners' problem behaviors, it is useful to consider whether any of the three groups of variables is significantly more influential on a regular basis and to consider the nature of the reciprocal interactions that may be exacerbating a situation (see In the

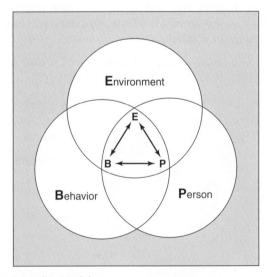

FIGURE 12.3 Triadic Reciprocality Model

Source: Adapted From Kauffman & Landrum, CHARACTERISTICS OF EMOTIONAL AND BEHAVIORAL DISORDERS OF CHILDREN AND YOUTH, Figure 3.1 "Triadic reciprocality in social-cognitive theory," p. 79, 2009. Reproduced by permission of Pearson Education, Inc.

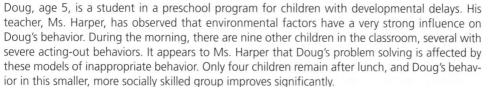

Reciprocal Ecological Interactions

Doug, age 5, is a student in a preschool program for children with developmental delays. His teacher, Ms. Harper, has observed that environmental factors have a very strong influence on Doug's behavior. During the morning, there are nine other children in the classroom, several with severe acting-out behaviors. It appears to Ms. Harper that Doug's problem solving is affected by these models of inappropriate behavior. Only four children remain after lunch, and Doug's behavior in this smaller, more socially skilled group improves significantly.

Debbie is a fifth grader with a learning disability. Her special education class joins a general education class for music. An incident last week illustrates the use of the triadic reciprocal model to analyze events. Some of the girls in the music class told Debbie that she was from the "stupid class." Debbie didn't lash out at them or act inappropriately. She ignored them and then talked about it later to her teacher, who was able to help her articulate her feelings. Her teacher also reinforced her for using an effective response they had practiced in social skills lessons. In this case, Debbie's status as a student receiving special education services (a person variable) interacted with the taunting of the other girls (an event/behavior variable) in music class (an environmental variable), leading to Debbie's behavior, ignoring, which contained the problem. Her teacher is pleased that Debbie seems to be developing the social skills to deal with such events and to take care of things on her own, since her teachers cannot always be there to address problems for her.

Classroom 12.7). Functional behavioral assessment requires attention to all three variables and their interactions as well, with such analysis leading to intervention suggestions to enhance positive forces and reduce or limit negative aspects (Gable, 1996; Wehby & Symons, 1996).

Risk and Resilience

As noted throughout this chapter, most learners with mild disabilities exhibit some behaviors with social–emotional adjustment concerns, in addition to the learning concerns related to their primary areas of disability. It is not unusual to find a child with an intellectual disability who also exhibits immature social behavior, or an adolescent with a learning disability who experiences periods of depression. The simple fact of having a disability appears to put a young person at risk for a variety of intrapersonal and interpersonal problems (Bender & Wall, 1994). IDEA 1997 confirmed this by requiring that behavioral planning be considered as part of the planning process for every learner who exhibits problems in behavior and social interaction, regardless of the category of disability.

This understanding invites us to consider potential outcomes for such students from an ecological perspective. Central to these outcomes is the concept of *risk,* defined by Keogh and Weisner (1993) as a "negative or potentially negative condition that impedes or threatens normal development" (p. 4). Risk factors identified in the literature include these (Crews et al., 2007; Morrison & Cosden, 1997):

- *Individual (personal) factors*, such as developmental delays, poor academic achievement, early antisocial behavior, disturbed peer relations, difficult temperament, comorbid psychiatric conditions, and problematic biological or genetic factors
- *Family and community factors*, such as chronic poverty, problematic parenting skills, parental psychopathology, chronic family discord, family instability, severe punishment patterns, and lack of social supports for the learner and the family
- *School and peer group factors*, such as lack of bonding to school, school failure, dropping out of school, substance abuse, negative peer influence, lack of normative expectations for behavior, and alienation from school, family, or community

ON THE WEB

Court Appointed Special Advocates for Children: CASA (http://www. casaforchildren.org) is a national organization that assigns volunteer advocates to assist children caught up in court actions related to abuse and neglect until they are placed in safe and stable homes.

Research into the phenomenon of risk has also identified a variety of protective factors that are associated with positive outcomes, even in the presence of multiple risk factors. *Resiliency* is defined as the ability of an individual to resist the negative effects of stresses and to achieve a positive outcome (Condly, 2006; Meltzer, 2004). Protective factors commonly associated with resiliency include these (Crews et al., 2007; Wong, 2003):

- *Individual (personal) factors*, such as cognitive skills, temperament, positive self-concept, and social cognitive skills and competence
- *Family factors*, such as consistent parenting, supportive family environment, secure attachment to family, and high but reasonable expectations
- *School and community factors*, including positive role models, positive school climate, prosocial peers, appropriate curriculum, and availability of supportive adults

An important research question, and one asked every day by parents and teachers, is "Why do some children succeed despite all odds, while others travel a destructive path to negative outcomes?" There are no reliable links between any particular risk factor and an associated protective factor, and there is no magic answer that will assure a positive outcome for every child. Rather, outcomes are determined by complex interactions among the multiple risks and protective factors (Condly, 2006; Crews et al., 2007; Morrison & Cosden, 1997). The more risk factors present, the more likely the youngster will encounter difficulty. But even when the picture seems bleakest, some young people survive and even thrive (see In the Classroom 12.8). As special

IN THE CLASSROOM 12.8

Risk and Resiliency

Brad is a third grader whose learning disability makes learning to read, spell, and write difficult. He struggles with work that other classmates would find easy, but his classroom is rich in support from his classroom teacher, plus a consultant teacher for one period a day. His family is also supportive at home. On a recent school day, Mrs. Shore, the consultant teacher, noted two events of interest. During the reading lesson, Brad listened intently and eagerly went back to his seat to complete an independent sequencing assignment. Halfway through the exercise, Brad realized that he didn't have enough room to paste the sentences. When he told his teacher, Mr. Jones explained Brad's error and told Brad to redo the exercise. At first Brad displayed frustration, but he persisted with the task, completing it in the allowed time. His face shone with pride!

Later in the morning, Brad was engaged in editing a paragraph with a classroom volunteer. After Brad read the paragraph aloud, the volunteer asked him to pick out his introductory and concluding sentences. He quickly realized that he didn't have a concluding sentence, and he wrote one more sentence. The volunteer helped him see that his new sentence was just another detail, and they worked for a while longer, resulting in his finally composing an appropriate conclusion. Throughout the process, Brad persisted, with some frustration, but he persisted nevertheless.

As Mrs. Shore, the consultant teacher, reflected on these events, she was struck by Brad's resilience. Challenge after challenge, he kept on going. In spite of his learning difficulties, he persisted and achieved results. She wonders what keeps him going despite his misunderstandings and frequent errors.

One possibility is Brad's strong drive for competence. Completing a project gives him tangible evidence of his achievements, and he takes great pride in that. Another possibility is the assistance provided by both teachers. The school environment seems to work well for Brad, supporting his growth and achievement. Mrs. Shore then reflected on the supportive family Brad goes home to each day; expectations are high, but so is the love and encouragement to achieve those expectations. All in all, Brad's resilience appears to be the result of a number of protective factors working together to minimize the risk posed by his learning disability. Mrs. Shore's concern turns to those students whose risk factors overpower the available protective factors, and she wonders how she can help to improve the ratio.

educators begin to apply RTI and functional behavioral assessment frameworks to diagnosis and intervention planning, attention to the development of internal and external protective factors will be increasingly important. Sometimes the most important thing teachers can offer children at risk is the opportunity to learn in a safe environment (Lovitt, 2010).

MALADAPTIVE BEHAVIOR

Thus far, the discussion has focused on the development of adaptive behaviors, including social–emotional characteristics and social competence. With some learners, however, the problem is not the delay or absence of adaptive behavior but rather the presence of maladaptive behavioral responses to life events. McGrew and Bruininks (1990) concluded that although there is some overlap between the dimensions of adaptive and maladaptive behaviors, adaptive behavior seems more determined by the interactions among conceptual, practical, and social intelligences as well as physical competence, whereas maladaptive behaviors appear to derive more directly from problems in the area of emotional competence.

In describing maladaptive behaviors, it is important to acknowledge that the difference between a child with serious maladaptive behavior problems and the typical child is not necessarily the presence or absence of a particular behavior—such as hitting, being noncompliant, stealing, or crying—but rather the number of such occurrences and the time between instances (i.e., frequency). All children display episodes of problem behaviors as they grow and develop their social responses. However, most children exhibit significant reductions in aggressive behaviors as they mature and as they develop other more adaptive ways of coping with daily frustrations.

This is generally not true of children identified as having maladaptive behavior. Such children continue to demonstrate higher rates of problem behaviors and a more serious degree of those behaviors than do other children (Kauffman & Landrum, 2009; Rutherford & Nelson, 1995). Other relevant dimensions used to describe these behaviors are the degree to which they deviate from age-appropriate responses and their overt or covert nature.

Generally, youngsters with significant maladaptive behaviors are identified for special education purposes as having a primary behavioral disorder. It is important to remember, however, that such students may also have problems in academic learning. Conversely, it is possible that a child whose primary disability is intellectual disability, ADHD, autism, or a learning disability may also exhibit one or more serious maladaptive behaviors (Bryan, 1997; Reynolds & Miller, 1985; San Miguel, Forness, & Kavale, 1996). The degree to which the emotional needs of these students are met may depend on the extent to which additional programming is provided to develop their emotional competence, rather than focusing exclusively on academic activities.

Patterns of Maladaptive Behavior

Because problems with maladaptive behavior do sometimes occur in childhood and adolescence, it is important for teachers to have a basic understanding of the major types of maladaptive behaviors and the ways problems in emotional competence may manifest themselves in childhood and adolescence (Forness et al., 2003). Over the years, parents, teachers, and researchers have identified ways to group maladaptive behaviors in children and adolescents. Based on a statistical analysis of maladaptive behaviors presented in children and youth, Quay and Werry (1986) defined the following patterns, or groupings, of common maladaptive behaviors, which still apply today:

- *Undersocialized aggressive conduct disorders* are antisocial externalizing behaviors that are aggressive, disruptive, and noncompliant and that significantly interfere with everyday functioning and the rights of others, leading others to conclude that the individual is unmanageable. These behaviors typically begin in childhood and violate major age-appropriate societal norms and rules.
- *Socialized aggressive conduct disorders* are antisocial externalizing behaviors that include involvement with peers in illegal acts or in behaviors that violate normative expectations.

ON THE WEB

NASP, the National Association of School Psychologists (www.naspcenter.org), provides links to a variety of informational resources on children's mental health, behavior, and discipline—for school, home, and community.

Behaviors in this category tend to be covert and are meant to be hard to detect and document. These behaviors predominantly become a problem in older children and adolescents.

- *Anxiety-withdrawal-dysphoria disorders* consist of internalizing behaviors such as anxiety, fearfulness, panic, shyness, and depression.
- *Attention deficit disorders* are characterized by behaviors not in accordance with age- appropriate developmental expectations, including problems in concentration, attention, impulsivity, clumsiness, passivity, and lack of perseverance. (Attention-deficit/hyperactivity disorders were discussed in detail in Chapter 7.)

CONDUCT DISORDERS   Conduct disorders is the *DSM-IV-TR* category that includes both socialized and undersocialized aggressive behaviors. Youngsters identified with conduct disorders display a significant repertoire (at least three areas of problem behavior) of age-inappropriate aggressive acts over a wide range of social situations They exhibit frequent violations of socially appropriate standards of behavior. The actions of these children are contrary to adaptive patterns of behavior such as cooperation, positive concern for others, and mutually beneficial social interactions (APA, 2000; Rutherford & Nelson, 1995; Walker et al., 2004).

Although all children and youth engage in externalizing problem behaviors from time to time, youngsters with conduct disorders engage in such behaviors much more frequently and with greater intensity than their typical peers do (APA, 2000). These young people typically exhibit high rates of aggression at earlier ages, develop a larger repertoire of aggressive acts, exhibit aggression across a wider range of social situations, and persist in aggressive behavior for a longer period of time. Their behaviors lead them to be feared and rejected by peers, and they in turn perceive peers as hostile to them, setting up a vicious cycle of antisocial behavior. These learners exhibit a persistent pattern of antisocial behavior that impairs their everyday functioning at school and at home (see In the Classroom 12.9).

IN THE CLASSROOM 12.9

Conduct Disorders

Johnny is 5 years old and is enrolled in kindergarten. His problem behaviors have just resulted in his referral for special education evaluation. Recently, Johnny became angry because his mother wouldn't take him to the park. In his rage, he took a butcher knife and ran toward her saying he would kill her. She locked her baby and herself in the bedroom until help could be summoned. Meanwhile, Johnny continued to pound on the bedroom door with the knife. His mother reported to the teacher that Johnny had been exhibiting violent and destructive behaviors since age 2. At school Johnny is verbally and physically aggressive toward the other children. He uses profanity, and when he has trouble expressing his feelings verbally, he lashes out physically. This causes the other children to become frightened, but Johnny is completely unaware of his effect on them. He reacts to crisis in two very different ways. Sometimes he just gives up, throws his hands in the air, and says, "Forget it, I can't take it anymore." The other reaction is to hit, pull hair, spit, and say, "I hate you" over and over. When he is angry with the teacher, he frequently tells her in great detail how he intends to kill her.

Julia, age 14, has spent her entire school career in self-contained classes for students with behavioral disorders. At this time, her behaviors fall primarily within the category of conduct disorders. Her teacher, Mr. Thomas, reports that Julia is a compulsive liar, sets fires, smokes pot, and engages in vandalism at school. These behaviors mystify Mr. Thomas. It is not clear whether Julia is angry with particular individuals or whether she is just not able to control herself. Mr. Thomas thinks that Julia may believe that these actions will make her look "cool" to her friends. When Julia is confronted about these behaviors, she denies any connection to them, becoming enraged when she is not believed. Mr. Thomas reports that Julia hangs out with some other girls who also display inappropriate behaviors to some degree, and it has become very difficult to control this group.

The behaviors exhibited by these learners lead teachers and parents to identify them as incorrigible, unmanageable, and/or dangerous. The maladaptive behaviors are frequently accompanied by academic problems and may be related to social cognitive deficiencies (Walker et al., 2004; Wehby, 1994). Bullying behavior is a common manifestation of these conditions as well, with serious emotional implications for both the victims and the bullies (Elinoff, Chafouleas, & Sassu, 2004). For this reason, conduct disorders are more likely to result in referral for special education evaluation than are other types of emotional or behavioral disorders because conduct disorders are so disruptive to classroom environments (Landrum, 2000; Yell & Drasgow, 2000). In evaluating instances of aggressive behaviors associated with a conduct disorder, it is important to attempt to determine the needs that such behaviors might be meeting for the individual student (Etscheidt, 2006; McIntosh, 2008; Moreno, 2010; Rodriguez, Thompson, & Baynham, 2010; Rutherford & Nelson, 1995). Some students seek attention for bad behavior rather than risk receiving no attention at all.

By definition, behaviors associated with conduct disorders include behaviors such as the following (APA, 2000):

- Initiating aggression toward or responding aggressively to other people and animals (e.g., threats, bullying, intimidation, fighting, assault with weapons, physical cruelty to people or animals, mugging, sexual assault)
- Destroying property (e.g., deliberate property destruction, fire setting)
- Being deceitful (e.g., stealing, lying)
- Violating rules (e.g., serious noncompliance, disobedience, running away, truancy)

Delinquent, antisocial behavior in the context of an antisocial peer group may be viewed as socialized aggression or, alternatively, as social maladjustment. The behaviors (e.g., gang activity) are problematic for the school and community, but they often meet important relationship needs for the individuals involved, and they can be adaptive within the peer group. The combination of acting-out, externalizing behaviors and dependency on a deviant peer group presents particularly difficult intervention problems. Despite the problems presented by such young people, many school districts and states have begun to make the determination that these students are not eligible for special education services, basing this ruling on the IDEA exclusion of youngsters with social maladjustment from the IDEA classification of emotional disturbance. Such determinations tend to result in the exclusion of these learners from school, and in eventual incarceration.

OPPOSITIONAL DEFIANT DISORDERS   Another diagnosis that is increasingly being used with younger learners with externalizing behaviors is oppositional defiant disorder (ODD; APA, 2000). The *DSM-IV-TR* describes these learners as being hostile, disobedient, negative, and defiant in responding to authority figures, with a stable pattern of behavior diagnosed only after being in evidence for at least 6 months. These learners argue and refuse to comply with directives from adults, shifting blame to others and appearing to deliberately try to annoy others. They are described as stubborn and are unwilling to compromise. These manifestations are significantly more prevalent than they are in typical age peers, and they increase with age.

Research indicates that ODD seems to be related to temperament issues and is a significant risk factor for development of conduct disorders, anxiety, and mood disorders (Loeber, Burke, & Pardini, 2009). A study by Connor and Doerfler (2008) looked at comorbidity and differentiation of ADHD, ODD, and conduct disorders. They determined that learners with ADHD alone had less severe symptoms and that those with comorbid ADHD/ODD had less serious behaviors than those with ADHD and conduct disorders. Another study (Guttmann-Steinmetz, Gadow, & DeVincent, 2009) found similar overlaps with autism spectrum disorders, ADHD, ODD, and conduct disorders. This overlap among categories again illustrates the difficulty of applying diagnostic categories meaningfully for use in planning. Description of the specific behaviors of concern—whether they are inattentive, hyperactive, oppositional, or conduct-related problems—is a more useful guide to intervention.

IN THE CLASSROOM 12.10

Anxiety-Withdrawal-Dysphoria Disorders

Billy, age 13, is a fifth grader with mild intellectual disability and a history of parental neglect and abuse. He is currently placed in foster care. Billy shows no interest in things common to a 13-year-old. He is afraid to go to bed at night and sleeps with a teddy bear and a flashlight. Billy has learned not to trust others, and at times he does not even seem to trust himself. His nonverbal communication portrays a withdrawn, unhappy child who refrains from making eye contact and walks in a slightly slouched manner. He appears to daydream for long periods of time; and he will isolate himself by drawing for hours, as if to withdraw from the present. His foster mother says she has noticed that he seems to have defined periods of depressed mood. He frequently sleeps all day and then stays up all night. He becomes anxious in new situations, and at these times his behavior can become disruptive—he hits others and damages toys belonging to other children. On a recent behavioral evaluation, he achieved scores indicating clinical levels of deviance on the withdrawal and anxious-depressed scales. Although Billy clearly qualifies as a student with mild intellectual disabilities, the school district has just determined that the addition of services for depression is appropriate.

Maria is 18 years old and is in a transitional program for young adults with learning disabilities. Her teacher, Mr. Cutter, is concerned that without some sort of positive intervention, she will be lost as an adult. She appears to be extremely depressed, although this has never been formally diagnosed. She is wary of everything and seems socially withdrawn most of the time. When she first joined the class, her peers tried to include her in their activities. When she failed to respond, they began leaving her alone. She exhibits fearfulness that affects her ability to acquire the skills she will need for adult living because she is afraid to try. Mr. Cutter is afraid that Maria's wariness will deprive her of the opportunity to eventually participate fully in the normal activities most adults take for granted.

ANXIETY-WITHDRAWAL-DYSPHORIA DISORDERS   Individuals experiencing these disorders display extreme feelings of inferiority, embarrassment, self-consciousness, shyness, anxiety, or panic in normal situations—a fearfulness that is not based on a rational appraisal of a situation (APA, 2000). Children with depression may be reluctant to try new things, withdraw from social interaction, be irritable, and have a tendency to display hurt feelings. They may be viewed as socially inept or as social isolates. Some youngsters exhibit fears and phobias relating to school environments that interfere with their ability to function. These behaviors are described as internalizing behaviors, because the children turn inward, withdrawing into a shell (see In the Classroom 12.10). Such learners are reported to comprise about 15 percent of all students identified as having emotional or behavioral disorders, although such problems are found among students with other types of disabilities as well (Falk, Dunlap, & Kern, 1996; Morrison & Cosden, 1997; Reynolds & Miller, 1985; San Miguel et al., 1996).

Some of these youngsters—including some with learning disabilities (Bryan, 1997), intellectual disabilities (Reynolds & Miller, 1985) and autism spectrum disorders (Bellini, 2004)—are characterized primarily by social isolation, withdrawal, anxiety, and lack of social skills. They engage in behaviors that drive others away, or they have deficiencies in the behaviors needed to establish social relationships. Their social behavior is generally viewed by them and others as inadequate. They either lack social skill (i.e., have skill deficits) or fail to use the skills they have when appropriate (i.e., have performance deficits; Gumpel, 2007).

Other learners display fears (i.e., anxiety disorders) that interfere with normal activities of childhood and adolescence (Bellini, 2004). Some of these fears develop into full-scale phobias, fears that lead to total avoidance of the feared situation. When school is the object of the phobia, it becomes very difficult to help these children through the educational system; they exhibit definite signs of anxiety and even panic when required to attend school. Physical symptoms such as sweating, stomachaches, dizziness, and shortness of breath are very common. For these children, school becomes a threatening or aversive place, and they seek refuge at home (Kauffman & Landrum, 2009). It is important to note that children who are habitually truant are not considered school phobic, but rather as having a conduct disorder because their absence from school is generally an act of defiance of authority.

Obsessive–compulsive behaviors are included in the group of anxiety disorders. Obsessions are persistent, repetitive, intrusive impulses or thoughts. They are images that these individuals cannot get out of their minds, such as constant worrying and repeating nonsense phrases. Compulsions are repetitive behaviors performed over and over that have no utility and that interfere with normal functioning, such as repeated hand washing or checking locked doors. Such behaviors sometimes appear to perform an anxiety-reducing function for these individuals.

Depression and related conditions are internalizing conditions characterized by depressed mood and a lack of interest in productive activity (MacPhee & Andrews, 2006; Wright-Strawderman, Lindsey, Navarette, & Flippo, 1996). There are three major types of depressive disorders: major depressive episodes or disorders (a combination of symptoms that seriously interfere with ordinary activity), dysthymia (less severe but chronic symptoms that prevent optimal functioning), and bipolar depression (a condition characterized by extreme mood swings).

Depression results from a complex interaction of a number of factors, with no single cause (MacPhee & Andrews, 2006). It may be related to genetic or biochemical imbalances, or it may be a reaction to specific environmental events. School failure and depression may be reciprocal causal agents, given the importance placed on school performance. Factors that have been implicated include feelings of worthlessness, helplessness, hopelessness, isolation, experience of loss, disturbance in peer relationships, rejection, family disorganization, abuse, and fear of failure and humiliation (Guetzloe, 1988). Studies have found that students with learning disabilities, emotional or behavioral disorders (particularly with conduct problems), ADHD, ASD, or mild intellectual disabilities are more likely than their counterparts without disabilities to experience depressed mood symptoms, especially when placed in unsupportive classroom environments (Reynolds & Miller, 1985; MacPhee & Andrews, 2006; Wenz-Gross & Siperstein, 1997; Wright-Strawderman et al., 1996).

Because children's life experiences are qualitatively different from those of adults, adults and children may experience and exhibit depression differently as well. Childhood depression frequently results from, or leads to, academic problems and may also lead to unacceptable conduct, including aggression, stealing, and social withdrawal. Common manifestations of depression in children include being irritable, sad, and lonely. Learners experiencing depression may display apathy, low self-esteem, excessive guilt, school phobias, pessimism, avoidance of tasks or social experiences, physical complaints including lack of energy, and problems with eating or sleeping (Wright-Strawderman et al., 1996). Depression can be life-threatening; it is implicated in over 60 percent of suicides among young people. For this reason, and because depression is sometimes biochemical in origin, medical evaluation is indicated when depression is suspected. See Table 12.5 for the *DSM-IV-TR* indicators of the presence of depression.

Table 12.5 *DSM-IV-TR* Criteria for a Major Depressive Episode

- Depressed or irritable mood
- Lack of interest in and inability to feel pleasure
- Disturbance of appetite (gain or loss); failure to gain weight appropriately
- Disturbance of sleep (insomnia or hypersomnia)
- Psychomotor agitation or immobility
- Lack of energy, fatigue
- Feelings of worthlessness, self-reproach, inappropriate guilt
- Inability to concentrate; indecisiveness
- Recurring thoughts of death; suicidal ideation; suicide threats or attempts.

Source: Reprinted with permission from the *Diagnostic and Statistical Manual of Mental Disorders,* Text Revision, Fourth Edition. Copyright 2000. American Psychiatric Association.

At its most extreme, depression can result in suicidal thoughts or attempts (Guetzloe, 1988; Wright-Strawderman et al., 1996). It is suspected that some accidents are actually disguised or misreported suicides (Kauffman & Landrum, 2009). Although rare, there are documented cases of even preschool youngsters attempting or completing suicide. Depression in students with learning disabilities has been associated with as many as 50 percent of completed youth suicides (San Miguel et al., 1996). Youngsters displaying a combination of the following risk factors should be considered at risk for potential suicide:

- Sudden changes in usual behaviors or affect (mood)
- School problems (academic, social, or disciplinary)
- Family or home problems (separation, divorce, abuse)
- Disturbed or disrupted peer relationships (including peer rejection or romantic breakups)
- Health problems (insomnia, loss of appetite)
- Substance abuse
- Giving away prized possessions
- Talking about suicide, making plans
- Situational events relating to the student or the student's family, such as death of a family member or friend, pregnancy, abortion, arrest, loss of a job
- Sense of hopelessness

The presence of maladaptive behaviors, both externalizing (e.g., conduct disorders) and internalizing (e.g., anxiety-withdrawal-dysphoric disorders), creates significant problems for learners, schools, families, and communities. Early identification of patterns of problem behavior allows for more effective interventions. Problem behaviors often coexist with other disabilities, and it is hypothesized that the impact of other disabilities on the effectiveness of a learner's social cognitive functioning may exacerbate some of the emotional deficits (APA, 2000; San Miguel et al., 1996). A full and multidisciplinary approach is needed to identify and meet the needs of these learners.

IDEA 2004 AND SERIOUS DISCIPLINE PROBLEMS

When young people present challenging behaviors in school environments, teachers and administrators need to be able to respond quickly and effectively to restore and preserve an environment that is safe and conducive to learning. These responses frequently involve a "change in placement" involving suspension or expulsion from school. It is widely (although incorrectly) believed that the ability of school personnel to respond quickly and decisively to problem behaviors is severely limited if the targeted student happens to be one who receives special education services. Teachers and administrators frequently believe that, if a student with a disability reacts aggressively, there is nothing they can do about it. They believe that suspensions are not allowed and that the child is exempt from the disciplinary measures that apply to other students. The responses of some students in problem situations seem to indicate that they also have been led to that same belief.

ON THE WEB

Wrightslaw (http://www.wrightslaw.com) is the go-to site for information on legal requirements and rulings related to special educational services, including the full text of the *Honig* v. *Doe* decision.

The Supreme Court in *Honig* v. *Doe* (1988) did rule that, based on the IDEA principle of zero reject, schools may not expel or suspend students when their problem behavior is determined to be directly related to their disability. However, the court also ruled that in such cases schools should respond by reconvening the multidisciplinary team and reviewing the student's program and placement to determine what modifications might need to be made—modifications that might involve changes in services (Hulett, 2009).

In IDEA 1997 and 2004, Congress sought to clarify the requirements established in *Honig* v. *Doe* with regard to placement of students with challenging behaviors. IDEA created new options for school administrators who need to be able to deal quickly and authoritatively with serious aggressive behaviors when the safety of others in the school community is seriously threatened. These procedures are designed to protect a child's right to a free and appropriate education while giving school officials the means to preserve the right of others to a safe learning environment (Council for Exceptional Children, 2009, 2010; Hulett, 2009; Yell & Drasgow, 2000).

The fundamental IDEA requirement that every child receive a free and appropriate public education forms the basis of school responsibility for program planning and placement of children with challenging behaviors. Schools are required to respond in a timely manner to referrals by parents or others to determine whether a disability is present. In the response to challenging behaviors, a student is considered to be covered under the provisions of IDEA if it can be shown that the school had reason to know that a disability might be present. If the school had no knowledge of the possible disability, then implementation of a general code of conduct, including suspensions, is allowed (U.S. Department of Education, 2006a, § 300.534).

Once a child is identified as having a disability, the IEP team must consider and include in the IEP any interventions, strategies, and supports required for a child whose behavior impedes learning, regardless of disability classification. Congress intends that a functional behavioral assessment (FBA) be compiled for every student with problems with behavior, regardless of the nature of the disability, and that an individualized, proactive behavior intervention plan (BIP) be developed for all such students.

When a child with a disability engages in behaviors that would have resulted in disciplinary action if the child did not have a disability, school officials are allowed to impose such sanctions as are provided for in the general code of conduct as long as the discipline does not result in removal from the established school placement. Removal from school—including suspension, expulsion, and placement in an alternative setting—is regarded as a change in placement, which must be reviewed by the IEP team before it can be implemented. In addition, IDEA 2004 stipulates that children with disabilities cannot be deprived of educational services even if they have been suspended or expelled from school (U.S. Department of Education, 2006a).

The exception to this general provision is that school officials may order the immediate removal of a student to an alternative educational placement or suspension for up to 10 school days if continuation of the current placement presents a danger to the student or others. Students with disabilities who bring firearms to school or who possess, use, or sell illegal drugs may be placed in an alternative education setting for up to 45 school days (U.S. Department of Education, 2006a, § 300.530).

IDEA 2004 specifies procedural guidelines for evaluating the placements of children who have been removed from school under these provisions. Before the 10th day, the IEP team is required to have conducted a functional behavioral assessment and to have developed an appropriate behavioral plan (if one is not in place) or to have reviewed and revised any plan already in place. Should the school or parents disagree with the evaluation of the team, the law provides for procedural due process. IDEA 2004 further provides that these students should remain in the alternative educational settings pending the outcome of any due process proceedings (U.S. Department of Education, 2006a, § 300.530–533).

A hearing officer may order placement in an alternative interim educational setting for up to 45 school days if the school can show that continuation of the current school placement is likely to result in injury to the child or others. In addition, the hearing officer must review the student's current intervention program and placement to determine whether the school has made reasonable efforts to implement the current placement plan. Any alternative interim educational placement must meet the following requirements:

- The child continues to receive appropriate educational services, or FAPE.
- The alternative educational placement includes services and modifications designed to address the behavior of concern.

ON THE WEB

The **National Information Center for Children and Youth with Disabilities** (www.nichcy.org) provides information for families and educators on topics related to students with disabilities, including materials related to current discipline and behavioral issues.

Central to all of these reviews is the process of manifestation determination. If a change of placement is to exceed 10 school days, the IEP team must review the facts of the case and determine the relationship, if any, between the problem behavior and the disability. The team may determine that the behavior is not a manifestation of the disability and the child may be disciplined in accordance with the general code of conduct of the school if the following criteria are met (U.S. Department of Education, 2006a, § 300.530; Yell & Drasgow, 2000):

- The child's program and placement are found to be appropriate, designed to meet the child's needs, and are implemented appropriately.
- The disability does not impair the child's ability to understand the consequences of the behavior.
- The disability does not impair the child's ability to control his or her own behavior.

ON THE WEB

The **Center for Effective Collaboration and Practice** (http://cecp.air.org) provides resources on assessment of and services for students with problem behaviors, including functional behavioral assessments and design of positive behavior support plans.

An appropriate behavioral intervention plan and placement are the best protection for school officials and for students. Individualized behavioral intervention plans should be created and in force for any learners who present a pattern of maladaptive behaviors, regardless of disability category. Such plans, now required by IDEA 2004, identify the behavioral expectations, the inappropriate behaviors of concern, and the positive and negative consequences that are associated with both the expectations and the inappropriate behavior. The team should proactively consider interventions to ameliorate the problem behavior, as well as the disciplinary process that will be followed if misbehavior occurs. A general crisis response plan may also be established in advance. This kind of effective preparation assists students in managing their own behaviors and ensures that, in an emergency, an alternative plan is ready to be implemented.

Summary

Social–emotional characteristics can be studied from developmental and ecological perspectives. Erikson's theory of psychosocial development proposes that human behavior develops as the result of social challenges (e.g., trust, autonomy, initiative, industry, identity) that must be addressed and resolved for healthy adaptation to occur.

Emotions are indicators of psychological development. The core emotions of joy, pride, sadness, guilt, fear, and anger communicate much about what we value. The explanations given for particular feelings develop over time and provide clues to an individual's development as a social being. Selman discovered that the ability to take the perspective of another develops just as emotions do. Social cognitive skills are also essential to the development of socially skilled behavior.

Personal competence derives from the interaction of physical competence, conceptual intelligence, emotional competence, and social competence (composed of social intelligence and practical intelligence). Social intelligence includes social awareness and social skill. Emotional competence is related to personality characteristics, including character and temperament.

The ecological perspective holds that behaviors or behavioral patterns can be understood only by analyzing the interactions among the person, the environment, and any antecedent behavioral variables. Another example of research with an ecological focus is the work on the relationship of risk factors and protective factors that results in the resilience displayed by some learners.

Maladaptive behaviors are present in some learners with mild disabilities, including, but not restricted to, those with emotional or behavioral disorders. Conduct disorders include those with externalizing aggressive, disruptive behaviors. Anxiety-withdrawal-dysphoria disorders include internalizing behaviors such as anxiety and panic disorders, obsessions, compulsions, phobias, and depression.

IDEA 2004 addressed the special concerns related to the management of students with challenging behaviors. The law requires that a functional behavioral assessment be part of the planning for any learner with any disability who presents problems in behavior; those behavior issues must then be addressed in the IEP planning and placement process.

A Case Study   • Sammy

Sammy is 16 years old and of African American heritage. He lives in a small southern rural town with his mother, father, and younger brother. Sammy's mother and father are both employed in low-wage service jobs. Over the years, they have tried to arrange their work schedules so that one of them has been available when the children were not in school. Sammy's mother has been very involved with the children's education, attending conferences and seeking solutions to problems.

Sammy began his elementary schooling at Tate Elementary under the district's majority–minority transfer plan. His mother believed that an integrated school would provide her children with a better education than their local school would. During first grade, Sammy experienced difficulty with the beginning reading process and had trouble staying on task. A special education evaluation indicated that he was eligible for services as a child with a learning disability, and he was served in Tate's resource program for the next 2 years with minimal progress.

The next year, the school district opened a self-contained program for students like Sammy. His underachievement was severe enough, and he was transferred to that program. Ms. Cole, his teacher, reported that during the next 2 years, Sammy began to make some progress in reading, but mathematics was still difficult. He had difficulty completing his math assignments, frequently being off task and unable to sustain attention. He also experienced continuing problems with impulse control and displays of anger. However, Sammy impressed Ms. Cole as being a capable child despite his reading and behavior problems.

During his second year in Ms. Cole's class, he was mainstreamed for fourth-grade science. Academically he was passing, but his behavior was erratic. He had particular problems dealing with teasing. A behavior contract was initiated in which he earned a star for each class period that his behavior met stated guidelines, and this seemed to have some positive effect.

At the end of that year, it was decided that Sammy had made sufficient progress to return to Tate School in a regular fourth-grade class with resource help. It was suggested that he be put on an organizational behavior contract and receive instruction in anger management. Unfortunately, the fourth-grade teacher was not willing to provide any extra support and was, in fact, overtly negative and sarcastic toward Sammy. In addition, the resource position was vacant for the first 2 months of the year, so there was no transition support. Sammy's behavior deteriorated, and his academic progress evaporated. By January he was sent back to the self-contained class, where he stayed for the remainder of elementary school. It seemed as if Sammy had decided that life was easier in the self-contained classroom and that was where he wanted to be.

He moved on to another self-contained class in seventh grade, and his behavior became more violent. He was frequently involved in fights and was suspended a number of times. At 15 he was socially promoted to ninth grade at the high school. There he was involved in a fight and suspended. His mother asked that he be placed in the alternative program for out-of-school youth; she did not understand that by doing so she was removing him from coverage under IDEA. The school district said that because she had removed him from school, they no longer had an obligation to serve him. He was soon expelled from the alternative program because of fighting and was placed under the jurisdiction of the juvenile justice system.

Sammy's mother is at her wits' end. She can no longer handle his emotional outbursts at home, and she feels that the school and other agencies just want to get rid of him. She knows that Sammy needs help emotionally and academically. Sammy's mother and the advocacy representative have requested that the school revisit Sammy's case and evaluate the possibilities for reinstituting services. At the request of Sammy's mother, the following information was provided by Ms. Cole, Sammy's special education teacher in elementary school:

To Whom It May Concern

I have been asked by Sammy's mother to provide some historical information that may be useful in Sammy's future educational placement and planning. I served as Sammy's teacher in the self-contained class for students with learning disabilities when he was 9 to 11 years old. I have kept in touch with the family since and have followed Sammy's journey through the school system.

When Sammy was a student in my class, he was classified as a third grader. He was reading at an average second-grade level and had difficulty completing math assignments. His primary problems at the time were work-habit related, including attention to task, task completion, and goal setting. He also exhibited periodic problems with impulse control in unstructured settings. This manifested itself by his engaging in fighting on the playground when teased. His failure to control his impulses appeared to increase when he was under stress, such as during state testing periods. It is unclear to me now whether his learning disabilities led to the behavioral problems or whether the behavioral problems resulted in his difficulty profiting from instruction. In any case, both areas impeded his academic and social progress.

Under certain circumstances, Sammy demonstrated average to excellent cognitive abilities. When he was 10, Sammy was invited to join a community Odyssey of the Mind team. He was the only member of the team not identified by the school system as gifted and talented, but observation of his interactions in the group would not have called attention to this fact. Because the competition relied on nonverbal exhibition of creative thinking, his poor reading skills were not a problem. On the contrary, his capability in logical problem solving proved to be an asset to the team, resulting in their winning second place at the regional competition. In addition, although he was the only African American student on the team, he interacted well with the other members. This experience indicated to me that, given a challenging environment that did not present assaults on his self-esteem, Sammy had the cognitive ability to function well. It also demonstrated that he was able to control his behavior as well as any other child, given clear goals, supportive leadership, and interesting tasks. I saw him grow during that semester, growth that was evidenced in his work at school as well.

By the time he was 11, Sammy had made sufficient academic and behavioral progress that mainstreaming for fourth grade science was initiated. He had some difficulty with the work expectations at first, but with my assistance and oral testing, he earned passing grades. He then began to have lunch and recess with that class. Behavior was a recurrent problem, primarily when he would "lose it" on the playground. We initiated a behavioral contract to help him monitor his behavior and work habits, and there was improvement.

By the end of the year it was decided that he was ready for a less restrictive placement. His reading was at a lower third-grade level, and so he was recommended for placement in a regular fourth grade at his home elementary school. It was expected that his resource teacher and general education teacher would work closely with him during the transition to mainstream programming. Unfortunately, for a variety of reasons primarily related to staffing problems during that period, the needed close support and monitoring apparently did not occur. The reported negative behaviors increased, and Sammy was returned to a self-contained class in the spring of that year.

In summary, Sammy has manifested a number of problems in the past that have interfered with his progress in school. His problems have primarily involved his inability to set and work toward goals, to accept the restrictions placed on him, and to control his impulses. While he appears to have some perceptual and cognitive disabilities, it appears to me that the behavioral aspects were primarily responsible for his performance problems. He needed then—and likely still does need—assistance, coaching, and support to develop the social cognitive skills to accomplish what he needs to do and to refrain from actions that are detrimental to him and others. The frustration he must feel at this point, after all these years of being shuffled from program to program without developing the skills he needs, must be seriously undermining his self-esteem.

Sincerely,

Susan Cole

Susan Cole

The following psychoeducational testing report was prepared for the multidisciplinary team meeting at the request of Sammy's mother.

EVALUATION REPORT

Sammy is 16 years old and attended the senior high school until 3 months ago, when his mother withdrew him while he was under suspension for fighting. Sammy is currently on probation with Juvenile Services for fighting at school. Even though he was never expelled from school, he entered an alternative program for dropouts operated by the school district. Sammy was dropped from that program 2 weeks later, again for fighting. Up until his enrollment in the alternative school, Sammy had been suspended for 21 days this year. Formal evaluations over the last 8 years have all found Sammy to be functioning in the low-average range intellectually. Sammy is currently receiving counseling at the community mental health clinic.

Test Results and Interpretation

Wechsler Intelligence Scale for Children–IV (WISC-IV)

Full Scale (FSIQ):	**81 (low-average)**	**Perceptual Reasoning**	**87**
Verbal Comprehension (VCI)	82	Block Design	7
Perceptual Reasoning (PRI)	87	Picture Concepts	12
Working Memory (WMI)	80	Matrix Reasoning	8
Processing Speed (PSI)	78	(Picture Completion)	10
Verbal Comprehension	**82**	**Working Memory**	**80**
Similarities	6	Digit Span	6
Vocabulary	9	Letter-Number Sequence	7
Comprehension	8	(Arithmetic)	6
(Information)	7		
		Processing Speed	**78**
		Coding	4
		Symbol Search	8

Peabody Picture Vocabulary Test–Revised (PPVT)

Sammy's PPVT score indicates that his receptive language is comparable to his intellectual ability measure:

Standard Score	**84 (moderately low)**
Percentile	14

Peabody Individual Achievement Test-Revised

Sammy's reading recognition is significantly below his overall ability level, although his reading comprehension is comparable to ability level.

	Standard Score	**Grade Equivalent**
Total reading	74	5.1
Reading recognition	64	4.8
Reading comprehension	84	6.4

Wide Range Achievement Test–Revised (WRAT)

Subtest	**Standard Score**	**Grade Equivalent**
Decoding	65	3 end
Spelling	59	<3 grade
Arithmetic	62	4 end/

Evaluator Conclusions

This evaluation indicates that Sammy is functioning intellectually in the low-average range. His receptive language is comparable to his estimated mental age. His academic achievement in reading recognition, spelling, and arithmetic is severely deficient. Sammy appears to have poor listening skills, with stronger visual processing skills. Some adjustment problems are apparent in the school setting; however, Sammy's behavior throughout the evaluation was exemplary, indicating that he can control his emotions. Lack of academic achievement no doubt contributes to his frustration, leading to his inappropriate behaviors. The assessment indicates that Sammy should probably continue to be classified as a student with a learning disability.

Discussion

- From the historical and current evaluation information provided to you about Sammy, make a list of the strengths and needs indicated by this case material.
- Given this information, do you concur with the school psychologist's conclusions about classification?
- What are the implications of that classification?

- What are the programming implications in this information?
- What implications do you see in this case about the interaction between learning disabilities and behavioral disorders?
- How might the use of RTI have changed the course of Sammy's disability?

APPENDIX

Policy Statements

Council for Exceptional Children (CEC)
  Labeling and Categorizing of Children
  Inclusive Schools and Community Settings

National Association of School Psychologists (NASP)
  Appropriate Academic Supports to Meet the Needs of All Students
  Appropriate Behavioral, Social, and Emotional Supports to Meet the Needs of All Students

Labeling and Categorizing of Children (CEC, 1997)

The field of special education is concerned with children who have unique needs and with school programs that employ specialized techniques. As a result of early attitudes and programs that stressed assistance for severely handicapped children, the field developed a vocabulary and practices based on the labeling and categorizing of children. In recent decades, labeling and categorizing was extended to children with milder degrees of exceptionality. Unfortunately, the continued use of labels tends to rigidify the thinking of all educators concerning the significance and purposes of special education and thus to be dysfunctional and even harmful for children.

Words such as "defective," "disabled," "retarded," "impaired," "disturbed," and "disordered," when attached to children with special needs, are stigmatic labels that produce unfortunate results in both the children and in the community's attitudes toward the children. These problems are magnified when the field organizes and regulates its programs on the basis of classification systems that define categories of children according to such terms. Many of these classifications are oriented to etiology, prognosis, or necessary medical treatment rather than to educational classifications. They are thus of little value to the schools. Simple psychometric thresholds, which have sometimes been allowed to become pivotal considerations in educational decision making, present another set of labeling problems.

Special education's most valuable contribution to education is its specialized knowledge, competencies, values, and procedures for individualizing educational programs for individual children, whatever their special needs. Indeed, special educators at their most creative are the advocates for children who are not well served by schools except through special arrangements. To further the understanding and servicing of such children, special educators as well as other educational personnel should eliminate the use of simplistic categorizing.

No one can deny the importance of some of the variables of traditional significance in special education such as intelligence, hearing, and vision. However, these variables in all their complex forms and degrees must be assessed in terms of educational relevance for a particular child. Turning them into typologies that may contribute to excesses in labeling and categorizing children is indefensible and should be eliminated.

In the past, many legislative and regulatory systems have specified criteria for including children in an approved category as the starting point for specialized programming and funding. This practice places high incentives on the labeling of children and undoubtedly results in the erroneous placement of many children.

It is desirable that financial aids be tied to educational programs rather than to children and that systems for allocating children to specialized programs be much more open than in the past.

Special educators should enhance the accommodative capacity of schools and other educational agencies to serve children with special needs more effectively. In identifying such children, special educators should be concerned with the identification of their educational needs, not with generalized labeling or categorizing of children.

Decisions about the education of children should be made in terms of carefully individualized procedures that are explicitly oriented to children's developmental needs.

To further discourage the labeling and categorizing of children, programs should be created on the basis of educational functions served rather than on the basis of categories of children served.

Regulatory systems that enforce the rigid categorization of pupils as a way of allocating them to specialized programs are indefensible. Financial aid for special education should be tied to specialized programs rather than to finding and placing children in those categories and programs.

Source: From *CEC Policies for Delivery of Services to Exceptional Children*, 1997. Copyright © 2010 by The Council for Exceptional Children. Reprinted with permission.

Inclusive Schools and Community Settings (CEC, 1997)

The Council for Exceptional Children (CEC) believes all children, youth, and young adults with disabilities are entitled to a free and appropriate education and/or services that lead to an adult life characterized by satisfying relations with others, independent living, productive engagement in the community, and participation in society at large. To achieve such outcomes, there must exist for all children, youth, and young adults a rich variety of early intervention, educational, and vocational program options and experiences. Access to these programs and experiences should be based on individual educational need and desired outcomes. Furthermore, students and their families or guardians, as members of the planning team, may recommend the placement, curriculum option, and the exit document to be pursued.

CEC believes that a continuum of services must be available for all children, youth, and young adults. CEC also believes that the concept of inclusion is a meaningful goal to be pursued in our schools and communities. In addition, CEC believes children, youth, and young adults with disabilities should be served whenever possible in general education classrooms in inclusive neighborhood schools and community settings. Such settings should be strengthened and supported by an infusion of specially trained personnel and other appropriate supportive practices according to the individual needs of the child.

Policy Implications

SCHOOLS. In inclusive schools, the building administrator and staff with assistance from the special education administration should be primarily responsible for the education of children, youth, and young adults with disabilities. The administrator(s) and other school personnel must have available to them appropriate support and technical assistance to enable them to fulfill their responsibilities. Leaders in state/provincial and local governments must redefine rules and regulations as necessary, and grant school personnel greater authority to make decisions regarding curriculum, materials, instructional practice, and staffing patterns. In return for greater autonomy, the school administrator and staff should establish high standards for each child and youth and should be held accountable for his or her progress toward outcomes.

COMMUNITIES. Inclusive schools must be located in inclusive communities; therefore, CEC invites all educators, other professionals, and family members to work together to create early intervention, educational, and vocational programs and experiences that are collegial, inclusive, and responsive to the diversity of children, youth, and young adults. Policy makers at the highest levels of state/provincial and local government, as well as school administration, also must support inclusion in the educational reforms they espouse. Further, the policy makers should fund programs in nutrition, early intervention, health care, parent education, and other social support programs that prepare all children, youth, and young adults to do well in school. There can be no meaningful school reform, nor inclusive schools, without funding of these key pre-requisites. As important, there must be interagency agreements and collaboration with local governments and business to help prepare students to assume a constructive role in an inclusive community.

PROFESSIONAL DEVELOPMENT. And finally, state/provincial departments of education, local educational districts, and colleges and universities must provide high-quality preservice and contin-uing professional development experiences that prepare all general educators to work effectively with children, youth, and young adults representing a wide range of abilities and disabilities, expe-riences, cultural and linguistic backgrounds, attitudes, and expectations. Moreover, special educa-tors should be trained with an emphasis on their roles in inclusive schools and community settings. They also must learn the importance of establishing ambitious goals for their students and of using appropriate means of monitoring the progress of children, youth, and young adults.

Source: From *CEC Policies for Delivery of Services to Exceptional Children*, 1997. Copyright © 2010 by The Council for Exceptional Children. Reprinted with permission.

Appropriate Academic Supports to Meet the Needs of All Students (NASP, 2009)

The National Association of School Psychologists (NASP) is committed to ensuring that all children receive an appropri-ate public education, irrespective of race, culture and background, sexual orientation, socioeconomic status, or educational need. NASP maintains that all students learn best in inclusive environments that implement high quality, science-based instruction. Inclusive programs are those in which students with and without disabilities receive appropriate specialized instruction and related services in age-appropriate general education classrooms that are located in the schools that the students would attend if they did not have a disability. NASP believes:

- All children can learn. Schools have a responsibility to teach all children. School personnel and parents should work together to assure every child a free and appropriate public education in a positive and inclusive school environment.
- General education should include all children. General education instructional options and support services should be based on the individual psychoeducational needs of each student, and should be evidence-based. Such a system of instructional supports requires collaboration of general and special education personnel.
- It is imperative to recognize early which students are struggling academically and implement swift remediation of academic deficits through research-based interventions (Burns, Appleton, & Stehouwer, 2005).
- Psychoeducational needs of children should be identified through a multidimensional, nonbiased assessment process. Such a process evaluates the match between learners and their educational environment and deter-mines whether scientifically validated curricula are in place. Blame for failure should never be focused on the child. Assessment and intervention activities must always link directly to the needs of students.

NASP supports a multitiered model of evidence-based instruction and intervention, typically referred to as "Response to Intervention" (RTI; e.g., Brown-Chidsey & Steege, 2005), as an effective approach for meeting the learning needs of all students in inclusive environments. The delivery of services in a multitiered model supports inclusive instruction because it assures that all students in a population receive research-based instruction and all decisions are made using data documenting students' needs. Importantly, such models incorporate awareness of student diversity in race, culture and background, socioeconomic status, sexual orientation, and educational need. NASP endorses a comprehensive model of support for students with learning problems wherein academic instruction is linked to the needs of the student and does not require assigning students to categorical special education groups. These NASP positions are consistent with recent federal legislation in supporting a multitiered approach to delivering academic instruction including:

- The No Child Left Behind Act (NCLB, 2001), which supports the use of science-based instruction to meet the learning needs of all students. NCLB also requires that states establish accountability standards to ensure aca-demic progress for all students, particularly those from underrepresented groups, such as ethnic minorities and students in special education.
- The Individuals with Disabilities Education Improvement Act (IDEIA, 2004) mandates the use of science-based academic instruction for all students in general and special education. IDEIA 2004 also allows for the implemen-tation of a multitiered model to determine students' need for special education services and supports.

FEATURES OF A MULTITIERED MODEL OF ACADEMIC ASSESSMENT AND INSTRUCTION

In a multitiered model of academic assessment and instruction, students receive science-based instruction on a school-wide basis, and when necessary, receive additional instructional support on a small group or individual basis. Frequent formative assessments are used to monitor student progress and make decisions about the need for modified or additional instructional strategies. Such assessments take into account student race, culture and background, socioeconomic status, and educational need. In traditional special education service delivery models, students must meet predetermined criteria and be identified as having a disability before they can receive special education services. NASP believes that the use of a multitiered model makes it possible to simultaneously address all educational needs of any student, rather than narrowly focusing on either academic, or behavioral, or emotional problems (Batsche et al., 2005). Most multitiered models of academic instruction are organized along three levels of support referred to as Tiers 1 (universal), 2 (targeted), and 3 (intensive). Some national experts have advocated for fewer or greater numbers of tiers (e.g., 2, 4, or 5). Prior to implementing such a system, school psychologists can help to identify important stakeholders, conduct needs assessments, and deliver professional staff development.

Tier 1: School-Wide Screening and Instruction

In Tier 1, high quality instruction and support is provided for all students in the general education setting via a sound core curriculum. Observations are conducted periodically to ensure that science-based instruction is delivered as intended. Universal (i.e., school-wide) screenings are conducted routinely (e.g., three times per year) to ensure that all students make adequate progress and to identify students who may require additional academic support. Such universal assessments ensure that all students are able to access the general curriculum, regardless of race, culture and background, socioeconomic status, or educational need. These formative assessment procedures typically include curriculum-based measurement (CBM). CBMs are short, reliable general indicators of core academic skills that are highly sensitive to students' responses to instructional modifications. Roughly 80–85% of students in a given population should succeed with universal instruction alone.

Tier 2: Targeted Support and Progress Monitoring

At Tier 2, targeted supplemental services are offered for students whose performance and rate of progress are below what is expected for their grade and educational setting. Based on data from the school-wide screening given at Tier 1, school teams identify students in need of more intense science-based interventions. At Tier 2, teams select appropriate strategies to support student learning and develop a plan to implement interventions. Typically, evidence-based academic intervention and support is provided *in addition to* the Tier 1 core curriculum (Fuchs & Fuchs, 2005) and may be provided on a small group basis. School staff ensures that interventions are implemented as intended. Additionally, student progress is monitored more frequently than at Tier 1 (e.g., at least monthly) to document students' responses to the intervention(s). About 10–15% of students in a given population, who do not succeed at Tier 1, are successful with Tier 2 support.

Tier 3: Intensive Support and Continuous Progress Monitoring

At Tier 3, intensive interventions are designed and implemented based on data indicating insufficient student responsiveness to Tier 1 and 2 interventions. At this level, students require the most intensive and, sometimes, individualized instruction. More frequent progress monitoring (e.g., at least weekly) is also necessary to document progress toward grade level standards. Progress data allow for objective analysis of student learning regardless of race, culture and background, socioeconomic status, or educational need. A student's continued lack of responsiveness or progress with interventions at Tier 3 might signal the need for a comprehensive evaluation and consideration for special education. A student's inadequate response to interventions at all three tiers may be used as documentation for special education eligibility as part of the comprehensive evaluation, consistent with IDEA 2004 regulations.

ROLE OF THE SCHOOL PSYCHOLOGIST

School psychologists can be instrumental agents in the application of multitiered models of academic support, given their broad training in research-based practice, consultation, assessment and leadership that supports the needs of students from diverse backgrounds (NASP, 2007). School psychologists are trained to deliver a continuum of prevention and intervention services, consistent with a multitiered model of academic support (NASP). Specifically, school psychologists can:

- Lead teams in designing and implementing a school-wide universal screening system and using these data to help identify at-risk students, select science-based interventions, and plan progress monitoring components of Tier 2 and Tier 3 services.
- Provide professional development regarding the most effective ways to address the learning needs of all students. School psychologists also provide culturally competent services at all tiers of service delivery. School psychologists can work closely with teachers and school teams to enhance critical skills, including conducting formative assessments, interpreting data, selecting and using science-based interventions, and making data-based determinations about the efficacy of interventions.
- Consult with teachers and other school staff. Specifically, school psychologists can assist school staff in understanding and using benchmark and progress monitoring data to determine if students are making adequate progress and decide next steps.
- Evaluate new models of service delivery. School psychologists can help administrators determine the impact of multitiered approaches on school-wide student achievement, rates of special education referral and placement, and disproportionate placement.

Summary

NASP believes that all children learn best in inclusive environments that provide high quality instruction to all students, and that access to appropriate academic support services should not require that students be assigned to categorical special education groups. NASP also has advocated for alternatives to categorical labeling that typically reflect traditional approaches to service delivery. Recent research suggests that an effective education for students can be accomplished with alternative multitiered systems that incorporate evidence-based academic curricula and supplemental targeted and intensive interventions. School psychologists play important roles in implementing this model, including leading school teams and facilitating the design and delivery of multitiered, problem solving systems of academic support to all students.

References

Batsche, G., Elliott, J., Graden, J. L., Grimes, J., Kovaleski, J. F., Prasse, D., et al. (2005). *Response to intervention: Policy considerations and implementation.* Alexandria, VA: National Association of State Directors of Special Education, Inc.

Brown-Chidsey, R., & Steege, M. W. (2005). *Response to intervention: Principles and strategies for effective practice.* New York: The Guilford Press.

Burns, M., Appleton, J., Stehouwer, J. (2005). Meta-analytic review of responsiveness-to-intervention research: Examining field-based and research-implemented models. *Journal of Psychoeducational Assessment, 23,* 381–394.

Fuchs, D., & Fuchs, L. (2005). Responsiveness to intervention: A blueprint for practitioners, policymakers, and parents. *Exceptional Children, 38,* 57–61.

Individuals with Disabilities Education Improvement Act (IDEIA). (2004). Public Law 108-446 (CFR Parts 300 and 301).

National Association of School Psychologists (NASP). (July, 2007). NASP Strategic Plan. Retrieved April 20, 2008, at: http://www.nasponline.org/about_nasp/strategicplan.pdf

No Child Left Behind Act (NCLB). (2001). Public Law 107-110.

Appropriate Behavioral, Social, and Emotional Supports to Meet the Needs of All Students (NASP, 2009)

The National Association of School Psychologists (NASP) supports the use of multitiered problem-solving strategies to address the behavioral, social, emotional, and academic needs of all students. Problem-solving models provide needed supports to all students in inclusive environments when problems are first identified. When supports are provided in the general education environment, students have continued exposure to science-based core instruction.

In multitiered problem-solving models, interventions are linked to the social, emotional, or behavior *needs* of students. Approximately 17% of school-aged students require mental health services. However, only 1% of these students receive such services in special education (Merrell & Walker, 2004). A multitiered problem-solving model allows for early support before problems develop or worsen. Services provided through a multitiered model range from system-wide, preventative services that provide support for all students, to intensive, individualized supports for severely struggling students. To effectively implement problem-solving, multitiered approaches it is important to consider both the culture and context of the specific needs of students, as well as the schools they attend. Culturally competent practices and culturally responsive school-wide and classroom management should also be considered (Weinstein, Curran, & Tomlinson-Clarke, 2003). Providing a multitiered continuum of prevention and intervention services that are empirically based, data-driven, and culturally competent is consistent with NASP's Strategic Plan (NASP, 2007). Multitiered problem-solving models have the following common features:

- They are evidence-based. Intervention strategies are selected according to their proven effectiveness, implemented with fidelity, and student progress is monitored through objective and validated measures.
- They use a systemic multitiered problem-solving and data-based decision-making approach to support the needs of all students.
- There is a focus on prevention strategies that lead to positive behavior and social–emotional learning and high academic achievement.
- They are culturally responsive across the continuum.

In multitiered models, students with behavioral, social, emotional, and academic concerns are exposed to evidence-based practices at levels of increasingly intensive support. Following is one example of a multitiered model.

Tier 1: Universal Support

At the school-wide level, universal interventions are provided. All students are taught expected behaviors and reinforced for practicing them. Consistent with social–emotional learning (SEL) concepts, all students are also taught skills related to self-management, responsible decision making, empathy toward others, establishing positive interpersonal relationships, and determining positive goals (Greenberg et al., 2003). Students can be screened using the latest population-based assessment strategies (Doll & Cummings, 2008). Such data, often generated through already existing school-wide information (e.g., office disciplinary referrals) or through universal social–emotional and behavior screening (e.g., teacher rating scales), provides information indicating which students are at the greatest risk for social and/or emotional difficulties. At this level, population-based data would be used to identify school-wide needs and to directly teach positive social, emotional, or behavior skills. Typically, 80–85% of students in a building are successfully supported at this level.

Tier 2: Targeted Support

At the targeted level, groups of students are identified from Tier 1 screenings who struggle behaviorally, socially, or emotionally, despite systematic and evidence-based school-wide interventions that are implemented with fidelity. Teams review data to identify students and select appropriate targeted interventions to deliver in addition to Tier 1 strategies. In addition, staff selects procedures to objectively and frequently monitor student progress. Approximately, an additional 10–15% of students are successful in school when Tier 2 group level supports are provided in addition to Tier 1 supports.

Tier 3: Intensive Support

Students who continue to struggle behaviorally, socially, or emotionally despite high quality Tier 1 and 2 interventions require the most intensive and, sometimes, individualized intervention and progress monitoring. A problem-solving team typically determines the need for more intensive supports, based on a variety of assessments and a lack of prior responsiveness to less intensive science-based interventions delivered with fidelity. Tier 3 interventions involve more intensive supports and may require services from specialized personnel. For example, at Tier 3, services may include functional analyses of behavior, behavior intervention planning, and multi-systemic interventions (Weisz, Jensen-Doss, & Hawley, 2006). Additionally, students who require such intensive behavioral, social, and emotional support may need wraparound planning in which a collaborative child service team, including school and community service providers, plans and carries out an integrated program of behavioral, social, or emotional interventions.

Students who require the most intensive intervention and progress monitoring may also qualify for special education services. The amount and intensity of special education and related services are determined by the problem-solving team's ongoing evaluation of students' needs. Such evaluations, when conducted by a multidisciplinary team, meet the requirements of the recently reauthorized Individuals with Disabilities Education Improvement Act (IDEIA, 2004).

RATIONALE AND SUPPORT FOR A THREE-TIER MODEL

A significant body of literature over the last decade has evaluated the effectiveness of multitier problem-solving implementation. Results have included improved academic performance, reductions in office discipline referrals, and more positive attitudes toward school. Studies using single-cases methodologies and quasi-experimental methods have shown links to improved student behavior, social–emotional learning, and academic outcomes. Using problem-solving multitiered models to meet the behavioral, social, and emotional needs of students is consistent with recent federal and state legislation. IDEA 2004 requires schools to consider positive behavioral supports when disciplining all students, including those with behavioral needs who are not in special education. The U.S. Office of Special Education Programs (OSEP) has funded a National Technical Assistance Center on Positive Behavioral Interventions and Supports (PBIS; www.pbis.org).

ROLE OF THE SCHOOL PSYCHOLOGIST

School psychologists play a critical role at all levels of support for students with behavioral, social, and emotional concerns.

- Their training in data-based decision making allows school psychologists to facilitate school teams' reviews of data at all tiers, evaluation of research-based findings, and design of evidence based interventions. School psychologists can serve as facilitators of problem-solving teams and assist in the evaluation of student responses to intervention through program evaluation efforts.
- School psychologists collaborate with a range of individuals who impact the lives of youth with behavioral, social, and emotional challenges. By coordinating and delivering services to families with the most complex challenges, school psychologists can prevent the fragmentation of services that often impact children with the greatest need for intensive support.
- School psychologists assist in designing and delivering academic interventions and curricular modifications within multitier models of problem solving. The school psychologist can also help design methods of evaluating student progress and participating in implementing interventions at multiple tiers.
- School psychologists advocate for the mental health needs of all students by leading efforts at all tiers of problem-solving, including universal screening, the design and delivery of targeted interventions, and the implementation of intensive interventions for individual students.
- School psychologists advocate for evidence-based and culturally competent practices for all students and help schools reform practices that result in inequitable and ineffective outcomes. Too often, the behavioral challenges of students of color are handled with exclusionary discipline through suspension and expulsion, ultimately placing students with behavioral, social, and emotional challenges at risk for dropping out and entering the juvenile justice system (Skiba & Rausch, 2006).

Summary

NASP believes that effective education for all students, including those with behavioral, social, or emotional problems, can be accomplished when using a multitiered problem-solving system that incorporates evidence-based interventions. School psychologists play important roles in implementing these models, including leading school teams and facilitating the design and delivery of a multitiered, problem-solving system of behavioral and mental health support for all students and families.

References

Doll, B., & Cummings, J. A. (2008). *Transforming school mental health services.* Thousand Oaks, CA: Corwin Press in collaboration with the National Association of School Psychologists.

Greenberg, M. T., Weissberg, R. P., O'Brien, M. U., Zins, J. E., Fredericks, L. R., Resnik, H., et al. (2003). Enhancing school-based prevention and youth development through coordinated social, emotional, and academic learning. *American Psychologist, 58,* 466–474.

Individuals with Disabilities Education Improvement Act (IDEIA). (2004). Public Law 108-446 (CFR Parts 300 and 301).

Merrell, K. W., & Walker, H. M. (2004). Deconstructing a definition: Social maladjustment versus emotional disturbance and moving the EBD field forward. *Psychology in the Schools, 41,* 899–910.

National Association of School Psychologists. (July, 2007). NASP Strategic Plan. Retrieved April 20, 2008, from http://www.nasponline.org/about_nasp/strategicplan.pdf

Skiba, R. J., & Rausch, M. K. (2006). Zero tolerance, suspension, and expulsion: Questions of equity and effectiveness. In C. M. Evertson & C. S. Weinstein (Eds.), *Handbook of classroom management: Research, practice, and contemporary issues* (pp. 1063–1089). Mahwah, NJ: Lawrence Erlbaum Associates.

Weinstein, C., Curran, M., & Tomlinson-Clarke, S. (2003). Culturally responsive classroom management: Awareness into action. *Theory into Practice, 42,* 269–276.

Weisz, J. R., Jensen-Doss, A., & Hawley, K. M. (2006). Evidence-based youth psychotherapies versus usual clinical care: A meta-analysis of direct comparisons. *American Psychologist, 61,* 671–689.

GLOSSARY

academic learning disabilities specific learning disabilities that are manifested by difficulty in school learning in such areas as reading, written expression, spelling, handwriting, mathematics, and content learning

academic learning time the amount of time students actually spend actively engaged in learning activities with a high rate of success

academic responding time the amount of time students actually spend in responding to academic tasks/challenges as opposed to waiting or engaging in task management activities

accommodation the process of handling new information by altering existing schema to incorporate new and contradictory information and experiences

acquisition the first stage in learning, which takes learners from little or no knowledge to basic mastery of the concept or skill

adaptation the process by which existing schema are modified, using either assimilation or accommodation, to make changes to students' cognitive organizational structures

adaptive behavior skills and behaviors involving everyday functions used by individuals to meet environmental demands and to function in a competent manner

ADHD acronym for attention-deficit/hyperactivity disorder

affect the collected feelings, moods, or emotions displayed by an individual

affiliation one of the sources of intrinsic human motivation that involves the desire to join with others in a common interest or purpose

alertness the stage in the attention process in which an individual determines that attention is required; characterized by a readiness to attend to sensory input or to a cognitive task

alternative educational setting (AES) temporary placement allowed by the 1997 IDEA amendments for use when a student's behavior is a threat in the classroom

Americans with Disabilities Act legislation that prohibits discrimination based on disability; applies to employment, public accommodations, governmental services, transportation, and telecommunication services

anencephaly a congenital condition involving the absence of part or all of the brain

anxiety a psychiatric condition characterized by fear and excessive worries and resulting in demonstrated distress, tension, or uneasiness

aphasia the loss or absence of the ability to use spoken and written language; may refer to children who fail to develop oral language skills as expected (i.e., *developmental aphasia*), with the presumption that central nervous system dysfunction is the cause

apprehension catching or registering a stimulus in the sensory register for use in subsequent cognitive processing

appropriating the process by which a learner assumes the skills demonstrated by a teacher or guide

Asperger's syndrome a condition associated with autism spectrum disorders, characterized by impairments in pragmatic language and social relationships but without deficits in intellectual functioning and language development

assimilation the addition of new and complementary information to an individual's existing cognitive schema

atrophy the wasting away of a body part or skill due to lack of use or to degenerative processes

attention the strategic control function that allows a learner to focus on the relevant aspects of a task or concept long enough to process the information

attention-deficit/hyperactivity disorder a condition characterized by inattention and/or hyperactivity and impulsivity that compromises an individual's ability to process cognitive information and to learn

attributions for success or failure the reasons given by individuals for their success or failure

auditory association the ability to relate ideas, find relationships, make associations, and categorize information obtained by listening

auditory blending the ability to make a complete word by blending the individual phonological elements and to perceive the whole as a combination of the parts

auditory closure the ability to identify words and other auditory elements that have been presented in incomplete form or that have unclear elements

auditory discrimination the ability to recognize differences between sounds and to make distinct perceptual judgments of auditory stimuli with very similar sounds

auditory figure-ground discrimination the ability to distinguish a sound from its background

auditory memory the ability to recognize and recall previously presented auditory stimuli or a sequence of items presented auditorily

auditory perception the ability to interpret auditory stimuli and to attach meaning to what is heard

autism a developmental disability with deficits in verbal/nonverbal communication and social relationships; generally displays restricted or repetitive interests and behaviors

autism spectrum disorders functional developmental disorders affecting social interactions and language development, ranging in severity from severe to mild functional impairment

automaticity the stage of learning following acquisition, in which a learner's goal is to maintain accuracy while increasing the rate of accurate production and to perform tasks with little conscious cognitive effort

autonomy independence or freedom; the capability of acting in accordance with one's own will and effort

behavioral disinhibition deficiency in the ability to reflect before acting and to refrain from carrying out actions that, on reflection, would be seen to be undesirable or ineffective; a lack of tolerance for delay within tasks and a reduced ability to delay responses

behavioral flexibility the ability to adjust one's behavior to different situations, people, or settings

biological constructivism Piaget's theory that an individual learner is inherently predisposed to process stimuli and information in predictable patterns

borderline intellectual disability a term used in the past to describe individuals with measured IQs of 75–80 who display some indications of intellectual disability but whose performance approximates that of typical individuals

bound morpheme a unit of language (such as a prefix, suffix, or an inflected ending) that has meaning only when combined with a free-standing morpheme or word

cerebral hemispheric dominance the theory that each side, or hemisphere, of the brain controls particular functions and that one hemisphere is stronger than the other in most individuals, affecting individual performance

character the combined traits that shape a person's nature and contribute to the establishment of the individual's personality

chronicity the characteristic of being of long or indeterminate duration or of recurring frequently

chunk a collection of stimuli or symbols treated as a unit for ease in cognitive processing

chunking the process of subdividing content into subunits for easier cognitive processing

classification the process of assigning individuals to groups or categories by using agreed-upon criteria; also a Piagetian developmental task in which a learner is able to group items in categories

classification system the formal taxonomy of categories and levels of disability, combined with the criteria by which classification decisions are made

clustering the process of grouping elements to assist in cognitive processing

cognitive stages periods of development that are characterized by a specific level of cognitive sophistication

cognitive style the way in which learners typically approach and structure stimuli and derive meaning from their experiences

comorbidity the coexistence of two or more conditions in the same individual

comparison the cognitive process of determining whether two stimuli are the same or whether they are members of the same class of objects

competence possessing the skills needed for successful performance of expected functions

comprehension the process of interpreting and deriving meaning from oral or written communication

compulsion a condition characterized by an intrinsic need to perform repetitive actions that appear to others to be irrational or against one's will

conceptual intelligence the intellectual ability of an individual, including the ability to process information, solve abstract problems, and understand and use symbolic processes such as language

concrete operations Piaget's third stage of cognitive development, characterized by the growing ability of children to think logically about concepts in their own experience, while remaining unable to deal with abstractions

conditional knowledge a component of long-term memory consisting of the knowledge that an individual uses to determine when or whether to utilize a particular cognitive process or knowledge base

conduct disorders a pattern of behavior characterized by frequent occurrences of serious levels of aggression, destruction of property, and violations of family and community norms and standards

connotative relating to the meanings associated with words; used to refer to enhanced meanings beyond a basic definition

content the aspect of language that includes elements related to meaning, including morphology and semantics

context the combined variables that characterize the environment in which a pragmatic language or social event occurs

criterion-referenced assessment the process of gathering information about which skills a learner has mastered

cross-categorical programs a model of service delivery in which services are provided to children with different conditions in the same setting; uses interventions designed to meet student abilities and needs rather than a disability category

culturally fair the term used to describe instruments and assessment processes designed to accurately assess the performance of individuals from culturally and linguistically diverse backgrounds

culturally normative referring to the concept that behaviors must be evaluated in the context of the culture in which they occur; behaviors that are adaptive for an individual in a particular setting

culture the attitudes, beliefs, values, traditions, and customs shared by a group of people and derived from their shared heritage

curriculum-based assessment the process of creating assessment instruments related to the curriculum that has been taught in a particular school or classroom

declarative knowledge knowledge that deals with factual information and the acquisition of related concepts

declarative memory the long-term storage facility used for factual and conceptual information

definition the criteria used to establish the identity of a condition; may be conceptual, referring to the nature of the condition, or operational, used to place individuals in diagnostic categories

denotative referring to the explicit, primary meaning of a word, indicating the meaning generally held by most people in a given culture

depression a condition characterized by a prolonged depressed mood and lack of interest in ordinary activities, including those generally viewed as pleasurable

developmental delay a noncategorical classification defined in IDEA 1997 for use with children ages 3–9; identified by documented delay in development of physical, cognitive, communication, social-emotional, and/or adaptive skills

developmental disability a chronic condition characterized by significant impairment in functioning that results from mental and/or physical impairments, is manifested before age 22, and results in substantial functional limitations in three or more major life activities

developmental learning disabilities specific learning disabilities that affect functions such as attention, perception, memory, and language

developmental period that period of life during which rapid physical, intellectual, social, and emotional development is occurring, culminating in transition to adult status at about age 18

deviance a condition characterized by behavior that significantly departs from accepted and expected normative behavior

diagnosis the result of an evaluative process that describes an individual's condition, including etiology, current manifestation of the condition, treatment requirements, and prognosis

dichotomous belonging to one of only two possible and mutually exclusive categories

differentiated instruction a pedagogical framework that provides for varying levels of challenge with a lesson, including different levels of goals, materials, methods, and assessments based on students' functional levels

differentiation Piaget's theory that learning begins when individuals distinguish between and among various environmental stimuli and recognize specific stimuli as new information

disability a describable, measurable condition in which an expected, specific human ability is curtailed or absent

discrepancy a difference from expectations or an inconsistency

disequilibrium an unsteady cognitive state resulting when new information or experiences need to be incorporated into existing cognitive schema

displacement the phenomenon of losing specific cognitive information because of limited storage capacity during processing

distractibility a tendency to attend to multiple and irrelevant stimuli rather than to focus on the most relevant stimulus

Down syndrome a condition characterized by multiple physical abnormalities as well as by some impairment of intellectual functioning; results from a chromosomal defect in the twenty-third chromosomal pair

due process procedures set of procedures designed to protect the right to receive notice of and to challenge governmental actions

dyscalculia severe disabilities in mathematical processing

dysgraphia severe disabilities in written expression and in performing the motoric functions associated with handwriting

dyslexia severe disabilities in reading, including failure to learn to read or to read fluently and effectively

early intervening services interventions for at-risk general education students; uses research-validated practices to help these students succeed in the general education classroom

ecological assessment a process that considers behaviors in the context of an individual's environment and assesses the effect of the interactions between and among environmental factors and the individual's behaviors for the purpose of designing effective interventions

educable an obsolete term used to describe students with mild intellectual disabilities who were believed to be capable of becoming functionally literate and to lead independent or semi-independent lives

Education for All Handicapped Children Act legislation passed in 1975 as P.L. 94-142 that guarantees a free, appropriate, public education to all children in the United States

elaboration cognitive mnemonic strategies that strengthen the meaning of a stimulus through semantic or visual enhancements; supports storage of information in long-term memory

emotional competence the degree to which an individual is able to maintain an emotional steady-state

emotional disturbance the term used in IDEA 1997 for the condition of learners with emotional or behavioral disorders

emotional or behavioral disorders a disability characterized by the presence of problem behavior(s) that are markedly different from those of typical peers, have existed for a prolonged period of time, and are affecting educational performance

encephalitis inflammation of the brain related to an infection

encoding the component of the process of perception that involves the formation of a mental representation of a stimulus, including its attributes, associations, or meaning

equilibration the process by which a learner resolves the unsteady cognitive state created by new information; uses the cognitive functions of organization and adaptation to achieve a new level of equilibrium and cognitive competence

etiology study of the factors that appear to cause or contribute to a disability, including biomedical, social, and behavioral factors

eugenics philosophy that holds that it is possible to improve the characteristics of a population by discouraging reproduction by those believed to have inferior characteristics and encouraging procreation by those with desirable traits

executive functions cognitive functions involved in monitoring and evaluating the effectiveness of cognitive processing, directing the flow of information, and making resource allocations among the structural storage components of memory

expressive language communication process that involves speaking and writing for the purpose of transferring information from the communicator to the reader or listener

external locus of control belief of learners that their success or failure is due to factors outside themselves, such as chance, fate, or the actions of others

externalizing behaviors problem behaviors that are characterized by acting out, aggressive actions directed at a target outside the individual

extrinsic motivation motivation related to the desire to earn a reward or avoid punishment

FAPE acronym for free and appropriate public education

fetal alcohol effects (FAE) a condition related to fetal alcohol syndrome in which the effects of a mother's drinking on the developing fetus are present but less severe

fetal alcohol syndrome (FAS) a condition that results in a child's displaying intellectual disability, drooping eyelids and other facial abnormalities, heart defects, reduced physical size throughout life, and/or other evidence of central nervous system dysfunction; caused by the mother's ingestion of alcohol during the prenatal period

field dependence the degree to which an individual's perceptual and cognitive judgments are dependent on the surrounding environment

field independence the degree to which an individual is able to interpret perceptual information independently by attending to and considering relevant information from the environment and comparing it to internal standards

field sensitive an alternative term for field dependence, which recognizes the positive aspects of interpreting some perceptual information with reference to the surrounding environment and which is characteristic of individuals in some cultures

figure–ground discrimination the ability to distinguish an object or sound from its background

form components of language associated with its structure, including phonology, morphology, and syntax

formal operations Piaget's final stage in cognitive development, characterized by the ability to think abstractly and to use reasoning for learning

formative evaluation evaluation conducted in the context of ongoing activity for the purpose of making changes

fragile X syndrome a common inherited cause of intellectual disability, associated with a fragile site on the X chromosome; also characterized by other learning and behavioral problems and physical differences

free and appropriate public education (FAPE) the core right in IDEA, which guarantees to every child an education designed to meet his or her needs and provided at no cost to the child's parents

free morpheme the smallest unit of language that can exist by itself and convey meaning

functional behavioral assessment the gathering of information to accurately describe a problem behavior, the contexts in which it occurs, and the function or need it fulfills for the student

general education curriculum the curriculum established by a school, district, or state for use by all children; specifies the goals and objectives viewed as essential for later functioning; pertains to the content of instruction, not the way it is taught nor the setting in which it occurs

general education initiative (GEI) the philosophy that students with disabilities can and should be educated within the general education classroom setting, with supports and modifications to teaching strategies as needed; formerly called the regular education initiative

generalization the use of learned skills in settings or situations other than those in which the skill was trained

grapheme a written symbol used alone or in combination to represent sounds in a language; a phonogram

habilitation the process of providing training in necessary life skills to individuals who have not acquired those skills previously

handicap restriction in the performance of a desired function due to environmental barriers; results from interaction of a disability with an environment that cannot or will not be modified to accommodate the disability and permit the function

handicapism the attitude that any individual with a disability must also be handicapped, or unable to perform necessary life functions

haptic perception the ability to ascribe meaning to tactile (touch) and kinesthetic (movement) stimuli

hearing impairment an impairment in the ability to process auditory and linguistic information; if mild/moderate, allows use of oral language for learning with accommodations

heritability a characteristic of traits believed to be inherited or controlled by genetic components

HFA acronym for high-functioning autism

high-functioning autism an impairment in the less severe range of autism spectrum disorders, characterized by mild or borderline intellectual impairment

high-prevalence disabilities conditions that occur relatively frequently in society

hydrocephalus a condition characterized by a relatively large head; related to an increase in the amount of cerebrospinal fluid, which leads to increased pressure on brain structures

hyperactivity a condition characterized by an unusually high level of activity and restlessness

hypoactivity a condition characterized by an unusually low level of activity

hypoxia a condition characterized by inadequate oxygenation of the blood

IDEA acronym for Individuals with Disabilities Education Act

imagery memory strategy that involves pairing a concept with a visual image to enhance the strength of the concept in long-term memory

immediate memory structural component that includes the working and short-term memories and is devoted to active processing of information prior to storage or output

impulsivity a cognitive style that is characterized by failure to think about an action before taking it

incidence the percentage of individuals who will at some point in their lives develop a particular condition

inclusion educational practice of providing within the general education setting all the educational services students with disabilities require

individualized education program (IEP) written plan for individualized instructional services, developed annually for each child with a disability

individualized family service program (IFSP) written plan for individualized educational services, developed annually for each preschool child with a disability

individualized transition program (ITP) written plan developed annually for every student with a disability who is at least 14; identifies the student's needs with respect to ultimate transition to adult living

Individuals with Disabilities Education Act special education legislation that guarantees a free, appropriate public education to all children in the United States

inner language the use of language and linguistic concepts in internal cognitive processing of information

insight the skills involved in determining the meaning of social information and its relevance to an individual

intellectual disability the preferred term for conditions characterized by significantly subaverage intellectual functioning accompanied by impairments in the skills needed for everyday functioning; previously referred to as mental retardation

intelligence quotient (IQ) standard score from a norm-referenced intelligence test such as the WISC-III or the Stanford-Binet, with a score of 100 indicating average intellectual functioning

interference a cognitive condition resulting from the identification of a discrepancy between new information and previously stored material; leads to the modification or loss of information deemed inaccurate

internal locus of control belief of learners that their success or failure is due to the personal effort they have exerted

internalizing behaviors problem behaviors characterized by social withdrawal, including anxiety, depression, fears, and phobias

intrinsic motivation motivation related to needs within an individual for competence, belonging, and self-determination

involuntary attention an attribute of tasks that forces or commands an individual's attention

I-plans individualized education program (IEP), individualized family service program (IFSP), and individualized transition program (ITP)

IQ acronym for intelligence quotient

judgment skills used to determine the relevance and value of social information prior to framing a behavioral response

kinesthetic of or related to the sensation of bodily movement

labeling the process of attaching a name to the disability category to which a child has been assigned

language any method or code employing signs, symbols, or gestures that is used for communicating ideas meaningfully

language disabilities conditions characterized by impaired ability to develop, understand, and use language

learned helplessness the belief that one's own efforts are not sufficient to positively affect outcomes

learning the process by which experience and practice result in a stable change in an individual's behavior in a way that is not explained simply by maturation, growth, or aging; the process of moving from a state of not knowing to knowing

learning disability a condition attributed to deficits in the psychological process involved in understanding and using language; identified by achievement deficits that are unresponsive to intervention and are not accompanied by other disabilities that might be causing the learning problems

learning styles theory a theory that each person possesses certain characteristics that interact with specific learning experiences and environments and result in enhancing learning or in making it more difficult

least restrictive environment the term used in IDEA to refer to the principle that children with disabilities should be educated with their typical peers as often as possible and that removal to more specialized or restrictive settings should occur only when it is not possible, even with the provision of supplementary aids and supports, to serve such students in the general education setting

lexicon the vocabulary (collection of morphemes) used by an individual; the vocabulary of a language

locus of control the degree to which individuals perceive that there is a connection between their actions and the outcomes achieved

long-term memory main cognitive storage component, with virtually unlimited storage capacity; holds information considered to be permanent and, if stored effectively, accessible throughout life

LRE acronym for least restrictive environment

mainstreaming temporal, physical, instructional, and/or social integration of children with disabilities with their typical peers in settings or activities in which their disabilities are not a problem and the need for accommodations is minimal

maintenance the stage of learning that follows mastery and proficiencyand seeks to continue a high level of performance over time

maladaptive behavior behavior that interferes with normal interpersonal interactions and is personally unsatisfying or socially unacceptable

manifestation determination the procedural requirement of IDEA that the IEP team must review the facts of disciplinary cases involving students with disabilities and determine the relationship, if any, between the problem behavior and the disability before proceeding with disciplinary actions or interventions

Mendelian trait a characteristic related to genetic factors and governed by the laws of heredity

mental retardation older term for the disability now known as intellectual disability

metacognition awareness of one's own thinking processes and the accompanying ability to direct and monitor one's own cognitive processing

metacognitive regulation cognitive abilities involved in self-instruction, self-monitoring, and self-evaluation of the efficiency and accuracy of thinking behaviors

metacomprehension awareness of one's effectiveness in understanding oral or written language

microcephalus a congenital condition characterized by an abnormally small skull and resultant brain damage and intellectual disability

mild disabilities disabilities that impair some functions needed for learning and everyday activities but that nevertheless allow many functions to be performed normally

mild intellectual disability level of disability characterized by IQs generally in the 55–70 range

minimal brain dysfunction the term proposed by Task Force I for the condition now referred to as a learning disability

mnemonic of or pertaining to memory

mnemonics specific techniques involving the use of memory cues to assist storage in memory

mnemonic strategies cognitive procedures used to achieve the storage of information in long-term memory

moderate disabilities disabilities that more severely affect the ability of individuals to function and that may require more intensive and continuing supports

modified curriculum a curriculum in which modifications or substitutions are made in particular goals and objectives related to the content of instruction

morpheme smallest meaningful unit in a language; a word

morphology the study of morphemes

motivation force or drive from either intrinsic or extrinsic sources that leads an individual to act in a certain way

multiple intelligences the theory that each individual possesses a number of separate talents, or intelligences, and that learners may have a variety of ways to approach a learning task most meaningfully

multiple-gated screening multistep screening process for assessing children for possible disabilities

nature versus nurture the debate concerning the relative importance of inborn traits (nature) and environmental events (nurture) in determining the eventual functioning level of an individual

NCLB acronym for No Child Left Behind legislation (2001)

newcomer phenomenon the condition resulting when an individual returns to an environment after an absence and is unable to quickly resume activity because of missing information

newness panic a condition of anxiety in which a person responds inappropriately in a situation perceived as new

noncategorical programs service delivery models that base programming on identified strengths and needs of students instead of categorical labels

nondiscriminatory evaluation evaluation procedures using tests that do not discriminate against students with respect to racial, linguistic, or cultural background

normalization the philosophy that supports making services available to individuals with disabilities in ways that are as close as possible to the norms and patterns of mainstream society

norm-referenced tests tests that provide scores allowing comparison of the performance of a specific child to that of typical children of that age or grade

object recognition ability to recognize the essential nature of an object

obsessions repetitive and intrusive thoughts, impulses, or worries that are unrelated to real-life demands and interfere with an individual's ability to handle everyday tasks

oppositional defiant disorder a pattern of behavior characterized by active noncompliance and other forms of hostile response to requests by teachers and parents

ordering arrangement of items in some logical sequence as a means of facilitating storage and retrieval from long-term memory

organization the process by which individual learners are prompted by internal self-regulatory processes to fit new information into existing cognitive structures and to relate new concepts to previous learning

paired associates connection of a new concept with a concept already in the learner's repertoire

perception recognition and labeling of sensory stimuli; attaching meaning to auditory, visual, and haptic stimuli

perceptual integration the process used to match an encoded stimulus with a previously stored mental representation

perceptual overload tendency for information from one sensory input system to interfere with the processing of information coming in from another

perceptual speed efficiency with which an individual is able to attach meaning to relevant sensory stimuli

performance deficits social skill deficits relating to problems in the decision making required to activate appropriate social skills that are in the person's repertoire but are not activated by environmental cues

perinatal the period from the 20th week of pregnancy to the 28th day of the life of a newborn

perseveration a condition characterized by repetition of a behavior past the point of usefulness

personal competence an individual's ability to coordinate and effectively use a variety of skills to function in social contexts and to respond to environmental demands

personality the pattern of an individual's behavioral characteristics, including attributes of character and temperament

pervasive disorder a disorder that affects most aspects of development and functioning

phenylketonuria (PKU) a genetic condition that prevents the metabolism of the amino acid phenylalanine

phobia irrational fear that prevents an individual from performing necessary functions

phoneme smallest unit of sound in a language

phonogram written symbols used alone or in combination to represent sounds in a language; a grapheme

phonological awareness the recognition of sounds and the understanding that words can be segmented into individual phonemes and syllables

phonology the study of the linguistic system of a language, involving individual sounds and letters and the ways they are combined

physical competence adequacy of performance related to abilities in fine and gross motor skills, as well as physical development and health status

PKU acronym for phenylketonuria

P.L. 94-142 the Education for All Handicapped Children Act of 1975

placental insufficiency a condition involving the inefficient transfer of nutrients by the placenta to the fetus in the last trimester of pregnancy

positive behavioral supports a proactive approach to addressing problem behaviors by assuring that it is possible for learners to meet important needs while engaging in socially acceptable behavior

postnatal the period after childbirth

practical intelligence the ability to deal with the physical and mechanical aspects of life, including daily living and vocational skills

pragmatics the study of language within a social context; the functional use of language

predisposition a genetic tendency to develop a certain characteristic in response to conditions conducive to that development

prenatal the period beginning with conception and ending at birth

preoperational the second stage of Piaget's theory of cognitive development, in which a child begins to use symbols for thinking but does not use logic to process cognitive information

prereferral problem-solving process prior to formal referral that involves gathering information about a child's difficulty in performing necessary tasks and designing interventions to address those problems

prevalence the total number of individuals with a particular condition in the population at a given time

primary prevention changing the conditions associated with a disability so that it does not occur in the first place

proactive behaviors behaviors designed to cause something to happen; purposeful behaviors designed to achieve a desired end

procedural knowledge information related to the performance of specific tasks; a system of condition-action rules

procedural memory the long-term storage facility used for processes and skills

production the expressive channel of language, composed of speaking and writing

production channel communication processes used to transmit messages from one person to another by means of speaking or writing

productions condition-action rules stored in long-term memory as a string of connected steps in a process and used to facilitate access to procedural knowledge

proficiency stage of learning following demonstration of mastery, the goal of which is to achieve automatic and fluent skill performance

profound disability pervasive and severe level of impairment, resulting in significant restrictions of the abilities required to carry out typical functions

psychoactive drug substance that affects mental activity or behavior

psycholinguistics the study of the psychological processes involved in the understanding and use of language

psychometric thresholds cutoff scores on norm-referenced instruments, used to make classification decisions

psychotic disorder emotional or behavioral disorder that is characterized by extreme departures from typical behavior and that presents serious barriers to ordinary activities

reaction range potential range of expression of a genetically directed trait; the extent to which environment hinders or enhances the development of an innate capability

reactive behaviors behaviors that occur in response to a particular condition or stimulus

receptive language communication functions used to receive information from the environment, including the skills of listening and reading

reflectivity cognitive style characterized by the presence of an effective deliberative process in which an individual thinks about ane action before acting

regular education initiative (REI) older term for the general education initiative

rehabilitation process of restoring an individual to a prior level of skill and functioning; the activities needed to regain a function that was lost because of injury or disease

rehearsal cognitive strategy involving simple repetition, used to store less complex concepts in long-term memory

relatedness source of motivation connected to the human need for belonging and nurturing; includes the need or desire to develop affiliations, a sense of belonging, or friendships

reliability extent to which other evaluators would be expected to arrive at the same conclusion about a classification

resiliency ability of an individual to resist or overcome the negative effects of environmental stress and to achieve a positive outcome

response to intervention (RTI) a process that identifies and then uses a student's response to scientific, research-based interventions in determining whether the student has a disability and requires special education

reversion period of early learning in which students experience some measure of success but still make significant numbers of errors

risk negative or potentially negative situation that impedes or threatens the achievement of desired goals

RTI acronym for response to intervention

scaffolding instruction Vygotsky's term for the role of teachers and others in supporting learners' development

schema a concept or intellectual structure that organizes perceptions of the world in a systematic manner

schizophrenia pervasive and severe psychotic condition characterized by distortions in thinking and bizarre behaviors

secondary prevention changing the environment as early as possible so that a person is affected as little as possible by a disability and its duration is shortened

Section 504 of the Vocational Rehabilitation Act legislation that guarantees equal access for qualified persons with disabilities to all programs and services supported by federal funds

seizure disorder disorder characterized by temporary abnormalities in neurological activity and periods of unregulated electrical discharges in the brain

selective attention the ability to focus on relevant stimuli without being distracted by irrelevant environmental factors

self-concept an individual's sense of personal identity

self-determination ability to act as the primary causal agent in one's life and to make choices and decisions

semantic elaboration a memory strategy utilizing verbal enhancement of a concept(s) to be stored in long-term memory

semantic memory the unit in long-term memory storage that deals with factual information and the acquisition of related concepts; alternative term for declarative memory

semantics the component of spoken and written language that focuses on the meaning of phrases, sentences, and more complex and longer expressions

sensorimotor the first of Piaget's cognitive stages, in which an individual acquires knowledge through sensory input and motoric activity

sensory encoding process of translating sensory input into a representational form that can be manipulated in working memory and stored in long-term memory

sensory register the structural component that receives and stores sensory stimuli very briefly, prior to cognitive processing by the strategic control functions of attention and perception; also called the sensory store

seriation process of arranging or ability to arrange items in a series along a specific dimension

serious emotional disturbance the term used in P.L. 94-142 for students with emotional or behavioral disorders; changed to emotional disturbance in IDEA 1997

severe disabilities conditions that affect major life functions to the point that an individual is dependent on external and intensive supports to perform activities

short-term memory temporary storage device for information being processed for a specific cognitive purpose; storage buffer for auditory, visual, and/or other sensory stimuli; mediator between input, processing, and output

significantly subaverage referring to scores on a norm-referenced test that are more than two standard deviations below the mean and that indicate significant levels of difference

"six-hour retarded child" concept developed in the 1970s to describe children who appear to have intellectual disabilities only in school contexts and who are able to function outside the classroom in ways consistent with norms

skill deficits absence of needed social skills in an individual's repertoire

social awareness abilities that allow an individual to receive and process relevant social information from the environment

social cognitive delay delay in developing age-appropriate, functional social cognitive skills and in applying those skills in social contexts

social competence ability to respond appropriately in social situations and to carry out the functions associated with independent living

social constructivism Vygotsky's theory that learning occurs through participation in social or culturally embedded experiences

social Darwinism theory that the social order is a result of the natural selection of those individuals with social skills most conducive to effective social adaptation

social field dependence trait possessed by individuals who attend closely to and make use of social models and frames of reference in their immediate environment as they make decisions about how to act in a given situation; field sensitivity

social intelligence abilities associated with social awareness and social skill

social learning theory theory proposed by Bandura that learning occurs as an individual observes and imitates social models in the immediate environment

social skill ability to select and use behaviors that lead to socially acceptable and personally satisfying outcomes

socialized aggressive behaviors antisocial behaviors that are characterized by covertness and that frequently occur in the context of a negative peer culture

spatial relations ability to perceive the position of physical objects in space in relation to oneself and other objects

spina bifida congenital malformation of the spinal column in which the structures that protect the spinal cord do not fully develop, frequently resulting in some degree of paralysis

standard deviation a measure of the variability of scores

standard English the version of English that is used most widely in public oral and written discourse in the United States

stigma a condition that is viewed negatively and that causes an individual to be viewed negatively as well

strategic control components cognitive functions involved in using appropriate strategies for specific task completion; includes attention, perception, and storage and retrieval strategies

structural components storage elements of the cognitive model, including the sensory register, immediate memory, and long-term memory

summative evaluation evaluation performed at the conclusion of an activity or program for the purpose of making judgments about the outcome

surrogate parent person appointed to serve in place of biological parents to advocate for and protect a child's rights in due process and legal proceedings

sustained attention ability to maintain focus on incoming information over a sufficient period of time to allow effective cognitive processing while evaluating and withholding responses to incidental or nonrelevant stimuli

syntax component of language that involves knowledge and application of the rules governing the use of classes of words; the grammar of a language

tactile of or pertaining to the sense of touch

tactile defensiveness a condition characterized by extreme sensitivity and discomfort in response to the slightest tactile stimulation or touch

task analysis the process of identifying the prerequisite and component skills that must be mastered to achieve a specific terminal objective

TBI acronym for traumatic brain injury

temperament behavioral style relating to how an individual interacts with others

tertiary prevention actions taken to provide support in educational and social environments over an individual's life span in order to maximize the level of functioning and prevent a condition from deteriorating any more rapidly than necessary

theory of mind ability to attribute mental states to others and to be reflective of one's own cognition; relates to social perspective taking

Tourette's syndrome chronic, hereditary tic disorder characterized by multiple motor and vocal tics

trainable obsolete term to describe students with moderate levels of intellectual disability who were believed to be capable of learning basic self-care skills and working in unskilled jobs with supervision

traumatic brain injury (TBI) impairment subsequent to an assault to the brain (e.g., car accident, falls, violent attack) that results in variable effects on cognition and emotions

triadic reciprocality model conceptual framework that holds that a given behavior is a result of interactions among personal, environmental, and behavioral variables and that behaviors can be understood only in an ecological context

triangulate to use several sources to confirm the value and meaning of information

UDL acronym for universal design for learning

undersocialized aggressive behaviors antisocial behaviors characterized by acting out

universal design for learning (UDL) the principles that hold that curricular materials, instructional methods, and learning environments should be designed to flexibly support and challenge as many students as possible

use aspect of language that deals with the functional application of oral and written language skills

VAKT acronym for one of the multisensory teaching procedures that make use of input from visual, auditory, kinesthetic, and tactile sources to enhance the stimulus for learning

vigilance continuous monitoring of stimuli combined with evaluative capacity to reject those that are not relevant to the task at hand

visual acuity the degree to which visual capability allows discernment of objects at specific distances

visual closure ability to identify figures that are presented in incomplete form

visual discrimination ability to identify dominant features of objects and to use that ability to discriminate among a variety of objects

visual figure–ground discrimination ability to distinguish an object from its background, to lift the relevant visual stimulus from its visual background

visual impairment an impairment in the ability to process visual and print information; when mild/moderate, allows use of print with accommodations

visual memory ability to recall dominant features of a stimulus no longer physically present or to recall the sequence of items presented visually

visual perception ability to attach meaning to visual stimuli

visual–motor integration incorporation of the perception of visual stimuli with a particular motor activity, as in copying, drawing, and writing

voluntary attention acting consciously to focus on and control the cognitive processing of stimuli

working memory component of immediate memory, used for manipulation of information from incoming stimuli as well as information retrieved from long-term memory

written expression use of handwriting, spelling, and composition to communicate with others

zero reject the principle that all children must receive a free, appropriate public education (FAPE) regardless of the severity of their disabilities

zone of proximal development range of learnings that students can achieve when they are engaged in meaningful activities with competent others

REFERENCES

Aaron, P. G. (1997). The impeding demise of the discrepancy formula. *Review of Educational Research, 67*(4), 461–502.

Abell, M. M., Bauder, D. K., & Simmons, T. J. (2005). Access to the general curriculum: A curriculum and instruction perspective for educators. *Intervention in School and Clinic, 41*(2), 82–86.

Aber, M. E., Bachman, B., Campbell, P., & O'Malley, G. (1994). Improving instruction in elementary schools. *Teaching Exceptional Children, 26*(3), 42–50.

Acrey, C., Johnstone, C., & Milligan, C. (2005). Using universal design to unlock the potential for academic achievement of at-risk learners. *Teaching Exceptional Children, 38*(2), 22–31.

Adelman, H. S., & Taylor, L. (1990). Intrinsic motivation and school misbehavior: Some intervention implications. *Journal of Learning Disabilities, 23*(9), 541–550.

Aebi, M., Metzke, C. W., & Steinhausen, H.-C. (2010). Accuracy of the "DSM"-oriented Attention Problem Scale of the Child Behavior Checklist in diagnosing attention-deficit hyperactivity disorder. *Journal of Attention Disorders, 13*(5), 454–463.

Akiba, D., & Alkins, K. (2010). Learning: The relationship between a seemingly mundane concept and classroom practices. *The Clearing House, 83,* 62–67.

Alamolhodaei, H. (2009). A working memory model applied to mathematical word problem solving. *Asia Pacific Education Review, 10,* 183–192.

Algozzine, B., Morsink, C. V., & Algozzine, K. M. (1988). What's happening in self-contained special education classrooms? *Exceptional Children, 55*(3), 259–265.

Algozzine, B., & Ysseldyke, J. E. (1988). Questioning discrepancies: Retaking the first step 20 years later. *Learning Disability Quarterly, 11,* 307–318.

Allen, V. L., & Greenberger, D. B. (1980). Destruction and perceived control. In A. Baum & J. E. Singer (Eds.), *Advances in environmental psychology: Vol. 2. Applications of personal control* (pp. 85–109). Hillsdale, NJ: Erlbaum.

Alley, G., & Deshler, D. D. (1979). *Teaching the learning disabled adolescent: Strategies and methods.* Denver: Love.

Allsopp, D. H., Kyger, M. M., Lovin, L. A., Gerretson, H., Carson, K. L., & Ray, S. (2008). Mathematics dynamic assessment: Informal assessment that responds to the needs of struggling learners in mathematics. *Teaching Exceptional Children, 40*(3), 6–16.

American Academy of Pediatrics: Council on School Health. (2009). Policy statement: Guidance for the administration of medication in school. *Pediatrics, 124*(4), 1244–1251. Retrieved from http://aap-policy.aappublications.org/cgi/content/full/pediatrics;124/4/1244

American Association on Intellectual and Developmental Disabilities (AAIDD). (2008). *Self- Determination* (Position Statement). Washington DC: Author. Retrieved from http://www.aaidd.org/content_163.cfm?navID = 31

American Association on Intellectual and Developmental Disabilities (AAIDD). (2010). *Intellectual disability: Definition, classification, and systems of supports* (11th ed.). Washington, DC: Author.

American Association on Mental Retardation (AAMR/AAIDD). (1992). *Mental retardation: Definition, classification, and systems of support.* Washington, DC: Author.

American Association on Mental Retardation (AAMR/AAIDD). (2002). *Mental retardation: Definition, classification, and systems of support* (10th ed.). Washington, DC: Author.

American Educational Research Association (AERA). (1999). *Standards for educational and psychological testing.* Washington, DC: Author.

American Psychiatric Association (APA). (1968). *Diagnostic and statistical manual of mental disorders* (2nd ed.). Washington, DC: Author.

American Psychiatric Association (APA). (1980). *Diagnostic and statistical manual of mental disorders* (3rd ed.). Washington, DC: Author.

American Psychiatric Association (APA). (1987). *Diagnostic and statistical manual of mental disorders* (3rd ed. rev.). Washington, DC: Author.

American Psychiatric Association (APA). (1994). *Diagnostic and statistical manual of mental disorders* (4th ed.). Washington, DC: Author.

American Psychiatric Association (APA). (2000). *Diagnostic and statistical manual of mental disorders* (4th ed., text revision). Washington, DC: Author.

American Psychological Association. (2010). *Publication manual of the American Psychological Association* (6th ed.). Washington, DC: Author.

American Speech-Language-Hearing Association (ASHA). (2010). *Typical speech and language development.* Retrieved from http://www.asha.org/public/speech/development/default.htm

Anderson, G. M., & Hoshino, Y. (2005). Neurochemical studies of autism. In F. R. Volkmar, R. Paul, A. Klin, & D. Cohen (Eds.), *Handbook of autism and pervasive developmental disorders* (3rd ed., Vol. 1, pp. 453–472). Hoboken, NJ: Wiley.

Anderson, J. R. (1983). *The architecture of cognition.* Cambridge, MA: Harvard University Press.

Anderson, M., Beard, K., Delgado, B., Kea, C. D., Raymond, E. B., Singh, N. N., et al. (2003). Excerpts from working with culturally and linguistically diverse children, youth and their families: Promising practices in assessment, instruction, and personnel. *Beyond Behavior, 12*(2), 12–16.

Anderson, P. L., & Meie-Hedde, R. (2001). Early case reports of dyslexia in the United States and Europe. *Journal of Learning Disabilities, 34*(1), 9–21.

Angell, M. E., Stoner, J. B., & Fulk, B. M. (2010). Advice from adults with physical disabilities on fostering self-determination during school years. *Teaching Exceptional Children, 42*(3), 64–75.

Angoff, W. H. (1988). The nature-nurture debate, attitudes, and group differences. *American Psychologist, 43*(9), 713–720.

Appl, D. (2006). First-year early childhood special education teachers and their assistants: "Teaching along with her." *Teaching Exceptional Children, 38*(6), 34–40.

Apter, S. J., & Conoley, J. C. (1984). *Childhood behavioral disorders and emotional disturbance: An introduction to teaching troubled children.* Upper Saddle River, NJ: Prentice Hall.

Arent, R. P. (1992). *Trust building with children who hurt.* West Nyack, NY: Center for Applied Research in Education.

Ariel, A. (1992). *Education of children and adolescents with learning disabilities.* New York: Merrill/Macmillan.

Armstrong, T. (1994). *Multiple intelligences in the classroom.* Alexandria, VA: Association for Supervision and Curriculum Development.

Armstrong, T. (1995, October 18). ADD as a social invention. *Education Week, 44,* 33.

Arter, P. S. (2007). The positive alternative learning supports program: Collaborating to improve student success. *Teaching Exceptional Children, 40*(2), 38–46.

Artiles, A. J. (2003). Special education's changing identity: Paradoxes and dilemmas in views of culture and space. *Harvard Educational Review, 73*(2), 164–202.

Artiles, A. J., Kozleski, E. B., Trent, S. C., Osher, D., & Ortiz, A. (2010). Justifying and explaining disproportionality, 1968–2008: A critique of underlying views of culture. *Exceptional Children, 76*(3), 279–299.

Artiles, A. J., Rueda, R., Salazar, J. J., & Higareda, I. (2005). Within-group diversity in minority disproportionate representation: English language learners in urban school districts. *Exceptional Children, 71*(3), 283–300.

Ashbaker, M. H., & Swanson, H. L. (1996). Short-term memory and working memory operations and their contributions to reading in adolescents with and without learning disabilities. *Learning Disabilities Research and Practice, 11*(4), 206–213.

Asperger, H. (1944). Die autistichen Psychopathen im Kindesalter. *Archiv fur Psychiatrie und Nervenkrankheiten, 177,* 76–137.

Association of Children with Learning Disabilities (ACLD). (1986). ACLD description: Specific learning disabilities. *ACLD Newsbriefs, 166,* 15–16.

Attwood, T. (2007). *The complete guide to Asperger's syndrome.* London: Kingsley.

Auchenbach, T. M. (2001). *Child Behavior Checklist.* Burlington, VT: Research Center for Children, Youth, and Families.

Austin, V. L. (2003). Pharmacological interventions for students with ADD. *Intervention in School and Clinic, 381*(5), 289–296.

Autism—Why the increased rates? A one-year update: Hearings before the Committee on Government Reform, House of Representatives, 107th Cong. 1. (2001). Serial No. 107–29, U.S. Government Printing Office.

Baddeley, A. (2000). Short-term and working memory. In E. Tulving & F. I. M. Craik (Eds.), *The Oxford handbook of memory* (pp. 77–92). New York: Oxford University Press.

Baker-Ericzen, M. J., Brookman-Frazee, L., & Stahmer, A. (2005). Stress levels and adaptability in parents of toddlers with and without autism spectrum disorders. *Research and Practice for Persons with Severe Disabilities, 30*(4), 194–204.

Balk, D. (1983). Learned helplessness: A model to understand and overcome a child's extreme reaction to failure. *Journal of School Health, 53*(6), 365–369.

Banda, D. R., Matuszny, R. M., & Therrien, W. J. (2009). Enhancing motivation to complete math tasks using the high-preference strategy. *Intervention in School and Clinic, 44*(3), 146–150.

Bandura, A. (1977). *Social learning theory.* Upper Saddle River, NJ: Prentice Hall.

Bandura, A. (1986). *Social foundations of thought and action: A social cognitive theory.* Upper Saddle River, NJ: Prentice Hall.

Bardovi-Harlig, K., & Mahan-Taylor, R. (2003). Introduction to teaching pragmatics. *English Teaching Forum, 41*(3), 37–39.

Retrieved from http://exchanges.state.gov/englishteaching/forum/archives/2003/03–41-3.html

Barkley, R. A. (2006). *Attention-deficit hyperactivity disorder: A handbook for diagnosis and treatment* (3rd ed.). New York: Guilford Press.

Barkley, R. A., & Murphy, K. R. (2006). *Attention-deficit hyperactivity disorder: A clinical workbook* (3rd ed.). New York: Guilford Press.

Barnhill, G. P. (2001). What is Asperger Syndrome? *Intervention in School and Clinic, 36*(5), 259–265.

Barnhill, G. P. (2005). Functional behavioral assessment in schools. *Intervention in School and Clinic, 40*(3), 131–143.

Bashir, A. S., & Scavuzzo, A. (1992). Children with language disorders: Natural history and academic success. *Journal of Learning Disabilities, 25*(1), 53–65.

Bellini, S. (2004). Social skill deficits and anxiety in high-functioning adolescents with autism spectrum disorders. *Focus on Autism and Developmental Disabilities, 19*(2), 78–86.

Benaron, L. D. (2008). *Autism.* Westport, CT: Greenwood.

Bender, W. N., & Wall, M. E. (1994). Social-emotional development of students with learning disabilities. *Learning Disabilities, 17*(4), 323–341.

Benevento, J. A. (2004). *A self-regulated learning approach for children with learning/behavioral disorders.* Springfield, IL: Charles C Thomas.

Bereron, R., Floyd, R. G., & Shands, E. I. (2008). States' eligibility guidelines for mental retardation: An update and consideration of part scores and unreliability of IQs. *Education and Training in Developmental Disabilities, 43*(1), 123–131.

Bickel, W. E., & Bickel, D. D. (1986). Effective schools, classrooms, and instruction: Implications for special education. *Exceptional Children, 52*(6), 489–500.

Biklen, D. (1985). *Achieving the complete school.* New York: Columbia University Press.

Billingsley, B. S., & Wildman, T. M. (1990). Facilitating reading comprehension in learning disabled students: Metacognitive goals and instructional strategies. *Remedial and Special Education, 11*(2), 18–31.

Black, C. (1981). *It will never happen to me!* New York: Ballantine.

Blackman, H. P. (1989). Special education placement: Is it what you know or where you live? *Exceptional Children, 55*(5), 459–462.

Blackman, S., & Goldstein, K. M. (1982). Cognitive styles and learning disabilities. *Journal of Learning Disabilities, 15*(2), 106–114.

Blanton, R. L. (1975). Historical perspectives on the classification of mental retardation. In N. Hobbs (Ed.), *Issues in the classification of children* (Vol. 1, pp. 164–193). San Francisco: Jossey-Bass.

Bloom, L. (1988). What is language? In M. Lahey (Ed.), *Language disorders and language development* (pp. 1–19). New York: Macmillan.

Bogdan, R., & Taylor, S. J. (1976). The judged, not the judges. *American Psychologist, 31*(1), 47–52.

Bogdan, R., & Taylor, S. J. (1994). *The social meaning of mental retardation: Two life stories.* New York: Teachers College Press.

Booth, T., & Ainscow, M. (2002). *Index for Inclusion: Developing learning and participation in schools.* Centre for Studies on Inclusive Education. Retrieved from www.eenet.org.uk/resources/docs/Index%20English.pdf

Borkowski, J. G., & Kurtz, B. E. (1987). Metacognition and executive control. In J. G. Borkowski & J. D. Day (Eds.), *Cognition in special children: Comparative approaches to retardation, learning disabilities, and giftedness* (pp. 123–152). Norwood, NJ: Ablex.

Borkowski, J. G., Weyhing, R. S., & Turner, L. A. (1986). Attributional retraining and the teaching of strategies. *Exceptional Children, 53*(2), 130–137.

Bost, L. W., & Riccomini, P. J. (2006). Effective instruction: An inconspicuous strategy for dropout prevention. *Remedial and Special Education, 27*(5), 301–311.

Boston, C. (2002). *The concept of formative assessment: ERIC Digest.* (ERIC Document Reproduction Service No. ED470206)

Bouck, E. C. (2004). State of curriculum for secondary students with mild mental retardation. *Education and Training in Developmental Disabilities, 39*(2), 169–176.

Boutot, E. A. (2007). Fitting in: Tips for promoting acceptance and friendships for students with autism spectrum disorders in inclusive classrooms. *Intervention in School and Clinic, 42*(3), 156–161.

Bowen, J. M. (2005). Classroom interventions for students with traumatic brain injuries. *Preventing School Failure, 49*(4), 34–41.

Bower, E. M. (1960). *Early identification of emotionally handicapped children in school.* Springfield, IL: Charles C Thomas.

Bower, E. M. (1982). Defining emotional disturbance: Public policy and research. *Psychology in the Schools, 19*(1), 55–66.

Bownam-Perrott, L. (2009). Classwide peer tutoring: An effective strategy for students with emotional and behavioral disorders. *Intervention in School and Clinic, 44*(5), 259–267.

Bradley, L. J., & Meredith, R. C. (1991). Interpersonal development: A study with children classified as educable mentally retarded. *Education and Training in Mental Retardation, 26*(2), 130–141.

Bradley, R., Danielson, L., & Doolittle, J. (2007). Responsiveness to intervention: 1997–2007. *Teaching Exceptional Children, 39*(5), 8–12.

Brantlinger, E. A. (2006). *Who benefits from special education? Remediating (fixing) other people's children.* Mahwah, NJ: Erlbaum.

Brehm, S. S., & Brehm, J. W. (1981). *Psychological reactance: A theory of freedom and control.* New York: Academic Press.

Brice, R. G. (2004). Connecting oral and written language through applied writing strategies. *Intervention in School and Clinic, 40*(1), 38–47.

Brigance, A. H. (2010a). *Comprehensive inventory of basic skills II.* North Billerica, MA: Curriculum Associates.

Brigance, A. H. (2010b). *Inventory of early development II.* North Billerica, MA: Curriculum Associates.

Brigance, A. H. (2010c). *Transition skills inventory.* North Billerica, MA: Curriculum Associates.

Brigham, R., Berkley, P., Simpkins, P., & Brigham, M. (2007). A focus on reading comprehension strategy instruction. *Current Practice Alerts 12.* Division for Learning Disabilities and Division for Research (CEC). Retrieved from http://www.teachingld.org/ld_resources/alerts/default.htm

Brigham, R., & Brigham, M. (2001). A focus on mnemonic instruction. *Current Practice Alerts 5.* Division for Learning Disabilities and Division for Research (CEC). Retrieved from http://www. teachingld.org/ld_resources/alerts/default.htm

Bronfenbrenner, U. (1979). *The ecology of human development: Experiments by nature and design.* Cambridge, MA: Harvard University Press.

Brophy, J., & Good, T. L. (1986). Teacher behavior and student achievement. In M. C. Wittrock (Ed.), *Handbook of research on teaching* (3rd ed., pp. 328–375). New York: MacMillan.

Brown, H. K., Ouellette-Kuntz, H., Bielsks, I., & Elliott, D. (2009). Choosing a measure of support need: Implications for research and policy. *Journal of Intellectual Disability Research, 53*(II), 949–954.

Brown-Chidsey, R. (2007). No more "waiting to fail." *Educational Leadership, 65*(2), 40–46.

Brown-Chidsey, R., & Steege, M. W. (2005). *Response to intervention: Principles and strategies for effective practice.* New York: Guilford Press.

Bruce, S., & Muhammad, Z. (2009). The development of object permanence in children with intellectual disability, physical disability, autism, and blindness. *International Journal of Disability, Development and Education, 56*(3), 229–246.

Bruner, J. (1990). *Acts of meaning.* Cambridge, MA: Harvard University Press.

Bryan, T. (1991). Assessment of social cognition: Review of the research in learning disabilities. In H. L. Swanson (Ed.), *Handbook of the assessment of learning disabilities: Theory, research, and practice* (pp. 285–311). Austin, TX: Pro-Ed.

Bryan, T. (1997). Assessing the personal and social status of students with learning disabilities. *Learning Disabilities Research and Practice, 12*(1), 63–76.

Burack, J. A., Flanagan, T., Peled, T., Sutton, H. M., Zygmuntowicz, C., & Manly, J. T. (2006). Social perspective-taking skills in maltreated children and adolescents. *Developmental Psychology, 42*(2), 207–217.

Burke, P. J., & Ruedel, K. (2008). Disability, classification, categorization in education: A U.S. perspective. In L. Florian & M. J. McLaughlin (Eds.), *Disability classification in education: Issues and perspectives* (pp. 68–77). Thousand Oaks, CA: Corwin.

Burks, H. F. (2006). *Burks Behavior Rating Scales* (2nd ed.). Los Angeles: Western Psychological Services.

Burleigh, M. (1994). *Death and deliverance: "Euthanasia" in Germany c. 1900–1945.* Cambridge, England: Cambridge University Press.

Bursuck, W. D., Munk, D. D., & Olson, M. M. (1999). The fairness of report card grading adaptations: What do students with and without learning disabilities think? *Remedial and Special Education, 20*(2), 84–92.

Bursuck, W. D., Polloway, E. A., Plante, L., Epstein, M. H., Jayanthi, M., & McConeghy, J. (1996). Report card grading and adaptations: A national survey of classroom practices. *Exceptional Children, 62*(4), 301–318.

Cahill, S. M. (2009). Where does handwriting fit in? Strategies to support academic achievement. *Intervention in School and Clinic, 44*(5), 223–228.

Candler, A. C., & Hildreth, B. L. (1990). Characteristics of language disorders in learning disabled students. *Academic Therapy, 25*(3), 333–343.

Cannon, G. S., Idol, L., & West, J. F. (1992). Educating students with mild handicaps in general classrooms: Essential teaching practices for general and special educators. *Journal of Learning Disabilities, 25*(5), 300–317.

Carbo, M. (2009). Match the style of instruction to the style of reading. *Phi Delta Kappan, 90*(5), 373–378.

Cardell, C. D., & Parmar, R. S. (1988). Teacher perceptions of temperament characteristics of children classified as learning disabled. *Journal of Learning Disabilities, 21*(8), 497–502.

Carey, T. A., & Bourbon, W. T. (2004). Countercontrol: A new look at some old problems. *Intervention in School and Clinic, 40*(1), 3–9.

Carey, T. A., & Bourbon, W. T. (2006). Is countercontrol the key to understanding chronic behavior problems? *Intervention in School and Clinic, 42*(1), 5–13.

Carpenter, D. (1985). Grading handicapped pupils: Review and position statement. *Remedial and Special Education, 6*(4), 54–59.

Carroll, J. B. (1963). A model of school learning. *Teachers College Record, 64*(8), 723–733.

Carroll, J. B. (1976). Psychometric tests as cognitive tasks: A new "structure of intellect." In L. B. Resnick (Ed.), *The nature of intelligence* (pp. 27–56). Hillsdale, NJ: Erlbaum.

Carroll, J. B. (1981). Ability and task difficulty in cognitive psychology. *Educational Researcher, 10*(1), 11–21.

Carroll, J. B. (1989). The Carroll model: A 25-year retrospective and prospective view. *Educational Researcher, 18*(1), 26–31.

Carter, E. W., Trainor, A., Owens, L., Sweden, B., & Sun, Y. (2010). Self-determination prospects of youth with high-incidence disabilities: Divergent perspectives and related factors. *Journal of Emotional and Behavioral Disorders, 18*(2), 67–81.

Cartledge, G. (1999). African-American males and serious emotional disturbance: Some personal perspectives. *Behavioral Disorders, 25*(1), 76–79.

Case, R. E., & Taylor, S. S. (2005). Language difference or learning disability? Answers from a linguistic perspective. *Clearing House, 78*(3), 127–130.

Cassidy, D. (2004). Learning styles: An overview of theories, models, and measures. *Educational Psychology, 24*(4), 419–444.

Causton-Theoharis, J. N. (2009). The golden rule of providing support in inclusive classrooms: Support others as you would wish to be supported. *Teaching Exceptional Children, 42*(2), 36–43.

Center, D. B. (1989). Social maladjustment: Definition, identification, and programming. *Focus on Exceptional Children, 22*(1), 1–12.

Center for Applied Special Technology (CAST). (2008). *Universal Design for Learning guidelines (Version 1.0)*. Retrieved from http://www.udlcenter.org/aboutudl/udlguidelines/downloads

Centers for Disease Control and Prevention. (2009). Prevalence of autism spectrum disorders—autism and developmental disabilities monitoring network, United States, 2006. Surveillance summaries, 2009. MMWR 2009, 58(SS-10).

Chapman, D. A., Scott, K. G., & Stanton-Chapman, T. L. (2008). Public health approach to the study of mental retardation. *American Journal on Mental Retardation, 113*(2), 102–116.

Cheney, C. O., & Sampson, K. (1990). Issues in identification and service delivery for students with conduct disorders: The "Nevada" solution. *Behavioral Disorders, 15*(3), 174–179.

Childre, A., Sands, J. R., & Pope, S. T. (2009). Backward design: Targeting depth of understanding for all learners. *Teaching Exceptional Children, 41*(5), 6–14.

Chinn, S., McDonagh, D., van Elswijk, R., Harmsen, H., Kay, J., McPhillips, T., & Skidmore, L. (2001). Classroom studies into cognitive style in mathematics for pupils with dyslexia in special education in the Netherlands, Ireland, and the UK. *British Journal of Special Education, 28*(2), 80–85.

Chomsky, N. A. (1965). *Aspects of the theory of syntax*. Cambridge, MA: MIT Press.

Christensen, C. (2004). Disabled, handicapped or disordered: 'What's in a name?' In D. Mitchell (Ed.), *Special educational needs and inclusive education: Major themes in education: Vol. 1. Systems and contexts* (pp. 17–32). London: Routledge Falmer.

Christensen, L. (2008). Welcoming all languages. *Educational Leadership, 66*(1), 59–62.

Christenson, S. L., Ysseldyke, J. E., & Thurlow, M. L. (1989). Critical instructional factors for students with mild handicaps: An integrative review. *Remedial and Special Education, 10*(5), 21–31.

Clarizio, H. F. (1992). Social maladjustment and emotional disturbance: Problems and positions II. *Psychology in the Schools, 29*, 331–341.

Clarizio, H. F., & Klein, A. P. (1995). Assessing the severity of behavior disorders: Rankings based on clinical and empirical criteria. *Psychology in the Schools, 32*, 77–85.

Claxton, C. S., & Murrell, P. H. (1987). *Learning styles: Implications for improving educational practices* (ASHE-ERIC Higher Education Report No. 4). Washington, DC: Association for the Study of Higher Education.

Clements, S. D. (1966). Minimal brain dysfunction in children: Terminology and identification (*NINDB Monograph No. 3*, Public Health Service Publication No. 1415). Washington, DC: U.S. Department of Health, Education and Welfare.

Cline, D. H. (1990). A legal analysis of initiatives to exclude handicapped/disruptive students from special education. *Behavioral Disorders, 15*(3), 159–173.

Coghill, D., Nigg, J., Rothenberger, A., Sonuga-Barke, E., & Tannock, R. (2005). Whither causal models in the neuroscience of ADHD? *Developmental Science, 8*(2), 105–114.

Comstock, R., & Kamara, C. A. (2003). Adult language/learning disability: Issues and resources. (ERIC Document Reproduction Service No. ED 482 311)

Condly, S. J. (2006). Resilience in children: A review of literature with implications for education. *Urban Education, 41*(3), 211–236.

Connor, D. F., & Doerfler, L. A. (2008). ADHD with comorbid oppositional defiant disorder or conduct disorder: Discrete or nondistinct disruptive behavior disorders? *Journal of Attention Disorders, 12*(2), 126–134.

Connors, C. K. (2001). *Connors Rating Scales–Revised*. North Tonawanda, NY: Multi-Health Systems.

Conroy, M. A., Sutherland, K. S., Snyder, A. L., & Marsh, S. (2008). Classwide interventions: Effective instruction makes a difference. *Teaching Exceptional Children, 40*(6), 24–30.

Conte, R. (1991). Attention disorders. In B. Y. L. Wong (Ed.), *Learning about learning disabilities* (pp. 59–101). San Diego, CA: Academic Press.

Cooper, P. (2001). Understanding AD/HD: A brief critical review of the literature. *Childhood and Society, 15*, 387–395.

Cooper, P. (2005). ADHD. In A. Lewis & B. Norwich (Eds.), *Special teaching for special children? Pedagogies for inclusion* (pp. 125–137). Berkshire, England: Open University Press.

Copeland, R., McCall, J., Williams, C. R., Guth, C., Carter, E. W., Presley, J. A., & Hughes, C. (2002). High school peer buddies: A win-win situation. *Teaching Exceptional Children, 35*(1), 16–21.

Copeland, W., Shanahan, L., Costello, E. J., & Angold, A. (2009). Configurations of common childhood psychosocial risk factors. *Journal of Child Psychology and Psychiatry, 50*(4), 451–459.

Coster, W. J., & Haltiwanger, J. T. (2004). Social-behavioral skills of elementary students with physical disabilities included in the general education classroom. *Remedial and Special Education, 25*(2), 95–103.

Cotugno, A. J. (1987). Cognitive control functioning in hyperactive and nonhyperactive learning disabled children. *Journal of Learning Disabilities, 20*(9), 563–567.

Council for Children with Behavioral Disorders. (1990). Position paper on the provision of service to children with conduct disorders. *Behavioral Disorders, 15*(3), 180–189.

Council for Exceptional Children. (1997a). Inclusive schools and community settings. In *CEC policies for delivery of services to exceptional children: CEC policy manual* (Section 3, Professional policies, Part 1: Ch. 3, Special education in the schools). Arlington, VA: Author. Retrieved from www.cec.sped.org

Council for Exceptional Children. (1997b). Labeling and categorizing of children. In *CEC policies for delivery of services to exceptional children: CEC policy manual* (Section 3, Professional policies, Part 1: Ch. 3, Special education in the schools). Arlington, VA: Author. Retrieved from www.cec.sped.org

Council for Exceptional Children. (1998a). *IDEA 1997: Let's make it work.* Reston, VA: Author.

Council for Exceptional Children. (1998b). IDEA 1997: IDEA reauthorization: Focus on the IEP and performance assessment. (Teleconference, January 21, 1998).

Council for Exceptional Children. (2004). *The new IDEA: CEC's summary of significant issues.* Arlington, VA: Author.

Council for Exceptional Children. (2005a). *Universal design for learning: A guide for teachers and educational professionals.* Arlington, VA: Author.

Council for Exceptional Children. (2005b). *What's new in the new IDEA 2004: Frequently asked questions and answers.* Arlington, VA: Author.

Council for Exceptional Children. (2007). *Understanding IDEA 2004: Frequently asked questions.* Arlington VA: Author.

Council for Exceptional Children. (2009). *CEC's policy on physical restraint and seclusion procedures in school settings.* Arlington, VA: Author. Retrieved from www.cec.sped.org

Council for Exceptional Children. (2010). A primer on the IDEA 2004 regulations. Retrieved from http://www.cec.sped.org/AM/Template.cfm?Section = Home&CONTENTID = 7839&TEMPLATE = /CM/ContentDisplay.cfm

Council for Learning Disabilities. (1987a). CLD position statements: Use of discrepancy formulas in the identification of learning disabled individuals. *Learning Disability Quarterly, 9,* 245.

Council for Learning Disabilities. (1987b). Measurement and training of perceptual and perceptual-motor functions. *Journal of Learning Disabilities, 20*(6), 350.

Coutinho, M., & Malouf, D. (1993). Performance assessment and children with disabilities: Issues and possibilities. *Teaching Exceptional Children, 25*(4), 63–67.

Coutinho, M. J., & Oswald, D. P. (2005). State variation in gender disproportionality in special education: Findings and recommendations. *Remedial and Special Education, 26*(1), 7–15.

Coutinho, M. J., Oswald, D. P., & Best, A. M. (2002). The influence of sociodemographics and gender on the disproportionate identification of minority students as having learning disabilities. *Remedial and Special Education, 23*(1), 49–59.

Coutinho, M. J., Oswald, D. P., & Forness, S. R. (2002). Gender and sociodemographic factors and the disproportionate identification of culturally and linguistically diverse students with emotional disturbance. *Behavioral Disorders, 27*(2), 109–125.

Cowen, J. (2003). *A balanced approach to beginning reading instruction.* Newark, DE: International Reading Association.

Cox, M. L., Herner, J. G., Demczyk, M. J., & Nieberling, J. J. (2006). Provision of testing accommodations for students with disabilities on statewide assessments: Statistical links with participation and discipline rates. *Remedial and Special Education, 27*(6), 346–354.

Cox, P. R., & Dykes, M. K. (2001). Effective classroom adaptations for students with visual impairments. *Teaching Exceptional Children, 33*(6), 68–74.

Cranston-Gingras, A., & Mauser, A. J. (1992). Categorical and noncategorical teacher certification in special education: How wide is the gap? *Remedial and Special Education, 13*(4), 6–9.

Crews, S. D., Bender, H., Cook, C. R., Gresham, F. M., Kern, L., & Vanderwood, M. (2007). Risk and protective factors of emotional and/or behavioral disorders in children and adolescents: A mega-analytic synthesis. *Behavioral Disorders, 32*(2), 64–77.

Cruickshank, W., Bentzen, F., Ratzeburgh, F., & Tannhauser, M. (1961). *Teaching methodology for brain-injured and hyperactive children.* Syracuse, NY: Syracuse University Press.

Cruz, L. M., & Petersen, S. C. (2002). Reporting assessment results to parents. *Journal of Physical Education, Recreation & Dance, 73*(8), 20–24, 31.

Cullinan, D., Epstein, M. H., & McLinden, D. (1986). Status and change in state administrative definitions of behavior disorder. *School Psychology Review, 15*(3), 383–392.

Cummings, T. M. (2010). Using technology to create motivating social skills lessons. *Intervention in School and Clinic. 45*(4), 242–250.

Cummins, J. (1999). *BICS and CALP: Clarifying the distinction.* (ERIC Document Reproduction Service No. ED 438 551)

Cummins, J. (2009). Multilingualism in the English language classroom: Pedagogical considerations. *TESOL Quarterly, 43*(2), 317–321.

Danforth, S., & Navarro, V. (2001). Hyper talk: Sampling the social construction of ADHD in everyday language. *Anthropology and Education Quarterly, 32*(2), 167–190.

Darling-Hammond, L., & Friedlaender, D. (2008). Creating excellence and equitable schools. *Educational Leadership, 65*(8), 14–21.

Darwin, C. (1859). *The origin of species by means of natural selection or the preservation of favored races in the struggle for life.* New York: D. Appleton.

Davila, R. R., Williams, M. L., & MacDonald, J. T. (1991). *Clarification of policy to address the needs of children with attention deficit disorders within general and/or special education.* Washington, DC: U.S. Department of Education, Office of Special Education and Rehabilitative Services.

Dean, A. V., Salend, S. J., & Taylor, L. (1993). Multicultural education: A challenge for special educators. *Teaching Exceptional Children, 26*(1), 40–43.

Deci, E. L., & Chandler, C. L. (1986). The importance of motivation for the future of the LD field. *Journal of Learning Disabilities, 19*(10), 587–594.

Deci, E. L., & Ryan, R. M. (1985). *Intrinsic motivation and self-determination in human behavior.* New York: Plenum.

Dellarosa, D. (1988). A history of thinking. In R. J. Sternberg & E. E. Smith (Eds.), *The psychology of human thought* (pp. 1–18). Cambridge, England: Cambridge University Press.

Deming, A. M., & Lochman, J. E. (2008). The relation of locus of control, anger, and impulsivity to boys' aggressive behavior. *Behavioral Disorders, 33*(2), 108–119.

Denham, C., & Lieberman, A. (1980). *Time to learn.* Washington, DC: National Institute of Education.

Denning, C. B., Chamberlain, J. A., & Polloway, E. A. (2000). An evaluation of state guidelines for mental retardation: Focus on definition and classification practices. *Education and Training in Mental Retardation and Developmental Disabilities, 35*(2), 226–232.

Deno, E. (1970). Special education as developmental capital. *Exceptional Children, 37,* 229–240.

Deno, S., Maruyama, G., Espin, C., & Cohen, C. (1990). Educating students with mild disabilities in general education classrooms: Minnesota alternatives. *Exceptional Children, 57*(2), 150–161.

DePauw, S. S. W., & Mervielde, I. (2010). Temperament, personality and developmental psychopatholgy: A review based on the conceptual dimensions underlying childhood traits. *Child Psychiatry and Human Development, 41,* 313–329.

Derry, S. J. (1990). Remediating academic difficulties through strategy training: The acquisition of useful knowledge. *Remedial and Special Education, 11*(6), 19–31.

Deshler, D. D., Ellis, E. S., & Lenz, B. K. (1996). *Teaching adolescents with learning disabilities* (2nd ed.). Denver: Love.

Desmedt, E., & Valcke, M. (2004). Mapping the learning styles "jungle": An overview of the literature based on citation analysis. *Educational Psychology, 24*(4), 445–464.

Developmental Disabilities Assistance Act and Bill of Rights of 2000 (P.L. 106–402). Retrieved from http://www.acf.hhs.gov/programs/add/ddact/DDACT2.html

Dever, R. B. (1990). Defining mental retardation from an instructional perspective. *Mental Retardation, 28*(3), 147–153.

Dever, R. B., & Knapczyk, D. R. (1997). *Teaching persons with mental retardation: A model for curriculum development and teaching.* Madison, WI: Brown and Benchmark.

Devlin, P. (2008). Create effective teacher-paraprofessional teams. *Intervention in School and Clinic, 44*(1), 41–44.

Diament, M. (2010, October 5). Obama signs bill replacing "mental retardation" with "intellectual disability." *DisabilityScoop.com.* Retrieved from http://www.disabilityscoop.com/2010/10/05/obama-signs-rosas-law/10547/

Diehl, J. J., Bennetto, L., & Young, E. C. (2006). Story recall and narrative coherence of high-functioning children with autism spectrum disorders. *Journal of Abnormal Child Psychology, 34*(1), 87–102.

Diehl, S. F. (2003). Prologue: Autism spectrum disorder: The context of speech-language pathologist intervention. *Language, Speech, and Hearing Services in Schools, 34,* 177–179.

Dingman, H., & Targan, G. (1960). Mental retardation and the normal curve. *American Journal of Mental Deficiency, 64,* 991–994.

Division for Learning Disabilities. (1991, November). DLD statement on appropriate educational interventions for students identified as having attention deficit disorders. Paper presented at the hearing of CEC Task Force, New Orleans, LA.

Dockrell, J. E., Lindsay, G., Connelly, V., & Mackie, C. (2007). Constraints in the production of written text in children with specific language impairments. *Exceptional Children, 73*(2), 147–164.

Doll, E. A. (1941). The essentials of an inclusive concept of mental deficiency. *American Journal of Mental Deficiency, 46,* 214–229.

Dombrowski, S. C., Kamphaus, R. W., & Barry, M. (2006). The Solomon effect in learning disabilities diagnosis: Can we learn from history? *School Psychology Quarterly, 21*(4), 359–374.

Dorn, S. (2010). The political dilemma of formative assessment. *Exceptional Children, 76*(3), 325–337.

Dotson, W. H., Leaf, J. B., Sheldon, J. B., & Sherman, J. A. (2010). Group teaching of conversational skills to adolescents on the autism spectrum. *Research in Autism Spectrum Disorders, 4,* 199–209.

Dudley, A. M. (2005). Rethinking reading fluency for struggling adolescent readers. *Beyond Behavior, 14*(3), 16–22.

Dudley-Marling, C. (2004). The social construction of learning disabilities. *Journal of Learning Disabilities, 37*(6), 482–489.

Dunn, L. M. (1968). Special education for the mentally retarded: Is much of it justified? *Exceptional Children, 35*(1), 5–22.

Dunn, R., & Dunn, K. (2005). Thirty-five years of research on perceptual strengths: Essential strategies to promote learning. *The Clearing House, 78*(6), 273–276.

Dupont, H. (1989). The emotional development of exceptional students. *Focus on Exceptional Children, 21*(9), 1–9.

Duquette, C., Stodel, E., Fullarton, S., & Haggland, K. (2006). Teaching students with developmental disabilities: Tips from teens and young adults with fetal alcohol spectrum disorder. *Teaching Exceptional Children, 39*(2), 28–31.

Dyches, T. T., Wilder, L. K., Sudweeks, R. R., Obiakor, F. E., & Algozzine, B. (2004). Multicultural issues in autism. *Journal of Autism and Developmental Disabilities, 43*(2), 211–222.

Dykeman, B. F. (2006). Alternative strategies in assessing special education needs. *Education, 127*(2), 265–273.

Easterbrooks, S. R., & Baker, S. K. (2001). Enter the matrix! Considering the communication needs of students who are deaf or hard of hearing. *Teaching Exceptional Children, 33*(3), 70–76.

Edgemon, E. A., Jablonski, B. R., & Lloyd, J. W. (2006). Large scale assessments: A teacher's guide to making decisions about accommodations. *Teaching Exceptional Children, 38*(3), 6–11.

Edgerton, R. B. (1967). *The cloak of competence: Stigma in the lives of the mentally retarded.* Berkeley: University of California Press.

Eiden, R. D., Edwards, E. P., & Leonard, K. E. (2007). A conceptual model for the development of externalizing behavior problems among kindergarten children of alcoholic families: Role of parenting and children's self-regulation. *Developmental Psychology, 43*(5), 1187–1201.

Elinoff, M. J., Chafouleas, S. M., & Sassu, K. A. (2004). Bullying: Considerations for defining and intervening in school settings. *Psychology in the Schools, 41*(8), 887–897.

Elkind, D. (1981). *The hurried child: Growing up too fast too soon.* Reading, MA: Addison Wesley.

Elkind, D. (1998). Behavioral disorders: A postmodern perspective. *Behavioral Disorders, 23*(3), 153–159.

Elliott, S. N., Gresham, F. M., Frank, J. L., & Beddow III, P. A. (2008). Intervention validity of social behavior rating scales: Features of assessments that link results to treatment plans. *Assessment for Effective Intervention, 34*(1), 15–24.

Elliott, S. N., & Roach, A. T. (2007). Alternate assessments of students with significant disabilities: Alternative approaches, common technical challenges. *Applied Measurement in Education, 20*(3), 301–333.

Ellis, E. S. (1993). Integrative strategy instruction: A potential model for teaching content area subjects to adolescents with learning disabilities. *Journal of Learning Disabilities, 26*(6), 358–383.

Ellis, E. S., & Howard, P. W. (2007). A focus on graphic organizers: Power tools for teaching students with learning disabilities. *Current Practice Alerts 13*. Division for Learning Disabilities and Division for Research (CEC). Retrieved from http://www.teachingld.org/ld_resources/default.htm

Ellis, E. S., Lenz, B. K., & Sabornie, E. J. (1987). Generalization and adaptation of learning strategies to natural environments: Part 1. Causal agents. *Remedial and Special Education, 8*(1), 6–20.

Englert, C. S. (1984). Effective direct instruction practices in special education settings. *Remedial and Special Education, 5*(2), 38–47.

Epstein, M. A., Shaywitz, S. E., Shaywitz, B. A., & Woolston, J. L. (1991). The boundaries of attention deficit disorder. *Journal of Learning Disabilities, 24*(2), 78–86.

Epstein, M. H. (2004). *Behavioral and Emotional Rating Scale* (2nd ed.). Austin, TX: Pro-Ed.

Epstein, M. H., & Cullinan, D. (1983). Academic performance of behaviorally disordered and learning disabled pupils. *Journal of Special Education, 17*(3), 303–307.

Epstein, M. H., Cullinan, D., & Sabatino, D. A. (1977). State definitions of behavior disorders. *Journal of Special Education, 11*(4), 417–425.

Erikson, E. (1963). *Childhood and society* (2nd ed.). New York: Norton.

Espin, C., Shin, J., & Busch, T. (2000). A focus on formative assessment. *Current Practice Alerts 3*. Division for Learning Disabilities and Division for Research (CEC). Retrieved from http://www.teachingld.org/ld_resources/default.htm

Etscheidt, S. (2006). Behavioral intervention plans: Pedagogical and legal analysis of issues. *Behavioral Disorders, 31*(2), 223–243.

Fairbanks, S., Simonsen, B., & Sugai, G. (2008). Classwide secondary and tertiary tier practices and systems. *Teaching Exceptional Children, 40*(6), 44–52.

Falk, G. D., Dunlap, G., & Kern, L. (1996). An analysis of self-evaluation and videotape feedback for improving the peer interactions of students with externalizing and internalizing behavioral problems. *Behavioral Disorders, 21*(4), 261–276.

Farone, S. V., & Biederman, J. (1998). Neurobiology of attention-deficit hyperactivity disorder. *Biological Psychiatry, 44*, 951–958.

Faust, M. S., & Faust, W. L. (1980). Cognitive constructing: Levels of processing and developmental change. In B. K. Keogh (Ed.), *Advances in special education: A research annual: Basic constructs and theoretical orientations* (Vol. 1, pp. 1–54). Greenwich, CT: JAI Press.

Federenko, E., Gibson, E., & Rohde, D. (2006). The nature of working memory capacity in sentence comprehension: Evidence against domain-specific working memory resources. *Journal of Memory and Language, 54*, 541–553.

Feldman, K., & Denti, L. (2004). High-access instruction: Practical strategies to increase active learning in diverse classrooms. *Focus on Exceptional Children, 36*(7), 1–12.

Fennerty, D., Lambert, C., & Majsterek, D. (2000). *Behavior rating scales: An analysis*. (ERIC Document Reproduction Service No. ED 442 042)

Ferguson, D. L. (1994). Is communication really the point? Some thoughts on interventions and membership. *Mental Retardation, 32*(1), 7–18.

Fernald, G. (1943). *Remedial techniques in basic school subjects*. New York: McGraw Hill.

Ferri, B. A., & Connor, D. J. (2005). In the shadow of Brown: Special education and overrepresentation of students of color. *Remedial and Special Education, 26*(2), 93–100.

Fiedler, B. C. (2001). Considering placement and educational approaches for students who are deaf or hard of hearing. *Teaching Exceptional Children, 34*(2), 54–59.

Field, S., Hoffman, A., & Posch, M. (1997). Self-determination during adolescence: A developmental perspective. *Remedial and Special Education, 18*(5), 285–293.

Fields, E., Farmer, E. M. Z., Apperson, J., Mustillo, S., & Simmers, D. (2006). Treatment and posttreatment effects of residential treatment using a re-education model. *Behavioral Disorders, 31*(3), 312–322.

Fisher, J. B., Schumaker, J. B., & Deshler, D. D. (1995). Searching for validated inclusive practices: A review of the literature. *Focus on Exceptional Children, 28*(4), 1–20.

Flanagan, D. P., Ortiz, S. O., Alfonso, V. C., & Dynda, A. M. (2006). Integration of response to intervention and norm-referenced tests in learning disability identification: Learning from the Tower of Babel. *Psychology in the Schools, 43*(7), 807–825.

Fletcher, J. M., Coulter, W. A., Reschly, D. J., & Vaughn, S. (2004). Alternative approaches to the definition and identification of learning disabilities: Some questions and answers. *Annals of Dyslexia, 54*(2), 304–331.

Fletcher, J. M., Francis, D. J., Boudousquie, A., Copeland, K., Young, V., Kalinowski, S., & Vaughn, S. (2006). Effects of accommodations on high stakes testing for students with reading disabilities. *Exceptional Children, 72*(2), 136–150.

Fletcher, J. M., Lyon, G. R., Barnes, M., Stuebing, K. K., Francis, D. J., Olson, R. K., & Shaywitz, B. A. (2002). Classification of learning disabilities: An evidence-based evaluation. In R. Bradley, L. Danielson, & D. P. Hallahan, *Identification of learning disabilities: Research to practice* (pp. 185–250). Mahwah, NJ: Erlbaum.

Fletcher, J. M., Lyon, G. R., Fuchs, L. S., & Barnes, M. A. (2007). *Learning disabilities: From identification to intervention*. New York: Guilford Press.

Fletcher, J. M., & Vaughn, S. (2009). Response to intervention: Preventing and remediating academic difficulties. *Child Development Perspectives, 3*(1), 30–37.

Foley, R. M., & Epstein, M. H. (1992). Correlates of the academic achievement of adolescents with behavioral disorders. *Behavioral Disorders, 18*(1), 9–17.

Fombonne, E. (2005). Epidemiological studies of pervasive developmental disorders. In F. R. Volkmar, R. Paul, A. Klin, & D. Cohen (Eds.), *Handbook of autism and pervasive developmental disorders* (3rd ed., Vol. 1, pp. 42–69). Hoboken, NJ: Wiley.

Fore, C., Riser, S., & Boon, R. (2006). Implications of cooperative learning and educational reform for students with mild disabilities. *Reading Improvement, 43*(1), 3–12.

Forness, S. R., Freeman, S. F. N., & Paparella, T. (2006). Recent randomized clinical trials comparing behavioral interventions and psychopharmacological treatments for students with EBD. *Behavioral Disorders, 31*(3), 284–296.

Forness, S. R., & Kavale, K. A. (1991). Social skills deficits as primary learning disabilities. *Learning Disabilities: Research and Practice, 6*(1), 44–49.

Forness, S. R., & Kavale, K. A. (2000). Emotional or behavioral disorders: Background and current status of E/BD terminology and definition. *Behavioral Disorders, 25*(3), 264–269.

Forness, S. R., & Kavale, K. A. (2001). ADHD and a return to the medical model of special education. *Education and Treatment of Children, 24*(3), 224–247.

Forness, S. R., & Knitzer, J. (1992). A new proposed definition and terminology to replace "serious emotional disturbance" in Individuals with Disabilities Education Act. *School Psychology Review, 21*(1), 12–20.

Forness, S. R., Walker, H. M., & Kavale, K. A. (2003). Psychiatric disorders and treatments: A primer for teachers. *Teaching Exceptional Children, 36*(2), 42–49.

Forns-Santacana, M., Amador-Campos, J. A., & Roig-Lopez, F. (1993). Differences in field dependence-independence cognitive style as a function of socioeconomic status, sex, and cognitive competence. *Psychology in the Schools, 30*(2), 176–186.

Fox, L., Vaughn, B. J., Wyatte, M. L., & Dunlap, G. (2002). "We can't expect other people to understand": Family perspectives on problem behavior. *Exceptional Children, 68*(4), 437–450.

Frattura, E., & Capper, C. A. (2006), Segregated programs versus integrated comprehensive service delivery for all learners: Assessing all difference. *Remedial and Special Education, 27*(6), 355–364.

Frey, L. M., & Wilhite, K. (2005). Our five basic needs: Application for understanding the function of behavior. *Intervention in School and Clinic, 40*(3), 156–160.

Friedman-Narr, R. A. (2006). Teaching phonological awareness with deaf and hard-of-hearing students. *Teaching Exceptional Children, 38*(4), 53–58.

Friesen, S. (2008). Raising the floor and lifting the ceiling: Math for all. *Education Canada, 42*(5), 50–54.

Frith, U. (2004). Emanuel Miller lecture: Confusions and controversies about Asperger syndrome. *Journal of Child Psychology and Psychiatry, 45*(4), 672–686.

Frostig, M., Lefever, D. W., & Whittlesey, J. B. (1964). *The Marianne Frostig developmental test of visual perception.* Palo Alto, CA: Consulting Psychology Press.

Fuchs, D., & Deshler, D. D. (2007). What we need to know about responsiveness to intervention (and shouldn't be afraid to ask). *Learning Disabilities Research and Practice, 22*(2), 129–136.

Fuchs, D., Fuchs, L. S., & Stecker, P. M. (2010). The "blurring" of special education in a new continuum of general education placements and services. *Exceptional Children, 76*(3), 301–323.

Fuchs, D., Mock, D., Morgan, P. L., & Young, C. L. (2003). Responsiveness to intervention: Definitions, evidence, and implications for the learning disabilities construct. *Learning Disabilities Research and Practice, 18*(3), 157–171.

Fuchs, L. S., & Fuchs, D. (1986). Effects of systematic formative evaluation: A meta-analysis. *Exceptional Children, 53*(3), 199–208.

Fuchs, L. S., Fuchs, D., & Speece, D. L. (2002). Treatment validity as a unifying construct for identifying learning disabilities. *Learning Disability Quarterly, 25*(1), 33–45.

Gable, R. A. (1996). A critical analysis of functional assessment: Issues for researchers and practitioners. *Behavioral Disorders, 22*(1), 36–40.

Gadow, K. D., & Sprafkin, J. (1994). *Child Symptom Inventory–4 (CSI–4).* Stony Brook, NY: Checkmate Plus.

Gadow, K. D., & Sprafkin, J. (1997). *ADHD Symptom Checklist–4.* Stony Brook, NY: Checkmate Plus.

Gallagher, J. J., Beckman, P., & Cross, A. H. (1983). Families of handicapped children: Sources of stress and its amelioration. *Exceptional Children, 50*(1), 10–18.

Gallego, M. A., Duran, G. Z., & Reyes, E. I. (2006). It depends: A sociohistorical account of the definition and methods of identification of learning disabilities. *Teachers College Record, 108*(11), 2195–2219.

Galton, F. (1869, 1978). *Hereditary genius: An inquiry into its laws and consequences.* London: J. Friedman.

Garcia, E. (1994). *Understanding and meeting the challenge of student cultural diversity.* Boston: Houghton Mifflin.

Garcia, S. B., & Tyler, B. J. (2010). Meeting the needs of English language learners with learning disabilities in the general curriculum. *Theory into Practice, 49*(2), 113–120.

Gardner, H. (2006). *Multiple intelligences: New horizons.* New York: Basic Books.

Gardner, R., Nobel, M. M., Hessler, T., Yawn, C. D., & Heron, T. E. (2007). Tutoring system innovations: Past practice to future prototypes. *Intervention in School and Clinic, 43*(2), 71–81.

Gartin, B. C., & Murdick, N. L. (2005). IDEA 2004: The IEP. *Remedial and Special Education, 26*(6), 327–331.

Gartner, A., & Lipsky, D. K. (1987). Beyond special education: Toward a quality system for all students. *Harvard Educational Review, 57*(4), 123–157.

Gaskins, I. W., & Pressley, M. (2007). Teaching metacognitive strategies that address executive function processes within a schoolwide curriculum. In L. Meltzer (Ed.), *Executive function in education: From theory to practice* (pp. 261–286). New York: Guilford Press.

Gathercole, S. E., Alloway, T. P., Willis, C., & Adams, A. M. (2006). Working memory in children with reading disabilities. *Journal of Experimental Child Psychology, 93*, 265–281.

Gay, Lesbian and Straight Education Network (GLSEN). (2010). 2009 National school climate survey. Retrieved from http://www.glsen.org/cgi-bin/iowa/all/news/record/2624.html

Gazaway, R. (1969). *The longest mile.* New York: Doubleday.

Geiger, W. L. (2002). *Requirements for conventional licensure of special education teachers.* (ERIC Document Reproduction Service No. ED460563)

Geiger, W. L. (2006). *A compilation of research on states' licensure models for special education teachers and special education requirements for licensing general education teachers.* (ERIC Document Reproduction Service No. ED491706)

Geisthardt, C., & Munsch, J. (1996). Coping with school stress: A comparison of adolescents with and without learning disabilities. *Journal of Learning Disabilities, 29*(3), 287–296.

Gelbach, H. (2004). A new perspective on perspective-taking: A multidimensional approach to conceptualizing an aptitude. *Educational Psychology Review, 16*(3), 207–234.

Gerber, M. M. (2005). Response to tough teaching: The 2% solution. *Learning Disability Quarterly, 28*(3), 189–190.

Gerber, M. M., & Durgunoglu, A. Y. (2004). Reading risk and intervention for young English learners [Special issue]. *Learning Disabilities Research and Practice, 19*(4).

Gersten, R., Brengelman, S., & Jiménez, R. (1994). Effective instruction for culturally and linguistically diverse students: A reconceptualization. *Focus on Exceptional Children, 27*(1), 1–16.

Giangreco, M. L. (2007). Extending inclusive opportunities. *Educational Leadership, 64*(5), 34–37.

Giangreco, M. F., Edelman, S. W., Luiselli, T. E., & MacFarland, S. Z. C. (1997). Helping or hovering: Effects of instructional assistant proximity on students with disabilities. *Exceptional Children, 64*(1), 7–18.

Giangreco, M. F., Yuan, S., McKenzie, B., Cameron, P., & Fialka, J. (2005). "Be careful what you wish for . . .": Five reasons to be concerned about the assignment of individual paraprofessionals. *Teaching Exceptional Children, 37*(5), 28–34.

Gibbs, D. P., & Cooper, E. B. (1989). Prevalence of communication disorders in students with learning disabilities. *Journal of Learning Disabilities, 22*(1), 60–63.

Gillingham, A., & Stillman, B. (1940). *Remedial training for children with specific disability in reading, spelling, and penmanship.* New York: Sacketts and Wilhelm.

Giordano, G. (1984). Analyzing and remediating writing disabilities. *Journal of Learning Disabilities, 17*(2), 78–83.

Glasser, W. (1990). *The quality school: Managing students without coercion.* New York: Harper.

Glasser, W. (1998). *Choice theory: A new psychology of personal freedom.* New York: HarperCollins.

Goddard, H. H. (1912). *The Kallikak family: A study in the heredity of feeble-mindedness.* New York: Macmillan.

Goldstein, A. P., & McGinnis, E. (1997). *Skillstreaming the adolescent: New strategies and perspectives for teaching prosocial skills* (rev. ed.). Champaign, IL: Research Press.

Goodman, G., & Poillion, M. J. (1992). ADD: Acronym for any dysfunction or difficulty. *Journal of Special Education, 26*(1), 37–56.

Gorlewski, D. (2010). Overflowing but underused: Portfolios as a means of program evaluation and student self-assessment. *English Journal, 99*(4), 97–101.

Graham, L. (1991). Wild boys and idiots: The beginnings of special education. *B.C. Journal of Special Education, 15*(1), 76–95.

Graham, L. J. (2008). From the ABC's to ADHD: The role of schooling in the construction of behavior disorder and the production of disorderly objects. *International Journal of Inclusive Education, 12*(1), 7–33.

Graham, S. (1985). Teaching basic academic skills to learning disabled students: A model of the teaching-learning process. *Journal of Learning Disabilities, 18*(9), 528–534.

Grandin, T. (2006). *Thinking in pictures: My life with autism.* New York: Vintage (Random House).

Grandin, T., & Johnson, C. (2005). *Animals in translation: Using the mysteries of autism to decode animal behavior.* New York: Scribner.

Graves, A. W., & Alvarado, J. L. (2005). Teaching young English learners to read [Special issue]. *Remedial and Special Education, 26*(4).

Gray, C. (2004). Understanding cognitive development: Automaticity and the early years child. *Child Care in Practice, 10*(1), 39–47.

Green, T. D., McIntosh, A. S., Cook-Morales, V. J., & Robinson-Zanartu, C. (2005). From old schools to tomorrow's schools: The psychoeducational assessment of African American students. *Remedial and Special Education, 26*(2), 82–92.

Greenspan, I. S. (2005). The problem with traditional diagnostic labels. *Scholastic Early Childhood Today, 19*(6), 18–19.

Greenspan, S. (2006). Functional concepts in mental retardation: Finding the natural essence of an artificial category. *Exceptionality, 14*(4), 205–224.

Greenspan, S., & Granfield, J. M. (1992). Reconsidering the construct of mental retardation: Implications of a model of social competence. *American Journal on Mental Retardation, 96*(4), 442–453.

Gresham, F. M. (1991). Conceptualizing behavior disorders in terms of resistance to intervention. *School Psychology Review, 20*(1), 23–36.

Gresham, F. M. (2002a). Responsiveness to intervention: An alternative approach to the identification of learning disabilities. In R. Bradley, L. Danielson, & D. P. Hallahan (Eds.), *Identification of learning disabilities: Research to practice* (pp. 467–519). Mahwah, NJ: Erlbaum.

Gresham, F. M. (2002b). Social skills assessment and instruction for students with emotional and behavioral disorders. In K. L. Lane, F. M. Gresham, & T. E. O'Shaughnessy (Eds.), *Interventions for children with or at risk for emotional and behavioral disorders* (pp. 242–258). Boston: Allyn & Bacon.

Gresham, F. M. (2005). Response to intervention: An alternative means of identifying students as emotionally disturbed. *Education and Treatment of Children, 28*(4), 328–344.

Gresham, F. M., & Elliott, S. N. (1987). The relationship between adaptive behavior and social skills: Issues in definition and assessment. *Journal of Special Education, 21*(1), 167–181.

Gresham, F. M., & Elliott, S. N. (1990). *Social Skills Rating System.* Circle Pines, MN: American Guidance Service.

Gresham, F. M., & Elliott, S. N. (2008). *Social Skills Improvement System.* Minneapolis, MN: Pearson Assessments Guidance Service.

Gresham, F. M., MacMillan, D. L., & Bocian, K. (1996). "Behavioral earthquakes": Low frequency, salient behavioral events that differentiate students at-risk for behavioral disorders. *Behavioral Disorders, 21*(4), 277–292.

Gresham, F. M., MacMillan, D. L., Bocian, K. M., Ward, S. L., & Forness, S. R. (1998). Comorbidity of hyperactivity-impulsivity-inattention and conduct problems: Risk factors in social, affective, and academic domains. *Journal of Abnormal Child Psychology, 26*(5), 393–406.

Grice, H. P. (1989). *Studies in the ways of words.* Cambridge, MA: Harvard University Press.

Griffin, H. C., Williams, S. C., Davis, M. L., & Engleman, M. (2002). Using technology to enhance cues for children with low vision. *Teaching Exceptional Children, 35*(2), 36–42.

Grolnick, W. S., & Ryan, R. M. (1990). Self-perceptions, motivation, and adjustment in children with learning disabilities: A multiple group comparison study. *Journal of Learning Disabilities, 23*(3), 177–184.

Grossman, H. J. (Ed.). (1973). *Manual on terminology and classification in mental retardation.* Washington, DC: American Association on Mental Deficiency.

Grossman, H. J. (Ed.). (1983). *Classification in mental retardation: 1983 revision.* Washington, DC: American Association on Mental Deficiency.

Grusec, J. E. (1992). Social learning theory and developmental psychology: The legacies of Robert Sears and Albert Bandura. *Developmental Psychology, 28*(5), 776–786.

Guetzloe, E. (1988). Suicide and depression: Special education's responsibility. *Teaching Exceptional Children, 20*(4), 25–28.

Guetzloe, E. (1998). Proposed definition of emotional disturbance. *CCBD Newsletter, 11*(4), 1.

Gumpel, T. (1994). Social competence and social skills training for persons with mental retardation: An expansion of a behavioral paradigm. *Education and Training in Mental Retardation and Developmental Disabilities, 29*(3), 194–201.

Gumpel, T. P. (2007). Are social competence difficulties caused by the performance or acquisition deficits? The importance of self-regulatory mechanisms. *Psychology in the Schools, 44*(4), 351–372.

Guskey, T. (2002). *Perspectives on grading and reporting: Differences among teachers, students, and parents.* (ERIC Document Reproduction Service No.ED464113)

Guttmann-Steinmetz, S., Gadow, K. D., & DeVincent, C. J. (2009). Oppositional defiant and conduct disorder behaviors in boys with autism spectrum disorder with and without attention-deficit hyperactivity disorder versus several comparison samples. *Journal of Autism and Developmental Disorders, 39*, 976–985.

Haddon, M. (2003). *The curious incident of the dog in the night-time.* New York: Random House.

Hall, T., Meyer, A., & Strangman, N. (2006). UDL implementation: Examples using best practices and curriculum enhancements. In D. H. Rose & A. Meyer (Eds.), *A practical reader in universal design for learning* (pp. 149–197). Cambridge, MA: Harvard University Press.

Hall, T., Strangman, N., & Meyer, A. (2009). *Differentiated instruction and implications for UDL implementation.* Wakefield, MA: National Center on Accessing the General Curriculum. Retrieved from http://www.cast.org/publications/ncac/ncac_diffinstructudl.html

Hallahan, D. P., & Kauffman, J. M. (1977). Labels, categories, behaviors: ED, LD, and EMR reconsidered. *Journal of Special Education, 11*(2), 139–149.

Hallahan, D. P., Kauffman, J. M., & Lloyd, J. W. (1999). *Introduction to learning disabilities* (2nd ed.). Boston: Allyn & Bacon.

Hallahan, D. P., Keller, C. E., Martinez, E. A., Byrd, E. S., Gelman, J. A., & Fan, X. (2007). How variable are interstate prevalence rates of learning disabilities and other special education categories? A longitudinal comparison. *Exceptional Children, 73*(2), 136–146.

Hallahan, D. P., & Mercer, C. D. (2002). Learning disabilities: Historical perspectives. In R. Bradley, L. Danielson, & D. P. Hallahan (Eds.), *Identification of learning disabilities: Research to practice* (pp. 1–67). Mahwah, NJ: Erlbaum.

Hallahan, D. P., & Reeve, R. R. (1980). Selective attention and distractibility. In B. K. Keogh (Ed.), *Advances in special education: A research annual: Basic constructs and theoretical orientations* (Vol. 1, pp. 141–182). Greenwich, CT: JAI Press.

Hallenbeck, M. J. (1996). The cognitive strategy in writing: Welcome relief for adolescents with learning disabilities. *Learning Disabilities Research and Practice, 11*(2), 107–119.

Hammill, D. (1990). On defining learning disabilities: An emerging consensus. *Journal of Learning Disabilities, 23*(2), 74–84.

Hardman, M. L., & Dawson, S. (2008). The impact of federal public policy on curriculum and instruction for students with disabilities in the general classroom. *Preventing School Failure, 52*(2), 5–11.

Hardman, M. L., & McDonnell, J. (2008). Disability classification and teacher education. In L. Florian & M. J. McLaughlin (Eds.), *Disability classification in education: Issues and perspectives* (pp. 153–169). Thousand Oaks, CA: Corwin.

Haring, N. G., & Phillips, E. L. (1962). *Educating emotionally disturbed children.* New York: McGraw Hill.

Harper, G. F., & Maheady, L. (2007). Peer-mediated teaching and students with learning disabilities. *Intervention in School and Clinic, 43*(2), 101–107.

Hartley, S. L., & Sikora, D. M. (2009). Which *DSM-IV-TR* criteria best differentiate high-functioning autism spectrum disorder from ADHD and anxiety disorders in older children? *Autism, 13*(5), 485–509.

Hasselbring, T. S., Goin, L. J., & Bansford, J. D. (1988). Developing math automaticity in learning handicapped children: The role of computerized drill and practice. *Focus on Exceptional Children, 20*(6), 1–7.

Hayes, B. K., & Conway, R. N. (2000). Concept acquisition in children with mild intellectual disability: Factors affecting the abstraction of prototypical information. *Journal of Intellectual and Developmental Disability, 25*(3), 217–234.

Hayes, B. K., & Taplin, J. E. (1993). Development of conceptual knowledge in children with mental retardation. *American Journal on Mental Retardation, 98*(2), 293–303.

Hayes, J. R. (1989). *The complete problem solver* (2nd ed.). Hillsdale, NJ: Erlbaum.

Haywood, H. C. (2004). Thinking in, around, and about the curriculum: The role of cognitive education. *International Journal of Disability, Development, and Education, 51*(3), 231–252.

Hearne, D., & Stone, S. (1995). Multiple intelligences and underachievement: Lessons from individuals with learning disabilities. *Journal of Learning Disabilities, 28*(7), 439–448.

Heber, R. (1959). A manual on terminology and classification in mental retardation. *American Journal on Mental Deficiency, 62* (Monograph Supplement).

Heller, K. W., Forney, P. E., Alberto, P. A., Schwartzman, M. N., & Goeckel, T. M. (2000). *Meeting physical and health needs of children with disabilities: Teaching student participation and management.* Belmont, CA: Wadsworth/Thomson Learning.

Heller, K. W., Fredrick, L. D., Best, S., & Cohen, E. T. (2000). Specialized health care procedures in the schools: Training and service delivery. *Exceptional Children, 66*(2), 173–186.

Hendley, S. L. (2007). Use positive behavior support for inclusion in the general education classroom. *Intervention in School and Clinic, 44*(2), 225–228.

Hessler, G. L., & Sosnowsky, W. P. (1979). A review of aptitude-treatment interaction studies with the handicapped. *Psychology in the Schools, 16*(3), 388–394.

Heumann, J. E., & Warlick, K. R. (2000). Questions and answers about provisions in the Individuals with Disabilities Education Act Amendments of 1997 related to students with disabilities and state- and district-wide assessments (OSEP Memo 00–24). Retrieved from www.dssc.org/frc/AssessmentQ&A.html

Hewett, F. M. (1968). *The emotionally disturbed child in the classroom.* Boston: Allyn & Bacon.

Hill, E. L., & Frith, U. (2003). Understanding autism: Insights from mind and brain. In U. Frith & E. L. Hill (Eds.), *Autism: Mind and brain* (pp.1–19). New York: Oxford University Press.

Hinshelwood, J. (1917). *Congenital word blindness.* London: H. K. Lewis.

Hitchcock, C., Meyer, A., Rose, D., & Jackson, R. (2002). Access to the general education curriculum: Universal design for learning. *Teaching Exceptional Children, 35*(2), 8–17.

Hobbs, N. (1975a). *The futures of children: Categories, labels and their consequences.* San Francisco: Jossey-Bass.

Hobbs, N. (1975b). *Issues in the classification of children: Vol. 1.* San Francisco: Jossey-Bass.

Hobbs, N. (1975c). *Issues in the classification of children: Vol. 2.* San Francisco: Jossey-Bass.

Hodapp, R. M., Burack, J. A., & Zigler, E. (Eds.). (1990). *Issues in the developmental approach to mental retardation.* Cambridge, England: Cambridge University Press.

Hoerr, T. R. (1996). *Implementing multiple intelligences: The New City School experience.* Bloomington, IN: Phi Delta Kappa Educational Foundation.

Hoge, G., & Datillo, J. (1995). Recreation participation patterns of adults with and without mental retardation. *Education and Training in Mental Retardation and Developmental Disabilities, 30*(4), 283–298.

Holdnack, J. A., & Weiss, L. G. (2006). IDEA 2004: Anticipated implications for clinical practice: Integrating assessment and intervention. *Psychology in the Schools, 43*(8), 871–882.

Hollenweger, J. (2008). Cross-national comparisons of special education classification systems. In L. Florian & M. J. McLaughlin (Eds.), *Disability classification in education: Issues and perspectives* (pp. 11–30). Thousand Oaks, CA: Corwin.

Hoover, J. J., & Patton, J. R. (2005). *Curriculum adaptations for students with learning and behavior problems.* Austin, TX: Pro-Ed.

Hudson, R. F., Pullen, P. C., Lane, H. B., & Torgeson, J. K. (2009). The complex nature of reading fluency: A multidimensional view. *Reading and Writing Quarterly, 25,* 4–32.

Hulett, K. E. (2009). *Legal aspects of special education.* Upper Saddle River, NJ: Pearson.

Hyter, Y. D. (2007). Pragmatic language assessment: A pragmatics-as-social practice model. *Topics in Language Disorders, 27*(2), 128–145.

Idol, L. (2006). Toward inclusion of special education students in general education: A program evaluation of eight schools. *Remedial and Special Education, 27*(2), 77–94.

Immunization Safety Review Committee, Board of Health Promotion and Disease Prevention, Institute of Medicine. (2004). *Immunization safety review: Vaccines and autism.* Washington, DC: National Academies Press. Retrieved from http://www.nap.edu

Interagency Committee on Learning Disabilities (ICLD). (1987). *Learning disabilities: A report to Congress.* Bethesda, MD: National Institutes of Health.

Itard, J. M. G. (1801, 1962). *The wild boy of Aveyron.* (G. Humphrey & M. Humphrey, Trans.). Upper Saddle River, NJ: Prentice Hall.

Jackson, R., & Harper, K. (2001). *Teacher planning and the universal design for learning environments.* Peabody, MA: Center for Applied Special Technology. Retrieved from www.cast.org/publications/ncac/ncac_teacherplanning.html

Jackson, R., & Harper, K. (2006). Teacher planning for accessibility: The universal design for learning environments. In D. H. Rose & A. Meyer (Eds.). *A practical reader in universal design for learning* (pp. 101–123). Cambridge, MA: Harvard University Press.

Javorsky, J. (1996). An examination of youth with attention deficit/hyperactivity disorder and language learning disabilities: A clinical study. *Journal of Learning Disabilities, 29*(3), 247–258.

Jegatheesan, B., Miller, P. J., & Fowler, S. A. (2010). Autism from a religious perspective: A study of parental beliefs in South Asian Muslim immigrant families. *Focus on Autism and Developmental Disabilities, 25*(2), 98–109.

Jenkins, J. J., & O'Connor, R. E. (2002). Early identification and intervention for young children with reading/learning disabilities. In R. Bradley, L. Danielson, & D. P. Hallahan (Eds.), *Identification of learning disabilities: Research to practice* (pp. 99–149). Mahwah, NJ: Erlbaum.

Jenkins, J. R., Pious, C. G., & Peterson, D. L. (1988). Categorical programs for remedial and handicapped students: Issues of validity. *Exceptional Children, 55*(2), 147–158.

Jensen, A. R. (1969). How much can we boost IQ and scholastic achievement? *Harvard Educational Review, 39,* 1–123.

Jerger, M. A. (1996). Phoneme awareness and the role of the educator. *Intervention in School and Clinic, 32*(1), 5–13.

Johns, B., Crowley, E. P., & Guetzloe, E. (2008). Engaged time in the classroom. *Focus on Exceptional Children, 41*(4), 1–7.

Johnson, D. J., & Croasmun, P. A. (1991). Language assessment. In H. L. Swanson & S. R. Forness (Eds.), *Handbook on the assessment of learning disabilities: Theory, research, and practice* (pp. 229–248). Austin, TX: Pro-Ed.

Johnson, D. W., & Johnson, R. T. (1996). Peacemakers: Teaching students to resolve their own and schoolmates' conflicts. *Focus on Exceptional Children, 28*(6), 1–11.

Johnson, D. W., Johnson, R. T., Holubec, E. J., & Roy, P. (1984). *Circles of learning: Cooperation in the classroom.* Reston, VA: ASCD.

Johnson, R. L., Penny, J. A., & Gordon, B. (2008). *Assessing performance: Designing, scoring, and validating performance tasks.* New York: Guilford Press.

Johnston, C. L. (1984). The learning disabled adolescent and young adult: An overview and critique of current practices. *Journal of Learning Disabilities, 17*(7), 386–390.

Joint Committee on Testing Practices. (2004). Code of fair testing practices in education. Retrieved from http://www.apa.org/science/programs/testing/committee.aspx

Jordan, L. C., & Chassin, L. (1998). *Protective factors for children of alcoholics: Parenting, family environment, child personality, and contextual supports.* San Francisco: American Psychological Association. (ERIC Document Reproduction Service No. ED 425 383)

Joseph, J., Noble, K., & Eden, G. (2001). The neurological basis of reading. *Journal of Learning Disabilities, 34*(6), 566–579.

Jung, L. A., & Guskey, T. R. (2007). Standards-based grading and reporting: A model for special education. *Teaching Exceptional Children, 40*(2), 48–52.

Jung, L. A., & Guskey, T. R. (2010). Grading exceptional learners. *Educational Leadership, 67*(5), 31–35.

Kaderavek, J. N., & Rabidoux, P. (2004). Interactive to independent literacy: A model for designing literacy goals for children with atypical communication. *Reading and Writing Quarterly, 20,* 237–260.

Kagan, J. (1965). Reflection-impulsivity and reading ability in primary grade children. *Child Development, 36,* 609–628.

Kagan, J. (1966). Reflection-impulsivity: The generality and dynamics of conceptual tempo. *Journal of Abnormal Psychology, 71*(1), 17–24.

Kalyanpur, M., & Harry, B. (2004). Impact of social construction of LD on culturally diverse families: A response to Reid and Valle. *Journal of Learning Disabilities, 37*(6), 530–533.

Kanner, L. (1943). Autistic disturbance of affective contact. *The Nervous Child, 2,* 217–250.

Karger, J. (2006). What IDEA and NCLB suggest about curriculum access for students with disabilities. In D. H. Rose & A. Meyer (Eds.), *A practical reader in universal design for learning* (pp. 69–100). Cambridge, MA: Harvard University Press.

Katims, D. S. (2000). Literacy instruction for people with mental retardation: Historical highlights and contemporary analysis. *Education and Training in Mental Retardation and Developmental Disabilities, 35*(1), 3–15.

Kauffman, J. M. (1977). *Characteristics of children's behavior disorders.* Upper Saddle River, NJ: Merrill/Pearson Education.

Kauffman, J. M., & Landrum, T. J. (2006). *Children and youth with emotional and behavioral disorders: A history of their education.* Austin, TX: Pro-Ed.

Kauffman, J. M., & Landrum, T. J. (2009). *Characteristics of emotional and behavioral disorders of children and youth* (9th ed.). Upper Saddle River, NJ: Merrill/Pearson Education.

Kauffman, J. M., Landrum, T. J., Mock, D. R., Sayeski, B., & Sayeski, K. (2005). Diverse knowledge and skills require a diversity of instructional groups. *Remedial and Special Education, 26*(1), 2–6.

Kauffman, J. M., Mock, D. R., & Simpson, R. L. (2007). Problems related to underservice of students with emotional or behavioral disorders. *Behavioral Disorders, 33*(1), 43–57.

Kavale, K. A., & Forness, S. R. (1983). Hyperactivity and diet treatment: A meta-analysis of the Feingold hypothesis. *Journal of Learning Disabilities, 16*(6), 324–330.

Kavale, K. A., & Forness, S. R. (1985). Learning disability and the history of science: Paradigm or paradox? *Remedial and Special Education, 6*(4), 12–23.

Kavale, K. A., & Forness, S. R. (1996). Social skill deficits and learning disabilities: A meta- analysis. *Journal of Learning Disabilities, 29*(3), 226–237.

Kavale, K. A., & Forness, S. R. (2000). What definitions say and don't say: A critical analysis. *Journal of Learning Disabilities, 33*(3), 239–256.

Kavale, K. A., Hirshoren, A., & Forness, S. R. (1998). Meta-analytic validation of the Dunn and Dunn model of learning-style preferences: A critique of what was Dunn. *Learning Disabilities Research and Practice, 13*(2), 75–80.

Kavale, K. A., Holdnack, J. A., & Mostert, M. P. (2006). Responsiveness to intervention and the identification of learning disability: A critique and alternative proposal. *Learning Disability Quarterly, 29*(2), 113–127.

Kavale, K. A., & Mattson, P. D. (1983). "One jumped off the balance beam": Meta-analysis of perceptual-motor training. *Journal of Learning Disabilities, 16*(3), 165–173.

Kavale, K. A., Spaulding, L. S., & Beam, A. P. (2009). A time to define: Making the specific learning disability definition prescribe specific learning disability. *Learning Disability Quarterly, 32* (1), 39–48.

Kehle, T. J., Bray, M. A., Theodore, L. A., Zhou, Z., & McCoach, D. B. (2004). Emotional disturbance/social maladjustment: Why is the incidence increasing? *Psychology in the Schools, 41*(8), 861–865.

Keller, J., & Ripoll, H. (2004). Stability of reflective-impulsive style in coincidence-anticipation motor tasks. *Learning and Individual Differences, 14,* 209–218.

Keogh, B. K., & Bess, C. R. (1991). Assessing temperament. In H. L. Swanson (Ed.), *Handbook of the assessment of learning disabilities: Theory, research, and practice* (pp. 313–330). Austin, TX: Pro-Ed.

Keogh, B. K., & Donlon, G. M. (1972). Field dependence, impulsivity, and learning disabilities. *Journal of Learning Disabilities, 5*(6), 331–336.

Keogh, B. K., & Margolis, J. (1976). Learn to labor and wait: Attentional problems of children with learning disorders. *Journal of Learning Disabilities, 9*(5), 276–286.

Keogh, B. K., & Weisner, T. (1993). An ecocultural perspective on risk and protective factors in children's development: Implications for learning disabilities. *Learning Disabilities Research & Practice, 8*(1), 3–10.

Kephart, N. C. (1960). *The slow learner in the classroom.* Columbus, OH: Merrill.

Ketterlin-Geller, L. R., Alonza, J., Braun-Monegan, J., & Tindal, G. (2007). Recommendations for accommodations: Implications of (in)consistency. *Remedial and Special Education, 28*(4), 194–206.

Keyser-Marcus, L., Briel, L., Sherron-Targett, P., Yasudo, S., Johnson, S., & Wehman, P. (2002). Enhancing the schooling of students with traumatic brain injury. *Teaching Exceptional Children, 34*(4), 62–67.

Kidder, T. (1989). *Among schoolchildren.* Boston: Houghton Mifflin.

King-Sears, M. E. (2008). Differentiation and the curriculum: Facts and fallacies: Differentiation and the general education curriculum for students with special educational needs. *Support for Learning, 23*(2), 55–62.

Kirk, S. A. (1963). Behavioral diagnosis and remediation of learning disabilities. *Proceedings of the Conference on the Exploration into the Problems of the Perceptually Handicapped Child,* Chicago. Reprinted in S. A. Kirk & J. McCarthy (Eds.), 1975, *Learning disabilities: Selected ACLD Papers.* Boston: Houghton Mifflin.

Kirk, S. A. (1987). The learning disabled preschool child. *Teaching Exceptional Children, 19*(2), 78–80.

Kirk, S. A., & Chalfant, J. C. (1984). *Academic and developmental learning disabilities.* Denver, CO: Love.

Kirk, S. A., & Kirk, W. D. (1971). *Psycholinguistic learning disabilities: Diagnosis and remediation.* Urbana: University of Illinois Press.

Kirk, S. A., & McCarthy, J. (Eds.). (1975). *Learning disabilities: Selected ACLD papers.* Boston: Houghton Mifflin.

Kirk, S. A., McCarthy, J., & Kirk, W. D. (1968). *Illinois Test of Psycholinguistic Abilities* (rev. ed.). Urbana: University of Illinois Press.

Klin, A., Salnier, C., Tsatanis, K., & Volkmar, F. R. (2005). Clinical evaluation in autism spectrum disorders: Psychological assessment in a transdisciplinary framework. In F. R. Volkmar, R. Paul, A. Klin, & D. Cohen (Eds.), *Handbook of autism and pervasive developmental disorders* (3rd ed., Vol. 2, pp. 772–798). Hoboken, NJ: Wiley.

Klingner, J. K., Artiles, A. J., & Barletta, L. M. (2006). English language learners who struggle with reading: Language acquisition or LD? *Journal of Learning Disabilities, 39*(2), 108–128.

Klorman, R. (1991). Cognitive event-related potentials in attention deficit disorder. *Journal of Learning Disabilities, 24*(3), 130–140.

Knoblock, P. (1983). *Teaching emotionally disturbed children.* Boston: Houghton Mifflin.

Koegel, A. K. (2008). Evidence suggesting the existence of Asperger syndrome in the mid-1800s. *Journal of Positive Behavioral Interactions, 10*(4), 270–272.

Kofler, M. J., Rapport, M. D., & Alderson, R. M. (2008). Quantifying ADHD classroom inattentiveness, its moderators, and variability: A meta-analytic review. *Journal of Child Psychology and Psychiatry, 49*(1), 59–69.

Kohl, F. L., McLaughlin, M. J., & Nagle, K. (2006). Alternate achievement standards and assessments: A descriptive investigation of 16 states. *Exceptional Children, 73*(1), 107–123.

Kohn, A. (1993). *Punished by rewards: The trouble with gold stars, incentive plans, A's, praise, and other bribes.* New York: Houghton Mifflin.

Kortering, L. J., & Blackorby, J. (1992). High school dropout and students identified with behavioral disorders. *Behavioral Disorders, 18*(1), 24–32.

Kortering, L. J., McClannon, T. W., & Braziel, P. M. (2008). Universal design for learning: A look at what algebra and biology students with and without high incidence conditions are saying. *Remedial and Special Education, 29*(6), 352–363.

Kovaleski, J. K., & Prasse, D. P. (2004). Response to instruction in the identification of learning disabilities: A guide for school teams. *NASP Communique, 32*(5), insert.

Koyanagi, C. (with Boudreaux, R.). (2003). The federal government and interagency systems of care for children with serious mental disorders: Help or hindrance? (ERIC Document Reproduction Service No. ED 475 886)

Krupski, A. (1980). Attention processes: Research, theory, and implications for special education. In B. K. Keogh (Ed.), *Advances in special education: A research annual: Basic constructs and theoretical orientations* (Vol. 1, pp. 101–140). Greenwich, CT: JAI Press.

Krupski, A. (1981). An interactional approach to the study of attention problems in children with handicaps. *Exceptional Education Quarterly, 2*(3), 1–10.

Krupski, A. (1986). Attention problems in youngsters with learning handicaps. In J. K. Torgeson & B. Y. L. Wong (Eds.), *Psychological and educational perspectives on learning disabilities* (pp. 161–192). Orlando, FL: Academic Press.

Krupski, A. (1987). Attention: The verbal phantom strikes again—A response to Samuels. *Exceptional Children, 54*(1), 62–65.

Kubina, R. M., & Hughes, C. A. (2007). A focus on fluency instruction. *Current Practice Alerts 15.* Division for Learning Disabilities and Division for Research (CEC). Retrieved from http://www.teachingld.org/ld_resources/default.htm

Lahey, B. B., Applegate, B., McBurnett, K., Biederman, J., Greenhill, L., Hynd, G. W., et al. (1994). *DSM-IV* field trials for attention deficit hyperactivity disorder in children and adolescents. *American Journal of Psychiatry, 151*(11), 1673–1685.

Landrum, T. J. (2000). Assessment for eligibility: Issues in identifying students with emotional or behavioral disorders. *Assessment for Effective Intervention, 26*(1), 41–49.

Landrum, T. J., Tankersley, M., & Kauffman, J. M. (2003). What is special about special education for students with emotional or behavioral disorders? *Journal of Special Education, 37*(3), 148–156.

Lane, H. (1976). *The wild boy of Aveyron.* Cambridge, MA: Harvard University Press.

Lane, K. I., Kalberg, J. R., Lambert, E. W., Crnobori, M., & Bruhn, A. L. (2010). A comparison of systematic screening tools for emotional and behavioral disorders: A replication. *Journal of Emotional and Behavioral Disorder, 18*(2), 100–112.

Lapadat, J. C. (1991). Pragmatic language skills of students with language or learning disabilities: A quantitative synthesis. *Journal of Learning Disabilities, 24*(3), 147–158.

Larkin, M. J. (2001). Providing support for student independence through scaffolded instruction. *Teaching Exceptional Children, 34*(1), 30–34.

Lavoie, R. D. (1989). *Understanding learning disabilities: How difficult can this be? The F.A.T. city workshop* [DVD]. Alexandria, VA: PBS Video.

Lavoie, R. D. (2009). *Beyond F.A.T. city: A look back, a look ahead* [DVD]. Alexandria, VA: PBS Video.

Leal, L., & Raforth, M. A. (1991). Memory development: What teachers do does make a difference. *Intervention in School and Clinic, 26*(4), 234–237.

Lee, D. L. (2006). Facilitating transitions between and within academic tasks: An application of behavioral momentum. *Remedial and Special Education, 27*(5), 312–317.

Lee, I. L., Schacher, R. J., Chen, S. X., Ornstein, T. J., Charach, A., Barr, C., & Ickowicz, A. (2008). Predictive validity of *DSM-IV* and *ICD-10* criteria for ADHD and hyperkinetic disorder. *Journal of Child Psychology and Psychiatry, 49*(1), 70–78.

Lee, S. H., Wehmeyer, M. L., Soukup J. H., & Palmer, S. B. (2010). Impact of curriculum modifications on access to the general education curriculum for students with disabilities. *Exceptional Children, 76*(2), 213–233.

Leffert, J. S., & Siperstein, G. N. (1996). Assessment of social-cognitive processes in children with mental retardation. *American Journal on Mental Retardation, 100*(5), 441–455.

Lenz, B. K., Bulgren, J., & Hudson, P. J. (1990). Content enhancement: A model for promoting the acquisition of content by individuals with learning disabilities. In T. Scruggs & B. Y. L. Wong (Eds.), *Intervention research in learning disabilities* (pp. 122–165). New York: Springer-Verlag.

Lerner, J. W. (1993). *Learning disabilities: Theories, diagnosis, and teaching strategies* (6th ed.). Boston: Houghton Mifflin.

Lerner, J. W., & Lerner, S. R. (1991). Attention deficit disorder: Issues and questions. *Focus on Exceptional Children, 24*(3), 1–17.

Lerner, J. W., Lowenthal, B., & Lerner, S. (1995). *Attention deficit disorders: Assessment and teaching.* Pacific Grove, CA: Brooks/Cole.

Lewis, F., Murdoch, B. E., & Woodyatt, G. C. (2007). Linguistic abilities in students with autism spectrum disorders. *Research in Autism Spectrum Disorder, 1*(1), 85.

Licht, B. G., & Kistner, J. A. (1986). Motivational problems of learning disabled children: Individual differences and their implications for treatment. In J. K. Torgeson & B. Y. L. Wong (Eds.), *Psychological and educational perspectives on learning disabilities* (pp. 225–255). Orlando, FL: Academic Press.

Lidz, C. S., & Elliot, J. G. (Eds.). (2000). *Dynamic assessment: Prevailing models and applications.* New York: Elsevier Science.

Linn, A., & Myles, B. S. (2004). Asperger syndrome and six strategies for success. *Beyond Behavior, 14*(1), 3–9.

Lipsky, D. K., & Gartner, A. (1987). Capable of achievement and worthy of respect: Education for all handicapped children as if they were full-fledged human beings. *Exceptional Children, 54*(1), 69–74.

Lipsky, D. K., & Gartner, A. (1996). Inclusion, school restructuring, and the remaking of American society. *Harvard Educational Review, 66*(4), 762–796.

Lloyd, J. W. (1984). How should we individualize instruction—or should we? *Remedial and Special Education, 5*(1), 7–15.

Lloyd, J. W., & Hallahan, D. P. (2005). Going forward: How the field of learning disabilities has and will contribute to education. *Learning Disabilities Quarterly, 28*, 133–136.

Locke, J. (1690, 1959). *An essay concerning human understanding* (A. C. Fraser, Ed.). New York: Dover.

Loeber, R., Burke, J., & Pardini, D. A. (2009). Perspectives on oppositional defiant disorder, conduct disorder, and psychopathic features. *Journal of Child Psychology and Psychiatry, 50*(1–2), 133–142.

Loiacono, V., & Allen, B. (2008). Are special education teachers prepared to teach the increasing number of students diagnosed with autism? *International Journal of Special Education, 23*(2), 120–126.

Long, N. J., & Morse, W. C. (1996). *Conflict in the classroom: The education of at-risk and troubled students* (5th ed.). Austin, TX: Pro-Ed.

Long, N. J., Morse, W. C., & Newman, R. G. (Eds.). (1965). *Conflict in the classroom.* Belmont, CA: Wadsworth.

Lord, C., & Corsello, C. (2005). Diagnostic instruments in autistic spectrum disorders. In F. R. Volkmar, R. Paul, A. Klin, & D. Cohen (Eds.), *Handbook of autism and pervasive developmental disorders* (3rd ed., Vol. 2, pp. 730–771). Hoboken, NJ: Wiley.

Lovett, M. W., Barron, R. W., & Benson, N. J. (2003). Effective remediation of word identification and decoding difficulties in school-age children with reading disabilities. In H. L. Swanson, K. R. Harris, & S. Graham (Eds.), *Handbook of learning disabilities* (pp. 273–292). New York: Guilford Press.

Lovitt, T. C. (2010). What teachers can do for children living in difficult circumstances. *Intervention in School and Clinic, 45*(5), 317–320.

Lyon, G. R., Fletcher, J. M., Shaywitz, S. E., Shaywitz, B. A., Torgeson, J. K., Wood, F. B., Schulte, A., & Olson, R. (2001). Rethinking learning disabilities. In C. E. Finn, A. J. Rotherham, & C. R. Hokanson (Eds.), *Rethinking special education for a new century* (pp. 259–287). Washington, DC: Fordham Foundation and the Progressive Policy Institute.

MacArthur, C. A. (2009). Reflections on research on writing and technology for struggling writers. *Learning Disabilities Research & Practice, 24*(2), 93–103.

MacMillan, D. L. (1998). Unpackaging special educational variables in the study and teaching of children with conduct disorders. *Education and Treatment of Children, 21*(3), 234–245.

MacMillan, D. L., & Forness, S. R. (1998). The role of IQ in special education placement decisions: Primary and determinative or peripheral and inconsequential? *Remedial and Special Education, 19*(4), 239–253.

MacMillan, D. L., Gresham, F. M., & Siperstein, G. M. (1993). Conceptual and psychometric concerns about the 1992 AAMR definition of mental retardation. *American Journal on Mental Retardation, 98*(3), 325–335.

MacMillan, D. L., Gresham, F. M., & Siperstein, G. M. (1995). Heightened concerns over the 1992 AAMR definition: Advocacy versus precision. *American Journal on Mental Retardation, 100*(1), 87–97.

MacMillan, D. L., Keogh, B. K., & Jones, R. L. (1986). Special education research on mildly handicapped learners. In M. C. Wittrock (Ed.), *Handbook of research on teaching* (3rd ed., pp. 686–724). New York: Macmillan.

MacMillan, D. L., Siperstein, G. N., & Gresham, F. M. (1996). A challenge to the viability of mild mental retardation as a diagnostic category. *Exceptional Children, 62*(4), 356–371.

MacPhee, A. R., & Andrews, J. J. W. (2006). Risk factors for depression in early adolescence. *Adolescence, 41*(163), 435–466.

Macrine, S. L., & Sabbatino, E. D. (2008). Dynamic assessment and remediation approach: Using the DARA approach to assist struggling readers. *Reading and Writing Quarterly, 24*, 52–76.

Maheady, L. (2003). A focus on class-wide peer tutoring. *Current Practice Alerts 8.* Division for Learning Disabilities and Division for Research (CEC). Retrieved from http://www.teachingld.org/ld_resources/default.htm

Mahitivanichcha, K., & Parrish, T. (2005). The implications of fiscal incentives on identification rates and placement in special education: Formulas for influencing best practice. *Journal of Education Finance, 31*(1), 1–22.

Mamlin, N., Harris, K. R., & Case, L. P. (2001). A methodological analysis of locus of control and learning disabilities: Rethinking a common assumption. *Journal of Special Education, 34*(4), 214–225.

Mandlawitz, M. (2006). *What every teacher should know about IDEA 2004.* Boston: Allyn & Bacon.

Mann, V. A. (2003). Language processes: Keys to reading disability. In H. L. Swanson, K. R. Harris, & S. Graham (Eds.), *Handbook of learning disabilities* (pp. 213–228). New York: Guilford Press.

Marchant, M., Anderson, D. H., Caldarella, P., Fisher, A., Young, B. J., & Young, K. R. (2009). Schoolwide screening and programs of positive behavior support: Informing universal interventions. *Preventing School Failure, 53*(3), 131–143.

Martin, D. (2005). English as an additional language and children with speech, language and communication needs. In A. Lewis & B. Norwich (Eds.), *Special teaching for special children? Pedagogies for inclusion* (pp. 97–109). Berkshire, England: Open University Press.

Martin, R. P. (1992). Child temperament: Effects on special education and outcomes. *Exceptionality, 3*(2), 99–115.

Marton, I., Wiener, J., Rogers, M., Moore, C., & Tannock, R. (2009). Empathy and social perspective taking in children with attention-deficit/hyperactivity disorder. *Journal of Abnormal Child Psychology, 37*, 107–118.

Masland, R., Sarason, S., & Gladwin, T. (1958). *Mental subnormality.* New York: Basic Books.

Maslow, A. (1954). *Motivation and personality.* New York: Harper and Row.

Mastropieri, M. A., & Scruggs, T. E. (1991). *Teaching students ways to remember: Strategies for learning mnemonically.* Cambridge, MA: Brookline Books.

Mastropieri, M. A., Scruggs, T. E., & Berkeley, S. L. (2007). Peers helping peers. *Educational Leadership, 64*(5), 54–58.

Mastropieri, M. A., Scruggs, T. E., & Butcher, K. (1997). How effective is inquiry learning for students with mild disabilities? *Journal of Special Education, 31*(2), 199–211.

Mathias, J. L. (1990). Social intelligence, social competence, and interpersonal competence. In N. W. Bray (Ed.), *International review of research in mental retardation* (Vol. 16, pp. 125–160). San Diego, CA: Academic Press.

Mayes, S. D., & Calhoun, S. L. (2003). Analysis of WISC–III, Stanford-Binet: IV, and academic achievement test scores in children with autism. *Journal of Autism and Developmental Disorders, 33,* 329–341.

Mayes, S. D., Calhoun, S. L., Murray, M. J., Morrow, J. D., Yurich, K. K. L., Mahr, F., & Peterson, C. (2009). Comparison of scores on the Checklist for Autism Spectrum Disorder, Childhood Autism Rating Scale, and Gilliam Asperger's Disorder Scale for children with low functioning autism, high functioning autism, Asperger's disorder, ADHD, and typical development. *Journal of Autism and Developmental Disorders, 39,* 1682–1693.

McCabe, P. C., & Meller, P. J. (2004). The relationship between language and social competence: How language impairment affects social growth. *Psychology in the Schools, 41*(3), 313–321.

McCardle, P., Mele-McCarthy, J., Cutting, L., & Leos, K. (2005). Learning disabilities in English language learners: Research issues and future directions [Special issue]. *Learning Disabilities Research and Practice, 20*(4).

McCollin, M., & O'Shea, D. (2005). Increasing reading achievement of students from culturally and linguistically diverse backgrounds. *Preventing School Failure, 50*(1), 41–45.

McConnell, M. E., Hilvitz, P. B., & Cox, C. J. (1998). Functional assessment: A systematic process for assessment and intervention in general and special education classrooms. *Intervention in School and Clinic, 34*(1), 10–20.

McCormick, P. K., Campbell, J. W., Pasnak, R., & Perry, P. (1990). Instruction on Piagetian concepts for children with mental retardation. *Mental Retardation, 28*(6), 359–366.

McDuffie, K. A., Mastropieri, M. A., & Scruggs, T. E. (2009). Differential effects of peer tutoring in co-taught and non-co-taught classes: Results for content learning and student-teacher interactions. *Exceptional Children, 75*(4), 493–510.

McFarland, C. F., Jr., & Weibe, D. (1987). Structure and utilization of knowledge among special children. In J. G. Borkowski & J. D. Day (Eds.), *Cognition in special children: Comparative approaches to retardation, learning disabilities, and giftedness* (pp. 87–121). Norwood, NJ: Ablex.

McGinnis, E., & Goldstein, A. P. (1990). *Skillstreaming in early childhood: Teaching prosocial skills to the preschool and kindergarten child.* Champaign, IL: Research Press.

McGinnis, E., & Goldstein, A. P. (1997). *Skillstreaming the elementary child: New strategies and perspectives for teaching prosocial skills* (rev. ed.). Champaign, IL: Research Press.

McGrew, K. S., & Bruininks, R. H. (1990). Defining adaptive and maladaptive behavior within a model of personal competence. *School Psychology Review, 19*(1), 53–73.

McGrew, K. S., Bruininks, R. H., & Johnson, D. R. (1996). Confirmatory factor analytic investigation of Greenspan's model of personal competence. *American Journal on Mental Retardation, 100*(5), 533–545.

McGuinnes, A., Humphries, T., Hogg-Johnson, S., & Tannock, R. (2003). Listening comprehension and working memory are impaired in attention-deficit hyperactivity disorder irrespective of language impairment. *Journal of Abnormal Child Psychology, 31*(4), 427–443.

McGuire, J. M., Scott, S. S., & Shaw, S. S. (2006). Universal design and its applications in educational environments. *Remedial and Special Education, 27*(3), 166–175.

McIntosh, A. S. (2008). A focus on functional behavioral assessment. *Current Practice Alerts 16.* Division for Learning Disabilities and Division for Research (CEC). Retrieved from http://www.teachingld.org/ld_resources/default.htm

McIntyre, T. (1993). Reflections on the new definition: Who still falls through the cracks and why. *Behavioral Disorders, 18*(2), 148–160.

McIntyre, T. (1996). Guidelines for providing appropriate services to culturally diverse students with emotional and/or behavioral disorders. *Behavioral Disorders, 21*(2), 137–144.

McLeskey, J. (1992). Students with learning disabilities at the primary, intermediate and secondary grade levels: Identification and characteristics. *Learning Disability Quarterly, 15*(1), 13–19.

McLeskey, J., & Waldron, N. L. (1991). Identifying students with learning disabilities: The effect of implementing statewide guidelines. *Journal of Learning Disabilities, 24*(8), 501–506.

McLeskey, J., Waldron, N. L., & Wornhoff, S. A. (1990). Factors influencing the identification of black and white students with learning disabilities. *Journal of Learning Disabilities, 23*(6), 362–366.

McLoughlin, J. A., & Lewis, R. B. (2008). *Assessing special students* (7th ed.). Upper Saddle River, NJ: Merrill/Pearson Education.

McMaster, K., & Fuchs, D. (2005). A focus on cooperative learning for students with disabilities. *Current Practice Alerts 11.* Division for Learning Disabilities and Division for Research (CEC). Retrieved from http://www.teachingld.org/ld_resources/default.htm

McMillan, J. H., Myran, S., & Workman, D. (2002). Elementary teachers' classroom assessment and grading practices. *Journal of Educational Research, 95*(4), 203–213.

Meadan, H., & Monda-Amaya, L. (2008). Social competence for students with mild disabilities in the general classroom: A structure for providing social support. *Intervention in School and Clinic, 43*(3), 158–167.

Mehring, T. A., & Colson, S. E. (1990). Motivation and mildly handicapped learners. *Focus on Exceptional Children, 22*(5), 1–14.

Meichenbaum, D. (1977). *Cognitive behavior modification.* New York: Plenum.

Melton, L., & Pickett, W. (1997). *Using multiple intelligences in middle school reading.* Bloomington, IN: Phi Delta Kappa Educational Foundation.

Meltzer, L. (2004). Resilience and learning disabilities: Research on internal and external protective factors [Special issue]. *Learning Disabilities Research and Practice, 19*(1).

Meltzer, L. (Ed.). (2007). *Executive function in education: From theory to practice.* New York: Guilford Press.

Meltzer, L., Katzir, T., Miller, L., Reddy, R., & Roditi, B. (2004). Academic self-perceptions, effort, and strategy use in students with learning disabilities: Changes over time. *Learning Disabilities Research and Practice, 19*(2), 99–108.

Meltzer, L., & Krishnan, K. (2007). Executive function difficulties and learning disabilities. In L. Meltzer (Ed.), *Executive function in education: From theory to practice* (pp. 77–105). New York: Guilford Press.

Meltzer, L., Pollica, L. S., & Barzillai, M. (2007). Executive function in the classroom: Embedding strategy instruction into daily teaching practices. In L. Meltzer (Ed.), *Executive function in education: From theory to practice* (pp. 165–193). New York: Guilford Press.

Mental Health and Special Education Coalition. (1991). Fact sheets: Definition of "seriously emotionally disturbed" under Individuals with Disabilities Education Act; Overview of proposed alternative to definition of "seriously emotionally disturbed" under Individuals with Disabilities Education Act; Clarification of changes proposed to terminology and definition. Alexandria, VA: National Mental Health Association.

Meo, G. (2008). Curriculum planning for all learners: Applying universal design for learning (UDL) to a high school reading comprehension program. *Preventing School Failure, 52*(2), 21–30.

Mercer, C. D. (1987). *Students with learning disabilities* (3rd ed.). Upper Saddle River, NJ: Merrill/Pearson.

Mercer, C. D., King-Sears, P., & Mercer, A. R. (1990). Learning disabilities definitions and criteria used by state education departments. *Learning Disability Quarterly, 13*(3), 141–152.

Mercer, J. (1973). *Labeling the mentally retarded: Clinical and social perspective on mental retardation.* Berkeley: University of California.

Merrell, K. W., & Walker, H. M. (2004). Deconstructing a definition: Social maladjustment versus emotional disturbance and moving the EBD field forward. *Psychology in the Schools, 41*(8), 899–910.

Merrill, E. C. (1990). Attentional resource allocation and mental retardation. In N. W. Bray (Ed.), *International review of research in mental retardation* (Vol. 16, pp. 51–88). San Diego, CA: Academic Press.

Meyer, A., & Rose, D. H. (2006). The future is in the margins: The role of technology and disability in educational reform. In D. H. Rose & A. Meyer (Eds.), *A practical reader in universal design for learning* (pp. 13–35). Cambridge, MA: Harvard University Press.

Milford, T., & Harrison, G. L. (2010). Using the PLEASE strategy with a struggling middle school writer with a disability. *Intervention in School and Clinic, 45*(5), 326–332.

Miller, D. (2006). Students with fetal alcohol syndrome: Updating our knowledge, improving their programs. *Teaching Exceptional Children, 38*(4), 12–18.

Miller, G. A. (1956). The magical number seven, plus or minus two: Some limits on our capacity for processing information. *Psychological Review, 63,* 81–97.

Miller, J. F., Heilman, J., Nockerts, A., Inglesias, A., Fabiano, L., & Francis, D. J. (2006). Oral language and reading in bilingual children. *Learning Disabilities Research and Practice, 21*(1), 30–43.

Miller, S., Heafner, T., & Massey, D. (2009). High-school teachers' attempts to promote self-regulated learning: "I may learn from you, yet how do I do it?" *Urban Review, 41,* 121–140.

Miller, S. P., & Mercer, C. D. (1997). Educational aspects of mathematics disabilities. *Journal of Learning Disabilities, 30*(1), 47–56.

Mills, R. P. (1996). Statewide portfolio assessment: The Vermont experience. In J. B. Baron & D. P. Wolf (Eds.), *Performance-based student assessment: Challenges and possibilities: Ninety-fifth yearbook of the National Society for the Study of Education* (Part 1, pp. 192–214). Chicago: University of Chicago.

Ming, K., & Dukes, C. (2010). Gimme five: Creating a comprehensive reading lesson with all the essential elements. *Teaching Exceptional Children, 42*(3), 22–28.

Minshew, N. J., Sweeney, J. A., Bauman, M. L., & Webb, S. J. (2005). Neurological aspects of autism. In F. R. Volkmar, R. Paul, A.

Klin, & D. Cohen (Eds.), *Handbook of autism and pervasive developmental disorders* (3rd ed., Vol. 1, pp. 473–514). Hoboken, NJ: Wiley.

Mira, M. P., & Tyler, J. S. (1991). Students with traumatic brain injury: Making the transition from hospital to school. *Focus on Exceptional Children, 23*(5), 1–12.

Mitchell, D. (Ed.). (2004). *Special educational needs and inclusive education: Major themes in education: Vol. 2. Inclusive education.* London: Routledge-Farmer.

Mitchell, D. (2008). *What really works in special and inclusive education: Using evidence-based teaching strategies.* London: Routledge.

Moore-Brown, B., Huerta, M., Uranga-Hernandez, Y., & Pena, E. D. (2006). Using dynamic assessment to evaluate children with suspected learning disabilities. *Intervention in School and Clinic, 41*(4), 209–217.

Moran, S., & Gardner, H. (2007). "Hill, skill and will": Executive function from a multiple-intelligences perspective. In L. Meltzer (Ed.), *Executive function in education: From theory to practice* (pp. 19–38). New York: Guilford Press.

Moran, S., Kornhaber, M., & Gardner, H. (2006). Orchestrating multiple intelligences. *Educational Leadership, 64*(1), 22–27.

Moreno, G. (2010). No need to count to ten: Advocating for the early implementation of the functional behavioural assessment in addressing challenging behaviours. *Emotional and Behavioural Difficulties, 15*(1), 15–22.

Morgan, P. (2006). Increasing task engagement using preference or choice-making: Some behavioral and methodological factors affecting their efficacy as classroom interventions. *Remedial and Special Education, 27*(3), 176–187.

Morrier, M. J., Hess, K. L., & Heflin, L. J. (2008). Ethnic disproportionality in students with autism spectrum disorders. *Multicultural Education, 16*(1), 31–38.

Morrison, G. M., & Cosden, M. A. (1997). Risk, resilience and adjustment of individuals with learning disabilities. *Learning Disability Quarterly, 20*(1), 43–60.

Morsink, C. V., Soar, R. S., Soar, R. M., & Thomas, R. (1986). Research on teaching: Opening the door to special education classrooms. *Exceptional Children, 53,* 320–340.

Munk, D. D., & Bursuck, W. D. (1998). Report card grading adaptations for students with disabilities: Types and acceptability. *Intervention in School and Clinic, 33*(5), 306–308.

Munk, D. D., & Bursuck, W. D. (2001a). Preliminary findings on personalized grading plans for middle school students with learning disabilities. *Exceptional Children, 67*(2), 211–234.

Munk, D. D., & Bursuck, W. D. (2001b). What report card grades should and do communicate: Perceptions of parents of secondary students with and without disabilities. *Remedial and Special Education, 22*(5), 280–287.

Munk, D. D., & Bursuck, W. D. (2004). Personalized grading plans: A systematic approach to making the grades of included students more meaningful. *Focus on Exceptional Children, 36*(9), 1–11.

Murphy, E., Grey, I. M., & Honan, R. (2005). Co-operative learning for students with difficulties in learning: A description of models and guidelines for implementation. *British Journal of Special Education, 32*(3), 157–164.

Murphy, V., & Hicks-Stewart, V. (1991). Learning disabilities and attention-deficit-hyperactivity disorder: An interactional perspective. *Journal of Learning Disabilities, 24*(7), 386–388.

Murray, C., & Greenberg, M. T. (2006). Examining the importance of social relationships and social contexts in the lives of children with high-incidence disabilities. *Journal of Special Education, 39*(4), 220–233.

Myles, B. B., & Simpson, R. L. (2001). Understanding the hidden curriculum: An essential social skill for children and youth with Asperger syndrome. *Intervention in School and Clinic, 36*(5), 279–286.

Nabors, L. A., Little, S. G., Akin-Little, A., & Jobst, E. A. (2008). Knowledge of and confidence in meeting the needs of children with chronic medical needs: Pediatric psychology's contribution to education. *Psychology in the Schools, 45*(3), 217–226.

National Advisory Committee on Handicapped Children (NACHC). (1968). *Special education for handicapped children: First annual report.* Washington, DC: HEW.

National Association of School Nurses (NASN). (2003). Medication administration in the school setting [Position statement]. Silver Spring, MD: Author. Retrieved from http://www.nasn.org/Default.aspx?tabid = 230

National Association of School Psychologists (NASP). (2003). Students with attention problems [Position statement]. Bethesda, MD: Author. Retrieved from http://www.nasponline.org/about_nasp/position_paper.aspx

National Association of School Psychologists (NASP). (2009a). Appropriate academic supports to meet the needs of all students [Position statement]. Bethesda, MD: Author. Retrieved from http://www.nasponline.org/about_nasp/position_paper.aspx

National Association of School Psychologists (NASP). (2009b). Appropriate behavioral, social, and emotional supports to meet the needs of all students [Position statement]. Bethesda, MD: Author. Retrieved from http://www.nasponline.org/about_nasp/position_paper.aspx

National Association of State Directors of Special Education (NASDSE). (1997). *Comparison of key issues: Current law and 1997 IDEA amendments.* Washington, DC: Author.

National Association of State Directors of Special Education (NASDSE). (2004). The Individuals with Disabilities Education Act: A Comparison of P.L. 105–17 (IDEA '97) to H.R. 1350. Retrieved from http://www.nasdse.org/GovernmentRelations/IDEAReauthorization/tabid/439/Default.aspx

National Association of State Directors of Special Education (NASDSE). (2006). *Response to intervention: Policy considerations and implementation.* Alexandria, VA: Author.

National Center for Education Statistics (NCES). (2004). *Issue brief: English language learner students in U.S. public school schools: 1994 and 2000.* Retrieved from http://nces.ed.gov/pubsearch/pubinfo.asp?pubid = 2004035

National Center for Education Statistics (NCES). (2010). *The condition of education 2010* (NCES 2010–028), Indicator 5. Retrieved from http://nces.ed.gov/programs/coe/2010/section1/indicator05.asp

National Center on Educational Restructuring and Inclusion (NCERI). (1994). *National study of inclusive education.* New York: Author. (ERIC Document Reproduction Service No. 375 606)

National Institute of Mental Health (NIMH). (2008). *Attention-deficit hyperactivity disorder (ADHD).* Washington, DC: Author. Retrieved from http://www.nimh.nih.gov/health/topics/attention-deficit-hyperactivity-disorder-adhd/index.shtml

National Institute of Neurological Disorders and Stroke (NINDS). (2010). Autism fact sheet. Bethesda, MD: Author. Retrieved from http://www.ninds.nih.gov/disorders/autism/detail_autism.htm

National Joint Committee on Learning Disabilities (NJCLD). (1998). *Operationalizing the NJCLD definition of learning disabilities for ongoing assessment in schools.* Retrieved from www.ldonline.org/about/partners/njcld#position

National Joint Committee on Learning Disabilities (NJCLD). (2004). State- and district-wide assessments and students with disabilities: A guide for states and school districts. *Learning Disability Quarterly, 27*(2), 67–76.

National Joint Committee on Learning Disabilities (NJCLD). (2005). Responsiveness to intervention and learning disabilities. *Learning Disability Quarterly, 28*(4), 249–260.

National Reading Panel. (2000). *Teaching children to read: An evidence-based assessment of the scientific research literature on reading and its implications for reading instruction.* Washington, DC: National Institute of Child Health and Human Development. (ERIC Document Reproduction Service No. ED 444 127)

Neely-Barnes, S., & Dia, D. A. (2008). Families of children with disabilities: A review of literature and recommendations for interventions. *Journal of Early and Intensive Behavior Intervention, 5*(3), 93–107.

Nelson, C. M., & Kauffman, J. M. (2009). The past is prologue: Suggestions for moving forward in emotional and behavioral disorders. *Beyond Behavior, 18*(2), 36–41.

Nelson, C. M., Leone, P. E., & Rutherford, R. B. (2004). Youth delinquency: Prevention and intervention. In R. B. Rutherford, M. M. Quinn, & S. R. Mathur (Eds.), *Handbook of research in emotional behavioral disorders* (pp. 282–301). New York: Guilford Press.

Nelson, J. R., Duppong-Hurley, K., Synhorst, L., Epstein, M. H., Stage, S., & Buckley, J. (2009). The child outcomes of a behavior model. *Exceptional Children, 76*(1), 7–30.

Nelson, J. R., Stage, S., Duppong-Hurley, K., Synhorst, L., & Epstein, M. H. (2007). Risk factors predictive of the problem behavior of children at risk for emotional and behavioral disorders. *Exceptional Children, 73*(3), 367–379.

Nevin, J. A. (1988). Behavioral momentum and the partial reinforcement effect. *Psychological Bulletin, 103*(1), 44–56.

Nichols, J. G., McKenzie, M., & Shufro, J. (1994). Schoolwork, homework, life's work: The experience of students with and without learning disabilities. *Journal of Learning Disabilities, 27*(9), 562–569.

Nichols, P. (1992). The curriculum of control: Twelve reasons for it, some arguments against it. *Beyond Behavior, 3*(2), 5–11.

Nirje, B. (1969). The normalization principle and its human management implications. In R. B. Kugel & W. Wolfensberger (Eds.), *Changing patterns in residential services for the mentally retarded* (pp. 179–195). Washington, DC: President's Committee on Mental Retardation.

Norwich, B. (2007). *Dilemmas of difference, inclusion and disability: International perspectives.* London: Routledge.

Nunez, J. C., Gonzalez-Pienda, J. A., Gonzalez-Pumariega, S., Roces, C., Alvarez, L., Gonzalez, P., & Rodriguez, S. (2005). Subgroups of attributional profiles in students with learning difficulties and their relation to self-concept and academic goals. *Learning Disabilities Research and Practice, 20*(2), 86–97.

Obiakor, F. E., Utley, C. A., Smith, R., & Harris-Obiakor, P. (2002). The comprehensive support model for culturally diverse exceptional learners: Intervention in an age of change. *Intervention in School and Clinic, 38*(1), 14–27.

Olympia, D., Farley, M., Christiansen, E., Pettersson, H., Jenson, W., & Clark, E. (2004). Social maladjustment and students with behavioral and emotional disorders: Revisiting basic assumptions and assessment issues. *Psychology in the Schools, 41*(8), 835–847.

O'Neal, D., & Ringler, M. (2010). Broadening our view of linguistic diversity. *Phi Delta Kappan, 91*(7), 48–52.

O'Reilly, M. F., & Glynn, D. (1995). Using a process social skills training approach with adolescents with mild intellectual disabilities in a high school setting. *Education and Training in Mental Retardation and Developmental Disabilities, 30*(3), 187–198.

Orkwis, R., & McLane, K. (1998). *A curriculum every student can use: Design principles for student access* (ERIC/OSEP topical brief). Reston, VA: Council for Exceptional Children.

Orton, S. T. (1937). *Reading, writing and speech problems in children.* New York: Norton.

Oswald, D. P., Best, A. M., & Coutinho, M. J. (2006). Individual, family, and school factors associated with the identification of female and male students for special education. *International Journal of Special Education, 21*(3), 120–137.

Oswald, D. P., Coutinho, M. J., Best, A. M., & Nguyen, N. (2001). Impact of socioeconomic characteristics on the identification rates of minority students as having mental retardation. *Mental Retardation, 39*(5), 351–367.

Oswald, D. P., Coutinho, M. J., Best, A. M., & Singh, N. N. (1999). Ethnic representation in special education: The influence of school-related economic and demographic variables. *Journal of Special Education, 32*(4), 194–206.

Otto-Flynn, K. (undated). *When mainstreaming fails.* Unpublished manuscript.

Overton, T. (2009). *Assessing learners with special needs: An applied approach* (6th ed.). Upper Saddle River, NJ: Merrill/Pearson Education.

Owens, R. (2010). *Language disorders: A functional approach to assessment and intervention* (5th ed.). Boston: Allyn & Bacon.

Ozonoff, S., & Griffith, E. M. (2000). Neuropsychological function and the external validity of Asperger syndrome. In A. Klin, F. R. Volkmar, & S. S. Sparrow (Eds.), *Asperger syndrome* (pp. 72–96). New York: Guilford Press.

Ozonoff, S., & Schetter, P. L. (2007). Executive function in autism spectrum disorders. In L. Meltzer (Ed.), *Executive function in education: From theory to practice* (pp. 133–160). New York: Guilford Press.

Paris, S. G., & Winograd, P. (1990). Promoting metacognition and motivation of exceptional children. *Remedial and Special Education, 11*(6), 7–15.

Pasnak, R., Whitten, J. C., Perry, P., Waiss, S., Madden, S. E., & Watson-White, S. A. (1995). Achievement gains after instruction on classification and seriation. *Education and Training in Mental Retardation and Developmental Disabilities, 30*(2), 109–117.

Pastor, P. N., & Reuben, C. A. (2008). Diagnosed attention deficit hyperactivity disorder and learning disability: United States, 2004–2006. *Vital and Health Statistics* (National Center for Health Statistics), *10*(237). (ERIC Document Reproduction Service No. ED 502 147)

Patton, J. M. (1998). The disproportionate representation of African Americans in special education: Looking behind the curtain for understanding and solutions. *Journal of Special Education, 32*, 25–31.

Paul, R. (2005). Behavioral assessment of individuals with autism: A functional ecological approach. In F. R. Volkmar, R. Paul, A. Klin, & D. Cohen (Eds.), *Handbook of autism and pervasive developmental disorders* (3rd ed., Vol. 2, pp. 799–816). Hoboken, NJ: Wiley.

Payne, J. S., & Patton, J. R. (1981). *Mental retardation.* Upper Saddle River, NJ: Merrill/Pearson Education.

Payne, L. D., Marks, L. J., & Bogan, B. L. (2007). Using curriculum-based assessment to address the academic and behavioral deficits of students with emotional and behavioral disorders. *Beyond Behavior, 16*(3), 3–6.

Peacock Hill Working Group. (1991). Problems and promises in special education and related services for children and youth with emotional or behavioral disorders. *Behavioral Disorders, 16*(4), 299–313.

Pearl, R., Donahue, M., & Bryan, T. (1986). Social relationships of learning-disabled children. In J. K. Torgeson & B. Y. L. Wong (Eds.), *Psychological and educational perspectives on learning disabilities* (pp. 193–224). Orlando, FL: Academic Press.

Perner, J. (2000). Memory and theory of mind. In E. Tulving & F. I. M. Craik (Eds.), *The Oxford handbook of memory* (pp. 297–312). New York: Oxford University Press.

Perry, P., Pasnak, R., & Holt, R. W. (1992). Instruction on concrete operations for children who are mildly mentally retarded. *Education and Training in Mental Retardation, 27*(3), 273–281.

Piaget, J. (1960). *The psychology of intelligence* (M. Piercy & D. E. Berlyne, Trans.). London: Routledge & Kegan Paul.

Pinborough-Zimmerman, J., Satterfield, R., Miller, J., Bilder, D., Hossain, S., & McMahon, W. (2007). Communication disorders: Prevalence and comorbid intellectual disability, autism, and emotional/behavioral disorders. *American Journal of Speech-Language Pathology, 16*, 359–367.

Pinker, S., & Jackendoff, R. (2005). The faculty of language: What's special about it? *Cognition, 95*(2), 201–236.

Pisha, B., & Stahl, S. (2005). The promise of new learning environments for students with disabilities. *Intervention in School and Clinic, 41*(2), 67–75.

Pivik, J., McComas, J., & LaFlamme, M. (2002). Barriers and facilitators to inclusive education. *Exceptional Children, 69*(1), 97–107.

Plomin, R. (1995). Genetics and children's experiences in the family. *Journal of Child Psychology and Psychiatry, 36*, 33–68.

Podell, D. M., Tournaki-Rein, N., & Lin, A. (1992). Automatization of mathematics skills via computer assisted instruction among students with mild retardation. *Education and Training in Mental Retardation, 27*(3), 200–206.

Polloway, E. A., Lubin, J., Smith, J. D., & Patton, J. R. (2010). Mild intellectual disabilities: Legacies and trends in concepts and educational practices. *Education and Training in Autism and Developmental Disabilities, 45*(1), 54–68.

Polloway, E. A., Patton, J. R., Smith, J. D., Lubin, J., & Antoine, K. (2009). State guidelines for mental retardation and intellectual disabilities: A re-visitation of previous analyses in light of changes in the field. *Education and Training in Developmental Disabilities, 44*(1), 14–24.

Pomplun, M. (1997). When students with disabilities participate in cooperative groups. *Exceptional Children, 64*(1), 49–58.

Posner, M. I., & Boies, S. J. (1971). Components of attention. *Psychological Review, 78*(5), 391–408.

President's Commission on Excellence in Special Education. (2002). *A new era: Revitalizing special education for children and their families.* Washington, DC: U.S. Department of Education, Office of Special Education and Rehabilitative Services.

President's Committee on Mental Retardation (PCMR). (1970). *The six-hour retarded child.* Washington, DC: U.S. Government Printing Office.

Pressley, M., Mohan, L., & Raphael, L. M. (2007). How does Bennett Woods Elementary School produce such high reading and writing achievement? *Journal of Educational Psychology, 99*(2), 221–240.

Price, L., & Shaw, S. (2000). Adult education and learning disabilities: Why are we still seeing them as children? Using what we know about adult education to improve outcomes of adults with learning disabilities. *Career Development for Exceptional Individuals. 23,* 187–204.

Pruess, J. B., Vadasy, P. F., & Fewell, R. R. (1987). Language development in children with Down syndrome: An overview of recent research. *Education and Training in Mental Retardation, 22*(1), 44–55.

Prutting, C. A. (1982). Pragmatics as social competence. *Journal of Speech and Hearing Disorders, 47*(2), 123–134.

Prutting, C. A., & Kirchner, D. M. (1987). A clinical appraisal of the pragmatic aspects of language. *Journal of Speech and Hearing Disorders, 52*(2), 105–119.

Quay, H. C., & Werry, J. S. (Eds.). (1986). *Psychopathological disorders of childhood* (3rd ed.). New York: John Wiley.

Rangel, E. S. (2007). Time to learn. *Research Points: Essential Information for Education Policy, 5*(2), 1–4. (ERIC Document Reproduction Service No. ED500799)

Raymond, E. B. (1997). It's all in the family: Working with gays and lesbians in family contexts. *Reaching Today's Youth, 1*(3), 32–36.

Redl, F., & Wineman, D. (1951). *Children who hate.* New York: Free Press.

Reid, D. K., & Button, L. J. (1995). Anna's story: Narratives of personal experience about being learning disabled. *Journal of Learning Disabilities, 28*(10), 602–614.

Reid, D. K., Hresko, W. P., & Swanson, H. L. (Eds.). (1996). *Cognitive approaches to learning disabilities* (3rd ed.). Austin, TX: Pro-Ed.

Reid, D. K., & Stone, C. A. (1991). Why is cognitive instruction effective? Underlying learning mechanisms. *Remedial and Special Education, 12*(3), 8–19.

Reid, R., Epstein, M. H., Pastor, D. A., & Ryser, G. R. (2000). Strengths-based assessment differences across students with LD and EBD. *Remedial and Special Education, 21,* 346–355.

Reilly, T. F. (1991). Cultural bias: The albatross of assessing behavior-disordered children and youth. *Preventing School Failure, 36*(1), 50–53.

Reschly, D. J. (2002). Change dynamics in special education assessment: Historical and contemporary patterns. *Peabody Journal of Education, 77*(2), 117–136.

Reschly, D. J. (2005). Learning disabilities identification: Primary intervention, secondary intervention, then what? *Journal of Learning Disabilities, 38*(6), 510–515.

Reschly, D. J., & Hosp, J. L. (2004). State SLD identification policies and practices. *Learning Disability Quarterly, 27,* 197–213.

Reynolds, C. R., & Horton, A. M. (2008). Assessing executive functions: A life-span approach. *Psychology in the Schools, 45*(9), 875–892.

Reynolds, C. R., & Kamphaus, R. W. (2004). *BASC-2: Behavior Assessment System for Children* (2nd ed.). San Antonio, TX: PsychCorp.

Reynolds, M. C. (1989). An historical perspective: The delivery of special education to mildly disabled and at-risk students. *Remedial and Special Education, 10*(6), 7–11.

Reynolds, M. C., & Heistad, D. (1997). 20/20 analysis: Estimating school effectiveness in serving students at the margins. *Exceptional Children, 63*(4), 439–449.

Reynolds, M. E., & Fish, M. (2010). Language skills in low-SES rural Appalachian children: Kindergarten to middle childhood. *Journal of Applied Developmental Psychology, 31,* 238–248.

Reynolds, W. M., & Miller, K. L. (1985). Depression and learned helplessness in mentally retarded and nonmentally retarded adolescents: An initial investigation. *Applied Research in Mental Retardation, 6,* 295–306.

Richards, G. P., Samuels, S. J., Turnure, J. E., & Ysseldyke, J. E. (1990). Sustained and selective attention in children with learning disabilities. *Journal of Learning Disabilities, 23*(2), 129–136.

Richardson, V., & Anders, P. L. (1998). A view from across the Grand Canyon. *Learning Disabilities Quarterly, 21*(1), 85–97.

Rimland, B. (1964). *Infantile autism: The syndrome and its implication for a neural theory of behavior.* Upper Saddle River, NJ: Prentice Hall.

Rinaldi, C. (2003). Language competence and social behavior of students with emotional or behavioral disorders. *Behavioral Disorders, 29*(1), 34–42.

Rittschof, K. A. (2010). Field dependence-independence as visuospatial and executive functioning in working memory: Implications for instructional systems design and research. *Educational Technology Research and Development, 58,* 99–114.

Rivera, M. O., Al-Otaiba, S., & Koorland, M. A. (2006). Reading instruction for students with emotional and behavioral disorders and at risk of antisocial behaviors in primary grades: Review of the literature. *Behavioral Disorders, 31*(3), 323–337.

Roach, A. T., Niebling, B. C., & Kurz, A. (2008). Evaluating the alignment among curriculum, instruction, and assessments: Implications and applications for research and practice. *Psychology in the Schools, 45*(2), 158–176.

Roberts, G., Torgeson, J. K., Boardman, A., & Scammacca, N. (2008). Evidence-based strategies for reading instruction of older students with learning disabilities. *Learning Disabilities Research and Practice, 23*(2), 63–69.

Roberts, J. E., Price, J., & Malkin, C. (2007). Language and communication development in Down syndrome. *Mental Retardation and Developmental Disabilities Research Reviews, 13,* 26–35.

Robinson-Neal, A. (2009). "I know you are, but what am I?" A reflective essay on possible predispositions to autism spectrum disorders. *Exceptional Parent, 39*(4), 30–32.

Roccio, C. S., Hynd, G. W., Cohen, M. J., & Gonzalez, J. J. (1993). Neurological basis of attention deficit hyperactivity disorder. *Exceptional Children, 60*(2), 118–124.

Rock, M. L., Gregg, M., Ellis, E., & Gable, R. A. (2008). REACH: A framework for differentiating instruction. *Preventing School Failure, 52*(2), 31–41.

Rodriguez, C. M., & Eden, A. M. (2008). Disciplinary style and child abuse potential: Association with indicators of positive functioning in children with behavior problems. *Child Psychiatry and Human Development, 39*, 123–136.

Rodriguez, N. M., Thompson, R. H., & Baynham, T. Y. (2010). Assessment of the relative effects of attention and escape on noncompliance. *Journal of Applied Behavior Analysis, 43*(1), 143–147.

Rogers-Atkinson, D. L. (2003). Language processing in children with emotional disorders. *Behavioral Disorders, 29*(1), 43–47.

Rose, D. H., & Meyer, A. (2002). *Teaching every student in the digital age: Universal design for learning.* Alexandria, VA: ASCD. Accessible digitally at http://www.cast.org

Rose, D. H., & Meyer, A. (Eds.). (2006). *A practical reader in universal design for learning.* Cambridge, MA: Harvard University Press.

Rose, D. H., Meyer, A., & Hitchcock, C. (Eds.). (2006). *The universally designed classroom: Accessible curriculum and digital technologies.* Cambridge, MA: Harvard University Press.

Rose, D. H., & Rose, K. (2007). Deficits in executive function processes. In L. Meltzer (Ed.), *Executive function in education: From theory to practice* (pp. 287–308). New York: Guilford Press.

Rosenshine, B. V. (1986). Synthesis of research on explicit teaching. *Educational Leadership, 43*(7), 60–69.

Rosenshine, B. V., & Stevens, R. (1986). Teaching functions. In M. C. Wittrock (Ed.), *Handbook of research on teaching* (3rd ed., pp. 376–391). New York: Macmillan.

Ross, R. P. (1995). Impact on psychologists of state guidelines for evaluating underachievement. *Learning Disability Quarterly, 18*(1), 43–56.

Rotter, J. B. (1966). Generalized expectancies for internal versus external control of reinforcement. *Psychological Monographs: General and Applied, 80*(1), 1–28.

Rowitz, L. (1986). Multiprofessional perspectives on prevention. *Mental Retardation, 24*(1), 1–3.

Rozencwajg, P., & Corroyer, D. (2005). Cognitive processes in the reflective-impulsive cognitive style. *Journal of Genetic Psychology, 166*(4), 451–463.

Ruhl, K. L., Hughes, C. A., & Camarata, S. M. (1992). Analysis of the expressive and receptive language characteristics of emotionally handicapped students served in public school settings. *Journal of Childhood Disorders, 14*(2), 165–176.

Rupley, W. H., Blair, T. R., & Nichols, W. D. (2009). Effective reading instruction for struggling readers: The role of direct/explicit teaching. *Reading & Writing Quarterly, 25*(2–3), 125–138.

Russell, C. L. (2008). How are your person-first skills? A self-assessment. *Teaching Exceptional Children, 40*(5), 40–43.

Rutherford, R. B., & Nelson, C. M. (1995). Management of aggressive and violent behavior in schools. *Focus on Exceptional Children, 27*(6), 1–15.

Rutter, M. (2005). Genetic influences and autism. In F. R. Volkmar, R. Paul, A. Klin, & D. Cohen (Eds.), *Handbook of autism and pervasive developmental disorders* (3rd ed., Vol. 1, pp. 425–452). Hoboken, NJ: Wiley.

Ryan, A. L., Halsey, H. N., & Matthews, W. J. (2003). Using functional assessment to promote desirable student behavior in schools. *Teaching Exceptional Children, 35*(5), 8–15.

Ryan, E. B., Short, E. J., & Weed, K. A. (1986). The role of cognitive strategy training in the improving of academic performance of learning disabled children. *Journal of Learning Disabilities, 19*(9), 521–529.

Ryan, S., & Ferguson, D. L. (2006). On, yet under, the radar: Students with fetal alcohol syndrome disorder. *Exceptional Children, 72*(3), 363–379.

Sabornie, E. J., Cullinan, D., Osborne, S. S., & Brock, L. B. (2005). Intellectual, academic, and behavioral functioning of students with high-incidence disabilities: A cross-categorical meta-analysis. *Exceptional Children, 72*(1), 47–63.

Sabornie, E. J., Evans, C., & Cullinan, D. (2006). Comparing characteristics of high-incidence disability groups. *Remedial and Special Education, 27*(2), 95–104.

Safford, P. L., & Safford, E. J. (1996). *A history of childhood and disability.* New York: Teachers College Press.

Safford, P. L., & Safford, E. J. (1998). Visions of the special class. *Remedial and Special Education, 19*(4), 229–238.

Safran, S. P. (2001). Asperger syndrome: The emerging challenge to special education. *Exceptional Children, 67*(2), 151–160.

Safran, S. P. (2008). Why youngsters with autism spectrum disorders remain underrepresented in special education. *Remedial and Special Education, 29*(2), 90–95.

Salend, S. J. (1998). Using portfolios to assess student performance. *Teaching Exceptional Children, 31*(2), 36–43.

Salend, S. J. (2001). *Creating inclusive classrooms: Effective and reflective practices* (4th ed.). Upper Saddle River, NJ: Merrill/Pearson Education.

Salend, S. J. (2008). Determining appropriate testing accommodations: Complying with NCLB and IDEA. *Teaching Exceptional Children, 40*(4), 14–22.

Salend, S. J., & Garrick Duhaney, L. M. (2002). Grading students in inclusive settings. *Teaching Exceptional Children, 34*(3), 8–15.

Salend, S. J., Garrick Duhaney, L. M., & Montgomery, W. (2002). A comprehensive approach to identifying and addressing issues of disproportionate representation. *Remedial and Special Education, 23*(5), 289–299.

Salend, S. J., & Rohena, E. (2003). Students with attention deficit hyperactivity disorder: An overview. *Intervention in School and Clinic, 38*(5), 259–266.

Salend, S. J., & Salinas, A. G. (2003). Language differences or learning difficulties: The work of the multidisciplinary team. *Teaching Exceptional Children, 35*(4), 36–43.

Samuels, S. J. (1987). Information processing abilities and reading. *Journal of Learning Disabilities, 20*(1), 18–22.

Sánchez, M. T., Parker, C., Akbayin, B., & McTigue, A. (2010). *Processes and challenges in identifying learning disabilities among students who are English language learners in three New York State districts* (Issues & Answers Report, REL 2010–No. 085). Washington, DC: U.S. Department of Education, Institute of Education Sciences, National Center for Educational Evaluation and Regional Assistance, Regional Educational Laboratory Northeast and Islands. Retrieved from http://ies.ed.gov/ncee/edlabs

Sanders, J. L. (2009). Qualitative or quantitative differences between Asperger's disorder and autism? Historical considerations. *Journal of Autism and Developmental Disorders, 39*, 1560–1567.

Sands, D. J., Adams, L., & Stout, D. M. (1995). A state-wide exploration of the nature and use of curriculum in special education. *Exceptional Children, 62*(1), 68–83.

Sands, D. J., & Doll, B. (1996). Fostering self-determination: A developmental task. *Journal of Special Education, 30*(1), 58–76.

San Miguel, S. K., Forness, S. R., & Kavale, K. A. (1996). Social skills deficits in learning disabilities: The psychiatric comorbidity hypothesis. *Learning Disability Quarterly, 19*(4), 252–261.

Santangelo, T., Harris, K. R., & Graham, S. (2007). Self-regulated strategy development: A validated model to support students who struggle with writing. *Learning Disabilities: A Contemporary Journal, 5*(1), 1–20.

Santos, K. E. (1992). Fragile X syndrome: An educator's role in identification, prevention, and intervention. *Remedial and Special Education, 13*(2), 32–39.

Sapon-Shevin, M. (2008). Learning in an inclusive community. *Educational Leadership, 66*(1), 49–53.

Schalock, R. L., Luckasson, R. A., Shogren, K. A., Borthwick-Duffy, S., Bradley, V., Buntinx, D. L., et al. (2007). The renaming of mental retardation: Understanding the change to the term intellectual disability. *American Journal on Intellectual and Developmental Disabilities, 45*(2), 116–124.

Schlesinger, H. (2000/1972). A developmental model applied to problems of deafness. *Journal of Deaf Studies and Deaf Education, 5*(4), 349–361.

Schnitzer, S. (1993). Designing an authentic assessment. *Educational Leadership, 50*(7), 32–35.

Schnoes, C., Reid, R., Wagner, M., & Marder, C. (2006). ADHD among students receiving special education: A national survey. *Exceptional Children, 72*(4), 483–496.

Schoenbrodt, L., Kumin, L., & Sloan, J. M. (1997). Learning disabilities existing concomitantly with communication disorder. *Journal of Learning Disabilities, 30*(3), 264–281.

Schrunk, D. H. (1992). Theory and research on student perceptions in the classroom. In D. H. Schrunk & J. L. Meece (Eds.), *Student perceptions in the classroom* (pp. 3–23). Hillsdale, NJ: Erlbaum.

Schultz, G. P., & Switzky, H. N. (1994). The development of intrinsic motivation in students with learning problems: Suggestions for more effective instructional practice. *Preventing School Failure, 34*(2), 14–19.

Schultz, R. T., & Robins, D. L. (2005). Functional neuroimaging studies of autism spectrum disorders. In F. R. Volkmar, R. Paul, A. Klin, & D. Cohen (Eds.), *Handbook of autism and pervasive developmental disorders* (3rd ed., Vol. 1, pp. 515–533). Hoboken, NJ: Wiley.

Schumm, J. S., Vaughn, S., & Leavell, A. G. (1994). Planning pyramid: A framework for planning for diverse student needs during content area instruction. *Reading Teacher, 47*(8), 608–615.

Sciutto, M. J., & Eisenberg, M. (2007). Evaluating the evidence for and against overdiagnosis of ADHD. *Journal of Attention Disorders, 11*(2), 106–113.

Scott, K., & Carren, D. (1987). The epidemiology and prevention of mental retardation. *American Psychologist, 42*(8), 801–804.

Scott, S., McGuire, J., & Foley, T. (2001). *Universal design for instruction: An exploration of principles for anticipating and responding to student diversity in the classroom.* Storrs: University of Connecticut, Center on Postsecondary Education and Disability.

Seifert, T. L. (2004). Understanding student motivation. *Educational Research, 46*(2), 137–149.

Seligman, M. E. P. (1975). *Helplessness: On depression, development and death.* San Francisco: W. H. Freeman.

Selman, R. L. (1980). *The growth of interpersonal understanding: Developmental and clinical analyses.* New York: Academic Press.

Shattuck, P. T., Durkin, M., Maenner, M., Newschaffer, C., Mandell, D. S., Wiggins, L., & Cunniff, C. (2009). Timing of identification among children with an autism spectrum disorder: Findings from a population-based surveillance study. *Journal of the American Academy of Child and Adolescent Psychiatry, 48*(5), 474–483.

Shaw, S. R. (2008). Educational programming framework for a subset of students with diverse learning needs: Borderline intellectual functioning. *Intervention in School and Clinic, 43*(5), 291–299.

Shaywitz, B. A., Pugh, K. R., Jenner, A. R., Fulbright, R. K., Fletcher, J. M., Gore, J. C., & Shaywitz, S. E. (2000). The neurobiology of reading and reading disability (dyslexia). In M. L. Kamil, P. B. Mosenthal, P. D. Pearson, & R. Barr (Eds.), *Handbook of reading research* (Vol. 3, pp. 229–249). Mahwah, NJ: Erlbaum.

Shaywitz, B. A., Shaywitz, S. E., Fletcher, J. M., Pugh, K. R., Gore, J. C., Constable, R. T., & Lacadie, C. (1997). The Yale Center for the Study of Learning and Attention: Longitudinal and neurobiological studies. *Learning Disabilities, 8*(1), 21–29.

Shaywitz, S. E., & Shaywitz, B. A. (1988). Attention deficit disorder: Current perspectives. In J. Kavanagh & T. J. Truss (Eds.), *Learning disabilities: Proceedings of the national conference* (pp. 369–567). Parkton, MD: York Press.

Shea, V., & Mesibov, G. B. (2005). Adolescents and adults with autism. In F. R. Volkmar, R. Paul, A. Klin, & D. Cohen (Eds.), *Handbook of autism and pervasive developmental disorders* (3rd ed., Vol. 1, pp. 288–311). Hoboken, NJ: Wiley.

Shippen, M. E., Simpson, R. G., & Crites, S. A. (2003). A practical guide to functional behavioral assessment. *Teaching Exceptional Children, 35*(5), 36–44.

Shore, S. (2001). Understanding the autism spectrum: What teachers need to know. *Intervention in School and Clinic, 36*(5), 293–299, 305.

Short, E. J., & Evans, S. W. (1990). Individual difference in cognitive and social problem-solving skills as a function of intelligence. In N. W. Bray (Ed.), *International review of research in mental retardation* (Vol. 16, pp. 89–123). San Diego, CA: Academic Press.

Sicile-Kira, C. (2004). *Autism spectrum disorders: The complete guide to understanding autism, Asperger's syndrome, pervasive developmental disorder, and other ASDs.* New York: Pedigree.

Siegel, L. S. (2003). Basic cognitive processes and reading disabilities. In H. L. Swanson, K. R. Harris, & S. Graham (Eds.), *Handbook of learning disabilities* (pp. 158–181). New York: Guilford Press.

Sigafoos, J. (2000). Communication development and aberrant behavior in children with developmental disabilities. *Education and Training in Mental Retardation and Developmental Disabilities, 35*(2), 168–176.

Silliman, E. R., & Scott, C. M. (2006). Language basis of literacy disabilities: Emerging evidence from second-language learning and language impairment [Special issue]. *Learning Disabilities Research and Practice, 21*(1).

Silva, M., Munk, D. D., & Bursuck, W. D. (2005). Grading adaptations for students with disabilities. *Intervention in School and Clinic, 41*(2), 87–98.

Silver, L. B. (1990). Attention-deficit/hyperactivity disorder: Is it a learning disability or a related disorder? *Journal of Learning Disabilities, 23*(7), 394–397.

Simmons, D. C., Kameenui, E. J., & Chard, D. J. (1998). General education teachers' assumptions about learning and students with learning disabilities: Design-of-instruction analysis. *Learning Disability Quarterly, 21*(1), 6–21.

Simonsen, B., Sugai, G., & Negron, M. (2008). Schoolwide positive behavior supports: Primary systems and practices. *Teaching Exceptional Children, 40*(6), 32–40.

Siperstein, G. N. (1992). Social competence: An important construct in mental retardation. *American Journal on Mental Retardation, 96*(4), iii–vi.

Siperstein, G. N., & Leffert, J. S. (1997). Comparison of socially accepted and rejected children with mental retardation. *American Journal on Mental Retardation, 101*(4), 339–351.

Skeels, H. M., & Dye, H. B. (1939). A study of the effects of differential stimulation on mentally retarded children. *Program of the American Association of Mental Deficiency, 44*, 114–136.

Skiba, R. J., Poloni-Staudinger, L., Gallini, S., Simmons, A. B., & Feggins-Azziz, R. (2006). Disparate access: The disproportionality of African American students with disabilities across educational environments. *Exceptional Children, 72*(4), 411–424.

Skiba, R. J., Simmons, A. B., Ritter, S., Gibb, A. C., Rausch, M. K., Cuadrado, J., & Chung, C.-G. (2008). Achieving equity in special education: History, status, and current challenges. *Exceptional Children, 74*(3), 264–288.

Skinner, B. F. (1953). *Science and human behavior.* New York: Macmillan.

Skinner, B. F. (1974). *About behaviorism.* New York: Knopf.

Skrtic, T. M. (2005). A political economy of learning disabilities. *Learning Disability Quarterly, 28,* 149–155.

Slack, N., & Norwich, B. (2007). Evaluating the reliability and validity of a learning styles inventory: A classroom-based study. *Educational Research, 49*(1), 51–63.

Sleeter, C. E. (1986). Learning disabilities: The social construction of a special education category. *Exceptional Children, 53*(1), 46–54.

Smith, C. A. (1991). What's in a word? Acquisition of the term "language learning disability." *Teacher Education and Special Education, 14*(2), 103–109.

Smith, C. R. (1991). *Learning disabilities: The interaction of the learner, task and setting.* Boston: Allyn & Bacon.

Smith, C. R. (1998). From gibberish to phonemic awareness. *Teaching Exceptional Children, 30*(6), 20–25.

Smith, J. D. (1985). *Minds made feeble: The myth and legacy of the Kallikaks.* Rockville, MD: Aspen.

Smith, J. D. (1994). The revised AAMR definition of mental retardation: The MRDD position. *Education and Training in Mental Retardation and Developmental Disabilities, 29*(3), 179–183.

Smith, J. D. (1997). Mental retardation as an educational construct: Time for a new shared view? *Education and Training in Mental Retardation and Developmental Disabilities, 32*(3), 167–173.

Smith, J. D. (1998). The history of special education: Essays honoring the bicentennial of the work of Jean Itard [Special issue]. *Remedial and Special Education, 19*(4).

Smith, J. D. (2002). The myth of mental retardation: Paradigm shifts, disaggregation, and developmental disabilities. *Mental Retardation, 40*(1), 62–64.

Smith, J. D. (2003). Abandoning the myth of mental retardation. *Education and Training in Developmental Disabilities, 38*(4), 358–361.

Smith, T. E. C. (1998). Introduction to the special series. *Remedial and Special Education, 19*(4), 194–195.

Smith, T. E. C. (2005). IDEA 2004: Another round in the reauthorization process. *Remedial and Special Education, 26*(6), 314–319.

Smith, T. E. C., & Puccini, I. K. (1995). Position statement: Secondary curricula and policy issues for students with mental retardation. *Education and Training in Mental Retardation and Developmental Disabilities, 30*(4), 275–282.

Snell, M. E., Luckasson, R., Bradley, V., Coulter, D. L., Craig, E. M., Gomez, S. C., et al. (2009). Characteristics and needs of people with intellectual disability who have higher IQs. *Journal of Intellectual & Developmental Disabilities, 47*(3), 220–233.

Snider, V. E. (1992). Learning styles and learning to read: A critique. *Remedial and Special Education, 13*(1), 6–18.

Solanto, M. V., & Alvir, J. (2009). Reliability of *DSM-IV* symptom ratings of ADHD: Implications for *DSM-V*. *Journal of Attention Disorders, 13*(2), 107–116.

Sourup, J. H., Wehmeyer, M. L., Bashinski, S. M., & Bouvaird, J. A. (2007). Classroom variables and access to the general curriculum for students with disabilities. *Exceptional Children, 74*(1), 101–120.

Speece, D. L. (2008). Learning disabilities in the United States: Operationalizing a construct. In L. Florian & M. J. McLaughlin (Eds.), *Disability classification in education: Issues and perspectives* (pp. 227–243). Thousand Oaks, CA: Corwin.

Speece, D. L., Case, L. P., & Molloy, D. E. (2003). Responsiveness to general education instruction as the first gate to learning disabilities identification. *Learning Disabilities Research and Practice, 18*(3), 147–156.

Speece, D. L., & Harry, B. (1997). Classification for children. In J. W. Lloyd, E. J. Kameenui, & D. Chard (Eds.), *Issues in educating students with disabilities* (pp. 63–73). Mahwah, NJ: Erlbaum.

Spradley, J. P. (1979). *The ethnographic interview.* New York: Holt.

Sprafkin, J., Gadow, K. D., & Nolan, E. E. (2001). The utility of a *DSM-IV* referenced screening instrument for attention-deficit/hyperactivity disorder. *Journal of Emotional and Behavioral Disorders, 9*(3), 182–191.

Stainback, S., & Stainback, W. (1987). Integration vs. cooperation: A commentary on "Educating children with learning problems: A shared responsibility." *Exceptional Children, 54*(1), 66–68.

Stainback, W., & Stainback, S. (1984). A rationale for the merger of special and regular education. *Exceptional Children, 51*(2), 102–111.

Stainton, T. (2008). Reason, grace and charity: Augustine and the impact of church doctrine on the construction of intellectual disability. *Disability & Society, 23*(5), 485–496.

Stanley, G., & Baines, L. (2004). No more shopping for grades at B-Mart: Re-establishing grades as indicators of academic performance. *Clearing House, 77*(3), 101–104.

Stecker, P. M., Lembke, E. S., & Foegen, A. (2008). Using progress-monitoring data to improve instructional decision making. *Preventing School Failure, 52*(2), 48–58.

Stenhoff, D. M., & Lignugaris/Kraft, B. (2007). A review of the effects of peer tutoring on students with mild disabilities in secondary settings. *Exceptional Children, 74*(1), 8–30.

Sternberg, R. J. (1988). Intelligence. In R. J. Sternberg & E. E. Smith (Eds.), *The psychology of human thought* (pp. 267–308). Cambridge, England: Cambridge University Press.

Sternberg, R. J., & Grigorenko, E. L. (1997). Are cognitive styles still in style? *American Psychologist, 52*(7), 700–712.

Stevens, G. D., & Birch, J. W. (1957). A proposal for clarification of the terminology used to describe brain-injured children. *Exceptional Children, 23,* 346–349.

Still, G. F. (1902). Some abnormal psychical conditions in children. *Lancet,* 1, 1008–1012, 1077–1082, 1163–1168.

Stipek, D. J. (1993). *Motivation to learn: From theory to practice* (2nd ed.). Boston: Allyn & Bacon.

Stolzenberg, J., & Cherkes-Julkowski, M. (1991). ADHD and LD connections. *Journal for Learning Disabilities, 24*(4), 194–195.

Stone, C. A., & Reid, D. K. (1994). Social and individual forces in learning: Implications for instruction of children with learning difficulties. *Learning Disability Quarterly, 17*(1), 72–86.

Strauss, A. A., & Kephart, N. C. (1955). *Psychopathology and education in the brain-injured child: Vol. 2. Progress in theory and in clinic.* New York: Grune & Stratton.

Strauss, A. A., & Lehtinen, L. E. (1947). *Psychopathology and education in the brain-injured child.* New York: Grune & Stratton.

Strout, M. (2005). Positive behavioral support at the classroom level: Considerations and strategies. *Beyond Behavior, 14*(2), 3–8.

Sugai, G. A., & Horner, R. H. (2002). Introduction to the special series on positive behavior support in schools. *Journal of Emotional and Behavioral Disorders, 10*(3), 130–135.

Sugai, G. A., Horner, R. H., & Sprague, J. R. (1999). Functional-assessment-based behavior support planning: Research to practice to research. *Behavioral Disorders, 24*(3), 253–257.

Sunderland, L. C. (2004). Speech, language, and audiology services in public schools. *Intervention in School and Clinic, 39*(4), 209–217.

Sutherland, K. S., & Singh, N. N. (2004). Learned helplessness and students with emotional or behavioral disorders: Deprivation in the classroom. *Behavioral Disorders, 29*(2), 169–181.

Swain, K. D., Friehe, M. M., & Harrington, J. M. (2004). Teaching listening strategies in the inclusive classroom. *Intervention in School and Clinic, 40*(1), 48–54.

Swanson, H. L. (1987). Information processing theory and learning disabilities: An overview. *Journal of Learning Disabilities, 20*(1), 3–7.

Swanson, H. L. (1991). Cognitive assessment approach I. In D. K. Reid, W. P. Hresko, & H. L. Swanson, *A cognitive approach to learning disabilities* (2nd ed., pp. 251–273). Austin, TX: Pro-Ed.

Swanson, H. L. (1994). Short-term memory and working memory: Do both contribute to our understanding of academic achievement in children and adults with learning disabilities? *Journal of Learning Disabilities, 27*(1), 34–50.

Swanson, H. L. (2002). Learning disabilities is a specific processing deficit, but it is much more than phonological processing. In R. Bradley, L. Danielson, & D. P. Hallahan (Eds.), *Identification of learning disabilities: Research to practice* (pp. 643–651). Mahwah, NJ: Erlbaum.

Swanson, H. L., Cochran, K. F., & Ewers, C. A. (1990). Can learning disabilities be determined from working memory performance? *Journal of Learning Disabilities, 23*(1), 59–67.

Swanson, H. L., & Cooney, J. B. (1991). Learning disabilities and memory. In B. Y. L. Wong (Ed.), *Learning about learning disabilities* (pp. 103–127). San Diego, CA: Academic Press.

Swanson, H. L., & Howard, C. B. (2005). Children with reading disabilities: Does dynamic assessment help in the classification? *Learning Disability Quarterly, 28*(1), 17–34.

Swanson, H. L., & O'Connor, R. (2009). The role of working memory and fluency practice on the reading comprehension of students who are dysfluent readers. *Journal of Learning Disabilities, 42,* 548–575.

Swanson, H. L., & Saez, L. (2003). Memory difficulties in children and adults with learning disabilities. In H. L. Swanson, K. R. Harris, & S. Graham (Eds.), *Handbook of learning disabilities* (pp. 182–198). New York: Guilford Press.

Sweller, J. (2004). Instructional design consequences of an analogy between evolution by natural selection and human cognitive architecture. *Instructional Science, 32,* 9–31.

Swick, K. J., & Williams, R. D. (2006). An analysis of Bronfenbrenner's bio-ecological perspective for early childhood educators: Implications for working with families experiencing stress. *Early Childhood Education Journal, 33*(5), 371–378.

Switzky, H. N., & Schultz, G. F. (1988). Intrinsic motivation and learning performance: Implications for individual educational programming for learners with mild handicaps. *Remedial and Special Education, 9*(4), 7–14.

Tallmadge, G. K., Gamel, N. N., Munson, R. G., & Hanley, T. V. (1985). *Special study of terminology: Comprehensive review and evaluation report.* Mountain View, CA: SRA Technologies.

Tannock, R. (1998). Attention deficit hyperactivity disorder: Advances in cognitive, neurobiological, and genetic research. *Journal of Child Psychology and Psychiatry, 39*(1), 65–99.

Tarver, S. G. (1999). A focus on direct instruction. *Current Practice Alerts 2.* Division for Learning Disabilities and Division for Research (CEC). Retrieved from http://www.teachingld.org/ld_resources/default.htm

Taylor, R. L. (2009). *Assessment of exceptional students: Educational and psychological procedures* (8th ed.). Boston: Allyn & Bacon.

Teeter, P. A. (1991). Attention deficit hyperactivity disorder: A psychoeducational paradigm. *School Psychology Review, 20*(2), 266–280.

Thatcher, K. L., Fletcher, K., & Decker, B. (2008). Communication disorders in the school: Perspectives on academic and social success: An introduction. *Psychology in the Schools, 45*(7), 579–581.

Theodore, L. A., Akin-Little, A., & Little, S. G. (2004). Evaluating the differential treatment of emotional disturbance and social maladjustment. *Psychology in the Schools, 41*(8), 879–886.

Thomas, A., & Chess, S. (1977). *Temperament and development.* New York: Brunner/Mazel.

Thomas, A., & Chess, S. (1984). Genesis and evolution of behavioral disorders: From infancy to early adult life. *American Journal of Psychiatry, 141*(1), 1–9.

Thompson, J. R., Bradley, V. J., Buntinx, W. H. E., Schalock, R. L., Shogren, K. A., Snell, E., et al. (2009). Conceptualizing supports and the support needs of people with intellectual disability. *Journal of Intellectual & Developmental Disabilities, 47*(2), 135–146.

Thompson, J. R., Bryant, B., Campbell, E. M., Craig, E. M., Hughes, C., Rotholz, D. A., & Wehmeyer, M. L. (2004). *Supports Intensity Scale.* Washington, DC: AAMR.

Thompson, J. R., Hughes, C., Schalock, R. L., Silverman, W., Tasse, M. J., Bryant, B., et al. (2002). Integrating supports in assessment and planning. *Mental Retardation, 40*(5), 390–405.

Thompson, J. R., McGrew, K. S., & Bruininks, R. H. (2002). Pieces of the puzzle: Measuring the personal competence and support needs of persons with intellectual disabilities. *Peabody Journal of Education, 77*(2), 23–39.

Tomlinson, C. A. (2000). Differentiation of instruction in the elementary grades. *ERIC Digest.* (ERIC Document Reproduction Service No. ED443572)

Torgeson, J. K. (1991). Learning disabilities: Historical and conceptual issues. In B. Y. L. Wong (Ed.), *Learning about learning disabilities* (pp. 3–37). San Diego, CA: Academic Press.

Torgeson, J. K. (2002). Empirical and theoretical support for direct diagnosis of learning disabilities by assessment of intrinsic processing weakness. In R. Bradley, L. Danielson, & D. P. Hallahan (Eds.), *Identification of learning disabilities: Research to practice* (pp. 565–613). Mahwah, NJ: Erlbaum.

Torgeson, J., & Kail, R. V., Jr. (1980). Memory processes in exceptional children. In B. K. Keogh (Ed.), *Advances in special education: A research annual: Basic constructs and theoretical orientations* (Vol. 1, pp. 55–99). Greenwich, CT: JAI Press.

Torgeson, J. K., Kistner, J. A., & Morgan, S. (1987). Component processes in working memory. In J. G. Borkowski & J. D. Day (Eds.), *Cognition in special children: Comparative approaches to retardation, learning disabilities, and giftedness* (pp. 49–86). Norwood, NJ: Ablex.

Torgeson, J. K., Morgan, S. T., & Rashotte, C. A. (1994). Longitudinal studies of phonological processing and reading. *Journal of Learning Disabilities, 27*(3), 276–286.

Towles-Reeves, E., Kleinert, H., & Muhomba, M. (2009). Alternate assessment: Have we learned anything new? *Exceptional Children, 75*(2), 233–252.

Treiber, F. A., & Lahey, B. B. (1983). Toward a behavioral model of academic remediation with learning disabled children. *Journal of Learning Disabilities, 16*(2), 111–116.

Trent, S. C., Artiles, A. J., & Englert, C. S. (1998). From deficit thinking to social constructivism: A review of special education theory, research, and practice from a historical perspective. In P. D. Pearson & A. Iran-Nejad (Eds.), *Review of research in education* (Vol. 23, pp. 227–307). Washington, DC: American Educational Research Association.

Troia, G. (2004). A focus on phonological awareness acquisition and intervention. *Current Practice Alerts 10.* Division for Learning Disabilities and Division for Research (CEC). Retrieved from http://www.teachingld.org/ld_resources/default.htm

Truscott, S., Catanese, A. M., & Abrams, L. M. (2005). The evolving context of special education classification in the United States. *School Psychology International, 26*(2), 162–177.

Turnbull, H. R., Stowe, M. J., & Huerta, N. E. (2007). *Free and appropriate public education* (7th ed.). Denver, CO: Love.

U.S. Department of Education. (1981). *Technical amendment: Final rule.* 34 CFR Part 300, Assistance to States for Education of Handicapped Children, 46 FR 3865 (January 16, 1981).

U.S. Department of Education. (1992). *Implementation of the Individuals with Disabilities Education Act: Fourteenth annual report to Congress.* Washington, DC: Government Printing Office.

U.S. Department of Education. (1994). *Sixteenth annual report to Congress on the implementation of the Individuals with Disabilities Education Act.* Washington, DC: Government Printing Office.

U.S. Department of Education. (1997a). Assistance to states for the education of children with disabilities: Proposed rule. *Federal Register, 62*(204), 55026–55135.

U.S. Department of Education. (1997b). *Nineteenth annual report to Congress on the implementation of the Individuals with Disabilities Education Act.* Washington, DC: Government Printing Office.

U.S. Department of Education. (1999). Individuals with Disabilities Education Act: Part 300. Assistance to states for the education of children with disabilities. *Federal Register, 64*(8), 12418–12480.

U.S. Department of Education. (2001). *Twenty-third annual report to Congress on the implementation of the Individuals with Disabilities Education Act.* Washington, DC: Author.

U.S. Department of Education. (2002a). *No Child Left Behind: A desktop reference.* Washington, DC: Author.

U.S. Department of Education. (2002b). *Twenty-fourth annual report to Congress on the implementation of the Individuals with Disabilities Education Act.* Washington, DC: Government Printing Office.

U.S. Department of Education. (2005). *Twenty-fifth annual report to Congress on the implementation of the Individuals with Disabilities Education Act, 2003* (Vols. 1 and 2). Washington, DC: Author.

U.S. Department of Education. (2006a). Assistance to states for the education of children with disabilities and preschool grants for children with disabilities: 34 CFR Part 300 [Final regulations]. *Federal Register, 71*(156), 46540–46845.

U.S. Department of Education. (2006b). *Twenty-sixth annual report to Congress on the implementation of the Individuals with Disabilities Education Act, 2004* (Vols. 1 and 2). Washington, DC: Author.

U.S. Department of Education. (2009). *Twenty-eighth annual report to Congress on the implementation of the Individuals with Disabilities Education Act, 2006* (Vols. 1 and 2). Washington, DC: Author.

U.S. Office of Education. (1976). Education of handicapped children. *Federal Register, 41,* 52405.

U.S. Office of Education. (1977a). Assistance to the states for the education of handicapped children: Procedures for evaluating learning disabilities. *Federal Register, 42,* 65082–65085.

U.S. Office of Education. (1977b). Implementation of Part B of the Education of the Handicapped Act. *Federal Register, 42*(163), 42474–42518.

U.S. Office of Special Education and Rehabilitative Services (OSERS). (1993, February 10). Invitation to comment on the regulatory definition of "serious emotional disturbance" and the use of this term in the Individuals with Disabilities Education Act. *Federal Register, 58*(26), 7938.

U.S. Office of Special Education Programs (OSEP). (1999). Universal design: Ensuring access to the general education curriculum. *Research Connections in Special Education, 5,* 1–5.

U.S. Office of Vocational and Adult Education (OVAE). (2010). Developmental disabilities. Retrieved from http://www2.ed.gov/about/offices/list/ovae/pi/AdultEd/disdev.html

Vandervelden, M. C., & Siegel, L. S. (1997). Teaching phonological processing skills in early literacy: A developmental approach. *Learning Disability Quarterly, 20*(2), 63–81.

van Garderen, D., & Whittaker, C. (2006). Planning differentiated multicultural instruction for secondary inclusive classrooms. *Teaching Exceptional Children, 38*(3), 12–20.

Vannest, K. J., & Hagan-Burke, S. (2010). Teacher time use in special education. *Remedial and Special Education, 31*(2), 126–142.

Vannest, K. J., & Parker, R. I. (2010). Measuring time: The stability of special education teacher time use. *Journal of Special Education, 44*(2), 94–106.

van Swet, J., Wichers-Bots, J., & Brown, K. (in press). Solution-focused educational assessment: Rethinking labels to support inclusive education. *International Journal of Inclusive Education.*

Vaughn, S., & Fuchs, L. S. (2003). Redefining learning disabilities as inadequate response to instruction: The promise and the potential problems. *Learning Disabilities Research and Practice, 18*(3), 137–146.

Vaughn, S., & Schumm, J. S. (1995). Responsible inclusion for students with learning disabilities. *Journal of Learning Disabilities, 28*(5), 264–270, 290.

Vaughn, S., Zaragoza, N., Hogan, A., & Walker, J. (1993). A four-year longitudinal investigation of the social skills and behavior problems of students with learning disabilities. *Journal of Learning Disabilities, 26*(6), 404–412.

Venn, J. (2007). *Assessment of students with special needs* (4th ed.). Upper Saddle River, NJ: Merrill/Pearson Education.

Vermont Developmental Disabilities Council. (2007). Choosing words with dignity. Retrieved from http://www.ddc.vermont.gov/publications-outreach

Verstraete, P. (2005). The taming of disability: Phrenology and bio-power on the road to the destruction of otherness in France (1800–60). *History of Education, 34*(2), 119–134.

Villa, R. A., & Thousand, J. S. (1988). Enhancing success in heterogeneous classrooms and schools: The powers of partnership. *Teacher Education and Special Education, 11*(4), 144–154.

Volkmar, F. R., & Klin, A. (2005). Issues in classification of autism and related conditions. In F. R. Volkmar, R. Paul, A. Klin, & D. Cohen (Eds.), *Handbook of autism and pervasive developmental disorders* (3rd ed., Vol. 1, pp. 5–41). Hoboken, NJ: Wiley.

Volkmar, F. R., State, M., & Klin, A. (2008). Autism and autism spectrum disorders: Diagnostic issues for the coming decade. *Journal of Child Psychology and Psychiatry, 50*(1–2), 108–115.

Volpe, R. J., Gadow, K. D., Blom-Hoffman, J., & Feinberg, A. B. (2009). Factor-analytic and individualized approaches to constructing brief measure of ADHD behaviors. *Journal of Emotional and Behavioral Disorders, 17*(2), 118–128.

Vygotsky, L. S. (1978). *Mind in society.* Cambridge, MA: Harvard University Press.

Vygotsky, L. S. (1987). Thinking and speech. In R. Rieber & A. S. Carton (Eds.), *Collected works of L. S. Vygotsky: Vol. 1. Problems of general psychology* (pp. 39–285). New York: Plenum.

Wadsworth, D. E. D., & Knight, D. (1999). Preparing the inclusion classroom for students with special physical and health needs. *Intervention in School and Clinic, 34*(3), 70–75.

Wahlstedt, C., Thorell, L. B., & Bohlin, G. (2009). Heterogeneity in ADHD: Neuropsychological pathways, comorbidity and symptom domains. *Journal of Abnormal Child Psychology, 37*(4), 551–564.

Walker, H. M., Ramsay, E., & Gresham, F. M. (2004). *Antisocial behavior in schools: Evidence-based practices.* Belmont, CA: Wadsworth.

Walker, H. M., & Severson, H. H. (1992). *Systematic Screening for Behavior Disorders (SSBD): User's guide and administration manual* (2nd ed.). Longmont, CO: Sopris West.

Walker, H. M., Severson, H., Stiller, B., Williams, G., Haring, N., Shinn, M., & Todis, B. (1988). Systematic screening of pupils in the elementary age range at risk for behavior disorders: Development and trial testing of a multiple gating model. *Remedial and Special Education, 9,* 8–14.

Wallace, T., Anderson, A. R., Bartholomay, T., & Hupp, S. (2002). An ecobehavioral examination of high school classrooms that include students with disabilities. *Exceptional Children, 68*(3), 345–359.

Wang, M. C., Reynolds, M. C., & Walberg, H. J. (1986). Rethinking special education. *Educational Leadership, 44*(1), 26–31.

Warnes, E. D., Sheridan, S. M., Geske, J., & Warnes, W. A. (2005). A contextual approach to the assessment of social skills: Identifying meaningful behaviors for social competence. *Psychology in the Schools, 42*(2), 173–187.

Webster, R. E., Hall, C. W., Brown, M. B., & Bolen, L. M. (1996). Memory modality differences in children with attention deficit hyperactivity disorder with and without learning disabilities. *Psychology in the Schools, 33*(3), 193–201.

Wegsheider, S. (1981). *Another chance: Hope and health for the alcoholic family.* Palo Alto, CA: Science and Behavior Books.

Wehby, J. H. (1994). Issues in the assessment of aggressive behavior. *Preventing School Failure, 38*(3), 24–28.

Wehby, J. H., Lane, K. L., & Falk, K. B. (2003). Academic instruction for students with emotional and behavioral disorders. *Journal of Emotional and Behavioral Disorders, 11*(4), 194–197.

Wehby, J. H., & Symons, F. J. (1996). Revisiting conceptual issues in the measurement of aggressive behavior. *Behavioral Disorders, 22*(1), 29–35.

Wehmeyer, M. L. (1992). Self-determination and the education of students with mental retardation. *Education and Training in Mental Retardation, 27*(4), 302–314.

Wehmeyer, M. L. (1994). Perceptions of self-determination and psychological empowerment of adolescents with mental retardation. *Education and Training in Mental Retardation, 29*(1), 9–21.

Wehmeyer, M. L. (2003). Defining mental retardation and ensuring access to the general curriculum. *Education and Training in Developmental Disabilities, 38*(3), 271–282.

Wehmeyer, M. L., Agran, M., & Hughes, C. (1998). *Teaching self-determination to students with disabilities: Basic skills for successful transition.* Baltimore: Paul Brookes.

Wehmeyer, M. L., Buntinx, W. H. E., Lachapelle, Y., Luckasson, R. A., Schalock, R. L., Verdugo, M. A., et al. (2008). The intellectual disability construct and its relation to human functioning. *Journal of Intellectual and Developmental Disabilities, 46*(4), 311–318.

Wehmeyer, M. L., Kelchner, K., & Richards, S. (1996). Essential characteristics of self-determined behavior of individuals with mental retardation. *American Journal on Mental Retardation, 100*(6), 632–642.

Wehmeyer, M. L., Lance, G. D., & Bashinski, S. (2002). Promoting access to the general curriculum for students with mental retardation: A multi-level model. *Education and Training in Mental Retardation and Developmental Disabilities, 37*(3), 223–234.

Wehmeyer, M. L., & Schwartz, M. (1997). Self-determination and positive adult outcomes: A followup study of youth with mental retardation or learning disabilities. *Exceptional Children, 63*(2), 245–255.

Weiner, B. (1985). An attributional theory of achievement motivation and emotion. *Psychological Review, 92*(4), 548–573.

Weiner, B. (1986). *An attributional theory of motivation and emotion.* New York: Springer Verlag.

Weiner, B. (2010). The development of an attribution-based theory of motivation: A history of ideas. *Educational Psychologist, 45*(1), 28–36.

Wenz-Gross, M., & Siperstein, G. N. (1997). Importance of social support in the adjustment of children with learning problems. *Exceptional Children, 63*(2), 183–193.

Werner, H., Garside, E. B., & Murphy, G. (1940). *Comparative psychology of mental development.* New York: Harper.

Whalen, C. K., & Henker, B. (1991). Social impact of stimulant treatment for hyperactive children. *Journal of Learning Disabilities, 24*(4), 231–241.

Whitelock, S. (2010). It's not your grandmother's school: Leadership decisions in RTI. *Communique, 38*(5), 1, 26–27.

Whitney-Thomas, J., & Moloney, M. (2001). "Who I am and what I want": Adolescents' self-definition and struggles. *Exceptional Children, 67*(3), 375–389.

Wiggins, G., & McTighe, J. (2001). *Understanding by design.* Upper Saddle River, NJ: Merrill/Pearson Education.

Wilkoff, W. L., & Abed, L. W. (1994). *Practicing universal design: An interpretation of the ADA.* New York: Van Nostrand Reinhold.

Will, M. C. (1986). Educating children with learning problems: A shared responsibility. *Exceptional Children, 52*(5), 411–415.

Williams, K. (2001). Understanding the student with Asperger syndrome: Guidelines for teachers. *Intervention in School and Clinic, 36*(5), 287–292.

Willows, D. M. (1991). Visual processes in learning disabilities. In B. Y. L. Wong (Ed.), *Learning about learning disabilities* (pp. 163–193). San Diego, CA: Academic Press.

Wing, L. (1981). Asperger's syndrome: A clinical account. *Psychological Medicine, 11*(1), 115–129.

Wing, L. (2005). Problems of categorical classification systems. In F. R. Volkmar, R. Paul, A. Klin, & D. Cohen (Eds.), *Handbook of autism and pervasive developmental disorders* (3rd ed., Vol. 1, pp. 583–605). Hoboken, NJ: Wiley.

Wing, L., & Gould, J. (1979). Severe impairments of social interaction and associated abnormalities in children: Epidemiology and classification. *Journal of Autism and Developmental Disabilities, 9*(1), 11–29.

Wing, L., & Potter, D. (2002). The epidemiology of autistic spectrum disorders: Is the prevalence rising? *Mental Retardation and Developmental Disabilities Research Review, 8*(3), 151–161.

Winzer, M. A. (1993). *The history of special education: From isolation to integration.* Washington, DC: Gallaudet University Press.

Winzer, M. A. (1998). A tale often told: The early progression of special education. *Remedial and Special Education, 19*(4), 212–218.

Winzer, M. A. (2007). Confronting difference: An excursion through the history of special education. In L. Florian (Ed.), *The Sage handbook of special education* (pp. 21–33). London: Sage.

Witkin, H. A., Moore, C. A., Goodenough, D. R., & Cox, P. W. (1977). Field-dependent and field-independent cognitive styles and their educational implications. *Review of Educational Research, 47*(1), 1–64.

Witte, R. H. (1998). Meet Bob, a student with traumatic brain injury. *Teaching Exceptional Children, 30*(3), 56–60.

Wodrich, D. J., & Joy, J. E. (1986). *Multidisciplinary assessment of children with learning disabilities and mental retardation.* Baltimore: Paul H. Brookes.

Wodrich, D. L., Stobo, N., & Trca, M. (1998). Three ways to consider educational performance when determining serious emotional disturbance. *School Psychology Quarterly, 13*(3), 228–240.

Wolfensberger, W. (1972). *The principle of normalization in human services.* Toronto, Canada: National Institute on Mental Retardation.

Wolff, S. (2004). The history of autism. *European Child and Adolescent Psychiatry, 13*, 201–208.

Wong, B. Y. L. (1991). Relevance of metacognition to learning disabilities. In B. Y. L. Wong (Ed.), *Learning about learning disabilities* (pp. 231–258). San Diego, CA: Academic Press.

Wong, B. Y. L. (2003). General and specific issues for researchers' consideration in applying the risk and resilience framework to the social domain of learning disabilities. *Learning Disabilities Research and Practice, 18*(2), 68–76.

Wood, F. (1982). Defining disturbing, disordered, and disturbed behavior. In F. Wood & K. Laken (Eds.), *Disturbing, disoriented, or disturbed?* (pp. 3–16). Reston, VA: CEC.

Wood, M. M. (1975). *Developmental therapy.* Baltimore: University Park Press.

Wood, M. M., & Long, N. J. (1991). *Life space intervention: Talking with children and youth in crisis.* Austin, TX: Pro-Ed.

World Conference on Special Needs Education: Access and Equality. (1994). *The Salamanca statement and framework for action on special needs education* (UNESCO). Retrieved from http://www.unesco.org/education/pdf/SALAMA_E.PDF

World Health Organization. (2001). *International classification of functioning, disability, and health (ICF).* Geneva, Switzerland: Author.

World Health Organization. (2007a). *Atlas: Global resources for persons with intellectual disabilities.* Geneva, Switzerland: Author.

World Health Organization. (2007b). *International Statistical Classification of Diseases and Related Health Problems, 10th revision (ICD-10): Chapter 5. Mental and behavioral disorders: F90 hyperkinetic disorders.* Geneva, Switzerland: Author. Retrieved from http://apps.who.int/classifications/apps/icd/icd10online/

Wright, D., Pillard, E. D., & Cleven, C. A. (1990). The influence of state definitions of behavior disorders on the number of children served under P.L. 94–142. *Remedial and Special Education, 11*(5), 17–22, 38.

Wright-Strawderman, C., Lindsey, P., Navarette, L., & Flippo, J. R. (1996). Depression in students with disabilities: Recognition and intervention strategies. *Intervention in School and Clinic, 31*(5), 261–275.

Wurst, D., Jones, D., & Luckner, J. (2005). Promoting literacy development with students who are deaf, hard-of-hearing and hearing. *Teaching Exceptional Children, 37*(5), 56–62.

Wyer, R. S., & Srull, T. K. (1989). *Memory and cognition in its social context.* Hillsdale, NJ: Erlbaum.

Yates, S. (2009). Teacher identification of student learned helplessness in mathematics. *Mathematics Education Research Journal, 21*(3), 86–106.

Yell, M. L., & Drasgow, E. (2000). Legal requirements for assessing students with emotional and behavioral disorders. *Assessment for Effective Intervention, 26*(1), 5–17.

Yell, M. L., Katsiyannis, A., & Hazelkorn, M. (2007). Reflections on the 25th anniversary of the U.S. Supreme Court's decision in Board of Education v. Rowley. *Focus on Exceptional Children, 39*, 1–12.

Yell, M. L., Rogers, D., & Rogers, E. L. (1998). The legal history of special education: What a long, strange trip it's been! *Remedial and Special Education, 19*(4), 219–228.

Yell, M. L., Ryan, J. B., Rozalski, M. E., & Katsiyannis, A. (2009). The U.S. Supreme Court and special education: 2005–2007. *Teaching Exceptional Children, 41*(3), 68–75.

Yell, M. L., & Shriner, J. G. (1997). The IDEA Amendments of 1997: Implications for special and general education teachers, administrators, and teacher trainers. *Focus on Exceptional Children, 30*(1), 1–19.

Ysseldyke, J. E., Algozzine, R., & Thurlow, M. L. (2000). *Critical issues in special education* (3rd ed.). Boston: Houghton Mifflin.

Ysseldyke, J. E., Burns, M. K., Scholin, S. E., & Parker, D. C. (2010). Instructionally valid assessment within response to intervention. *Teaching Exceptional Children, 42*(4), 54–61.

Ysseldyke, J. E, Nelson, J. R., Christenson, S., Johnson, D. R., Dennison, A., Triezenberg, H., et al. (2004). What we know and need to know about the consequences of high-stakes testing for students with disabilities. *Exceptional Children, 71*(1), 75–94.

Zentall, S. S. (2005). Theory- and evidence-based strategies for children with attentional problems. *Psychology in the Schools, 42*(8), 821–836.

Zigler, E., & Hodapp, R. M. (1986). *Understanding mental retardation.* Cambridge, England: Cambridge University Press.

Zigler, E., Hodapp, R. M., & Edison, M. R. (1990). From theory to practice in the care and education of mentally retarded individuals. *American Journal on Mental Retardation, 95*(1), 1–12.

Zirkel, P. A., & Krohn, N. (2008). RTI after IDEA: A survey of state laws. *Teaching Exceptional Children, 40*(3), 71–73.

NAME INDEX

SUBJECT INDEX

Page references followed by *f* and *t* indicate figures and tables respectively.